England (Parish) Dewsbury, Samuel Joseph Chadwick

The Registers of Dewbury, Yorkshire

England (Parish) Dewsbury, Samuel Joseph Chadwick

The Registers of Dewbury, Yorkshire

ISBN/EAN: 9783741186738

Manufactured in Europe, USA, Canada, Australia, Japa

Cover: Foto ©ninafisch / pixelio.de

Manufactured and distributed by brebook publishing software (www.brebook.com)

England (Parish) Dewsbury, Samuel Joseph Chadwick

The Registers of Dewbury, Yorkshire

THE

REGISTERS OF DEWSBURY,

YORKSHIRE.

Vol. 1.

1538 to 1653.

EDITED BY

SAMUEL JOSEPH CHADWICK, F.S.A.

Honorary Secretary of the "Record Series" of the Yorkshire Archæological Society.

PRINTED BY JOSEPH WARD AND CO., CAXTON SQUARE, DEWSBURY.

PREFACE.

This volume is a reprint from the *Dewsbury Parish Magazine*. It contains the first three volumes of the Registers of Dewsbury, and covers the period from 1538 to 1653. There are a few intervals in the first volume, which, until it was bound and its leaves were mounted at the Public Record Office a few years ago, was in a very bad state, all the leaves being loose, and some of them being much frayed.

I am responsible for the transcript of the first volume, and for comparing the proof sheets of the first and second volumes with the originals. I also compared the proof sheets of the third volume of the Registers with the transcript. The second and third volumes were transcribed by Miss PATTIE OSLER at the British Museum, where they were under the care of Mr. J. P. ANDERSON until they were copied; and the transcript of the third volume, which in parts is much faded, was compared with the original by Mr. W. PALEY BAILDON, who kindly volunteered his services.

The Index has been partly prepared by Mr. W. W. YATES and his daughter, Miss YATES, and has been completed by two of my daughters. It contains some peculiar names, and records many varieties in the spelling of the more common names. On the whole, however, the entries are not particularly interesting. We find frequent references to Lee Fair, and Care Sunday is often mentioned. Some Accounts of the Churchwardens appear on page 29. The Plague is mentioned on pages 50 and 51. Then we find Crosse Week, page 92; Plowe Day, page 100; Seane Day, page 106; Fastens Even, page 108; Exercise Day, page 117 and elsewhere; and there is frequent mention of Shire or Shear Thursday, Collop Monday, the New Park, &c. I commenced to prepare a General Index; but it appeared to be such a list of unimportant matters that I abandoned the idea.

S. J. CHADWICK.

DEWSBURY PARISH REGISTERS.

Notice to our Readers.

It is proposed to devote a leaf of the Magazine each month to the Old Registers of the Parish Church, and to other matters of local interest which it may be possible to print. As considerable expense will be incurred in carrying out this scheme, it is hoped that the members of the Parish Church Congregation and other friends who may be interested in local history will do their best to increase the sale of the Magazine, so as in some measure to meet the expense. Much interesting information can easily be printed if sufficient funds can be raised for the purpose. Among the most valuable records of the past are the Parish Registers, which date back to the year 1538, and which on the whole are in very good order. The first volume extends from 1538 to 1599, and owing to the leaves being loose for many years and having become very friable, they have crumbled away at the edges and some of the writing has perished. This volume was, however, in the year 1840, copied by Mr. H. J. Hemingway, Surgeon, Dewsbury, into a small 4to. volume, which is now kept in the vestry, and from which some words can now be made out which have disappeared in the original register. Implicit reliance cannot, however, be placed on the copy, as there are many errors in it, apparently owing to the difficulty which was experienced in reading the original. These errors will be corrected as far as possible in the copy printed in this Magazine. Mr. Hemingway tells us that he copied the first two pages of his transcript "from an old copy of the Registry, some fragments of which are now (1840), along with the original Registry, loose in old backs." A great part of the first two pages of the original has disappeared, and the remainder consists of an almost circular part of the centre of the leaf from which it has been possible to check and correct part of Mr. Hemingway's copy. This copy has the following note on the first page :—

Copy

of Book A (from 1538 to 1599) of the Registry of Marriages, Baptisms, and Burials within the Parish of Dewsbury, transcribed and given to the Parish Church of Dewsbury by Henry Johnson Hemingway, Surgeon, Dewsbury, A.D. 1840, et Anno Regni Reginæ Victoriæ Quarto. Revd. Thomas Allbutt, M.A., Cantab,

Vicar. Revd. William Milton, A.B., Oxon, Curate.

P.S.—This book has been gratuitously bound by Mr. Wilkinson, Stationer, Market Place, Dewsbury.

The original "Book A" was carefully re-bound at the Public Record Office in London 4 or 5 years ago, and every leaf was carefully mounted and protected, so that with ordinary care it will now last for many years.

The Register is as follows :—

The month of July.
Robert Longely had a child buried the first day named William.
Richard Nettleton buried his wife the xjth day named Genitt.
John Audesley was buried the xijt day of July.
Alis Baldon was buried the same daye.

The month of November Anno Di 15xxxviijt*
Imprimis Matthew Speight had a child christened the xxijiijt day of November named Alice.†
John Boltone and Elizabeth Mansfeld weare married the xxvjt day of November.
Nycolas Walker had a child christened the same day named iohana.
Edward Tomsone had a child christened the xxx day named Henry.†

The monithe of December.
Henyt Medley had a child christened the vijt day named Richard.
Wilforan Walker had a child christened the xx day named Sybell.
Stewine Tomsone had a child christened the xxixth day named Richard.

The monithe of Januarij.
Thomas Browne was buried the xvijt day of Januarij.
Robarte Longeley and Agnes‡ Gibsone was weddyd ye xix day
Agnes Turton widowe late wife Thomas Turton was buried the xxvijth daye of January.

The monithe of Februarij.
†† Willm Richardson and Margaret Kythley was weddyd ye fyrst day.
†† Richard Speight had a child christened the iiijt day named Elizabeth.
†† Willm Audesley had a child christened the iiijt day named Wilha.
§ Item. Edward Byerle had a child christened the xth day named Alexander.

---

* This date and all the preceding entries have disappeared from the original Register. They are taken from Mr. Hemingway's copy.

† The name and date are taken from Mr. H.'s copy.

‡ All the entries for December and January down to the word Agnes are taken from Mr. H.'s copy.

†† These men's names have disappeared from the original and are taken from Mr. H.'s copy.

§ The word "Item" occurs at the beginning of each entry, but is omitted afterwards for the sake of brevity.

Sir Henry Savell, Knyghtt, had a child christened ye xvith day named Edward.*
Wm. Wormall had a child christened ye xvijth day named Robert.
Elles Greyne had a child christened ye xxiij day named iohana.
John Boyy had a child christened ye xxvth day named iohana.
Elles Greyne had a child buried ye xxviijth day nay named iohana.

March.
Gilbert Wilkyngson had a child buried ye second day named esabell.
Thomas Matling (alias Flader) had a child christened ye vijth day named iohana.
Richard Aldersson had a child christened ye ten day named . . . . †
Thomas Stede had a child christened ye same xth day named . . . . †
Edward Byerle had a child buried ye xxth day named . . . . †
Richard Flader had a child buried ye same xxth day named . . . . †
John Greyne had a child christened the xxiiijth day named Alexander.

Aprile.
Robert Bawll had a child christened the fyrst day named William.
John Dyshfyrth had a child christened the xth day named yannet (Janet).
John Blakbourne had a child christened ye xith day named Esabell.
Gilbert Wilkyngson had a child christened ye xiijth day named Alexander.

Hereafter followth the names of eny (every) pson weddyde christened and buriede wthn the pish of Dewsbury maid syth (since) the xvth day of Aprile

---

* The Sir Henry Savell, or Savile, here mentioned was made a Knight of the Bath at the coronation of Queen Anne Boleyn, 30th May, 25th Henry VIII. He was High Sheriff of Yorkshire 29th and 33rd Henry VIII., and was Steward of the Honor of Pontefract and of the Manor of Wakefield. At the time of his death he was the owner of 30 manors in the county of York. By his marriage with Elizabeth, daughter and co-heiress of Thomas Soothill of Soothill, Esquire, he greatly increased his estate, the Manor of Soothill Upper being part of the property so acquired by him. Edward Savell, whose baptism is here recorded, was the eldest son of this marriage and his father's heir. He was of weak intellect, and died in the year 1604 without issue, having been twice married. Sir Henry Savile had an illegitimate son, Robert, who was the first of the Saviles of Howley Hall, a not very reputable family, who became extinct in 1671, when Howley and the accompanying estates passed to the Earls of Cardigan. Sir Henry Savile took an active part in the suppression of the Pilgrimage of Grace; and the Constable of Dewsbury and his fellow officials having attempted to assess the people of that place for the purpose of equipping two soldiers on behalf of the Commons or rebels, Sir Henry Savile, on All Hallows Day, 1536, caused the Constable and his assistants to be brought before him in Dewsbury Church, threatened them, and made them pay the money back under pain of being hanged as traitors.

† Name destroyed.

in the year of our lord god m⁰ iiiii xxxixth. Recordyde by the Wardeynes of the said church of Dewsbury that ys to say Richard Byrkbey Wyllm Richardson Thomas Methley Robt Janyn (alias Haywyerd) Richard Wormall and Thomas Gomersall. In yo xxxjt year of the Reign of or souaine (our sovereign) lord King Henry eight supreme head of the church of England.

Aprile.
Robert Lee of Gawthorrpe had a child buried the xxth day named Robert.
Alice Ramsden widdow (late wife of John Ramsden) was buried the xxiiijth day of Aple.

Maij.
Robert Wrightt and Johan Tomson was weddid the fourt day.
Richard Browne and Agnes Sykes was weddid ye same fourt day.
John Sekar had a child christened ye viiith day named Alexander.
John Nayler was buried the xjth day of Maij.
James Roberd had a child buried ye xiiijth day named Agnes.
Mathew Spight had a child buried ye xxiiijth day named Alic.
Edward Huchinson had a child christened ye same xxiiij day named Richard.
John Flader had a child christened ye same xxiiij day named Alexander.

June.
Robert Lee of Soothill had a child buried the xxvth day of Junij named John.
Agnes Bradford wyddow (late wiffe of Wm. Bradford) was buried ye xxvj day.

Julij.
John Greyn and Agnes Tailyor was weddid ye xxviit day.

August.
Wm. Rawson and Agnes Bright was weddid ye iij day.
Elizabeth Oxley (late wiff of Wm. Oxley) was buried ye xth day.
Robert Walkar was buried ye xxxjt day of August.

September.
John Methley had a child christened ye fyrst day named Agnes.
John Walkar had a child christened ye forth day named iohana.
John Awtie had a child buried ye viijt day named Anna.
Richard Dyshforth had a child christened ye ixt day named iohana.
Richard Dransfeld and Sille Boylle was weddyd ye xth day.
John Robynson (alias Townend) had a child christened ye xiijth day named iohana.
James Scolar had a child babtised named Thomas the . . . . yerste by the . . . .
Jenett Methley had a bastard child buried ye xxjt day named iohana, ann ye father of ye same child ys unknowne.

DEWSBURY PARISH REGISTERS.

[The entries in the January and February numbers of the Magazine were given in full, in order to show the form in which the Register was kept. But it would have involved a useless expenditure of time and money to print the whole of the volumes in this manner. Therefore the subsequent entries are summarised as much as possible, but the original spelling of surnames and place names will be retained, and anything worthy of notice will be printed *verbatim et literatim.*]

Alice Haldsworth widdow (late wiff of Robert Haldsworth) was buried ye xxixt day of Septembre.
John Acrod had a child christened ye same xxixth day named isabell.

October.
Willam Gybson had a child christened ye fyrste day named Alexander.
John Ramsden had a child christened the vjth day named Alexander.
Richard Lee had a child christened ye same vjth day named Agnes.
Richard Wode and Johana Tailyer was weddyd ye xijth day.

Nov. 3—Alice Carlynghow (late wife of John C.) was buried.
,, 8—William Dykanson and Alice Hall were married.
,, 9—Wm. Tyas had a child christened named esabell.
,, 11—John Hepworth and Alic (*i.e.*, Alice) Wytley were married.
,, 15—John Alen had a child christened named iohana.
,, 25—yames (James) Robynson and Agnes Wode were married.
,, 26—Thomas Barbar had a child buried named iohana.
,, 29—Nycolas Sekar had a child christened named Anna.
,, 29—Wm. Tyas had a child buried named esabell.
,, 30—Richard Tomson had a child christendd named elizabeth.

Dec. 7—Nycolas Walkar had a child christened named edward.
,, 8—Thomas Hall had a child christened named William.
,, 8—Thomas Barber had a child buried named John.
,, 8—Gilbert Wode had a child christened named Elizabeth.
,, 15—John Bradford* had ij children christened, the one named Margaret and the other Esabell.

---
* The name of Bradford occurs frequently in the early Registers of Dewsbury. The family were the owners of Horth Hall, near Wakefield, and afterwards (about the middle of the 16th Century) went to reside at Stanley, near

Dec. 25—John Aylen† had a child buried named Elizabeth.
Dec. 25—Wm. Dykanson had a child christened named William.
,, 26—Mathew Spight had a child christened named Elizabeth.

1540.
Jan. 4—Thomas Syko was buried.
,, 4—Richard Dyshforth had a child buried named Johana.
,, 5—Robert yanyn (alias Haywyerd) had a child christened named Anna.

Wakefield. The members of the family whose names appear in the Dewsbury Registers resided at Ossett. See *Testamenta Eboracensia* (Surtees Society), vol. iv. p. 108, and vol. v. p. 283, for further information. John Bradforth, of Ossett, made his will 20th June, 1506, and directed that he should be buried in the Church of Allhallows of Dewsbury. He bequeathed 1s. 3d. "to the makyng of a pixe (the box in which the host was kept)te ye hye awter of Dewisbory," and he mentions John Bradford the elder, and Thomas his son, John Bradford the younger, and William his brother. The three latter are probably identical with the persons of the same names who are mentioned so frequently in the Dewsbury Registers.

† The Allens were a numerous family residing at Ossett, Horbury, and Dewsbury. The name is spelt in many ways in the Register. The John Aylen here mentioned was probably the son of John Alayn of Ossett, an abstract of whose will, dated 13th May, 1509, is printed in the 5th vol. of the Test. Ebor., p. 2. This will is very interesting, not only for its quaint wording and spelling, but also for the bequests contained therein and the directions given by the testator. The following is an abstract:—"My soule to God Almightie, our Lady Sent Mary, and all ye fair felliship of hevyn. My best gud to be my mortuary. It is my wyll that my wyff be content with her feffment and her third parte of all my boght landes. It is my wyll that John my son abyde styll upon my fader's bowis with my fader ; and it is my wyll that William my broder be ther husband (*i.e.*, husbandman) and that thei do wit to him for his labor. It is my wyll that my fader and John my son give to Alison my doghter xxli nowbuls (*i.e.*, nobles, coins worth 6s. 8d. each) unto her marriage, and that she be with my suster Alyson, for she will teche her sunne gude. It is my wyll yt Robert my broder have at harvest half a quarter rye, also it is my will yt Elizebeth my sister be well seen to amanges youe. Also, fader, if ye have any troubull (trouble) for my boght land go to M. Sotteli (Mr. Southill) and pray hym to be gud m. (good man) to my son and youe, and let hym have ye ferme of Hammond ilj yere. And, father, if my wif be with an other childe, ye must melide her sumwhate (make some further provision for her). And all other thynges I leve with God and youe, as my triste is in youe. The residue of all my gudes shall be at ye disposicion of John my son, father, by your oversyght ; and John my son shall be mym executor : and for Gode's sake, rule all wisely as I have done, and ye shall have much menske (honour or credit) thereof." The date of probate of this will is not given. There is in the York Registry another will of John Alan of Ossett also dated 13th May, 1509, and which was proved on the 21st July following. It is possible that it may be the will of the father of the above-named testator. The will is as follows:—

In the name of God, Amen. The xiijth day of May, ye yere of or Lord mvcix. I John Alan of Ossett of ye pishe of Dewslbury holle of mynd make my testament in yis wyse first I gif my saul to almyghtic Gode our lady Seynt Mary and all the son' felishlip of hevyn and my body to be buried in ye church garth of Dewesbury and my best ox to be my mortuary. Also I gyfh to Alyson my doghter x mare' to her maryage also to Willm Alan my broder a met of whete (a bushel of wheat). Ye residue of all my gudes my dettes payd I giff to Elizabeth my wif whom I mak myn executrix to dispus for ye helth of my saule. thes witnesseth John townend John Alan and other.

Jan. 18—Wm. Wode and Elizabeth Wormall were married.
„ 25—Agnes Sharp, widow of Wm. Sharp, was buried.
„ 25—Richard Dransfeld had a child christened named William.
„ 30—Wm. Richardson had a child christened named William.
„ 31—Edward Greyn had a child christened named Thomas.
Feb. 4—Johana Tomson (late wife of Ric. Tomson) was buried.
„ 5—Robert Longley had a child christened named Richard.
„ 10—Richard Wade had a child christened named Nycolas.
„ 11—Agnes Taylyer (late wife of Wm. Tailyer) was buried.
„ 12—John Awdsley had a child christened named Esabell.
„ 15—Johana Baildon, widow (late wife of John Baildon) was buried.
„ 17—Wm. Gauntt had a child christened named Alexander.
„ 20—Elles Greyn had a child christened named Margaret.
March 4—Margaret Bruke was buried.
„ 10—Johana Byrkenshey (late wife of John Byrksnshey) was buried.
„ 10—Alie Forest (late wife of John Forest Elder) was buried.
„ 20—Wm. Smeth had a child christened named William.
„ 21—Richard Wamsley had a child christened named Alexander.
„ 22—John Bradford had a child buried named Esabell.
„ 27—Robert Lee of Dewisbury had a child christened named Elizabeth.
„ 31—Margaret Roids was buried.
April 1—Richard Byrkbey had a child christened named Elizabeth.
„ 3—Robert Wrightt had a child christened named Robt.
„ 3—John Sykes had a child christened named Johana.
„ 5—Agnes Hesshall, widow (late wife of Ric. Hesshall) was buried.
„ 6—Robert Lee of Gawthorpp had a child christened named Johana.

Hereafter followeth the names of euy (every) psone weddyd, christened, and buried within the pish (parish) of Dewisbury made synnyss April vijt in the year of our Lord God in iiiij xlt Recordyd by the Wardynes of the said church of Dowisbury thatt ys to say Richard Byrkbey Willm Richardson Thomas Methley Robert yanyn (alias Haywyerd) Richard Wornall and Thomas Gomersall. In the xxxij' year of the reigne of o' sonaine (sovereign) lord King Henry the eigth supreme head of the church of England.

April 11—yames Robert had a child christened named yames.
„ 11—Robert Sharpons and Esabell Bruk were wedded.
„ 13—John Sykes had a child buried named Johana.
„ 15—Robert Wytakers* had a child christened named Johes (John).
„ 25—William Longley and Elizabeth Lee were wedded.
„ 29—Richard Hanson had a child christened named Richard.
May 2—Thomas Richardson and Agnes Greyn were wedded.
„ 6—Robert Spightt had a child christened named Nycolas.
„ 9—William Kyttson was buried.
„ 9—Brian Tomson was buried.
„ 10—Elizabeth Nayler, widow (late wife of John Nayler) was buried.
„ 24—Richard Flader had a child buried named Robert.
„ 25—Roger Dawsson had a child christened named Johana.
„ 30—Gilbert Olred and Agnes Browne were married.
June 3—Laurence Baildon was buried.
„ 9—Margaret Bruke (late wife of Wm. Bruke) was buried.
„ 12—John Bruke had a child buried named Johana.
„ 15—John Nowell younger had a child christened named Esabell.
„ 16—John Awtie had a child christened named Johes (John).
„ 19—Wm. Wytaker had a child christened named Robert.
„ 20—Robt. Goodfelow (alias Brught) and yayne Hall were wedded.
„ 26—Ric. Dykanson had a child christened named Johes (John).
„ 27—Edward Tomson had a child christened named Alice.

*This is the first of a long series of Whitaker entries. The family has been seated at Ossett for something like 400 years, the last of the name resident at that place being the late Joshua Whitaker, Esq., J.P. His nephew, John Arthur Whitaker, Esq., resides at West Grinstead Park, Horsham, Sussex, and another nephew, Joshua Whitaker, Esq., resides at Palermo. Another member of the family is Benjn. Ingham Whitaker, Esq., of Hesley Hall, Tickhill. Mrs. Carr, the wife of Wm. Carr, Esq., of Gomersal House, J.P., and her sister, Mrs. M. S. Scholefield, were nieces of the above-named Mr. Joshua Whitaker, J.P. Another branch of the family is settled in America, and a member of It alleges that the original stock was settled in Warwickshire so far back as the year 1100. Another member of the family was Dr. Wm. Whitaker, an eminent Calvinistic divine and controversial writer in Queen Elizabeth's reign. He was Professor of Divinity at Cambridge and Chancellor of St. Paul's Cathedral, and subsequently Master of St. John's College, Cambridge. Other connections of the Whitakers are the Brookes of Honley (the Ven. Archdeacon Brooke's family), the Sykes family of Dunningley and Soothill, and the Woodens of Rouse Mill. The present Lord Crewe also is connected with the family through an ancestress.

DEWSBURY PARISH REGISTER.
(Continued.)

Edited by S. J. Chadwick, F.S.A.

1540.
- July 2—Robert Adamson had a child christened named Alexander.
- „ 2—Jenet Methley had a child christened named Henry, being a bastard child and the father of hit unknown.
- „ 4—Esabell Dey, widow (late wife of John Dey), was buried.
- „ 16—Thomas Pekar had a child christened named Robert.
- „ 19—Wm. Oxley had a child buried named Johes.
- „ 25—Robt. Spightt had a child buried named Oswold.
- „ 25—yames Blakburne and Elizabeth Wode were wedded.
- Aug. 3—An Oxley (wife of Wm. Oxley) was buried.
- „ 13—John Forest had a child christened named Richard.
- „ 16—John Boyll younger had a child christened named Lawrance.
- „ 22—Thomas Barbar had 2 children christened, the one named Agnes and the other named Iohana.
- Sept. 6—Johana Dishforth (late daughter of Rauffe Dishforth) had a child christened, being bastard begotten, and named Ric.
- „ 9—Agnes Robynson, widow (late wife of Wm. Robynson), was buried.
- „ 13—Johana Dishforth aforesaid had a child buried named Richard.
- „ 16—Robt. Lee (of Sotehill Comon) had a child christened named Johenes.
- Oct. 2—Stewyn Tomson had a child christened named Elizabeth.
- „ 3—Ric. Kytson & Esabell Rosell were wedded.
- „ 3—Robt. Byngley and Elizabeth Richardson were wedded.
- „ 7—John Walkar had a child christened named Johana.
- „ 10—Katheryn Tyas (wife of Thomas Tyas) was buried.
- „ 10—John Peas and Elizabeth Dishforth were wedded.
- „ 19—Ric. Browne had a child buried named Elizabeth.
- „ 20—Wm. Tyas had a child buried named Agnes.
- „ 22—Sir John Gillott,* Pst (priest) was buried.

* Probably Curate of Dewsbury. The Vicar of Dewsbury was accustomed to keep a curate, as we find from the certificate given in the 1st or 2nd year of King Edward VI. of the value of the suppressed "Chantry of our Lady" in the Parish Church; where it is stated that "the vicar fyndeth one preist to serve the Cure besyde hymself. The number of houslyng people (communicants) is viij^c (800) and the pysh (parish) ys wyde." It is proposed to print these Chantry Certificates in subsequent numbers of the Magazine. Possibly the curate had charge of the chapel of ease at Ossett.

1540.
- Oct. 23—John Townend (alias Robynson) had a child christened named Johes (John).
- Nov. 19—Ric. Dyshforth had a child christened named Mgaret.
- „ 22—Mgaret Hill was buried.
- „ 20—Johana Bruke, widow (late wife of Robt. Bruk), was buried.
- „ 30—yames Robard had a daughter buried named Anna.
- Dec. 19—Robt. Goodfelow (alias Browghtt) had a child christened named Johana.
- „ 24—Mathew Spight had a child christened named Robt.
- „ 24—Thomas Musgrav had a child christened named Anna.
- „ 31—Richard Spightt had a child christened named Sible.
- „ 31—Robert Bawll had a child christened named Agnes.
- „ 31—yayne Scot wife of John Scot was buried.
- Jan. 1—Christofer Nayler was buried.
- „ 8—Alice Robynson (wife of old John Robyson) was buried.
- „ 13—Robt. Lee (of Sotchill Comon) had a child buried named Johes.
- „ 22—Old Katheryn Dishforth was buried.
- „ 23—Old Elizabeth Hagh was buried.
- „ 28—Johana Sykes, widow (late wife of Thomas Sykes), was buried.
- „ 28—Thomas Nowell had a child christened named Esabell.
- „ 29—Wm. Gybson had a child christened named Thomas.
- „ 30—John Aylane had a child christened named Helyn.
- Feb. 1—Nycolas Wyttlay and Alic Aldsworth were wedded.
- „ 2—Ric. Aldersson had a child christened named Thomas.
- „ 6—John Romer and Alice Bayldon were wedded.
- „ 7—Ric. Hyrst and Elizabeth Dykanson were wedded.
- „ 8—Thomas Hall had a child christened named yannett.
- „ 12—Charles Bayldon had a child christened named Agnes.
- „ 26—Juliana Starbrowghtt had a child christened named William (base begotten).
- March 2—Wyllum Kyttson of Ossett was buried.
- „ 6—Gylbert Wylkyngson had a child christened named Alice.
- „ 20—Edward Wrightt was buried.
- „ 20—Alice Hall (wife of John Hall) was buried.
- „ 20—Richard Dransfold had a child christened named Elizabeth.

George Mawde, curate, was one of the witnesses to the will of Richard Bradford, of Ossett, dated 24th September, 1539, and "the chapell" is mentioned in the will of Robert Bradforthe, of Ossett, dated 30th May, 1542. Our readers no doubt know that "Sir," Latin "Dominus," was the customary title of a priest at this period, and they will recollect Sir Hugh Evans, the Welsh parson in the "Merry Wives of Windsor."

1540.
March 25—John Greyn had a child christened named Thomas.
  „ 26—Nycolas Wyttlay had a child christened named Agnes.
April 1—Anna Wryghtt late wife of Edward Wryghtt was buried.
  „ 11—John Robynson of New parke had a child christened named Agnes.
  „ 16—the said John Robynson buried the said child named Agnes.

> Hereafter folowith ye nam of euy pson beyng weddyd christened and buried wthn ye Pysh of Dewisbury from ye xxvijt day of Aprile in ye year of oor lord god m iiiii xli Reordyd by the Wardeynes of the said church of Dewisbury than beyng, that ys to say, Richard Hall Richard Wod Thomas Methley Robt. yanyn (alias Hayvyerd) John Aylen and Richard Wormall, in the xxxiijt year of the reigne of oor souaine lord King Henry the Eight suprem head of ye Church of England.

April 29—Henry Robynson had two children christened, a son named Thomas and a daughter named iohana.
  „ 29—John Ellyson had a child christened named Ric.
May 2—Robert yanyn (alias Hayvyerd) had a child christened named iohana.*
  „ 8—Thomas Bradford had a child christened Dorithe.
  „ 9—John Bayldon and Jenet Wormall were wedded.
  „ 9—John Forest (elder) was buried.
  „ 19—Ric. Kyttson had a child christened named Edward.
  „ 26—Robert Wryghtt had a child christened named Esabell.
June 4—John Acrod had a child christened named Johanna.
  „ 11—John Methley had a child christened named William.
  „ 24—Nycolas Tempes, Esquyer,† had a child christened named yayn.
July 3—Herre Robynson had a child buried named Johanna.
  „ 7—Gilbert Olred had a child christened named Agnes.
  „ 15—John Baildon (younger) had a child christened named Elizabeth.
  „ 19—William Oxley and yayn Druke were wedded.
  „ 19—Richard Hyrst had a child christened named Thomas.
  „ 20—Richard Kyttson had a child buried named Jolies.

* Many of the names, both christian and surnames, commence with a small letter in place of a capital. Henceforward they will be printed with capitals except in special cases.

† Third son of Sir Richard Tempest of Bracewell and Bolling (Bowling, near Bradford) by his wife, Rosamund Bolling. He was born about 1502, and was married before 20th June, 1516 to Beatrice, daughter of John Bradford

1541.
July 25—John Sykes had a child christened named Richard.
  „ 31—William Taylyar had a child christened named William.
Aug. 7—Christofer Scott and Johan Stawnay were wedded.
  „ 17—Richard Fayrbarne was buried.
  „ 18—William Whythed was buried.
  „ 20—John Raner had a child christened named Margaret.
  „ 28—Yames Wod and Johan Dishforth were wedded
  „ 30—Thomas Sted had a child christened named Anna.
Sept. 3—Wm. Williamson had a child christened named Johana.
  „ 9—Hugh Monssell was buried.
  „ 9—Gilbert Wod had a child christened named Richard.
  „ 22—Richard Dransfeld had a child buried named Elizabeth.
  „ 24—Edward Byerlo had a child christened named Margaret.

of Hetho (Heath, near Wakefield), a note of whose will is given in the Test. Ebor. iv. 169. His father, Sir Richard T., left to him by will the leases which he (th[e] father) held in Wakefield and the premises brought from the abovenamed John Bradford. An undated bill of complaint before the Star Chamber was brought by Nicholas Tempest as King's farmer of all the toll of the town of Wakefield and lordship (under a demise made o Henry VIII. to Sir Richard, his father, at a rent of £99 0 7½), who said that Thomas Savell of Clyfton, in the lordship of W[a]kefield, had about 31st March last past drowned himse[l]f, and Nicholas Tempest claimed £30 of his goods unjustly removed. He (Nicholas) served on the grand jury at Doncaster, 24th November, 1541, who found a true bill against Queen Catherine Howard, Lady Rochford, Francis Dereham, and Thomas Culpeper, when an indictment was prepared against them before the King's Justices for acts of criminality alleged to have taken place at Pontefract Castle. He was bailiff of Wakefield in 1543-4, and still bailiff in 1549, and in the latter year he paid 20s. to the lay subsidy for £20 worth of goods in the Ossett Division. His first wife, Mrs. Beatrice (or "Betterys") Tempest, was buried at Dewsbury 8 December 1550. In 1551 he had married again, as in that year he (described as of Wakefield) and Isabel his wife, late wife of Hen. Kyghley, of Inskipp, in Lancashire, Esq., deceased, sued Henry the son for certain goods at Inskipp Hall. On the 20th June, 1562, he and his son Robert sold certain lands in Tong to Henry Batt (the first of that name at Oakwell Hall, the former owner having been Charles Brandon, Duke of Suffolk). On the 7th September, 1554, he was a party to the marriage articles of Richard, his son and heir, with Eleanor, daughter of Lord Scrope of Bolton. Both his elder brothers having died without issue, he succeeded to the estates of Bracewell and Bolling and other family estates, which at his death, about 24th December, 1579, devolved on his above-mentioned son Richard. Genealogists have sometimes confused him with his uncle Nicholas Tempest, who on the 25th May, 1537, in company with Sir John Bulmer, Sir Stephen Hamerton, and the abbot of Jervaux and others, was hanged, drawn, and quartered for participating in the Pilgrimage of Grace. Nicholas the nephew seems, however, to have been more discreet or more fortunate than his uncle, and to have died in his bed, which was rather uncommon in the time of the Tudors. For a great part of the information contained in this note the writer is indebted to an obliging communication from Mrs. Arthur Tempest, of Coleby Hall, Lincoln, and to a paper by that lady on Nicholas Tempest published in the Yorkshire Archaeol. Journal, Vol. XI.

DEWSBURY PARISH REGISTERS.

1541.
Sept. 24—John Flader had a child christened named Richard.
,, 25—Richard Tomson yongr was buried.
,, 28—John Cartter (fole* to Sʳ Yames Whaytt quondam of Pomfrett) was buried.
Oct. 11—Elizabeth Hyrst was buried
,, 16—Edward Greyn and Johan Hall were wedded.
,, 16—Edmund Hey and Margaret Browne were wedded.
,, 25—John Acrod had a child buried named Johana.
Nov. 2—Agnes Methley (wife of Thomas Methley) was buried.
,, 2—Thomas Greyn had a child christened named Thomas.
,, 3—John Dawsson had a child christened named William.
,, 4—Bryan Bradford Gentilman begat a child with Alic yanyn which was christened Thomas, being base begotten.
,, 14—Richard Fallay and Issabell Gryffyn were wedded.
,, 19—Alic Nowell, widow (late wife of Robt. Nowell), was buried.
,, 20—Wm. Tayiyer and Sibill Hall were wedded.
,, 21—John Hall and Agnes Brok were wedded.
,, 24—Bryan Horton had a child christened named Johes.
,, 25—John Sekar had a child christened named Richard.
,, 26—Roger Thournes and Alic Hearhold were wedded.
,, 27—Bryan Bradford, Gentilman, had a child buried named Thomas, being a bastard and begotten of Alic yanyn.
Dec. 2—Richard Browne had a child buried named Johes.
,, 29—John Dyshforth had a child christened named Elizabeth.
Jan. 15—Thomas Ramsden and Elizabeth Methley were wedded.
,, 19—Robt. Longley had a child christened named Baterisse.
,, 20—Wm. Wytakerr had a child christened named Elizabeth.
,, 31—Edward Huchodson had a child christened named Nycolas.
Feb. 4—Thomas Synson and Margaret Tomson were wedded.
,, 6—Bennett Methley had a child christened named Robert.
,, 26—Lawrance Walton was buried.
,, 27—Wm. Peas had a child christened named Dorythe.
March 8—John Bradford yongr had a child christened named Edward.
,, 10—John Tyas had a child christened named Thomas.
,, 21—Nycolas Walkar had a child christened named Elizabeth.
,, 22—Wm. Awdslay had a child christened named Richard.

1541.
March 25—John Bradford yongr had a child buried named Edward.
,, 26—Edward Tomson had a child christened named Edward.
,, 28—John Peas of Sowd (qy., Sowood) was buried.
,, 29—John Carlynghow was buried.
,, 30—Wm. Brnk had a child christened named Johana.
April 2—Nycolas Sekar had a child christened named Dorythe.
,, 3—John Bruk had a child christened named Johana.
,, 8—Wm. Richardson had a child christened named Agnes.
,, 9—Yames Wodo had a child christened named Alic.
,, 17—Edward Greyne had a child christened named Edward.
,, 19—John Peas had a child christened named Richard.

Hereafter folowith the name of euy psone beyng weddid christened and buried wᵗʰⁿ the pysch of Dewisbury from the xviij day of Aprile in the year of oor lord god in iiiii xlii and in the xxxiiij year of the Reigne of oor sonaine lord Kyng Henry the eight supreme head of the church of ynglland and yreland next under Christ Recordyd by us sex psons Ric. Hall Ric. Wod Robt. Wylkyngson John Brok Thoas. Sted and John Townend alias Robynson being the churchwardens.

April 22—William Byorle had a child christened named Johana.
,, 22—Bennet Methley begat a child with Alic Boyth, being christened the same 22nd day, bastard begotten and named Dorythe.
,, 23—John Browne was buried.
May 1—yong yames Browne, late the son of Thoas. Brown, deceased, was buried.
,, 3—Edward Tomson had a child buried named Edward.
,, 4—Elles Greyn had a child christened named Agnes.
,, 7—Steywyn Tomson had a child christened named Issabell.
,, 10—Jenet Tomson, widow (late wife of Ric. Tomson, deceased), had a child christened named Agnes.
,, 21—Mathew Spight had a child christened named Issabell.*
,, 23—Issabell Hellywell had a child christened named Johana, being bastard begotten, and as it is said Richard Ellys of Wakfeld is the said child father.
June 9—John Walkar had a child christened named Richard.
,, 12—Richard Dransfeld had a child christened named Roger.

---

* i.e. fool.

*This entry seems to have been interlined.

1542.
June 26—John Byrk and Katheryn Hanson were wedded.
July 2—John Hynchclyff and Elizabeth Kyttson were wedded.
  ,, 25—Margaret Dyshforth, widow (late wife of Wm. Dyshforth), was buried.
       Nihil*
Aug. 19—Thomas Ramsden had a child christened named Johana, and the said child was buried also the said 19th day.
  ,, 26—William Richardson had a child buried named Agnes.
  ,, 30—Wm. Taylyar of Batley Car had a child christened named Richard.†
Sept. 4—Richard Browne had a child christened named Johes, and the same child was buried upon the said 4th day.
  ,, 19—Nycolas Wyttley had a child buried named (Margaret which he had to nourish of on Psyvall Sayvell, deceased).‡
Oct. 1—Wm. Barker and Elizabeth Hall were wedded.
  ,,   6—Wylliam Gauntt had two children (? christened), the one of them named Isabell; and the other named Margaret.
  ,,   7—Old John Robynson Smeth was buried.
  ,,   8—John Awdslay had a child christened named yames.
  ,, 13—Robt. Aylen (being a bastard sonne of Thomas Tattarsall) was buried.
  ,, 17—Thomas Netleton had a child christened named Wyllam.
Nov. 5—Agnes Bradford, wyddow (late wife of Thos. B.), was buried ye fywth day.
  ,, 21—Thomas Clathon and Elizabeth Dawson were wedded.
  ,, 24—John Townend otherwise called Robynson had a child christened named Richard.
  ,, 24—Margaret Greyn, wyddow (late wife of John G.), was buried.
  ,, 27—Wm Dykanson had a child christened named Alice.§
  ,, 28—Hamar Fox and Issabell Broke were wedded.
  ,, 29—John Townend (alias Robynson) had a child buried named Richard.
  ,, 29—Roger Swallow had a child christened named Roger.
Dec. 14—Wyllam Smith had a child christened named Elizabeth.
  ,, 19—Margaret Barkar, wyddow (late wife of Wyllam Barkar, deceased), was buried.
  ,, 20—Thomas Synson had a child christened named yayn.

1542.
Dec. 22—Thomas Sykes had a child christened named Thomas.
  ,, 30—Anna Wythed, wyddow (late wife of William Wythed, deceased), was buried.
Jan. 2—Elizabeth Bradford, wife of old John Bradford, was buried.
  ,,   8—Robert* Goodfelow (alias Drowght) had a child christened named Roger.
  ,, 11—Robart Wytayker had a child christened named Auna.
  ,, 13—Robert Bawll had a child christened named Nycolas.
  ,, 13—Robert Wryghtt had a child christened named Agnes.
  ,, 16—Adam Tynglo and Alic Fayrbarn were wedded.
  ,, 17—William Gaunt had a child buried named Margaret.
  ,, 20—Robert Robynson and Agnes Olred were wedded.
  ,, 20—Richard Wode had a child christened named Alexander.
  ,, 28—John Mylnes had a child christened named Robert.
Feb. 2—Robt. Lee of Dewisbury had a child christened named Alic.
  ,, 10—Roger Dawson had a child christened named Robert.
  ,, 13—Richard Hyrst had a child christened named Robert.
  ,, 26—John Bayldon had a child christened named Agnes.
March 4—William Barbar had a child christened named Roger.
  ,, 15—Richard Spight had a child christened named Marmaduke.
  ,, 23—Thomas Clayton had a child christened named Roger.
    Hereafter foloyth the name of euy pson beyng wedded christened & buried wᵗⁱⁿ the parysh of Dewisbury in the countie of York from the fywth day of Aprile in the xxxiiij ᵗ yer of the reigne of oor souerayng lord Henry the eightt by the grace of God Kyng of England Fraunce & Ireland defender of the faith & in earth of the church of England & Ireland supreme head & in ye year of oor lord God m ͥ iiiiͨ xliij ᵗ Recordyd by us sex psones yt ys to say Wm. Spyghtt Robt. Whytaker John Awdsley laurence Gyll Richard lee & Robt. Bawll then beyng the church wardens of Dewysbury.

1543.
April 5—Alic Olred had a child christened named Margaret (beyng a bastard).
  ,, 10—Bennett Metlilay had a child christened named . . . . †

---

* So in original. The above two entries for July appear to have been originally entered as for June, and the word July has been interlined immediately above them.

† This entry has evidently been added after the next entry has been made.

‡ The words within brackets are in a different handwriting from the first part of the entry. The Persyvall Sayvell here mentioned may possibly have been a younger son of Thos. Savile of Luplet. See Foster's *Yorkshire Pedigrees*.

§ This entry has been interlined.

* Mr. Hemingway gives this word as "Ric." in his copy, but the correct reading is "Robt.," I think. The date of this christening is partly rubbed away in the original and now stands as "iij." It is possible the date may have been originally "viij."

† It is impossible to make out this name, which has been interlined and blotted. Mr. Hemingway reads it "Gesea."

1543.
April 12—Thomas Nayler had a child christened named Anna.
" 15—John Fayrbarn and Dorithe Nayler were wedded.
" 17—Richard Bawll had a child christened named Robert.
" 22—William Boith and Issabell Goodayll were wedded.
" 23—Nycolas Whytlay had a child christened named Thomas.
" 29—Bateress Lee (wife of Ric. Lee) was buried.
" 30—Thomas Sted had a child christened named yaym.
May 1—John Methley had a child christened named Elizabeth.
" 3—John Acrode had a child christened named Geffray.
" 19—William Richardson had a child christened named Alic.
" 20—Edward Thomson had a child christened named Agnes.
" 27—Johan Olred and Elizabeth Wylkyngson were wedded.
" 28—John Saxton had a child christened named Johana, and the child was buried the same day.
June 1—Hamer Fox had a child christened named Agnes.
" 3—Wilfryd Walkar and Johana Boyth were wedded.
" 7—Alic Hyrst, widow (late wife of Wm. Hyrst) was buried.
" 21—Wm. Wormall had a child christened named Elizabeth.
" 24—Gilbert Olred had a child christened named Dorythe.
" 27—William Taylyar had a child christened named Nycolas.
July 1—Robert Smith and Elizabeth Bradford were wedded.
Aug. 9—Robert yanyn (alias Havyerd) had a child christened named Mary.
" 16—Ric, Brown had a child christened named Agnes.
" 23—Yong John Bradford had a child christened named Elizabeth.
" 24—William Tyas had a child christened named Margaret.
Sept. 6—Yong John Bolle had a child christened named Robert.
Sept. 27—Ric, Dishford had a child christened named Agnes.
Oct. 5—Nycolas Clark had a child christened named yaym.
" 5—John Wod had a child christened named John.
" 8—John Lee had a child christened named George.
" 12—Robert Lee of Gawthorpp had a child christened named Agnes.
" 13†—John Townend (alias Robynson) had a child christened named Christopher.

† This is the date given in Mr. Hemingway's copy, and is probably correct. In the original Register the "x" has

1543.
Oct. 14‡—Edward Ramsden and Elizabeth Jagger were wedded.
" 25—William Broke had a child christened named Johanna.
Novembre Auo Dni. m. D, xliij⁰
Nov. 4—William Robynson had a child christened named Robert.
" 4—Richard Hall and Elizabeth Broyke were married.
" 22—William Tyas had a child buried named Margaret.
" 28—Thomas Bradforth had a child christened named Annes.
" 25—A poore woman and a straunger was buried the xxvt day named Jenet Hawley.
" 26—John Bradforth and Elizabeth Byarell were married.
Dec. 3—Christofer Nayler had a child christened named rychard.
" 8—William Robynson had a child buried named Johana.
" 9—John Peas wyff was buried, named Agnes.
" 14—William Gybson had a child christened named Elizabeth.
" 23—Thomas Hyrst had a child christened named James.
" 26—relicta Dransfeld had a child christened named rychard.
" 30—John Townend (alias Robynson) had a child buried named Christofer.
" 30—William Tailyer of Gawthorp had a child christened named Jenett.
Jan. 6—Richard Flayther had a child christened named Richard.
" 8—Margarie Haull had a child christened named Elizabeth, a basterd.
" 21—John Fairbarn had a child christened named John.
" 23—Robert Robynson had a child christened named Robert.
" 23—John Forest had a child christened named Isabell.
" 25—Richard Dyshforth had a child buried named Agnes.
" 26—Margariti Wryght, widow, was buried.
Feb. 4—Thomas Nowwell of the streite§ had a child christened named Thomas.
" 5—Dawson wyff widow was buryed.
" 6—Robert Smyth of Dewisbury had a child christened.
" 13—Thomas Granison was buried.
" 13—Richard Anderson had a child buried named John.
" 17—George Stuythley was buried.

disappeared, the paper having been worn away, and only "iljth" can now be seen.
‡This is the date given in Mr. Hemingway's copy. The original Register reads "xiii," the final "jth" having probably disappeared with the paper which has been worn away.
§ Probably Ossett Street Side.

1543.
Feb. 17—Mathew Speight had a child christened named Nycolesse.
" 19—William Whyteacres had a child christened named Dorythe.
" 21—Gylbert Wood of Ossyt had a child christened named Alice.
" 26—William Fox was buried.
Ano Dm. mo Do xliiijo.
March 1—Henry Robynson had a child christened named Esabell.
" 2—James Wood had a child christened named Richard.
" 3—Gylbert Wylkynson of Osset had a child christened named Thomas.
" 4—Wylm Whytacres had a child buried named Dorethe.
" 4—John Olerede had a child christened named John.
" 17—Thomas Hall had a child christened named Nycoles.
" 18—Richard Sagar was buried.
" 18—Wilm Boyth had a child christened named Anne.
" 30—Wilfryde Walkar had a child christened named John.
April 1—John Greyn had a child christened named Robart.
" 7—John Awtie had a child christened named Elizabeth.
" 10—Wilm Peace had a child christened named Jane.
" 12—Robert Longley had a child christened named Elizabeth.
" 12—Wylyn Failyo of ye care (? Carr) had a child christened named John.
" 14—Robert Carter was buried.
" 15—John Saxton had a child buried named John.
" 23—John Alane had a child christened named George.
" 27—Thomas Gaunt had a child christened named Annes.
May 8—Nycolas Walkar had a child christened named John.
" 15—Roger Hutchynson was buried.
" 24—Robert Sharpulls had a child christened named Dorithe.
June 10—William Nowell was buried.
" 12—Nycoles Whitley was buried.
" 15—Robert Wryght of Gawthorp had a child buried named Isabell.
" 26—William Denton was buried.
July 3—Steuen† Tomson had a child christened named Sybell.
" 8—John Greyn of Osset had a child chrisnamed Robert.
" 6—Robert Byrtton and Mgt Medley were married.
Aug. 10—Thomas Nailer and Elisabeth Hall were married.
" 13—Annes Awtie (wife of John Awtie) was buried.

1544.
Aug. 18—Edward Greyne had a child christened named Chris. ‡
" 25—Thomas Gryffyn had a child christened named Thomas.
" 26—George Tootehill had a child christened named Thomas.
" 26—William Barber had a child christened named Annes.
The wyfe of Rychard Drancefeld had a child buried the (no date given).
Sept. 14—The wylf of Rychard Drancefeld had a child buried.
" 14—Edward Byarle had a child buried.
" 17—Richard Hall yongr. had a child buried.
" 21—William Scolfelde and Annes Hutchynson were married.
" 24—John § Greyn wylfe of Osset was buried.
Oct. 18—William Methley of Osset was buried.
" 19—William Whitley and Sybill Drancefeld were married.
Nov. 4—William Broike of Osset had a child christened named William.
" 6—John Baldon was buried.
Dec. 14—John Kent yongr. had a child christened named Agnes.
" 16—George Rychardson was buried.
" 19—John Kent younger had a child buried.
" 27—Edward Hutchynson had a child christened named Annes.
" 28—Robert Wryght was buried.
" 29—George Toithyll had a child buried.
January Ano. dm. 1545.
Jan. 16—Thomas Wylson was buried.
" 26—Thomas Scade had a child christened named Ely. ‖
" 25—Robert Crosbe and Jenet Speight were married.
" 27—James Walkar and Alyson Whitley were married.
Ano. Dm. mo Do xlvo.
Feb. 1—Robert Janyn had a child christened named Rosamunde.
" 7—Robert Lee of Dewsbury had a child christened named Roger.
March 6—Elis Grene of Hetton had a child christened named William.
" 6—John Bruk of Hetton had a child christened named Margaret.
" 22—Jenet Smyth of Dewsbury had a child christened named Thomas.
" 22—Robert Boult had a child christened named Thomas.
" 25—Robert Janyn had a child christened named Roysamond.
" 29—John Dishforth had a child christened named William.

‡ Mr. Hemingway gives this name as Christofer. The last two syllables have disappeared in the original.
§ This christian name is inserted in a much later hand. It was evidently left blank when the entry was first made. It is also blank in Mr. Hemingway's copy.
‖ Mr. Hemingway gives this christian name as Elyn. It is very probable that the letter "n" has been worn away in the original.

† This word is partly worn away, but Mr. Hemingway gives it as Steuen, which is probably correct.

1545.

April 1—William Tyas had a child christened named William.

,, 1—Richard Haudsley had a child christened and buried named John.

,, 3—William Tyas had a child christened named John.

,, 2—Thomas Grane was buried.

,, 5—Thomas Barber had two children christened named Dorethe and Grace.

,, 9—William Gawnte had a child christened named William.

,, 13—William Whitacres had a child christened named Margery.

,, 15—William Lee, John Lee of Ossett sone, was buried.

,, 19—Robert Wryght of Gawthorp had a child christened named John.

,, 28—James Barber had a child christened named Alice.

,, 28—John Walkar of Osset had a child christened named Nycoles.

May 1—William Scolefeld was buried.

,, 4—Rycharde Hyrst had two chyldre christened, one named Rychd the other Jenet.

,, 5—Robert Jagger and Margrete Saxton were married.

,, 15—John Townend had a child christened named Thomas.

,, 16—Rychard Hyrst had a child buried named John.

,, 19—Thomas Sykes had a child christened named William.

,, 23—William Scolfeld had a child christened named Annes.

June 8—John Saxton had a child christened named John.

,, 21—Gylbert oylerhiade (? Oldroyd) had a child christened named William.

,, 23—William Dyeconson had a child christened named Anne.

July 19—Robert Whytacres had a child christened named Elsabeth.

,, 23—John Seckar had a child christened named Elsabeth.

,, 28—William Boith had a child christened named Elsabeth.

Aug. 13—Mr. Francke.* Mr. Nycolas Tempest sone in lawe, had a chylde chrystened the xiijth day named Elsabeth.

,, 13—Am: Foxe had a child christened named Margrete.

,, 16—Roger Swallow had a child christened named William.

1545.

Aug. 26—Robert Goodfelow (alias Borghe) had a child christened named Annes.

ano dni. mº Dº xl . . . º †.

,, 27—John Fairbarne had a child christened named Richard.

,, 28—John Baldon of Heaton, yongr, had a child christened named Edward.

Sept. 3—William Wood of Chydsell had a child christened named Margrete

,, 5—Christofer Thorpe of Osset was buried.

,, 6—William Tailyer of Dewisbury had a child christened named Thomas.

,, 7—John Allanson of Halyfax was buried.

,, 12—Edward Byarle had a child christened named James.

,, 12—William Tailyer had a child buried named Thomas.

,, 18—Rychard Wood of Gawthrop had a child christened named William.

,, 20—Robert Sharpuls had a child buried.

,, 26—Wyllm Hawidsley had a chyld crystened namyd Elsabeth.

Oct. 7—Richard Hall ‡ was buried.

1546.*

,, 11—William Carter and Anne Copley were married.

,, 13—William Hall and Elsabeth Robynson were married.

,, 14—Benet Medley had a child christened named William.

,, 25—Edward Tomson of Osset had a child christened named Esabell.

Nov. 1—John Grynton was buried.

,, 2—Rychard Olerede was buried.

---

* Would this be Mr. Antony Frank, of Alwoodley? See the pedigree of this family in Foster's edition of St. George's Visitation of Yorkshire, page 519. Mr. Antony Frank had a child named Margaret, buried at Dewsbury on the 26th November, 1550. He had a child christened on the 11th August, 1551, named Agnes, and he had a child named Betterysse, buried 23rd July, 1548. Betterysse or Beatrice was the name of Nicolas Tempest's wife.

† The letters after "1" are blotted so that they cannot be read. This date is at the top of the page of the Register.

‡ The will of Richard Hall of Dewesberie was proved at York, 26th January, 1545/6. It is dated 25th Sept., 37 Hen. VIII.

For the wills or letters of administration of the following persons, whose names appear in the preceding pages, see Index of Wills in the York Registry, Vol. XI. of the Record Series of the Yorkshire Archæological Association, viz.:

Richard Draunecfelde of Dewsberie, married 10th Sept., 1539, and see entry for 26th Dec., 1543. Letters of administration granted 29th Jan., 1544/5.

Thomas Syke, or Sikes, of Ossett, buried 4th Jan., 1543/4. Will proved 8th Jan., 1543/4.

Christopher Nayler, of Chidswell, buried 1st Jan., 1540/1. Will proved 18th Feb., 1540/1.

Johana Sykes (otherwise Joan Sikes), of Ossett, buried 25th Jan., 1540/1. Will proved 18th Feb., 1540/1.

Wyllam Kyttson (otherwise Wm. Kitson), of Ossett, buried 2nd March, 1540/1. Will proved 30th March, 1541.

Richard Fayrbarne, buried 17 Aug., 1541. Will proved 12th Sept., 1541.

Laurence Walton, of Dewsbury, buried 26th Feb., 1541/2. Will proved 9th Aug., 1542.

Robert Carter, of Dewsberie, Tanner, buried 14th April, 1544. Will proved 21 July, 1544.

Wm. Nowell, of Dewsberie, buried 10th June, 1544. Will proved 15th July, 1544.

Nicholas Whitley, of Dewesberie, buried 12 June, 1544. Will proved 21st July, 1544.

* This date is written in figures at the top of the page. It appears to be a mistake for 1545.

1545.
Nov. 8—. . . . Brodebent and Alis Frank were married.
 ,, 10—Isabell Gybson, William Gybson dought: (daughter), was christened.
 ,, 15—Jamys Walker hayd ij chyldryng chrystened, one named Nycolis a nother genet.
 ,, 18—Crest. Naller (? Christopher Naylor) had a child christened named Thomas.
 ,, 20—Isabell Wyttakarys of Chykynley was buried.
 ,, 24—Adam Thyngyll and Ane Medley were married.
 ,, 26—Ric : Greyn and Agnes Hall were married.
Dec. 5—Steyne Tomson had a child christened named Elsabeth.
 ,, 10—Mathe Speyght had a child christened named Alys.
 ,, 20—Edward Hall had a child christened named Jamy (? James or Janet).
 ,, 23—Ryc. Hall had a child buried named John.
 ,, 24—Ryc. Speyght had a chyld christened named Robert.
Jan. 4—James Wayd was buried.
 ,, 4—John Clak had a child christened named Genet.†
 ,, 5—John Flat had a child christened named Jenet.
 ,, 15—William Walker had a child christened named Ane.
 ,, 18—Angnes (? Agnes) Wallis (? Naller) was buried.
 ,, 19—ane Ryc : son (? Richardson) of baud : rod (? Boothroyd) was buried.
 ,, 20—John Greyne had a child christened named William.
February anno dni. mo do xlvjo.
Feb. 1—Robert genynge had a child christened named Christopher.
 ,, 2—The forsayd child was buried.
 ,, 3—William Wytteley had a child buried named William.
 ,, 7—William Fernley and Genett Wryght were married.
 ,, 16—William Ryeson ‡ was buried.
 ,, 16—Mr. Nycolys Tempes had a child christened named Alys.
 ,, 17—Ric : hayldeysley was buried.
 ,, 21—William Carter had a child christened and buried named Genete.
 ,, 23—John Richardson was buried.
 ,, 24—Angnes Pyckerrynge was buried
 ,, 24—William Tyes had a child buried named Genet.
 ,, 27—William Tyes had a child buried named William.

† This entry has been interlined in very bad writing, and is partly struck out. It is doubtful whether it was intended to stand.
‡ The will of William Richardson of Dewisburie was proved at York. 13th May, 1546.

1545.
March 6—Thomas Bradforthe had a child christened.
 ,, 6—On (one) Isabell Medley had a child christened.
 ,, 7—Margaret Sterkey was buried.
 ,, 8—Thomas Clayton had a child christened named Jamys.
 ,, 11—Wylfra Walker had a child buried named Ane.
 ,, 12—William Booth had a child buried named Robert.
 ,, 17—Richard Sterkey was buried.
 ,, 19—Thomas Berbre had a child buried named Grace.
 ,, 21—John Bradforthe had a child christened named Alyce.
 ,, 26—William Werwell had a child christened named John.
April 2—John Gren had a child buried named Thomas.
 ,, 17—Genet Wythed, wedo (? widow) was buried.
May 2—Robertthe Smythe had a child christened named Elsabeth.
 ,, 8—Margaret Hooll was buried.
 ,, 17—Alis Coupe was buried.
 ,, 20—Nycolis Seker had a child christened.
 ,, 21—William Wytley had a child christened named John.
 ,, 22—William Rychardson had a child christened named Thomas.
ano. dni. mo Do xlo vjo. §
Robert ginyngs had a chylde chrystened the xxiiij day named xpof. ‖
June 4—Richard Greyne had a child christened named John.
 ,, 5—The same child was buried.
 ,, 7—Jenkyn Hawdysle had a child christened.
 ,, 8—Alis Cyllynbroke ¶ had a child christened named Dorithe.
July 11—Thyane Crowder and Agnes Naler were married.
 ,, 18—Robert Rockley and Alis Scott were married.
 ,, 20—Christopher Baldon wyff was buried named Agnes.
 ,, 27—Wyllm Franke* was chrystyned the xxvij day havre to m : (Mr.) Franke.
Aug. 20—John Holred had a child christened named Angnes.
Sept. 3—Christopher Naler had a child buried named William.
 ,, 19—Richard Naler and Issabel Clappam were married.
 ,, 26—Johan Holred and Isabell Scolfeld were married.

§ This date is at the top of the page.
‖ This entry has been lightly struck through with a pen, and the line of ink has almost faded away. See entry for 1st February, 1546.
¶ This name is difficult to make out. The writing in the Register is bad about this period, and many of the surnames cannot be easily read.
* See note to entry of christening of Mr. Frank's daughter, on 13th Aug., 1545.

DEWSBURY PARISH REGISTERS.

1546.
Sept. 28—John Dyscheforthe had a child christened.
Oct. 3—John Greyn and Margaret Richardson were married.
" 17—Richard Gyll and Genet Norythes were married.
" 20—John Grane had a child christened named John.
" 21—William Tailyer had a child christened.
" 21—Robert Ley had a child buried named Anes.
Nov. 12—Richard Bradforthe wyff was buried named Jenet.
" 21—Nycolis Walker had a child christened named Sebell.
" 21—Genet Staforthe was buried.
" 23—John Forrest had a child christened named Jamys.
Dec. 1—John Robinson was buried.
" 3—Richard Brown had a child christened named Richard.
" 8—John Pese was buried.
" 18—Nycolis Clark had a child christened named Alis.
" 20—Richard Smyth was buried.
Jan. 4—John Holred had a child buried.
" 7—Edward Byerle had a child christened called Thomas.
" 16—William Barber had a child christened called James.

January an°. dni. m° D° xlvijo. †

" 16—Matho Boyll and Elsabethe Lee were married.
" 25—Robert Megson and Alis Nowell were married.
" 26—Anges (? Agnes) Boithe was buried.
March 3—John Greyn had a child christened named Richard.
" 5—The same child was buried.
" 12—Jamys Wytacar ‡ was buried.
" 18—Matho Speyght had a child buried named William.
" 19—Johon Hallan had a child christened named Jamys.
" 25—Steuen Tolson had a child christened named Alis.
" 25—Jamys Wood had a child christened named Bettryss.
April 3—Roger Dawson had a child christened named Ane.
" 7—John Bradforthe was buried.
" 11—George Robynson was buried.
May 14—William Talyer had a child christened named John.
" 5—Steavenn Tompsonn had a child christened named William.

Junij anno dni m° quingintissemo xlvij°.

June 12—Henry Tolson and Alice Lee were married.

† This date is at the top of the page.
‡ The Will of James Whitakers of Chekenley, parish of Dewisberie, was proved at York, 5th July, 1547.

1547.
June 13—John Alane was buried.‖
" 12—Christopher Steid had a child christened named Robert.
" 15—Thomas Heyrst had a child christened named John.
" 18—William Browke had a child christened named Christopher.
" 19—John Nowell and Agnes Bawme were married.
" 30—Mathois Barker hayd a chyld xpyned the layste day named Roger.
July 20—Robert Longley had a child christened named Thomas.
" 24—William Scolfeld had a child christened named Jenet.
Aug. 10—Thomas Halley and Alice Hesselwod were married.
" 15—Rye. Naller had a child christened named Battryse.
" 17—Chayrles Daldon had a child christened named Antone.
" 17—Wylfra Walkar had a child christened named yszabell.
" 19—Mr. Peter Franke had a child christened named Betterysse.
" 24—Benet Medley had a child christened named Bartelmen.
Sept. 4—John Jakson and Genet Lynay were married.
" 6—Wyllm Greyn was buried.
" 10—Wyllm. Wytley had a child christened named Necolese.
" 11—Wyllm Lee had two children christened, one named Genet the other Robert.
" 12—Thomas Clatone had a child christened named Agnes.
" 16—Wylm Carter wyff was buried named Agnes.
" 18—Bryan Crowder had a child christened named Issabell.
" 19—Christoffr Naller had a child christened named Ane.
" 25—Robert Goodfeloy had a child christened named Ane.
" 25—Robert Goodfeloy had a child christened named Ane.

M̃d yt syxe schelengs viijd is forfet of the chyrcho wardens for omyttyn tow Sondays wtout Record of thᵣ ptie yt is to say ix day of Octobre & syxten day off the saym. *

‖ The will of John Allayn of Ossett, husbandman, was proved at York, 5th July, 1547. The testator directs " My bodie to be buried within the hallowed ground of All Hallows in Dewsberie and messe and dirigie song for my soull the day of my buriall."

* In September, 1538, Thomas Lord Cromwell issued an Injunction " That every parson, vicar, or curate within this diocese for every church keep one Book or Register wherein he shall write the day and year of every wedding, christening, and burial made within your parish, and so every man succeeding you likewise . . . . And for the safe keeping of the same book, the parish shall be bound to provide of their common charges one sure coffer with two locks and keys, whereof the one to remain with

1517.

The Regest Boike of all the weding xpynning & burialls aynd in the fyrst yere off the Regne off Kynge Edward the sixt Wherin is inserted evy pson name so wedyd xpyned & buryed Recorded by the Wardens or els on off therm at leste yt is to say Roberte Lee Mathew Barbar John Wornhall Robert Wytacar Rye Naller & Thomas Gomsawlle.

Oct. 2—Wyllm Farrar and Genete Naller were married.
,, 2—Wyllm Jagar and Agnes Talyer were married.
,, 3—Wyllm Gybson had a child christened named Agnes.
,, 4—Rye: Kytson had a child christensd named Dorite.
,, 7—Wyllm Wilson had a child christened named Elzabethe.
,, 10—Rye. Kytson had a child buried named Dorythe.
,, 18—George Hobkynson had a child christened named Mgret.
,, 24—John Touened (Townend) had a child christened named Antonye.
Nov. 12—Robert Tyes had a child christened named Genet.
,, 13—Thomas Wod and Elzabeth Smith were married. Testis (witness) Jhn Worhall.
,, 14—Thomas Wayd and Elzabeth Smyth were married.
,, 15—John Fayrbarne had a child christened named Iszabell.
,, 19—Alis Raner had a child christened named Agnes. Testis Matho Barbar.
,, 20—Thomas Akroid and Alis Holred were married.
,, 25—Robert Tyese had a child buried called Jenet.
,, 26—Matho Speyght had a child christened m (the remainder of the word is frayed away). Testis Robertus Wytacar.

December Anno Dni. m° D xlvij°.

Dec. 2—Thomas Ramsden wyff was buried named Izabell.
,, 13—Wyllm Gante had a child christened named Gylbert.
,, 21—Robert Bowkeht † had a child buried named Agnes.

you, and the other with the wardens of every parish wherein the said book shall be laid up, which book ye shall every Sunday take forth, and in the presence of the said wardens or one of them write and record in the same all the weddings, christenings, and burials made the whole week afore; and for every time that the same shall be omitted the party that shall be in the fault thereof shall forfeit to the said church iij iiij to be employed on the reparation of the said church."

A somewhat similar injunction was issued by Edwd. VI. in 1547, but it directs that the penalty "be employed to the poore men's box of the parishe." See further, as to the institution of Parish Registers, Burn's "History of Parish Registers," and "Parish Registers in England," by R. E. Chester Waters.

† This name is difficult to read. Mr. Hemingway gives it Pamluht.

1547.

Jan. 9—John Baldon had a child christened named Robert.
,, 15—Issabell Slake was buried.
,, 17—Wyllm Smythe had a child christened named Pet:
,, 18—Genet Boythe was buried.
,, 24—Wyllm Schepherde had a child christened named Wyllm.
,, 24—Gylberte Wholreyde had a child christened named Rye:
,, 26—John Nowell was buried.

Februarie.

Wylm Woode hayd a child xpyned the theyrtie † day named Edward.

Feb. 8—Wyllm Wod had a child buried named Edward.
,, 9—Thomas Grefyne had a child christened named Elsabeth.
,, 16—John Saxton had a child christened named Elzabeth.
,, 16—Thomas Akeroid had a child christened named Jane.
March 3—John Hollored had a child christened named Elzabeth. ||
,, 3—Rye: Darkston had a child christened named John.
,, 8—Edward Tolson had a child buried named John.
,, 11—John Dyschforth had a child christened named Wylm.
,, 11—Ham: Foxe had a child christened named Roberthe.
,, 15—Thomas Barbare had a child christened named Margery.
,, 21—Mathew Bood had a child christened named Johne.
April 4—John Greyne had a child christened named Wyllm.
,, 4—Wyllm Boythe had a child christened named Agnes.
,, 5—Edward Hochynson had a child christened named Wyllm.
,, 6—Genet Boy was buried whose husband was Johan.
,, 28—Roberte Wyttakar and Genete Alane were married.
May Genet Ryeson (Richardson) was buried. §
June Anno. Dni. M° D° xlviij°.
June 10—Wylm Horner and Ane Bryge were married.
,, 11—John Seker had a child christened named James.
,, 27—Wylm Rycharson had a child christened named Ane.
July 10—Elzabeth Syke was buried.
,, 11—Agnes Carlynhall was buried.

‡ Probably should be 30th January. The word February appears to have been interlined after the entries for the month were made and to have been written above instead of below this entry by mistake.

§ The name Elzabeth is taken from Mr. Hemingway's copy. It has disappeared from the original.

¶ The day of the month and the rest of this page have been torn off or worn away.

DEWSBURY PARISH REGISTERS.

1518.
July 12—John Haldesworth was buried.
,, 23—Mr. Antony Franke had a child buried named Betterysso.
,, 29—Thomas Ryeson (Richardson) and Agnes Fynche were married.
Aug. 6—Wylm Farunde had a child christened named Elizabeth.
,, 7—Wylm Speyght and Ane Haudsley were married.
,, 28—Rye. Heyrste had a child christened named Margaret.*
Sept. 16—Wylm Wyttacar had a child christened named Edward.
,, 18—Wylm Smyth had a child christened named Antonye.
,, 24—Rye Hayll had a child christened named Agnes.
Oct. 6—Mr. Antony Franke had a child christened named Margaret.
,, 18—Thomas Bradfortbe had a child christened named Thomas.
,, 30—Necoles Clarke had a child christened named Agnes.
Nov. 12—Genet oits had a child christened named Margaret.
,, 11—Junys Hayge and Margaret Ryeson (Richardson) were married.
,, 13—John Pence and Mgaret Deton were married.
,, 13—Thomas Nowell had a child christened named Wyllm.
,, 15—Thomas Hochynson had a child christened named John.†
    Januarie Anno Dni. M° D° xlviij°.
Jan. 14—Roberte Tyase had a child christened named Christopher.
,, 15—Another child christened named Roberte.
,, 22—Issabell Tins was buried.
,, 22—John Toson‡ was buried being Hery Toson child.
Feb. 3—Rye Lee and Mgaret Syk were married.
,, 9—John Grane had a child christened named Thomas.
,, 10—Rye Dekenson and Alice Walkar were married.
,, 10—Thomas Syke and Alice Boythe were married.
,, 11—Gylbert Crowder had a child christened named Mgt.
,, 13—Wyllm Barbar had a child christened named James.
,, 15—Wyllm Wytley had a child christened named Rye.
,, 16—Agnes York had a child christened bast: gottynge named Rye:

* The rest of this page has been torn off or worn away, except that the next entry seems to have been a christening on the 30th.
† The rest of this page has been torn off or worn away, with the exception of portions of the entries of a wedding and a christening, the wedding being on the 13th.
‡ Judging from the mark of abbreviation this name is probably Tolson.

1548.
    Wyfray Walkar . . . .
    namyd §
    Robert §
    R §
1549. anno Dni. M° D° xlviijo.
March 1—Margaret Carter was buried.
,, 1—Roger Dawson had two children christened, the one named Mary the other Grace.
,, 3—Robert Balle had a child christened named Jane.
,, 8—John Forrest had a child christened named Thomas.
,, 12—Genet Walkar was buried.
,, 13—Thomas Medley was buried.
,, 16—Edward Toson had a child christened named Ellyng.
,, 18—Thomas Wayd had a child christened named Genett.
,, 21—Thomas Gant had a child christened called Alice.
,, 25—Thomas Jaggar had a child christened named Genet.
,, 25—Wylm Talyero had a child christened named Rychard.
April 1—Mr. Nicoles Tempest had a child christened named Ane.‖
,, 1—Thomas Sykes had a child christened named Agnes.
,, 3—Rye: Browno had a child christened named Thomas.
,, 5—Wylm Tyas had ij children christened, the one named Genet the other Doryte.
,, 6—The same children were buried.
,, 7—Rye: Hall had a child buried.
,, 8—Rye: Lee had a child christened named Rye:
,, 10—Alice nurce to Mr. Tempest was buried.
    anno Dni. M° D° xlviiij.
,, 12—Rye: Whytley had a child christened named Sebell.
,, 12—Robert Janynge had a child christened named Doryte.
,, 20—Wyllm Wormwall had a child buried named Ro.
,, 22—Thomas Jagar was buried.
April 22—John Dyshforthe had a child christened named Genet.
,, 23—Robert Wytacars had a christened named Doryte.
,, 25—Rye: Dyckonson had a child christened named Necoles.

The Regist: book of Dewisburye maid the iiij day of mai the year of or lord god m. D. xlviiij wherin is wryttin euy Parson name wedded xpyned & buryed wt the day & the year Recorded by the warden of the same church yt is to say Necoles Seekar Rob: Banll Rob: Wylkynson John Brouk John lee John Barbarne.

§ The rest of this page has been torn off or worn away.
‖ See note to entry for 24th June, 1511.

1549.
May 6—John Bradforthe had a child christened named Genett.
 „ 14—Rye: Lee was buried.
 „ 19—Wylm Ferneley had a child christened named Rye:
 „ 18—John Walkar had a child christened named Dorythe.
 „ 21—Robt. Musgrave and Sebell Kent were married.
 „ 27—Henry Naller and Sobell Haull were married.
June 3—John Greyne had a child christened called Elyzabeth.
 „ 19—Thomas Sykes had a child christened called Wylm.
July 1—Agnes Gant was buried.
 „   3—Wylm Boull had a child christened called Ane.
 „ 28—Rye: Symson had a child christened named Genet.
ug. 4—Ric: Slak and Elizabeth Lee were married.
 „ 17—Robert Musgrave had a child christened called Necoles.
 „ 19—Anes Wayd was buried.
 „ 23—Gyllt Holred had a child christened called Elzaleth.
 „ 26—Jamis Ryeson had a child buried called John.
 „ 28—Benet Medley had a child christened called Sebell.
 „ 29—John Haull had a child christened called Agnes.
Sept. 26—Rye: Bradforthe * was buried.
Oct. 6—Thomas Seker and Agnes Musgrave were married.
 „   7—Wylm Scolfelde had a child christened named Elzabeth.
      Anno Dni, Mo Do xlviiijo.
 „ 11—John Fayrbarne had a child christened called Wyllm.
 „ 11—Wylm Peace had a child christened called Wyllm.
 „ 13—Jamis Colyer had a child christened named Rye:
 „ 15—Thomas Stansfeld and Agnes Barbaro were married.
 „ 19—John Dynnyson had a child christened named Rye:
 „ 23—Mathewe Speyght had a child christened called Jamys.
 „ 24—Challes Baldon had a child christened called John.
 „ 27—Wylm Gybson had a child christened called Ane.
Nov. 5—John Bradforthe and Margaret Baldon were married.

 * Ric. Bradford, of Orsett, made his will 24th Sept., 1549. The following is an extract:—" I bequeath and pifftth my soull to god and my bodie to be buried within the churcheyrde of Dewesberie nie to the Diall. Also I bequeath to the hie altar of Dewesberie for my tithes and oblacons forgotten 12d." He also mentions his sons, Robert, John, William, and Ric. And he appoints Robert his executor, who proved the will 15th Nov., 1549.

1549.
Nov. 7—Robt. Lawley had a child christened named Leonard.
 „   9—Mr. Standley had a child christened called Frances.
 „ 10—Gylbt Wood had a child christened named Wylm.
Dec. 11—Rye: Dickenson had a child buried called Necoles.
 „ 12—Agnes Baildone was buried.
 „ 15—Mathew Barbre had a child christened called Mary.
 „ 17—John Peace was buried.
 „ 19—Necoles Walkar had a child christened called Alyc.
 „ 24—John Byrkyngshey was buried.
 „ 25—Iszabell Waltone was buried.
 „ 28—Charles Baldone had a child buried called John.
 „ 28—Stewene Tomsone had a child christened named Magarett.
Jan. 7—Rye: Greyne had a child christened named Robt.
 „   9—Thomas Nettyltone was buried.
 „ 23—Rye: Heyrst was buried.
Feb. 11—Jamis Barbar and Bettaryse Seckar were married.
 „ 11—Wylm Lee and Alice Dawson were married.
 „ 25—Thomas Sacor had a child christened named Elzabeth.
 „ 28—xpof Nayller had a child christened named Alice.
March 4—Robt. Goodfeloy had a child christened named John.
 „   7—Wylm Clarkson was buried.
 „ 11—Ralf Borton was buried.
 „ 11—Edward Greyne had a child christened called Alice.
 „ 13—Mgaret Pyckaryng had a child christened being last gottyng called Necoles.
 „ 27—John Hollered had a child christened named Jenet.
April 2—Alice Medley had a child christened named Edward bast: gotten.
1550.   Anno Dni. mo Do lo.
April 3—John Baildon had a child christened named John.
 „   3—Agnes Stott was buried.
 „   9—xpof Naller had a child buried called Alice.
 „ 17—Genet Bayldone was buried.
 „ 13—Necoles Seccar had a child christened named Edwarde.
 „ 20—Rye: Lee had a child christened named Betteris.
 „ 24—John Dyshforth had a child christened named Mathew.
 „ 26—Thomas Talyer was buried.
 „ 28—Thomas Clatone had a child christened called Thomas.
 „ 30—Robert Smyth had a child christened called Rye:
May 5—Wylm Saxtone and Mgaret Aykroyd were wedded.
 „ 11—Henry Alcoke and Issabell Hyrstt were wedded.

1550.
May 12—Wylm Audysley had a child christened called Dorythe.
,, 12—Jamys Barbar had a child christened named Alice.
,, 17—John Saxtone had a child christened named Ralff.
,, 19—Elzabeth Barstone was buried.
,, 20—* child christened named Elzabeth.

Anᵒ Dni, Mᵒ Dᵒ Iᵒ.

June 16—Johon Dyshefourth had a child christened named Alice.
,, 17—Thomas Gaunt had a child christened named Wylm.
,, 21—Thomas Stansefeld had a child christened named Alice.
July 1—Wylm Lee had a child christened named Roger.
,, 1—Iszabell Scott was buried.
,, 13—Elzabeth Wood Browne was buried.
,, 22—Wylfryd Walcar had a child christened called Agnes.
,, 27—Robert Tins and Genet Wylkynson were wedded.
Aug. 5—John Bayldon and Alice Graro were wedded.
,, 2—Amar Foxe had a child christened called Wylm.
,, 14—Roberth Robynsou had a child christened called Wylm.
,, 15—The same Wylm Robensone was buried.
,, 17—Wylm Nowell and Elzabeth Bayldone were wedded.
,, 21—James Hochynsone had a child christened named Wylm.
,, 22—Genet Slak was buried.

Anno Dni. mᵒ Dᵒ Iᵒ. 1550.

,, 25—Margarete Forrand was christened.
,, 26—Agnes Wormwall was buried.
Aug. 30—Wylm Smythe had a child christened called Genet.
,, 31—Rye: Hyrste wife had a child christened called Elzabeth.
Sept 21—Henry Alcoke had child christened called Nycoles.
,, 28—Rychard Horsfall was buried.
Oct. 7—Nycoles Alcoke was buried.
,, 7—John Townend had a child christened called yszabell.
,, 8—John Bradforthe had a child buried called Roger.
,, 11—Wylm Wylson was buried.
,, 12—Thomas Beamond and Elzabeth Wode were wedded.
,, 14—Wylm Nowell and Dyonis Baildone were wedded.
,, 19—Genet Walcar was buried.
Nov. 16—John Wylsone and Agnes Talyer were wedded.
,, 16—John Medley had a child christened named Agnes.
,, 25—Thomas Baildone was buried.

* The first part of this entry has been worn away.

1550.
Nov. 20—Mr. Antony Franke had a child buried called Mgaret.
Dec. 8—Maysterys Betterys Tempest was buried.†
,, 9—Thomas Mather and Alice Tomson were wedded.

Anᵒ Dni. mᵒ D. lj.

Jan. 4—Rye: Kytson wife mother was buried called Margaret. ‡
,, 15—Robt. Bradforthe had a child christened called Robt.
,, 18—Wylm Barbar had a child christened called Amous. §
,, 18—Genet Smyth had a child christened called John, bast: gottyng.
,, 22—Rychard Nayller had a child christened called Elzabeth.
,, 22—Robt. Adame wyfe was buried called Genet.
,, 26—Wylm Whytley had a child christened called Sebell.
Feb. 1—John Wormwalt ‖ was buried.
,, 12—Chareles Bayldone had a child christened named Rosamond.
,, 19—Wylm Wormall had a child christened named Wylm.
,, 22—John Jowet had a child christened named Agnes.
,, 23—Rye: Whytley had a child christened called Thomas.
,, 23—John Boye was buried.

mᵒ D. lj̇ᵒ.

,, 26—Agnes Medley was buried.
March 1—Jamys Walcar had a child christened named Mgaret.
,, 2—Bryane Crouder had a child christened named Mgaret.
,, 4—Thomas Crabtre had a child buried called Alyce.
,, 8—Wylm Colyer was buried.
,, 16—Wylm Nowell had a child christened called John.
,, 18—Robt. Dey had a child christened called Marye.
,, 19—Wylm Boyth had a child christened called Genet.
,, 20—Wylm Speyght had a child christened called Genet.
,, 23—John Dybson (possibly Bylson) was buried.

†See note to entry for 24th June, 1541.

‡This Christian name is partly worn away. It looks more like Mary than Margaret in the original. Mr. Hemingway gives it Margaret.

§ The reading of this christian name is taken from Mr. Hemingway's copy. The original is badly written and difficult to read. The second letter may be either "m" or "n," and the word ends with a flourish which may be intended for a sign of abbreviation. The name may be intended for Ambrose.

[The will, dated 2nd July, 1548, of John Wormall, of Erles Heton, was proved at York 14th Feby., 1550. The apparent discrepancy in dates is caused by the year 1551 in the Register commencing in January instead of in March.

1551.
June 28—Nycoles Wylbe and Elzabeth Speyght were married.
July 31—Wyllm Ryeson had a child christened called Ellen.
„ 31—Gylbt Woode had a child christened called Rye:

m⁰ D⁰ Ij⁰.

Aug. 4—Ane Lee was buried.
„ 7—Robt. Whyttacars had a child christened called Margaret.
„ 8—Robt. Baull had a child christened called Rye:
„ 9—Benet Medley was buried.
„ 11—Mastr Antony Franke had a child christened called Agnes.
„ 13—John Medley ‡ was buried.
„ 22—Alyce Boltone was buried.
„ 23—Wyllm Whyttacars had a child christened named Dorythe.
„ 23—John Farbarne had a child christened named Dorythe.
„ 27—John Grave had a child christened called Genet.
Sept. 12—Wylm Chelfeld had a child christened named Iszabell.
„ 13—Mathew Boull had a child christened named Edward.
„ 20—Thomas Aykrod had a child christened called Roger.†
„ 25—John Walcar Smyth had a child christened called Alyce.
„ 28—Genet Allen was buried.

October Ann⁰ Dni. M⁰ D⁰ Ij⁰.

Oct. 6—Agnes Farbarne was buried.
„ 11—Thomas Syke was wedded.
„ 17—John Walcare was wedded.
„ 27—John Bradforth had a child christened called Thomas.
„ 29—James Wode had a child christened called Genet.
„ 21†—Wyllm Pulle had a child christened called Robt.
„ 24†—Jams Colyer had a child christened called Mgaret.
Dec. 13—Rye: Nayller was buried.
„ 22—Robt Lee was buried.
Jan. 4—Agnes Sykes was buried.
„ 8—Henry Savyll was buried.
„ 19—John Longley and Betteres Wood were wedded.
„ 27—Elzabeth Antye was buried.
„ 27—Thomas Smythe Rye: Wood Elzabethe Grene and Ellen Janyng were christened.
Feb. 8—Wyllm Talyer had a child christened called John.

* The will, dated 12th Aug., 1551, of John Medley, of Chidsell, was proved at York 23rd Sept., 1551. The will of Thomas Medley, of the same place, who was buried 13th March, 1549, was proved at York 1st April, 1549.
† Original Illegible. The name is taken from Mr. Hemingway's copy.
‡ The month is not given in these two entries. Probably it should be November.

1551.
Feb. 16—Robt. Allen and Genet Batley were wedded.
„ 26—Agnes Whyttacar was buried.
„ 23—Margaret Gybson was buried.
„ 26—Thomas Besmonde had a child christened called Thomas.
March 1—Alyce Gomersall was buried.
Feb. 27—John Longley had a child christened called John.
March 8—John Saxton had a child christened called John.
„ 13—Thomas Stansfeld had a child christcned called Marye.
„ 19—Robrte Musgrave had a child christened called Roberte.
April 4—Robt. Bradforthe had a child christened called Robt.
„ 23—Grace Bule was buried.

Ano Dni. M⁰ D⁰ Lij⁰.

May 1—George Walcar was christened son unto Nycholas Walcar.
„ 1—Wyllm Smyth had a child christened called Antony.
„ 23—Agnes Yhorke was buried.
„ 26—Thomas Secker had a child christened named Margret.
June 5—John the son of Wyllm Taylyer was christened.
„ 17—Wyllam Boot was buried.
„ 26—Hary Haloode had a child christened called Doryt.
„ 29—Thomas Greyn was wedded.
July 3—Roger Roulles was wedded.
„ 8—Necoles Clark had a child buried named Mgarette.
„ 19—Wyllam Whitley had a child christened named George.
„ 24—Wyllam Barbur had a child buried named Ambrose.
Aug. 9—Uxor Jamys Barebar was buried.
„ 12—Willm Dyshforth had a child buried named John.
„ 18—John Walkar had a child buried named Jane.
„ 30—Uxor Jamys Richadson was buried.
Sept. 4—Willm Smyth was married.
„ 5—Ric: Browne had a child baptised named Jenett.
„ 5—Jamys Huchonson had a child baptised named Alice.
„ 20—John Hawle was buried.
Oct. 7—Willm Whitlay had a child buried named George.
„ 8—John Browne was buried.
„ 12—Willm Fayrebarne had a child baptised named John.
„ 17—Ric: Slacke had a child baptised named John.
„ 21—Willm Syke had a child baptised named John.
„ 27—Willm Lee had a child baptised named Marie.
„ 30—Uxor Nicoles Woode was buried.

DEWSBURY PARISH REGISTERS. 19

1552.
Nov. 5—Thomas Grene had a child baptised named Ric:
 „ 8—John Wade and Annes were married.
 „ 10—Ric: Browne was buried.
 „ 15—John Schapilthorpe and Jenett were married.
 „ 29—Uxor Willm Richardson was buried.
Dec. 4—Willm Aykrodd and Jenett Lee were married.
 „ 5—Jamys Shepard and Anc were married.
 „ 9—Willm Tomson was buried.
 „ 10—Thomas Pyckard and Jane were married.
 „ 12—Mychaell Alan had a child buried named Leonard.
 „ 20—Willm Hustlar and Margrate were married.
 „ 21—Ric: Hawlo had a child baptised named Elsabeth.
 „ 25—Robart Dey had a child baptised named Annes.
Januarie Auo : Dni. mo Do lijo.
Jan. 6—Uxor Ric: Hawlle was buried.
 „ 10—Georg Grayveson and Margrete were married.
 „ 21—Mathewe Boyle had a child baptised named Annes.
 „ 28—Mathewe Barebar had a child baptised named Alice.
 „ 28—Alice Lee had a child baptised named Jenett.
 „ 28—Peter Grene had a child baptised named Thomas.
 „ *30—Willm Nowell had a child baptised named Willm.
Same day—John Olleroyd had a child baptised named Marie.
Same day—John Bayldon had a child baptised named Rosamund.
Feb. 1—Uxor Willm Kytson was buried.
 „ 2—Mathew Speyght had a child baptised named Marie.
 „ 11—John Medley had a child buried.
 „ 12—John Walkar had a child baptised named John.
 „ 19—Richard Lee had a child baptised named Robart.
 „ 19—Nycoles Nayler had a child baptised named Jounne.
 „ 19—Amar Fox had a child baptised named Elene.
 „ 20—Willm Richardson had a child buried.
 „ 20—John Walkar was buried.
Mar. 5—Robart Mathewe had a child baptised named Robart.
 „ 8—Annes Longley was buried.
 „ 12—Richard Dyckonson had a child baptised named Alys.
 „ 12—John Broke wife was buried.
 „ 12—John Grene wife was buried.
 „ 20—Thomas Grene had a child buried.
 „ 27—Thomas Gomersalle was buried.

*This date is clearly XXXV, in the original. Mr. Hemingway gives it 30, but why is not clear.

1553. Anno Dni. Mo Do Liijo.
April 1—Willm Lee had a child baptised named Mary.
 „ 2—Willm Aykrod had a child baptised named Willm.
 „ 4—Eadmund Oke had a child baptised named Alys.
 „ 11—Willm Lee had a child buried.
 „ 16—Thomas Peaker wife was buried.
 „ 23—John Morvell had a child baptised named Margret.
 „ 29—Thomas Tyas was buried.
May 1—Johanna Lee a bastard was baptised.
 „ 2—Edward Gomersall and Margret were married.
 „ 2—Robart Wittikars had a daughter buried.
Oct. 29—*Richard Bentesone and Margaret Pecarde were married.
 „ 29—Christopher Tyass and Annes Walker were married.
 „ 30—Jane the daughter of Thomas Peykerd was buried.
 „ 30—Peter son of Willm Barber was christened.
The month of November, 1556.
Nov. 4—Henry Carlingchawe was buried.
 „ 4—John Wilbe had a son christened named George.
 „ 13—Issabell Maukmyeholis was buried.
 „ 18—John Walker had a child christened named John.
 „ 30—Edward Gomsaill had a child christened named Margaret.
Dec. 4—John Beadfourthe† had a child christened named Willm.
 „ 14—Thomas Seiker had a child christened named Annes.
 „ 16—Robert Dey had a child christened named Thomas.
 „ 22—Robarte Ollerrede had a child christened named Sybell.
 „ 27—Willm Richardsone had a child buried named Annes.
 „ 29—Richard Haulle had a child christened named Edward.
Jan. 19—Maister Aberan Copley, Esquire,‡ and Mistris Grace Beadfourthe were married by Mr. Rud, vicar, B.D.||

*This entry (for Oct. 29th) and the following entries down to the 28th June, 1557, inclusive, are copied from Mr. Hemingway's copy. He has made a note in his copy to the effect that he transcribed these entries "from an old copy of the Registry, part of which copy is with the original in loose backs." This copy is not now to be found, and, although it is many years since I first examined the Registers, I have never seen it nor have I been able to hear anything of it. There are no entries in the original Register from the 2nd May, 1554, to the 25th July, 1557. —S. J. C.

† This name is certainly Beadfourthe in Mr. Hemingway's copy. It may be intended for Bradfourthe or Bradford. There was a John Bedford living at Crow Nest about this time.

‡ This gentleman was no doubt Alveray Copley, of Batley Hall, owner of the Batley estate, now belonging to the Earl of Wilton. His first wife was Joanna or Jane, daughter of Richard Beaumont, Esq., of Whitley Hall, His second wife is said to have been Grace, daughter of

1556.
Jan. 23—Thomas Sykes had a child christened named George.
,, 31—Joseph Arnall and Elizabeth Tyas were married.
,, 31—Anne Nowell was buried.
Feb. 2—Nicolis Clarke had a child christened named Dorytie.
,, 6—Willm Burnet was buried.
,, 8—John Disfourthe had a child christened named Annes.
,, 11—Anthony Awtie and Jenyt Graisone were married.
,, 15—Alys Robinsone was buried.
,, 16—Annes Secker was buried.
,, 19—Jenyt Haulle was buried.
,, 23—John Robinsone had a child christened named Annes.
,, 28—Thomas Secker had a child christened named Elisabeth.
,, 28—The said Thomas had a child buried the same day named Johana.
Mar. 1—William Speight, of Chittshell (Chidswell), was buried.
,, 2—Elizabeth Sykes was buried.
,, 10—Thomas Greyne had a son christened named John.
,, 12—Thomas Musgrave was buried.
,, 14—Thomas Sharpus had a child christened named Robert.
,, 15—Richard Whitley had a child buried named John.
,, 21—Christofer Nayler had a child christened named Mihiell.
,, 21—James Waide had a child buried named Nicholis.
,, 22—Annes, wife of Willm Nayler, was buried.
,, 22—Elizabeth, the daughter of John Morvill, was buried.
,, 24—Margaret Hallrede was buried.
,, 25—Mihill Nayler, son of Christofer Nayler, was buried.
,, 30—Willm Foxe, son of Annes Foxe, was buried.
April 1—John Gowitt was buried.
,, 3—Willyam Musgrave wife was buried.
,, 11—John Greyne, son of Thomas Greine, was buried.
,, 28—Christofer Bradfourthe was buried.

Bryan Bradford, of Stanley. The lady's surname in Mr. Hemingway's copy of the Register is written Bradfourtie, and not Bradfourthe.

" The Rev. John Rudd was instituted to the Vicarage of Dewsbury, 30th Dec., 1554, he having previously brought letters from the Bishop of London and the Vicar-General of the Diocese of Lichfield, to shew that he had been divorced from Isabella Welden, his late wife, that he was penitent, and that he had been restored to his priestly orders.—Yorkshire Archæol. Journal, vol. 10, page 94. He had no doubt been in trouble on account of his marriage, the Queen having in March, 1553-4, sent a series of articles into the dioceses authorising the deprivation of clerks who were married contrary to the state of there order, and the laudable custom of the Churche." He probably re-married after the Queen's death, for he had a child christened at Dewsbury Church on the 24th December, 1561.

1556.
May 15—John Dayo was buried.
,, 18—Robert Lo was buried.
,, 19—Jenyt, wife of John Baldone, was buried.
,, 22—Annes Disforthe was buried.
June 3—John Beadfourthe was buried.
,, 3—Willm Smithe had a child christened named Willm.
,, 6—John Keynit was buried.
,, 6—Anthony Awtie had a child christened named Anthonie.
,, 10—Margaret, wife of Rogar Barker, was buried.
,, 12—Thomas Stannefeld had a child buried named Mgaret.
,, 20—Richard Lo had a child buried named Robart.
,, 20—Gilbert Hollered had a child buried named Thomas.
,, 22—Willm Lee had a child christened named Elizabeth.
,, 28—John Kent was buried.
,, 28—Thomas Secker had a child buried named Margaret.

Julij, Anno Dni M ccccc lvij.
The 25 day of Julij & in the yeare fourth and fyft of Philipp & Mary by the Grace of God kyng and qwen of England Fraunce Jerusalem and Hireland defenders of the faith &c, Thomas Wade had a child bapt named James the same day.'

July 25—Jenet Chayffe had a child baptized named Jenet.
,, 28—Uxor Warton had a child buried named Annes
Aug. 1—Rye: Neteyllton was buried.
,, 8—Jogred Colpo wife was buried named Marg.
,, 10—John Grayff had a child baptised named Mary.
,, 14—Thomas Mansfeld was buried. †John Benley and Mergret Dawson was married. *John Beldon and Mary Wylkyngson was married.
,, 17—Jamys Wallker was buried.
,, 18—Uxor Tomson was buried.
Sept. ‡—Annes Tomson, late wife of Stevine Tomson, was buried.
,, 2—Elizabeth Nayler, wife of Christofer Nayler was buried.
,, 3—Uxor Okrede was buried.
,, 6—Rye: Wood, of Gawthourpe, was buried.
,, 8—Rye, son of Robert Dey, was buried.
,, 8—Alyson Maulcoll was buried.
,, 9—Rye: Nayler had a child buried named Mychaell.

* After this entry comes the following note in Mr. Hemingway's copy, viz.:—"Here ends the transcription from the copy.—H. J. H."

† These two entries are crowded in after the entry of Thomas Mansfeld's death, and are in a different hand writing.

‡ The day of the month is worn away.

DEWSBURY PARISH REGISTERS.

1557.
Sept. 9—Rye: Disforth had a child christened named Mary.
,, 10—Elsabeth Medley, wife of John Medley, was buried.
,, 11—James Woode was buried.
,, 13—Rye: Grenno was buried.
,, 14—Michael Alane had (a child) christened named Anne.
,, 19—Thomas Gryfyng was buried.
,, 19—Mary Rude was buried.
,, 19—John Diche and Ezabell Estwoode was married.
,, 20—Alyson Flather was buried.
Oct. 10—Rye: Wormwall had a child christened named Thomas.
,, 10—Jenet Olred was buried.
,, 20—Roger Tayliyer had a child buried named Janne.
,, 27—Wyllm Peace was buried.
Nov. 4—John Fayrnbarne had a child christened named Elsabeth.
,, 9—Christofer Nayler and Annes were married.
,, 9—John Arnalde had a child christened named Isbell.
,, 12—Margret Longley was buried.
,, 13—Alice Hepworthe was buried.
,, 14—Alice Helisston had a child christened named Sybell.
,, 15—Robert Scharpus was buried.
,, 16—Annes Scharpus was buried.
,, 21—Robert Burlby and Annes Seeker were married.
Nov. 22—Wyllm Bradforth was buried.
Dec. 9—John Farowe had a child christened named Cath . . . . .
,, 18—James Walcar had a child christened named James.
,, 22—Wyllm Mavnsell was buried.
,, 22—Rye: Tyas was buried.
,, 27—John Wood was buried.

1558.
Jan. 7—In the year of our Lord God M.D. lviijt and in the vijt day off January, Wyllm Dickynson was buriede the same day.
,, 18—Roger Clayton and Angnes Haigh were married.
,, 20—Thomas Seeker had a child christened named Edwarde.
,, 27—John Dickyngson was buried.
Feb. 4—Wyllm Wittelay had a child christened named Margret.
,, 6—John Walcar, of Ossett, had a child christened named Mychaell.
,, 13—Peter Grene, of Osset, had a child christened named John.
,, 16—Thomas Barkesston was buried.
,, 19—Rye: Battson had a child christened named John.
,, 25—Thomas Sykes, of Osset, had a child christened named Rye:
Mar. 1—Mathew Bull had a child buried called Sibell.
,, 2—Briane Vicars was buried.
,, 16—Antony Scharpule was buried.

1558.
Mar. 16—Elsabeth Haldersley was (? buried).
,, 23—Emer Foxe had a child christened named Emer.
,, 26—Auno Totte, wife of Robert Totto, was buried.
,, 26—Aune Alen, daughter of Mychaell Alan, was buried.
Appriell Ao. Dni. 1558.
April 10—Agnes Grayfsson was buried.
,, 25—The Ryght Wyrshipfull Sir Henry Sayvell depted the xxvt day off Appriel 1 In the year off our lord god A.Mdl viijt.
,, 28—Edward Beamunde was buried.
May 3—Randalle Nytylton and Angnes Greno were married.
,, 3—Rye: Naylor had a child buried named Margret.
,, 8—John Soniar and Elsabeth Beamonde were married.
,, 8—Rye: Walcar was buried.
,, 11—John Hepworth and Margreat Wharton were married.
,, 14—Angnes Tomson, wife of Edward Tomson, was buried.
,, 16—Edward Haull was buried.
July 2—Lenard Dickyngson and Sybell Smyth were married.
,, 3—John Smyth was buried, the son of Robert Smyth.
,, 7—John Hobkyngson was buried.
,, 9—John Hobkyngson was buried.
,, 12—Elsabeth Smythe was buried.
,, 16—Mr. John Gastou had a child christened named Mgret.
July 16—Edward Tomson had a child christened named Christoffer.
,, 17—Thomas Barbar was buried.
,, 22—Antone Aute was buried.
,, 23—Wyllm Gyle had a child christened named Dorythe.
Aug. 7—John Gommersall was buried.
,, 8—Robert Tyas was buried.
,, 12—Thomas Wornnawill had a child christened.
,, 16—John Grayne and Elizabethe his wife were buried.
,, 20—Rye: Cofyne had a child christened named . . . .
,, 23—George Grayfson had a child christened named Jenet.
,, 24—Annes Jowet was buried. *Thomas.
,, 27—, ... Casson had a child christened named John.
Sept. 7—Alison Grayne was buried.
,, 10—John Arnauld had a child christened named Alis.†
,, 10—John Walcar had a child christened named Margret.
,, 11—John Kytchengman was buried.
,, 19—Angnes Seeker was buried.
,, 21—Esabell Kent was buried.

* So in original.

† This name is taken from Mr. Hemingway's copy. It has disappeared from the original.

1558.
Sept. 26—Annes Wylkyngson wife was buried.
 ,, 29—Rye: Slack had a child christened named Rye:
Oct. 1—Nycoles Wood was buried.
 ,,   6—Wyllm Smyth had a child christened named Esabell.
 ,, 10—John Alot and Sebell Speght were married.
 ,, 10—Wm Childe had a child christened named John.‡
 ,, 10—Wyllm Lee had a child christened named Robert.
 ,, 12—Matthew Speght had a child buried named James.
 ,, 15—..... Dawson was buried.
 ,, 16—Rye: Wormwall was buried.
 ,, 19—Thomas Wade had a child christened named Anne.
 ,, 19—John Beldon was buried.
 ,, 22—Thomas Barbar and Alis Secker were married.
 ,, 23—Robert Brock had a child christened named Jane.
 ,, 24—Wyllm Brock and Anne Seck were married.
 ,, 27—Rye: Haule had a child christened named John.
Nov. 9—Wyllm Ayckrod had a child christened named Eliz.
 ,, 18—Mathew Barbar had a child christened named .....
 ,, 20—Robert Olred wife was buried.
 ,, 20—John Bradforth had a child christened named Anne.
 ,, 21—Wm Olred had a child christened named John.
 ,, 21—Thomas Secker and Margaret Barker were married.
Dec. 3—Rye: Both had a child buried named John.
 ,, 11—Robert Smyth had a child christened named .....
 ,, 19—John Hepworth had a child christened named Elyne.
 ,, 21—Thomas Bradforth was buried.
 ,, 23—Briane Hagh was buried.
 ,, 27—Alison Baull was buried.
Jan. 2—Georg Brok had a child christened named Anne.
 ,,   8—Alyson Bull had a child christened named Dorite, and as she saith yt one Caye is the Father of it.
 ,, 13—Thomas Secker had a child christened named Edward.
 ,, 16—John Le, of Gawthorpe, had a child buried named Martyne.
 ,, 17—Peter§ Grene had a child christened named Essabell.
 ,, 18—Robert Smythe had a child buried named Mary.
 ,, 29—Arthur Longley and Jenet Barbar were married.

‡ This name is taken from Mr. Hemingway's copy.
§ Taken from Mr. Hemingway's copy.

1558.
Feb. 1—Wyllm Sleth, otherwise called Skot, had a child buried named John.
 ,,   6—Lawrance Bothman and Elizabeth Copley were married.
 ,, 19—Briane Hagh had a child christened named Briane.
 ,, 20—Wyllm Brocke had a child christened named Nycoles.
 ,, 22—Elizabeth Tomson was buried.
Mar. 9—Rye: Wittelay had a child christened named Alice.
 ,, 17—Jenet Mylls, wife of John Mylls, was buried.
 ,, 18—Jenet Schayf had a child buried named Jenet.
 ,, 19—Jenet Boy was buried.
 ,, 22—Christofer Nayler had a child christened named Helene.‖
In the year off our Lord God mdlx., this is the Register Bock for this year. †
1560.   Abrille (first day of).
April 1—Adame Fayrbarne had a child christened named ....
 ,, 11—James Hagh had a child christened named James.
 ,, 23—James Barber had a son christened named Jams.
May   1—John Beldon had a child christened named Anne.
 ,, **—Robert Wykyngson and Sebell Beldon were married.
 ,, 29—John Denyson was buried.
June 7—Robert Byrkby had a child christened named Elisabeth.
 ,, 11—Thomas Ricson, Osset, had a child buried named Thomas.
 ,, 19—John Le, of Sowwood, had a child christened named Sybell.
 ,, 23—John Wood, late wife of Ric Wood, was buried.
 ,, 24—John Diche had a child christened.
 ,, 25—Thomas Langfeld and Augnes Audsley were married.
July 7—John Lee, of Gawthorpe, had a child christened named Edward.
 ,, 12—James Hagh had a child buried named James.
 ,, 13—Roger Inyllizar had a child buried named John.
 ,, 13—..... wane Alanson had a child christened named Wyllm.
 ,, 17—Wyllm* Beldon had a child buried named John.
 ,,   †—John Fayrbarne had a child christened named Edward.
 ,, 22—Nycoles Clark had a child christened named Ane.
 ,, 24—Robert Saxton had a child christened named Grace.
 ,, 26—Rye: Disforth had a child christened named John.

‖ Taken from Mr. Hemingway's copy.
** The date has disappeared.
* Taken from Mr. Hemingway's copy.
† The date has disappeared.
‡ The entries for 1559 are wanting.

1560.
July 30—Thomas Barbar had a child christened named Elsabeth.
  „ 31—Alis Ayckrod, wife of Thomas Ayckrod, was buried.
Aug. 8—John Wylson had a child christened named John.
  „ 11—Robert Olred and Jane Speght were married.
  „ 21—John Walcar had a child christened named Esabell.
  „ 28—John Wylson was buried.
  „ 29—Nycoles Nayler had a child christened named Nycoles.
  „ 30—John Excame had a child christened named John.
Sept 1—John Clayton had a child christened named Rychard.
  „ 6—Edward Gommersall had a child christened named Thomas.‡
  „ 11§—Thomas Secker and Margret Gybson were married.
       The same day Rye. Betthson had a child christened named Rye.
  „ 13—Rye Both had a child christened named . . . . .
Sep. 13—John‖ Oired had a child christened. . . . . Agnes Worm . . . ll.
Oct. 9—Robert g . . de . . had a child christened named Iszabell.
  „ 9—Thomas Secker had a child christened named Nycoles.
  „ 12—Thomas Sharpus had a child christened named Fraunces.
  „ 14—Thomas Sharppus had a child buried named Frannces.
  „ 18—John Robynson had a child christened named Issabell.
  „ 19—Wyllm Kynto was buried.
  „ 29—John byrtaun** was buried.
Nov. 8—Lawrance Bothman had a child buried named Johua.
  „ 12—Mathew Speght had a child christened named Willym.
  „ 18—Thomas Lidbetter had a child christened named Margret.
  „ 21—Roger Dawson was buried.
Dec. 2—Anne Wornwall was buried.
  „ 6—Rye. Hall had a child christened named Dorite.
  „ 10—Thomas Rowbotham was buried.
Jan. 1—Christofer Nayler had child christened named . . . .
       The year of our lord god A. m. d. (remainder torn off.)
       Rye Bothe had a child buried (remainder torn off.)
  „ 13—Willm Carter and Jenyt Scafe had a child (? christened) bayst. gotten named . . . .

‡ The child's name is taken from Mr. Hemingway's copy.
§ The date has disappeared from the original. It is taken from Mr. Hemingway's copy.
‖ The christian name is taken from Mr. Hemingway's copy.
** Bycame in Mr. Hemingway's copy.

1560.
Feb. 1—Mychaell Alane had a child christened (remainder torn off.)
  „ 2—Wyllm Robynson and Agnes Grayve were married.
  „ 5—Annes Greune was buried.
  „ 10—Robert Broune of Leds and Agnes Byerell of Dewsbury had a child christened bast. gotten named Robert.
  „ 13—Thomas Secker had a child christened named Wyllm.
  „ 19—Rye. Nayler had a child christened named Dorite.
  „ 19—Thomas Ryeson had a child christened named Esabell.
March 9—Henry Gybson had a child christened named . .
  „ 10—Robert Walcar had a child christened named Elizabeth.
  „ 12—Robert Olered had a child christened named John.
  „ 13—Robert Olred had a child buried named John.
  „ 15—John Disforth was buried.
  „ 18—Ann Gybson was buried.
  „ 17— . . . . Kent had a child christened named Wyllm.
  „ 21—Wyllm Wytteley had a child christened named Annes.
  „ 26— . . . . . llson was buried.
1561.
April 4— . . . . ecker had a child christened named Wyllm.
  „ 5— . . . . anderson was buried.
  „ 9— . . . Walcar had a child christened named Wyllm.
  „ 14— . . . llm Audesley was buried.
  „ 15—Roger Knowels had a child christened named Nycoles.
  „ 25—Annes Rawson was buried.
May 4—Thomas Taylyer and Alye Dych had a child christened named Thomas and bast: gotyne.
  „ 9—Robert Walcar had a child buried named Elizabeth.
  „ 9—Rye. Spyght had a child christened.
  „ 18—Edward Worwall had a child christened named Edward.
June 2—Robert Bradforth was buried.
  „ 3—Wyllm Andrue was buried.
  „ 4—Christofer Nayler had a child christened named . . .
  „ 4—Robert Brocke had a child christened named . . .
  „ 8—Thomas Taylyer had a child buried named Thomas.
  „ 29—Wyllm Lee had a child buried named Fraunces.
July 3—John Soniarde had a child christened named Wyllm.
  „ 4—John Mylls had a child christened named Roberte.
  „ 6—John Dishforth and Ezabell Le were married.
  „ 28—Wyllm Scote had a child christened named Anne.
  „ 29—Edward Wornwall was buried.

1561.

Aug. 2—James Haigh had a child christened named Tho . . .
„ 3—Robert Strynger and Agnes Grenno were married.
„ 10—Thomas Ayckrod and Sybell Hagh were married.
„ 29—Wyllm Lee had a child christened named Sybyll.
Sept. 15—Roger Clayton had a child christened.
Oct. 19—John Wylson had a child christened named Thomas.
Dec. 3—Edward Tomson had a child christened named Wyllm.
„ 9—John Gaston had a child christened named Mary.
„ 20—John Arnald had a child christened named Doryte.
„ 21—Robert Mathew and Esabell Clark were married.
„ 24—Mr. John Rudd Bacheler of Divinite and Vicar of Dewisbury had a child christened named Elsabethe.
„ 28—Thomas Barbar had a child christened named Alis.
Jan. 3—Nycoles Sayvell and Elizabeth Barbar had a child christened named John and bast : gotyne.
„ 6—Thomas Sharpus had a child christened named Esabell.
„ 13—Robert Longley was buried.
Jan. 17—Wyllm Sylleswyck was buried.
Feb. 1—George Brocke had a child christened named Isabell.
„ 9—Rye : Wood was buried.
„ 10—Emer Fox was buried.
„ 15— . . . . Bradforth was buried.

1562.

Oct. 19*—John Ayckerod was buried.
„ 22*—Beatrice Fayrebarne a child was buried.
„ 25*—Thomas Grene had a child baptised named Margrete.

Novembre 1562.

Nov. 1*—Nicholais Clarke had a child baptised named Rychard.
„ 3*—Rye : Clarke a innocent was buried.
„ 6*—Robert Olleroid a ladde was buried.
„ 11*—Thomas Aickerod had a child baptised named Averay.
„ 11*—James Barebar had a child baptised named Martyn.
„ —Arthure Hyrst had a child bapt : named†
„ 22*—Arthure Hyrste and Margrete Kytchin were married.
„ 22*—John Walcar had a child baptised named Elizabeth.
Dec. 1*—Rycharde Awdsloi and Beatrice Wurnall were married.
„ 6—Chrystofer Nailer had a child baptised named John.
„ 13—John Lee had a child buried named Jamys.
„ 21—Thomas Marshe and Elizabeth Stead were married

* The day of the month is taken from Mr. H.'s copy.
† The last five words of this entry are struck through with a pen.

1562.

Januarie 1562.

Jan. 3*—Margrete Fyncho was buried.
„ 6*—John Dyshforth had a child baptised named Thomas.
„ 8*—Rychard Slacke was buried.
„ 10*—John Lee had a child baptised named John.
„ 14—John Crowder wife was buried.
„ 24—Rychard Nailer had a child baptised named Thomas.
„ 25—Rychard Speyght had a child baptised named Rychard.

Februarie 1562.

Feb. 10—Willm Whytley had a child baptised named Ezabell.
„ 14—Thomas Secker had a child baptised named Nicholas.
„ 16—Genet Otes was buried.
„ 27—Willm Lee wife was buried.
March 1—Willm Rawson had a child baptised named Annes.
„ 4—Roger Gawnt had a child baptised named Annes.
„ 7—Edmnd Earlo had a child baptised named Robart.
„ 7—Robart Deie had a child baptised named Jane.
„ 25—George Broke had a child baptised named Christofer.

1563.

Aprille 1563.

April 4—Roger Bryggo had a child baptised named Robart.
„ 7—Wyllm Chylde wife was buried.
„ 7—George Pyckend was buried.
„ 7—George Deie wife was buried.
„ 9—John Conyer had a child baptised named Thomas.
„ 10—Rychard Wylcocke had a child baptised named Edward.
„ 11—Edward Gomersall had a child baptised named Edward.
„ 16—John Grene had a child buried.
„ 18—Rychard Beatson had a child baptised named Kateryn.

Anno Dni. Mo Do sexagesimo iijo.

May 4—Ezabell Whitles a child was buried.
„ 4—Wyllm Lee and Annes William were married.
„ 9—Willm Burnet and Jane Godraie were married.
„ 13—Elizabeth Hall a child was buried.
„ 14—Michaell Alan had a child baptised named Henrie.
„ 14—Beatrice Fayrebarne a child was buried.
„ 23—Henrie Gybson and Elsabeth Spyvie were married.
„ 23—Alexander Byrle was buried.
„ 23—John Walcar had a child baptised named Joanne.
„ 25—John Robynson and Elsabethe Wornall were married.
June 15—Edwarde Dawson and Genett Sykes were married.

1563.
June 19—Robarte Broke had a child baptised named Robarte.
July 4—Rychard Cosyn had a child baptised named Ric.
" 4—Robart Saxton had a child baptized named Elzabeth.
" 5—Willm Walker and Margrete Rychardson were married.
" 6—John Northoppe and Alys Stansfeld were married.
" 7—Robarte Brygge a child was buried.
" 8—Francys Secker an Innocent was buried.
Aug. *5—John Dyshforth had a child baptised named Wyllm.
" *5—Robarte Walshaie had a child baptised named Alice.
, *22—Wyllm Stotte had a child baptised named Barbare.
" *2..—Edmunde Dawson had a child baptised named Ezabel.
Sept. †9—Kateryn Beatson a child was buried.
" 9—John Hyrste had a child baptised named Grace.
" 9—John Huchonson had a child baptised named Sibylle.
" 21—Esabell Mylner had a bastard baptised named Annes.
Oct. 3—Rycharde Awdysley had a child baptised named Rychard.
" 12—Rycharde Hopton and Genett Bayldon were married.
" 24—Wyllm Aickerod had a child baptised named Rychard.
" 25—Rychard Stansfeld and Genett Dawson were married.
Nov. 7—Edwarde Barebar had a child baptised named Henrie.
" 14—Antonie Pook had a child baptised named Robart.
" 15—Robarte Myllnars‡ was buried.
" 21—Annes Mylner a bastard was buried.
" 29—John Clayton had a child baptised named Henrie.
" 30—Rycharde Boythe had a child baptised named Rycharde.
Dec. 5—John Stocks had a child baptised named Lawncelette.
" 12—John Mylues had a child baptised named John.
" 19—Roger Clayton had a child baptised named James.
" 19—John Exame had a child baptised named Genet.
" 26—Edwarde Tomson had a child baptised named Robart.
" 26—John Sharpe had a child baptised named Doritye.

* The day of the month is taken from Mr. H's copy.
† It is doubtful whether the day of the month is IX or XIX in the original.
‡ This is Mr. H's reading. I think the word is more like Wytthars.—S. J. C.

1563.
Jan. 1—Benet Medley was buried.
" ||—Margrete Rayner had a child baptised named Genett.
" ||—Willm Bayldone had a child baptised named Grace.
Feb. ||—Robart Byrkbe had a child baptised named Robart.
" 13—Wyllm Lee had a child baptised named Willm.
" 13—Robart Walcar had a child baptised named Rychard.
" 16—John Lee had a child baptised named Robert.
" 20—Rychard Whytlaye had a child baptised named Margrete.
" 20—Nicholes Duxburie had a child baptised named John.
" 22—Robart Earle a child was buried.
March 5—Thomas Mawnsell had a child baptised named Annes.
" 5—Wyllm Burnett had a child baptised named Willm.
" 25—Robart Olleroid had a child baptised named Robart.
1564. Apryll anno Dni. Mᵒ Dᵒ sexagesimo iiijᵒ.
April 1—Thomas Barebar had a child baptised named Edward.
" 4—Willm Dawson had a child baptised named Dorothie.
" 2—Henre Clayton a child was buried.
" 22—Annes Colier was buried.
May 5—Margrete Otes an old woman was buried.
" 12—John Dyshforth had a child baptised named Willm.
" 14—James Haghe had a child baptised named Alice.
" 15—John Bayldon had a child baptised named June.
" 29—John Lynlay and Annes Whitticars were married.
" 29—Anne wyffe of Willm Bayldon was buried.
June 11—John Fayrebarne had a child baptised named Anne.
" 13—Genett Jannyns had a bastard baptised named John.
" 23—Margerie wyfe of Ric. Diconson was buried.
July 2—John lasles and ezaboll late wyfe amer Fox were married.
" 13—Richard Nayler an old man was buried.
" 16—John Robynson had a child baptised named Henrie.
" 17—John Jannys a child was buried.
" 17—Rychard Boythe a child was buried.
Aug. 6—Thomas Secker had a child baptised named Averaie.
" 13—Margrete Dyeson had a child baptised named Willm.
" 20—Rychard Beatson had a child baptised named June.
" 28—Rycharde Beatson was buried.

|| The day of the month has disappeared.

DEWSBURY PARISH REGISTERS.

1564.
Sept. 3—Mathwe Barebar had a child baptised named Gregorie.
,, 3—Robart Asheton had a child baptised named Elizabeth.
,, 10—*John Hepworth had a child baptised named Thomas.
,, 15—*John Dyshforth had a child buried.
,, 17—Thomas Quill† and Elsabeth Quill† were married.
,, 20—*Agnes Syks a child was buried.
‡—Mr. John Rud had a child baptised named Marc.
‡—Wyllm Broke had a child baptised named Mychaell.
Oct. 3—John Deie and Esabell Milnes were married.
,, 15—Willm Baildon and Ganett Scayve were married.
,, 17—Alexaundre Broke an innocent was buried.
,, 26—Robart Walkar had a child baptised named Henrye.
,, 26—Peter Grene had a child baptised named Elyzabethe.
,, 26- Chrystofer Nayler had a child baptised named Robert.
Nov. 5—Rye. Stansfeld had a child baptised named Agnes.
,, 8—Thomas Sharpus wyfe was buried.
,, 12—Wyllm Rawsonne had two children baptised, the one named Alice the other Margrete.
,, 12—Thomas Wormall had a child baptised named John.
,, 12—Alexander Gybson had a child baptised named Thomas, bastard gotten.
,, 19—John Wylson had a child baptised named John.
,, 19—Henrye Nayler and Elizabeth Barbure were married.
Dec. §—Wylliame Farrande had a child baptised named Elizabeth.
,. 17—John Daie had a child baptised named John.
,, 17—Jamys Barebar had a child baptised named Robart.
,, 21—Alice Rawson a child was buried.
,, 24—John Dyshforth had a child baptised named Edmunde.
Jan. 10—Elizabeth Grene a child was buried.
,. 14—Thomas Seeker had a child baptised named Marmaduke.
,, §—Thomas Leadbeater and Agnes Helyfeld were married.
,, §—John Scayfe and Genett Smith were married.
Februarie Anno Dni. no Do sexagesimo quinto.
Feb. 2— arte Ballo had a child baptised named Marie.

* The christian names are taken from Mr. Hemingway's copy.
† It is difficult to decide whether the first letter of the surname is g or q in the original.
‡ The day of the month has disappeared.
§ The day of the month has disappeared.

1565.
Feb. 4—Thomas Sharpus and Annes Fearnlay were married.
,, 26—Robarte Bedforth had a child baptised named Grace.
,, 24—James Barebar an innocent was buried.
March 3—Leonard Dyeonson had a child baptised named Alice.
,, 6—Roger Gaunte had a child baptised named Elsabeth.
,. 10—Richard Speight had a child baptised named Willm.
,, 25—Robert Gylle had a child baptised named George.
,, 25—Roger Hyrste had a child baptised named Elizabeth
,, 28—John‖ Wormall was buried.
April 15—Willm Gylle had a child baptised named Elsabethe.
,, 21—Richard Booithe had a child baptised named Ric.
,, 22—Robart Allen was buried.
,, 29—Thomas Ayeredde had a child baptised named Rachell.
,, 29—Thomas Grene had a child baptised named Anne.
May 20—Robart Lee and Alis Haghe were married.
,, 31—Richard Torquell had a child baptised named Bryan.
June 9—Willm Smythe had a child baptised named Annes.
,, 24—John Bradforth had a child baptised named Esabell.
,, 25—Rychard Byrkebie was buried.
July *—Robert Lea had a child baptised named Rychard.
,, ,,—Janys Haldisworth and Alis Walcar were married the same day.
,, 6—John Grene was buried.
,, 7—John Alan was buried.
,, 8—Randall Nettylton had a child baptised named Janys.
,, 10—John Olroid was buried.
,, 11—Brian Torquell was buried.
,, 15—Robart Marshall and Genett Burghe were married.
Aug. 1—Frauncys Fayro† Larne an innocent was buried.
,, 9—Genett Nettylton an innocent was buried.
,, 12—Jane Nettilton an innocent was buried.
,, 12—Roger Knolles had a child baptised named Genett.
,, 13—Willm Baildon wyfe was buried.
,, 19—Willm Arundell had a child baptised named Annes.
Sept. 4—Genett Knolles a child was buried.
,, 9—John Huchonson had a child baptised named John.
,, 16—Richard Boothe a child was buried.
,, 22—John Huchonson a child was buried.
,, 29—Andrew Pickeryng had a child baptised named Grace.

‖ The christian name is taken from Mr. Hemingway's copy.
* The day of the month has disappeared.
† Two words in the original.

1565.

Sept. 29—John Hyrst had a child baptised named Margrete.
Oct. ‡1—John Arnold had a child baptised named Francis.
,, 1—John Dyshforth had a child baptised named Robart.
,, 8—John Secker was buried.
,, 11—John Hyrst wife was buried.
,, 21—John Lee had a child baptised named John.
,, §18—Robart Robynson had a child baptised named Rychard.
,, 18—Edward Phylype had a child baptised named Katheryn the same day.
Nov. 30—Robert Walsheye had a child baptised named Johan the last (day).
,, 25—Rychard Hall and Esabeth Byrkebe were married.
Dec. 25—Margaret Allan widow was buried.
Jan. 15—Robart Wormall had a child baptised named Elzabeth.
,, 15—Thomas Sykes and Dorathye Secker were married.
,, 20—John Mylne had a child baptised named Henrye.
,, 20—Agnes Olred had a child baptised named Thomas a bastard.
,, 26—Robart Byrkebe had a child baptised named John.
Feb. 3—Esabell Beamound had a child baptised named Wyllm a bastard.
,, 4—Thomas Wormall had a child buried named Esabell.
,, 4—Thomas Whyttacars and Margaret Ayerode were married.
,, 3—Esabell Dyshefurth was buried.
,, 7—Esabell Beamound had a child buried named Wyllm a bastard.
,, 9—Thomas Horsefurth and Agnes Barbur were married.
,, 10—‖George Broke had a child baptised named Myghaell.
,, 10—Thomas Syke had a child baptised the same day named Elizabeth.
,, ...‖Stocks had a child baptised named Dorytye.
Date gone.....Robart Byrkebe had a child buried named Robart.
Feb. 19—Robart Denton was buried.
Date gone....James Hemmyngwaye had a child baptised named Agnes.
,, ¶21—James Barbur was buried.
Date gone.....Chrystofer Nayler had a child baptised named Chrystofer.

Marche 1566.

Mar.**2—Robart Marshall had a child baptised named Wyllm.

‡The day of the month has disappeared.
§It is doubtful whether the day of the month is xviij or xxviij.
‖Taken from Mr. Hemingway's copy. The original is very indistinct.
* Date taken from Mr. Hemingway's copy. I think it ×××× in the original.—S. J. C.
** Date taken from Mr. Hemingway's copy.

1566.

Mar. 6—Adam Fayrebarne was buried.
,, 6—Margrett Pyckeringe was buried.
,, 17—Omneferayo Dyeson had a child baptised named Ales.
,, 23—Edward Barbur had a child baptised named Sybell.*
,, 23—John Hepworthe had a child baptised named John.*
,, 23—John Wulker had a child baptised named Henrye.
,, 23—Robart Suxtonn had a child baptised named Esa...*
,, 6—Thomas Sharpus was buried.
,, 31—Wyllm Dawsonn had a child baptised the last day named..........

Apryll 1566.

April 7—Thomas Sharpus had a child baptised named..........
,, 7—John Exunn had a child baptised named ....
,, 10—Agnes Hyrst was buried.
,, †27—Chrystofer Nayler had a child buried.
May 13—Roger Claytonn had a child baptised named Genett.
,, 13—Agnes the wife of Wyllm Bug was buried.
,, 17—Omneferayo Elys had a child baptised named John.
,, 17—Edmunde Earle had a child baptised named James.
,, 20—Edward Gomersall had a child baptised named Anne.
,, 27—Robart Dey had a child buried named Dorathy.
June 1—Robart Ollredd had a child baptised named Grace.
,, 1—Wyllm Burnett had a child baptised named Jane.
,, 3—Genett Walker was buried.
,, 9—Rychard Lyusedge and Agnes Olredd were married.
,, 9—Rychard Awdesleye had a child baptised named Johnna.
,, 9—Dorathy ..... ⎱ had a child baptised James Shaw ⎰ named Katheryne.
,, 16—Robart Hyrst and Margarett Grene were married.
,, 18—Roberte Kaye‡ and Alys Barbur were married.
July 2—Edward Walker and Elizabethe Speyght were married.
,, 9—Wyllm Roger and Agnes Wod were married.
,, 21—Mychaell Allann had a child baptised named Agnes.
Aug. 4—John Beldon had a child baptised named Marc.
,, 5—Jane Baull was buried.
,, 15—Essabell Walker was buried.
,, 18—Wyllm Ayerodde had a child baptised named Awerray.

* The child's name is taken from Mr. Hemingway's copy.
† The date is taken from Mr. Hemingway's copy.
‡ "Laye" in Mr. Hemingway's copy.

1566.
Aug. 18—Rychard Lee had a child baptised named Dorathye.
 „ 25—Rycharde Chossyn† had a child baptised named John.
Sept. §1—John Dycanson had a child baptised named Frances.
Date gone......Thomas Mawnsfeld had a child baptised named Thomas.
Sept. 15—Edward Walkar had a child baptised named Sabbell.
 „ 15—Edward Tomson had a child baptised named Elsabett.
Sept. 15—John Boothe had a child baptised named John.
 „ 20—Rychard Chollar was buried.
 „ 21—Robert Walkar had a child baptised named John.
 „ 24—Wyllam Bull and Elsabet Ball were married.
Oct. 6—Wyllm Brouke had a child baptised named Elisaboth.
 „   8—Rychard Awdesleye and Elisabethe Walker were married.
Date gone......Genet Dyshefurthe the wife of John Dyshfurthe was buried.
Oct. 21—Rychard Thompsonn had a child baptised named Mychaell.
 „ 28—John Nettiltone had a child baptised called John.
Nov. 1—John Suuyer had a child baptised named Rychard.
 „ 10—Thomas Barbur had a child baptised named Johanne.
 „ 11—Wyllm Bayldonn had a child buried named Maduke.
 „ 16—Christopher Nayler had a child buried named............
 „ 20—Thomas Whyttacars had a child baptised named ....
 „ 26—Willm Hansonne and Elsabeth............ were married.
Dec. 18—Alys Bull was buried.
Jan. 18—Sir Richard North‖ was buried.
Date gone......Thomas Sekker had 2 children baptised ....
Jan. ¶21—Thomas Seeker had a child buried.
 „ **22—............Nettilton and Annes Sharpus were married.
 „ 24—Thomas Seeker had a child buried called Thomas.
 „ 26—Alis the daughter of Edward Tombsonn had a child baptised named Elizabethe.
Feb. 4—Roger Boutt†† was buried.

‡ This name is written over an obliteration and is very indistinct. The first letter may be a small "t," and there are traces of a sign of abbreviation at the end of the word.
†It is doubtful whether the day of the month is 1st or 5th. It is partly worn away.
¶This name is doubtful. It is very indistinct.
* This entry is taken from Mr. H.'s copy, it has almost entirely disappeared from the original.
** The day of the month is taken from Mr. H.'s copy.
†† This name may be Bent. It is in a handwriting different from the adjoining entries.

1567.
Feb. 24—Rychard Speight of Heaton had a child baptised named John.
 „ 24—Robert Walker of Boudroude had a child baptised named Elzabet.
1567.
 „ 26—Wyllm Witticars clarke of Dewisbere had his wife buried named Elsabith.
 „ 26—John Morvell of Ousset had his wife buried.

Marche 1567.
March 2—Wyllm Wytley of Batley Car had a child baptised named John.
 „   8—Thomas Acrode had a child baptised named Thomas.
 „ 24—Edmund Jepson had a child baptised named Edmund bast gottin with Jennett Haveor.
April 6—*Wyllm Dysfurthe had a child baptised named Esabell.
 „ 13—............ had a child baptised ....
 „ 27—............ cristene named Doryte.
May   2—Roger Claton had his daughter Annes Claton buried.
 „ 15—Wyllm Grene was buried.
 „ 18—John Robynson had a child christened called Elisaybeth.
 „ 27—John Prince and Jenyt Taylyer were married.
June 1—Willm Lee had a child christened named ....
 „ 15—John Hucchinsone had a child baptised named Elsabethe.
 „ 21—John Goodfelow was buried.
 „ 22—Richard Hadesley had a child baptised called Elsabeth.
July 6—Leonard Diconsone had a child baptised called Leonard.†
 „   6—Wyllam Bedforth had a child baptised called Elsabeth.
 „ 13—‡Thomas Juct and Esabell Skott were married.
 „ 16—‖Johen Pence of Osset had his wife buried called Margaret.
 „ 16—‖Roger Tayllyer had a son buried.
 „ .... of Sutell had a child christened called Rychard.
 „ 20—Roberte Grene had a child baptised named Johan gotten with Betteres Ronesley.
 „ 31—............ was buried.
Aug. 3—§Ball of Over Boudred was buried.
 „   3—............ Day had a child baptised.
 „   5—‖Wyllm Witticar the clarke had his son Robert buried.
 „   5—Thomas Gant the elder was buried.
 „ 27—Willm Wyttikars was buried.

* The day of the month and the Christian name are taken from Mr. H.'s copy.
† Name taken from Mr. H.'s copy.
‡ This man's name is taken from Mr. H.s copy. It is illegible in the original.
§ This reading is doubtful. The name is almost illegible.
‖ Date taken from Mr. H.'s copy.

1567.
Aug. 31—John Deye had a child baptised named Anne.
  ,, 31—Ryehard Beateson had a child baptized named Anne.
Sept. 13—¶Laurence Bull and Elsabethe Gibson were married.
  ,, 14—John Leye had a child baptised named Jayne.
  ,, 15—Ryehard Seeker was buried.
  ,, 21—Wyllm Bull had a child baptized named Averaye.

Monie wch the church wardanns laid out.
Imprimis at the visytations - - xij^d
Item for mendinge of the clocke - xij^d
Item for mendind of the beles (bells) ij^s viij^d
Item at one communion (on part**) - viij^d
Item at a other communions· - ij^s
Item for ringinge on the crowneration day - - - - - - xx^d
Item for paintinge the queenes armes iiij^s
Item to the ronges (ringers - - - ij^s
Item to the clarke for the clocke keepinge - - - - iij^s iiij^d
Item for wyne at Ester - - ij^s
  and xij^d to Edward Seeker at an other communon
Item to the Rogers (ringers) agane - xx^d
Item for the table cloths   ,,   iij^d
Item for bread at Ester and all other tymes - - - - vj^d††
Item our charges at the laye layinge of ourselves and the iiij men - x^d
Item to Willm Ackrood for stoms leadinge - - - - - xij^d††
Item paid for writinge - - iiij^d

1571.

Here followyth^o all the burialls xines (christenings) and weddings wch weare in the yeare of our lord godd 1571 Anno Regni Regine Elizabethe Decimo Quarto. This yeare weare Willm Dawson Robarte Bedfourthe younger (younger) John Claiton Mathew Speight Thomas Waide and Richard Clarke churchewardens. A^o d^i 1571.

1571.
Mar. 16—Inpmis Sibiell Walker was buried.
  ,, 29—George Allande had a child christened named Elisabethe.
April 12—Roger Monssefeld had a child christened named Issabell.
  ,, 17—Edwarde Gomersaule had a child buried named James.
  ,, 19—Uxor Monssefeld was buried called Eliz:
May 15—Richard Whiteheade was buried.
  ,, 20—Thomas Gomersaill buried his wife named Margaret.
  ,, 20—Mr. George Gascoyne had a child christened named Nicholis.
  ,, 29—Robarte Wornemull buried his wife named Jenit.

* Date taken from Mr. H.'s copy.
** The words in brackets are struck out.
†† These sums have disappeared from the original and are taken from Mr. H.'s copy.

1571.
May 30—Richard Bradfourthe buried his wife named Issabell.
  ,, 30—Andrew Pickeringe had a child christened named Edwarde.
June 2—Richard Hurst of Ossit buried a child named Thomas.
  ,,   3—John Wornemalde buried his wife named Alee.
July 14—John Wilbore had a child baptised named John.
  ,, 21—Thomas Tyas had a child baptised named Thomas.
  ,, 27—Richard Audesley had a child baptized named John.
Aug. 10—John Walker of Ossyt had a child baptised named Doritie.
  ,, 14—*Thomas Ramesden of Ossitt was buried.
  ,, 18—Willm Lunde was buried.
Sept. 13—Willm Acroode had a child buried named Willm.
  ,, 21—John Mylnes had a child christened named John.
Oct.   6—Mihicll Alland had a child christened named Willm.
  ,, 13—Noper (Christopher) Nailer had a child baptised named Margaret.
  ,, 18—Jeferaye Acrode and Margaret Ramesden were married.
  ,, 28—John Disfourthe of Gauthrope had a child christened named Thomas.
  ,, 30—John Stocks and Annes Haines were married.
Nov.   9—Edwarde Greine and Doritie Whittikers were married.
  ,, 16—Richarde Haule and Annes .... were married.
  ,, 23—Thomas Seeker of Heaton had a child christened named Robarte.
  ,, 23—John Dickinsone of Ossit had a child christened named Elizabethe.
Dec.   7—Mr. Hughe Casson had a child christened named Willm.
  ,, 17—Robarte Dawson had a child christened named Thomas.
  ,, 17—Willm Tottie was buried.
  ,, 20—Edwarde Walker was buried.
  ,, 22—Robarte Dawson had a child buried named Thomas.
  ,, 27—John Stocks had a child christened named Henrye.
  ,, 30—George Walker was buried.
  ,, 30—Jefferay Ackeroid had a child christened named Margaret.
Jan.   3—Alison a baldon was buried.
  ,,   3—Jeferay Ackeroide had a child buried named Margaret.
  ,,   4—John Walker of Ossit was buried.
  ,,   7—Nicholis Walker was buried.
  ,, 14—Lawrance Bull had a child christened named Richarde.
  ,, 14—Thomas Whittikers had a child christened named Robarte.
  ,, 14—Willm Burnet had a child baptised named Rowlande.

* The day of the month is taken from Mr. H.'s copy.

1571.

Jan. 16—John a bentley had his servant buried named ....
„ 23—Willm Berkinge had a child christened named Brigyt.
„ 23—Willm Gill had a child christened named Willm Gill.
Feb. 7—Rogar Clayton had a child christened named ....
„ 7—Sander Gibsone had a child christened named Grace.
„ 7—Willm Harison had a child christened named Edwarde.
„ 11—The said Willm Harrison had a child buried named Nightetinggaile.
„ 12—Edward Secker and Margere Barber were married.
„ 17—Sander Gibsone buried his child named Grace.

Anno Di 1572.

1572.
Mar. 1—Richard Bows, Reder, of Ossit was buried.
„ 8—Thomas Barber had a child christened named Anne.
„ 12—Robarte Walkar of Bowteroid was buried.
„ 15—Hughe Nettilton had a child christened named Rychard.
„ 15—John Tobby of Caverlaie prishe (parish) had a child christened named Grace.
„ 22—Robarte Saxton had a child buried named John.
„ 25—Richard Audeslay of Gawthrope had a child christened named Elizabeth.
„ 25—Mr. Willm Haworthe Vicar had a child christened named Marye.
„ 26—Richard Audeslay had a child buried named Elizabethe.
„ 27—James Haige alitr (otherwise) Collier buried his wife called Jenet.
„ 30—Xoper (Christopher) Denton had a child christened named Issabell.
„ 30—Thomas Shepperd aliter (otherwise) Leadebeater had a child christened named John.
„ 31—John Lee the elder was buried.
April 13—John Wilby buried his wife named Kaitherine.
„ 17—Robarte Clarkesone had a child christened named Issabell.
„ 23—John le (Lee) of Gawthrop had a child christened named Thomas.
„ 30—John Bothe had a child christened named Kaitherine.
May 11—Nicholis Secker of Dewisburie was buried.
„ 14—John Disheforthe of Gawthrop had a child christened named Richard.
„ 26—Henry Robinsone was buried.
June 3—Imprimis John Auty younger (younger) had a child base begotten with Alison Bradforth weh weare buried and xined (christened) in the house the night before and buried upon the iij day of June named John.

1572.

June 7—Robarte Ollared had a child christened named Marmaduke.
„ 7—Edward Arundall had a child christened named Robarte.
„ 9—Robarte Speighte and Jane Ackeroid were married.
July 11—Thomas Nowill and Doritie Lobley were married.
„ 16—Richard Haull had a child christened named Willm.
„ 18—The same child was buried.
„ 24—Willm Dawson had a child christened named Jenyt.
Aug. 7—John Litellwod and Alce Walker were married.
„ 14—George Grene and Elizabethe Burrell were married.
„ 19—John Hurst had a child christened which was base begotten with Janyt Jeninge named Issabell.
„ 22—John Bentley had a child buried which was baptised at home named John.
„ 29—Uxor Robarte Walker was buried.
„ 30—Edmonde Jebsone had two children christened which were base begotten with Brigge wife the one named Jenyt the other Marye.
Sept. 3—Willm Bradforth was buried.
„ 7—John Sandell and Margaret Peace were married.
„ 14—Richard Exsome had a child christened named Rowland.
„ 15—Hughe Monsfield was buried.
„ 16—Gylbert Hiddesdell buried his wife named Sybell.
„ 18—Gylberd Hiddessdell himself was buried.
„ 18—John Litelwod had a child christened named Alce.
„ 19—The said child was buried.
„ 23—Henry Hepworthe and Jenit Austley were married.
„ 26—Robarte Wormell and Betteris Lee were married.
„ 28—John Forest and Uxor Johann Walker de Ossit were married.
„ 29—Arthur Tomsone and Issabell Crowder were married.
„ 30—Willm Bull had a child christened named Grace.
Nov. 11—Robarte Threpeland and Alyce Barbar were married.
„ 16—Robarte Speight had a child christened named James.
„ 29—Thomas Ackeroid had a child christened named Jenytt.
„ 29—Roger Clarksonne had a child christened named Dorytye.
Dec. 7—James Haulle and Elizabethe Smithe were married.
„ 14—Roger Hurst had a child christened named Margarett.
„ 14—John Lee of Gawthrope had a child christened named Richard.
„ 18—Robarte Byrkby had a child christened and buried named Robarte.

DEWSBURY PARISH REGISTERS.

1572.
Jan. 4—Edward Philip had a child christened named Briande.
" 4—John Stocks had a child christened named Willm.
" 15—John Dey had a child christened named Edwarde.
" 18—Thomas Peace and Elizabeth Audesley were married.
" 20—Ambrose Unbye and Grace Speight were married.
Feb. 4—Willm Broke had a child christened named ....
" 11—Richard Boithe of Ossit had a child christened named Jams.
" 15—Willm Arrandell had a child christened named Willm.
" 30—Andrew Pickeringe had a child christened the xxx^t day named Thomas.
" 30—John Huchinsone had a child christened the same day named Edwarde.
" 30—Thomas Secker had a child christened the same day named Robart.

The monithe of Marche Anno Di. 1573.

1573.
Mar. 19—Robarte Askelonne had a child christened named Marmaduke.
" 26—James Hurst had ij children christened the one named Thomas and the other named Grace.
" 27—James Hurst buried one of his said children named Thomas.
" 30—Richard Audesley of Gauthroppe had a child christened named Anne.
April 8—James Hurst had a child buried named Grace.
" 9—Willm Whitley had a son buried named ....
" 23—George Grene buried a child which was christened in the house named John.
May 1—Thomas Shepherd aliter Leadebeater had a child christened n. Annes.
" 3—Uxor Secker was buried named ....
" 8—Uxor Kitchinge of Gawthropp was buried.
" 11—Allexsander Gibsonne had a child christened named Anne.
" 15—Uxor Warde of Ossit was buried named Annes.
" 16—Willm Cartar of Dewisburie was buried.
" 18—Richard Nayler of Ossit was buried.
" 19—John Wilbe and Uxor Elizabethe Walker late wife of Edwarde Walker deceased were married.
" 27—Thomas Franne* and Elizabethe Gaunte were married.
" 27—Willm Dawsone had a child buried named Edyc.
" 27—Richard Peace of Ossit had a child christened named Dorite.
June 1—John Bradley and Jenit Le were married.
" 1—Edmonde Earle buried his wife named Annes.
" 3—Elizabeth Dinysone daughter of Richard D. was buried.

1573.
June 14—Richard Bradfourth had a child christened named Richarde.
" 14—Robart Wornnell had a child christened named Betteris.
" 15—The said child was buried.
" 21—John Ollerede had a child christened named John.
" 21—Jayne Peace had a child xined (christened) wch weare begotten of her brother whome fled his way upon ye same ye child named John.
" 23—............ Wilbye widow was buried.
July 4—John Litelwod had a child christened in the house which weare buried the iiijt day named ....
No date.—Jeferay Ackeroide had a child christened named Annes.
" 12—Robert Bradforth and Dority Audesley were married.
" 14—Richard Dynisone and Elizabeth Maude were married.
" 19—John Forest of Osset had a child christened named Issabel.
" 20—Edwarde Kitsone and Elizabethe Boith were married.
Aug. 25—John Claiton had a child christened named John.
" 26—Richard Cowsinge had a child christened named Robart.
" 29—Willm Greine son of Richard was buried.
" *2—John Knowles had a child christened named Annes.
Sept. 3—James Secker had a child christened named John.
" 4—The same child was buried.
" 6—Hughe Casson had a child christened named Dorytye.
" 11—Uxor Speight of Sotehill was buried.
" 20—Uxor Ward of Ossit was buried.
" 26—Uxor Monsfeild was buried named Alyce.
" 28—Robart Nailer was buried.
Nov. 7—John Forest and Uxor Walker were married.
" 20—Thomas Peace had a child christened named John.
" 26—Christopher Denton had a child christened named Elizabeth.
" 30—Thomas Broke of Ossit had a child christened named John.
Dec. 7—Christofer Nailer had a child christened named Sybell.
" 13—John Ollerede had a child christened named Robart.
" 18—Richard Bradforthe had a child buried named Robart.
" 18—John Clayton had a child christened named Alce.
" 20—Sr. Hughe Casson Curait of Dewisburie had a child buried named Dorytie.
" 27—Jeferay Ackeroide had a child christened named Elizabeth.

* This entry is under August in the Register, possibly it should be under September.

* Possibly Franco.

DEWSBURY PARISH REGISTERS.

1573.
Dec. 27—Robarte Ollerede had a child christened named ....

The monithe of January Anno Dni. 1573.
Jan. 7—John Robinsone had a child christened named Robart.
Jan. 17—Thomas Greine had a child christened named Agnes.
„ 28—Leonarde Dixesone had a child christened named Alce.
„ 30—Allexsander Gareladie and Margaret Le were married.
Feb. 22—James Nettyltone of Ossit had a child christened named Robte.
Mar. 6—Willm Gill of Ossit christened a child named Francis.
„ 13—Edwarde Greine had a child christened named Edwarde.
„ 13—George Allande had a child christened named Annes.
„ 15—Robart Haveycarde buried his wife.
„ 20—Uxor Hurst was buried.

The monithe of Apriell Anno. Dni. 1574.
1574.
April 4—Thomas Monsfeild had a child christened named Willm.
„ 4—John Bradley had a child christened named Anne.
„ 8—Edwarde Greine had a child buried named Edward.
„ 8—John Robinsone had a child christened named Abrose.
„ 10—James Hurst buried his wife named Alisone.
„ 12—John Wilbe had a child christened named Robart.
„ 13—George Greue had a child christened named Francis.
„ 20—John Beamonde was buried.
May 13—John Dishforth of Gawthrope was buried.
„ 20—Edward Tomson was buried.
„ 26—John Dishforth had a child christened named Elyzabeth.
June 3—John Hurst and Jenet Nayler were married.
„ 13—Nicholis Nayler was buried.
„ 22—John Wilson and Jenyt Smyth were married.
July 13—Willm Gyll was buried.
„ 21—John Sumyart had a child buried named John.
„ 29—Agnes Birle had a child buried named Edward.
Aug. 3—Thomas Whitacares had a child christened named Edward.
„ 3—Rychard Dinison had a child christened named Thomas.
„ 8—Agnis Boyth had a child christened named Dorytye.
„ 9—Rychard Forrest and Agnis Walker were married.
„ 9—Thomas Lankefeld and Jenet Hall were married.

1574.
Aug. 13—Thomas Backhouse had a child christened named Thomas.
„ 18—George Stringer and Mary Spight were married.
„ 18—John Marshe had a child christened named Mary.
„ 22—Thomas Backhouse had a child buried named Thomas.
„ 28—Lorance Bull had a child christened named Annis.
Sept. 21—James Audisley and Jenet Wade were married.
„ 21—Willm Dauson had a child christened named Mathew.
„ 25—John Nayler was buried.
„ 30—Alexander Gibson had a child buried named Annis.
Oct. 3—John Walker had two children christened the one named Franncis the other Jenet.
„ 3—John Lyttellwood had a child christened named Elizabeth.
„ 10—Willm Brocke had a child christened named Edward.
Nov. 15—Franncis Grene had a child christened named Robart.
„ 25—Roger Mannsfeld had a child christened named Elizabeth.
Dec. 1—Willm Fearneley of Gawthrope buried his wife.
„ 20—Mr. Wyllm Shirlley had a child christened named ....
„ 25—Hught Nettleton had a child christened named John.
Jan. 6—Rychard Audeslye had a child christened named Rychard.
„ 6—Thomas Sickes had a child christened named Jenet.
„ 13—John Stockes had a child christened named Edwarde.
„ 13—Rychard Forrest had a child christened named Dorytye.
„ 25—Olde Spight wife of Chidsell was buried.
„ 25—Christopher Tenaunte and Jenet Jegger were married.
Feb. 8—*John Gooddall and Alis Bradforde were married.
„ 9—Nicholis Walker and Annis Audisley were married.
„ 10—Alexaunder Gibson had a child buried named Alis.
„ 12—Gorge Blagburne had a child christened named Gorge.
„ 13—Richard Nayler had a child christened named Thomas Nayler.
„ 26—Mathew Ball had a child christened named Willm.
Mar. 1—Robart Spight had a child christened named Margreat.
„ 6—Robart Wormall had a child christened named Robart.
„ 20—Uxor Jacson was buried.

---

* There is an "x" before the "viij" in the original. It is doubtful whether it forms part of the date or not.

1575.

Heare after folletho the names of all such p'sones as weare maryed christined and buryed wythin the prishe of† from ye xxvt day of Marche in the year of our Lord God 1575. These beinge Churchewardenes for Dewisbury Richard Whitley Roger Clayton Thomas Gante sistant‡ for Settell John Farnell Robart Nayler for Osset John Forrest Thomas Peace.

Mar. 29—Thomas Secker had a child christened named Elizabeth.
April 6—Christopher Denton had a child christened named Willm.
  ,, 12—Robart Lee had a child buryed named Agnis.
  ,, 20—John Lee had a child buryed named Dorytye.
  ,, 18—Thomas Langfeld had a child christened named Dorytye.

The monythe of May.

Nycolis Hucheson and Agnis Lee were married the ix day of April.
May 16—Willm Burnet had a child christened named Jefferaye.
  ,, 17—John Robinson and Elizabeth Greno were married.
  ,, 26—Thomas Laughtfeld had a child buried named Dorytye.
June 7—Willm Storye and Elizabeth Bull were married.
  ,, 13—John Hurst and Annis Huchason were married.
  ,, 18—Rychard Audesley had a child buried named Rycharde.
  ,, 22—John Steade was buried.
July 4—Willm Tayler wife was buried.
  ,, 12—Robarto Dyshforth and Esabell Tomson were married.
  ,, 18—Thomas Barber had a child christened named Thomas.
  ,, 18—John Lee had a child christened the same day.
  ,, 19—John Bull and Elizabeth Glydall were married.
  ,, 24—Andrew Pickeringe had a child christened named Annis.
  ,, 30—John Oldrode had a child christened named Tobie.
Aug. 17—Roger Hurst had a child buried named John.
  ,, 21—Alixaunder Gibson had a child christened.
  ,, 21—Thomas Nowell had a child christened named Dorytye.
Sept. 14—Old Wilcoke wife was buried.
  ,, 21—Robart Peaker had a child christened named Roger.
  ,, 30—John Dishforth had a child buried named John.

† Name of parish omitted.

‡ This word is not easy to read. Mr. H. has left a blank for it in his copy. There is a blank space left after Robert Nayler's name sufficient to contain another name.

1575.
Oct. 2—Robart Naylor had a child christened named Jenet.
  ,, 9—John Hurst had a child christened named Athomye.
  ,, 9—Rychard Ashton had a child christened named ....
  ,, 15—James Audesley had a child christened named Esabell.
  ,, 16—John Slacke had two children buried.
Nov. 6—Edward Greno had a child christened named Dorytye.
  ,, 12—John Bayldon was buried.
  ,, 19—John Gooddall had a child christened named Edward.
  ,, 20—John Bentley had a child christened named Mercye.
  ,, 26—Thomas Peace had a child christened named Thomas.
Dec. 4—John Grawe and Elizabeth Oldrode were married.
  ,, 4—Nicholis Pickeringe had a child christened named Annis.
  ,, 18—Roger Knowoles had a boye buried being xij yeares the xviij day of December named Nicholas.
  ,, 24—Rychard Spight wife was buried.
  ,, 26—John Walker of Osset had a child buried.
  ,, 30—Robart Greno had a wenche buryed of the age of xij yeares named Anna.
Jan. 7—Old Shepherde wife was buried.
  ,, 8—Thomas Birle had a child christened named Elizabethe.
  ,, 8—John Hucchason had a child christened and was buried the xiij day of the same month named Anne.
  ,, 15—John Bradley had a child christened named Willm.
  ,, 26—Edward Arrandell had a child christened named Willm.
Feb. 10—Ather Tomson Wild* was buried.
  ,, 16—Thomas Chaster had a child christened named Edward.
  ,, 19—Willm Dawson and Elizabeth Dishforth were married.
  ,, 22—James Haughe and Esabell Hepworthe were married.
  ,, 22—Robert Haveyardd was buried.
  ,, 26—Nicholas Huchason had a child christened.
  ,, 28—Christopher Brought and Esabell Wood were married.
  ,, 28—John Lyttellwoode had a child christened named Joyce.
  ,, 28—Franncis Greno had a child christened named Grace.
Mar. 10—John Forrest had a child christened named Anne.
  ,, 18—John Bull had a child christened named Margoryt.

1576.
The monithe of Aprill Ao dni 1576.
April 13—Rychard Autye had a child christened named Edwarde.

* Query—Is Wild a mistake for wife?

1576.
April 22—Thomas Grene had a child christened named ....
May 6—Rychard Audesley had a child christened named Edwarde.
 „ 13—Thomas Grene had a child buried.
 „ 13—Athour Tomson and Alis Bradforth were married.
 „ 17—Margreat Grayson was buried.
 „ 20—Old Ellis wife was buried.
 „ 20—John Wilbe had a child christened named John.
 „ 27—Wyllm Dawson of Gawthrope had a child christened named Alixaunder.
 „ 27—Robert Daye was buried.
 „ 29—Roger Knowles was buried.
June 4—Thomas Sheppard buried his wife.
 „ 4—Edward Walker son of John Walker was buried.
 „ 10—Thomas Shepparde had a child christened named Willm.
July 8—Willm Dawson had a child christened named Edward.
 „ 8—Thomas Pickard and Jenet Bingley were married.
 „ 1—George Gamell and Dorytye Nayler were married.
 „ 15—John Robinson had a child christened named Margaret.
 „ 16—Rowland Owen Keeper of New Parke† had a child buried named Leonard.
 „ 22—John Hurst had a (child) christened named John.
 „ 25—Christopher Nayler had a child christened named Robart.
 „ 25—Edward Kitson buried his wife.
Aug. 6—Loraunce Bull had a child christened named Loraunce.
 „ 6—Rychardo Arnalde and Ann Dawson were married.
 „ 16—Gorge Grene had a child buried named ....
 „ 19—Gorge Allin had a child christened named ....
Sept. 19—Sur Roger Nayler was buried.
 „ 23—Roger Hurst had a child christened named Robarte.
 „ 23—John Knowles had a child abristened named Anne.
 „ 23—Hary Hepworth had a child christened named Willm.
Oct. 7—Roger Swallow and Margreat Acroode were married.
 „ 7—John Diconson had a child christened named Annis.
 „ 7—Robart Wornall had a child christened named Edwarde.
 „ 8—John Barker was buried.
 „ 21—Mr. Rowlande Owen Keeper of the New Park had a child christened named John.
Nov. 11—Thomas Pace had a child christened named Thomas.

† The New Park of Wakefield, situate in Ossett and Alverthorpe.

1576.
Nov. 15—James Dison had a child christened named Thomas.
 „ 25—Franncis Ellis was buried.
Dec. 9—Rychard Forrest had a child christened named Elizabethe.
 „ 10—Thomas Maunsfelde had a child christened named Rychard.
 „ 16—Thomas Wormall had a child christened.
 „ 16—John Lee had a child christened named Abraham Lee.
 „ 24—Grace Daye was buried.
 „ 26—Willm Gill wife was buried.
 „ 29—Old Bothe wife was buried.
Jan. 5—Marmaduke Mason had a child christened named John.
 „ 13—James Haigh had a child christened named Grace.
 „ 20—Thomas Gill and Anis Nayler were married.
 „ 20—John Forrest had a child christened named Willm.
 „ 20—John Robinson had a child christened named Alis.
 „ 21—John Spight and Anis Claiton were married.
 „ 22—Thomas Sickes had a child buried named John.
 „ 27—Leonarde Diconsone had a child christened named Alan.
 „ 29—Margreat Oiles was buried.
Feb. 3—Henry Ellis had a child christened named Edwarde.
 „ 11—Thomas Backhouse had a child christened named Willm.
 „ 11—Hught Nettelton had a child christened named Alexaunder.
 „ 12—Elis Grene was buried.
 „ 25—Robart Robinson had a child christened named ....

1577.
The moneth of Marche 1577.
Mar. 14—John Farburne was buried.
 „ 17—John Spight had a child christened Katherine.
 „ 23—Thomas Willboro had a child christened bast gotten named Thomas
 „ 28—Peter Fairebarne was buried.
April 5—James Audesley had a child christened named Jenett.
 „ 7—Christopher Broughe had a child christened named ....
 „ 8—Christopher Nayler had a child buried.
 „ 13—John Forrest buried his wife.
 „ 25—Thomas Gyll buried his wife and had a child christened the same day named Agnes.
May 1—Thomas Grene had a child christened named Agnes.
 „ 6—Willm Haule and Catheryn Dieson were married.
 „ 19—John Boye and Mary Gybson were married.
 „ 19—Willm Smythe alias Wood and Margaret Byrle were married.
 „ 20—Thomas Ramsoden was buried.

DEWSBURY PARISH REGISTERS.

1577.
May 24—Rye Nayler was buried.
" 24—John Stocke had a child christened named Francis and buried another named John.
June 2—Robt Olroyd had a child christened named John.
" 14—Richard Ashetonne had a child buried named John.
" 15—Robt Dysforthe son of John Dysforthe was buried.
" 16—Nycholas Kykley (Keighley) and Margarett Bradforthe were married.
" 16—Robarte Bedforthe had a child christened named Edward.
" 16—Wyllm Storye had a child christened named John.
" 20—Edward Seekar had a child christened named Nycholas.
" 23—George Brooke had a child christened named ....
July 13—John Nettleton had a child christened named Beterys.
" 15—Robart Dawson had a child christened named Roger.
Aug. 11—John Scayle was buried.
" 31—Robart Bayldon had a child christened named Thomas.
Sept. 1—Edward Bull and Dyanye Craven were married.
" 6—Edward Philyppe had a child christened named Dorytie.
" 8—George Grene had a child buried named John.
" 14—George Gamoll had a child buried named John.
" 18—John Hirste had a child christened named Nycholas.
" 20—John Grayse had a child christened named Elyzabeth.
Oct. 13—Andrew Pickeringe had a child christened named Fraunces.
" 20—John Bull had a child christened named Edwarde.
Nov. 9—Jenet Wood was buried.
" 9—Lorance Pickeringe had a child christened named Margret.
" 10—Willm Walker and Agnes Rychardson were married.
" 12—Robart Spight had a child christened named Edward.
" 14—Thomas Birle had a child christened named Samvell.
" 19—Thomas Powell buried his wife.
" 25—Robart Peaker had a child christened named John.
" 29—Thomas Ball had a child christened named Abraham.
" 30—John Mylnes had a child christened named Thomas.
Dec. 2—Old Dynison wife was buried.
" 10—John Wilbe had a child christened named Samvell.
" 15—John Olrood had a child christened named Sarac.
" 16—Robart Bradforth and Jenet Brooke were married.

1577.
Jan. 16—Rychard Newsom had a child christened named Alixaunder.
" 16—Lorance Pickeringe had a child buried named Margreat.
" 19—Willm Brooke and Dorytye Fairbarne were married.
" 26—Nicholis Pickeringe had a child christened named Marye.
Feb. 2—Alis Wood had a child christened bast gotten weh she sayd one John Brealhay was the father named John.
" 3—John Goodall had a child christened named John.
" 3—Gorge Blagburne had a child christened named John.
" 10—Edward Rydall and Anne Edmesall were married.
" 10—Rychard Beatson wife was buried.
" 13—Andrew Pickeringe. had a child buried named Agnis.
" 17—John Lyttelwoode had a child christened named John.
" 17—Frauncis Grene had a child christened named ....
" 27—Rychard Whitlay had a child christened named Elizabeth.

1578.
The monith of March Ao Dni. 1578.
Mar. 8—Richard Cussinge had a child christened named Willm.
" 13—John Grene was buried.
" 13—Alexander Gibson had a child christened named ....
" 14—Matthew Bull was buried.
" 18—Robart Clarkeson buried his wife.
" 24—John Autye buried his wife.
April 1—Edward Bull had a child christened named Elyzabethe.
" 7—John Hurst had a child christened named ....
" 16—Old Kent wife was buried.
May 3—Willm Bull had a child christened named ....
" 4—Ooldo Dysfurth wife was buried.
" 7—Nicholas Kighley had a child christened named Grace.
" 11—Edward Moore and Agnis Wade were married.
" 18—Robarte Lee had a child christened named Margreate.
" 21—Christofer Denton had a child christened named James.
" 21—Rychard Speight was buried.
" 25—Willm Bornet had a child christened named James.
" 27—Thomas Pickard had a child christened named Thomas.
June 8—Wyllm Addie and Elyzabeth Ellmsall were married.
" 11—Rychard Dynison had a child buried named John.
" 13—Old Ball wife was buried.
" 14—Thomas Sickes had a child christened named Jenet.
" 16—Nicholis Walker and Elyzabeth Seeker were married.

1578.
June 17—Wyllm Sharppus and Elizabeth Grene were married.
,, 17—Robart Burkbye had a child buried.
,, 18—Rychard Ashton had a child christened named Robart.
July 3—Nycholas Walker of Ossett had a child christened named Elyzabeth.
,, 6—Wyllm Walker had a child buried.
,, 9—Nicholas Walker of Dewseburye had a child christened named John.
,, 25—Edward Arandell had two children christened the one named Thomas ye other Mary.*
,, 26—Rychard Bradforth had a child christened named Agnis.
Aug. 6—John Marshe had a child christened named Mary.
,, 7—Thomas Smyth and Jenet Ellis were married.
,, 13—James Hage had a child christened named Elyzabeth.
,, 13—Edward Moore had a child christened named Edward.
,, 26—Thomas Wade was buried.
Sept. 7—Nicholas Hucchason had a child christened named Agnes.
,, 9—Edward Grene had a child christened named Alis.
,, 10—Thomas Caresforth and Margaret Saxton were married.
,, 12—Elyzabeth Tayler was buried.
,, 17—Thomas Peace had a child christened named Thomas.
,, 22—Gorge Gamell had a child christened named Thomas.
,, 23—Rychard Ashton had a child buried named John.
,, 25—Edward Arrandell had a child buried named Marye.
Oct. 1—Robert Dischforth had a child christened named Elyzabethe.
,, 8—John Forest had a child christened named Wyllm.
,, 9—Ather Tomson had a child christened named Dorytie.
,, 19—Thomas Forrest and Elyzabeth Walker were married.
,, 25—John Boytman and Elizabeth Haveyard were married.
,, 28—Robert Bradforth had a child christened named John.
,, 29—John Lytellwood had a child buried named Elyzabeth.
Nov. 6—Robert Spight was buried.
,, 9—Lorance Boylle had a child christened named ....
,, 9—Elyzabeth Bradforth had a child christened named Elyzabeth.
,, 12—Rychard Autie had a child christened named Antonye.
,, 12—Robart Nayler had a child christened named Nicholas.

* The following note is in the margin opposite this entry, viz:—"but 4d. for churchinge."

1578.
Nov. 18—Edward Seeker had a child christened named Edward.
,, 26—Rychard Peace had a child buried named John.
Dec. 2—Thos. Barber had a child buried.
,, 3—Rycharde Auddisley had a child buried named Willm.
,, 6—Mathew Spight was buried.
,, 26—John Walker of Ossett had a child christened named . . . .
Jan. 11—Wyllm Smythe was buried.
,, 18—John Walker of Dewsburie had a child christened named Edward.
,, 21—Robert Threapeland had a child christened named Elizabeth.
,, 31—Thomas Grylline had a child christened named John.
Feb. 8—Willm Dawson had two children christened named Willm and Elizabeth.
,, 9—John Smith alias Wood had a child christened named Isabell.
,, 9—Rychard Wood and Agnis Robinson were married.
,, 19—Rychard Wood had a new born child buried.
,, 21—Wyllm Spight was buried.
1579.
The monithe of Marche A^o Dni. 1579.
Mar. 4—Willm Whitley was buried.
,, 7—Rowland Owen Keper of New Parke had a child christened named Willm.
,, 12—Willm Sharppus had a child christened named Agnis.
,, 13—John Auddisley was buried.
April 1—James Auddisley had a child christened named Thomas.
,, 13—Agnis Bull had a child christened bast: begotten named Agnies.
May 10—Wyllm Brooke had a child christened named Agnes.
,, 20—Wyllm Sharppus had a child buried named Agnes.
,, 26—George Allyne had a child christened named Edward.
,, 31—John Robinson had a child christened named John.
June 4—Thomas Sheppard had a child christened named Marye.
,, 5—Wyllm Dawson had a child buried named Elyzabeth.
,, 10—Thomas Whyttakeres had a child buried named Agnes.
,, 29—Thomas Whyttakeres had a child christened named Agnes.
July 6—John Tomson had a child buried.
,, 10—Robart Spight had a child buried named Edward.
,, 18—Willm Addie had a child christened named Agines.
,, 27—Old Slacke wife was buried.
Aug. 16—John Mallinson and Margreat Smyth were married.
,, 23—John Pease was buried.
,, 28—Dorytie Lee was buried.

1579.
Sept. 6—Robart Musgreve had a child christened named Elyzabeth.
,, 8—Willm Walker had a child christened named Rychard.
,, 13—Rainebrowne Wright and Elizabeth Oldred were married.
Oct. 3—Thomas Whytikeres had a child buried.
,, 4—Rychard Burnet and Avice* Grene were married.
,, 4—John Bull had a child christened named Avice.*
,, 6—Syr Omfray Armitage Vicar of Warmefield and Jenet Smyth were married.
,, 12—Rychard Gybson and Margreat Dinison were married.
,, 12—John Philipe and Bettruse Raunsley were married.
,, 12—Frauncis Grene had a child christened named Willm.
,, 25—Christofer Houlte had a child christened named Jane.
,, 30—Edward Whytley had a child christened named John.
,, 30—Thomas Grene had a child baptised named Agnes.
Nov. 2—Thomas Ball had a child baptised named ....
,, 3—Willm Draunsfeld and Esabell Thornton were married.
,, 7—Peter Philipe and Elyzabeth Lee were married.
,, 10—Peter Philipe had a child christened named John.
,, 13—John Dicconson had a child christened named Christofer.
,, 17—Thomas Bachouse had a child christened named Thomas.
,, 21—Thomas Hurst buried his wife.
,, 26—John Saxton buried his wife.
,, 28—Christofer Hoult had a child buried named Jane.
,, 29—Thomas Robinson and Agnes Raunseley were married.
,, 30—Rychard Whittley had a child baptised named Rychard.
,, 30—Rychard Newsom had a child christened named Marmaduke.
Dec. 3—Willm Draunsfeld had a child baptised named John.
,, 6—George Fenche and Jenet Spight were married.
,, 10—Wilm Draunsfeld had a child buried named John.
,, 12—John Hurst had a child baptised named Elyzabeth.
,, 13—Rychard Peace had two children baptised, the one named Isabell and the other Ellen.
,, 18—John Lettlewood had a child baptised named John.
,, 25—Christofer Brooke had a child baptised named Christofer.
Jan. 13—John Bentley and Agnis Harison were married.

* Mr. Hemingway reads this name "Alice."

1579.
Jan. 14—Willm Harto and Margreat Brigge were married.
,, 18—Elyzabeth Atkinson was buried.
,, 20—Rycharde Woode had a child christened named Anne.
,, 20—Willm Harte had a child christened named Edward.
,, 24—Robart Burkebe had a child buried.
,, 29—John Bull had a child buried named Avice.
,, 30—Rychard Newsome had a child buried named Marmaduke.
Feb. 5—Willm Draunsfeld was buried.
,, 5—Old Bedforth wife was buried.
,, 12—George Fenche had a child baptised named Willm.
,, 16—Henry Elyse had a child baptised named Elyzabeth.
,, 20—Old Robinson wife was buried.
,, 27—John Wylbe had a child baptised named Elyzabeth.
Mar. 12—John Hurst had a child christened named Margreat.
1580.
April 25—Mr Wyllm Shirley had a child christened named Marke.
,, 27—Old Catryne of Osset was buried.
May 10—Henry Ellies had a child buried named Elysabeth.
,, 15—Andrew Pickeringe had a child buried named Elyzabeth.
,, 24—John Oldrode had a child christened named ....
,, 24—Thomas Pickard had a child christened named Robart.
,, 24—Thomas Sickes had a child buried.
June 10—Andrew Pickeringe had a child baptised named ....
,, 11—John Wormall and Margreat Wilson were married.
,, 12—Old Perker was buried.
,, 19—Elizabeth Armytage had a child base begotten christened named Willm was fathered upon Willm Whittley.
,, 21—John Doye had a child christened named Willm.
July 11—Thomas Gill and Elyzabeth Ackroode were married.
,, 16—Rychard Forrest had a child christened named John.
,, 24—Thomas Brigge and Sibbell Oldrood were married.
,, 26—Robart Lee of Sotell Comon buried his wife.
,, 30—Old Nettleton wife was buried.
Aug. 28—Omfraye Watterhouse had a child baptised named Elyzabeth.
,, 28—Robart Dawson had a child baptised named Rychard.
,, 31—Thomas Forrest had a child baptised named Christofer.
Sept. 1—Ric. Burnett had a child christened named Eliz.
Nicholas Walker had a child christened named Eliz.

1580.
Sep. 12—Mr. Willm Shyrley had a child buried named Marke.
,, 12—John Roper had a child buried.
,, 13—Alixaunder Barber and Isaboll Draunsfeld were married.
,, 15—Willm Brooke had a child christened named Elyzabeth.
Oct. 9—John Parker and Agnis Whitley were married.
,, 15—Rychard Aske and Esabell .... had a child baptised base begotten named Robarte.
,, 16—Edward Barber and Elyzabeth Willie were married.
,, 16—John Philipe had a child baptised named Dorytie.
,, 20—Rychard Wood had a child buried.
,, 30—Hughe Nettleton had a child baptised named Thomas.
,, 31—Rychard Ashton had two children christened, the one named Jane the other Robart.
Nov. 4—Thomas Whytakeres had a child buried named Edwarde.
,, 7—Bryan Lumble and Dorythe Skidlingthorpe were married.
,, 9—Nicholas Armytage had a child baptised named Robart.
,, 10—Rychard Oldred was buried.
,, 11—Andrew Pickeringe buried his wife.
,, 13—Thomas Robinson had a child buried.
,, 21—Old Beamonde wife was buried.
,, 29—Jeffray Ackrood had a child buried—this child was not christened the duetyo ....iijd
Dec. 13—John Robinson had a child baptised named James.
,, 18—Robert Gest had a child baptised named Susanna.
,, 18—Robart Musgreve had a child baptised named Rychard.
,, 25—John Bentley had a child baptised named Michell.
,, 26*—Nicholas Armitage had a child baptised named Robert.
,, 25—Edward Arrundell had a child baptised named Marmaduke.
Jan. 1—Rychard Pickeringe had a child baptised named Willm.
,, 2—John Dishforth had daughter buried named Elyzabeth.
,, 3—Edward Arrundell had a child buried named Marmaduke.
,, 10—Edward Kitson had a child baptised named Dorytie.
,, 11—Thomas Whytykeres had a child baptised named Elyzabeth.
,, 11—John Forrest had a child baptised named Christofer.
,, 15—The said John buried a child the same child.
,, 15—Rychard Jacson had a child baptised named Elyzabeth.

* This entry is interlined between the two lines of the preceding entry.

1580.
Jan. 18—Thomas Ackrood had a child baptised named Elyzabeth.
,, 19—Rychard Autie had a child christened named Thomas.
,, 25—Jefray Robinson and Alis Grene were married.
,, 30—Kateringe Nayler was buried.
Feb. 6—James Haghe had a child baptised named James.
,, 9—Edward Secker had a child baptised named Elyzabeth.
,, 9—Thomas Ackrood had a child buried named Elyzabeth.
,, 10—Rychard Wood had a child buried named Rychard.
,, 13—Lorans Bull had a child baptised named Alis.
,, 13—John Spight had a child baptised named Alis.
,, 13—Robart Goodalle had a child baptised named Margreat.
,, 15—Thomas Gryffine had a child baptised named Robart.
,, 16—John Wornall had a child baptised named John.
,, 21—John Marshe had a child baptised named Thomas.
,, 23—Andrew Pickeringe had a child buried.
,, 24—John Littlewood buried his wife.
,, 25—Roger Hurst had a child baptised named Rosamond.

1581.
Mar. 4—Thomas Griffinge had a child buried.
,, 10—Mr. Rowland Owen had a child baptised named Grace.
,, 5—John Marshe had a child buried named Thomas.
,, 29—Robert Lee was buried.
,, 31—Francis Grene had a child buried.
April 12—John Wornall was buried.
,, 23—Agnes Bull had a child buried.
May 7—Willm Lee and Agnis Armytage were married.
,, 7—Robart Neyler had a child buried named John.
,, 9—.........* and Agnis Peaker were married.
,, 16—Robart Neyler had a child buried named Jenet.
,, 23—Thomas Birle had a child baptised named Willm.
June 10—Willm Spight wife was buried.
,, 12—Leonard Diccenson had a child buried.
,, 13—Nycholas Nailer and Elyzabeth Ackrood were married.
,, 17—Edmond Arrundell was buried.
,, 20—John Sheard had a child baptised named Christofer.
,, 28—John Jackson and Marie ....† were married.
July 1—Robart Wornall had a child baptised named Dorite.
,, 2—Willm Longley and Maude Daye were married.

* The husband's name is omitted in the Register.
† Blank in the Register.

1581.
July 9—Nicholas Atkinson had a child baptised named Marie.
,, 22—Mr. Blacke had a child baptised named Jason.
,, 23—John Sheppard had a child baptised named John.
Aug. 6—Thomas Gill had a child baptised named Elizabeth.
,, 13—Thomas Sekesf had a child baptised.
,, 16—Axixaunder Berbar had a child baptised named Thomas.
,, 20—Eward Whitley had a child baptised named Elizabeth.
Sept. 10—Abraham Garret had a child baptised which was base gotten named Thomas Garrett.
,, 15—George Finche had a child baptised named Elizabeth.
,, 17—Nicholas Huchuson had a child baptised named ....
,, 17—Thomas Robinson had a child baptised.
,, 23—Syr Rychard Loord had a child baptised named Susann.
,, 24—Thomas Gaunt and Margreat Chickeley were married the xxiiij day (this day).
Oct. 1—Alis Grene was buried.
,, 3—Thomas Harpine and Jenet Ramsdine were married.
,, 3—James Secker had a child baptised which was base gotten named Elyzabeth.
,, 9—Lorance Boythman and Alis Carter were married.
,, 8—Mr. Willm Shirley had a child baptised named John.
,, 8—Rychard Whitley had a child baptised named Elyzabeth.
,, 12—Willm Addie had a child baptised named Willm.
,, 20—Willm Saxton had a child baptised named Elyzabeth.
,, 26—Frauncis Grene had a child baptised named Elyzabeth.
Nov. 6—Willm Bull had a child baptised named Adam.
,, 17—John Sandie wife was buried.
,, 18—Willm Bull buried a child named Adam.
,, 19—Richard Bradforth had a child baptised named Elyzabeth.
,, 19—John Law and Alis Dikson were married.
,, 20—John Huchuson had a child baptised named Sibbell.
,, 21—Robart Bradforth had a child baptised named Elizabeth.
Dec. 2—James Secker and Agnes Diccouson were married.
,, 7—Elyzabeth Bradforth was buried.
,, 7—Willm Addie buried a child named Willm.
,, 17—John Walker had a child baptised named Marmaduke.
,, 25—Willm Brooke had a child baptised named Willm.

‡ So in the Register.

1581.
Jan. 1—Henrie Ellis had a child baptised named Anne.
,, 6—Willm Lee had a child baptised named Wyllm.
,, 6—John Bull had a child baptised named Sibell.
,, 6—Jeffray Ackeroode had a child baptised named John.
,, 12—John Tomson had a child baptised named Thomas.
,, 17—Lorance Boythman was buried.
,, 22—John Antie had a child baptised named John.
,, 24—Rychard Wood had a child christened named Jonie (? Joine).
,, 25—Christofer Brooke had a child baptised named Doritie.
,, 26—Edward Barber had a child christened named Henrie.
,, 27—George Grene buried his wife
,, 30—Christofer Kirke and Ellinge Nayler were married.
,, 31—John Ellis and Susanna Gooddall were married.
,, 31—James Audesley had a child baptised named John.
Feb. 2—John Forrest had a child baptised named Thomas.
,, 2—Thomas Archer had a child baptised named ....
,, 2—John Pickard had a child baptised named John.
,, 2—Edward Barber buried a child named Henrye.
,, 2—Old Boulton wife was buried.
,, 7—Christofer More had a child baptised named Doritie.
,, 13—John Lastlesse buried his wife.
,, 15—Rychard Audesley had a child christened named Christofer.
,, 15—Antonio Smithe had a child baptised named Agnies.
,, 18—Thomas Gryfinge had a child baptised named Anne.
,, 22—Athor Tomson had a child baptised named Rychard.
1582.
Mar. 4—John Walker had a child baptised named Agnis.
,, 4—Frauncis Grene buried his wife.
,, 4—Old Raundesley wife was buried.
,, 11—Rychard Spight had a child baptised named Philemon.
,, 16—Rychard Burnet had a child baptised named Avice.
,, 28—Thomas Wright had a child baptised named Marie.
April 14—Christofer Denton had a child baptised named Thomas.
,, 13*—John Hurst had a child baptised named Agnies.
,, 14—Robart Nayler son of Robart Nayler Under Banke was buried.

* This date has been altered and is not very distinct.

1582.
- April 16—Robart Baldon had a child baptised named Alis.
- ,, 17—Willm Longley had a child baptised named Nicholas.
- ,, 22—Christofer Freckleton had a child baptised named Agnis.
- ,, 29—Andrew Pickeringe had a child baptised named George.
- ,, 30—Thomas Smyth and Ann Brooke were married.
- May 6—John Robinson had a child buried named Jane.
- ,, 19—Thomas Peaze had a child baptised named Agnes Peace.
- ,, 21—John Walker and Jane Hurst were married.
- ,, 20—Edward Grene had a child baptised named Agnis.
- ,, 24—John Diconson had a child baptised named Thomas.
- ,, 27—John Gamnell had a child baptised named Agnis.
- ,, 30—Thomas Ackrood had a child baptised named Edward.
- June 2—Thomas Baull had a child baptised named Mercie.
- ,, 9—Willm Burnete had a child baptised named John.
- ,, 12—Robart Sharppus and Upsilie (qy. Ursilie) Tayller were married.
- ,, 12—John Hurst buried a child.
- ,, 19—Thomas Smyth had a child baptised named Agnes.
- ,, 20—Robart Auddislay and Anne Steade had a child baptised which was base gotten named Robarte.
- ,, 26—Franncis Grene and Jane Ireland were married.
- July 1 *Nicholas Ryghlay had a child baptised named Doritie.
- ,, 3—Robart Burkebe had a child baptised named Isabell.
- ,, 11—Robart Auddeslay had a child buried named Robert.
- ,, 15—John Beldon and Alis Tayller were married.
- ,, 15—John Blagburne had a child baptised named Elyzabeth.
- ,, 22—George Spight and Jenet Oldrood were married.
- Aug. 10—Omfray Watterhouse had a child buried.
- ,, 18—Edward Arraundell had a child baptised named Elyzabeth, and was buried the xx day.
- ,, 24—John Hurst had a child baptised named Margerye.
- ,, 24—Rychard Dynison had a child buried named Rycharde.
- ,, 30—Rychard Wood had a child buried.
- Sept. 2—Willm Knowles and Agnis Bryggo were married.

* This entry seems, when inspected by daylight, to read "Nicholas Ryghlay" &c., and not "Nicholas Ryghlay." The first letter of the surname is indistinct, Mr. Hemingway reads the surname "Dighlay."

1582.
- Sept. 9—Robart Sharpus had a child christened named Margerie.
- ,, 16—Robarte Bedforth was buried.
- ,, 29—Nicholas Nayler had a child baptised named Elyzabethe.
- Oct. 13—Willm Dawson had a child baptised the thurteth (? thirteenth) day named Elyzabeth.
- ,, 14—James Robinson buried his wife.
- ,, 16—Edward Bull had a child baptised.
- Novr. 4—Robart Addie had a child baptised named Elyzabeth.
- ,, 28—Edward Kytson had a child baptised named Willm.
- Decr. 5—Robart Audeschay and Alis Goodfellow were married.
- ,, 7—John Ellis had a child baptised named Isabell.
- ,, 18—Robart Spight had a child baptised named Elyzabeth.
- ,, 18—John Robinson had a child baptised named Grace.
- ,, 18—Edward Barber had a child baptised named Elyzabeth.
- ,, 19—Nicholas Huchason buried his wife.
- ,, 25—John Bentlay had a child baptised named Robart.
- Jan. 1—Edmond Ellis and Isabell Daye were married.
- ,, 1—Margreat Pyckeringe was buried.
- ,, 6—Thomas Ball was buried.
- ,, 9—Mr. R. Lord had a child baptised named Elyzabeth.
- ,, 13—Robarto Clarkeson had a child baptised named Elyzabeth.
- ,, 14—John Oldreed had a child baptised named Edwarde.
- ,, 16—Nicholas Walker had a child baptised named Edward.
- ,, 23—Robart Clarkeson had a child buried.
- ,, 29—Edward Arrandell had a child buried.
- Feb. 7—Richard Myllear and Margreat Daye were married.
- ,, 8—James Haghe had a child baptised named John.
- ,, 9—John Lyttlewood and Agnes Stansfeld were married.
- ,, 20—Old Byrele wife was buried.

Marche Ano Dni. 1583.
- Mar. 2—Rychard Bradforth had a child baptised named Willm.
- ,, 2—John Spight had a child baptised named Willm.
- ,, 2—John Grane (or Grave) had a child baptised named Thomas.
- ,, 2—George Spight had a child baptised named James.
- ,, 5—Edward Dicconson had a child baptised named Abraham.
- ,, 7—Rychard Antie had a child baptised named Marie.
- ,, 16—James Rychardson wife was buried.
- ,, 23—Nicholas Armytage had a child baptised named Esther.
- ,, 19—Hugh Nettleton was buried.
- ,, 25—Willm Sharppus had a child baptised.

DEWSBURY PARISH REGISTERS.

1583.
April 3—John Rayner was buried.
,, 6—Thomas Whytakeres buried his wife.
,, 9—Robarte Spyght buried his wife.
,, 9—Roger Lee had a child baptised named John.
,, 13—John Lawe was buried.
,, 13—John Robinson had a child baptised named John.
May * —Willm Brooke had a child baptised named Elyzabeth.
,, 14—Thomas Gyll had a child baptised named ....
,, 27—Nicholas Walker had a child baptised named Elyzabeth.
June 1—Thomas Watson was buried.
,, 2—Edward Phylipe had a child baptised named Willm.
,, 2—John Lytlewood had a child baptised named John.
,, 3—James Secker had a child baptised named James.
,, 9—W. Saxton had a child baptised named............
,, 9—James Auddisley had a child buried named............
,, *—Ric Myllner had a child baptised.
,, *—Nicholas Walker of Ossett had a child baptised.
,, *—Ric Denyzon had a child baptised named............
July 14—John Hurst had a child baptised named............
,, 13—Omphrey Waterhouse had a child buried.
,, 20—Andrew Pickeringe had a child baptised named Marie.
Aug. 10—Rychard Newsom alias Jackson had a child baptised named John. †
,, 25—Thomas Forrest had a child buried.
Sept. 15—Mr. Rowland Owen had a child baptised. †
,, 30—Rychard Forrest had a child baptised.
Oct. 12—Willm Addie had a child baptised named Robarte.
Nov. 10—John Hurst was buried.
,, 26—John Sunyear and Margreat Hurst were married.
Dec. 6—Richard Sowood had a child baptised named Anne.
,, 13—James Audeslay had a child buried named Rycharde.
,, 22—John Gooddall had a child baptised named Robarte.
,, 29—John Bentlay had a child baptised.
Jan. 12—John Blagburne had a child baptised named John.
,, 16—Willm Bull had a child baptised named............
Feb. 9—John Hayworth was buried.
,, 13—Mr. Hoyle and Alis Ackeroode were married.

* No date given in the original.
† The entries for August and September are almost illegible.

1583.
Feb. 21—Willm Wormall and Issabell Farrande were married.
,, 26—George Wilbye and Anne Lee were married.
1584. Marche Anº Dni 1584.
Mar. 3—Olde Nycholas Secker wife was buried.
,, 7—Thomas Grayne (or Grayve) had a child baptised named Thomas.
,, 13—Olde Thomas Gaunt wife was buried.
,, 19—Rychard Speight had a child baptised named Brice.
Apr. 4—Gauwen Meatcalfe had a child baptised named Edwarde.
,, 6—Henrye Whytehead and Agnis Saxton were married.
,, 18—Thomas Whytakeres and Agnies Hurst were married.
,, 21—Arthour Tomson had a child baptised named Margreate.
June 10—John Walker had a child baptised named Nicholas.
,, 10—Edward Whytlay had a child baptised.
,, 15—George Wilbee had a child baptised.
,, 25—Alixaunder Barber had a child baptised named John.
July 4—Rychard Dynison had a child buried.
,, 8—Robart Threapland had a child buried.
,, 10—John Willie had a child baptised named Edward.
,, 12—James Rychardson had a child baptised named Alis.
,, 13—James Rychardson buried his wife.
,, 23—Henry Headeley and Jenet Ratcliff alias Boyth were married.
Aug. 2—John Boye had a child baptised.
,, 2—Thomas Sickes had a child baptised.
,, 20—Christofer Broocke had a child baptised.
,, 22—John Sheppard had a child baptised.
,, 24—Robart Carter had a child baptised named Alis.
Sept. 5—John Speight had a child baptised named Elyzabeth. '
—Richrd Lord Curat had a child baptised the xxiiij of Februarii called Debora id est Abn. Aº Dni 1581. '
Jan. 3—W. Wormall was buried.
,, 12—Ric Newsom alias Jackson had a child baptised named Willm.
,, 8—Rich Griffine was buried.
,, 16—Ric Burnett had a child baptised named Alexander.
,, 16—Willm Sharpus had a child baptised named Thomas.
,, 25—John Bull had a child baptised named Lucee.
,, 28—Mathew Robinson had a child baptised named Annes.
,, 29—Thomas Pyckerde had a child baptised named Edward.
,, 29—Rycharde Cowood had a child baptised named Elizabeth.

* These two entries are written at the top of a page on which there are no other entries. There are no entries for October, November, or December.

1584.
Jan. 20—Nicholas Nayler had a child baptised named Robarte.
Feb. 8—Lorance Bull had a child baptised named Henry.
" 9—James Gornall alias Sharpe and Margreate Gaunte were married.
" 10—Lorance Bull had a child buried named Henry.
" 14—Thomas Gyll had a child baptised named Luce.
" 16—Richard Ashton had a child baptised named Luce.
" 26—Robart Cossinge was buried.
1585.
Mar. 3—Mr. Nicholas Wilbie had a child baptised named Joseph.
" 3—Old Lee wife was buried.
" 5—Persyfull Bingley was buried.
" 6—George Wilbie had a child baptised named Nicholas.
" 12—Rychard Hall was buried.
" 15—Edward Whytley had a child baptised named Rychard.
" 15—John Oldroode had a child baptised named Luce.
" 25—Willm Wormall had a child baptised named Abraham.
" 29—Robart Scolfeld was buried.
" 30—John Ellies was buried.
April 2—Mr. Roger Acroode had a child baptised named Margreat.
" 3—Robart Carter had a child baptised named Elyzabeth.
" 6—Bryan Crother and Isabell Wadesworth were married.
" 7—Rychard Whytley was buried.
" 14—Thomas Green had a child baptised named Robarte.
" 16—Edward Bull had a child baptised named Omfray.
" 24—Edward Wilcocke was buried.
" 24—John Robinson wife of Osset was buried.
June 21—Jenet Rychardson had 2 children buried base gotten.
" 26—John Robinson had a child baptised named Marie.
July 2—Rycharde Brigge had a child baptised named Margreat.
" 8—Thomas Birle had a child buried named Elyzabet.
" 8—John Crosfeld and Alis Mylnes were married.
" 9—Rychard Pickersgill and Sebell Whitley were married.
" 16—Edward Barber had a child baptised named Joyce.
" 16—George Barnbye had a child baptised named Ann.
" 23—John Parker had a child baptised named Mageryc.
Aug. 10—Thomas Birle was buried.
" 19—John Bayldon buried his wife.
" 19—Old Ellies Grene wife was buried.
" 22—Jeffray Acroode buried a child.
" 27—Rychard Sunyer and Agnes Exomo were married.

1585.
Aug. 27—Nicholas Huchingson had a child baptised named Elyzabeth.
" 27—John Grane (or Grave) had a child baptised named Agnies.
Sept. 2—Rychard Wood had a child baptised named Alixander.
" 2—Edward Roydes had a child baptised named Anne.
" 20—Nicholas Huchingson had a child buried named Elyzabeth.
Oct. 9—Willm Bradforth and Allis Law were married.
" 9—Adame Wheatley had a child baptised named Robarte.
" 15—John Wade had a child baptised named John.
" 28—Thomas Archer had a child baptised named Elline.
Nov. 3—Old John Audesley wife was buried.
" 7—Alixaunder Barber had a child baptised named Robarte.
" 10—John ....* and Isabell Nayler were married.
" 13—Andrew Pickeringe had a child baptised named Robarte.
" 20—Nicholas Arinytage had a child baptised named William.
" 20—Rychard Sunyeare had a child baptised named Thomas.
" 29—Thomas Fearneley and Agnes Dishforthe were married.
Dec. 11—Willm Gaunte had a child baptised named Susanna.
" 18—Willm Brooke had a child baptised named Dorytie.
" 28—Mr. Lowlande (Rowland) Owen had a child baptised named Kateringe.
Jan. 1—John Goodall had a child baptised named ....*
" 1—Omfray Watterhouse had a child buried.
" 6—Marmaduke Spight had a child baptised named Susann.†
Feb. 4—Thomas Pelles had a young child buried.
" 6—Wyllin Fayrebarne was buried.
Feb. 11—Thomas Wade wife was buried.
" 11—Christofer Brooke had a child buried.
" 13—John Sheppard had a child baptised named James.
" 16—Robarte Wormall had a child buried named Agnis.
" 19—Oulde Rycharde Lee was buried.
" 26—Olde Brooke wife was buried.
" 27—Thomas Hurst was buried.
1586.
Mar. 1—John Oldroode had a child buried named Mychell.
" 4—Christofer Brooke had a child baptised named Dorytie.
" 9—John Hurst had a child baptised named Edwarde.
" 12—Thomas Sheppard was buried.
" 16—Thomas Grayve had a child buried named Robarte.

---
* Blank in original.
† "Luce" struck out.

1586.
Mar. 18—Willm Bayldone was buried.
 ,, 21—Thomas Tyas buried his wife.
April 9—George Nayler had a child baptised named Jenne.
 ,, 18—William Speight had a child baptised named Rychard.
 ,, 22—George Lee had a child baptised named Luce.
 ,, 28—William Saxton had a child baptised named William.
 ,, 30—William Speight had a child buried.
May 2—Gylbart Oldrood buried his wife.
 ,, 5—Rychard Ashton buried his wife.
 ,, 7—Rychard Dynison had a child baptised named Agnies.
 ,, 28—Robart Sharpus had a child baptised named Elyzabeth.
June 4—John Lockewood was buried.
 ,, 12—Agnis Clayton was buried.
 ,, 25—Elyzabeth Arrandell was buried.
July 1—Rychard Bradforth of Ossett had a child baptised named Lyonell Bradforthe.
 ,, 11—John Brodley was buried.
 ,, 13—William Fearneley was buried.
 ,, 24—Mr. William Shirley had a child baptised named Mychell.
Aug. 7—Rychard Bradforth of Dawgrene had a child baptised named Agnis.
 ,, 24—Sr John Hoyll had a child baptised named Jeremye Hoyle.
 ,, 25—Rychard Speight and Margreat Clayton were married.
 ,, 26—John Dyconsou buried his wife.
 ,, 29—John Saxton was buried.
Sept. 9—Robart Bull was buried.
 ,, 13—John Walker had a child baptised named Josephe.
 ,, 16—Robarte Mysgreve had a child buried named ....‡
 ,, 22—Edward Boyll had a child buried named Agnies.
 ,, 25—John Oldrood of Hiuging Heatou had a child baptised named Jenet.
 ,, 28—Robart Musgrove was buried.
Oct. 4—John Bentley of Osset had a child baptised named William.
 ,, 7—James Lee was buried.
 ,, 15—John Cordingley had a child baptised named John.
 ,, 18—Old Nycholas Walker wife was buried.
 ,, 19—John Farnell buried his wife.
 ,, 31—John Feether was buried.
Nov. 5—Lorance Bull had a child baptised named Thomas.
 ,, 6—Old James Walkes (Walker's) wife was buried.
 ,, 8—Rychard Cossinge was buried.
 ,, 11—Thomas Audsley was buried.
 ,, 12—Elyzabeth Andesley was buried.
 ,, 14—Thomas Audesley wife was buried.
 ,, 14—Thomas Graveson (or Graneson) and Janet Elmesall were married.
 ,, 18—John Audesley was buried.

1586.
Nov. 19—Edward Lee his wife was buried.
 ,, 21—Robarte Audesley and Dorytie Allinn were married.
 ,, 24—Elyzabeth Stanninge (?) was buried.
 ,, 30—John Oldrood had a child baptised named Isabell.
Dec. 3—Rychard Medley had a child baptised named John Medlaye.
 ,, 3—Alis Bradforth was buried.
 ,, 7—John Dyshforth was buried.
 ,, 9—Agnis Birle was buried.
 ,, 10—Rychard Armytage had a child baptised named Anne Armitedge.
 ,, 12—John Saxton and Anne Clarke alias Haryson were married.
 ,, 12—Edwarde Whytley was buried.
 ,, 16—Alis Rychardson was buried.
 ,, 17—Thomas Grayson had a child baptised named Agnies.
 ,, 17—John Bentley had a child buried named William.
 ,, 19—Alixander Brooke was buried.
 ,, 19—John Feather had a child buried named Elyzabeth.
 ,, 20—Thomas Peace was buried.
 ,, 20—Robarte Grene was buried.
 ,, 23—Elyzabeth Longley was buried.
 ,, 25—............* Diceonson (?) buried his wife.
 ,, 25—John Audesley was buried.
 ,, 25—Agnies Alline was buried.
 ,, 26—Mr. Nicholas Sayvell was buried.
 ,, 27—Jenet Dawson was buried.
 ,, 27—Rychard Armytage buried his wife.
Jan. 1—Nicholas Wood had a child christened base begotten named Rychard.
 ,, 2—Willm Brooke was buried.
 ,, 2—Thomas Maunsfield was buried.
 ,, 6—Rychard Whytley buried his wife.
 ,, 10—Andrew Pickeringe was buried.
 ,, 12—John Hurst had a child baptised named Agnies.
 ,, 12—John Cossinge was buried.
 ,, 12—John Farnell and Jenet Sickes were married.
 ,, 12—Elyzabeth Cossinge was buried.
 ,, 16—Thomas Sickes buried his wife.
 ,, 19—Rychard Peace buried his wife.
 ,, 21—Willm Longley had a child baptised named Susanna.
 ,, 21—Onfraye Waterhouse buried his wife.
 ,, 21—George Barmeely had a child baptised named Elyzabeth.
 ,, 25—Athonr Tomson buried his wife.
 ,, 27—Henrye Nowell buried his wife.
 ,, 28—John Denton buried his wife.
Feb. 1—Willm Dawson was buried.
 ,, 1—Lorance Bull had a child buried.
 ,, 7—John Wade was buried.
 ,, 7—Jon Ellis had a child christened named Susanna.
 ,, 9—John Bentley was buried.
 ,, 10—Thomas Dawson was buried.
 ,, 11—Edward Dawson was buried.

‡ Blank in original.   * Illegible in original.

1586.

Feb. 11—John Wroo and Margreat Gill were married.
,, 17—John Wyllson buried his wife.
,, 18—George Gammell had a child buried.
,, 19—Mr. Willm Hauworthe,† Vicar, was buried.
,, 24—Willm Bull was buried.
,, 25—Chrystofer Nayler was buried.
,, 25—Gylbart Lepton buried his wife.

† 1587.

Mar. 2—Thomas Peace wife was buried and a young child that she was delivered of was buried the same day.
,, 3—James Rychardson was buried.
,, 9—Christofer Mychell buried one of his maid servants.
,, 9—Old John Wade wife was buried.
,, 15—Dorithye Peace was buried.
,, 18—George Gammell buried his wife.
,, 30—Thomas Pickard had a child baptised named Agnes.

§ 1588.

April 6—Thomas Barber was buried.
,, 7—Raphe Lynley had a child buried base gotten in his house.
,, 12—Robart Stansfeld buried his wife.
,, 13—John Dyconson buried his wife.
,, 15—Rychard Audesley was buried.
,, 16—George Grayveson was buried.
,, 18—John Slacke buried his wife.
,, 19—Rychard Cowood was buried.
,, 19—John Feather had a child baptised named Elline.
,, 21—George Spight had a child baptised named Grace.
,, 22—John Goydall was buried.
,, 24—Willm Tayller of Gawthroppe was buried.
,, 25—Robart Wallshay was buried.
,, 28—John Dent and Jenet Rychardson were married.
,, 29—James Girnall alias Sharpe buried his wife.
May 8—Rychard Speight had a child baptised named Ethelldre......*.
,, 8—Rychard Sunnyeare buried his wife.
,, 16—Robart Nayler was buried.
,, 18—John Kente was buried.
,, 20—Thomas Wilson and Janie Baildon were married.
,, 25—Willm Boyll had a child buried named John.
,, 27—Rychard Peace wife was buried.
,, 31—John Lytlewood had a child baptised named Agnis.
,, 31—Thomas Pickeringe was buried.

---

† This name is also spelt Hayworth and Haworth in other documents.

‡ The year has been altered in the original from 1588 to 1587, and a similar alteration has been made each year back to 1586, which was originally written 1581.

§ This year has not been altered.

* The latter part of this Christian name is frayed away.

1588.

June 4—Thomas Gill had a child baptised named William.
,, 27—Mary Musgreve was buried.
,, 30—Thomas Grenewood buried his wife.
July 3—Richard Newsom alias Jackson had a child baptised named Edward.
,, 13—Thomas Grave had a child baptised named Thomas.
,, 16—Robart Saxton was buried.
,, 21—Ann Stead was buried.
,, 26—John Autye had a child baptised named William.
Aug. 11—Rychard Sunyeare and Allis Hepworthe were married.
,, 13—John Forrest had a child baptised named Elyzabeth.
,, 14—Rychard Wade had a child baptised named Jenet.
,, 15—John Letlewood had a child buried named Elyzabeth.
,, 18—Lorance Pickeringe was buried.
,, 21—John Slacke and Agnis Beamond were married.
,, 25—Alis Wornall was buried.
,, 28—John Robinson was buried.
,, 31—Athor Tomyon was buried.
Sept. 1—William Walker was buried.
,, 8—William Lanscare had a child baptised named John.
,, 10—Robert Wornall was buried.
,, 12—Robert Wornall his wife was buried.
,, 13—Marmaduke Speight had a child baptised named William.
,, 16—Lynell Barker had a child base gotten baptised named Agnis.
,, 17—John Speight wife was buried.
,, 22—Robart Carter had a child baptised named Robarte.
,, 22—Edward Reedall had a child baptised named Marie.
Oct. 6—Thomas Fearneley had a child baptised named Beatrice.
,, 6—Alixaunder Gibson buried his wife.
,, 6—Jaine Peace was buried.
,, 13—Richarde Wood had a child baptised named Brgete.
,, 13—Thomas Wilson had a child baptised named Thomas.
,, 13—Edward Ouldroyd and Grace Bayldon were married.
,, 20—Fraunces Exley and Margaret Stansfeld were married.
,, 20—Williame Hunt a pyper had a son buried named Robart.
,, 21—Grace daughter of George Speight buried.
,, 28—John son of Thomas Fell baptised.
,, 28—Edee daughter of Rychard Rychemond baptised.
,, 28—Elizabethe daughter of Robart Awdsley the elder baptised.
,, 31—Nicolas Clarke alias Harrisonn buried.
Nov. 3—Grace daughter of Rychard Kirton baptised.
,, 5—Agnes daughter of Rychard Ashton baptised.

DEWSBURY PARISH REGISTERS.

1588.
Nov. 5—Elizabethe Smithe buried.
,, 5—Xpofer Freelton had a child buried.
,, 24—David son of Williame Wurmall, "clarke of this churche," baptised.
,, 26—Nicholas Walker and Elizabethe Osburne married.
Dec 1—Williame Boothe and Jane Dey married.
,, 2—Williame Ellis and Alice Ellis both of Bradfurthe parish married here.
,, 2—Rychard Slacke and Grace Haworthe married.
,, 3—Uxor Bradforthe buried.
,, 3—Agnes daughter of John Litlewoode buried.
,, 6—Rychard Stansfeild buried his wife.
,, 10—Williame son of Anthonye Smithe baptised.
,, 10—Williame son of Edward Roydes baptised.
,, 14—Averye More buried.
,, 18—David son of Williame Wurmall buried.
,, 23—Edward Wilkinson and Isabell Sharphouse had a child base gotten baptised and buried.
,, 26—Agnes daughter of Rychard Ashton buried.
Jan 6—Alexander Gibson and Marye Netleton married.
,, 9—Williame Dishforthe buried.
,, †—Williame son of Williame Lee baptised and buried.
,, 28—James Kent and Elizabethe Lee married.
,, 28—Henry Robinson and Grace Ouldroyd married.
,, 28—Robert son of John Boye baptised and buried.
Feb. 2—John son of William Lauscarre buried.
,, 3—Xpofer son of George Nayler baptised.
,, 5—John son of Williame Gaunt baptised.
,, 9—John Cowpas and Margerett Whitley married.
,, 13—Williame Rychardson a boy buried.
,, 13—Anne daughter of Thomas Acrod "yonger" baptised.
,, 14—Margaret daughter of Edward Grene baptised.
,, 16—Robert son of John Bentley of Osset buried.
,, 23—Anne daughter of Thomas Graysonn baptised.
,, 27—John Dishforthe buried his wife.
Mar. 2—Dorithye daughter of Williame Sharpus baptised.
,, 5—Jone Barstoe a stranger buried here.
,, 10—Annes daughter of Williame Gill "yonger" baptised.
,, 10—Williame Sharpus buried his wife.
,, 11—Rychard son of John Dickenson baptised.
,, 11—Robert son of John Dent baptised.
,, 11—Rychard Brigge buried his wife.
,, 12—Marye daughter of George Lee baptised.
,, 15—Uxor Kent of the Daw grene buried.

† Day of month omitted.

1588.
Mar. 16—Anne daughter of John Grene baptised.
,, 22—Robert son of Robert Hudsonn baptised.
,, 30—Marye daughter of George Blackburne baptised.
1589.
April 1—............s son of James Forrest buried.
,, 11—Margeret Fox buried.
,, 14—Thomas Langfeild buried.
,, 14—............ daughter of John Robinson baptised.
,, 23—............ son of Thomas Clayton baptised.
,, 27—............ Stansfeild and Elsabethe Saxton married.
,, 29—Rychard Brigge and Mary Brodlaye married.
May 2—Rychard son of Rychard Sonyerd baptised.
,, 4—............ base daughter of Robert Ramsden baptised.
,, 4—............ daughter of John Sllacke baptised.
,, 11—............ daughter of Georg Wilbye baptised.
,, 12—............ son of Williame Speight baptised.
,, 14—............ daughter of John Berrye baptised.
,, 18—............ daughter of Thomas Rychardson and Anne Carter wife .... Carter of Lincolne, baptised.
June 8—Elizabethe daughter of Edward Ouldroyd baptised.
,, 10—Thomas Rodlaye and Anne Whitlaye married.
,, 14—Robert son of Rychard Medlay baptised.
,, 14—William son of John Beamond baptised.
,, 15—Robert Mawde and Agnes Sykes married.
,, 15—Michaell son of James Nicolson baptised.
,, 27—Isabell daughter of Lyonell Barker baptised.
,, 27—Betheris daughter of Robert Sharpus baptised.
,, 24—Elizabethe daughter of Robert Bleisbee baptised.
July 1—Robert Barton and Isabell Hall married.
,, 13—John son of Rychard Slacke baptised.
,, 15—Henrye Nowell and Alice Adam married.
,, 25—Robert son of Frances Exlay baptised.
,, 30—Jenet Scott buried.
,, 31—Isabell daughter of Lyonell Barker buried.
Aug. 1—James son of Nicholas Walker baptised.
,, 10—Rychard son of Thomas Archer baptised.
,, 15—Jane daughter of Edward Lee "yonger" baptised.
,, 19—Averye Whitakers and Mary Grenwoode married.
,, 29—William son of Xpofer Brooke baptised.
Sept. 3—Omphray son of Rowland Owen baptised.
,, 4—William son of William Tayler baptised.
,, 6—John Dey buried his wife.
,, 14—Dorithye daughter of Rychard Wade baptised.
,, 21—Isabell daughter of Rychard Bradforthe younger baptised.

1589.

Sept. 21—Thomas Monsfeld buried.
" 25—William Gyles *senex* buried.
" 26—Jane daughter of Edward Le yonger buried.
" 29—Thomas son of Thomas Rodley baptised.
" 29—Rychard son of Edward Walton of Caverley parish buried here.

Oct. 5—Thomas Fox and Agnes Hemingway married.
" 5—Elizabethe daughter of Rychard Forrest baptised.
" 8—Margeret daughter of Christofer Denton baptised.
" 12—Lowrance Ecclesfeild and Jane Exam married.
" 18—Alice Ouldroyd buried.
" 19—Agnes Ouldroyd buried.
" 26—Robert son of Robert Dawson baptised.
" 26—Rychard son of Rychard Fernlaye baptised.
" 26—John son of John Stubley baptised the same day and was buried the 30th day.

Nov. 2—Elizabethe daughter of William Saxton baptised.
" 3—Dorithye daughter of Edward Barbar younger baptised.
" 9—William son of William Lanscare baptised.
" 9—Isabell daughter of John Cordingley baptised.
" 14—Henry Nayler buried.
" 23—John Speight and Margrett Shuttleworthe married.
" 25—Lawrance Pickering and Agnes Walker married.
" 29—Marye daughter of George Blackburne buried.
" 30—Edwin son of James Clayton baptised.

Dec. 7—Mary daughter of George Speight baptised.
" 14—............ Parker buried his wife.
" 16—............ Rushforthe and Alice Dickenson married.
" 21—............ daughter of Rychard Awtye baptised.
" 26—............Clayton had a daughter being not baptised buried and the same day the mother of the child was buried with it.
" 28—............Tayler of carles henton buried.

Jan. 4—William Wurmall clarke of this parish was buried.
" 4—Edward Bull had a son baptised named George and the same George was buried the next day after.
" 4—Renould Tayler *senex* was buried.
" 11—John Dishforth and Katharyn Lockwood married.
" 11—Robert Speight admitted clarke of Dewsbury.
" 11—John Litlewoode had a son baptised named Robert.
" 10—Elizabethe Ryding *sener* was buried.
" 12—William Bradforthe buried his wife.
" 15—William Boothe had a son baptised named Rychard.

1589.

Jan. 21—William Sharpus had a daughter buried named Dorithye.
" 25—John Ouldroyd of Hanging Heaton had a daughter baptised named Sara.

Feb. 1—Robert Blagburne and Alice Phillipe married.
" 2—Emar Fox and Isabell Brigge were married.
" 4—John Grene of Ossett was buried.
" 5—William Grene, *senex*, of Dewsbury was buried.
" 8—William Lee of Gawthorpe had a daughter baptised named Angela.
" 10—John Wade of Sowood Grene buried his wife.
" 15—Christopher Freckleton had a son baptised called Averye.
" 15—Rychard Bradforthe of Dewsbury had a son baptised called Edward.
" 17—John Dey and Jane Tayler were married.
" 21—John Dickenson of Ossett had a child buried named Rychard.
" 22—John Shepperd of Ossett had a son baptised named William.
" 23—Thomas Chaster and Alice Rawnslaye were married.
" 28—William Storye was buried.

Mar. 1—Rychard Grayve and Margerot Gryme were married.
" 1—John Shepperde of Ossett had a son buried named William.
" 4—Robert Barton had a son baptised called William.
" 6—John Boyes had a daughter baptised named Marye.
" 8—Edward Wilkinson had a son baptised named George.

Mar. 14—Robert Barton had a son buried named William.
" 19—Nicholas Walker had a son buried named Henry.
" 20—Thomas Chaster had a child buried which was not baptised.

1590.

Mar. 25—Thomas Ouldrood had a daughter baptised named Grace.
" 28—John Boothe of Ossett buried his wife.
" 31—Rychard Hoole and Jane Jackson married.

April 5—Rychard Ashton had a son baptised named Rychard.
" 12—Fynias son of William Shirley keeper of the New Parke baptised.
" 16—Allice daughter of Robert Bradfurthe baptised.
" 15—Uxor Bradforthe was buried.
" 22—Margrett wife of Nicholas Kighleye buried.
" 26—John Deye, *senex*, buried.
" 27—Uxor Bingley wife of Perceveille Bingley buried.
" 29—Thomas son of Thomas Wilson buried.

May 2—George son of Thomas Walshey alias Gooddrood baptised.
" 7—Peter son of Peter Warren buried.

1590.
May 10—Robert Smythe and Isabell Wormall married.
„ 11—Jenet daughter of Richard Speight baptised.
„ 17—Jenet daughter of Christopher Dickson baptised.
„ 17—Grace daughter of Alexander Barber baptised.
„ 17—Richard Michell and Ann Bradford married.
„ 27—John Awtie *senex* buried.
June 4—William son of James Kent baptised.
„ 14—Margrett Whytticars daughter of Enery Whyttakers baptised.
„ 14—Alverny Hoyle son of Richard Hoyle baptised.
„ 16—Matthew Parker and Elizabeth Whitleye married.
„ 17—John son of Richard Slack buried.
„ 22—Bettrice daughter of Robert Sharpus buried.
„ 26—George son of Edward Wilkinson buried.
„ 27—James Speight *senex* buried.
July 10—Richard son of John Cowpas baptised.
„ 14—William Richardson and Ann Soward (? Coward) married.
„ 19—Thomas Lee buried.
„ 20—John Speight buried his wife.
„ 25—Uxor Whytley buried.
„ 25—Elizabethe daughter of John Boyes baptised.
„ 30—Rychard son of Rychard Wood baptised.
Aug. 1—Thomas Greenwood was buried.
„ 3—Jenet wife of Roger Mounsfeld buried.
„ 4—John son of Alexander Gibsonne baptised and the same daye a daughter of the sayd Alexander Gibsonne buryed beinge not christened, borne at the same tyme.
„ 5—Thomas Grayve buried.
„ 6—John sonne of Alexander Gibsonne and the mother of the sayd child was buryed the sixt daye.
„ 12—Gilbert Ouldroyd *senex* was buried.
„ 16—Marye daughter of Rychard Grayve baptised.
„ 16—Lucie daughter of Rychard Ashton was buried.
„ 20—John Marshall a stranger was buried.
„ 25—James Lee the elder was buried.
„ 23—John the son of William Gill junior baptised.
„ 23—Johane the daughter of Robert Mawde baptised.
„ 27—Anne the daughter of Matthew Parker baptised.
„ 30—William Sharpus had a daughter not baptised buried.
Sept. 2—Margeret Beamond a mayd was buryed.
„ 22—Ellen daughter of Henry Nayler buried.
„ 22—John son of Robert Mawde buried.
„ 27—Emmett daughter of Rychard Richmonde baptised.
„ 28—Massoley a maid of Mr. Rowland Owans a washwoman buried.
„ 28—William Burnet buried his wife.

1590.
Sept. 30—John son of Robert Awdisley younger baptised.
„ 23—Rychard son of Edward Arrandell buried.
Oct. 16—Annes daughter of John Speight buried.
„ 22—Uxor Carter buried.
Nov. 1—Margeret daughter of John Dent buried.
„ 3—James Wade and Elsebethe Barbar married.
„ 5—Rychard Wilson son of Thomas Wilson baptised.
„ 5—Rogor Pickerd son of Thomas Pickerd baptised.
„ 8—Humphraye Dickson and Margeret Stansfeld married.
„ 29—Annes daughter of Nicolas Armitage baptised.
Dec. 1—William Croft and Jenet Wilbye married.
„ 1—Thomas son of Thomas Gill baptised.
„ 4—Robert son of Robert Awdslaye the elder baptised.
„ 7—William Walker and Jenet Ouldroyde married.
„ 12—Jenye daughter of Emar Fox baptised.
„ 13—Frances Saxton buried.
„ 15—Anne the daughter of John Lee of Gawthorpe had a child buried not baptised.
„ 15—William Clayton buried his wife.
„ 22—Margeret daughter of Edward Green buried.
„ 25—Elizabethe daughter of William Longlaye baptised.
„ 26—Fyneas son of Willme Sherlaye keeper of the new Park buried.
Jan. 4—Isabell Shutleworthe buried.
„ 20—Dido daughter of Thomas Rychardson buried.
„ 24—Rychard son of Robert Priestlay baptised.
„ 25—Rowland Owen keper of ye new Parke buried.
Jan 25—Thomas Dishforthe buried.
„ 25—Emmet daughter of Rychard Rychmond buried.
„ 28—Thomas son of James Wade baptised.
Feb. 2—William son of Edward Arrandell buried.
„ 2—Agnes wife of Thomas Grene of Spynkewell buried.
„ 6—William Lee of Dewsbury buried.
„ 14—Elsabethe daughter of Humphraye Dixson baptised.
„ 25—Margeret daughter of John Hurst baptised.
„ 27—Robert Brown a stranger buried.
„ 27—Mary daughter of John Grenewood baptised.
„ 27—............ daughter of Robert Carter baptised.
„ 27—............ Speight of Chidsell buried a child not baptised.
Mar. 2—Alice Dishforthe buried.
„ 7—Alice daughter of Robert Barton baptised.
„ 12—Robert Robinson of Chickenlaye buried.
„ 14—Grace daughter of Robert Carter buried.
„ 14—Edward son of William Barlow baptised.
„ 15—Grace wife of Thomas Slacke buried.
„ 16—Elizabeth Ouldroyd buried.
„ 18—William Hall buried his wife.

1590.
Mar. 19—John Sayvill buried.
,,   23—Marye Marshe daughter of John Marshe of Chidsell buried.
,,   25—John Ouldroyd son of Edward Ouldroyd baptised.

1591.   Anno Dni. 1591
Mar. 25—Thomas son of John Shepperd baptised.
,,   28—Thomas Gryfine buried.
April 11—Thomas son of Edward Roydes baptised.
,,   13—John Knowles buried.
,,   20—Margerye Whiteheade buried.
,,   18—Thomas son of Robert Sharphowse baptised.
,,   23—Thomas Grene buried.
May 2—Elizabeth daughter of Rychard Jenkinson baptised.
,,   6—Thomas son of John Dey baptised.
,,   19—Frauncis wife of Rychard Jenkinson buried.
,,   24—Edward son of Rychard Bradforthe of ye Dawgrene buried.
June 2—Esther daughter of Thomas Clayton baptised.
,,   8—Robert Speight and Agnes Grayve married.
,,   8—Thomas Langefeild and Sibell Lee married.
,,   11—Agnes wife of Christopher Freelton buried.
,,   20—John Warde buried.
July 3—Elizabethe daughter of Henry Nayler baptised.
,,   7—Edward Arrandell buried.
,,   11—Henry son of John Saxton baptised.
,,   15—Rychard son of George Nayler baptised.
,,   20—Rychard Michell and Ann Fayrboune married.
,,   23—Elizabeth daughter of Thomas Langefield baptised.
,,   25—Michaell son of James Clayton baptised.
Aug. 1—Symeon son of William Sherley keeper of the new parke baptised.
,,   8—Margeret daughter of Robert Smith baptised.
,,   14—Elizabeth daughter of Thomas Langefeild buried.
,,   17—Peter Myrfeild and Elizabeth Stead married.
,,   27—Henry son of John Saxtone buried.
,,   29—Marye daughter of John Boye buried.
,,   31—James son of Nicholas Walker buried.
Sept. 2—Elizabethe daughter of Rychard Medlaye baptised.
,,   5—John Milnes and Elizabethe Walker married.
,,   8—Uxor Clayton of Ossett buried.
,,   17—Willme Lee of Earls heaton buried.
,,   23—Jane daughter of Willme Sheifeld clerke buried.
,,   30—Uxor Ball wife of Willme Ball buried.
Oct. 3—John son of Willme Rowse baptised.
,,   8—Ellen Lee a mayde was buried and a younge child that she was delivered of not baptised buried with her.
,,   9—Willme Sherlay keeper of the new parke buried.

1591.
Oct. 10—Willme son of Nicholas Woode alias Smithe baptised.
,,   12—Edward Ramsden and Ann Pickeringe married.
,,   12—Marye daughter of Rychard Jacksonn alias Newsome baptised.
,,   17—Grace daughter of Willme Gaunt baptised
,,   18—Henrye son of Rychard Wodde baptised.
,,   19—Willme Kent and Elizabeth Hurst married.
,,   23—John Forrest of Ossett buried
,,   26—Willme Hall and Elizabethe Mosseley married.
,,   31—Christofer son of Henrye Nayler buried.
Nov. 7—Thomas son of Henrye Whitehead baptised.
,,   13—............ Barbar the elder buried.
,,   14—John son of Henrye Robinsonn baptised.
,,   16—Georg son of John Baylye baptised.
,,   17—John son of John Craven baptised.
,,   24—Betteris daughter of Rychard Fernlye baptised.
,,   25—Margerye daughter of John Parker buried.
,,   28—Thomas son of James Gurnall alias Sharpe baptised.
Dec. 13—Raphe Linley of Hanging Heaton buried
,,   26—Roberte son of Rychard Robinson baptised.
,,   29—Robert son of Rychard Rychmond baptised.
Jan. 4—Dorithye Pickering buried.
,,   6—Willme son of Rychard Wade baptised.
,,   11—Janet Brigge a maid was buried.
,,   12—Frauncis Lee a young infante a mayd baptised at home was buried.
,,   13—Thomas Fernlaye was buried.
,,   15—Uxor Lee wife of Rychard Lee of Dewsburye was buried.
,,   16—Thomas son of Thomas Fox baptised
,,   23—Sibell daughter of Willme Gill the younger baptised.
,,   24—John Boothe and Katherin Phillippo married.
,,   26—Anne daughter of Rychard Bradforthe the younger baptised.
,,   31—John Cowpas the elder and Jane Feather married.
Feb. 2—Marye daughter of Thomas Ouldroyd baptised.
,,   3—Averye son of Christopor Freelton buried.
,,   3—Agnes daughter of Rychard Denysonn buried.
,,   5—Thomas son of Thomas Fox buried.
,,   11—Henrye Pollerd of Birle (Bierley) within the Parishe of Bradfor the died and was buried here at Dewsburye.
,,   13—George son of Robert Mawde baptised.
,,   13—Ann daughter of Willme Rychardsonn baptised.
,,   16—Gorge Gill a boy buried.
,,   20—Dorithye daughter of Thomas Goodroyd alias Walshay baptised.
,,   27—Isabell daughter of Thomas Graysonn baptised.

1591.
Mar. 5—Sibell daughter of John Cowpas the elder baptised.
,, 5—Alice Brigge a mayde buried.
,, 14—Margrett Nutt alias Bradlay buried.
,, 15—Annc daughter of Fraunces Whitleye baptised
,, 15*—Elizabethe daughter of Rychard Sonyere baptised.
,, 17*—Ann daughter of Willme Rychardsonn buried.
,, 23*—Marye daughter of Robert Speight baptised.

The year beginnethe at this daye Anno Dm. 1592 Ano Eliz. Regine 34to.

1592.
Mar. 25—Elsabethe daughter of Rychard Sonyear buried.
,, 26—Esther daughter of Nicholas Nayler baptised.
April 16—Robert son of John Nayler baptised.
,, 21—Valentyne son of Rychard Speight baptised.
,, 23—Robert Willee and Sibell Pickar-gill married.
,, 26—Robert son of John Nayler buried.
,, 30—Agnes daughter of Robert Harrisonn alias Clarke baptised.
,, 30—Sibell daughter of John Slacke baptised.
May 8—James Brouke and Isabell Saxton married.
,, 13—Willme son of Willme Barlee baptised.
,, 14—Willme son of Rychard Wade buried.
,, 15—John Speight buried.
,, 16—Willme Gaunt buried
,, 21—Grace daughter of Willme Tayler baptised.
,, 31—Agnes daughter of John Milnes the younger baptised.
June 2—Uxor Bull wife of Matthew Bull buried.
,, 13—Anne daughter of John Parker buried.
,, 27—James son of James Brouke baptised.
,, 25—Nicholas son of Adam Wheatlye baptised.
,, 28—James son of James Brouke buried.
,, 29—Robert son of Edward Barbar baptised.
July 9—Robert son of Robert Bleisbye baptised.
,, 19—John son of Robert Carter baptised.
,, 21—Alice daughter of John Ouldroyd baptised.
,, 25—John Dawson and Jenet Bedforthe were married.
,, 23†—Agnes daughter of Emar Fox baptised.
,, 30—Danyell Gledall and Elizabethe Walker married.
Aug. 2—A young boy son of Thomas Fox of Hanging Heaton not baptised buried
,, 7—John Robinsonn of Ossett buried.
,, 13—Robert Wilsonn and Agnes Law married.
,, 13—Rychard son of John Cordingley baptised.
,, 20—John Rychardsonn and Elizabethe Leo married.

* These dates are illegible in the original and are taken from Mr. Hemingway's copy.
† So in original register.

1592.
Aug. 20—Margarett daughter of Willme Knowles baptised.
Sept. 3—Dorithie daughter of Thomas Barke (qy. Barker or Burke) baptised.
,, 4—A young child of Thomas Rodlay not baptised buried.
,, 10—Willme son of Rychard Grayve baptised.
,, 14—Allan Ellery and Mary Haighe married at Hartheade.
,, 17—Jennett daughter of Lyonell Barker baptised.
,, 18—Grace Dishforthe a mayde buried.
,, 26—Roger Hurst buried his wife.
,, 27—Elizabeth daughter of Rychard Medlay buried.
Oct. 2—Roberte Lee and Jennett Langfeld married.
,, 3—Rychard Acrod and Elizabethe Whitlay married.
,, 7—Robert Carter buried.
,, 9—Ellen base daughter of Percivall Stead of the Parishe of Otley baptised, mother of ye child Grace Ramsden.
,, 11—Marye daughter of Averye Whitakers baptised.
,, 15—Averye son of Robert Milnes baptised.
,, 16—Willme son of Rychard Acrode baptised.
,, 22—Jenet Ramsden buried.
,, 22—Rychard Hudeswell and Jenett Barbar married.
,, 23—John Batlay and Alis Kent married.
,, 25—Betheris daughter of Edward Wurmall baptised.
,, 28—Marye base daughter of Willme Aldersley of Ollerton in Bradforthe Parishe and Jane Johnsonn of the same parishe was baptised here in this churche.
,, 29—Rychard Ouldroyd and Elizabethe Robinson married.
,, 29—George son of Thomas Pickerd baptised.
,, 31—Thomas son of Willme Speight baptised.
Nov. 1—Marye daughter of John Boy baptised.
,, 1—Thomas son of Willme Speight buried.
,, 7—John son of John Littlewood buried.
,, 11—Robert Ouldroyd the elder buried.
,, 11—Marye base daughter of Willme Peaker and Dorithie Savile baptised.
,, 19—John Robinsonn a boy buried.
Dec. 21—John son of Edward Midlebroughe baptised.
,, 24—Susann daughter of Thomas Archer baptised.
,, 24—Marye daughter of Thomas Wilsonn baptised.
,, 26—Uxor Hurst wyfe of Rychard Hurst buried.
,, 28—Elizabethe daughter of Allan Ellerye baptised.
Jan. 2—Katheryne wyfe of John Dishforthe buried.
,, 21—Anne daughter of John Saxtonn baptised.
,, 23—Grace daughter of John Cowpas baptised.
,, 27—Thomas Horstorthe buried.
,, 28—Marye daughter of Willme Lanscarre baptised.

1592.
Feb. 2—Elizabeth daughter of John Grenewoode baptised.
 ,, 3—Edward son of Willme Barlow buried.
 ,, 4—Margrett daughter of Mrs.* Willm buried.
 ,, 4—Averye son of Edward More baptised.
 ,, 10—Agnes daughter of Rychard Medlay baptised at Horbury and the same Agnes
 ,, 11— was buried here the xij^the daye.
 ,, 13—Robert Dey and Dorithye Walker married.
 ,, 21—George Walker and Isabell Forrest married.
 ,, 25—George son of Gorge Lee baptised.
 ,, 26—Rychard Gepsonn and Agnes Gaunt married.
 ,, 27—James Awdsley the younger was buried.
Mch. 11—Michaell son of John Berrye baptised.
 ,, 11—Henrye son of Christopher Brouke baptised.
 ,, 11—Philemon son of Christopher Dixsonn baptised.
 ,, 18—Willme son of John Deye baptised.
 ,, 23—Michaell Warde was buried.
The beginnige of the yeare Ano Dni 1593.
1593.
Mch. 25—Perigryne son of Mr. Wilkinsonn baptised.
 ,, 28—Jonnye daughter of Willme Hall baptised.
April 12—Rychard son of Robert Awdesley the elder baptised.
 ,, 14—Uxor Linley of Hanginge Heaton was buried.
 ,, 17—Dorithie daughter of Raphe Slator baptised.
 ,, 22—Nicolas son of Nicholas Walker baptised
 ,, 22—A young son of Willme Barloe not baptised buried.
 ,, 29—Edward and John sons of Willme Rycharsonn both baptised.
May 13—John son of Edward Oublroyd baptised.
 ,, 13—Gorge son of Willme Gill the younger baptised.
 ,, 20—Willme Tyas and Agnes Smithe married.
 ,, 20—Ellen daughter of Lawrance Wamsley baptised.
 ,, 27—Thomas son of Willme Burnett baptised.
June 2—Edward son of Willme Rychardsonn buried.
 ,, 8—John Robinsonn buried his wyfe.
 ,, 10—John base son of John Jagger and Margrett Exam baptised.
 ,, 10—Jonye daughter of Robte Smithsonn baptised.
 ,, 14—Josephe son of Robert Dey baptised.
 ,, 20—Elizabethe daughter of Rychard Brigge buried.
 ,, 24—Rychard son of John Nayler baptised.
 ,, 26—Willme Thomsonn and Elizabethe Carter married.
 ,, 30—Averye son of Edward More buried.
July 1—Jenye daughter of Willme Hall buried.
 ,, 3—A young daughter of Nicholas Wood not baptised buried.

* The word is not distinct in the original.

1593.
July 14—Robert base son of John Harrope and Jenet Clayton baptised.
 ,, 18—Christopher Denton elder buried of the plague at his own house.
 ,, 19—Josephe son of Robert Dey buried.
 ,, 21—Merrye Arrandell buried.
 ,, 25—Rosamond daughter of Rychard Forrest baptised.
 ,, 26—John son of John Dawsonn baptised.
 ,, 26—Alice daughter of James Kent baptised.
 ,, 30—John Craven buried of the plague in the leighes.
 ,, 31—Christopher Denton younger buried of the plague.
 ,, 31—William Denton buried of the plague at their father's house.
Aug. 3—Isabell Denton buried of the plague at home.
 ,, 3—James Dentonn buried of the plague at home.
 ,, 3—Thomas Dentonn buried of the plague at home.
 ,, 3—Alice Dentonn buried of the plague at home.
 ,, 3—Margrett Dentonn buried of the plague at home.
 ,, 3—Joanye Brouke buried at Denton's of the plague.
 ,, 3—Ann Ward buried at Denton's house of the plague.
 ,, 8—Alice Hudsonn buried of the place in the leighes.
 ,, 9—Thomas son of Thomas Langefeild baptised.
 ,, 10—Alice Nowell buried of the plague at Denton's house.
 ,, 10—Agnes Ward buried of the plague at Denton's house.
 ,, 11—John son of Edward Wilkinsonn baptised.
 ,, 14—Thomas Acrod and Ann Tebbe married being Tuesday.
 ,, 15—Uxor Craven widow died of the plague and buried at home in the leighes.
 ,, 15—John Craven a young child buried of the plague in the leighes.
 ,, 19—Isabell daughter of James Brouke baptised.
 ,, 20—Agnes Hudsonn buried of the plague at home in the leighes.
 ,, 21—James Brodley and Sibell Lee married.
 ,, 26—Dorithye daughter of Robte Barton baptised.
 ,, 26—Thomas son of Robte Awdesley the younger baptised.
 ,, 27—Thomas Sykes buried at his own house at Sowode Grene.
Sept. 10—John Nowell and Edan Boothe married.
 ,, 16—Dorithye daughter of Henrye Nayler baptised.
 ,, 21—John Boothe buried of the plague at Denton's house.
 ,, 28—Dorithye daughter of Robte Barton buried.
Oct. 2—Edward Megsonn and Grace Acrod married.

DEWSBURY PARISH REGISTERS.

1593.
Oct. 5—Frances* son of Thomas Gill baptised.
" 4—Gorge son of Gorge Nayler baptised.
" 4—Sibell base daughter of Averye Gill and Jenet Awdsley baptised.
" 7—Sibell daughter of Marmaduke Speight baptised.
" 7—Grace daughter of Marmaduke Speight baptised.
" 10—Elizabethe daughter of Robte Smithe baptised.
" 15—John Westerman and Dorithye Sharphouse married.
" 21—Grace daughter of Rychard Sonyare baptised.
" 21—Gorge son of Gorge Wilbye baptised.
" 22—Elizabethe daughter of Robte Smithe buried.
" 23—Sibell daughter of Marmaduke Speight buried.
" 28—Willme son of Henry Whitheade baptised.
Nov. 2—Marye daughter of James Sharpe baptised.
" 11—Willme Jacksonn and Agnes Hutchinsonn married.
" 11—Danyell son of Willme Tyas baptised.
" 14—Grace daughter of Rychard Sonyare buried.
" 20—Averye Gill and Jenett Awdesleye married.
" 20—Edmond Gepsonn and Alice Lee married.
" 20—Thomas son of Rychard Bradforthe the younger baptised.
" 21—John Walker of Dewsburye the younger buried.
" 21—Sibell daughter of Henrye Barbar baptised.
" 25—Sibell base daughter of Averye Gill buried.
" 25—Henrye son of Willme Tayler baptised.
" 25—Robert Grayve buried at night.
" 30—Elizabethe daughter of Robte Dishforthe buried.
" 30—John son of Rychard Oulroyd buried.
Dec. 1—Isabell wife of Robert Dishforthe buried.
" 4—Rychard Thornes and Alice Tyas married.
" 16—Marye daughter of Willme Varnont gentleman baptised.
" 16—Willme son of Willme Rowse baptised.
" 16—Thomas Tayler buried his wife.
" 18—Rychard Graver and Margrett Barbar married at Osset.
" 18—Jane Wilsonn buried at Ossett of the plague at home.

*So in original

† In 1606 the rectories of Wakefield, Dewsbury, Calverley, Bardsey, and Collingham were granted by King James I. to William Vernon, of Southill, gentleman, and Christopher Naylor, of Wakefield, gentleman, as trustees for Sir George Savile. (See Article 111 in the *Dewsbury Reporter* on the "Parish of Dewsbury.") William Vernon seems to have been buried at Wakefield Parish Church, 21st October, 1623, and his wife, "Frezwell," was buried at the same church, 24th January, 1618. (See Taylor's "History of Wakefield Rectory Manor, 311th".)

1593.
Dec. 18—Uxor Pickeringe buried at Ossett of the plague.
" 19—Rychard son of Robert Priestlaye buried.
" 19—Ann Forrest buried *of the plague.*
" ‡—Robert Dishforthe buried.
" 23—Ann base daughter of Rychard Hoyle and Ann Sydall baptised.
" 30—Robert son of Edward Roydes baptised.
" 31—Jane daughter of Rychard Bradforthe the older buried.
Jan. 5—John son of Edward Wilkinsonn buried.
" 6—Elizabethe wife of John Walker of Dewsburye buried.
" 7—Willme son of Willme Gill the younger baptised.
" 9—Alice daughter of Edward Ouldroyd baptised.
" 9—Ann daughter of Edward Ouldroyd baptised.
" 12—Dorithie daughter of Omphraye Dicksonn baptised.
" 22—Jonett daughter of John Westerman baptised.
Feb. 3—Willme Tayler and Ann Yeaden married.
" 3—Esther daughter of Rychard Jepsonn baptised.
" 5—Jane daughter of Willme Tayler of Chidsell baptised.
" 9—John son of James Clayton baptised. } twynes.
" 9—Averye son of James Claytonn baptised.
" 9—A young son of Thomas Goodrode alias Walshaw not baptised buried.
" 10—Jane daughter of Willme Tayler of Chidsell buried.
" 12—Averye son of James Claytonn buried.
" 13—Margrett daughter of Willme Jacksonn baptised.
" 13—Ann daughter of Willme Lee of Gawthorpe baptised.
" 16—Rychard Whitley of Dewsburye buried Satterdaye.
" 17—Agnes daughter of Thomas Ouldroyd baptised.
" 17—Agnes wife of George Nayler buried of the plague at night here.
" 24—Lucye daughter of John Bull buried.
" 24—Grace daughter of Rychard Aerode baptised.
" 25—Robert Barton buried.
" 27—Rychard son of Willme Speight of Chidsell baptised.
Mar. 3—Dorithie daughter of Rychard Fernlay baptised.
" 4—John Milnes the older was buried being Mondaye.
" 5—Rychard son of Willme Speight of Chidsell buried.
" 6—Averye son of Robert Hassard and Margret Aspinal baptised base gotten.

*The three words in italics are taken from Mr. Hemingway's copy, having disappeared from the original.
‡ The date is frayed away.

1593.
Mar. 6—John son of Robte Hassard and Margret Aspinal baptised base born.
„ 7—Marye daughter of Thomas Ouldroyd buried.
„ 16—Elizabethe daughter of Emar Fox baptised.
„ 20—John son of Gawen Metcalfe baptised.
„ 24—John son of Robert Hassard and Margrett Aspinall base gotten buried, being Palm Sondaye.
„ 24—Willme son of Robert Speight baptised.
„ 25—Willme son of Edward Midlebroughe baptised.

1594.
April 1—John Jagger and Margrett Exam married.
„ 7—Averye Milnes and Grace Claytonn married.
„ 11—A young son of Averye Milnes not baptised buried.
„ 15—John Blakey and Elizabethe Clarsonn (qy. Clarkson) married.
„ 21—John son of Gorge Speight baptised.
„ 25—Edward son of James Brodlaye baptised St. Marke's daye.
„ 26—A young son of Henry Robinson's not baptised buried.
   Elizabeth daughter of Richard Graver.§
May 2—............ daughter of Edward Lee the younger baptised.
„ 9—Elizabeth daughter of Richard Graver baptised.
„ 14—Willme son of Rychard Thornes baptised.
„ 15—Edward son of James Broadley buried.
„ 26—Robert son of John Milnes baptised: trinitie.
„ 26—John son of James Walker baptised.
„ 26—Willme son of James Walker baptised.
„ 29—Thomas son of Rychard Woode baptised.
June 12—Marye daughter of John Shepperd baptised.
„ 15—Willme Rychardsonn buried his wife.
Julye 9—Willme Lee and Marye Walker married.
„ 14—John son of George Speight buried.
„ 14—Willme son of Frauncis Whitley baptised.
„ 21—Averye son of Thomas Pickerd baptised.
„ 29—Averye Acrod and Margrett Steade married.
„ 30—Humphraye Waterhowse and Isabell Walker married.
„ 30—Uxor Walshaw was buried.
Aug. 4—Margrett daughter of Nicholas Nayler baptised.
„ 7—Arthure son of Nicholas Smithe alias Woode baptised.
„ 9—A young son of John Hurst of Dewsbury not baptised buried.
„ 11—Mereye daughter of Thomas Acrod of Earleshenton the younger baptised.
„ 11—Jenett daughter of Thomas Fox baptised.
„ 12—Thomas Whitakers the younger and Jane Southe married.

§ This entry is imperfect, and may be incorrect, as it occurs again on the 5th May following.

1594.
Aug. 20—Thomas son of James Wade buried.
„ 22—Uxor Barbar of Ossett buried.
„ 25—Edward son of Robert Preistlaye baptised.
„ 27—John son of John Littlewoode baptised.
Sept. 12—John base son of John Awdesley and Susann Boothe baptised.
„ 18—A young child of Dorithie Savill and John Lockwoode not baptised was buried.
„ 21—Robert son of Robert Bartonn baptised. St. Mathew daye.
„ 22—Averye son of Rychard Sonyare baptised.
„ 28—Robert son of James Wade baptised.
Oct. 6—Nicholas son of Robert Haveyard baptised.
„ 6—Margrett daughter of Thomas Graysonn baptised.
„ 8—John Awdesleye and Susann Boothe married.
„ 9—Agnes daughter of Rychard Grayve baptised.
„ 13—Agnes daughter of Edmonde Jepsonn baptised.
„ 17—Michaell son of Robert Dey baptised.
„ 27—............ daughter of Robert Millnes baptised.
„ 28—............ Parker and Ann Roodes married.
Nov. 5—John Peace and Ann Maunsfeld married.
„ 10—Elizabethe daughter of John Ouldroyd baptised.
„ 11—Michaell son of Rychard Speight baptised.
„ 17—Jonye daughter of Averye Gill baptised.
„ 25—Gorge Wilbee buried his wife.
„ 26—Thomas Wilkinsonn and Dorithye Dawsonn married.
„ 28—Agnes wife of Hughe Cassonn Parson of Hartill buried.
Dec. 1—Andrewe son of Robert Smithe baptised.
„ 8—Betheris daughter of Rychard Rychemond baptised.
„ 8—John son of John Deye baptised.
„ 15—Betheris daughter of John Slacke baptised.
„ 22—*William son of William Varnon Gentleman baptised.
„ 22—Venicia daughter of John Nayler baptised.
„ 26—Jenet daughter of Robte Harrisonn baptised.
„ 28—Edward son of Robte Preistley buried.
„ 28—Robert base son of Robte Lee of Ollerthorpe (qy. Alverthorpe) and Betheris Seeker married.
„ 29—Jonye daughter of Robte Brouke the younger baptised.
Jan. 20—Gorge son of Gorge Wilbye buried.
„ 21—Willme Harrisonn and Elizabethe Dawsonn married.
„ 22—A young daughter of Rychard Jacksons not baptised buried.

* See note to entry for 16th December, 1593.

1594.
Jan. 26—Rachell daughter of Averye Whitakers baptised.
" 30—Abraham son of Willme Wurmall buried.
Feb. 11—Abraham Lee and Dorithye Savill married.
" 15—Alice wife of Thomas Chaster buried.
" 23—Agnes daughter of Rychard Draper baptised.
Mar. 2—Mathew son of Willme Lanscarre baptised.
" 10—John Newell was buried.
" 19—Grace daughter of Avery Acrode baptised.
" 28—Thomas son of John Awtye baptised.
" 30—Jane daughter of Thomas Wilsonn baptised.
" 31—Andrew son of Roberte Smithe buried
1595.
April 2—Weniffride daughter of Henrye Barbar baptised.
" 2—Alice daughter of John Robinsonn baptised.
" 2—Elizabethe daughter of Willme Gill the youngest baptised.
April 4—John son of James Kent baptised.
" 8—Willme son of Willme Varnon Gentleman buried.
" 12—Mathew son of Willme Speight baptised.
" 15—Grace daughter of James Brouke baptised.
" 16—Ann daughter of James Nicolls baptised.
" 24—Elizabethe daughter of Thomas Walshawe baptised.
" 26—A young son of Thomas Langfelde not baptised buried.
May 6—John Townend alias Robinsonn the elder buried.
" 8—Thomas Exam buried.
" 18—John son of John Speighte baptised.
" 26—Rychard Fernlaye buried. Rogation Monday.
" 29—Elizabethe daughter of Averye Milnes baptised.
June 3—John Boothe and Katheryn Fow married.
" 7—Roberte son of James Brodlaye baptised.
" 22—Thomas son of Willme Tayler baptised.
July 14—Edward Pollerd and Ellen Stevensonn married.
" 23—Marye daughter of John Peace baptised.
" 26—Elizabethe daughter of Marmaduke Speight buried.
" 27—........bell daughter of Thomas Barghe baptised.
" 29—Robert Smithe and Margrett Pollerde baptised.
Aug. 11—Henrye Nowell and Dorithye Brouke married.
" 13—John Netleton buried.
" 29—John son of John Jagger buried.
" 31—Willme son of Edward Wilkinsonn baptised.
Sept. 7—Willme son of Willme Longeley baptised.
" 14—A young daughter of Rychard Bradforthe the younger buried.
" 16—Ambrose Robinsonn and Frannces Grene married.

1595.
Sept. 16—Thomas Chaster and Margrett Robinsoun married.
" 18—Edye daughter of George Lee baptised.
" 21—Robert Leadbeater and Frauncis Peace married.
" 22—Rychard Bradforthe younger buried his wife.
Oct. 7—Thomas Dickensonn and Isabell Wilbye married.
" 12—Martyn son of John Boye baptised.
" 14—Arthure son of Lawrance Wamesley baptised.
" 14—Rychard son of Lawrance Wamesley baptised.
" 26—Jonye daughter of Abraham Lee baptised.
Nov. 9—Anne daughter of Robert Ledbeater baptised.
" 16—A young child of Edwarde Pollerd not baptised buried.
" 20—Uxor Harrisonn buried.
" 21—A young son of Rychard Jepson's not baptised buried.
" 28—John Mowbraye buried his wife.
" 30—Marye daughter of Thomas Boothe baptised.
" 30—Mercye daughter of Christopher Dicksonn baptised.
Dec. 2—Edmond Dishforthe and Elizabethe Walker married.
" 2—Thomas Ashtonn and Margrett Milnes married.
" 2—Elizabethe daughter of Raphe Slater baptised.
" 11—Agnes daughter of Gorge Nayler baptised.
" 14—John son of James Gurnall alias Sharpe baptised.
" 17—John son of Ambrosse Robinsonn baptised.
" 17—John son of Rychard Wright alias Grave baptised.
" *—Michaell Walker and Jane Boothe married.
Jan. 3—Roger Hurst was buried.
" 11—Raphe base son of Robte Sonyare and Alice Mosseley baptised.
" 18—John son of Rychard Awtie buried.
" 24—Elizabethe daughter of Averye Milnes buried.
" 25—Marye daughter of John Boothe baptised.
" 29—Gorge son of Edmond Dishforthe baptised.
" 31—Willme son of Willme Tayler buried.
Feb. 3—Willme Rychardsoun and Alis Smythe married.
" 3—Robte son of Rychard Thornes baptised.
" 15—Averye son of Willme Bowse baptised.
" 16—Agnes daughter of Willme Harrisonn baptised.
" 17—Gilbert Leptonn buried.
" 18—Etheldrede Speight buried.

* This date has disappeared.

1595.
Feb. 21—Willme Harrisonn buried his wife.
 ,, 22—Rychard Bradforthe the younger and Grace Grenewood married.
 ,, 22—Josephe son of Henrye Nayler baptised.
 ,, 22—Grace daughter of Robert Smithsonn baptised.
 ,, 23—Willme Lambe and Sibell Bayldonn married.
 ,, 23—Willme son of Michaell Walker baptised.
 ,, 25—Mathias son of Henrye Whitchede baptised.
 ,, 25—Willme son of Robert Tomlinsonn baptised.
 ,, 25—Isabell daughter of Henrye Nowell baptised.
 ,, 25—Jenett daughter of Thomas Archer baptised.
 ,, 28—Ann daughter of Willme Knowles baptised.
Mar. 3—Rosamond daughter of Emar Fox baptised.
 ,, 5—Willme son of Willme Lee of Gawthorpe buried.
 ,, 14—Agnes daughter of Willme Lee of Dewsburye baptised.
 ,, 14—Willme Lee of Gawthorpe buried.
 ,, 15—Alice daughter of Edwarde Ouldroyde buried.
 ,, 17—Robert son of Robert Awdesley the younger baptised.
 ,, 19—Anne daughter of Rychard Acrode baptised.
 ,, 20—Edward son of John Saxtonn baptised.
 ,, 20—Agnes daughter of John Saxtonn baptised.
 ,, 22—Bryan Crowder buried.
 ,, 28—John Wilbye of Dewsburye buried.
 ,, 28—Agnes daughter of Willme Lee of Dewsburye buried.
 ,, 31—Edward son of John Saxtonn buried.
 ,, 31—A young infant of Edward More not baptised buried.
1596.
April 2—Elizabethe daughter of Willme Longlay buried.
 ,, 3—John son of Willme Rychardsonn buried.
 ,, 5—James Dallahaye buried.
 ,, 8—Agnes wife of Abraham Adcocke buried.
 ,, 13—John Peaker buried.
 ,, 13—Peter son of Willme Rowso buried.
 ,, 16—Gorge son of John Walker the younger of Ossett buried.
 ,, 17—Uxor Peaker buried.
 ,, 19—Uxor Tayler buried.
 ,, 21—Robte Awdsley the elder buried.
 ,, 19—John Few buried.
 ,, 25—Elizabethe daughter of Willme Gill the younger baptised.
May 1—John son of Ambrose Robinsonn buried.
 ,, 1—Grace daughter of Robte Smithe baptised.
 ,, 4—Marmaduke Ellis and Margrett Acrod married.
 ,, 14—Phillippe son of John Berrye baptised.
 ,, 28—Robte son of Robte Awdsley the elder buried.

1595.
May 30—Alice daughter of Willme Saxtonn baptised.
June 6—Elizabethe daughter of Edward Roydes baptised.
 ,, 15—Thomas Robinsonn and Jane Scott married.
 ,, 16—Elizabethe daughter of Rychard Graver buried.
July 4—Averye son of Nicholas Armitedge baptised.
 ,, 6—Edward Hutchinsonn and Margrett Nayler married.
 ,, 6—Thomas Slacke and Isabell Sharphouse married.
 ,, 6—Henry son of James Claytonn baptised.
 ,, 10—Ellen daughter of John Dawsonn baptised.
 ,, 11—Nicholas Seeker and Agnes Wood married.
 ,, 13—Robte Robinsonn and Dorithie Sykes married.
 ,, 14—Marye daughter of Rychard Graver baptised.
 ,, 17—Margrett wife of Thomas Seeker buried.
 ,, 25—Thomas Bayley and Isabell Ouldroyd married.
 ,, 28—Elizabethe daughter of Thomas Ashtonn baptised.
Aug. 18—Jenett daughter of Thomas Langfelde baptised.
 ,, 21—Roger son of Thomas Gill baptised.
 ,, 22—Willme Lea and Elizabethe Poolay married.
Sept. 12—Susann daughter of Willme Tyas baptised.
 ,, 17—Elizabethe daughter of Robte Ouldroyde baptised.
 ,, 18—Elizabethe daughter of Robte Ouldroyd buried.
 ,, 18—Margrett daughter of Robte Ouldroyd baptised.
 ,, 18—Margrett daughter of Robte Ouldroyd buried.
 ,, 26—Elizabethe daughter of Rychard Ouldroyd baptised.
 ,, 29—Willme son of Willme Tomsonn baptised.
 ,, 30—Marye daughter of Rychard Graver buried.
Oct. 7—Grace daughter of Thomas Chaster baptised.
 ,, 10—Dorithye daughter of Averye Gill baptised.
 ,, 10—Ann daughter of Robte Robinsonn alias Man baptised.
 ,, 17—Willme son of John Westerman baptised.
 ,, 17—Alice daughter of Willme Rychardsonn baptised.
 ,, 24—Elizabethe daughter of Willme Varnon gentleman baptised.
 ,, 24—Edward son of Willme Lea alias Symne* baptised.

* This name is very difficult to decypher. Mr. Hemingway reads it as "Symare."

1596.

Oct. 28—Alice daughter of Willme Rychardsonn buried.
,, 29—Margerye wife of Robte Wrighte buried.
,, 31—Averye son of Averye Acrode baptised.
,, 31—Michaell son of Robte Brooke the younger baptised.
Nov. 2—Margery wife of John Dickensonn buried.
,, 7—Nicholas son of John Milnes baptised.
,, 14—Robte son of Robert Dey baptised.
,, 28—Elizabethe daughter of Thomas Ouldroyde baptised.
,, 30—Jeryeme son of Willme Lambe baptised.
,, 30—Edwarde Hurst and Dorithie Fernlaye married.
Dec. 3—Gorge Warren of Gawthorpe buried.
,, 7—Rychard Acrode and Sibell Barbar married.
,, 19—Rebecca daughter of Robte Smithe baptised.
,, 19—Agnes daughter of Willme Clark alias Harrisonn buried.
,, 25—............ daughter of Willme Knowles buried.
,, 27—Elizabethe daughter of John Nayler baptised.
Jan. 1—Alice daughter of Rycharde Wooddo baptised.
,, 2—Jennett Hoptonn buried.
,, 6—Robert son of John Parker baptised.
,, 8—Willme base son of Bryan Collier and Agnes Mawde baptised.
,, 10—Uxor Dawsonn of Dewsburye buried.
,, 14—Elizabethe daughter of John Nayler buried.
,, 19—Robert Lee of Dewsburye buried his wife.
,, 19—Robert Bradforthe the younger buried his wife.
,, 19—Robert son of Edwarde Ouldroyde baptised.
,, 19—Agnes daughter of Thomas Whitakers the younger baptised.
,, 19—Elizabethe daughter of Mr. Varnon buried.
,, 24—Nicholas Nayler buried his wife.
,, 25—Grace daughter of Marmaduke Ellis baptised.
,, 25—Anthouye Hepworthe and Agnes Allen married.
,, 26—Alice daughter of Edwarde Grene buried.
,, 27—Lyonell Barker was buried.
,, 30—Elizabethe daughter of Edward Hutchinsonn baptised.
,, 30—Susann daughter of Nicholas Secker baptised.
,, 31—Nicholas Armitedge buried his wife.
Feb. 6—Nicholas Nayler buried his mother.
,, 6—James son of James Walker baptised.
,, 6—Ellen daughter of James Walker baptised.
,, 8—James son of James Walker buried.
,, 8—Ellen daughter of James Walker buried.
,, 20—Robert Awdesley the younger of Ossett buried.

1596.

Feb. 26—Bryan Collyer was buried.
,, 27—Henrye son of Ambrose Robinsonn baptised.
,, 27—John son of Rychard Dentonn baptised.
Mar. 6—Willme son of Willme Lee baptised.
,, 7—Thomas Secker of Chickenlaye buried.
,, 9—Grace daughter of Averye Milnes baptised.
,, 17—Roger Gaunt was buried.
,, 17—Thomas son of Christopher Brouke baptised.
,, 20—Agnes daughter of Edwarde Midleborough baptised.
,, 20—Alice daughter of Henrye Barkar baptised.
,, 25—Dorithye daughter of John Dey baptised.
,, 26—Hester daughter of Rychard Sonyare baptised.

An°. Eliz. 39. A creatióne Mundi, 5559.

1597.

April 3—Thomas son of Thomas Slacke baptised.
,, 7—A young son of Peter Amblers and Eden Newell not baptised that was base born buried.
,, 7—Alice daughter of Rychard Bradforthe the younger baptised.
,, 8—Henrye son of Ambrose Robinsonn buried.
,, 10—Willme son of Anthonye Hepworthe baptised.
,, 15—Dorithie daughter of Humphraye Dicksonn buried.
,, 30—John son of Rychard Dentonn buried.
May 11—Margrett Croslay servant to Christofer Mitchell buried.
,, 10—Willme base son of Bryan Collier and Agnes Mawde buried.
,, 16—Bryan Phillippe and Agnes Roydes married.
,, 19—John Lee of Gawthorpe buried his wife.
,, 22—Ellen daughter of James Kent baptised.
,, 27—Nicholas son of John Milnes buried.
,, 27—Rychard Graver buried his wife.
,, 29—Mercye daughter of James Broodlaye baptised.
June 7—Robert Wright and Ann Leptonn married.
,, 12—Willme son of Rychard Speight baptised.
,, 19—Nicholas son of Gilbert Mortonn baptised.
,, 19—Marye daughter of John Ouldroyd baptised.
,, 26—Willme Wilsonn and Isabell Rychardsonn married.
July 5—Ann daughter of Humphray Dixsonn baptised.
,, 10—Gorge Blackburne the elder buried.
,, 12—John Lambe and Ellen Kighlaye married.
,, 25—Rychard son of Thomas Fox baptised.
,, 25—Averye son of Franccis Whitley baptised.
Aug. 1—Rychard son of Thomas Fox buried.
,, 21—Marye daughter of Averye Bull baptised.
Sept. 11—Jeremye son of Willme Lambe buried.

DEWSBURY PARISH REGISTERS.

1597.
Sept. 17—Ann daughter of Rychard Jepsonn baptised.
,, 25—Edward Wilcocke and Elizabethe Best married.
,, 25—Agnes daughter of Robert Pighells baptised.
Oct. 2—Averye son of John Lambe baptised.
,, 3—Willme Thomas a stranger was buried.
,, 5—Francis wife of John Lacye of Woodchurche was buried here in this parish of Dewsburye.
,, 7—Tobias Ouldroyd buried.
,, 6—A young infant of James Wade not baptised buried.
,, 9—Alice daughter of Thomas Graysonn baptised.
,, 12—Agnes daughter of Willme Gill the youngest baptised.
,, 13—James Awdesleye buried.
,, 20—Jeffearaye Boothe and Isabell Bradforthe married.
,, 23—Betheris daughter of Martynn Lister baptised.
,, 26—Robert Bedforthe buried his wife.
,, 30—Thomas son of John Peace baptised.
Nov. 1—John Deye was buried.
,, 3—Thomas Wheelewright and Agnes Bentlay married.
,, 6—Abrahame Adcocke and Edan Nowell married.
,, 23—Jonye daughter of Edward Fayerbarne baptised.
,, 29—Agnes daughter of Henrye Nowell buried.
Dec. 2—Agnes daughter of Robte Pighells buried.
,, 7—Thomas son of Gorge Nayler baptised.
,, 18—Ellen daughter of John Nayler baptised.
,, 18—Alice daughter of Willme Speight baptised.
,, 27—Rychard son of Willme Rychardsonn baptised.
,, 31—Arthure Tomsonn was buried.
Jan. 1—Robert son of Robert Ouldroyd baptised.
,, 7—Edward son of Rychard Rychemond buried.
,, 8—Thomas son of Willme Rychardsonn baptised.
,, 9—Robte son of Rychard Bradforthe the younger buried.
,, 9—Thomas son of Willme Rychardsonn buried.
,, 15—Rychard Speight was buried.
,, 17—Christopher Pickersgill buried.
,, 19—Elizabethe wife of John Bull buried.
,, 20—Ann daughter of James Nicolls buried.
,, 22—Willme Awdesleye and Agnes Maunsfelde married.
,, 22—John son of Rychard Thornes baptised.
,, 23—Michaell son of Robte Brouke the younger buried.
,, 24—Francis son of Willme Gill the eldest buried.
,, 24—Alice daughter of John Slacke buried.
,, 26—Willme Burnett buried his wife.

1597.
Jan. 27—Agnes daughter of Thomas Maunsfeld's wife buried.
,, 31—John son of Rychard Thornes buried.
,, 31—Thomas son of Willme Burnett buried.
,, 31—Edward son of John Speight buried.
Feb. 5—Willme son of Rychard Thornes buried.
,, 6—Willme Burnett was buried.
,, 7—Thomas Boothe was buried.
,, 8—Uxor Johis (of John) Walker of Ossett was buried.
,, 10—Elizabethe Speight the younger was buried.
,, 12—Elizabethe Gryffyne was buried.
,, 14—Agnes Lee of Ossett was buried.
,, 16—Averye son of John Lambe buried.
Feb. 17—Isabell Wade of Ossett was buried.
,, 18—John Bentlaye of Ossett buried his wife.
,, 24—Jennett daughter of Abrahame Lee buried.
,, 26—Gorge Gamble buried his wife.
,, 28—Thomas Boothe his wife was buried.
Mar. 5—John son of Luke Sykes baptised.
,, 8—Isabell daughter of Willme Wilsoun baptised.
,, 14—............ daughter of Rychard Rychemond buried.
,, 17—Rychard Rychemond buried.
,, 18—Uxor Johis (of John) Acrode was buried.
,, 20—Betheris daughter of Rychard Rychemond buried.
,, 21—Gorge Gamble buried.
,, 28—Willme Sharphowse buried his wife

1598.
April 1—Marmaduke son of Willme Varnon gentleman baptised the first day and
,, 3—was buried the third day of this month.
,, 9—Grace daughter of Henrye Whitcheade baptised.
,, 12—Uxor Robinsonn of Ossett buried.
,, 23—Beniamyn son of Rychard Acrode baptised.
,, 24—Gorge son of Gorge Nayler buried.
May 2—Kathevyn Hall buried.
,, 7—Isabell daughter of Emar Fox baptised.
,, 24—Thomas Norton of Sandall and Rosamond Awdsley of this parish were married here with a licence.
,, 25—Robert son of Jefferye Boothe baptised.
June 25—Elizabethe daughter of Averye Whitakers baptised.
July 12—Rychard son of John Littewood baptised the 12th day, and the same was buried
,, 13— the 13th day.
,, 15—Ann daughter of John Bayldonn buried.
,, 23—Robert Robinsonn and Alice Wilbye married.
,, 25—James son of Willme Lambe baptised.
,, 27—Ann daughter of Edmond Jepsonn baptised.
Aug. 1—Mr. Acrod Vicar of Dewsburye and Isabell Forrest married.
,, 2—Isabell daughter of Gorge Lee baptised.
,, 4—Sara daughter of Lawrance Wamsley baptised.
,, 7—Venitia daughter of John Naylor buried.

DEWSBURY PARISH REGISTERS.

1598.
Aug. 8—Robert Netletonn and Rachell Acrodo married.
,, 13—A young infant not baptised of Gawen Metcalfe buried.
,, 20—Willmo Wilbye and Agnes Forrest married.
,, 24—Willmo son of Thomas Wilsonn baptised.
,, 29—Ann Sandersonn dying at Lyversedg was buried here.
Sept. 3—Thomas Bradforthe and Marye Burnell married.
,, 3—Alice daughter of Edmond Dishforthe baptised.
,, 4—Uxor Tayler alias Renoulde buried.
,, 5—............ son of Edward Ouldroyd buried.
,, 10—Thomas Greue of Ossett in the Street buried here.
,, 17—Jonye daughter of Edward Fayerbarne buried.
,, 20—Willmo Rychardsonn of Ossett was buried.
,, 27—Uxor Milnes was buried.
,, 27—Willme Awdesley of Ossett buried.
,, 27—Alisonn Doye widow was buried.
,, 28—Jennett daughter of Robte Pighells baptised.
,, 30—Agnes daughter of Robert Bradforthe the elder buried.
Oct. 1—Henrye Whitheade buried his wife.
,, 6—Alexander Secker buried his wife.
,, 7—Alice daughter of Edmonde Dishforthe buried.
,, 12—Marye daughter of Edwarde Lee baptised.
,, 15—Robert Walker and Francis Sayill married.
,, 18—Willmo son of Willme Awdsley of Ossett baptised.
,, 21—Grace daughter of Rychard Acrode the younger baptised.
,, 25—A young infant of John Milnes not baptised buried.
,, 28—John son of Thomas Langofelde baptised.
,, 28—Grace daughter of Rychard Draper baptised.
,, 29—Robert son of Roberto Brouke the younger baptised.
Nov. 2—...........uye daughter of Averye Gill buried.
,, 5—............ daughter of Thomas Fox baptised.
,, 12—Robert son of Robte Smith baptised.
,, 12—Alice base daughter of Ann Lee and John Dishforthe baptised at evening prayer.
,, 19—Dorithye daughter of Robte Wright baptised.
,, 20—John Milnes buried his wife.
,, 22—Dorithye daughter of John Saxtonn baptised.
,, 30—Willmo son of Robte Shepperd baptised.
Dec. 3—Jonye daughter of Edward Wilcocke baptised.
,, 3—Sibell daughter of Averye Gill baptised.

1598.
Dec. 10—Dorithye daughter of John Westermann baptised.
,, 17—Edward son of Edward Roydes baptised.
,, 17—............ daughter of Robte Maw baptised.
,, 17—Edwarde son of Averye Acrod baptised.
,, 18—Ann daughter of Abraham Adcocke baptised.
,, 19—Dorithye daughter of John Saxtonn buried.
,, 21—Agnes daughter of Thomas Ashtonn baptised.
,, 24—Willme son of Robte Shepperd buried.
,, 28—Robte son of Willmo Wilbye baptised.
,, 29—A young infant of Gabriell Lambe's not baptised buried.
Jan. 1—Agnes daughter of Edward Midlebroughe buried.
,, 7—Robert base son of Anthonye Fisher alias Gripper and Agnes Pence baptised.
,, 22—John base son of John Dishforthe and Elizabethe Hurst baptised.
,, 23—John Nowell and Alice Rychardsonn married.
,, 27—A young infant of Bryan Phillipps not baptised buried.
Feb. 13—Alexander Secker and Merioll Robinsonn married.
,, 14—Isabell daughter of Rychard Thomas baptised.
,, 15—Elizabethe daughter of Marmaduke Ellis baptised.
,, 22—John Whitlaye of Sowood Greue the elder buried.
,, 25—Isabell daughter of Thomas Nortonn baptised.
,, 28—Alice daughter of Thomas Bonthe baptised.
Mar. 4—Jenet daughter of Willmo Rowse baptised.
,, 11—John son of Henrye Nayler baptised.
,, 11—Edward son of Thomas Ouldroyd baptised.
,, 11—Elizabethe daughter of Thomas Barghe baptised.
,, 11—Elizabethe daughter of Rychard Sonyare baptised.
,, 11—Edward son of John Dawsonn baptised.
,, 18—Robert son of Roberte Smithsonn baptised.
,, 21—Marye daughter of John Berrye baptised.
,, 25—Thomas son of James Claytonn baptised.
,, 25—Edward son of Michaell Walker baptised.
,, 25—Marye daughter of John Crosfeld baptised.
,, 26—A young infant a son of Robte Smithe not baptised buried.
,, 28—Betheris daughter of Rychard Graver baptised.
,, 28—Katheryn daughter of Rychard Musgrave baptised.
,, 30—Marye daughter of Rychard Marshall baptised.

1599.
April 5—Robert son of Willme Wilbye buried.
  „   8—John Slacke buried his wife.
  „ 18—Elizabethe daughter of Nicolas Secker baptised.
May 1—Leonerde Dickinsoun and Ann Moro married.
  „   6—John Ouldroyd and Grace Bull married.
  „   8—John son of Henrye Nayler buried.
  „ 16—Oswalde Midletonn buried.
  „ 19—Elizabethe daughter of Rychard Souyeare buried.
  „ 20—Gorge Ootes and Rachell Ouldroyde married.
  „ 20—Edwarde son of Edwarde Hutchinsoun baptised.
  „ 29—Jenet Awdesley was buried.
June 5—Roberte Thorpe and Mereye Bull married.
  „ 10—James son of Martynn Lister baptised.
  „ 10—Willme son of Thomas Wilsonn buried.
  „ 17—Robert son of Abraham Lee baptised.
  „ 17—Samuell son of Willme Winnersley baptised.
  „ 24—Thomas son of Edwarde Wilkensonn baptised.
  „ 21—Agnes daughter of Willme Tyas baptised.

1599.
  „ 24—Sara daughter of Willme Gill the younger baptised.
July 1—Michaell son of Thomas Whelewrighte baptised.
  „   1—Roger Scott and Elizabethe Arrandell married.
  „   3—Rychard Dishforthe and Margrett Sharphowse married.
  „   7—Margrett daughter of John Litlewoode baptised.
  „   8—Margrett daughter of John Litlewoode buried.
  „ 11—John son of Edwarde Fayerbarne baptised.
  „ 15—Michaell son of Gorge Otes baptised.
  „ 22—Marye daughter of Henrye Barbar baptised.
  „ 22—Henrye son of John Speight baptised.
  „ 29—Uxor Lee of Dewsburye buried.
Aug. 1—Margrett daughter of Edward Wurmall baptised.
  „   5—Thomas son of Rychard Wright baptised.
  „   5—Rychard son of Robert Dey baptised.
  „   5—Ann daughter of James Kent baptised.

End of the First Volume.

VOLUME II.

The Second Volume of the Parish Registers extends from 25th March, 1600, to 29th January, 16⅜⅞. It is a narrow folio volume of vellum with five paper leaves inserted at the commencement and one paper leaf added at the end of the volume. The first and last of the paper leaves contain miscellaneous notes, and the other four leaves contain the names of the Churchwardens of Dewsbury from Easter, 1599 to 1653, inclusive, with the addition of further miscellaneous notes on the last page of the fourth leaf.

The volume has been copied in full with all the quaint spelling and will be so printed. The first leaf has writing on the second page only, which consists largely of scribble, and the few entries on it are not consecutive and are in many different hands.

The entries are as follows:—
Michaell Smyth and Marye Pickarde marryed at Ossett Chapel the xijth of Novem. 1639.
Martyn Lyster Jos. Dewsberie.
[These two names appear to be autographs; it is doubtful if they have any reference to the foregoing entry. Just above is the date 1599.]
24 Martii dyed quene Elizabethe 1602 anno eius regni 44.
She raigned fortye fower yeares 18 weekes.
Averye Acrode viccar of Dewsburye.
[This signature seems to be the autograph of the Vicar. It occurs again at the top of the first page of the Register.]
Richard Bedforthe buryed ye xvjth of Februarye 1614............day and a Thursday.
Mris Ratcliffe of Thornhill was buried there the fourth daye of Julye beinge Fridaye 1626.
Mathew Robinson ⎱ Mense Martii.
Ann Ledgarde   ⎰
Williame Autie *alias* Anderton an° Dⁿⁱ 1613.
Richard (?) Robinson.
Januarie 1637.
Mr. John Copley being drowned upon Tusdaie and buried the last daie above expresste at Batley.
A note of all the churche wardens from anno Dni 1599.

5 Martij 1599	Martyn Lister,
Anno creationis	Thomas Whittakers, ju.,
5560 1599	Rychard Cartar,
easter dayo	Willme Rowso,
8 Aprilis	Thomas Nortonn,
Eliz. 41.	John Peace.
1600	John Claytonn,
Easter day	Francis Whitlaye,
2d Marche	Thomas Wurmall,
	Edward Kitsonn,
Eliz. 42.	John Whitlaye of ossott,
	Xpofer Brouke, ju.
Easter daye	1601.
12 Aprille	John Awtye, se.,
1601	James Claytonn,
Eliz. 43.	Roberte Dickensonn,
	Rychard Acrode, ju.,
	John Robinson alias Townende,
	Roberte Pighells, s.
Easter daye	Henrye Robinsonn,
4 Aprill	Thomas Rudlaye, sc.,
an° Dni. 1602	Rychard Marshall,
Eliz. 44.	Thomas Archer,
	Thomas Pickerde,
	Edward Fayrbarne.
Easter daye	Averye Milnes,
24 Aprill	Adam Wheatlye,
ann° Dni. 1603	Roberte Nethetonn,
Jacobi primi	John Westerman,
anno ejus primo.	John Maunsfelde,
	Rycharde Awdsleye, se.
Easter daye	Robert Willbye,
octavo Aprill	John Bentlaye,
anno Dni 1604	Rychard Cartare,
Anno Jacobi	Willme Brouke, ju.,
secundo	John Fayerbarne,
Magno Britanico	Thomas Fox.
anno Regis Jacobi	John Dawson,
tertio	Edmonde Jepsonn,
Easter daye	John Grave, sc.,
ultimo Martij	Rychard Wilkensonn,
31mo eiusdem diei	Robert Bradfortho, ju.,
anno Dni.	Eunar Fox.
1605	
Easter dayo	John Hurst,
vicessimo die	Robert Ouldroide,
aprill	John Goodall,
Jacobi regis	John Ouldroide,
quarto	John Phillipps,
	John Rawson.
	Dewsbarie.
Easter	Thomas Barbar,
quinto Aprill	Willme Shepley,
1607	Edward Kitsonn,
Jacobi regis quinto	Gorge Speight,
	Rycharde Thornes,
	Roberte Brouke, ju.
Easter	James Sharpe,
27mo martij	Nicholas Hirst,
1608	Thomas Wurmall,
Jacobi regis	Thomas Archer,
scotie 41.	Henrie Whitheade,
	Parcivall Tirrye.
Easter 16	Phillippe Slade,
Aprilis 1609	Willme Knowles,
Jacobi regis	Mr. Whittakers, j.,
Septino	Anthonye Hurst,
Scotie 42°	Willme Gill, elder,
	Willme Hurst.
Easter 8	John Milnes,
Aprilis 1610	Robert Thorpe,
Jacobi regis	Rycharde Roydes,
anno octavo	John Westerman,
Scotie 43°	Robert Bradfortho, youngest,
	Edmonde Fox.

	1611.		1620.
Easter	Nicholas Mitchell,	Easter	James Claytonn,
Martij 24	Jefferay Acrode,	ann° Dni. 1620	Willme Pollerde,
1611	Philemon Speight,	16 Aprill	Alexander Netleton,
Jacobi regis	Rychard Goodall,	Jacobi regis	James Speight,
nono.	Thomas Nayler,	decimo octavo	John Stead of ye street,
Scotiœ ann° 44 to	Edwarde Midlebroughe.		John Awdslaye.
quadragessimo		primo die Aprilis	Henric Robinson,
quarto.		Easter	Adam Wheatlaye,
Easter	John Bedforde,	an° Dni. 1621	Robert Netleton,
ann° Dni	Michaell Wheatlay,	Jacobi regis	Willme Westerman,
1612	Frances Fernlay,	decimo nono.	father son and holye ghost amen
Jacobi regis	Robert Boothe,		......godes father.
decimo	Willme Saxtone,		Edward Roydes,
Scotiœ 45.	Roberte Pickerde.		Rychard Nayler.
		Easter 1622	Mr. Hemyngewaye,
quarto aprilis	Michaell Bentlay, se.	Jacobi regis	Abraham Grenewoode,
Easter ann° Dni.	Abram Grenewood,	vicesimo.	John Stockes,
1613	Rychard Cartar,		Nicholas Hurst,
Scotiœ 46 Angliœ	John Owldroide,		Thomas Gill,
undecimo.	Roger Beatsonn,		John Nayler.
	John Bradfortho.		
		Easter 1623	Anthonye Hurst,
24 Aprilis	Richard Acrode, se.,	Jacobi regis	John Milnes,
Easter an° Dni.	Nicholas Walker,	vicesimo primo.	James Broadlaye,
1614	Rychard Mayhall.		John Denisonn,
Scotiœ 47	Willme Speight, ju.		Thomas Peace,
Angliœ	John Medley.		Willme Paslaye.
...nodecimo.	(The last name worn off.)		
		Easter 28	John Dawsonn,
	Dewsburio 1614.	Aprill 1624	Thomas Rodlaye,
		Jacobi regis	Roberte Speight,
Easter	Thomas Netletonn,	22	Thomas Netleton,
9no die aprilis	John Houldswortho,	Dewsburie.	of Hoyle milne,
1615.	Gilbert Whelowright,		Rychard Thornes,
	John Saxtonn,		Thomas Marshall.
	Edward Kitsonn,		
	Willme Speight, se.	Easter an°	Thomas Barbar,
		Dni. 1625	Robert Wheatlaye,
Easter	Thomas Kitsonn,	22 Aprill	Carey Morishe,
vltimo die	Willme Acrode,	* 17 Jacobi regis.	Robert Roydes,
Martij	Roberto Beckwithe,	Caroli regis	Thomas Langefelde,
1616.	Robert Breayaye,	primo.	James Pickerde.
	Roberte Mitchell,		
	Roger Pickarde.	Easter 1626	Rychard Dawsonn, ju.,
		ix^{no} Aprill	Robert Naylor,
Easter	Willme Sheplaye,	Caroli regis	Rychard Dawsonn, se.,
20 Aprill	Robert Robinsonn,	secundo.	Francis Fernlaye,
1617.	Thomas Wurnnall,		Willme Thornes,
	Anthonye Hurst,		Abraham Hemyngwaye.
	Rycharde Fayrbarne,		
	Rycharde Nayler, se.	Easter 1627	Henric Barbar,
		Martij 25	John Dickesonn,
Easter	Averie Whitakers,	Caroli regis	John Tilsonn,
an° Dni. 1618	Rychard Whitlaye, of ye carre,	tertio.	Samuell Foxcroft,
quinto Aprill	Francis Fernlaye,		John Peace,
Jacobi regis	Henric Bowlinge,		Edwarde Langefelde.
decimo sexto.	Samuell Tattersall,		
	Willme Robucke.	Easter 1628	Robert Wade,
		Aprilis 13	Robert Touson,
Easter	Walter Cordinglaye,	Caroli regis	Symeon Grenewoode,
an° Dni. 1619	Josepho Owldroide,	quarto.	Rycharde Wilkinson,
28 Martij	John Owldroide,		Willme Gill,
Jacobi regis	Rycharde Archer,		John Fox.
decimo septimo	John Forrest,		
	Averie Pickerde.		* So in the Register.

DEWSBURY PARISH REGISTERS. 61

	1629.		1638.
Easter 1629 5 Aprill Caroli quinto	Nicholas Mitchell, Rychard Whitlaye, ju., John Stocke, Thomas Acrode, Rychard Molingdale, Rychard Fernlay.	Easter daie the xxvth daie of March 1638 Visitacons the 8th of Maie 1638 Anno R.Re.Caroli Angli. decimo quarto.	Nicholas Wheatley, Willm Autie, Robert Nettleton, James Speight, James Simpson, Thomas Nailor, junior.
Easter 1630 Marcho 28 Caroli sexto.	Michaell Bentley, ju., Thomas Awtie, Robert Nettleton, John Tayler, Michaell Wheelwright, John Haghe.	Easter daie the 14th of Aprill 1639.	
		Visitacons at Pontifracte ye xviijth of Aprill 1639	Michael Bentley, senior, Tho. Whitakers, Robert Greene, Robert Dickson,
Easter 1631 Aprill x Caroli septimo.	Michaell Bentley, sc., Philemon Dixon, Richard Archer, Robert Audsleye, John Richardson,	Anno R. Re. Caroli nunc Anglie decimo quinto.	Tho. Hepworth & Willm Rayner.
1631	Robert Audsley de Ossett.	Anno Regni Regis Caroli decimo sexto 1640.	Robert Wheatley, Robert Peaker, Willme Roodes, Philemon Dickson, Christopher Audsleye, Rychard Dyson,
Easter 1632 Aprill firsto Caroli octo.	Michaell Wheelwrighte, James Fearnleye,! Richard Hemingwaye, Willme Speighte, John Gill, Richard Spurre.	Anno Regni Regis Caroli decimo septem 1641.	Thomas Webstar, Mich. Parker, Thos. Hemingwaye, Robt. Audsleye, John Freckleton, Willme Middlebrongh.
Easter 1633 Aprill xxjth Caroli regis nono 1633 1633.	Rychard Whitleye de car, Willme Williamson. Henrye Allen, John Nettleton, Christopher Audsleye, Robert Barghe.	Anno Regni Regis Caroli decimo octavo 1642.	Nicholas Mitchell, Robt. Barbar, Thomas Acrode, Robt. Goodall, Robt. Bradforthe, Thomas Audsleye.
Easter April 6 1634 Caroli regis decimo.	Thomas Nettleton, George Towleson, Thomas Audsleye, Willme Burnleye, Franscis Gill, Anthonio Curtice.	Anno Regni Regis 1643 Caroli decimo nono	Rych. Dawson, John Ashleye, John Tailier, Tho. Marshall, Paull Lumsden, Robt. Fairbarne,
1635 Easter March 29 1635 Caroli regis vndecimo.	Robert Bedforth, James Clayton, Wilhae Westerman, James Bradley, Thomas Nayler, sc., Willme Audsleye.	Anno Regni Regis 1644 Caroli viginti.	Martin Parker, Abra. Greenwoode, George Allen, Tho. Fox, Anthonye Shearde, Parcinall Terrie.
the 13 of October 1636		Anno Regni Regis Caroli viginti vno. 1645.	Michaell Wheatleye, Willme Leezhe, John Tilson, Robt. Westerman, Willme Gill, John Nayler.
Easter daye 17 of Aprill 1636 Anno R. Re Caroli Anglie duodecimo.	Richard Whitley, Robert Mythes, Richard Nettleton, John Dynison, Robert Roydes & Joseph Armitage.		
Easter daie the 9th of Aprill 1637		1646 *	Andrew Claton, Nicholas Naylor, Richard Nettleton, Willme Billesden, James Wilson, John Forrest.
Anno R. Re. Caroli Angli. decimo tertio.			
the xxiijth of Maye 1637			
	Joseph Oldroid, senior, Robert Broadley, Anthonio Fearnley, Nicholas Booth, George Leigh, Richard Terrie.		

* It will be noted that with this year all mention of Charles I. ceases. On 5th May, 1646, the King having lost all hope of success against the parliamentary force, placed himself in the power of the Scotch army at Southwell, and became a captive.

DEWSBURY PARISH REGISTERS.

1617.

1647 — Nicholas Mitchell,
Michaell Bentley,
John Nettleton,
Timothie Kitson,
John Sugden,
Willim Reynor.

1648 — James Fearneley,
Lawrence Whittakers,
Willm. Broodley,
Willm Burneley,
Francis Brooke,
Edward Thornes.

1649 — Joseph Jepsonne,
Edmunde Copley,
Richard Archer,
Symeon Greewoode, senior,
George Nalor,
Anthony Curteous.

1650 — Willme Williamson,
Israell Owldroyd,
John Roydes,
Thomas Awty,
John Gill,
John Spurr.

1651 — Richard Whitley of the Dawgreen,
Richard Holdsworth,
Robert Nettleton,
Joseph White,
John Worsdall,
Thomas Awdsley of Gawthrop.

1652 — Dewsbury Church wardens,
Robt. Ouldroide,
Willim Whitley,
(The rest is broken away).

1653 — Henry Barber,
Lawrence Whitaker,
Symeon Greenwood, jun.,
Willim Rodes,
Michaell Wheatley,
George Otley.

The xth of Aprill 1626.

It is agreed of by the Churchwardens of this parish that George Pickhard shall have for keepinge and upholdinge of the Clocke the some of   iijs. overie yeare after this yeare be expired.

Marche 9 1634.

Arthure Kaye and Edward Kaye beinge brethren was drowned in calder ath' top of ye annams (Aldams) heade the 9 of March 1634.
Sara daughter of Tho. Nayler jn. of Ossett baptized the xxijth daye of Septem. 1635 sera nocte (late at night).
Mr. Haworth vicar of Batley Buryed the 30th daye of Septem. anno Dni. 1635 Caroli xith.
Rycharde Gibson & Eliz. Womersley marryed at Mourley Chappell the xxvth daye of Noue 1635 by Mr. Pearson.
Robert Westerman & Eliz. Atkinson was marryed at Batley Churche the same daye.

1635.

Robert son of Willm Champney of Ossett townshippe Baptized at Wakefield Churche the xvijth daye of October anno Dni. 1635.

July 1636.
Henrie Adam was induckted vicar of Dewsburie the xijth daie by Roger Audsley vicar of Batley no RRe Caroli Anglie &c. duo decimo 1636.
Thomas Banne of Ossett had a childe Baptized in Horburye Churche the 4th of Januarye anno 1634 named Nathaniell.

1628.
a mundi creatione 5619.
* synce brute entred this Iland, 2735.
synce England first receaved ye christian faythe 1448, synce ye conquest by duke William 562.
carles rebellion in ye northe 59.
printing invented 168.
Rychard Whitley & Easter France married at Mirfeilde the vijth of Aprill anno Dni. 1635.
Robert Bradforth & Eliz. Boothe married at Hartsheade the vth of May anno 1635.

1627.
tymes of mariages prohibited
from
advent sondaye and † ye thirtenthe of Januarie being hillarie day.
septuagesima sondaye and † lowe sondaye.
betwixt sonday next before ascention daye and trinitie sondaye an° Dni. 1627
46 article at visitacons of
the (lord)archbishoppe an° Dni. 1627.
Rychard Willinson of this parishe of Dewsburie was buried the xiijth daye of December 1628 then sondaye.........s afore St. Thomas Daye that yeare 1628.
Francis Nettleton & Alice Bradle married at ....the.....................634.
‡ Avery Acrode   multu(m) et diu,
Vicear   modice et modico.
Here beginethe this register of Dewsburye upon ye 25th daye of Marche anno Dni. 1600 of all mariages burrialls and christenings within this parishe of Dewsburye anno Eliz. regine 42; anno a creatione mundi 5562.

Marche 1600 Imprimis.
Rychard sonn of Rychard Acrod baptised ye xxxth daye.
Agnes daughter of John Peace baptised ye same daye.
Margret daughter of Edmonde Dishforthe baptised ye same daye.

---

*Brutus or Prydain, by Welsh tradition said to have been the natural son of Sylvius, grandson of Æneas, and to have visited England after he was expelled from Italy. Tradition has it that in England he founded a city called Troai-Newydd (New Troy) which name was subsequently changed to Caerludd, and afterwards to Lundun.—See Notes and Queries, 8th Series, V. 351-2.

† The word "untyll" has been interlined after "and" in each of these places, and has afterwards been struck out.

‡ The Register on vellum commences here with the Vicar's signature and what would seem to have been his motto, viz.—*multum et diu*, much and long; *modice et modice*, moderately and quietly—a very good motto for a parish priest.

DEWSBURY PARISH REGISTERS. 63

Aprill 1600.
Edwarde sonn of Thomas Wilson baptised ye sixt daye.
Ann daughter of Xxpofer Brouke, ju. baptised ye same daye.
Ann daughter of Raphe Slator baptised yo same daye.
A yonge sonn of Thomas Wilsons being not baptized was buried the same daye.
John Sonyare buried his wyfe the xxjth daye.

May 1600.
Roberto sonn of Humphrye Dixon baptised ye xiijth daye.
A yong infante of Roberte Smithe of Dewsburie not baptised was buried the xiijth daye.
Willmo Tomsonn buried his wyfe the xxiijth daye.
Henrie Rayner and Jenet Awdsley maried ye xxvijth daye.

June 1600.
Sibell daughter of Willmo Gill yongest baptised ye forth day.
Roberte sonn of Humphry Dixon buried ye sixt daye.
Thomas sonn of Thomas Graysonn baptised yo eight daye.
Thomas sonn of John Slacke baptised ye xxijth daye.
Sara daughter of Thomas Wholewright baptised ye xxijth daye.
Roberto sonn of Lawrence Wamesley baptised yo xxvjth daye.
Ann daughter of Averye Bull baptised the xxixth daye.
Jennet daughter of Roberte Thorpe baptised ye same daye.

Julie 1600.
Mercie daughter of John Ouldroyd baptised ye second daye.
Thomas soun of Francis Tebbe baptised ye vthe daye.
Roberto sonn of Ambrosse Robinson baptised yo vjthe daye.
Rychard Barbar was buried ye same daye.
John Fornell was buried ye seaventhe daye.
Thomas Peace and Ann Taylier maried yo eight daye.
Roberte sonn of Edward Secker of York baptised ye xijth daye.
Gorge Lee was buried the thirtenthe daye.
Mathew sonn of John Dickenson baptised yo thirtene daye.
Isabell daughter of Richard Harrish baptised yo xxthe daye.

August 1600.
John sonn of Roberte Dey baptised the third daye.
Thomas sonn of Willmo Lansfearre baptised ye tenthe daye.
Henrye Robinsonn buried his wife ye xxv daye.
Emar sonn of Emar Fox baptised ye xxxjth daye.
Phillippe sonn of John Gibsonn baptised ye xxxjth daye.

September 1600.
Mercie daughter basse borne of Willmo Sheplaye and Elizabethe Allen baptised ye vijthe daye.
Phillip sonn of John Gibsonn buried ye same daye.
Ann daughter of John Litlewood baptised ye vijth daye.

1600.
Rychard son of Rychard Thornes baptised ye xiiijth daye.
Thomas sonn of Averio Gill baptised ye same daye.
Edwarde Lee and Agnes Barber married ye xxjth daye.
Thomas sonn of Willmo Speight baptised ye same daye.
Willmo Hawden and Flanell Dixon beinge of Leedes parishe were married here the xxviijth daye.
John sonn of John Mannsfelde baptised ye xxviijth daye.
Elizbethe daughter of Thomas Peace baptised ye same daye.

Eliz. regine 42. The monethe of October 1600.
Easter daughter of Thomas Ashtonn baptised ye vth daye.
Robert Allott of Wursbroughe and Dorithie Kitsonn of this parishe were married at Wursbroughe ye vjth daye.
Willmo Brouke of Allmanburie parishe and Agnes Gill of this parishe were married here the xxjth daye.
Thomas sonn of Willmo Speight buried yo xxijth day.
Uxor Boothe of Ossett was buried the xxviijth day.
Phillippe sonn of Edward Barbar baptised ye same daye.

Eliz. 42. The monethe of November 1600.
James sonn of Francis Whitlay baptised ye first daye.
Edmonde Exam and Jenett Clayton maried ye second daye.
Jane daughter of Henrye Bedfortho of Emlay beinge drowned in Calder here was buried the third daye.
Edward sonn of Averie Whittakers baptised ye vthe daye.
James sonn of Fraunces Whitlaye buried yo xjth day.
Jennett wyfe of Edmond Exam buried yo xijth day.
Edwarde sonn of Averye Whittakers buried yo xvjth daye.
Alice daughter of Roberte Ouldroyde baptised ye same daye.
Elizabethe daughter of Uxor George Lee baptised yo same day.
Jennett daughter of Averye Acrod baptised ye same daye.
Henrie Bull and Alice Robinson maried ye xxiijth day.
Johu sonn of George Nayler baptised yo xxiijth day.
Alice daughter of Willmo Lambe baptised ye xxiijth day.
Fryssell daughter of Rychard Marshall baptised ye xxxth day.

Eliz. 43. December 1600, a creatione anno 5363.
Elizabethe daughter of Mr. Aerode vicar beinge borne the fourtho daye was baptised the seaventho daye.
Grace daughter of Willmo Gill yonger baptised ye xxjth daye.

1600.

Jennet daughter of Averye Aerod buried ye xxiijth daye.
A yonge daughter of Rychard Musgrave beinge not baptised was buried the xxvth daye.
Dorithie daughter of Averye Milnes baptised ye xxvth day.
Agnes Gryphyn a maide buried the xxvjth daye.

Eliz. 42.* Januarye 1600.

Rychard sonn of Willme Taylier baptised ye xjth daye.
Rychard sonn of Willme Tayler buried ye xvth daye.
Jennett daughter of Henrye Bull baptised ye xvijth daye.
Gorge Barmbye was buried the xixth daye.
Thomas Ashtonn & Agnes Hinchcliffe maried ye xxvjth day.
Edward sonn of Edward Ouldroyd baptised ye xxviijth day.
Alice daughter of Edward Midlebroughe buried xxxjth daye.

Februarye 1600 ano Eliz. 43.

Ann daughter of Martynn Lister baptised ye first daye.
John sonn of Rychard Tyas baptised ye same daye.
Jane daughter of Thomas Ouldroid baptised ye same daye.
Rychard sonn of Rychard Ashtonn buried the third daye.
Rychard Bullman and Ann Lee maried ye xiijthe daye.
Isabell daughter of Abraham Lee baptised ye viijth daye.
Ann daughter of Marmaduke Ellis baptised ye same daye.
Thomas Barbar and Elizabethe Scott maried ye xvijth day.
Samuell Grenwoode and Isabell Newsome maried ye same daye.
John basse son of Rychard Slacke and Uxor Rychmond beinge borne ye eight daye was baptised ye xxijth daye.
John sonn of Thomas Jagger baptised ye same daye.
Ann daughter of Edward Fayrbarne baptised ye same daye.
Rychard sonn of Thomas Hinchlyffe baptised ye xxiijth daye.

Marche 1600.

John Lee of Gawthorpe buried ye third daye.
Gorge sonn of John Westermann baptised ye viijth day.
Brygett daughter of Roberte Smithe baptised ye same day.
Elizabethe daughter of Thomas Rychardson of Liversedge dyinge at Ossett was buried here ye xxth daye.
Willme Sharphowse buried his wyfe ye xxjth daye.
Thomas sonn of Thomas Boothe baptised ye xxijth daye.
Marye daughter of Humphrye Dixon baptised ye same daye and the same Marye was buried ye xxvithe daye.

* So in original. Should be 43.

1600.

John basse son of Richard Slacke and Uxor Rychemond was buried the xxixthe day.

Aprill 1600.

Thomas sonn of Roberte Broake, ju, baptised ye vth daye.
Easter daughter of Henrye Barbar baptised ye xijth day.
Thomas sonn of Thomas Nortonn baptised ye xiijth daye.
A yonge infant of Samuel Greenwoode beinge not baptised was buryed the xviijth daye.
Thomas sonn of Roberte Pighells baptised ye xxvjth day.
Roberte sonn of Edward Lee baptised ye same daye.

Maye anno Dni 1601.

Elizabethe daughter of John Fox dying at the new parke was buried the second daye.
Isabell daughter of Abraham Adcocke baptised ye third daye.
Ann daughter of Edward Hutchinsonn baptised ye xxjth daye.
Leonard sonn of Willme Rowse baptised ye xxiijth daye.
Thomas sonn of Francis Tebbe buried ye xxvthe day.

June Ano Dni. 1601.

Willme Walker alias Piper buried ye first daye.
John sonn of John Ouldroid yonger baptised ye second daye.
Francis sonn of Thomas Ashton yonger baptised ye same daye.
Isabell daughter of Rychard Thornes buried ye tenthe daye.
A yonge daughter of Thomas Slacke being not baptised was buried here the xijthe daye.
Thomas son of Willme Leadbeater alias Sheppard was here baptised the xxjthe daye.
Jane daughter of Thomas Ouldroide buried ye xxvijth Daye.
Edwarde Wurmall and Jennett Bradforthe married ye xxixth day.
John Bradforthe and Marye Sladenn married the xxixth daye.

The monethe of Julie 1601.

Robte Lockwood and Elizabethe Grene mar'ed ye vijthe day.
Edmunde Dishforthe was buried ye second daye.
Henrie sonn of John Speight buried the fourthe daye.
John sonn of John Ouldroide ju., buried ye vthe daye.
Elizabeth daughter of John Milnes baptised ye xvth daye.
Elizabethe daughter of John Milnes buried ye xxijth daye.
Dorithie daughter of Rychard Awdsley, ju, baptised ye xxvjth day.
Juditho daughter of Edward Roides baptised ye same daye.
John Walker and Ellen Grendall maried ye xxviijth day.

The monethe of August 1601.
Emmott wyfe of Samuell Scollfelde of Liversedge dying there was buried here at Dewsbury ye vijth daye.
Alice Smithe was buried the same day.
Marmaduke Speight was buried ye xvjth daye.
Ann daughter of Edward Hutchinsonn buried the xixth daye.
Willme Tomsonn and Anne Speight maried the xxxth daye.
Joseph sonn of John Nayler baptised ye same daye.
Grace daughter of Gorge Oetes baptised yo same daye.

Eliz. 43. The monethe of September 1601.
Henrye Robinsonn of this parishe and Ann Mawde of Churcheaton (Kirkheaton) was maried here the tenthe daye.
Alice Dishforthe was buried the ixthe daye.
Robte sonn of Thomas Barbar baptised ye xiiijth daye.
Agnes daughter of Edward Wurmall baptised ye xxth daye.
Willme sonn of John Dawsonn baptised ye xxth daye.
Susann daughter of John Walker of Mirffelde was here baptised the one and twentye daye.
Alice daughter of Jefferay Boothe buried ye xxvjth day,
Edwarde sonn of Robte Allott baptised ye xxvijth daye.

Eliz. 43. The monethe of October 1601.
Willme sonn of John Dawsonn buried ye sixth daye.
Martyn sonn of Francis Whitlay baptised ye xxvth day.

The moneth of November 1601.
Alice daughter of Averye Acrod baptised ye first daye.
Thomas sonn of Willme Wilbye buried ye same daye.
Grace daughter of Averye Whittakers baptised ye vjth daye.
Francis daughter of Thomas Barghe baptised ye eight daye.
Joaye daughter of Edward Hiddlebroughe* baptised ye xthe daye.
Jenett daughter of Henrye Robinson baptised ye xjth daye.
Robte sonn of Robert Netletonn baptised ye same daye.
Christopher Birkill and Margerie Bull maried ye xvijth daye.
Willme Roebucke of Horburye and Alice Lee of this parishe were maried the xxijth daye.
Charles Helves of Horbarye and Elizabethe Hutchinsonn of this parishe were married ye xxixth day.
Mary daughter of Willme Wimersley baptised the same daye.

Eliz. 44. December Anno dni. 1601.
Maye daughter of Lawrence Barom baptised ye xijth daye.

---

* This name may be "Hinelebroughe." It is very indistinct.

1601.
Nicholas Hutchinsonn buried his wyfe ye xvjtho daye.
Rosamond daughter of Henry Nayler baptised ye xxvjth day.

Januarye anno dni. 1601.
Margrett daughter of John Speight buried ye xxij daye.

Februarye anno dni. 1601.
Edward Gibsonn of Huddersfeld and Beatryce Fearnley of this parishe maried here the xvjthe daye.
Uxor Ouldroid of Hanging Heaton buried ye sixth daye.
Robt sonn of Rychard Wright baptised ye xxth daye.
Grace daughter of Willme Gill yonger buried ye xxvjth daye.
Agnes daughter of John Peace buried ye same daye.

Marche anno Dni. 1601.
Alexander sonn of Robte Smithsonn baptised ye xxjth daye.

Aprill anno Dni. 1602.
Alice daughter of Jefferye Boothe baptised ye vthe daye.
Jane daughter of Humphrye Dixsonn baptised ye vjthe daye.
Mary daughter of Willme Wymersley buried ye xjth daye.
John Fairbarne and Elizabethe Walshaw maried ye xxthe daye.
John sonn of Rychard Woode baptised ye xvijth daye.
Uxor Robinsonn of Dewsbury more syde buried yo xxjth daye.
Edward sonn of Willme Grene baptisd ye xxvth daye.
A yonge sonn of Thomas Chaster being not baptised was here buried the xxvijth daye.

Maye anno Dni. 1602.
Thomas Chaster buried his wyfe the first daye.
Edward Ellis and Anne Grene maried ye fourthe daye.
A yonge sonn of John Rawsonn being not baptised was here buried the xijth daye.
Rychard sonn of Thomas Hyncheliffe buried ye xxth daye.
Alice daughter of Rychard Thornes baptised ye xxiijth daye.
Alice daughter of James Claytonn baptised ye xxijth daye.
Agnes Rowse was buried the xxiiijth daye.
Alisonn Rayner was buried the xxvijth daye.
Alice daughter of Samuell Grenewood baptised ye same day.

June anno Dni. 1602.
Anthonye Hurst and Isabell Bartonn maried ye first daye.
Wilme Barnett and Ellen Pell maried ye xvijth day.
Randal Netletonn buried his wyfe the xxth day.
Robte Stansfeld buried his wyfe the xxvjth daye.

Eliz. 44. Julie anno Dni. 1602.
Elizabethe Clayton was buried ye first daye.
Thomas son of Rychard Acrode baptised ye eight daye.
Alexander sonn of Robte Smithsonn buried yo xirthe daye.
Isabell daughter of Willme Speight baptised yo same daye.
Thomas Acrode of Earles Heatonn buried ye xvijth daye.
Grace daughter of Robert Smithe buried xvijth daye.
Alice daughter of Thomas Fox baptised yo xviijth daye.
Nicholas Longleye of Earls Heaton buried yo xxvijth daye.
Marie daughter of Henrie Barbar buried yo xxixth daye.

The monethe of August 1602.
Thomas sonn of Godfray Fox baptised yo first daye.
Alice daughter of John Milnes baptised yo xijth daye.
John sonn of Willme Dey baptised yo xvthe daye.
Robert sonn of Thomas Barbar buried yo xviijth daye.
Willme Sothill and Agnes Robinsonn maried yo xxijth daye.
James Dishforthe was buried yo xxiiijth daye.
John son of Rychard Wilson baptised ye xxixth daye.
Agnes daughter of Willme Wilbye baptised yo same daye.
Jenett daughter of Averie Gill baptised ye same daye.

The monethe September anno Dni. 1602.
Henrie sonn of John Dawson baptised yo fift daye.
Thomas Chaster and Jennett Arnoulde maried ye xijth daye.
Gorge sonn of Robert Smithe baptised ye xvth daye.
A yonge daughter of Willme Sharphowse being not baptised was here buried the xvjthe daye.
Nicholas Hutchinsonn and Elizabethe Atkinson bothe of this parishe married ye xxjthe daye.
Michaell sonn of John Parker baptised ye xxixthe daye.
Ann daughter of Thomas Peace baptised ye same daye.

The monethe of October 1602.
Josephe sonn of Willme Gill younger baptised yo third daye.
Jennett daughter of John Cowpar baptised ye third daye.
Christopher Birkill was buried ye vthe daye.
A yonge infant of Willme Lambe beinge a sonn not baptised was buried the xjthe daye.
Jennett wyfe of Robte Lee of Heaton buried ye xjthe daye.
Rosamond daughter of Edward Warmall baptised *xxijth daye.

* This date may be "xvijth." Several of the entries on this page of the Register are much faded.

1602.
Alice daughter of Nicolas Secker baptised yo xxviijth daye.

The monethe of November 1602.
Elizabethe daughter of Edward Ellis baptised ye vijth daye.
Ann daughter of Marmaduke Ellis buried ye xiijth daye.
Ell n (?) daughter of Martyn Lister baptised ye xxjth daye.
Francis daughter of John Ouldroide baptised yo xxxthe daye.

Eliz. regine 45. The monethe of December 1602.
Alice daughter of Willme Roebucke baptised ye vthe daye.
Ann daughter of Bryan Phillips baptised ye xijthe daye.
Christopher Yarwood buried his wyfe ye xvijthe daye.
Roberte son of Thomas Bradforthe baptised yo xixth daye.
Alice daughter of Thomas Barbar baptised ye xxvjth daye.
Ann daughter of Rychard Ouldroide baptised ye same daye.
Rosamond daughter of Edward Nayler buried ye xxxth daye.

The monethe of Januarye 1602.
Willme son of Rychard Marshall baptised the second daye.
Jane daughter of Rychard Marshall baptised ye same daye.
John sonn of Thomas Graysonn baptised ye vjthe daye.
Beatrice daughter of Rychard Graver buried ye viijth daye.
John sonn of John Saxtonn baptised the ixthe daye.
Willme son of Rychard Dishforthe baptised the xxiijth daye.

Eliz. 45. The monethe of February 1602.
Alexander Newsome and Ellen Scooles married ye vjthe daye.
Edwarde Fletcher and Jennett Barnbye married ye vjthe daye.
Willme sonn of Rycharde Marshall buried ye xth daye.
John sonn of Robert Brouke yonger baptised ye viijth daye.
Wilne sonn of Thomas Ashtone baptised ye xxthe daye.
Elizabethe daughter of Edwarde Lee baptised ye same daye.
Michaell sonn of Robert Thorpe baptised ye xxiijthe daye.
Mereye daughter of Robert Thorpe baptised ye same daye.
Thomas sonn of Thomas Wilsonn baptised ye same daye.
John Bradforthe of Ossett was buried ye xxvthe daye.
Susann daughter of Anthonye Hurst baptised ye xxvijthe daye.

1602.

Willmo sonn of Edward Midlebroughe buried ye xxviijth daye.
Willmo Musgrave and Dorithie Arnould married ye xxviijthe daye.

Marche anno Dni. 1602.

Mercie basse daughter of John Masonn of Churche Heaton parishe and Sibeel Leake of this baptised ye vtho daye.
William sonn of Averye Bull baptised ye vijthe daye.
John Awtie and Elizabethe Seeker married ye same daye.
Easter daughter of Nicholas Armitedge buried ye same daye.
Grace daughter of George Oetes buried ye same daye.
Mereye daughter of Robert Thorpe buried ye xvthe daye.
Robto sonn of Robto Shepperd alias Leadbeater baptised ye xxth daye.
Grace daughter of Henrie Barbar baptised ye same daye.
Michaell son of Robert Thorpe baptised ye xxijthe daye.
Ann daughter of Ambrosse Robinson baptised ye xxvthe daye.
Margrett wyfe of Thomas Crowle dying at Liversedge was buried here ye xxxjthe daye.

Anno primo regni regis Jacobi primo.
Aprill anno Dni. 1603.

Rychard sonn of Thomas Hynchliffe baptised ye third daye.
Alice daughter of John Boothe baptised ye vjthe daye.
Rychard sonn of Thomas Hynchliffe buried ye sixt daye.
Peter Barrett was buried ye viijthe daye.
Uxor Bradforthe of Ossett Butts buried ye xxvthe daye.
Willmo Capps of Batlaye parishe and Jane Masern alias Gillome of this parishe were married here by lycence ye xxvijthe daye.

Maye 1603.

Elizabethe daughter of John Rawsonn baptised ye first daye.
Jane daughter of Thomas Wilsonn buried ye vijthe daye.
Edwarde Cox dyinge at ye Newe parke was here buried the xiijthe daye.
Thomas Barbar and Marye Lee married ye xvthe day.
Mary daughter of Willmo Rowse baptised ye same daye.
Nicholas Armitedge of this parishe and Agnes Bronke of Birstall were (? married) there at Birstall the xxiiijthe daye.
Thomas Leadbeater alias Shepperd and Margrett Musgravo married the xxixthe daye.
Mereye basse daughter of John Masson and Sybell Leake buried the same daye.

June 1603.

John sonn of John Antye yonger baptised ye second daye.

1603.

John Sonnyar and Jane Ouldroide married ye vijthe day.
James Speight and Elizabethe Clay alias Allen married ye vjthe day.
Mr Wilkinsonn dyinge at Chidsell the xjthe day was buried at Allmanburie the xijthe daye.
Alice daughter of Thomas Ouldroide baptised ye same daye.
Nicholas Hurst and Elizabethe Williamsonn were here married the xiiijthe daye.
Rychard Hemyngeway and Ann Acrod married ye xxthe day.
Willmo Kitsonn of this parishe and Margery Lee of Churche Heaton were married at Churche Heaton ye same day.

Jacobi regis primo. Julye 1603.

Jennet daughter of John Berrye baptised ye ixthe day.
Rychard Nayler and Dorithie Grene married ye xthe day.
Xpofer sonn of Willmo Winnerslay baptised ye xthe day.
Willmo son of Robte Doy baptised ye same daye.
Alice daughter of John Mannsfield baptised ye same daye.
Edwarde sonn of Edwarde Wilcocke baptised ye xvijthe daye.
John sonn of Rychard Sonnyare baptised ye xxthe daye.
Alice wyfe of the sayd Rychard Sonyar buried ye xxiij day.
Robto Chappell and Jennet Grene married ye xxiiijth daye.
James sonn of James Speight baptised the xxvthe daye.
Easter daughter of Rychard Sonnyar buried ye xxviijthe day.
John sonn of Rycharde Sonyare buried the last daye.
Willmo sonn of Roberto Netletone baptised ye same daye.
Mereye daughter of Thomas Whelewright baptised yt daye.

August 1603. Anno Jacobi primo.

Alice daughter of John Mannsfeld buried ye third day.
Edwarde sonn of Robto Smithsonn baptised ye vijthe day.
Ann daughter of John Litlewood buried ye xviijthe day.
Martha daughter of Averie Whittakers baptised ye xxjth day.
Dorithie daughter of John Nayler baptised ye xxvijthe day.
Jennett daughter of Thomas Leadbeater alias Shepperd was baptised ye same daye.

September 1603.

Edwardo Hurst was buried yo fift daye.
Mary daughter of Marmaduke Ellis baptised ye viijthe day.
John Tyas and Alice Goodaill maried ye xiijthe daye.
Isabell daughter of Robto Pigbells baptised ye xxvthe day.

1603.

Alice daughter of Thomas Chaster baptised ye same daye.

October 1603.

Jennett daughter of Thomas Leadbeater alias Shepperd was buried the second daye.
Thomas sonn of Rychard Harrishe baptised yo ixth day.
Elizabethe daughter of Xpofer Brouke was baptised the same daye.
Elizabethe daughter of Averye Milnes was here baptised ye same daye.
A yonge sonn of Mr. Acrode viccar being not baptised was buried the xjthe *daye.
Averye son of Henrie Bull baptised ye same day.

Anno Dni. 1603.

Thomas sonn of Rychard Awdsley Jn. baptised yo xviij day.
Isoboll daughter of Robte Pighells was buried here the xvjthe daye.

The monethe of November 1603.

Willme sonn of Willme Sharphowse baptised ye second day.
Grace wyfe of Willme Sharphowse buried ye same day.
Henrye sonn of Henry Robinsonn baptised ye xvjtho day.
Edwarde sonn of Edward Fayrbarne baptised yo xxtie daye.
John Bedforthe of this parishe and Alice Savill of the parishe of Wakefielde maried there yo xxijtie daye.
Rychard sonn of Averye Acrod baptised ye xxvijthe day.

The monethe of December 1603.

John Hueden and Jennett Haldsworthe maried ye vijthe daye.
Willme Gill eldest buried the vjthe daye.
Elizabethe daughter of John Milnes baptised ye xjthe daye.
Willme sonn of Robert Smithe baptised ye xviijthe daye.
Robert Hepworthe and Dorithie Bradforthe maried ye xixthe daye.
Willme sonn of Edward Midlebronghe baptised ye xxvjthe daye.
Alice daughter of John Tyas baptised ye same daye.

The monethe of Jannarye 1603.

A yonge sonn and being not baptised of Edward Roydes was here buried ye first daye.
Henrye Fishe was buried the xiiijthe day.
Ellenn daughter of Raphe Slater baptised ye xvijth daye.
Thomas Sonnyare under ye hill was buried ye xxvjthe daye.
Willme sonn of James Broadlaye baptised ye xxixthe daye.
Averie sonn of Averie Gill baptised ye xxixthe daye.
Robert Smithe was buried the xxxthe daye.
John Milner alias Shepperd and Agnes Bull maried ye xxxjth day.

* This date is indistinct. It may be xvjthe.

February anno Dni. 1603.

Thomas Fournesse and Elizabethe Dickensonn were here maried the vthe daye.
Samuell Wilbye and Elizabethe Howsonn were maried at Wakeffeldo ye vijtho daye.
Franncis daughter of James Coossinge baptised ye same daye.
Uxor Dent of Ossett buried ye tenthe daye.
Janye daughter of Henrye Dowlinge baptised ye xijthe daye.
Alisonn wyfe of Roger Gaunte buried ye xiiijthe daye.
Jennett daughter of John Berrye buried ye same daye.
Isabell daughter daughter of Willme Speight buried ye xvjthe daye.
John sonn of John Saxtonn buried ye xixthe daye.
Willme sonn of Thomas Jagger baptised yo xxvjthe daye.
Edwarde Hamesdenn buried ye xxixthe daye.
John Goodall buried his wyfo ye same daye.

The monethe of Marche 1603.

Nicholas Scollfeild alias Pickeringe buried ye third daye.
Thomas sonn of Thomas Barbar of Osset baptised ye fourthe daye.
Rychard sonn of Thomas Ashtonn baptised ye seaventhe daye.
Jennet daughter of John Bradforthe baptised ye ixthe daye.

Anno Dni. 1604.

Thoma sonn of Rychard Hemyngeway baptised ye xjth daye.
Marye daughter of Willme Lambe baptised yo same daye.
Isabell daughter of Samuell Grenewoode baptised ye xviijth day.
John Benthye elder was buried ye xtxthe daye.
Dorithie Bull was buried the xxiijthe daye.
John Fox sonn of John Fox of the newe parke was here buried the xxxth daye.
James Forrest was buried the xxxjthe daye.

Aprill 1604.

Elizabethe daughter of John Milner alias Shepperd was here baptised the first daye.
and the sayd Elizabethe daughter of John Milner alias Shepperd was buried the third daye.
Ellin daughter of James Kent buried the fift day.
Grace daughter of Henry Barbar buried ye vijth day.
John sonn of Nicholas Armitedge baptised ye vijth day.
Alexander sonn of Alexander Newsome alias Jackesonn was baptised the ixthe daye.
Roger Dawsonn and Agnes Haldsworthe maried ye xvijth day.
Elizabethe daughter of Uxor Sonnyare late wyfe of Thomas Sonnyare baptised ye xxijthe daye.
Nicholas Armitedge was buried ye xxiijthe daye.
Rychard Sonnyare and Essabell Smithe were maried at Hertsheade by a licence ye xxvtie day, being St Mark's day.
Willme Crofte was buried ye xxixtie daye.

DEWSBURY PARISH REGISTERS. 69

May anno Dni. 1604.

Edward Awtye and Marye Joy maried ye first daye.
John Hurst and Jennett Arrundell maried yt daye.
Alexander sonn of Alexander Newsome buried ye iiijth daye.
Thomas sonn of John Gibsonn baptised ye xiijth daye.
Gorge sonn of Robert Smithe of Dewsburie buried ye xxjtie day.
Randall Netletome was buried ye xxijtie daye.
Phillippe Barbar was buried ye xxvjtie daye.

Jacobi regis secundo. June anno Dni. 1604.

Willme sonn of Willme Grene baptised ye ixth daye.
Alice basse daughter of Willme Croft and Alice Jowithe buried the tenthe daye.
John Houldsworthe and Alice Barbar maried ye xjth daye
A yong sonn of Willme Leadbeater alias Shepperd being not baptised was buried the xijth daye.
Ann daughter of Rychard Thornes baptised ye xvijth daye.
Michaell sonn of Robert Thorpe baptised ye xxiiijth daye.

Julye anno Dni. 1604.

Willme Walker and Margrett Wilsonn maried ye first day.
Willme Shepley and Elizabethe Acrode maried the third day.
Uxor Nayler was buried the xijthe daye.
Francis Staynecliffe and Susann Dickenson maried ye xvth day.
Robte sonn of Willme Wilbye baptised yt daye.
Grace daughter of Willme Gill elder baptized yt daye.

Anno Dni. 1604.

Rychard Hemyngewaye and Frauncis Archer maried ye xvijthe daye.
George basse sonn of Giles Beisbey and Dorithy Scolfelde alias Pickeringe baptised ye xxijthe daye.
Samuell Wilbye was buried ye xxvthe daye.
Alice daughter of Godfray Fox baptised ye same daye.
A yonge daughter of Thoms Hynchlyffe being not baptized was buried the xxvijthe daye.
Robert Houlte and Alice Fox married ye xxixtie daye.
Robert sonn of John Westerman baptised ye same daye.

August 1604.

Henrie Ju. Ellis and Ann Horsforthe married ye fift daye.
Willme sonn of Willme Gill yonger baptised ye same daye.
Roger Claytonn was buried ye xiiijtene daye.
Uxor Lee of Earles Heatonn was buried ye xvjtene daye.
Willme sonn of John Mansfelde baptised yt daye.
Isabell daughter of Roger Dawson baptised ye sixth daye.

1604.

Thomas sonn of Edwarde Wurmall baptised ye xxvjth daye.
Marye daughter of Jefferye Booth baptised yt daye.
Thomas Tyas was buried ye xxvijth daye.
Margery daughter to John Cowpas baptised ye xxviijtie daye.
Agnes Barbar was buried the xxixthe daye.

September anno Dni. 1604.

Isabell daughter of Roger Dawsonn buried ye third daye.
A yonge basse daughter of Lyonell Kay and Ann Birkhead being not baptised was buried ye vijth daye.
John sonn of John Sonnyarre baptised ye ixth day.
Marye daughter of John Berrye buried ye xvjth daye.
Robert son of Thomas Burghe baptised ye xxiijth daye.
Thomas sonn of Rychard Hemyngway baptised ye xxiiijth day.
James base sonn of Rychard Sonnyare and Agnes Peace was here baptised ye xxvtie daye.
A yonge daughter of James Claytonn beinge not baptised was buried the same daye.
Robert sonn of Thomas Barbar baptised ye xxxtie daye.

October anno Dni. 1604.

Michaell Bentlye* Ju. of this parishe and Elizabethe Crowder of Hallifax maried there ye second daye.

---

* At a Court of the Rectory Manor, held 23rd December, 31 Elizabeth, Marmaduke Speight, of London, Merchant and Mary his wife, by Michael Bentley senr., surrendered lands in the fields called Crackenedge and the Northfield to the use of Michael Bentley, son of John Bentley, of Ossett.
At the same Court (23rd December, 31 Elizabeth), Richard Briggs surrendered all his right and title to a cottage in Dewsbury to the use of Michael Bentley of Batley, yeoman, for the residue of a term of 21 years.
Michael Bentley is also mentioned in the Court Roll of 30th March, 33 Elizabeth, as an owner of land, and also as lending to Marmaduke Speight the sum of twelve pence on mortgage of two selions of land in the "Crockoynes."
(Crook Ing) Dewsbury.
At a Court held 8th October, 30th Elizabeth, Michael Bentley was amerceed 4d. for that he being a tenant of the Manor and owing suit had not appeared at that Court; and at the same Court John Bentley was amerced 12d. for "keepenige and goatinge his cattall upon the common when the corne was growing there," and Thomas Greenwood and Michael Bentley were ordered to "sett their accustomed steeles (stiles) betweene the Bentheysides for the foote way before All Saints day then next" under a penalty of 3s. 4d. each for default.
At a Court held 15th April, 30th Elizabeth, Michael Bentley of Batley, appears as lending to Marmaduke Speights and his wife £80 on mortgage of land in Dewsbury, and Michael Bentley also appears as buying several pieces of land and as selling another piece.
It will be seen from the list of Churchwardens already printed that Michael Bentley, senr., and Michael Bentley, jun., were churchwardens of Dewsbury several times. The former gave 20s. per annum to the poor in 1617, and the latter 21s. 8d. per annum in 1621 for the same object. These sums called "Bentley's Doles" are still received by the Vicar and Churchwardens for the use of the poor. The two Bentleys also gave stone cottages in Dewsbury to be occupied rent free by poor people.

1604.

Parcivall Terry and Ann Sharphowse married yt daye.
A young sonn of John Hurst Junior being not baptised was buried yt day.
Rychard sonn of Robert Pighells baptised ye vijth daye.
Lawrence Bull yonger and Alice Cantuar† maried ye ixth day.
Rychard sonn of Avery Acrod buried yt daye.
A yonge daughter of John Bedfortho being not baptised was buried the xiiijth daye.
Agnes daughter of Lawrence Barome baptised ye xxjtie day.
Robert sonn of Willmo Wilbye buried ye xxvtie daye.

November 1604.

Margrett daughter of Lawrence Bull Junior baptised the fourthe daye.
Ann daughter of Rychard Thornes buried ye xvithe daye.
Michaell Oglethorpe of Thorner and Elizabethe Speight of this parishe maried ye xixtie daye.
Rychard Kedinge was buried yt daye 1604.
Thomas Secker and Margerie Birkhill were maried the xxtie daye.
Willme Richardson and Annie Robinsonn maried ye xxvtie daye.
Margerie wyfe of Edwarde Secker buried yt daye.
Rycharde Fernsyde and Anne Speight married ye xxvjtie day.
Willme sonn of John Awtie yonger baptised ye xxvjtie day.
Thomas sonn of Edwarde Awtie baptised ye xxvijtie day.
Thomas sonn of Edwarde Awtie buried ye xxvijtie daye.

December 1604.

Thomas sonn of Rycharde Naylor baptised ye second day.
Rychard sonn of Willme Shepley baptised the vthe daye 1604.
Henrie sonn of Henrie Ellis yonger baptised ye xjth day.
A yonge sonn of John Parkers beinge not baptised was buried the xijth day.
Thomas sonn of Rychard Naylor buried ye xiiijtene day.
Alice daughter of Godfray Fox buried ye xvjth daye.
A yonge daughter of Willme Sharphowse being not baptised was buried ye xxvijtie daye.
Willme Claytonn was buried ye xxxtie daye.

January anno Dni. 1604.

Elizabethe daughter of Thomas Whelewright baptised ye thirtenthe daye anno Dni. 1604.
Ann daughter of Rychard Wright baptised yt daye.
John sonn of Willme Speight baptised ye xvjthe daye.

† This name may be Cantuar or Cantuar.

1604.

Marie daughter of Robert Bronke the yonger baptised the twentie daye.
Alice daughter of Thomas Secker baptised the xxvtie daye.

February 1604.

Alice daughter of John Dawson was baptised the second daye.
Rosamonde daughter of Mr. Acrode viccar was baptised the thirde daye, being born ye first daye.
Willme sonn of Willme Haldonn baptised yt daye.
John sonn of Willme Barnard baptised yt daye.
Sara daughter of Robte Gill baptised ye vijth day.
John Pickerd and Ann Waterhowse maried ye xth day.
Gorge Haye and Catheryn Speight maried yt day.
Clemont Hay and Sibell Awdsley maried yt daye.
Phœbe daughter of John Ouldroid baptised yt day.
Frauncis Gibsonn and Agnes Scolfeld married ye xjth day.
Dorithie daughter of Rychard Marshall was baptised the xvijth day.
Rosamond daughter of Edward Roydes was baptised the xvijth daye.
Agnes daughter of Bryan Phillippe baptised ye xxiiijtie daye.

The monethe of Marche.

Anno Dni. 1605. Jacobi tertio.

John basse son of John Rylay of Normanton and Susan Forrest alias Bull was here baptised the sixt daye.
Mercye daughter of Thomas Leadbeater alias Shepperd yonger was baptised the tenthe daye.
Margrett wyfe of Thomas Leadbeater alias Shepperd yonger was buried the xvjth daye.
John Joye was buried the xxixtie daye.
Willme Tayler buried his wyfe ye xxxtie daye.
Willme son of Averie Bull buried yt day.

Aprill anno Dni. 1605.

Edward son of Humphry Dixson baptised ye first day.
Easter daughter of Willme Casson baptised yt day.
Edwarde Hansonn of Rastricke within Ealande parishe was buried here the sixt daye.
Agnes daughter of Francis Stayneliffe was here baptised ye xxviijth daye.
John sonn of John Milner alias Shepperd was baptised that daye.
John Goodall and Alice Ingle maried ye last day.

May anno Dni. 1605.

John Beatsonn buried his wyfe ye second daye.
Ann daughter of Rycharde Owldroid buried yt day.
Nicholas Musgrayve was buried the vthe daye.
Peter sonn of Willme Rychardson baptised yt daye.
Nicholas Flather and Agnes Whitlay maried ye vijth day.
Thomas Glover and Jonye Nayler maried ye xiijth daye.
Bettheris Secker buried ye xvthe day.

1605.

John sonn of Gorge Harrisonn baptised ye sixth day.
Marye daughter of Francis Gibsonn baptised yt day.
Averye sonn of Willme Walker baptised ye xxvjth day.

June anno Domini 1605.

Thomas sonn of Thomas Fox baptised ye second daye.
Issabell daughter of Rychard Acrode of Earles Heatonn was baptised ye ixthe daye.
Edwarde sonn of Edwarde Ellis baptised ye xijth daye.
A yong sonn of John Goodall being not baptised was here buried the xiiijth daye.
Dorithie daughter of Thomas Peace baptised ye xvjth day.
Susann daughter of Gorge Hage baptised ye same day.
Rychard Roydes and Alice Hutchinsonn maried yt day.
Elizabethe daughter of Thomas Wheelewright buried ye xxvth daye.
Robert Beckwithe of Wakefielde and Elizabethe Threapland of this Parishe maried ye last day.
John Rychardsonn of Thornhill and Grace Gill of this parishe maried yt daye.
Robte sonn of Rychard Hemyngwaye, Ju. baptised yt daye.
Grace daughter of Willme Lambe buried yt daye.

Julie 1605.

Elizabethe daughter of John Cowpas buried ye first day.
Ann daughter of John Tyas baptised ye vijth day.
Dorothie daughter of Thomas Peace buried ye viijth daye.
Thomas sonn of Percivall Terrye baptised ye xiiijth day.
Thomas Leadbeater yonger and Jane Claypam maried ye xxjtie day.
Issabell daughter of John Milnes baptised ye xxviijth day.

August 1605.   Jacobi regis tertio.

Ambrosse sonn of Ambrosse Robinson baptised ye second day.
Jennett daughter of Thomas Grayson baptised ye xjth daye.
Alice daughter of Edwarde Lee baptised ye same daye.
Mercye daughter of John Berye baptised ye xvth daye.
Rychard Forrest was buried the xvjthe daye.
Edward sonn of Rychard Thornes baptised ye xxvtie daye.
Sara daughter of Robte Gill buried ye xxviijth day.

September 1605.

John lasse sonn of Mathew Scorer and Elizabeth Barbar being borne the last of August was baptised the vijthe of this monethe of September.

1605.

A yong infant a sonn of John Hurst yonger being not baptised was buried ye viijth daye.
Jennet wyfe of John Hurst yonger was buried the xijthe daye.

Jacobi tertio.   October 1605.

Edward Seeker of oure parishe and Jane Bradley of Woodkirke were maried there the first daye.
Willme Musgrave and Alice Pickering were maried ye vjthe daye.
Robte sonn of Martynn Bentlay baptised ye sixt day.
Elizabethe daughter of Michaell Bentlay yonger baptised ye same daye.
Alice daughter of Averie Gill was baptised the same daye.
Robert Lee of Earles Heaton buried the viijth day.
Rychard sonn of Rychard Dishforthe baptised ye tenth day.
John sonn of John Ouldroid Junior baptised ye viijthe day.
Alice daughter of Robte Hoult baptised yt daye.
Roger sonn of Willme Doy baptised ye xxtie daye.
A yong son of Alexander Newsame alias Jacksonn being not baptised buried the xxvjthe daye.
Francis son of Robte Netleton baptised ye xxvijth daye.
Gorge son of John Nayler baptised yt day.
Margrett daughter of Averie Acrod was baptised that same daye.
Thomas Hage of Horburie and Dorithie Goodall of this parishe maried ye xxixtie daye.

November 1605.

John Ellis and Elizabethe Womersley maried yo third day.
John sonn of Thomas Wilsonn baptised ye xvijthe daye.
Willme Speight and Marye Saltinstall maried ye sixth daye.
Ann daughter of Marmaduke Ellis baptised ye xxiiijtie daye.

December 1605.

Marye daughter of Godfray Fox baptised ye first day.
Gorge Ouldfeild of Hallifax parishe and Mercye Bentlay of this parishe maried the thirde daye.
Robert sonn of John Bedforthe baptised ye xvth day.
Henrie son of Henrie Barbar baptised yt daye.
Marie daughter of Thomas Hyneliffe baptised ye xvijth day.
Robert Carrier was buried the xxjtie day.
Alice daughter of Averie Gill buried ye same daye.
Agnes wyfe of John Clayton of ye more side buried ye xxij day.
Thomas sonn of Robert Leadbeater alias Shepperde was baptised the same day.
Elizabethe daughter of Rychard Hemyngewaye of Earles Heaton was baptised the xxixtie daye.

Januarie 1605.

Samuell sonn of Robte Dey baptised ye first day.
A yonge daughter of James Coossinge being not baptised was buried the third daye.
John sonn of Averie Milnes baptised ye xijth day.
Willme sonn of Mr. Glover minister at Ossett was baptised the xvtho day.
A yonge childe of Edwarde Awtyes being not baptised was buried the xix'he day, ano Dni. 1605.
Josephe sonn of Willme Lambe baptised ye xxtie daye.
John Walker of this parishe and Ann Shillitoe of Kirkthorpe were maried the xxjtie daye.
Nicholas sonn of Thomas Leadbeater alias Shepperd the yonger was baptised the xxtho day.
James sonn of James Claytonn baptised ye xxvjthe day.
Ellen daughter of Willhae Gill elder baptised yt day.
Nicholas son of Thomas Leadbeater alias Shepperd the yonger was buried yt daye.
Michaell sonn of John Litlewooldo baptised yt day.
Rychard Awdsley of Gawthorpe buried ye xxviijth day.

Februarie 1605.

Agnes daughter of Thomas Bradforthe baptised ye second day.
Edwarde Bull of Ossett buried his wyfe yo fourthe day.
Elizabethe daughter of Robert Pickerd baptised yo same daye.
John sonn of Rychard Roydes baptised ye ixth day.
Willme son of John Ellis baptised yt day.
Francis Norfolke and Agnes Pickerd maried ye xvjth day.
Rychard sonn of James Speight baptised yt day.
John Walker of Ossett buried the xxijtie day.
Willme sonn of Willme Grene buried yt day.

Jacobi regis tertio.   Marche 1605.

Alice daughter of Edward Wurmall baptised ye second day.
Rychard Wilkinsonn of this parishe and Sibell Bradlay of Woodchurche maried there yo second day.
Agnes daughter of Rychard Nayler baptised ye xvjth day.
Willme sonn of Thomas Glover buried yo xxjtye day.
Robte sonn of Raphe Slator baptised ye xxijth day.

1605.

Robte sonn of John Rawsonn baptised ye xxvtie.
Willme Broadlay was buried ye xvjth daye.
Thomas Leadbeater alias Shepperd the elder was buried the xxvijth daye.

Aprill 1606.

Alice daughter of Robert Beckwithe ye xvijth day was here baptised.
John sonn of Francis Stayneliffe baptised ye xxjtie daye.
Henrie Barbar was buried the xxijtie day.
Thomas son of Thomas Netleton baptised ye xxvijth day.

May 1606.

Robert sonn of Willme Grene baptised ye fourthe day.
Edmond Oxelay of Claytonn and Elizabethe More of the same maried here the xjth daye by a lycence.
Christopher sonn of Christopher Brooke the yonger was baptised the xviijth day.
Alice daughter of Willme Musgrave baptised yt day.
Rychard sonn of John Boothe baptised ye xxvth day.

June 1606.

Francis Fearnlay and Agnes Armitedge maried ye third day.
Thomas Sykes and Elizabethe Kenling maried ye ixth day.
Thomas Nayler and Jenett Bradforth maried ye xvijth day.
Henrye sonn of Henrie Guyeslay buried ye same day.
Ann wyfe of Thomas Bent within ye countye of Leister dying at the howse of Willme Saxton within this parisho was buried ye xvjth daye.
Edward Bull and Ann Walker maried ye xvijth day.
Willme Shepperde buried his wyfe that daye.
Willme sonn of Willme Gouldsborowe baptised ye xxijth day.
Ann daughter of John Pickerd baptised yt day.
Willme sonn of Edward Barbar baptised ye xxiijtie day.
Edwarde Dey and Elizabethe Wilbye maried ye xxixtie day.
Elizabethe daughter of Thomas Barbar baptised yt day.

Jacobi regis quarto.   Julyo anno Dni. 1606.

Cotton Broadlay and Susann Ingle maried ye first day.
Edward sonn of Thomas Chaster baptised ye xxvtie day.
Sibell daughter of Nicholas Seeker baptised ye xxvijth day.
Robert Ouldroid was buried the xxxtie day.
A yonge childe basse sonn of Esabell Wilbye and John Whitlaye borne at Heckmondwyke not baptised was buried yt day.

August 1606.

Willme Hurst of Ardslaye and Elizabethe Forrest of this parishe were maried ye third day.
Thomas sonn of Thomas Jagger baptised ye same day.
Willme sonn basse borne of Ellen Andertone and Willme Awtye was baptised ye same daye.
Issabell daughter of Thomas Peace baptised ye vth daye.
Edward Bachowse and Elizabethe Wilbye maried yt daye.
Willme Arrandell was buried ye vjthe day.
Henrie sonn of Henrie Bull baptised yt daye.
John Saxtone buried his wyfe the xxjtie daye.
Luke sonn of Francis Norfolke baptised ye last day.

DEWSBURY PARISH REGISTERS. 73

September 1606.
Robert sonn of John Rawsonn buried the thirde day.
Elizabethe daughter of Willmo Sheplay baptised ye vijth day.
Lawrance Bull elder was buried ye xijth daye.
Christopher Mitchell buried his wyfe the xiijth day.
Edwarde Phillippe and Issabell Nayler maried ye xiiijth day.
Grace daughter of Willmo Speight yonger baptised yt day.
Mathew sonn of Robte Smithe baptised ye xxjtio dayo.
Willmo Leadbeater alias Shepperd of this parish and Ann Brent of Church Heaton maried here yo xxviijtie daye.

October 1606.
Nicholas Walker and Botheris Allan maried yo vth day.
Elizabethe daughter of John Goodall baptised ye vijth day.
Alice wyfe of Edward Midlebroughe buried ye xth day.
Alice daughter of Edwarde Midlebroughe baptised yt day.
Thomas Awdslay and Agnes Peace maried yo xiiijth day.
Willmo Taylior and Agnes Fox maried yo xixth dayo.
Luke sonn of Rychard Grayve alias Wright baptised yt day.

November 1606.
Elizabethe daughter of Rychard Harrishe baptised ye second day.
John Lee and Marye Scolfelde maried yt dayo.
Jennett daughter of Robert Brouke, Ju. baptised ye xvjthe daye.
Gorge Allan buried his wyfe the xixth day.
John sonn of Averie Gill baptised ye same day.
Margrett daughter of Henrie Bowling baptised ye xxiijth day.
Margrett daughter of Willmo Walker baptised yt day.
Agnes daughter of Willmo Rowse baptised yo last dayo.

Jacobi regis quarto. December anno Dni. 1606.
Edwarde Roebucke and Agnes Brouke maried ye second day.
John Hurst and Alice Hutchinsonn maried ye vijth day.
Mathewe son of Robte Man baptised yt day.
Elizabethe daughter of Robte Gill baptised yt day.
Marye daughter of Robte Lee baptised yt day.
Willmo sonn of John Milner alias Shepperd was baptised yo xiiijthe daye.
Willmo sonn of Roger Dawsonn baptised ye xvjth day.
Willmo sonn of Willmo Wilbye baptised ye xxjt dayo.
Alice Colbecke of Leedes dying at Rychard Marshalls of Chidsell, within this parishe was buried yo xxvjth day.
Franncis daughter of Willmo Gill, Ju baptised yo xxvijth day.

Januarie 1606.
Michaell son of Henrie Ellis, Ju. baptised ye first day, and the same childe was buried ye fourthe day.
Margrett daughter of Edward Ellis baptised yo vjth daye.
Ann wyfe of Willmo Bronke buried ye xviijth day.
Rychard sonn of John Tyas baptised yt day.

Jacobi regis quinto (sic) Angliae.
Februarye anno Dni. 1606.
Henrie Naylor of Ossett buried ye second day.
James sonn of John Dawsonn baptised yt day.
Thomas sonn of Averie Whittakers baptised ye vjth day.
Josua Wilson of Allmanburie parishe and Lucy Ouldroide of this parishe maried ye tenthe daye.
Robert Saxtonn of this parishe and Ann Oxelay of Hoyland maried yre the same daye.
Rychard son of Martyn Bentlay baptised yt day.
Thomas son of Edward Awtye baptised yo xvth day.
Michaell son of Michaell Bentlay, Ju. baptised yo xxij day.

Jacobi regis quarto. Marche 1607.
Willmo son of Willmo Royds baptised the first day.
Grace daughter of Alexander Newsonne alias Jackesonn was baptised yt day.
Rychard son of John Gibsonn baptised the xjtho daye.
Willmo son of Edwarde Barnerd alias Roebucke baptised the xvthe daye.
Jenett daughter of Samuell Mitchell alias Grenewoode baptised the xxijth daye.
Edwarde son of Nicholas Walker baptised yt day.
Robte son of Robert Thorpe baptised yt day.
Willmo sonn of Jefferay Boothe baptised ye xxvth day.
Agnes daughter of John Lee of Gawthorpe was baptised the xxixth day.

Jacobi regis quinto. Aprill 1607.
Rychard son of Parcivall Terrye baptised yo second day.
Thomas Whelewright buried ye third day.
Rychard Speight buried ye fourthe day.
Rosamond daughter of Rychard Thornes baptised yo vth day.
Thomas son of John Awtye yongr baptised ye vjth daye.
Edmonde Hycke and Dorithie Tyas maried the fourthente daye.
Ann daughter of Robte Dey baptised yo xxvth day.
Mereye daughter of Francis Fernlay baptised yo xxvjth day.
Elizabethe daughter of John Mannsfeld baptised yt day.
James Wade was buried yo same daye.
Averie son of Averie Bull baptised yo same day.

May 1607.
Thomas sonn of Thomas Nayler baptised ye third day.

1607.

Rychard sonn of Francis Gibson baptised ye same day.
Thomas sonn of Thomas Whelewright baptised ye xth day.
Rychard basse sonn of John Waltonn and Ann Kyrkbye bothe within Bradforthe parishe buried here the xijth day.
Sibell daughter of Rychard Roydes baptised the xiiijth day.
John sonn of Thomas Barghe baptised ye xvijth daye.
Elizabethe wyfe of Leonarde Patricke of Leedes dying at John Dickensons of Ossett was buried ye xviijth daye.
Willme Dawsonn of Batlay and Elizabethe Gill of this parishe maried here the xixth day.
Thomas sonn of Robte Pickerde baptised ye xxth daye.
Thomas Robinson and Elizabethe Grayve maried ye xxvth daye.
Rychard Whitlaye and Alice Rychardson maried ye xxvjthe day.

June 1607. Jacobi regis quinto.

Agnes daughter of Willme Leadbeater alias Shepperde baptised ye viijth day.
Rychard sonn of John Lee buried ye ixth daye.
Ann daughter of Edwarde Phillippe baptised ye xvjth day.
Jennet daughter of Sammuell Mitchell buried ye xvijth day.
Grace daughter of Cotton Broadlay baptised ye xxixth day.

Julye anno Dni. 1607. Jacobi regis quinto.

Edwarde Lee of Earles Heatonn buried his wyfe the xijth day.
Rycharde sonn of Rychard Wilkinsonn baptised yt day.
Thomas Awbraye and Ann Warde maried ye xixth day.
Uxor Awdslaye of Gawthorpe elder buried yo xxvjth daye.
Jennett daughter of Willme Taylier baptised ye same day.
Rycharde sonn of Francis Gibsonn buried ye xxvijth day.
Thomas son of Robte Pickerde buried ye xxviijth daye.

August 1607.

James sonn of John Hurst under ye hill, Ju. baptised ye xvjth day.
James son of John Sonnyare baptised ye xxiijth day.
Uxor Mannsfelde of Ossett buried ye xxixth daye.
John Dickensonn of Ossett buried the xxxth daye.
Elizabethe Wilbye buried the xxxjth daye.

September 1607.

Willme Pollerd and Marye Ouldroide maried yo viijth daye.
Elizabethe daughter of Willme Rychardson baptised ye xiijth day.

1607.

Mereye daughter of Francis Fearnlay buried yo xxijth day.
Alice wyfe of John Hutchinsonn buried the xxiiijtie day.
Elizabethe daughter of Bryan Phillippe baptised ye xxvijth day.
Nicholas White and Elizabethe Walker maried yt day.
A yonge daughter of Thomas Fox not baptised was buried here ye xviijth daye.

November (sic) 1607.

Agnes wyfe of Thomas Fox mother of this child was buried here the xxjtie daye.
Jenet daughter of Robert Thorpe buried ye xxvth day.
Thomas sonn of Rycharde Marshall baptised yt daye.

November 1607.

Issabell wyfe of John Dickenson buried ye third day.
James sonn of Robte Netleton baptised ye vth daye.
Mary daughter of John Ellis baptised ye viijth day.
Jane daughter of John Nayler baptised ye same day.
Dorithie daughter of Averie Acrode baptised yo xijth day.
Ann daughter of James Coosinge baytised yt day.
Marye daughter of Thomas Graysonn baptised ye xxijth day.
Alice daughter of Ambrosse Robinson baptised ye xxiiijtie day.
John Dickeson and Ann Ellis maried yt day.

December 1607. Jacobi regis quinto.

Elizabethe basse daughter of Gorge Brouke of Mirffelde and Alice Arrandell of this parishe baptised ye first day.
A yongo sonn of John Rawson being not baptised was buried the same day.
Nicholas Wood buried his wyfe the vijth day.
Gorge Brouke of Mirffelde and Alice Arrandell of this parishe maried ye viijth day.
A yonge sonn of Edwarde Backhowse not baptised was buried here the tenthe daye, Thursdaye.
Ellen daughter of Nicholas White baptised ye xiijth day.
Rychard Wibsye of Harthead Chappellry and Elizabethe Archer of this parishe were maried here the xvthe daye.
Alice daughter of Henrie Robinson baptised ye xxtie day.

Januarye 1607.

Elizabethe basse daughter of Gorge Brouke alias Sykes and Alice Arrandell buried ye third day.
Jenet Acrode wydowe buried ye tenthe day.
Jennett wyfe of Robte Bayldon buried ye xiijth day.
Thomas son of Thomas Secker baptised ye xvijth day.
Agnes Allan wyfe of Michaell Allan dying at Liversedge was buried here the xixth day.

1607.

Agnes wyfe of Thomas Wurmall of Highe Sothill was buried the xxjth daye.
Edward Lee and Elizabethe Rodlay maried ye xxiiijth day.
Edward Secker and Dorithie More maried that dayo.
Robte Boothe and Grace Nayler maried ye xxvjthe.
Mary daughter of Robte Saxton baptised ye xxiiijth day.
John son of Thomas Wilsonn buried ye same day.
Thomas son of Thomas Secker buried ye xxvth day.

Februarye 1607.

Thomas France and Agnes Greene maried ye second day.
Nicholas son of John Westerman baptised ye vijth day.
John son of Gorge Hage baptised the same day.
Rycharde son of Rychard Hemyngeway baptised ye xvijth day.
Agnes wyfe of Edwarde Lee of Gawthorpe buried ye xviijth day.
Josephe son of John Ouldroide Ju. baptised ye xxjtie day.
Thomas Coosen buried the xxiiijtie day.
John son of Thomas Robinsonn Jn. baptised ye xxviijth day.
Betheris daughter of Edward Wurmall baptised yt day.

Marche 1607.

John son of Henrie Ellis Ju. baptised ye sixt day.
Averie son of Averie Bull buried ye seaventhe day.
A yonge son of Robte Beckwithe not baptised buried ye xth day.
John son of Thomas Awdslay baptised ye xiijth day.
Uxor Wilcocke buried ye xviijth day.
Edwarde Lee of Gawthorpe buried ye xxtie day.

Aprill 1608.

Alice daughter of Thomas Hyncliffe baptised ye iijth day.
John son of John Cowpas baptised yt day.
Willme sonn of John Lee baptised ye xxiiijtie day.
Grace daughter of Robte Pighells baptised yt day.
Marke sonn of Mr. Acrode vicar baptised ye xxvth day beinge Monday and Saint Markes day.
Mercye daughter of Rychard Hemyngeway was baptised the same day.
Roger Mannsfelde was buried the xxxtie dayo ye last daye.

Jacobi regis sexto. May anno Dni. 1608.

Thomas Graysonn buried the first day May daye.
John sonn of Marmaduke Ellis baptised ye xvth day.
Ann daughter of Willme Lambe baptised ye same day.
Margrett daughter of John Dixsonn baptised yt day.
Susann daughter of John Owldroid baptised yo xvijth day.

1608.

Sara daughter of Averye Milnes baptised ye same day.
Alice daughter of Rychard Whitlay baptised yt daye.
John Medlay and Alice Bradforthe married ye xxiiijth day.
Nicholas Mitchell of this parishe and Elizabethe Allan of Burstall maried at Burstall yo same day.
Robert Brouke of Ossett the elder buried yo xxviijth day.
Jane daughter of Thomas Wilsonn baptised ye xxixth day.
John Wade and Jenett Whitlay maried ye last daye.

Jacobi regis anno sexto. June anno Dni. 1608.

Samuell soun of Samuell Grenewood baptised ye first day.
Rycharde sonn of Rycharde Thornes buried ye thirde day.
Margrett daughter of Xpofer Honlay of St. Katherins in Yorke baptised the vthe daye.
Tymothie Hall of Swillinghtone parishe and Margrett Lockwoode of oure parishe of Dewsburie maried ye vijth day.
Elizabethe daughter Rychard Thorpe of the parish of Baulne or Bawne baptised the viijth day borne at Wilbye wyfe her howse.
A yonge daughter of John Goodall beinge not baptised was buried here the tenthe day.
Robert sonn of Robte Bradforthe yongest baptised ye xijth day.
John sonn of Rychard Dishforthe baptised yt day.
Samuell son of Samuell Grenewood buried the xxth daye.
Michaell Wheatlay and Margrett Smithe were maried the xxjth day being Tuesdaye before Midsmer day.
Rycharde Slacke was buried the xxiijtie day.
A yong son of Robert Gill being not baptised was here the same day buried.
John Bingley of the parishe of Thornhill and Agnes Awdslay of this parishe maried by lycence the xxvjth day being Sondaye betwixt eight and nyne of ye clocke in ye morninge that day.
Phillippe sonn of Willme Roydes baptised the same day.
Alice daughter of Thomas Graysonn buried ye xxxtie day.

Jacobi regis sexto. Julye 1608.

John sonn of Willme Grene baptised the thirde day.
Rychard Whitlay and Elizabethe Newsom alias Jacksonn was married the vthe daye.
Marye daughter of Robert Pickerd baptised ye vjthe day.
Robert Phillippe and Ann Hyncliffe maried ye xth day.
Dorithie daughter of Willme Taylier baptised ye xvijth day.
John Rawsonn an oulde man buried the xviijthe daye.
Alice daughter of Edwarde Lee of Heaton buried yo same day.

1608.

Marye daughter of James Speight baptised ye xxjtie daye.
Robert Scorer and Ann Brouke maried ye xxiijtie day.
John sonn of Willme Greene buried ye xxvtie daye.
Willme son of Willme Lee of Batlay Carre was baptised here the same day at evenyng prayer.
Uxor Rodlay an oulde woman buried ye xxvijt day.
Susann daughter of Gorge Hage buried ye xxixth daye.
Robert Hage and Jane Illingworthe maried yo last day.

August 1608.

Thomas Oxelay and Grace Dishfoithe maried ye seaventhe day.
John Scorer of Hanginge Heaton buried ye xjth day.
Francis daughter of Willme Musgrave baptised ye xiiijth day.
Robert sonn of Edwarde Bull baptised ye xxjth day.
Edwarde Hurst and Elizabeth Acrode maried ye xxiijth day.
John sonn of Michaell Bentlay yonger baptised ye xxviijth day.
Bertle sonn of Gorge Bocmar baptised yt day.
Robert Speight of Chickenlay was buried ye last day.

September 1608.

Mychaell Allan dyinge at Lyversedge was here at Dewsburie buried the viijth daye Ladye day.*
John Fletcher of Hallyfax and Susann Longelay of this parishe maried here the xjth day.
Rychard sonn of Willme Rowse baptised ye same day.
Robert sonn of Robte Lee of Chidsell baptised ye xviijth day.
Issabell daughter of Edwarde Ellis baptised ye xxjth day.
Thomas sonn of John Wade baptised ye xxvth day.

October 1608.

John Tomsonn and Elizabethe Hutchinson maried here the second daye.
Willme sonn of Robte Brouke baptised the same day.
Jervice son of Humphray Dixsonn baptised ye ixth day.
Jervice son of Humphray Dixson buried ye xixth day.
Edmonde Sonnyare and Alice Cartar were maried here the xxiijth day Sonday after St. Luke his daye.

Jacobi regis sexto. November 1608.

John sonn of Edwarde Phillippe baptised ye first daye.
Nicholas Scolfelde and Jonye Cooke maried ye same day.

---

* The 8th September, being the Feast of the Nativity of the Virgin, was called Latter Lady Day; and the 15th August, being tue Feast of the Assumption, was called First Lady Day.

1608.

Uxor Jacobi Lee of Sawoodgrene buried ye vtho day.
Jefferay Boothe buried his wyfe that daye.
Thomas son of John Pickerde baptised ye vjtho day.
Dorothie daughter of Willme Walker baptised yt day.
John Claghtonn of Giesley parishe and Elizabethe Whitakers of this pari-he maried ye viijtho day.
John Croft of Burstall parishe and Katheryne Bradforth of this parishe maried that day.
John Owldroyd of the More syde the elder was buried here the eleventhe daye.
Thomas Barbar of Ossett was buried the xijthe day.
John sonn of Edwarde Lee baptised ye xiijth day.
Elizabethe daughter of John Shepperd baptised yt day.
Elizabethe daughter of Robte Shepperd baptised yt day.
Dorithie daughter of Willme Sheplay baptised yo xxthe day.
A yonge sonn of Dorithie Pickering and Giles Heisbye basse gutten not baptised buried ye same daye.
Robte Man buried his wyfe the xxvjth daye.
Willme sonn of Edwarde Secker baptised yo xxvijth day.
Xpofer sonn of Thomas Jagger baptised that daye.
Thomas Wornnall and Susan Speight maried ye xxxtie day being St. Andrew his day and Wednsdaye in ye weeke.

December 1608.

Gofferaye Boothe dyinge at Wakefeld was there buried at Wakenfelde the thirde day.
Robert sonn of Robte Phillippe baptised ye fourtho day.
Ann daughter of Edward Wurmall baptised yt day.
Robert sonn of Francis Gibsonn baptised ye xjth day.
Ann daughter of John Milnes baptised yt day.
Elizabethe daughter of Rychard Thornes baptised yt day.
Thomas son of Thomas Rodlay younger baptised ye xviijth day.
Nicholas Woodheade of Hallifax parishe and Dorithie Whelewright of this parishe maried ye xxtie daye.
Elizabethe daughter of Francis Whitlay was baptised the xxjtye daye.
Agnes daughter of Averie Gill baptised ye xxvtho daye.

Januarye 1608.

Willme son of Edmonde Sonnyar baptised ye first daye.
Josephe Lister a piper was buried the xjtho day.
Elizabethe daughter of Lawrance Bull baptised the xvthe day anno regis jacobi sexto.
Willme sonn of Willme Pollerd baptised ye viijtho daye.
Anne daughter of Willme Dey baptised at Batlaye ye xxixth daye of this monethe at eveninge prayer there.

DEWSBURY PARISH REGISTERS. 77

1608.
Edwarde Mildborowe and Alice Brouke maried the xxxjth daye the last day.

Februarye 1608.
Issabell daughter of Robte Milnes buried ye vthe day.
Sara daughter of Thomas Peace baptised ye vth day.
John sonn of Nicholas Mitchell baptised ye xijth daye.
Rychard sonn of Thomas Leadbeater alias Shepperde was baptised the xxiiijth daye.
Thomas Boothe buried his wyfe the xxvthe daye.

Jacobi regis sexto. Marche 1608.
Susann daughter of John Ouldroide of Hanginge Heatonn buried ye third daye.
Ann daughter of Thomas Allan baptised ye vthe day.
Robert sonn of Willme Leadbeater alias Shepperd was baptised the same day at evening prayer.
Mereye daughter of Robert Thorpe was baptised the xijth daye being Sondaye at evening prayer.
Elizabethe daughter of Willme Sheplaye was buried the xiiijthe daye.
Mereye daughter of Robert Smithe baptised the xixth daye.
John Rawsonn was buried the xxtie daye.
Thomas Slacke buried his wyfe the xxviijth daye.

April 1609.
Rychard Bradforthe buried his wife the vijth daye.
Michaell son of John Litlewood buried the same day.
John sonn of Thomas Bradforthe baptised ye ixth day.
Franncis daughter of Thomas Secker baptised ye xvijth day.
A yonge sonn of Averie Bull buried ye same day.
Ann daughter of Robte Beckwithe baptised ye xviijth day.
Marye wyfe of Rychard Brigge buried the xxjth daye.
John sonn of John Bedforthe baptised the xxiijth daye being Low Sondaye.
Uxor Willme Smithe of Ossett was buried the xxixth daye Satterday.
Willme Fell and Margrett Hall maried the xxxtie day.
Rycharde son of Alexander Jackson alias Newsome was baptised the xxxtie daye.

Jacobi regis septimo.   May anno Dni. 1609.
Martha daughter of Henrye Bull baptised ye vthe day.
John Whittlay and Agnes Roydes maried ye xiiijth day.
Ann daughter of Gorge Nayler baptised ye same daye.
Elizabethe daughter of Thomas Barbars wyfe of Ossett was buried the xxthe daye Satterday.
Nicholas Wood alias Smithe buried ye xxith day.

June 1609.
Phillippe sonn of Mathew Cooke baptised ye thirde day being Whitson even in ye after noone.
Thomas sonn of Gorge Brooke alias Sykes baptised ye fourthe daye Whitsonday
Agnes daughter of Robert Hage yonger was baptised that day.
Elizabethe daughter of Rychard Grayve alias Wright baptised that day.
Margrett daughter of Willme Fells was baptised the vjthe daye Tuesday in Whitsonweeke.
Rychard sonn of Rychard Whitlaye yonger baptised the same day at eveninge prayer Tuesdaye.
Elizabethe daughter of Samuell Grenewode baptised ye xijthe daye.
Robert Robinsonn alias Mawe of this parishe and Issabell Bankes of Leedes parishe were maried here the xiijth daye beinge Tuesday after Trinitye Sondaye.
Edwarde Wilcocke buried the xijth daye beinge Monday after Trinitye Sondaye.
John Bentlay sonn of Michaell Bentlay yonger was buried the xiiijthe daye.
Agnes daughter of Gorge Brooke his wyfe now wyfe of Francis Fearnlaye buried ye xxiijth daye.
A yonge daughter of Humphrye Dixsonn being not baptised was buried the xxiijth day mid-anner daye otherwise caled Saynete John Day 1609.

Jacobi regis septimo.   Julie 1609.
Issabell daughter of Nicholas White baptised ye second day.
John Beamonde of Ossett was buried ye sixt daye.
Rychard Bradforthe of Ossett buried ye xjthe day.
Rychard Helvishe of Horberye and Margerye Rychemond of this parishe maried ye xjth daye.
Gilbert Hawkeyerde of Myrffeilde and Margerie Hurst of this parish maried ye xvjth daye.
Thomas sonn of Willme Wilby baptised ye same daye.
John Speight of Ossett buried his wyfe ye xvijth day.
Robert son of Parcivall Terry baptised ye xxxtie day.
Willme son of John Dawson baptised ye same day.

Jacobi regis Anglie septimo et Scotie 42.
August 1609.
Thomas son of Thomas Rodlay Ju. buried ye ixth daye.
Ann daughter of Robert Saxton buried ye xijth daye.
Marmaduke son of John Fletcher baptised ye xiijth day.
Thomas son of John Mannsfelde baptised ye xxvjth day.
Elizabeth daughter of Thomas Barbar baptised yt day.

September 1609.
Uxor Jacobi Wade was buried ye seconde day.
Nicholas son of John Tomsonn baptised ye tenthe day.
Jennet daughter of Edmond Fox baptised yt day.
Willme son of John Sonnyate baptised ye xvijth day.

1609.

Elizabethe daughter of Thomas Wurmall baptised the same day.
Elizabethe daughter of Willme Speight Ju. baptised the xxiijtie day.
Willme sonn of Robte Bronke buried ye xxvjth day.
Elizabethe daughter of Willme Speight Junior buried the xxvijth daye.

October 1609.

Margret wyfe of Phillippo Slade buried ye vthe day.
Thomas Boothe and Jonye Fox maried ye viijth day.
Thomas Walker of Herberye and Alice Boothe of this parishe maried ye xvthe day.
John Bentlaye and Jenett Awdslaye maryed by a lycence the xxvjth day Thursdaye.
Robte son of Rychard Roydes baptised ye xxixth day.
Rychard son of John Hurst yonger baptised yt daye.

November 1609.

John sonn of John Tyas baptised ye first daye.
John sonn of John Ellis baptised ye vthe day.
Robert sonn of Robert Saxtonn baptised yt day.
Rychard sonn of John Hurst yongest buried ye xth day.
John son of Philemon Speight baptised ye xijth daye.
Rychard son of John Owldroide yonger baptised yt day.
Sibell Bentlaye an ould woman buried ye xvthe day.
Robert son of John Goodayll baptised ye xixth day.
A yonge daughter of Mr. Wilsonn beinge not baptised was buried the xxvthe daye.
Ann daughter of Thomas Peace buried yt same day.
Mathew Houldsworthe and Elizabethe Todde maried the xxxtie daye.
Uxor Dishforthe buried the same daye.

December 1609.

Elizabethe Speight sister to Marmaduke Speight deceased buried the first day.
John sonn of Philemon Speight buried ye third day.
Abraham Heape and Grace Turner maried ye fourth day.
Uxor Robinsonn of Chickenlay buried ye tenthe day.
Rycharde Rolland and Elizabethe Wilcocke maried ye xviijth daye.
John Claytonn of ye More-side buried ye xxijth day.
Elizabethe daughter of Edwarde Midlebroughe baptised the xxviijtho day.

Januarie.

Alice daughter of Rychard Wilkensou baptised ye first day.

1609.

Robert sonn of Edwarde Awtie baptised ye vjth day.
Dorithie daughter of Thomas Nayler baptised yt day.
Issabell wyfe of Rycharde Sonnyare parishe clarke of Dewsburie was buried ye ixthe daye.
Uxor Bradforthe mother of Robte Bradforthe ye yonger buried that daye.
Nicholas son of John Tomsonn buried ye xijth daye.
Jennet daughter of Thomas Netleton baptised ye xxijth day.
Eliz: daughter of John Nayler baptised yt day.
Mary Kellam daughter of John Kellann of Rypon buried here the same day.
Martha daughter of John Wade baptised ye xxviijth daye.
Rychard son of Averie Acrode baptised at eveninge prayer the same daye.
John Fayerbarne of Sowood grene buried ye last daye.

Februarye 1609.

Dorithie daughter of Willme Roides baptised ye seconde daye.
John Awtie of Dewsburie more side thelder buried the second day being Frydaye.
John sonn of Mathew Holdsworthe baptised ye fourthe day.
Willme Wilsonn Schoolemaster buried ye vijth daye.
John Hurst of Dewsburie buried ye same daye.
Ann Nowell an ould woman buried ye xjth day.
John sonn of Thomas Chaster baptised ye xiijth day.
Robte Stansffelde and Issabell Baylie maried that day.
Rychard son of Rychard Marshall baptised ye xviijth day.
George Collyer and Grace Turner maried ye xixth day.
Thomas Pickerde of Sowood elder buried ye xxth day being Shrove Tuisdaye.
Ann daughter of Michaell Wheatlay baptised the xxiijtho daye St. Mathias day eveninge prayer.
Henrie Croslande beinge slayne bye Willme Greue the xxvthe daye was buried at Thornhill the xxvjtho daye.

Jacobi regis octavo. Marche 1609.

Ann daughter of Michaell Wheatlay buried ye third daye.
Robte son of Edward Awtie buried ye vijth day.
Elizabethe daughter of Roger Dawsonn baptised yt day.
Dorithie daughter of Henrie Ellis youger was baptised the xvjthe daye being Friday at one of ye clocke.
Dorithie Wade daughter of Rychard Wade Ossett was buried the xviijth day Sonday before care* Sonday and the fourthe Sondaye in Lent.
George Hage buried ye xxiiijtie daye.

---

* Mid-Lent Sunday, otherwise Carling or Mothering Sunday.

DEWSBURY PARISH REGISTERS.

1609.

Josephe sonn of Rycharde Harrishe baptised yo xxvth day.
Agnes daughter of John Mardlay (? Madley) baptised yt daye.
Alice daughter of Averie Whitakers baptised that daye.
Issabell daughter of John Dixon baptised yt daye.
John Walker of Dewsburie buried yo xxvijtie daye.
Grace daughter of Henrie Bowlinge baptised yo xxviijth day.
A yonge sonn of John Milnes not baptised was buried the xxxtie daye.

Jacobi regis octavo. Aprill 1610.

Martha daughter of John Wade buried yo fourthe day.
Elizabethe daughter of Thomas Awtie baptised yo xvthe daye.
John Mowbraye* was buried the xvjth daye.
A yonge childe of Margrett Riplyn a stranger not baptised was buried the xviijth daye.
George Nayler buried his wyfe the xxijtie day.
Grace daughter of Michaell Bentlay yougest baptised yt day.
Edward Awtie son of John Awtie yonger baptised yt daye at evening prayer.
A yonge sonn of Willme Tayler of Gawthorpe being not baptised was buried the xxiiijtie daye Tuesdaye.
John sonn of Willme Lee of Batlay Carre baptised at Batlay the xxvth day being St. Marke Day.
Mychaell sonn of John Hewden baptised ye xxixthe day.
Eliz. daughter of Ambrosse Robinson baptised yt daye.

May 1610.

John Speighte buried ye first daye Tuesday.
John Morehowse and Issabell Bradforthe maried ye sixt day.
Robert Castley of Wakeffeld and Edithe Hurst of Dewsburie maried here by a lycence the vijthe daye.
Murmaduke son of Robert Dey baptised ye xvijth day being ye Asention daye.
Alice daughter of Robert Pickerde baptised ye xxtie day.
Thomas Walker of Batlay parishe and Mary Barbar of this parishe maried here the xxijtie daye.

June 1610.

Alice daughter of Rycharde Thornes buried yo third day.
Uxor Owldroide of Dewsburie More side buried ye viijth day.
Rosamond daughter of Robert Robinsonn alias Mawe baptised the tenthe daye.
Robert Speight and Jouye Cartar maried ye xijth daye.
Michaell sonn of Willme Gill Ju. baptised ye xvijth daye.
John Freckleton and Francis Gill maried ye xviiijtie daye.

* The gravestone of this man is now placed in the Church at the west end of the north aisle.

Jacobi regis octavo. Julie 1610.

John Willi and Ann Acrode maried ye thirde daye.
John son of Edwarde Lee buried the viijth daye.
John Fayrbarne and Jonye Lee maried ye xxijtio daye.
Susann daughter of Robte Brooke baptised yt day.
Ann daughter of Willme Rychardson baptised yt daye.
Edwarde son of Rycharde Goodall baptised ye xxixtb day.
John Acrode and Margrett Bar ie maried ye xxxjth day.

Jacobi regis octavo. August 1610.

Elizabethe daughter of Rycharde Thornes was buried the seconde daye.
Rycharde Sonnyare of this parishe and Jennett Lee of Mirtfelde maried there yo sixt daye.
Margrett daughter of Thomas Boothe baptised yo fift daye.
Dorothie daughter of Robte Bradforthe the yonger baptised ye same daye.
Eliz. daughter of Nicholas Walker baptised yt day.
Eliz. daughter of Thomas Awtye buried ye vijth day.
A yonge son of John Whitlay beinge not baptised was buried the viijth daye.
Thomas son of John Morchowse baptised ye 19th daye.

Jacobi regis octavo. September 1610.

Uxor Owldroide of Bowderoide buried ye first day.
Michaell sonn of John Bentlaye of Gawthorpe was baptised ye ixth daye of September anno deo.
Elizabethe wyfe of John Fayrbarne of Sothill Smithies was buried ye xxvijth daye.
Robert Wilbye and Frideswoode Cooke maried yt daye.
Elizabethe daughter of Roberte Stansfelde yonger baptised ye xxixth daye Michaellmas day.
Rycharde Bull and Alice Wilboro maryed ye xxxtie day.

Jacobi regis octavo. October anno 1610.

John Tomson buried elder ye tenthe daye.
Merioll wyfe of Allexander Secker buried ye xiijth daye.
Rosamonde daughter of John Shepperd baptised ye xvijth day.
Willme son of Gorge Collier baptised ye xxvijth daye.
A yonge sonn of Edwarde Barnarde not baptised was ye tenthe day of November* buried.

November 1610.

John son of Bryan Phillippe baptised ye xjth daye.
Ann daughter of Edward Ellis baptised ye xjth daye.
Robert Threaplande was buried ye xvjthe daye.
Jonye daughter of Edwarde Bull baptised ye xviijth day.
Willme sonn of John Acrode baptised ye xxijtie daye.

* So in Register.

1610.

John son of Robte Brearay baptised yo xxixth day.
Edithe daughter of Nicholas White baptised xxxtie daye beinge Saynete Andrewe day at eveninge prayer.

December 1610.

Margrett daughter of John Fletcher baptised yo second day.
Ann daughter of Robte Phillippe baptised yt day.
Ann daughter of Tho. Radleye Ju. baptised ye third daye.
Ann Baraclonghe was buried ye seaventhe day.
Henrie son of Stephen wyfe (? Wyse) baptised yo xvjth day.
Robte son of James Speight baptised yt daye.
John son of Edwarde Awtye baptised yt daye.
Merceye daughter of Tho. Robinsonn baptised yt daye.
Thomas son of Rychard Whitlay of yo Carre baptised yo xxiijtie day.
John son of John Tomsonn baptised yo xxvjth day.
Jonye daughter of Rycharde Fell baptised ye xxviijth day.
John Beamonde dyinge at Uxor Barbar howse in this parishe was buried at Mirfelde there the xxxtie daye Sonday before New Year's daye.

Januarie 1610.

Edwarde son of Edwarde Phillippe baptised yo vjth daye.
Marye daughter of Nicholas Mitchill baptised yt day.
Margrett daughter of Lawrance Bull buried yt day.
Thomas son of Averye Bull baptised yt day.
Eliz. daughter of Rychard Hemyngway Ju. baptised yt day.
Willme sonn of Gorge Collyer buried ye viijth daye.
Margrett Whitakers a mayde dyinge at Exelay was buried at Hallifax the ixth daye being Wednesday after twelve daye.
Jane daughter of John Lee baptised ye xiijth daye.
John sonn of Robert Netletonn baptised ye xxtie day.
Abraham sonn of Rycharde Hemyngeway elder baptised yt daye.
Ann daughter of Willme Musgrave baptised yt daye.
Josephe Owldroide and Margrett Knowles maried the xxijtie daye.
John Sharpe and Elizabethe Barbar maried ye xxvijtie day.
Willme Speight and Dorithye Coplay maried yo xxixth day.
Alexander Seeker and Elizabeth Bull maried the same day.

Jacobi regis octavo. Februarye 1610.

John sonn of Edwarde Awtie buried the first daye.
Percivall son of Rycharde Dishforthe baptised yo third day.
Jouye daughter of Rycharde Fell buried yo fourthe daye.

1610.

Issabell daughter of Willme Fell baptised yt daye.
Margrett daughter of Thomas Boothe buried yo ixth day.
Alice daughter of Robte Lee baptised yt daye.
John son of John Wade baptised the xijtho daye.
Jane daughter of Averye Milnes baptised yo xvijth.
Eliz. daughter of Tho. Allan baptised yt daye.
Thomas sonn of Thomas Awdslay baptised ye xxiiijtie daye.
Ann daughter of John Wilbye baptised ye same daye.

Marche 1610.

Uxor Brouke widowe of Ossett buried ye vth daye.
Gorge son of Willme Grene baptised tenthe daye.
Thomas son of Abraham Lange baptised ye xvijthe daye.
Margrett daughter of Marmaduke Ellis was baptised that daye at evening prayer.
Eliz. daughter of John Westerman baptised the xxiijtie daye.
Rychard Juwitt of Bradforthe parishe beinge drowned in calder was buried the xxvthe day.
John Scriven was buried the xxvjth day.
John Bower was buried ye same daye.

April 1611.

Grace daughter of Robert Speight of Chickenlay baptised ye vijth daye second Sunday after Easter anno regis Jacobi nono.
John son of Thomas Bradforth buried yo xjth daye.
Willme Speight a yonge man of Osset was buried the xiijth daye Satterday.
Robert son of Robert Pighells baptised yo xiiijtie day.
Eliz. daughter of John Freckltonn baptised yo xvjthe day.
Rychard sonn of Rycharde Thornes baptised the xxiijtie day.
Willme son of Francis Fernlay buried yo xxiiijtie day.
Eliz. daughter of John Parker baptised at home in her father's house the xxiijtie daye.
Eliz. daughter of John Parker buried the xxvijth daye.
Thomas son of Edwarde Secker baptised yo seconde daye of May.*

Jacobi regis nono. Maye 1611.

John Bayldon and Francis Leake maried ye vthe daye.
Mychaell Wheatlaye son of Michaell Wheatlay baptised the same day at eveninge prayer.
A yonge daughter of Robert Hage yonger not baptised was buried the xijthe daye.
Rycharde son of Thomas Awtie baptised yo xijth day.
Willme Saxtonn of Sowoode Grene buried his wyfe the xvijth daye Fryday before Trinitye Sonday.
John Greave and Eliz. Comsmithe maried ye xxtie day.

* So in Register.

1611.

Susann daughter of Rychard Brigge was baptised the xxvjthe daye first Sonday after Trinityo Sonday"
Willme Nowsom alias Jackesonn and Catheryne Wright maried the xxxth day Thursday.
Ann daughter of John Wilbye buried yo same day.

June 1611.

Dorithye basse daughter of Willme Downes of Normanton parishe and Susann Forrest of this parishe baptised the second day.
Christopher Mitchell buried the vthe daye.
Willme Lyversedge of Hallifax parishe and Anne Hurst of this parishe maried the xjth daye.
Thomas son of Abraham Lange buried yo xxiijtio day.

Julyo 1611.

Agnes wyfe of Thomas Whitakers elder was buried the vjthe daye Satterday.
Alice Barton daughter of Robert Bartonn deceased buried the ixthe day.
Rycharde Wade buried ye cleaventh daye.
Abraham Grenewoode and Ellen Archer maried yt day.
John son of Thomas Nayler baptised yo xiiijth daye.
A yonge son of Alexander Nowsome not baptised buried the xiiijth day.
Edwarde son of Edwarde Midlebroughe was baptised the xxviijtie day.
Rycharde son of John Sharpe baptised yt day.

August 1611.

Ann daughter of Thomas Peace baptised the fourthe daye.
Elizabethe daughter of Xpofer Kirke baptised the vijth daye.
Susann daughter of John Hurst Ju. baptised the xjth daye at eveninge prayer.
Willme son of John Fayrbarne baptised yo xviijth day.
Willme son of Willme Broadlay baptised ye xxviijth day.

September 1611.

Thomas son of John Morehowse buried yo tenthe day.
A yonge sonn of Edwarde Wurmall not baptised was buried tho xiijth daye.
Michaell son of Gorge Domar baptised yo xxixtie day beinge Michaellmas day.
Jane daughter of Thomas Somestar of Wakeffelde gent. was buried the last day Monday 30 day.

October.

Ellen daughter of Willme Lambe baptised ye vjth day.
Grace daughter of Rycharde Whitlay Ju. baptised yt day.
John Newsome of this parishe and Jennett Duckeworthe of Emlay parishe were maried here bye lycence the xiijth daye Sondaye.

1611.

Robert Sharphowse and Alice Linlay were maried the xvthe daye Tuesdaye.
Rycharde Mittonn and Francis Hare were maried the xvijth day Thursday.
Michaell sonn of Gorge Boemar buried yo xijth daye.
Jonet daughter of Robte Smithe baptised yo xxvij day.

November 1611.

Eliz. daughter of Edmonde Sonnyare baptised the first day All Hallowe Day Friday.
Issabell daughter of Nicholas White buried the second day Satterday.
Rosamond daughter of John Whitlay baptised yo third day Sonday after All hallowe day.
Mercy daughter of Willme Roides baptised yt day.
John Denison and Ann Bayldon maried yo vth day.
Edwarde son of Willme Newsome alias Jackesonn baptised the tenthe daye Martynmas even Sonday.
Robert Dawsonn buried the xxjtie daye Thursday.
Josephe sonn of Willme Lambe buried yt day.
John sonn of Samuell Grenewood baptised the xxiiijth day.

December 1611.

Thomas sonn of John Dickenson baptised yo first day first Sonday of Advent.
A yonge childe of Willme Taylior of Gawthorpe being a daughter not baptised buried yo third day.
Rosamond daughter of John Whitlay buried yo vthe day.
A yonge sonn of Edwarde Lee not baptised buried ye xjth day.
Edwarde son of Willme Jackeson alias Newsome was buried the xiiijth day Satterday 1611.
Martha daughter of Willme Shepperde baptised yo xxijtie day.
Jenett daughter of Willme Wilbye baptised yo xxvjth day: another yonge daughter of his being not baptised was buried that daye.

Januaryo 1611.

Josephe son of Josephe Owldroide baptised the vthe.daye first Sondaye in yo newe yeare anno Dni. 1611. Jacobi regis nono.
Willme Broadlay was buried the ixth day Thursday.
Eliz. daughter of John Morehowse baptised ye xiijth daye.
Robert sonn of Willme Speight baptised yo xiiijth day: this is Willme Speight yongest of Earles Heaton.
Michaell son of Willme Gill Ju. buried ye xxjtie day.
Robert son of Willme Speight of Earles Heaton yonger was buried yo same day Tuesday.
Robert Stansfelde buried yo xxvjth day Sonday.
Rychard son of Rycharde Roydes baptised yt day Sonday before candlemas day at morning prayer.
A yonge child of Robert Saxton not baptised was buried yo xxvjth day.

Februarye 1611.

Rachell daughter of Mr. Acroile vicar was baptised the second day Sonday beinge candlemas day.
Edwarde son of Edward Barnarde baptised yt day.
Rychard son of Rycharde Wright baptised yt day.
Eliz. daughter of John Dawson baptised yt day.
Sibell daughter of Willme Gill senior of Sowoode Grene buried the tenthe daye Monday.
Edwarde Fayrbarne of this parishe and Brigett Walker of Thornhill pishe maried the xjth day Tuesday.
A yonge son of Averie Gill not baptised was buried the xiiijth daye.
Grace daughter of Rycharde Goodall buried ye xvth day.
Michaell son of Robte Brouke baptised the xvjth day.
Ann daughter of John Ellis baptised ye same day.
Robert Son of Robert Sharphowse yonger baptised the same day at eveninge prayer yt day.
Robert Walker of Thornhill and Eliz. Fayerbarne of this parishe maried here xixth daye Wednesdaye.
Eliz. daughter of John Grayve Ju. baptised ye xxiijth day.
Rowlande Knowles and Alice Beamond maried yt day.
John son of Robte Thorpe baptised ye same day.
Gilbert Firthe of Wakeffelde and Jennett Hull (? Hall) of Dewsburio parishe maried here the xxiiijtie day colloppe Monday in the morninge.
Phillippe Slade and Ann Broadlay maried ye xxvth day.
Thomas Wade son of Rychard Wade buried yt day St. Mathie day and Shrove Tuesday.
Susann daughter of Willme Dey baptised ye xxvth daye Shrove Tuesday at eveninge prayer.

Marche anno Dni. 1611.

Eliz. wiffe of Willme Kent was buried ye first day first Sonday in Lent.
Eliz. daughter of Abraham Grenewood being baptised at Batlaye ye seaventhe day was buried here the ixth day at Dewsburie.
Uxor Howly wife of Averye Howly of Batlay dyinge at Rychard Goodall of Sothill Smithies was buried at Batlay the eleaventhe day.
Eliz. daughter of Robert Leckwithe (? Beckwithe) baptised ye xxijth day.
Dorithie daughter of John Goodall baptised yt day.
John son of John Robinsonn Ju. baptised yo same day; this is John Robinson of Dewsburio Moresyde yonger in the afternoone at evening prayer.
Edwarde son of John Tyas baptised ye xxixtie day.

Jacobi regis decimo. Aprill anno Dni. 1612.

Ann wyfe of Robert Wright of Dewsburio was buried the second day Thursdaye.
Ann daughter of Rychard Marshall baptised yo xiiijth daye.
John son of Percivall Terrye baptised ye xixth day.
Willme son of Gorge Ingram alias Brooke baptised yt day.

1611.

Alice daughter of Thomas Barghe buried ye xxijth day.
Eliz. daughter of John Willbye baptised that day.
Robert Wright was buried the xxiiijtie day Friday.
Eliz. daughter of Bryan Phillippe buried ye xxviijth day.

Jacobi regis decimo. May anno Dni. 1612.

Mercye daughter of Henrye Bull baptised ye third day.
Willme sonn of John Sonyare buried yt day.
Marye daughter of Abraham Lange baptised ye xiiijth day.
John Forrest and Agnes Rawson maried ye xvijth day.
Sara daughter of Rychard Fell baptised yt day at eveninge prayer.
Marmaduke Longelay and Mary Sayer maried ye xixth day being St. Dunston's day anno instanti.
Alice wyfe of Abraham Lango buried ye xxijtie day.
Willme son of Edwarde Langefelde baptised ye xxiiijth day.
Issabell daughter of Thomas Boothe baptised ye same day.
Issabell wyfe of Willme Wilsonn buried ye xxvth day being Monday.
Gregory sonn of Thomas Jaggar baptised ye xxxjth daye.
James son of Thomas Netleton baptised yt day White Sonday in ye afternoone before evening prayer.
Sara daughter of Rychard Fell buried yt day.

June 1612.

Katheryne wyfe of Gorge Hage buried ye vthe day.
Agnes daughter of Thomas Wurmall Ju. baptised vijth day trinitye Sonday in ye after noone.
A yonge son of Humphrye Dixon buried ye xiijth day being not baptised before ye buriall.
Thomas son of Henrie Robinson baptised ye xiiijth day.
Edwarde Grene buried his wyfe the xvjth day.
Anthonye son of Edwarde Awtye baptised ye xxijtie day also a yonge daughter of the same Edwarde Awtye not baptised was buried the same tyme at eveninge prayer Sonday before Midsumer daye.
Thomas Wurmall of Highe Sothill buried ye xxijtie day being Monday before Midsmer day.

Julye 1612.

Sara daughter of John Nayler baptised ye vthe day.
Jennett daughter of John Nayler baptised ye same day.
Edwarde Grene was buried the vijth day Tuesday.
Mercye daughter of John Owldroid baptised ye xijth day.
Willme Benn and Angelus Lee maried yt daye.
Rychard Allan was buried ye xvjth day Thursday.
Edwarde basse son of Edwarde Brouke and Issabell Smithe of Bustall pishe buried ye xxiijtie day St. James eveninge at night Fryday 1612.

DEWSBURY PARISH REGISTERS.

1612.

John son of John Denison baptised ye xxxtie day also another son of ye same John Denisons being not baptised was buried yt day Friday.

The monethe August 1612.

Jenett daughter of Nicholas Walker baptised the xxiijtie day Sonday at eveninge prayer and Bartholomew even that yeare an° Dni 1612.

The monethe September 1612.

Eliz. daughter of Nicholas White baptised yo vjth day being Sonday later Leo fayer even at eveninge prayer ann° Dni. Dco. 1612.
Edwarde More of Osset buried his wyfe the tenthe day beinge Thursday.
Thomas Forrest buried the xvjth day Wednesday.
Willme son of Robert Bradforthe yongest baptised ye xxtie day St. Mathew his even.
Thomas Coplay of Ardeslaw and Jane Smithe of this parishe were maried the xxvijth day.

October.

Jenett daughter of John Naylor buried ye third day being Satterday in ye after noone at eveninge.
John son of Edmond Fox baptised ye xjth daye.
Eliz. daughter of Ambrosse Robinson buried ye xvjth daye.
Marye daughter of John Mannsfelde baptised ye xviijth daye St. Luke daye.
Uxor Secker under ye Highe banke buried ye xixthe day.
Sara daughter of Willme Longelay of Horburye was buried the last day Satterday All hallowes even.
John son of Robert Stansfeld baptised ye xxvth day Sonday before All hallowes day ann° Dni. 1612.

November.

Jane Blacker beinge drowned in Calder betwixt the milnes the vthe day was buried at Thornhill the vjth day being Fryday drowned on Thursday 1612.
Marye daughter of Gorge Bomar baptised the xvijth daye Tuesdaye in ye after none.
John son of John Forrest baptised ye xxijth day.
John Norton of Pomfrett and Ann Birkehead of this parishe maried the xxith day.
Marye daughter of Michaell Bentlay Ju. baptised the xxixth day St. Androwe even and Sonday.

December.

Eliz. wyfe of Willme Broadlay Sr. buried ye ixth daye.
Grace Lee buried the tenthe daye Thursday anno regni Jacobi regis, &c. decimo.
Eliz. daughter of Ambrosse Robinson baptised ye xiijth day Sonday in ye after noone at evening prayer ann° Dni. 1612.
Rychard son of Nicholas Mitchell baptised ye xxtie day Sonday before Christenmas Day 1612.

1612.

Mr. Whitakers parson of Thornhill was buried there ye xxijtie day Tuesday before Christenmas day ann° Dni. 1612.
Rychard son of Willme Casson baptised ye xxiijtie day.
Uxor Arnould wyfe of John Arnould buried ye xxvjth day St. Stephen his daye.
Willme son of Edwarde Ellis baptised that day at eveninge prayer ann° Dni. 1612.
Jenett daughter of Willme Rychardson was baptised the xxvijth day St. John day at eveninge prayer.

Jacobi regis decimo. Januarye 1612.

Nicholas son of Nicholas Walker elder deceased was buried the first day Newe year's day.
A yonge son of John Cowpas not baptised was buried the second day Saterday in after noone.
Rychard Awdslay of Ossett buried ye vth of January being ye twelfe night Tuesday.
Eliz. daughter of Rychard Goodall baptised ye tenthe day Sonday at eveninge prayer.
Thomas son of Robert Phillippe baptised ye xiiijth day.
A yonge childe of Thomas Allen not baptised was buried the xvth day.
John Broadlay and Dynyse Scorar was maried ye xxvjth day Tuesday.
A yonge son of Phillippe Slade not baptised was buried the xxxtie day Satterday in ye after noone.
Agnes daughter of Edwarde Fayerbarne yonger was baptised ye last day Sonday.
Brigett daughter of Robert Turpen was baptised the same day at eveninge prayer.

A creatione mundi 5562. Ab ingressu Bruti in Augliam 2720.

Februarye ann° Dni. 1612.

Rychard Drybecke of Hallifax parishe and Grace Whelowright of this parishe maried ye second day Candlemas day.
Willme son of Edwarde Lee baptised yt day.
Robert son of John Walker baptised ye vijth day.
Tobye sonn of Willme Lee of ye Carre baptised ye xiiijth day.
Eliz. daughter of Tho. Chaster baptised yt daye beinge Shrove Sondaye in the after noone.
Michaell sonn of Willme Speight Ju. baptised ye xvjth daye Shrove Tuesdaye.
Phillippe son of John Howden baptised ye xxjtie day first Sonday in lent at eveninge prayer.
Mawde wyfe of Willme Longelay buried ye xxvijth beinge seconde Sonday in lent.
Thomas son of Henrye Ellis Ju. baptised yt day at evening prayer.

Marche 1612.

Willme Longelay of Earles Heaton was buried ye first day.
Jane daughter of John Robinson of Ossett yonger was baptised ye vijth day third Sonday in lent.
Rychard son of Edwarde Phillippe baptised ye xiiijth day.
Robte son of John Wade baptised yt daye fourth Sonday in lent.

1612.

Christopher son of John Dixon baptised yt day at the eveninge prayer.
Rychard Fayrbarne of Sowoode Grene buried his wyfe the xvth daye Mondaye.
Edwarde son of Edwarde Phillippe buried ye xxtie daye beinge the day before Care Sonday.
Sibell wyfe of James Broadlay buried ye xxjtie day being Care Sonday.
James Kent of Dewsburie buried ye xxijtie day Mondaye.
A yonge soun of John Broadlay not baptised was buried that day.
Mychaell sonn of ye same John Broadlay was baptised that day in yo after noone and the same childe was buried yt day ano Dni. 1613.
Marye daughter of John Whitlay baptised yo xxvtie day oure Ladyo day and Thursday ano Dni. 1613.
A yonge daughter of Willmo Taylier not baptised was buried yo xxvijtie day of Marche Palmo Sonday even.

Jacobi regis undecimo. Aprill ano Dni. 1613.

John son of Gorge Hage buried ye fourth day on Easter day in yo after noone.
Easter daughter of Willmo Newsome alias Jacksoun was baptised yo vtho day Monday in Easter wecke.
Eliz. daughter of Willmo Greue baptised yo vjth day Tuesday in Easter wecke.
Sibell Denison was buried the vijth day Wednsday.
A yonge daughter of Robte Hage yonger not baptised was buried the ixthe day.
Easter daughter of John Wilbye baptised yo xjth day on low Sonday at eveninge prayer.
Willme Rychardson and Jenet Dixeson maried yo xiijth day being Tuesday.
Alice daughter of Cotton Broadlay baptised yo xiiijth day being Wednsdaye.

May 1613.

Rychard son of Robert Cartar baptised ye ixth day Sonday before Ascension day Holie Thursday.
Thomas Peace buried ye xiijth day Ascension day.
Gorge Toulsonn and Eliz. Cartar maried ye xviijth day Tuesday before Whitsonday.
Willme son of Tho. Rodlay yonger was baptised yo xxiijth (? xxiiijth) day Whitsonday in yo after noone.
Thomas son of Marmaduke Longlay baptised ye xxvth day Tuesday in Whitsonday wecke.
Rychard Medlay buried his wyfe yo xxvjth daye Wednsday in Whitsonday wecke.
Agnes daughter of Stephen Wyse buried yt day.
Rychard son of Robert Cartar buried yo xxvijth day Wednsday in Whitsonday wecke.

June 1613.

Edwarde Whitlaye and Alice Leo maried ye first day Tuesday after Trinitye Sonday.
Jonothan Crowder of this parishe and Patience Smithe of Huddersfelde maried there the same day.

1613.

Judithe daughter of Averie Gill baptised ye vjth day first Sonday after Trinitie Sonday ano Dni. 1613.
Robert Robinson and Judith Croft maried ye viijth daye beinge Tuesday.
Willme Aerode and Eliz. Berry maried ye xixth day boinge after St. Barnabe day.
Mary daughter of Robert Brear baptised the xxtie day Sonday before Midsmer day.
Thomas Townend alias Robinson and Jonye Saxtone were maried ye xxjte day Tuesday before Midsmer day.
Edwarde Pickerde and Agnes Fox maried ye xxviith day Sonday after Midsmer day.
Mereye daughter of Rychard Brigge baptised yt day.

Julie. Jacobi regis 11.

Eliz. daughter of Willme Grene buried ye first day.
Eliz. daughter of Robert Speight baptised ye fourthe day vth Sonday after Trinityo Sonday.
Thomas Secker buried ye vjth day Tuesday after Sayncte Peter day.
Rychard Ridlsdon was buried ye xjth day.
Eliz. daughter of Abraham Grenewoode alias Mitchell baptised the same day.
Friscwythe daughter of Robert Wilbye baptised that day at eveninge prayer.
Rychard Castle and Margrett Hurst maried ye xiijth day Tuesday.

August.

Jenet Peace buried ye second day.
Willme son of Willme Rychardson alias Boy baptised the vthe day Thursday.
Dorithie daughter of John Medlay baptised the viijth daye Sonday after Lammas day.
Robert Medlay and Margrett Bramham maried the xijth Frydaye ye Lee fayre day the first bye a licence. Post meridem* hora quinta.
Michaell son of Thomas Secker baptised that day at eveninge prayer the xvtho day.
Willme son of Christopher Bronke of Ossett older was buried the xixth day being Tuesdaye.
John son of James Speight baptised yo xxijth day Sonday before Bartholomew day.
Rycharde Owldroide of Chidsell buried ye xxiiijth day Tuesday and St. Bartholemew day.
Willme Awtye and Francis Denyso maried on Tuesday the last daye of August viz: 31 day a seaventho after Bartholomew day being ye xxiiijth day or a wecke.

September anno Dni. 1613.

John Sonyare late of Dewsburie dyinge at Churche Heaton was buried there ye vth day Sonday before yo Lady day ye later.
Josephe son of Edwarde Midlebroughe baptised the xijth daye.
Ann daughter of John Morehowso baptised that day at eveninge prayer.
Uxor Grene wyfe of Thomas Grene of ye Street in Ossett was buried the xxijtie day, day after St. Mathew daye being Wednsday.

* So in Register.

1613.

Edward Fayrbarne of Ossett dyinge at Wakefelde the xxvjth daye was buried there ye xxvijth day Monday before Michellmas day.

October.

Edwarde son of Edwarde Wurmall of Ossett baptised the thirde daye Sonday after michelmas daye.
Ann daughter of Uxor Peace buried ye fourthe day.
Alice daughter of Rychard Thornes baptised ye next daye.
A yonge daughter of Robert Dey not baptised buried yt daye.
John son of Robert Pighells baptised ye tenthe day.
Thomas son of Marmaduke Ellis baptised ye xviijth day being St. Luke his day.
Eliz. daughter of Robert Lee baptised ye xxviijthe day Thursday Symon and Jude day. This Lee dwellethe in Chidsell.
Thomas son of Thomas Robinson baptised ye last day.
Thomas Roydes of this parishe and Eliz. Heywood of Glossuppe maried that day.

November 1613.

Thomas Robinson under ye hill buried his wyfe the second day Tuesday day after all Hallowe day.
Eliz. daughter of John Acrode baptised ye vijth day Sonday before Martenmas day.
Rychard Wood of Ossett was buried ye xvth day Monday after Martynmas day.
Alice daughter of Willme Awtye baptised ye xxjthe day.
Robert Pighells of Gawthorpe buried ye xxiijth day Wednesday before St. Andrewe day.
Thomas son of Willme Roades baptised ye xxvijth day Sondaye advent.

December 1613.

Margrett wyfe of Michell Bentlay eldest was buried ye first daye Monday.
Willme son of Edwarde Le buried that day.
Eliz. daughter of John Wilby buried ye second day.
Alice daughter of Willme Awtye buried ye fourth day Satterday after St. Andrew day.
Agnes daughter of Edward Wurmall buried the xth daye St. Lucye even Fryday before.
Roger Hurst and Marye Forrest maried ye xijth day.
Rychard Whiteheade buried yt day.
Phillippe son of John Awtie baptised yt day beinge St. Lucye even.
Willme son of Willme Fell baptised yt day.
Thomas son of Thomas Robinson buried ye xvth day.
Thomas son of Robte Sharphowse baptised yo xixth day Sonday before St. Thomas day.
Isabell daughter of Thomas Netletonn baptised that day at eveninge prayer.
Thomas son of Willme Roades buried ye xxjtie daye St. Thomas daye.

1613.

Robert Ashton buried his wyfe the xxiijtie day Thursday before Xristemmas day.
Robert son of John Sharpe baptised ye xxvijth day St. John day in Christenmas.

January 1613.

Eliz. daughter of Willme Musgrave baptised the first daye Satterday.
Grace daughter of Thomas Allen baptised ye second day first Sonday in ye New yeare.
Robert son of Robert Mawe alias Robinson baptised yt day.
Robert son of Robert Pickerde baptised yt day.
Marye daughter of Robert Brear buried ye third day Monday.
Rychard son of Michaell Wheatlay baptised ye vjth day ye Epiphany or twelfe day.
Phillipe son of Phillippe Sladc baptised ye ixth day.
Issabell daughter of Rychard Fell baptised yt day.
Eliz. daughter of Willme Acrode baptised the ixth daye.
Eliz. daughter of Ed. Lee buried ye xvjth day.
Robert son of Rychard Dishforthe baptised ye xxiijtie day.
Bryan son of Bryan Phillippe baptised yt day.
John son of John Fayrbarne baptised ye xxxtie day Sonday before Candlemas day.
John Milner alias Shepperd buried yt day at eveninge prayer.

Jacobi regis undecimo. Februarye 1613.

Thomas son of John Grayve yonger baptised the sext day Sonday after Candlemas day.
Xpofer son of Nicholas Gunsonn baptised yt day in ye morninge prayer tyme.
Md. that a stranger whose name was not knowne at eveninge prayer that daye buriede.
Rycharde sonn of John Denisonn baptised ye xiijth day.
Rosamond daughter of Robert Smithe baptised yt day on Sonday before Valentyne day ano Dni.
Robert son of John Tomson baptised ye xvth day.
Eliz. daughter of John Owldroid baptised ye xxiiijth day.

Marche ano Dni. 1614.*

Alice daughter of John Tyas buried ye first day.
A yonge son of Robert Saxton not baptised was buried ye second day Wedusday 1614.
Robert son of Rychard Dishforthe buried yt day.
John Exam of Chidsell buried ye viijth day upon Shrove Tuesdaye.
Rychard son of Willme Roebothom baptised ye xiijth day first Sonday in Lent 1613.*
Eliz. daughter of Robert Bronke baptised ye xxth day.
John Cowpas yonger buried ye xxvjth day.

* So in Register.

Aprill 1614.

Thomas son of Thomas Robinsonn baptised yo third daye fourthe Sonday in Lent.
John Sonn of Rychard Castle baptised that day at eveninge prayer.
Robert Hawkesworthe of Penystone and Ann Nowell of Dewsburye maried there at Dewsburye bye a licence upon Mondaye ye fourthe of Aprill bye Mr. Tyngle.* Circa hora† undecimam.
Issabell daughter of Robte Thorpe baptised the tenthe daye Care Sonday 1614.
Robert son of Edmonde Sonnyare baptised the xvijth day Palme Sonday.
Edward Bradforthe and Jenet Forrest maried on Monday in Easter weeke St. Markes day bye a licence yo xxvth day of Aprill 1614.
Rychard son of John Denyson buried yt day.

May.

Easter daughter of John Wilbye buried ye first day Low Sonday.
Willme Townende and Agnes Robinsonn maried yt day.
Ellen daughter of Tho. Netletonn baptised yo fourth day.
Michaell son of Robert Dey buried ye vijth day.
Nicholas son of Nicholas White baptised ye viijth day.
Lawrance son of Lawrance Bull baptisd yt day second Sonday after Easter.
Ann daughter of Thomas Awtye baptised ye xvth day.

Jacobi regis duodecimo, Scotico 47mo.

June 1614.

Marye daughter of Rycharde Bull baptised ye vth day Sonday after Ascension day evening prayer.
Eliz. daughter of John Hurst Ju. baptised yt daye at eveninge prayer.
Christopher Dixon of Ossett was buried yo ixth of May Thursday before Whitsonday.
Mychaell son of John Broadly baptised ye xijth day Whitsonday at eveninge prayer.
Edwarde Seekar of Ossett buried the xiiijth day Tuesday in Whitsonday weeke.
Rychard Davesonn and Ann Bradforthe maried that day.
Robte son of Gorge Towlson baptised ye xxvjth day first Sonday after Trinitye.
James Speight and Betteris Fernlay maried ye xxviijth day Tuesday before St. Peters day.
Robte Hemyngway and Mercye Acrod maried last daye.

---

* This is the Mr. Thomas Tingle who is mentioned in Hunter's "Ecclesiastical History of Dewsbury" as having written a piece of doggerel verse, "In praise of Dewsbury," a full copy of which is among the Hunter MSS. in the British Museum, but is too long to be printed here. Dr. Nathaniel Johnston, of Pontefract, took down the verses from the mouth of the Parish Clerk of Dewsbury about the year 1670, and he calls Mr. Tingle "Minister of Dewsbury," probably meaning that he was Curate.

† So in Register.

Julye 1614.

Henrye son of Thomas Boothe baptised yo third day Sonday after Peters day.
Gamaliell sonn of Robert Brearay baptised that day at eveninge prayer.
Henrie son of Thomas Boothe buried sixt day.
Grace daughter of John Freeleton baptised the tenthe day third Sonday after Trinitye Sonday.
Alice daughter of Roger Dawson baptised ye same Sonday at eveninge prayer.
Thomas sonn of Rychard Roydes baptised ye xiiijth day.
Uxor Leadbeater buried ye xvth daye.
Ann daughter of John Gibson bapt ye xvijth day.
Rychard Acrode of Earles Heatonn dyinge on ye xxth day was buried ye xxjth daye Thursday before St. James day.
Averie Pickerd and Eliz. Roodes maried ye xxiiijth day St. James even 1614 and Sonday.
Marye wyfe of Rychard Marshall was buried the same daye.
Botheresse daughter of Rychard Marshall baptised ye xxiiijth daye.
Marye daughter of John Pickerd baptised yo same day.

August 1614.

Edwarde Lee of Earles Heaton buried ye vijth day Sonday before ye first Lady day.
And a child of one Thomas Morebye buried then a stranger at Ossett.
Grace wyfe of Rychard Cartar buried ye xiijth day the first Lady day and Satterday.
Edmond Jepsonn dyinge that day was buried the xiiijth day Sonday after ye Ladye day.
Willme Wilsonn and Eliz. Ellery maried yt day.
Edmound Bothomlay and Grace Hanson maryed yo xxviijth day.

September 1614.

Sara daughter of Robte Medlay baptised ye 4th day.
Sara daughter of Josephe Ouldroide baptised tho xjth daye.
Willme son of Rychard Hemyngway Ju. baptised the xviijth day.
Robert Wheatlay of this parishe and Mereye Smith of Batlay parishe maried here ye xxvjth day Monday before Michelmas day.
Uxor Gryphyn buried ye xxvjth day.
Mychaell son of Willme Shepheard baptised the xxixth day Mychelmas day at eveninge prayer.

October.

Mychaell son of Willme Shepperd buried ye vth day.
Willme basse son of Gorge Pickerd and Eliz. Wroe baptised that day Wednesday after michelmas daye.
Willme son of Rychard Hemyngway buried ye vijth day Satterday after Mychelmas day.
Samuell son of John Ellis baptised ye ixth day.
Josephe son of Tho. Nayler baptised yt day.
Agnes daughter of John Shepperd baptised yt day Sonday after Michelmas day.
John Rayner and Eliz. Sharphowse maried bye a licence the tenthe daye.

1614.

Martha daughter of Willmo Shepperd buried the xvth day Satterday.
Juditho daughter of Edwarde Leo deceased baptised the xvjth day Sonday before St. Luke day.
Eliz. daughter of Roger Hurst baptised that day in ye tyme of morning prayer.
Thomas Robinsonn and Alice Sykes maried the xviijth day St Luke day.
Robert son of John Wade buried ye xxiijth day Sonday before Symon day and Jude.
Willmo Knowles and Jony Swynden maried ye xxiiijth day Monday before Symon day and Jude.

November.

Rychard Keighlay and Issabell Owldroid maried the first day All Sancts' day.
Eliz. wyfe of Willmo Roides was buried ye vth day at ten of ye clocke in ye night Satterday.
Issabell daughter of ye same Roydes baptised the vjth day Sonday.
Uxor Leo of Gawthorpe buried ye ixth day.
Francis daughter of Edmonde Fox baptised the xiijth day Sonday after Martynmas day.
John Bradford buried ye xvjth day.
Uxor Awdsley of Ossett buried the xxiiijth day being Thursday.
Issabell daughter of Rychard Davison baptised xxvijth day Advent Sonday in ye morninge.
John Cowpar and Ellyn Whiteylaye maried ye last day St. Andrewe day Wednsday.

December.

Robte Cowpar and Eliz. Hepworthe were maried here by a lycence ye fourthe daye being Sonday after St. Andrew daye.
Parsivall son of Parsivall Terry baptised that day at morning prayer.
Uxor Threapland buried the xvth daye.
Susan daughter of Michaell Bentlay Ju. baptised the xviijth day Sonday before St. Thomas day.
Willmo Spoight of Earles Heaton was buried the xxiijth day Friday after St. Thomas day.
Thomas son of John Wilby baptised ye xxvth day being Christenmas day at eveninge prayer.

Januarye 1614.

A yong daughter basso borne of Mary Hurst and Josephe Crowder bothe of Mirfelde not baptised was buried ye fourthe day Wednsday.
Willmo son of Edward Phillippe baptised ye ixth day.
Ann daughter of Edmonde Jepson deceased buried that day Menday after ye twelfe day.
Margrett daughter of Nicholas Mitchell baptised the xjth day.
Henry Ellis elder was buried yt day.
Betheris daughter of Rychard Marshall was buried ye xiiijth day Satterday.
Margerye wyfe of Thomas Fell buried ye xvth day.
John son of Edward Langefeld baptised yt day.
Ellin daughter of John Morehowse baptised yt day at evening prayer.
Willmo son of Edward Phillippe buried ye xxth day.
Eliz. daughter of Rychard Whitlay of ye Carre baptised ye xxijth day Sonday before St. Paule day.

1614.

Issabell daughter of Willmo Roydes buried ye xxvijth day Fryday after St. Paule day.
John Leo of Gawthorpe a collier buried his wyfe yt day in ye after noone.
Margrett daughter of Nicholas Mitchell buried the xxixth day Sonday after St. Paule day.
John son of Robte Bradfortho yongest baptised yt day.
Thomas son of John Dickensonn buried ye last day.
Alice daughter of Edward Bedfortho baptised yt day.

Februarye 1614.

Sibell wyfe of Thomas Acrode of Earles Heaton was buried ye third day; day after Candlemas day Fryday.
Alice daughter of Thomas Robinsonn of ye moresyde baptised ye vthe daye Sonday after Candlemas day and ye mother of ye sayd childe buried yt night.
Thomas Hawkycard and Ellen Fell maried ye vjth day.
Robte Clarke and Issabell Forrest maried ye xiiijth daye being Tuesday.
Edwarde Bedforthe was buried ye xvjth daye after Valentyne daye and Thursday o.
Rychard son of Robert Phillippe baptised ye xixth day Sonday being Shrove Sonday.

Marcho 1615.

Mercye daughter of Robte Hemyngwaye baptised ye vth daye second Sonday in Lent.
Elizabeth wyfe of John Shepperde elder buried yt day in the afternoon 1614* second Sonday in Lent.
Raphe Tomson a piper was buried ye ixth day beinge Thursdaye in atter none.
Ann daughter of Mr. Acrode vicar was baptised on Fryday ye xth day after noone.
Issabell daughter of ye same Mr. Acrode baptised yt day in ye after noone.
Juditho daughter of Willmo Day baptised ye xijth day third Sonday in Lent.
A yonge childe of Willmo Acrode not baptised being a daughter was buried ye xvijth day Fryday in after noone.
Issabell daughter of Mr. Acrode buried ye xxijth day of this monethe Wednesdaye before ye Lady day in Lent.
Ann daughter of Mr. Acrode buried yt day.
John Hutchinsonn buried the xxixth day Wednsdaye.

Aprill 1615.

Eliz. daughter of John Forrest baptised ye tenth daye Monday in Easter weeke.
Edwarde son of John Goodall baptised at home ye sextene daye Satterday and ye same childe buried the same day in ye after noone.
Robert son of John Wade baptised ye xvjth day on Low Sonday.
Josephe Walker and Agnes Graysonn maried ye xxiijth day Sonday after Low Sunday.

---

* The year 1614 is given after most of the entries for this month.

1615.

Richard son of Willme Jackesonn baptised that day in the after noon.
Mark son of John Robinsonn Ju. baptised the xxvth day St. Marke day Tuesdaye.

May 1615.

Willme Roydes and Alice Bull married yo xiiijth day Sonday before Ascention daye.
George Maude and Kyrstabell Pell maried yo xxjth day Sonday after Ascention day.
Robert son of Robert Stansfelde baptised yt day.
Thomas Kyrke and Eliz. Hall maried yo xxiijth day being Tuesday after Ascention day Holy Thursday.
Alice daughter of Richard Dishforthe baptised yt day.
John son of John Fell baptised yo xxviijth day on Whitsonday at eveninge prayer.

June 1615.

Rychard Goodall buried yo vth day Monday after Trinitye Sondaye.
Margrett daughter of John Milnes baptised ye xjth day first Sunday after Trinity Sunday.
George Castle and Francis Gamble maried yt day.
Grace daughter of Rychard Goodall baptised yt day at eveninge prayer.
Robert son of Thomas Porsonn of Askerigge in Wensedall baptised yo xiijth day Tuesdaye.
Agnes wife of John Hurst under hill buried ye xviijth day Fryday before Midsmers day.
Rychard Marshall and Margrett Speight maried at Yorke bye a licence on Monday yo xixth day.
Robert Birkebeyo was buried yo xxvijth day Tuesday after Midsmer day.
Thomas Robinson and Grace Speight maried yt day.

Jacobi regis 13º. Julye 1615.

John Broadlay and Eliz. Owldroide maried ye iiijth daye beinge Tuesday.
John Coa and Thomison Iles maried yo ixth day.
Alice daughter of Robert Wroe baptised yo xvjth daye after St. Swithmes daye.
Lawrence Issott and Judithe Brouke maried ye xvijth day Monday.
Robert Rayner and Grace Aerode maried yo xxth day Thursday anº Dni. 1615.

August.

A yonge childe of John Robinson alias Townende not baptised buried the first day Tuesday Lamas day.
John Malinson buried his wife the third day Thursday after Lamas day.
Anthonye son of Richard Castle baptised ye vjth day at eveninge prayer 1615.
Dorithie daughter of Edwarde Midlebrouke baptised the xxiiijth day Bartlemew day Thursday.
John Kay and Agnes Grayson maried yo xxvijth day Sonday after Barthellmew daye.
Eliz. daughter of Averye Pickerde baptised yt day.
Ann daughter of Henrie Bull baptised yt day at eveninge prayer.

September 1615.

Margrett daughter of Thomas Boothe baptised the third daye St. Giles Sondaye.
Margrett daughter of Thomas Boathe buried yo vijth day on Thursday after ye Lee fayer day yo later.
Eliz. daughter of George Maude baptised yo xvijth daye Sonday before St. Mathow daye.
John Mallinsonn and Grace Taylier maried the xixth day Tuesdaye before St. Mathew day.
Willme Mansfeld buried yo xxiijth daye Satterday after St. Mathewe daye.
Mercye daughter of Willme Rychardsonn alias Boye baptised ye xxiiijth day at eveninge prayer.
Issabell daughter of John Kay alias Gawen baptised the xxixth day Michellmas day at eveninge prayer.

October.

Christopher son of Richard Nayler elder baptised the first daye Sondaye after Michellmas day.
James Broadlaye and Marye Whelewright maried ye third day Tuesday after Michellmas daye.
Grace daughter of Robte Pickerde baptised yo ixth daye on Mandaye.
Ann daughter of Gorge Collier baptised yo xviijth day St. Luke his day Wednesdaye.
John Son of Willme Knowles baptised yo xxijth day at eveninge prayer Sonday before Symon and Jude.
John Lee and Issabell Arrandell maried ye xxiiijth day beinge Tuesday before Symon day and Jude.
Ann daughter of Thomas Nettetonn baptised yo xxixth day Sonday before All Saynts daye.

November.

Robte son of Robte Brearay baptised ye vth day.
Mercye daughter of Robte Bekwithe baptised yt day.
Nicholas son of Edwarde Ellis baptised yt daye.
Rychard son of Edward Ellis baptised yt daye.
Philemon Dixon and Jenett Bouton maried the vijth day Tuesdaye.
John son of John Houldsworthe baptised yo xijth daye.
Roger Pickerde and Rosamond Forrest maried the xixth daye Sonday sennight before Andrewe daye.
Samuell son of Marduke Longelay baptised yt day

December.

Robte son of Samuell Mitchell baptised yo third day Sonday after St. Andrewe daye.
A yonge daughter of John Dixon not baptised buried the ixth day Satterdaye.
John son of Willme Knowles Ju. buried yo tenthe day.
Elizabethe daughter of Willme Speight baptised yt daye.
Philemon son of James Speight Ju. baptised yo xvijth day Sonday before St. Thomas day.
Marye daughter of John Shepperde baptised yt day Sonday before St. Thomas day.
Nicholas Seeker an ould man was buried the xxvijth day Wednesday in Christenmas Holy dayes and St. John day.

1615.

Marye wyfe of John Mannsfeld buried the tenthe daye Satterday before New Years daye.
Agnes daughter of Edwarde Pickerd baptised ye last day Sonday and New years even.

Januarye 1615.

Robert Mannsfelde and Mary Bradforthe wyfe of John Bradforthe deceased maryed the ixth day Tuesday after twelfe daye.
Philemon sonn of James Speight Ju. buried yt day in the after noone.
Alexander Barbar buried ye xiiijth daye beinge Sonday after ye Epiphanye the seconde day after Hilary day.
Rycharde sonn of Philemon Dixon baptised yt day.
Susan daughter of Richard Hemyngway baptised yt day.
Deboray daughter of Marmaduke Ellis baptised yt daye.
Christopher son of John Tyas baptised ye xxjth day.
Robert son of Roble Brearay buried ye xxijth day and Monday in ye after noone.
Thomas son of Edward Phillippe baptised ye xxvjth day.
Robte son of Edwarde Phillippe baptised ye same day beinge Fridaye.
Elizabeth Seckar was buried ye xxvijth day Satterday before Candlemas day.

Februarye 1615.

Christopher Fox buried the third day being the day after Candlemas day and Satterday.
Thomas Hepworthe of Horberye and Ciceli Bentlay of this parishe maried here ye vjth day Tuesday after Candlemas day.
John sonn of Edwarde Fayerbarne Ju. baptised ye xjth daye being Shrove Sondaye.
Richard sonn of Josephe Walker baptised that day at eveninge prayer.
Samuell sonn of Nicholas Mitchell baptised xiijth daye, and Shrove Tuesdaye.
Ursula daughter of Robert Sharphowse baptised ye xviijth first Sonday in Lent.
Thomas Cloughe of Hallifax was buried here the xxjthe day Wednsdaye.
Mathew sonn of George Boemar baptised ye xxiiijth daye beinge Satterday and in ye after noone.
Willme Saxtonn was buried the xxvth daye being St. Mathias daye in the after noone.
John sonn of Rychard Fayerbarne buried ye xxixth daye.
George son of Rychard Marshall baptised ye same day.
Ellen daughter of Rychard Marshall baptised yt day.

Marche 1615.

George son of Willme Lee of Batlaye Carre baptised ye third daye third Son. of Lent.
Clemett Sheplaye of Clyftonn dyinge at Ossett was buried here at Dewsburie ye tenthe daye.
Elizabethe daughter of Henrye Ellis baptised ye xiijth day Wednsdaye anno Dni 1615.

1615.

Edward sonn of Xpofer Kirke baptised ye xvijth day on Care Sundaye.
Lawrance sonn of Edward Barnard baptised yt day.
Sybell Hey widowe was buried ye xixth daye.
A yonge sonn of Robte Tompson not baptised buried the xxjth daye Thursday in ye after noone.
Thomas sonn of Thomas Allan baptised ye xxiiijth daye Palme Sonday in ye after noone.
Ann Brooke widowe buried ye xxixth day Good Frydaye.
Phillippe son of Phillipe Slade buried ye xxxjth daye being Easter daye 1616 in ye morninge.
Robert son of Willme Roydes baptised yt day at eveninge prayer Easter day 1616.

April 1616.

Dorithie wyfe of Edwarde Fayerbarne dyinge at Medlaye was buried here ye first daye Monday in Easter weeke 1616.
Uxor Claytonn wydowe buried ye iiijth daye Thursday.
Robert sonn of Nicholas Gunsonn baptised ye vijth daye Low Sondaye or first Sondaye after Easter day.
Mercye daughter of John Owlroyd buried ye vthe daye.
Marye daughter of Samuell Dobsonn baptised the xiiijth daye.
Marke sonn of Thomas Robinsonn baptised the xxvijth daye Sonday before May day.
Sara daughter of John Walker of Ossett collier baptised the same day.
Ann daughter of Rychard Bull baptised ye same daye at eveninge prayer.

Maye.

Ann daughter of John Lee of Gawthorpe collier buried ye second daye Thursdaye.
Rycharde son of Edwarde Awtye baptised ye thirde day Frydaye and St. Ellen daye 1616.
Richard sonn of Edward Awtye buried ye vth day Sonday.
John sonn of John Goodall baptised that daye Sondaye.
Susann daughter of Rycharde Brigge buried ye vjth daye being Monday before ye Ascention day.
Willme sonn of Robert Lee baptised the ixth daye Ascention day or Holye Thursdaye.
Willme Broadheade an oulde man buried yt daye.
Rebecca daughter of Willme Fell baptised ye xijth day Sonday after Ascention daye or Holy Thursday.
Rychard son of Willme Leadbeater baptised yt daye.
Eliz. daughter of Thomas Rodlaye Ju. baptised yt daye.
Edwarde Newsome and Mercye Dixon maried the xiiijth daye beinge Tuesday.
Thomas Rodlay yonger beinge slayne at Wakefelde ye xvijth buinge Fryday was buried here at Dewsburie ye xvijth day being Satterday and Whitsunday his even.
Willme son of Robert Brooke of Ossett baptised ye xxjth day Tuestiaye in Whitsonweeke.
A yonge son of George Brooke not baptised buried the xxvthe day Trinityo even Satterday.

1616.

Thomas Grayve yonger and Marye Rychardsonn maried ye xxviijth day Tuesday after Trinityo Sonday.

June.

Elizabethe daughter of John Hurst Ju. under ye hill buried yo third day Mondaye.
John Fayrbarne was buried ye vijthe daye beinge Fryday in ye after noone.
Elizabethe daughter of Robert Saxton baptised the ixth daye: second Sonday after Trinityo Sonday.
Nicholas Hutchinsonn of Earles Heatonn buried ye xijth day: the day after Saynt Barnabye day Wednesday.
Averaye son of John Whitlaye baptised ye xvjth daye Sondaye sennight before Midsmer day.
Thomas son of John Fletcher baptised yt day.
Sibell daughter of John Owldroide of ye More syde baptised that daye at ye eveninge prayer.
Edward Allan and Elizabethe Crofte maried ye xviijth day: Tuesday before Midsmer day.
Jonye wyfe of Adam Wheatlaye buried ye xxth daye Thursdaye before Midsmers daye.
Thomas Gamble and Ann Tyrpen maried ye xxiijth day Sonday and Midsmers even.
Jonye daughter of Rychard Brigge baptised yt daye at eveninge prayer.
Elizabethe daughter of John Cowpar baptised ye xxiiijth day Mondaye and Midsmers daye.
Marye daughter of Willme Acrode baptised last daye vthe Sonday after Trinitye Sondaye at evening and day after Peters daye.

Jacobi regis xiiij^{tn.} July.

Elizabethe daughter of Thomas Rodlay Ju. deceased was buried ye viijth daye Mondaye.
Edwarde sonn of Xpofer Kyrke buried yt day at night.
A yonge daughter of Gregorye Castle buried ye xijth daye beinge Frydaye.
John sonn of James Webster baptised ye xxviijth daye Sondaye after St. James daye.
Dorithye daughter of John Sharpe baptised yt daye.
Willme sonn of Willme Longelay buried ye last daye beinge Wednsdaye.

August.

John sonn of John Grayve yonger baptised ye iiijth day Sonday after Lammas daye.
Rycharde Dawsonn and Ellen Dawsonn maried the vjth daye Tuesdaye after Lammas daye.
Ann daughter of Edmounde Brouke sonn of Edmonde of Hudersfelde parishe and Susan Norcliffe of ye same parishe base borne baptised ye xjth daye borne at ye house of John Bentlaye in Cawthorpe in this parishe.
Jenett daughter of Robte Smithe buried ye xviijth day Sondaye before Bartholomew day.
Willme Rayner and Susann Archer maried ye xxth daye Tuesday before Bartholomew daye.
Thomas Claytonn of Thornhill and Elizabethe Gill of this parishe maried that daye.
Rychard sonn of Thomas Chaster baptised yo xxvth daye Sonday after Bartholomew daye at eveninge prayer.

1616.

Willme Liley of Churche Heaton and Grace Acrode maried here the xxvijth daye Tuesday after Bartholmew daye.

September.

Margrett wyfe of John Cowpas buried ye second daye Tuesday before the later Ladye daye.
Anne daughter of Michaell Wheatlay baptised the vth daye and Thursdaye: exercyse* first yt daye.
Agnes daughter of Henrye Bull buried the xviijth day Wednesday before St. Mathew day.
John sonn of Nicholas Walkar buried ye xxijth day Sonday and day after St. Mathew day.
Rychard Wilson and Elizabethe Wilson maried the xxijthe daye and Sonday.
John sonn of Thomas Boothe baptised ye xxijth daye Sonday: and day after St. Mathew day.
Issabell daughter of Willme Fell buried ye xxvth daye beinge Wednsdaye.
John sonn of Thomas Boothe buried ye xxvjth day: Thursday before Michellmas day.
Michaell son of James Broadlay baptised ye xxixth day and Michelmas day.
Jennett wyfe of Rychard Sonnyare dyinge on ye xxixth day being Michaellmas day was buried yo xxxth daye being Mondaye: day after Michellmas day.

October.

John Netletonn of Thorpe of ye hill in Rothewell parishe and Jennett Pighells of this parishe maried here bye a licence on Tuesday the viijth daye.
Rychard Marshall of Chidsell was buried ye ixth day beinge Wednsdaye.
Rycharde Hurst and Eliz. Lee maried ye xvijth day: being Thursday and St. Luke his even: in ye after none.
A yonge sonn of Edwarde Hurst not baptised buried the xxvth daye being Fryday before Symon day and Jude.
Elizabethe daughter of John Robinsen baptised ye xxvijth day Sonday and Symon day and Jude his even.

November.

Elizabethe daughter of Thomas Nayler baptised ye xxiiijth day.
A yonge sonn of Rychard Fell not baptised buried ye xxiiijth daye Frydaye in ye afternoone.

---

* Exercises were assemblies of the clergy held by leave of their bishop, for the interpretation of texts of Scripture, "one speaking to it orderly after another;" these were called prophesyings from the apostolical direction. I. Cor. xiv. 31,—"Ye may all prophesy one by one that all may learn and all be comforted." Neal's History of the Puritans, Vol. I., c. 5,—These exercises were held early in Queen Elizabeth's reign, but the Queen did not approve of them, and in May, 1577, she issued letters to all the bishops commanding them peremptorily to put the exercises down. Archbishop Grindal ventured to remonstrate with her imperious Majesty, who was so enraged that she ordered him to be confined to his house and sequestered him from his archiepiscopal functions for six months. The exercises were again held after the death of Elizabeth. Archbishop Grindal's letter to the Queen in defence of prophecies is printed in Fuller's Church History, Book ix. sec. 4.

1616.

Rychard Beatson and Marye Hollinbridge maryed yo xxiiijth day: Sonday before St. Andrew daye.
John son of John Hurst baptised ye last daye beinge St. Andrew day at eveninge prayer.
Robert son of John Hurst baptised that tyme at eveninge prayer.

December.

John son of John Wilbye baptised tho first daye at eveninge prayer.
Robert son of John Hurst buried the second daye Tuesdaye.
John son of John Hurst buried ye third day Wednsdaye.
Sara daughter of John Fayerbarne baptised the vijth daye.
Sara daughter of Willme Musgrave baptised yt day.
Ann daughter of George Towlsonn baptised yo xvth day Sonday before St. Thomas day at eveninge prayer.
Marye daughter of Thomas Netletoun baptised the xxijth day Sonday before Christenmas daye 1616; this was Thomas Netleton of the Towne of Dewsburie.
John son of John Wilbye buried ye xxiijth daye Monday before Christenmas daye.
Abraham son of Abraham Grenewoode baptised the xxvjth daye St. Stephen daye Thursdaye.
John sonn of Robte Mawe baptised yt daye.
Marye daughter of Robert Smithe baptised yt day and Mondaye in the morninge.

Januarye 1616.

Elizabethe daughter of John Saxtone baptised tho vth daye being ye twelfe night.
Philippe sonu of Robert Wilbye baptised yt day at eveninge prayer and Sondaye.
Elizabethe Walker wyfe of Nicholas Walker deceased buried on Monday and ye twelfe daye or feast of yo Epiphanye.
Jenett daughter of Rycharde Davison baptised ye vjth day being ye Epiphanye, or twelfe day and Monday.
Abraham sonn of Robert Hemyngwaye baptised ye xiijth daye Sonday after ye Epiphanye.
Grace daughter of Rychard Roydes baptised yt day.
Grace wyfe of Thomas Robinson yonger of Earles Heaton buried on Thursdaye yo xvjthe daye.
Elizabethe daughter of John Wade baptised yo xixth day third Sonday after ye Epiphanye or twelfe daye.
Thomas sonn of Rycharde Wilkensonn baptised yo xxijth day and Wednsdaye.
Margrett wyfe of Jefferay Acrode buried yo xxvth day Sancto Paulo day and Satterday.
Issabell daughter of Ambrosso Robinsonn baptised ye xxvjth day, day after St. Paule day and Sonday.
A woman beinge a stranger dyinge at Gawthorpe was buried here on Tuesdaye yo xxviijth daye.

Jacobi regis decimo quarto. Dewsburia.
Februaryo 1616.

Mercye daughter of John Mallinson baptised yo secondo day Candlemas day fourtho Sonday after yo Epiphanyo.

1616.

Marye daughter of Nicholas White baptised yt day at eveninge prayer Candlemas day.
Issabell Owldroido alias Bayly widowe buried yo sixt day and yo first Thursday after Candlemas daye.
Robert Phillippo was buried yo vijth daye beinge Fryday after Candlemas daye.
Uxor Gill of Sowoode Grene wthin Ossett towne buried the viijth daye Saterday.
Grace daughter of John Medlaye baptised ye xvjth day Sonday after Valentyne day Septuagessima Sonday.
John Fox of Wakeffeildo and Susann Mitchell of this parisho maried here yo xviijth daye Tuesdaye.
Edwarde Backehowse buried ye xxth day Thursday Thursday before St. Mathias day.
Thomas son of Thomas Wurnall baptised yo xxiijth day Sonday before St. Mathias day.
Sara daughter of Michaell Bentlay Ju. baptised yt day.
Sara daughter of Josephe Owldroide baptised yt day.

Dewsburie. Marche anno Dni. 1617.

George sonn of Thomas Robinsonn alias Townende baptised yo secondo daye Shrove Sonday.
Martyn Barbar Junior was buried yo viijth day beinge Satterday after Shrove Sonday.
Marye daughter of Edwarde Newsome alias Jackeson baptised ye ixth daye first Sonday in Lent.
John sonn of John Freeletonn baptised yo same day.
Sibell daughter of John Owldroide buried yo xviijth (? xxiijth) daye beinge Tuesdaye before ye Ladye day in Lent.
Willme sonn of James Speight senior baptised tho xxiijth day Sonday before yo Ladye daye.
Rycharde sonn of Edwarde Ellis buried yo xxiiijth daye Monday and ye Ladye even ; or yo Anunciation of Marye.
Xpofer son of John Tyas buried yo xxvjth day yo day after ye Anunciation of yo Virgyn Marye.
Marmaduke Ellis was buried the xxvijth daye Thursday after the Ladyo daye or Anunciation of yo Virgyn Marye.
Willme son of Bryan Phillippe baptised yo xxxth day Sonday after ye Ladye day and fourth Sonday in Lent.
Margerie Leadbenter alias Shepperd buried ye last day and Monday after yo Ladye daye.

Aprill ano Dni. 1617.

Willme Sharphowse buried his wyfe on Tuesdaye then before Care Sonday beinge Tuesdaye.
George son of John Ellis baptised ye vjth daye and Care Sondaye.
Henrie Whitcheade buried his wyfe the same day at eveninge prayer.
Jennet daughter of Rychard Davisonn buried ye xviijth daye good Frydaye in ye after noone.
Edwarde sonn of Edwarde Whitlayo baptised yo xixthe daye Easter even.
Josephe sonn of Robert Phillippo deceased baptised yo xxjth daye Monday in Easter weeke in morninge.
Easter daughter of John Pickerdo baptised then and yt daye Monday in Easter weeke at morninge prayer.

1617.

Alice daughter of Thomas Awtye baptised yo xxijth daye Tuesdaye in Easter Holye dayes in after noone. Elizabethe daughter of John Dixesson baptised yo xxvijth day first Sonday after Easter day Low Sonday.

Maye.

Uxor Exam buried the first daye May day.
Issabell daughter of Robert Cartar baptised ye xjth day third Sondaye after Easter at evening prayer.
Willme Day and Ann Wright maried ye xiijth day Tuesdaye after ye third Sondaye in ye morninge.
Thomas Blagburne buried ye xiiijth daye Wednsdaye.
Ursula wyfe of Robert Sharphowse of Gawthorpe buried ye xviijth daye Sondaye yo fourthe after Easter.
Agnes daughter of Robert Robinsonn of Earles Heaton baptised the xviijth daye fourthe Sonday after Easter.
Parcivall basse sonne of Thomas Sharphowse and Prudens Terrye baptised ye xxth daye Tuesdaye before rogation Sonday or ye crosse week.*
Alice wyfe of John Tyas buried ye xxjth daye Wednsdaye in yo after noone.
Parcevall basse son of Thomas Sharphowse and Prudens Terrye buried ye xxijth daye Thursday before rogation Sondaye.
Thomas Slacke buried ye xxixth day on Holye Thursday at night, hora septa.

June.

Robert Taylier and Elizabethe Ouldroide maried the third day Tuesdaye before Whitsondaye.
Elizabethe Dey buried ye vjth day Fryday before White sonday.
Thomas son of Robert Bradfortho Junior baptised ye eight daye White sondaye in ye fore nooue.
Jane wyfe of John Berrye buried the ixth day Monday in Whitsondaye weeke 1617.
Thomas Acrode of Dewsburie buried ye xvth daye on Trinitye Sondaye.
Willme sonn of James Speight buried ye same day at eveninge prayer.
Robert son of Edwarde Phillippe buried yt day also at eveninge prayer.
Elizabethe daughter of Thomas Grayve yonger baptised the xxijth daye Sonday before Midsmer daye.
Thomas son of Thomas Secker baptised the xxiiijth daye Tuesday and Midsmer daye.
Jenett daughter of Edwarde Fayerbarne baptised yt daye.

*Cross Week, Rogation Week, or Gang Week, so called because on Monday, Tuesday, and Wednesday of that week Rogations and Litanies were used, and the clergy having crosses borne before them and accompanied by their churchwardens, choristers, and others, went in procession round the bounds of their parishes. The boundaries of a parish were in some instances marked at certain points by Gospel Trees, so called from the custom of having the Gospel read under or near them by the clergyman attending the perambulation: and in other instances small crosses cut in stone or wood were used to mark the boundaries. Ultimately the Thursday in Rogation Week, i.e. Holy Thursday or Ascension Day became the more usual day for beating the bounds. The churchwardens' accounts of the parish of Mirfield contain many entries of payments made when beating the bounds, or "rambling" as it was called.

1617.

Thomas Whittakers of Chickenlay dyinge at Ecclesfelde in Bradfortho parishe was buried there xxvjth daye beinge Thursdaye after Midsmer daye.

Jacobi regis decimo quarto. Julye.

John son of John Acrode baptized ye vjth daye.
Issabell wyfe of Robert Maw buried ye same daye beinge Sondaye after Peter's day third Sonday after Trinitye.
Ann daughter of John Earle dying at Ossett was buried here the tenthe daye being Thursdaye.
Mychaell sonn of Rychard Whitlaye of the Carre baptized ye xiijth daye fourthe Sonday after Trinitye
John sonn of Willme Wilbye baptised ye xxth day Sondaye before St. James' daye.
Lawrance Wannesdaye was buried ye xxiijth day Wednsdaye before St. James' daye.
Josepho son of Christopher Kyrke baptised ye xxvijth Sonday after St. James' day.

Jacobi regis 14. August.

Robert Wilbye was buried ye first daye Lamas daye and Frydaye in yt weeke.
John Saxton ye yonger of Sowoode Grene was buried ye second day beinge Satterdaye o day after Lamas daye.
Marye daughter of John Houldsworthe baptised the tenthe day Sonday before ye first Lee fayer day.
Elizabethe basse daughter of Marye Lanscarre and Thomas Mortonn baptised ye xjth daye.
Allexander Secker buried ye xvjth day Satterdaye after ye first Ladye daye.
Elizabethe daughter of Edward Allen baptised ye seaventynthe daye Sonday before Bartholomew day.
Merioll wyfe of Robert Lee of Chidsell buried ye xixth daye Tuesday before Barthelmew daye.
Valentyne Speight and Eliz. Hunter maried by licence the vth of August.
John Mannsfelde was buried the xxjth daye Thursdaye before Barthellmew daye.
Issabell daughter of Rycharde Harrishe buried yo xxijth daye Frydaye before Barthellmew even beinge Satterday.
Edwarde sonn of Percivall Terrye baptised ye last daye Sondaye before the latter Layde day.

September.

Robert Barbar and Elizabethe Richardsonn maried on Tuesdaye ye second daye Tuesday before the later Ladye daye on Lee fayer daye.
A yonge daughter of Rycharde Dishfortho not baptised buried ye eight daye later Ladye daye.
Robert Leadbeater alias Shepperd buried Francis his wife the xiijth daye Sonday before St. Mathew day.
A yonge sonn of John Mannsfelde not baptised buried ye sextene daye and Tuesdaye.
Ann daughter of John Broadlaye baptised ye xxijth daye and St. Mathew daye, tempore vespertino.
Robert Leadbeater alias Shepperd buried ye xxvth daye Thursday after St. Mathew daye.
Sara daughter of Edwarde Midlebroughe baptised that daye.

DEWSBURY PARISH REGISTERS.   93

1617.

Rychard sonn of Robert Stansfeldo baptised ye xxviijth daye and St. Michaell his even at eveninge prayer.
Betheris daughter of James Speight Junior baptised the xxixth day Monday and Michellmas daye.
Michaell son of Willme Dey baptised ye last day ye day after Michaell's day.
Mathew White and Easter Broadlaye maried yt same day beinge Tuesdaye next after St. Michaell's daye.

October.

Debora daughter of Marmaduke Ellis deceased buried the vjth daye Mondaye after Michaell's daye.
Willme Taylier alias Renoulde was buried ye xjth day beinge Saterday at night.
Grace daughter of John Nayler of ye Parke syde baptised ye xijth day Sondaye before St. Luke his daye.
Jennett daughter of Willme Taylier alias Renoulde buried ye same daye in ye after noone.
Ann daughter of John Slacke buried ye xviijth daye St. Luke his day and Satterdaye.
Josua sonn of George Brouke alias Sykes baptised the xixth daye and daye after St. Luke's day.
Ann daughter of Thomas Boothe baptised yt day being Sonday and day after St. Luke his day.
Sara daughter of Edwarde Midlebroughe buried on Monday ye xxth daye.
Samuell son of John Ellis buried ye xxijth day Wednesday after St. Luke his daye.

November.

Averie son of Thomas Netletonn of ye Hoyle Milne baptised ye second day after all Sayntes day and Sonday.
Edwarde son of Edwarde Pickerde baptised yt day.
Dorithye daughter of Nicholas Wheatlay baptised yt day being Sonday and day after All Sayntes day.
Ann wyfe of Willme Rychardson buried ye third daye.
Edwarde Robinsonn of Barnslaye and Ann Hyeke of this parishe maried ye fourthe day and Tuesdaye in ye weeke.
A yonge childe a sonn of Rychard Hurst alias Fox not baptised buried ye vthe day Wednesdaye in ye after noone.
James Speight of Ossett ye elder was buried on Fryday ye xliijth daye Fryday after Martynmas daye.
Michaell son of Willme Sheplay of Bowdroide baptised ye sextene daye Sondaye after Martynmas daye.
Willme son of ye same Willme Sheplay baptised yt day in ye morninge prayer tyme.
John Longclay of Rothewell and Beatrice Harrison of this parishe were maried here the xviijth daye Tuesdaye.
Dorithye wyfe of Robert Dey buried the xxiij and yt day in the afternoone and Sonday before St. Andrew daye.
Agnes daughter of Rychard Castle baptised that daye at eveninge prayer.
Brigett daughter of Roger Hurst baptised ye xxvjth daye Wednesday before St. Andrew day.

1617.

Jennett daughter of Roger Hurst also baptised that daye Wednesday before St. Andrew daye.
Thomas Kitsonn buried his wyfe the xxviijth day and Frydaye before St. Andrewe daye.
Robert Smithe of Ossett was buried ye xxixth daye beinge St. Andrewe his even and Satterdaye.

December.

A yonge daughter of Francis Slacke not baptised buried on Monday ye first day and day after St. Andrewe daye.
Lidia daughter of ye same Francis Slacke baptised that same daye, day after St. Andrewe day Mondaye.
Thomas sonn of Willme Taylier alias Renoulde was buried the second day Tuesday after Andrew daye.
Willme Knowles was buried ye fourthe daye Thursday.
Marye daughter of George Mawde baptised on Satterdaye ye vjth daye at night.
A yonge daughter of Averie Pickerde not baptised was buried that tyme of yt daye at night.
John Westerman was buried ye vijth daye Sonday after Andrewe daye tempore matutino.
A yonge sonn of Willme Williamsonn not baptised buried the tenthe day Wednesday before St. Lucey day.
Thomas sonn of Edwarde Ellis baptised ye xiiijth daye Sondaye on daye after St. Lucye day at night.
Elizabethe daughter of Robte Barbar yt day at night or at eveninge prayer was baptised.
Jennett daughter of Roger Hurst buried ye xvijth daye Wednesdaye before St. Thomas daye.
Grace daughter of John Steade of Ossett in ye streete baptised ye xxjth daye Sonday and St. Thomas day.
Ellen daughter of Rycharde Dawson baptised the xxviijth day and Innocent's day and Sonday before Newe Year's daye or Circumcision of Christ.
Elizabethe wyfe of Thomas Forrest deceased wydowe was buried ye xxixth day Tuesdaye before Newe Year's day or Circumcision of Christ.

Jacobi regis decimo quinto. Januaryo 1617.

Ellen daughter of Rychard Dawsonn buried on Monday ye vthe day and ye twelfe even or even of ye Epiphanye.
George Allan of Heatonn was buried on Frydaye the ixth daye Fryday after ye Epiphanye or twelfe day.
Willme Richardson and Marye Walker maryed the xjth daye Sonday after ye twelfe day in ye morninge.
Henrie Ellis was buried ye xiijth daye Wednesday.
Robert Robinsonn of Nedder Bowdroide buried his wyfe on Wednesday ye xxjthe daye whose name was Elizabethe Robinsonn.
Martha daughter of Edwarde Croslay baptised the xxvth day St. Paule day.
Willme sonn of Willme Jacksonn baptised that same day at eveninge prayer.
Agnes daughter of Willme Richardson alias Boy baptised that day at eveninge prayer.

1617.

A yonge childe of Roger Dawsonn not baptised buried on Fryday before Candlemas day being the xxixth daye.
Robert Mitchell of Ossett buried his wyfe that day.
Jonye daughter of Rychard Brigge buried ye xxxth day Satterday before Candelmas daye.

Februarye 1617.

Bryan basse son of Gregorye Hudsonn and Agnes Gibson baptised ye first day Candelmas even and Sondaye in the morninge.
Willme sonn of Willme Sheplay buried ye second day Candlemas day and Tuesdaye.
June wyfe of Nicholas Pickeringe buried the same day in the after noone.
Uxor Wholewright wyfe of Gilbert Wholewright of Gawthorpe was buried ye eight day Sunday next after Candlemas daye.
Willme Hall of Thornhill and Elizabethe Denis of this parishe maried here ye ixth day Monday sennight after Candlemas day.
John Croslaye of Almanburie and Elizabethe Socker of this parishe maried ye xth day Tuesdaye.
Edwarde Wilsonn of Myrfelde and Agnes Awtye of this parishe maried here ye same day.
Edwarde Higgyn and Rebecca Wilcocke maried the same daye.
Alexander Newsome alias Jacksonn buried ye tenthe day Tuesday sennight after Candlemas daye.
John sonn of Edwarde Millebrouke buried ye xth day being Tuesdaye before Shrove Sonday.
Nicholas sonn of Nicholas Mitchell baptised the xijth daye and Thursdaye.
Thomas sonn of John Forrest baptised ye xvth day beinge Shrove Sondaye.
Marye daughter of Robert Brearay baptised ye xvijth day on Shrove Tuesdaye.
Marye daughter of Thomas Wilson of Ossett buried that day in ye after noone.
Nicholas sonn of Joseph Walker baptised ye same tyme in the after noone Shrove Tuesdaye.
Alice daughter of Edmound Sonyare baptised ye xxijth day at eveninge prayer first Sonday in Lent 1617.
Robert Ashtonn was buried on Monday in ye after noone beinge ye xxiijth day St. Mathias his even.

Marche anno Dni. 1618.

Ann Wade an oulde woman of Ossett was buried on Fryday the vjth daye.
Robert Mitchell of Ossett was buried ye vijth day Satterday anno Dni. 1618.
John Knowles sonn of Willme Knowles of ye more syde baptised the viijth daye third Sonday in Lent.
Edwarde Kitsonns wyfe of Hanginge Heaton was buried ye xjth day and Wednesdaye anno Dni. 1617.*
Willme Milner an oulde man buried yt daye anno Dni. 1617.*
Jane wyfe of Thomas Wilson buried ye xvijth daye beinge Tuesdaye before Care Sondaye.
Issabell daughter of John Cay beinge drowned ye xvijth day beinge Tuesday was buried ye xviijth day Wednesday at five of the clocke at night.

* So in Register.

1618.

Anthonye basse sonn of Roberte Byrkeheade and Margrett Marshall baptised ye sixth day Thursday before Care Sondaye.
Margrett basse daughter of ye same Robert Byrkehead and Margrett Marshall baptised yt day.
James Webstar of ye street buried ye xxth day Fryday before Care Sondaye.
Martyn Barbar an oulde man buried ye xxvth daye beinge ye Ladye day in Lent and Wednesday before Palme Sondaye eodem anno 1618.
Margrett wyfe of Rycharde Marshall deceased was on Fryday before Palme Sondaye beinge ye xxvijthe daye buried yt day in the after noone.
Thomas Robinsonn of Earles Heatonn the elder was buried ye xxxixthe daye beinge Palme Sondaye.
Uxor Ellis ye eldest was buried ye xxxthe daye on Mondaye after Palme Sondaye at night that daye anno Dni. 1618.

April 1618.

Dorithie daughter of Willme Roydes buried ye fourth day Easter even in ye afternoone, 1618.
Thomas Wilson of Ossett was buried ye vijth day beinge Wednsdaye in Easter weeke anno Dni. 1618.
Sara daughter of John Nayler buried ye xjth day being Satterdaye and low Sonday his even.
Marye daughter of James Broadlaye baptised ye xijth daye beinge Low Sonday.
Robert Greno of ye Hoyle Milne beinge burned to deathe there was buried ye xvth day Wednsdaye after Low Sonday in ye after noone.
Agnes Robinsonn wydowe late wyfe of Thomas Robinson of Earles Heatonn elder deceased buried ye xviijth daye Satterdaye after Lowe Sondaye.
Marye wyfe of Thomas Bradforthe of Ossett was buried ye same daye Satterdaye after Low Sondaye.
Elizabethe wyfe of Edwarde Barbar buried the xxijthe daye Wednsdaye before St. Marke daye and St. George even.
Elizabethe daughter of Willme Fell baptised yt daye beinge Wednesday before St. Marke daye St. George even.
John Willbye was buried ye xxvth daye Satterday and St. Marke daye in the after noone.
Willme Leadbeater alias Shepperde buried his wyfe one Monday ye xxvijth daye Monday after St. Markes daye.

Maye.

Elizabethe daughter of Robert Nayler baptised the third daye beinge St. Ellen daye.
John son of John Wilbye deceased baptised ye vijth being Thursday in the after noone.
Dorithie wyfe of Robte Bradforthe elder buried on Saterday ye ixth day.
Elizabethe daughter of Rycharde Bull baptised ye tenthe day Sonday before Ascention day in ye after noone.
Rychard Sonyare parishe clarke of Dewsbarie dyinge upon Sondaye beinge ye Sondaye after Ascention day and the xvijth daye was buried on Mondaye ye xviijth daye.
Tymothie sonn of Willme Kitsonn baptised ye xxiijth daye beinge Whitesondaye.
Phillippe Slade dyinge on Whitesondaye ye xxiiijth day in ye nighte was buried ye xxxthe daye beinge Monday in Whitesonday weeke.

1618.

Thomas Robinsonn of ye More Syde and Elizabethe Roodes maried yo xxvith day Tuesday in Whitsun weeke.
Uxor Wilbye elder was buried yo xxxth day beinge Satterdaye and Trinitye even.

June.

Uxor Heamount of Ossett was buried yo eight day beinge Mondaye.
Issabell daughter of Edwarde Phillippe baptised the xiiijth daye second Sondaye after Trinitye.
Ann daughter of John Cowpar baptised yo xxixth day beinge St. Peters day at eveninge prayer.

July.

Jennett wyfe of Thomas Chaster buried ye third day beinge Frydaye ye Frydaye after St. Peters day.
John Robinsonn of the Moresyde yo eldest buried yt day beinge Fridaye after St. Peters day.
Elizabethe daughter of Thomas Robinsonn of ye more syde baptised ye vthe day Sunday after Peters day at eveninge prayer.
Anne wyfe of Roger Beatsonn of Ossett was buried ye vijth day beinge Tuesdaye sennight after St. Peters daye.
Thomas Leadbeater alias Shepperde was buried on Satterdaye ye xviijth daye a Seaventhe before St. James daye.
Edwarde More of Ossett was buried yt daye.
Averie sonn of Philemon Dixsonn baptised ye sixth day Sonday before St. James day at evening prayer.
Mychaell Chambers and Isabell Higgyns of this Parishe maried yo xxjth daye Tuesday before St. James daye.

August.

Issabell wyfe of Averie Bull buried on Satterday the first of August on Lamas day.
Grace daughter of Willme Speight of Earles Heaton baptised ye second day after Lamas daye.
Samuell son of Robert Pickerde baptised yt daye.
Thomas Chaster buried ye fourthe day Tuesday after Lammas daye.
Averie Whittakers buried yo viijth day Satterday after Lamas daye.
A yonge sonn of John Fell not baptised buried yt day being Satterday after Lamas daye yt day sennight after Lamas daye.
Alice daughter of John Robinsonn of ye More Syde baptised ye ixth day Sonday before ye first Leo fayer or first Ladye daye.
Anne daughter of John Cowpar buried ye xiiijth daye beinge Fryday and ye first Ladye even.
Willme Kitsonn of Hanginge Heatonn buried ye xxjth day being Fryday before Barthelmew day in after noone.
Margrett wyfe of Marmaduke Ellis deceased was buried ye xxvjjth day Thursday after Barthellmew daye.
Rycharil Awtye of the water lane buried on Satterday after Barthelmew daye xxixth day.

September.

Sara daughter of Edwarde Langffeld baptised ye next daye Sonday before ye later Ladye daye.

1618.

John sonn of Mathew White baptised yt day at eveninge prayer.
Ann daughter of Valentyne Speight baptised ye xiijth day Sondaye after ye later Ladye daye.
Danyell sonn of Gilbert Furthe deceased buried ye xxvijthe daye Sonday before Michelmas daye.
James son of James Webstar deceased baptised yt daye.
Margrett daughter of Rychard Fell baptised yt daye.
Elizabethe daughter of George Towlsonn baptised that daye at eveninge prayer.

October.

Thomas Jewethe of Thornhill and Dorithie Ferndaye of this parishe maried on Tuesday ye xjth daye.
John Rychardsonn alias Boyo buried ye tenthe daye being Satterdaye.
Robert Harrope and Issabell Graysonn maried the eleaventhe daye Sonday before St. Luke daye.
John Mittonn of Wakelffelde and Agnes Ellis of this parishe maried ye xiijth day Tuesdaye before St. Luke daye.
Michaell Bentlay oldest buried ye xxjth daye.
Alice daughter of Robert Rayner baptised on Satterday the xxiiijth daye.
Grace wyfe of the same Robert Rayner was that day buried ye Satterday after St. Luke daye.
Robert Bradforthe elder and Elizabethe Parkinsonn maried at Ossett Chappell on Thursday ye xxxth day the day after Symon and Jude by a lycence.

November.

Willme son of Marmaduke Longelay baptised the first daye beinge All hallowe daye.
Margrett daughter of Edwardo Newsome alias Jakesonn baptised that day at eveninge prayer.
Thomas Collier and Elizabethe Headelay maried on Monday ye day after All hallow day second day.
Willme Broadheade buried that day.
John Battye and Ann Acrode maried on Tuesday after All Hallowe daye the third daye.
John Stayneliffe and Marie Browne bothe of this parishe maried here ye same daye.
Henrie Bowlinge was buried the vijth day Satterday before Martynmas daye.
Elizabethe wyfe of John Awtye buried on Monday the ixth of November Mondaye before Martynmes day.
Henryo Greaves of Leedes parishe and Anne Brooke of Dewsburie maried here the tenthe day beinge Tuesdaye before Martynmas daye bye a licence from mye lorde archebushoppe.
Margrett daughter of Edwarde Newsome alias Jackesonn buried yo xiijth day Fryday after Martynmas daye.
Elizabethe daughter of Rycharde Archer baptised ye xvth day Sonday after Martynmas daye.
Elizabethe daughter of Rycharde Hurst baptised yt daye.
Mereye daughter of John Fletcher baptised yt day being Sonday after Martynmas day.
George Broadheade and Marye Newsome maried the last daye beinge Sancto Andrew daye and Mondaye.

December 1618.

John Smithe and Marye Bentlay maried ye first day and day after St. Andrewe daye.
Willme Acrode of Earles Heatonn and Marye Robinsonn of Chickenlay maried yt daye.
Uxor Awtye of the more syde buried ye firste daye being Tuesdaye.
Agnes wyfe of Rycharde Harrishe buried yt daye at night.
Charles sonn of Symeon Grenewoode of Sothill Hall baptised on Tuesdaye ye eight daye and Tuesdaye after ye second Sondaye of Advent.
Uxor Knowles wyfe of Willme Knowles deceased buried ye nynthe daye being Wednesdaye.
Rychard sonn of Rychard Thornes buried on Thursday before St. Thomas daye ye xvijth daye.
Willme Sharphowse an ould man buriedd ye xxth daye Sonday before Christenmas day St. Thomas his even.
John Wilsonn of Ossett an oulde man buried yt daye.
Marye daughter of Rychard Wilkenson baptised yt daye.
Marye daughter of Richard Wilkenson buried the xxiijth daye; day before Christenmas even being Wednesday Christenmas day on Fryday after.
Dorithye daughter of Thomas Gamble baptised the xxvijth day boinge Saynete Johns day in Christenmas Holye dayes.
Alice daughter of Willme Roydes baptised yt day at eveninge prayer Sonday after Christenmas daye and St. Johns daye in Christenmas weeke.
Thomas sonn of Robert Wheatlaye baptised the xxviijth daye beinge Monday and Inocents daye in Christenmas Holye dayes.

January anno Dni. 1618.

Alice daughter of Henrye Bull baptised ye first daye beinge Sonday and Newe Years daye or ye feast of Circumcision.
Mathewe Holderithe of Chidsell buried on Wednesdaye the sext daye and the feast of ye Epiphanye or twelfe daye.
Alice daughter of Thomas Wurmall baptised ye tenthe daye Sondaye after ye Ephiphanye or twelfe daye.
Sara daughter of John Wade baptised yt daye.
Grace daughter of John Hurst under ye hill baptised ye last daye Sondaye before Candlemas day Sexagesima Sunday at morninge prayer that daye.
Ann daughter of John Howden baptised yt day at eveninge prayer.

Februarye 1618.

John Stapletoun and Grace Smithson maried on Tuesday the second day being Candlemas daye.
Rychard son of Willme Shepperde alias Leadbeater buried that daye.
Elizabethe daughter of Willme Lee of Bowderoide baptised that daye.
Thomas Smithe surgeon and Ann Bynnes were here maried by a licence the seaventhe day beinge Shrove Sondaye.
Marye daughter of Thomas Greave yonger baptised that daye being Shrove Sondaye.

1618.

John Litlewoode an oulde man buried ye ixthe day beinge Tuesday and Shrove Tuesdaye that yeare.
Elizabethe daughter of Rychard Dawsonn baptised ye xjthe daye beinge Thursdaye after Shrove Tuesdaye.
Marye daughter of Uxor Smitho of Ossett buried that daye.
Elizabethe daughter of Rychard Hurst alias Fox buried ye xiijth day Satterday after Ashe Wednsday.
Abraham son of Rychard Hemyngeway baptised that day at nighte.
Marye daughter of Willme Acrode of Earles Heaton baptised ye xiiijth day first Sonday in Lent.
Willme Fell of Ossett buried ye xxjthe daye being second Sonday in Lent Sonday before St. Mathias day in ye after noone.
Sara daughter of John Wade buried ye xxijth daye being Monday before St. Mathias daye.
Alice daughter of John Stapleton baptised ye xxiiijth daye St. Mathias daye and Wednsdaye.

Marche 1618.

Robert Medlaye of Ossett buried on Frydaye then the vthe daye Fryday before mid lent Sondaye.
Peter Harrisonn an oulde man of Ossett was buried on Monday being ye day after Midlent Sonday eight daye.
Margrett wyfe of Averie Acrode buried on Tuesdaye before Palme Sonday sextene daye.
Robert son of John Dickensonn of Ossett baptised the xxth daye and Palme Sonday his even.
Phebe daughter of John Owldroide of Hanginge Heatonn buried ye xxvth day Thursday before Easter daye.
Agnes Naylor widowe wyfe of Henrye Naylor deceased buried on Easter daye ye xxviijth day.
Jennett daughter of Averye Pickerde baptised on Tuesday in Easter Holidays and ye xxxth day.

Aprill 1619.

George Waltonn of Ossett a woode * collier buried ye first daye Thursdaye after Easter day.
Rycharde Naylor elder of the streete buried the second daye being Fridaye after Easter daye.
John sonn of John Whitlay of Ossett baptised the fourthe day being Lowe Sondaye.
Grace daughter of Willme Acrode of Dewsburie towne baptised yt daye at eveninge prayer.
Robert Bradforthe of Osset yougest buried the vjth day Tuesday after Low Sondaye.
Willme son of George Broadheade baptised the xjth day beinge Sondaye after Low Sonday in the after noone that daye.
John Bradlaye dyinge at Edwarde Seekers of Dewsburie was buried on Thursday sennight after Low Sonday xvth day.
Robert sonn of Robert Cartar of Ossett baptised ye xvijthe daye beinge Satterdaye in the after noone.
John Parker yonger and Dionise Crawshaw maried on Tuesdaye ye xxth daye Tuesday before St. Markes day.

* Probably a burner or seller of charcoal.

1619.

Sara daughter of John * Tilsonn of Sothill Hall baptised the xxvijth daye Tuesday after St. Markes daye.

May.

Francis Aglande of Wakeffelde and Martha Innes of this parishe maried there at Wakeffelde ye second daye then beinge daye after Maye daye.
John sonn of Thomas Netletonn of Hanginge Heatonn baptised that daye daye after May daye vth Sonday after Easter.
Margrett daughter of John Greave yonger baptised that daye day after Maye daye vth Sonday after Easter.
John Wade of Ossett buried on Tuesday day after St. Ellens daye in ye after noone the iiijth daye.
John sonn of Edwarde Midlebrouke baptised ye ixth daye Sonday after ye Ascention daye or holye roode daye.
John sonn of Michaell Bentlay yonger baptised the xijth daye Tuesdaye before Whitsondaye.
Marye daughter of Nicholas Gunsonn baptised the xvjth day beinge Whitsonday bye Mr. Sonyare.
John Knowles of this parishe and Elizabethe Denn of Burstall maried there the xviijth day Tuesday in Whitsondaye Holye dayes.
Thomas Awtye of Dewsburie more syde and Jennett Archer maried on Trinitye Sonday the xxiijth daye in the morninge that daye.
Elizabethe daughter of Henrye Fletcher of Hallifax buried on Wednsdaye after Trinitye Sonday ye xxvjth daye.
Ann wyfe of Edwarde Wilkensonn of Ossett buried on Thursday after Trinitye Sondaye ye xxvijth daye.
Michaell basse sonn of Michaell Speight and Martha Rodlay baptised ye same daye Thursday after Trinitye Sondaye.
Willme Eastewoode and Katheryne Smyrthett bothe of this parishe were maried the xxxth day beinge then ye Sonday after Trinitye Sondaye.
Robert sonn of Robert Beckwithe baptised yt day also at morninge prayer.
John son of John Parker yonger baptised yt daye at the eveninge prayer.
John Pickerde of Ossett was buried ye thirtye and one daye beinge Mondaye ye last of Maye.

Jacobi 17. June 1619.

Willme Pasleye of Ossett and Issabell Lee of the same towne and of this parishe bothe maried ye viijth daye beinge Tuesdaye.
Willme Grene of Ossett street syde buried yo ixth daye Wednsdaye.
George sonn of Thomas Allan of Earles Heaton baptised the xiijth daye Sonday after Barnabye daye.
John sonn of Robert Robinsonn alias Mawe buried ye xxvth daye beinge Frydaye and daye after Midsmer daye.
Thomas sonn of Robert Robinson of Earles Heaton baptised the xxvijth day Sonday after Midsmer daye.

* Probably a relative of Bishop Tilson, but I cannot trace the connection.

Julye 1619.

John sonn of John Battye baptised ye fourthe daye at eveninge prayer.
Rycharde Waynwrighte and Marye Milner maried the xxvth daye and St. James daye and ye ixth Sondaye after Trinitye Sondaye.
James sonn of Robert Bradforthe yonger late of Dewsburie parishe deceased borne at Woodchurche was baptised the xxvth day St. James daye.
Joyce daughter of John Sharpe baptised the same day at eveninge prayer.
John sonn of John Tomsonn of Ossett buried on Tuesday after St. James the xxvijth day of this monethe.

August.

Alice daughter of John Houldsworthe baptised ye first day.
Willme son of Robert Jackesonn alias Hunt a piper was buried the xjth daye beinge ye daye before the first Ladye daye her even.
Elizabethe daughter of widowe Fell wyfe of Willme Fell deceased buried ye xijth day Thursday and ye first Ladye even.
Rycharde Fearnlaye and Dorithio Awdslay maried the xvijth daye Tuesdaye sennight before Barthlemew daye.
Agnes wyfe of Nicholas Secker buried yt daye in the after noone beinge Tuesdaye that yeare.
Ellen wyfe of Valentyne Topcliffe was buried beinge Mondayo the xxiijth daye Barthlemew even.
Willme sonn of John Boothe baptised ye xxixth day.
John basse son of Raphe Sarocolo and Susan Forrest baptised that day Sonday after Barthlemew day and that same child was buried the day after.

September.

Alice daughter of Rycharde Roydes baptised ye vth day.
Michaell sonn of Thomas Procter alias Jewett baptised the xijth daye.
Elizabethe daughter of Robert Tounsonn of Ossett was baptised the xixth day Sonday before St. Mathew daye.
Willme sonn of Willme Cassonn baptised the xxjth daye beinge St. Mathewe daye and Tuesdaye that year.
Dorithye daughter of Thomas Procter alias Jewithe baptised the xjth * daye.

October.

Jenett daughter of Rycharde Fernlay baptised ye thirde yeare.
Isabell daughter of Robert Harrope baptised yt day at eveninge prayer.
Agnes daughter of Robert More buried ye sixt daye beinge Wednesdaye.
John Alverey and Elizabeth † maried the xth daie.
Robert sonn of George Gill of Ossett baptised the same daye.
Susane daughter of Robert Hemyngway baptised ye xijth day beinge Tuesdaye being St. Luke dayed.

* So in Register.
† Blank in Register.
‡ St. Luke's day is on the 18th October.

1619.

John Townende alias Robinsonn ye elder was buried ye xviijth daye beinge Mondaye and St. Luke daye.
Sara daughter of Willme Pasley baptised ye xxiiijth day.
Mary Wroe buried yo same daye.
Margret daughter of Michaell Wheatlay baptised yt day.
Jennet daughter of Rychard Casle baptised yt daye.
Willme sonn of Edwarde Newsome baptised yt daye.
Willme Awtye was buried ye xxxth daye being Satterday before All Sayntes daye or day before All Hallowe even.

November.

Alice daughter of Nicholas White baptised on Mondaye beinge the first daye Ann° Dni. 1619.
John Norcliffe of Hallifax and Eden Thorpe of Dewsburie were here lawfullye maried the vjth daye beinge Satterdaye before Martynmas daye bye a lycence.
Josephe son of John Fell baptised ye vijth day Sonday next before Martynmas day.
Elizabethe daughter of Thomas Awtye elder baptised that daye at eveninge prayer.
Ambrosse sonn of Edwarde Ellis baptised that daye.
Josephe sonn of Mychaell Hardye baptised ye xiiijth day Sondaye after Martynmas daye.
Edwarde Stable and Marye Rodlay maried yo xvjth day Tuesday after Martynmas daye.
John sonn of John Speight Baptised that daye.
Adam sonn of Nicholas Wheatlay baptised ye xxjth day Sonday before Advent Sonday.
Israell son of Josephe Owldroide baptised yt daye beinge Sondaye before Advent Sondaye wch was on ye next Sondaye followinge viz. ye xxviijth of this November.
Martyn sonn of Robert Barbar baptised that daye at eveninge prayer.
Willme Lambe of Ossett was buried ye xxiiijthe daye beinge Wednesdaye before Andrewe daye.
Rycharde Fayerbarne of Ossett was buried ye xxvijthe daye beinge Satterday before Andrewe daye Advents eve.
James son of John Cowpar baptised ye xxviijth day being Advent Sonday in ye after noone at eveninge prayer.

December.

Thomas Milner alias Shepperd and Ellen Gunsome were maried ye second day Thursday after Andrew day in ye after noone second day after the goinge out of mariage.*
Grace daughter of Willme Lee yonger baptised the xijth day second Sondaye of Advent.
Susan daughter of Thomas Netletonn of ye hoyle Milne baptised ye xixth day Sonday before St. Thomas day.

* See note of the "tymes of mariage prohibited" at the commencement of this volume (2nd) of the Register, after the list of Churchwardens.

1619.

Willme sonn of Willme Musgrayve baptised yt day at eveninge prayer.
Edwarde Wilkensonn of Ossett buried ye xxvth daye beinge Satterday and Christenmas day this year.

Januarie an° Dni. 1619.

Ann daughter of Thomas Milner alias Shepperd baptised ye sixt daye twelfe day and Thursdaye.
Agnes Speight wyfe of Robert Speight elder deceased was buried ye ixth daye Sonday after the twelfe daye.
Robert Boothe of ye Hayebecke within this parishe his wyfe was buried that daye in ye after noone and first Sonday after ye Epiphanye or twelfe daye.
Roger sonn of Edwarde Pickerde baptised the xvjthe daye third Sonday after the twelfe daye.
Edwarde Denyse and Frithewyde Wilbye maried the xxth daye beinge Thursdaye this yeare.
Bryan Healde and Agnes Owldroyd maried the xxiijth daye Sonday sennight before the purification or candlemas daye.
Josephe son of Mychaell Hardye buried yt daye at eveninge prayer.
Thomas sonn of Uxor Phillippe buried the xxvjth daye Wednesdaye this yeare.
Willme sonn of Thomas Boothe baptised the last daye Sunday before Candlemas daye.

Februarye 1619.

Josephe son of Willme Gill oldest buried ye sext daye Sonday after Candlemas daye.
Robert Tomsonn of this parishe and Alice Robinson of this parishe also maried on the Tuesday sennight after Candlemas day being ye viijth day.
Susan Whitakers daughter of Thomas Whitakers yonger deceased buried ye vijth daye Monday.
Holeana sonn of Nicholas Mitchell baptised ye xvthe daye beinge Tuesdaye.
Elizabethe daughter of John Croslande baptised the xxth daye Sonday before St. Mathias daye.
John sonn of Thomas Robinsonn of ye water rate baptised that day at eveninge prayer.
Elizabethe basse daughter of Jacobe Wood and Elizabethe Ashtone baptised ye xxiijth daye Thursday before Shrove Sonday.
Agnes daughter of John Robinsonn of Ossett baptized ye xxvjthe daye Shrove Sondaye.
A yonge daughter of John Dixeson not baptised buried ye xxviijth day beinge Shrove Mondaye.
Averie Truelove and Grace Bradforthe maried the last daye beinge Shrove Tuesdaye.

March an° Dni, 1620.

Elizabethe daughter of John Crosland buried the fourthe daye Saterday in ye after noone.
Dorithie daughter of Willme Dey baptised the vth day first sonday in Lent.
Elizabethe daughter of John Ellis of Ossett baptised ye xijth daye second Sonday in Lent.
A yonge daughter of Gregorye Castle not baptised buried the xxth day Mondaye before the Annunciation of Marye or Ladye day in Lent.
Willme Lea an oulde man of Gawthorpe was buried ye xxiiijth Fryday and ye Lady even.

1620.

Alice wyfe of George Gill of Osset was buried ye xxvjth daye fourthe Sonday in Lent and day after ye Ladye daye.
Thomas son of Thomas Awdslay of Ossett yonger baptised the xxixth day being Wednsday before Care Sondaye and Wednsday after ye Ladye daye in Lent.

Aprill.

Alice daughter of Thomas Wurmall buried the vijth daye Fryday before Palme Sondayo in the after noone.
Willme Lawscarre of Chickenlay an oulde man buried the eight daye Satterday Palme Sonday even.
Margrett daughter of Rychard Fell, buried ye xvth daye being Easter even in ye after noone.
Easter daughter of Edmonde Sonyare baptised ye xvijthe daye Mondaye in Easter weeke.
Mary wyfe of Roger Hurst buried ye xxijth day beinge Satterdaye and Lowe Sonday even at night.
Marmaduke Iles an oulde man dyinge at Xpofer Broukes of Ossett yonger buried ye xxviijth day Frydaye after St. Markes daye.
Margrett daughter of John Knowles baptised ye last daye second Sondaye after Easter.

Maye.

A yonge childe of George Mawde not baptised buried ye fourthe daye ye Seane (Synod) day at Yorke.
Rychard Hall and Elizabethe Fox maryed ye xiiijth daye.
Robert sonn of Averye Truelove baptised yt daye.
John senn of Thomas Awtye of the More syde baptised yt day.
A yonge daughter of John Medlay not baptised buried the xvjth day in ye after noone at nighte.
George Bentonm of Wakeffelde and Jennet Westerman of this parishe maried here ye xvijth day beinge Wednsdaye sennight before Ascension day.
James Willans and Jennett Healde maried the xxjth daye Sondaye before Ascention daye or Rogation Sondaye.
Rycharde son of Rycharde Whitlaye of ye Carre baptised that daye.
A yonge daughter of Thomas Robinsonn of Ossett not baptised buried the xxijth day Mondaye in ye Rogation weeke.
Edwarde sonn of Edwarde Allan baptised the xxviijth daye Sonday after ye Ascention daye or holye Thursday.
Thomas Sharphowse and Prudence Terrye maried the last daye beinge Wednsdayo before Whitsondaye.

Jacobi regis decimo octavo. June.

Elizabethe Bull wyfo of Lawrance Bull older deceased was buried the second daye beinge Frydaye before Whitsondaye that yeare.
Robert sonn of George Gill of Ossett buried ye third daye being Satterday and Whitsonday oven in the after noone.
Thomas Woode and Elizabeth Taylor maried ye vth day beinge Monday in Whitsondaye weeke.
Silvester son of Silvester Ilbishye baptised the vjtho daye Tuesdaye in Whitsonday weeke.

1620.

A yonge sonn of Thomas Sharphowse not baptised buried the xthe of June beinge Trinitye oven and in the after noone that daye.
Nicholas sonn of Robert Nayler baptised the xjtho daye being Trinitye Sonday and St. Barnabye day in the after-noone that daye.
A yonge daughter of John Kighlaye not baptised buried the xviijth daye Sondaye after Trinitye Sonday at eveninge prayer that daye.
John Northe and Agnes Robinsonn maried ye xxvjth daye beinge Mondaye after Midsmers daye.

Julye.

John sonn of John Awdslay baptised the iiijth daye beinge Tuesdayo after Peters daye.
Rychard Ashtonn was buried ye tilt daye being Wednsdaye after Peters daye.
John Holde dying at John Naylers of Ossett wthin this parishe was buried the vth day Wednsday after Peters day.
Thomas son of Thomas Wurmall buried the sext daye beinge Thursdaye after Peters daye.
Willme Dey was buried yo xxvtho beinge St. James daye and Tuesdaye.
Easter daughter of Edmonde Sonyare buried ye xxvjth daye day after St. James daye and Wednsday in that weeke.
Rycharde Wright alias Greave and Margrett his wyfe bothe buried then together the xxixth daye being Satterday after St. James daye.
Willme sonn of Edwarde Barbar buried the xxxtie beinge Sondaye after St. James daye.
James son of Rycharde Bull baptised the xxxtie day beinge Sonday after St. James daye in ye after noone.
Robert Fayrbarne of Ossett buried ye xxxjth daye Mondaye after St. James daye.

August.

Rychard Pollard and Issaboll Milner maried ye xiijth daye being Sondaye before ye first Ladye daye.
Alice daughter of Nicholas White buried ye xviijth daye being Frydaye before St. Bartholomew daye.
Robert sonn of John Denysonn baptised ye xxth day Sondaye before Bartholomews daye.
Marye daughter of Rycharde Waynewright baptised yt daye.
Uxor Kent of ye Daw Grene buried on Tuesdaye ye xxijth daye daye before Bartholomew his even.
Peter Thornton of Hallifax and Anne Franckland of this parishe were maried ye same daye being Tuesdaye before Bartholomew daye.

September.

Robert Leaver of Boultonn in ye mores in Lankeshire and Frauncis Daulton of this parishe were maried ye fourthe daye beinge Mondaye before ye first Laday daye or Lee fayer.
Thomas Marshall of Ledsham and Marye Clayton of this parishe maried ye tenthe daye Sondaye after ye first Lee fayer.

1620.

Mawde wyfe of Francis Whitlay buried ye *xvjth daye of September beinge Saterday before St. Mathew day.
A yonge daughter of Thomas Nayler of Ossett not baptised buried the *xvthe daye in ye after noone.
Willmo sonn of George Toulsonn baptised ye xvijth day and Sonday before St. Mathewe daye.
Elizabethe daughter of Robert Stansfelde baptised the same daye at eveninge prayer.
Elizabethe daughter of John Stapletonn baptised ye xxiiijth daye being Sondaye after St. Mathewe daye.
Roger Hurst and Jennett Wayde maried yt daye.
Thomas Boothe was buried ye xxvjth daye being Tuesday before Michellmas daye.

October.

Josua son of Robert Brearaye baptised ye first daye being Sonday after Michellmas daye.
Elizabethe wyfe of Rycharde Wilsonn buried ye thirde daye Tuesdaye after Michellmas daye.
George Bynnes and Marye Hurst maried here yt daye Tuesdaye after Mychellmas daye.
Rycharde Wilsonn of Dewsburie Milner buried on Fryday the vjth daye and Fryday sennight after Michellmas daye.
Roger Metcalfe and Ellen Wynterburne bothe of Leedes parishe maried here ye vth daye beinge Thursdaye after Michellmas daye after noone bye a lycence directed accordinglye.
John Bould and Jouye Smitheson maried ye xxixth daye.
Marye daughter of James Speight baptised the viijth daye.
Walter son of Bryan Healde baptised ye xxixth daye being Sondaye before all Sayntes daye at eveninge prayer.
Willmo son of Rycharde Fearnlaye baptised yt day at morninge prayer.
Josua sonn of John Frecleton baptised yt day also at morninge prayer.
Willmo Rychardson buried the xxxth day being Monday before all Saynetes daye.

November.

John son of Willmo Rychardson alias Boy baptised the vth daye Sondaye after all Saynetes daye and ye Kynges Holye daye of Gonne Powder Treasonn.
Uxor Ridlesdenn of Hanginge Heatonn buried ye vjth daye beinge Mondaye after all Saynetes daye.
Dorithye wyfe of Henrye Nowell buried ye xijth daye.
Elizabethe daughter of George Boomar baptised yt day.
Jenet daughter of ye same George Boomar baptised the same daye at eveninge prayer.
Rychard Spurre and Issabell Webstar maried the xiijth daye being Mondaye.
Elizabethe daughter of Thomas Nayler buried that daye.
Grace daughter of Edward Denise baptised ye xxviijth daye Tuesday before St. Andrewe daye.

December 1620.

Alice wyfe of Christopher Dixon buried ye first daye and ye next daye after Andrewe daye and Frydaye.
John Malinson buried ye third daye and Sondaye after Andrewe daye.
Susan daughter of Philemon Dixon baptised that daye at eveninge prayer.
James son of Rycharde Bull buried the ixth day beinge Satterdaye.
Henrie son of John Mallinson baptised ye tenthe daye.
Dorithie daughter of Thomas Jowithe baptised yt daye.
Thomas Barbar yonger buried ye xjth daye.
John Townend and Jenet Speight maried yt daye.
John Berrye buried ye xiiijth daye daye after St. Lucye daye.
Uxor Jepsonn dyinge the xxiiijth daye being the Christenmas even was buried ye xxvth daye being Mondaye and Christenmas daye.
Robert Beckwithe was buried that daye beinge Mondaye and Christenmas daye.
Grace daughter of John Hurst under ye Hill buried ye xxvjth daye St. Stephens daye and Tuesdaye.

Januarye.

Rychard sonn of Valentyne Speight baptised the first daye being Mondaye.
Brygett daughter of Roger Hurst buried the viijth daye Mondaye and ye plowe * daye or the daye after ye first Sondaye after ye twelfe daye.
A yonge daughter of John Acrode not baptised buried the xijth daye and Frydaye in ye after noone.
Thomas sonn of Thomas Grayve yonger baptised the xiiijth daye.
Uxor Rayner alias Ramsden buried yt daye in the after noone.
Josua sonn of Robert Pickerde baptised the xviijthe daye beinge Thursdaye.
Alexander sonn of Willme Newsome alias Jacksonn baptised ye xxjth daye third Sonday after twelfe daye.
Issabell daughter of Parsevall Terrye baptised ye xxviijth daye Sondaye before ye purification or Candlemas daye.
Francis Gill and Ann Pickerd maried the last daye being Wednsdaye and daye before the Candlemas even.

Februarye 1620.

Thomas sonn of Rychard Dishforthe baptised ye fourthe daye Sondaye after Candlemas daye.
Robert son of Rychard Hall baptised yt daye.
Ann daughter of Willmo Acrode of Earles Heaton baptised that daye.
Issabell daughter of John Tomson of Ossett baptised yt daye.
Robert Robinson and Agne Shepperd alias Leadbeater maried ye sixt daye Tuesdaye before Shrove Sondaye.
Xpofer sonn of Xpofer Saxtonn of Ossett baptised the xjth daye beinge Shrofte Sunday.

---

* So in Register.

* See Brand's Popular Antiquities:—Notes on "Fool Plough and the Sword Dance."

1620.
Francis Slacke sonn of Francis Slacke baptised the same daie.
William sonn of Thomas Audsley elder baptised the same daie.
Sara daughter of Francis Gill baptised the xiijth daye Shrove Tuesdaye.
John sonn of John Kaye baptised the xixth daye Mondaye before St. Mathias daye.
Henrye Hepworthe buried his wyfe the xxvth daye Sondaye after St. Mathias daye and the second Sondaye in Lent.
Elizabethe daughter of Josephe Walker baptised that daye at eveninge prayer.

Marche 1621.
Willme son of Thomas Awdslaye elder buried the third daye beinge Satterdaye after St. Mathias daye.
Robert sonn of John Parkar yonger baptised the fourthe daye beinge Sondaye the thirde in Lent.
Samuell Tattarsall buried the xthe daye beinge Saterdaye after St. Mathias daye.
A yonge sonn of Tho. Robinson of Ossett not baptised buried the tenth daie beinge Satterdaie in the after noone.
Edmonde son of Michaell Hardye baptised the xjth daye fourthe Sonday in Lent or midlent * Sondaye in ye after noone.
Willme son of Willme Knowles baptised the xviijth daye beinge Care * Sondaye.
Robert son of Thomas Gamble baptised yt daye beinge Care * Sondaye or Sondaye before Palme Sondaye.
Philemon Speight of Earles Heatonn buried the xixth daye beinge Mondaye after Care Sondaye.
Joann son of Robert Brearaye buried the xxiiijthe daye beinge Palme Sondaye his even.
John Crosfelde was buried the xxvthe daye beinge Palme Sondaye or the Ladye daye in Lent.
Willme son of Robert Tomsonn baptised the same daye in the after noone being Palme Sondaye.
Thomas son of Willme Roydes baptised the xxviijth daye Wednsdaye before Easter daye.
Anne daughter of Rychard Beatsonn baptised that daye beinge Wednsdaye in the Passion weeke or Wednsdaye before Easter daye.
Alice daughter of Willme Speight elder baptised the xxixth daye being Shear Thursdaye. †

Aprill 1621.
Ann daughter of Rychard Beatson buried the first daye being Easter daye in ye after noone.
Ester daughter of Mathewe White baptised the third daye Tuesdaye in Easter weeke.
Josephe son of Roger Hurst baptised ye eight daye beinge Low Sondaye.
Alice wyfe of Edwarde Midlebroughe buried the ixth daye beinge Mondaye after Low Sonday.
A yonge sonn that she was delivered of at that tyme beinge not baptised was buried then withe her.

---
* Inadvertently in the note to the entry for the 18th March, 1562, Midlent Sunday and Care or Carling Sunday have been treated as synonymous. The note should be cancelled.

† Otherwise Maundy Thursday.

1621.
A yonge son of Edwarde Walker not baptised was buried the xijth daye beinge Mondaye.
John son of Thomas Peace baptised the xvthe daye beinge ye second Sondaye after Easter.
Dorithie daughter of Gregorye Castle baptised the same daye.
Marie wyfe of Marmaduke Longelay and a yonge son yt she was delivered of not baptised buried the xxth daye being Frydaye in ye after noone.
Gregorye Castle of Ossett buried his wyfe on Wednsdaye the xixthe daye.
Marye daughter of Rycharde Hutchinson baptised ye xxijth daye and ye third Sonday after Easter.
Marye daughter of John Fletcher baptised that daye or ye Sondaye before St. Markes daye.
Richard sonne of Thomas Smyth Surgion of this Towne baptised the xxixth daie beinge the Sundaie before Maye daie.

Maye.
Rycharde Woode of Hallifax being drowned in Calder the vth daye being Satterdaye was buried on Monday the vijth daye beinge Monday before Ascention daye or Holye Thursdaye.
Willme Speight of Earles Heaton Ju. and Agnes Jepsonn of Dewsburie maried the viijth day Tuesdaye after Ascention daye.
Thomas sonn of Rycharde Archer baptised ye xiijth daye beinge Sondaye after Ascention daye or Holye Thursdaye.
Josephe basse son of Rycharde Thorpe alias Smithe and Alice Saxton baptised that daye being the xiijth daye or Holye Thursdaye.
John son of Thomas Peace buried the xvjth daye Wednsdaye before Whitsondaye.
John son of Edwarde Barnerdo alias Robucke baptised ye xxjtie daye being Mondaye in Whitson weeke.
Willme Cawthorne and Jonye Fayerbarne marryed that daye.
Henrie Darwyn and Elizabethe Ouldroide maried that daye.
Robert Owldroide and Rachell Whitakers maryed the xxijth daye Tuesdaye in Whitsondaye Holydayes or Whitsonday weeke.
Abraham sonn of James Broadlaye baptised ye same daye in the after noone being Tuesdaye in Whitson weeke or holye dayes.
John sonn of Richard Spurre baptised ye xxvijth daye beinge Trinitye Sondaye in ye fore noone.
Alice daughter of John Boulde baptised ye same daye at the eveninge prayer beinge Trinitye Sondaye.
George sonn of Thomas Allan buried the xxxjth daye beinge the last daye and Thursdaye after Trinitye Sondaye.

June.
Alice daughter of Thomas Woode baptised ye third daye first Sondaye after Trinitye Sondaye.
Rycharde son of Thomas Smithe Surgeon buried ye ixth daye beinge Satterdaye before Barnabye daye.
Robert sonn of Thomas Marshall baptised ye tenthe daye Sondaye before St. Barnabye daye.

1621.

Susan daughter of Thomas Allan baptised that daye at morninge prayer.
Rycharde Hutchinson buried his wyfe the xjth daye beinge St. Barnabe daye and Mondaye.
Rycharde Smithe alias Thorpe and Alice Saxtone maried ye xijth daye beinge St. Barnabye daye and Tuesdaye yt weeke.
Roger More of Rothewell and Elizabethe Mitchell of this parishe maried ye xvijth daye Sondaye before Midsmer daye.
Gilbert Son of John Houldsworthe baptised that daye.
John Horsfortho of Huddersfelde and Margrett Brigges of this p̕she maried ye xxth daye Wednsday before Midsmer daye.

Julye.

Tempest sonn of Robert Wheatlaye baptised ye first day fitt Sondaye after Trinitye Sondaye.
Ann wyfe of Howlande Burnett buried ye second daye.
Dorithie daughter of Gregorie Castle buried yt day.
John son of Nicholas White baptised yt daye beinge Mondaye in ye after noone.
John sonn of Rychard Dawsonn baptised ye iiijth daye beinge Wednsdaye.
Averye Tomlinson and Ann Acrode maried ye eight daye.
Agnes Wilsonn of ye Spynkewell widowe buried ye tenthe daye beinge Tuesdaye.
Ann daughter of Henrie Dunhill baptised ye xvth daye ye seaventhe Sondaye after Trinityo St. Swithun his daye.
John sonn of John Goodall buried on Wednsdaye the xviijth daye and Wedusday before Magdalen her daye.
Elizabetho daughter of John Northe baptised ye xxijthe daye being Marye Magedolene daye and Sondaye before St. James day.
A yonge sonn of John Dixon not baptised was buried ye xxvjth daye Thursdaye and ye daye after St. James daye at night yt day.
Grace daughter of Robte Tomson baptised the xxixth daye beinge Sondaye after St. James daye.
John Arrowsmithe of Woodchurche and Jane Lewes of this parishe maried here by a Lycence on Tuesdaye ye last daye of Julie and daye before Lammas daye.

August.

Thomas sonn of John Horsforthe baptised ye first daye being Wednsdaye and Lammas day in ye after noone.
George sonn of ye same John Horsforthe baptised yt daye.
Carye Morris and Jonye Boothe bothe of this parishe maried here bye a lycence upon Satterdaye beinge the xjthe daye being Satterdaye before ye first Lee fayer or Ladye daye.
George sonn of John Horsforthe buried ye xvjth daye beinge Thursdaye in the after noone.
Thomas sonn of John Horsforthe buried ye xviijth daye beinge Satterdaye before Bathlemewe daye.
Elizabethe daughter of John Medlaye baptised ye xixth daye and Sondaye before Barthomowe daye.

1621.

Ann daughter of Thomas Milnor alias Shepperde buried ye xxth day Mondaye before Barthlemewe daye.
A yonge sonn of John Battye not baptised buried ye xxvjth daye Sonday after Bartlemew daye.
Ann daughter of Thomas Sharpehowse baptised yt daye being Sondaye after Barthlemewe daye.
Rychard Helvishe an oulde man of Ossett buried that daye in ye afternoone.
Nycholas Aveyende of Woodchurche and Marye Boothe of this parishe maried ye xxvijth daye beinge Mondaye then after Barthlemewe daye.
John Stocke of Hallifax and Margorye Kitsonn maried here the xxviijth daye beinge Tuesdaye after Barthlemewe daye.
Willme Claytonn of Ossett and Ann Bull of Dewsburie maried the xxixth daye beinge Wednsdaye after Barthlemew daye in the morninge.
Robert Ellis an oulde man of Gawthorpe was buried ye xxixth daye being Wednsdayo after Barthlemew daye.

September.

Uxor Rychardsonn dyinge at Nicholas Hurst was buried the eleaventho daye beinge Tuesdaye after the later Ladye daye.
John sonn of John Kaye buried ye xvijth daye beinge Mondaye before St. Mathewe day.
A yonge childe of Thomas Robinsonn Sc. not baptised was buried ye xxth daye being Thursdaye and St. Mathew his even this was Thomas Robinson his childe of Dowderode.
Susane daughter of Mr. Homyngeway baptised ye xxjth daye Fryday and St. Mathew daye.
A yonge sonn of John Nayler of the streete not baptised buried that daye.
Marye daughter of John Howden baptised ye xxiijth daye Sonday before michelmas dayo at evouingo prayer.
Marmaduke Langeleye and Rosamonde Fox maried the xxvth daye Tuesdaye before Michelmas daye.

October.

John sonn of James Pickerde baptised ye vth daye beinge Frydaye after Michellmas daye.
Thomas Cartar of Earles Heaton within this parishe and Jane Fisher of the same towne and parishe maried the ixtho daye Tuesdaye after Michellmas daye.
Willme sonn of Willme Westerman baptised ye xiiijth daye beinge Sondaye before St. Luke daye.
Willme son of Robert Barton baptised yt daye.
Rycharde Denysonn of Earles Heaton buried ye xvth daye being Mondaye before St. Luke daye.
George Woode of Myrfielde and Agnes Greave of Ossett within this parishe maried yt daye.
Roger Lee and Grace Sykes bothe of this parishe maried yo xvjth daye being Tuesday before St. Luke daye.
Jane daughter of Thomas Milnor alias Shepperde baptised the same daye.
Alice daughter of George Mawde baptised ye xxjth daye beinge Sondaye after St. Luke daye.
John sonn of John Tilson baptised ye xxiiijth daye beinge Wednsdaye after St. Luke daye.

1621.

Thomas son of Thomas Chaster being drowned ye xxijth day at Myrffeldo was buried here at Dewsburie ye xxiiijth daye.
Susan daughter of Arcuio Tomlinson baptised ye xxviijth being ye xxijth Sondaye and Symon day and Jude.
Willme son of Robert Barton buried the xxxth daye Tuesdaye after Symon day and Jude.

November.

Willme Speight of Chidsell elder buried ye fourthe daye beinge Sonday after All Sayntes daye.
Anno wyfe of John Battye yonger milner buried ye vth daye Monday after All Sayntes day ye Kyngs holye daye.
Rychard sonn of Nicholas Gunson baptised ye xjth daye Sonday after Martynmas day.
Dorithie daughter of John Knowles baptised yt daye.
George son of George Broadheade baptised yo xvijthe daye beinge Satterdaye.
Alice daughter of Gorge Mawde buried ye xxixth daye Thursdaye and Andrewe even.
Elizabethe daughter of John Robinson of Osset buried ye last daye.

December.

Edwarde sonn of Edwarde Allan buried yo first daye beinge Mondaye after Andrewe daye.
John Fox of Wakefielde and Jane Mathewgill alias Lea maried ye fourthe of this monethe Tuesdaye after Androw day and ye first Tuesdaye in Advent.
Dorithie daughter of Willme Pasley baptised ye viijth daye second Sondaye in Advent.
Dorithie daughter of Willmo Awdsley of Osset baptised yt day.
Dynise daughter of Edwarde Pickerde baptised yo xvjth day third Sondaye of Advent.
Elizabethe daughter of John Sharpe baptised yt daye at the eveninge prayer.
Arthure Woode otherwise called Arthure Smyth of this parish and Margret Wroe of the parishe of Wakefield maried the eighteenth daie being Tuesdaye before Sancte Thomas daye before Christenmas by a licence dated at Yorke the xijth of December instant.
Willme Wilsonn of Ossett was buried ye xxiiijth daye beinge Monday and Christenmas even.
Adam sonn of John Speight of Osset baptised yo xxxth day being Sonday after Christenmas Holye dayes or ye Sondaye before new years daye.

Januarye an⁰ Dni. 1621.

John son of John Pollerd of Hallifax dying at Thomas Jagger his howse in Ossett was buried here the second day.
Francis Slacke of Ossett buried yo third day being Thursday.
Jonas sonn of John Fell baptised yo vjth daye beinge the Epiphanye or Twelfe daye.
Robert basse sonn of George Brear of Hallifax and Marye Boothe of this parishe baptised yo viijth day being Sonday after the twelfe daye.

1621.

Marye daughter of Thomas Awtye of yo Preist Lane* baptised that daye at eveninge prayer.
Adam son of John Speight buried yt day at eveninge prayer.
Henrie Hepwortho an oulde man was buried the xvth daye being Tuesday.
Willme Gill of Sowoodo Groue neare Osset yo elder was buried ye xxth daye being ye second Sonday after ye twelfe daye.
Edwarde sonn of Rycharde Hurst alias Fox baptised yt day.
Dorithie daughter of Willmo Awdslay of Osett buried ye xxijth daye beinge Tuesdaye.
Robert son of George Woode baptised the xxvijth day Sonday before Candlemas daye.
Grace daughter of Thomas Netleton of Hanging Heaton baptised that daye.

Februarye 1621.

Jefferaye sonn of John Acrode baptised ye second daye beinge ye feast daye of the purification of Marye or Caudlemas daye.
Thomas sonn of Nicholas Wheatlaye baptised ye third daye beinge ye daye after Candlemas daye.
Marye daughter of John Yewden buried ye fourthe day.
Jefferaye son of John Acrode buried ye tenthe daye beinge Sondaye before Valentyne daye.
Willme Ridlsdenn of Wakeffelde and Margret Bell of this parishe maried on Tuesday ye xijth daye.
Robert Dey was buried ye xiijth daye beinge Wednesday and Valentyne his even.
Edwarde sonn of John Whitlaye of Ossett baptised yo xvijth daye being Septuagesima Sondaye.
Robert sonn of Robert Robinsonn yonger baptised yt daye at eveninge prayer this is Robert Robinson son of Ambrosse Robinson whose son was this daye baptised.
John sonn of John Townende baptised ye xixthe daye being Tuesdaye.
Ellen daughter of John Greave yonger baptised yt daye.
John Cowpas and Elizabethe Backehowse maried yo xxvjth daye beinge Tuesdaye before Shrove Sondaye.
George Whelewright and Ann Broadlay maried yo last daye.

Marche 1622.†

John Claytonn and Marye Boothe maried ye third daye beinge Shrove Sunday ann⁰ Dni. 1622.†
Rosamond daughter of Averie Pickerd baptised yt day.
Agnes daughter of Smitho alias Comsmithe baptised yt day at eveninge prayer.
Roger son of John Sugdenn of Osset baptised ye xtho day first Sonday in Lent ann⁰ Dni. 1621.
Alice daughter of Willme Acrode of Dewsbarie baptised the same daye at eveninge prayer.
John sonn of Robert Nayler baptised ye xvijth daye beinge the seconde Sonday in Lent in fine an⁰ Dni. (at the end of the year of our Lord) 1621.

---

* Now Church Street.
† So in Register.

1621.

Robert sonn of Roger Leo baptised yt day at eveninge prayer being in line anno Dni. 1621.
Robert son of Robert Robinsonn of Earles Heaton baptised the xxijth daye and Frydaye before yo Ladye daye in Lent, called yo anunciation of Maryo ano Dni. 1621.

Anno Dni. 1622, Ano Jacobi regis vicesimo.

Lawrance son of Edwardo Barnardo alias Robucke buried the xxviijth daye Wednsdayo after yo Ladye daye in Lent 1622.
Maryo Robinsonn of ye More Sydo buried ye xxviijth daye.
Samuell sonn of Edwardo Allan baptised ye last daye.
Alice daughter of Edwardo Ellis baptised yt day.

Aprill.

Edwardo sonn of Thomas Robinsonn baptised ye second daye beinge Tuesdaye before Care Sondaye.
Jane daughter of Rychardo Wilkensonn of Chidsell baptised the teuthe day Wednsday before Palme Sondaye.
Sara daughter of Thomas Nayler baptised the xiiijth daye beinge Palme Sondaye.
Esay son of Josephe Owldroide baptised ye xvijth daye beinge Shere Thursdaye in ye Passion weeke.
Grace daughter of Roger More baptised yo xxjth daye beinge Easter daye.
Robert Hunt a piper was buried ye xxiiijth day beinge Wednsdaye after Easter Holy dayes.
Edwarde Secker of Dewsburie an ould man was buried on Satterdaye ye xxvijth daye beinge Low Sonday his even.

Maye.

Anna daughter of Nicholas Mitchell baptised yo first daye beinge Wednsdaye May daye.
Elizabethe daughter of ye same Nicholas Mitchell baptised that daye.
Grace daughter of Roger More buried yo second day being Thursdaye.
Uxor Barrett un oulde woman buried yo eleaventh day.
Dorithie daughter of Thomas Jewithe buried that day.
Grace daughter of Robert Harropo baptised yo xijth daye beinge the thirde Sondaye after Easter at yo eveninge prayer.
Mr. George Shawe a preacher dyinge at Walter Cordingleye his howse one Satterdaye yo xviijth daye was buried ye same day in the after noone.
Elizabethe daughter of Robert Cartar baptised on Wednsday beinge yo xxijth daye Wednsday before rogation Sondaye.
Judithe daughter of Michaell Bentlaye baptised yo xxiijth day Thursday before Rogation Sondaye.
Elizabethe daughter of Caray Moris baptised yt daye.
John sonn of Robert Nayler buried ye xxvth daye beinge Satterdaye and the Rogation Sondaye his even.

June.

Maryo daughter of George Wheelowright baptised yo second daye Sonday after ye Ascension daye.

1622.

A yonge childe of Gorge Pickeringe not baptised buried the vijth daye beinge Fridaye before Whitsondaye.
Maryo daughter of Edwarde Hurst of Sothill Smithie baptised yo ixth daye beinge Whitsonday in yo after noone.
Issaboll daughter of Willmo Lee of ye Spynkewell yonger baptised yo tenthe daye Mondaye in Whitson weeke in the after noone.
Rychardo Harrishe and Margerie Helvishe maried ye eleaventhe daye being Tuesday in Whitson weeke and St. Barnabye daye.
Rycharde basse sonn of Rycharde Hutchinson and Sibell Slacke baptised that day in ye after noone.
Sara daughter of Willmo Lee baptised yo xxijth daye.
John sonn of Robert Hemyngeewaye baptised the xiijtho daye Thursdaye before Trinitye Sonday.

Julye.

Rycharde Scolfolde of Harteshoade and Maryo Marshall of this Parishe were maried ye ixth' daye.
James son of Marmaduke Longelaye baptised yo xxviijth daye beinge Sonday after St. James daye.
Thomas sonn of Rycharde Dishforthe buried ye xxxjth daye beinge Wednsdaye and Lamas even.

August.

Willme son of Rychard Fearnlaye buried ye first daye.
Xpofer Dixesonn an oulde man buried on Monday after Lamas daye being ye vth daye and ye kyng's holye daye.
Josua sonn of Rychard Roodes baptised ye xjth daye being Sondaye before ye first Ladye daye or Lee fayer.
Austine Dickensonn a yonge man of Hallifax dyinge at Michaell Wheatlay his howse was buried yo xijth being Mondaye and first Ladye even or Lee fayer even.

1622.

Averie sonn of John Claytonn baptised xviijth daye beinge Sonday before Barthlomewe daye.
Rycharde sonn of Willme Speight of Chickenlaye baptised the xxijth daye beinge thursday before Barthlomew daye.
Robert Netleton of Chidsell was buried ye xxvijtho daye beinge then Tuesdaye after Barthlomewe daye.

September.

†Dorithie daughter of Thomas Gamble buried ye second daye.
Easter daughter of Mathewe White buried ye xvijth daye beinge Tuesdaye before St. Mathewe daye.
Alice daughter of Robert Barton baptised yo xxijth daye Sonday seunight before Michelmas day or day after St. Mathewe daye.
Alice daughter of Edwarde Newsome alias Jackesonn baptised ye xxixth day Michellmas day and Sondaye.

---

* So in Register.

† This entry appears to have been interlined after the following entries were made.

DEWSBURY PARISH REGISTERS. 105

October 1622.

Robert Kaye and Alice Barbar maried ye viijth daye beinge Tuesdaye sennight after Michellmas daye.
John sonn of Edwarde Denise baptised yt daye.
Marye daughter of ye same Edwarde Denise baptised the same daye.
A yonge childe of Henrie Bull not baptised buried ye xjth day beinge Friday sennight before St. Luke his daye.
John Baconn and Margrett Pearsonn maried ye xxjth daye beinge Mondaye after St. Luke his daye.
Willme Whitlaye and Alice Speight maried the xxijth daye Tuesdaye after St. Luke daye.
John Tyas and Grace Bell maried yt daye.
Roger Beatsoun and Elizabethe Fayrbarne mariede ye xxixth daye at Ossett Chappell Tuesday before All Saynts day.

November.

John Saxtone an oulde man buried ye vthe day beinge then Tuesday and ye Kings holy daye about ye Gunpowder Treasonn pretended to be done.
Michael sonn of Philemon Dixonn baptised ye tenthe daye at eveninge prayer being St. Martyn ye Bushoppe his even and xxjth Sondaye after Trinitye.
Ann daughter of Rycharde Castle buried ye xvijth daye beinge Sonday after Martynmas day.
Robert sonn of Robert Owldroide of Dowderoide baptised that daye at eveninge prayer.
John sonn of John Stapleton baptised ye xxiiijth day beinge Sonday before St. Androwe day.

December.

Jonas sonn of Willme Dey baptised ye first daye beinge daye after Androwe day and Advent Sondaye.
Thomas sonn of Symeon Grenewoode baptised the vthe day beinge Thursdaye.
John sonn of John Hall of Gawthorpe baptised ye right daye Sonday before St. Lucye daye.
Robert sonn of Bryan Healde baptised yt daye at eveninge prayer.
Robert sonn of Rycharde Waynewright baptised ye xvthe day Sonday after St. Lucye daye.
Anthonye son of Rychard Whitlay of ye Carre baptised the xviijth daye Wednesdaye after St. Lucye day.
Elizabethe daughter of John Sharpe buried ye xixth day.
Dorothie daughter of John Sharpe buried ye xxth daye.
Joyce daughter of John Sharpe buried ye xxvth day and Christenmas daye and Wednesdaye yt yeare.
Uxor Harrison wyfe of Peter Harrisonn deceased buried ye xxvijth day St. John day in Christemas holy day and Fryday.
Marye daughter of Nicholas Fallinge baptised ye xxixth day.
Marye daughter of Thomas Peace baptised yt daye being Sonday after Christenmas holye dayes.

Januarye.

John sonn of John Robinsonn of Ossett baptised ye vjth daye twelfe daye and Monday.

1622.

Willme sonn of Willme Boy alias Rychardsonn buriede that daye being ye Twelve day in Christenmas holy dayes.
Elizabethe daughter of Rychard Castle baptised that daie at eveninge prayer.
Wynoffryde daughter of Willme Musgrave baptised the xthe daye being Thursdaye after Twelfe day.
John sonn of Robert Hemyngeway buried ye the xjtho daye.
Stephen son of Rychard Spur baptised ye xijth day.
George sonn of George Toulsonn baptised yt day.
Rosamund daughter of Henrie Greave baptised yt day.
Robert sonn of John Ellis baptised ye xxvjthe daye Sonday after St. Paulo daye.
Judithe daughter of ye same John Ellis baptised yt daye and that tyme at morninge prayer.
Robert sonn of George Mawde baptised at Horburie ye —— daye.

Februarie.

Grace daughter of John Boulde baptised ye seconde daye beinge Sonday and Candlemas day that yeare.
Alice Kent a mayde was buried the vthe daye beinge Wednsdaye after Candelmas day.
John lyn laye (Lindley) of Myrffelde being drowned at Ledgar Bridge by misadventure was here buried at Dewsburie on Monday the tenthe of Februarye.
Rychard son of Rycharde Fearnlay baptised ye xvjth day beinge Sonday after Valentyne daye.
John Smithe and Susann Cordinglay maried ye xviijth daye beinge Tuesdaye before St. Mathye daye.
Willme Speighte of Chidsell and Sara Whelewright maried the xxth daye being Thursdaye before Shrove Sondaye.
Edwarde sonn of Edwarde Fayerbarne baptised ye xxiijth day being Shrove Sondaye.
Thomas Woode of Batlaye and Jane Secker of this parishe maried ye xxiiijth daye beinge daye after Shrove Sondaye or colloppe Monday and St. Mathye daye.
A yonge childe of Rycharde Dishforthe not baptised buried yt day.
A yonge childe of John Dixon not baptised buried ye xxvth day being Shrove Tuesdaye.

Marche 1623.

Rychard Elvidge and Marye Paule maried here bye a lyconce ye vjthe daye ano Dni. 1623 being Thursdaye.
Marye daughter of Rychard Hemyngewaye on ye more syde baptised ye vijth day being Satterday in the after noone ano Dni. 1622.
Rosamund daughter of Willme Casson of Ossett baptised the ixth daye being second Sondaye in Lent 1622.
Robert son of Michaell Wheatlay baptised yt daye at the eveninge prayer ano Dni. 1622.
Uxor Thomas Terry buried ye tenthe daye beinge Mondaye.

1622.

Margrett daughter of Robert Brearaye baptised yo xixth daye beinge Tuesdaye before midlent Sondaye an° Dni. 1622.
Thomas Terrye buried ye xxxth day being Care Sondaye.

Aprill.

Willme sonn of Roger More baptised ye vjth daye beinge Palme Sondaye an° Dni. 1623.
James sonn of John Battye baptised yt day at morninge prayer.
Robert sonn of Robert Smithesonn yonger baptised the xiijth daye being Easter day in the after noone at ye eveninge prayer.
Thomas sonn of John Houldsworthe baptised ye xvth daye beinge Tuesdaye in Easter holy dayes.
Sara daughter of Willme Awdslaye of Ossett baptised yt daye being Tuesday in Easter holye dayes.
James Hunter of Myrffeldo and Jenet Robinsonn of our parishe maried ye xxth daye beinge Low Sondaye.
Thomas sonn of John Houldsworthe buried ye xxijth daye being Tuesdaye after Low Sondaye.

Maye.

Samuel Grenewoode alias Mitchell buried on Thursdaye beinge the first daye or Philip and Jacobe daye and ye Senue* daye at Yorke this yeare.
Thomas son of Thomas Robinson of Bowderoide baptised the fourthe day Sonday after Mayo daye or St. Ellen day.
Dorithie daughter of Thomas Jewithe alias Procter baptised that daye beinge Sonday after May daye or St. Ellen daye.
Issabell daughter of Robert Tomson baptised yt daye at ye eveninge prayer.
A yonge daughter of Thomas Netleton of ye Hoyle Milne not baptised was buried the vijth daye.
Marye wyfe of Averie Whitakers late deceased was buried on Frydaye being ye ixth daye of Maye.
Willme Dixon and Ellen Longelaye maried ye xiijth daye.
Alice Hoyle widowe was buried yo xiijthe daye being Tuesdaye.
Uxor Horsforthe was buried the xviijthe daye.
Mathew Lanscarre was buried ye nynetenthe daye.
Ann daughter of Thomas Marshall baptised yt daye.
Ellen daughter of Thomas Greave baptised yt daye.
Margrett daughter of John Brouke of Sowood Grene neare vnto Ossett baptised that daye.
A yonge sonn of John Forest not baptised buried ye xixth daye Mondaye before Ascention daye.
John Tayler of Honlaye and Marye Owldroide of this parishe maried here ye xxvijth daye beinge Tuesday after Ascention daye or Holy Thursdaye.
Grace wyfe of Thomas Oxelay buried yo xxxth day.

---

* Seane—also spelt seene, seyne, and seyn—a synod of the clergy. See the *Catholicon Anglicum*, s. v. Seyn for some examples of the use of the word. The word also occurs in the entry in the Register for 4th May, 1620, the latter part of which should read "buried ye fourthe, ye seane (synod) day at Yorke."

Jacobi regis, &c., vicesimo primo. June 1623.

Margrett wyfe of John Slacke of Ossett buried yo vjth daye beinge Fryday before Trinitie Sonday.
George son of Perigryne Wilkenson baptised ye xvth daye Sondaye after Trinitye Sonday.
Ann wyfe of Robert Byrkebye was buried ye xxjth daye Satterdaye after Trinitie Sondaye.
Charles Waltonn of Ossett was buried yo xxiiijth daye being Midsmer daye in ye after noone.
Elizabethe daughter of John Awdslaye baptised ye xxvjtho daye beinge Thursdaye after Midsmer daye.
Uxor Bentlaye of Stayneliffe was buried yo xxxth day being Monday and daye after Peters daye.

July.

Adam Wheatlaye was buried ye xjth daye beinge Saterday after St. Peters daye.
Alice daughter of Willme Claytonn baptised yt daye and the said Alice was buried ye same daye.

August.

Percivall Terrye was buried the first daye Lammas day and Frydaye.
Ann daughter of Mr. Hemyngewaye baptised ye thirde day being Sondaye after Lammas daye.
Edwarde Barbar was buried yo vthe daye being Tuesdaye and one of the Kynges holye dayes abouto Earle Gowrye* conspiricye in Scotlande.
Robert sonn of Michaell Wheatlaye buried yo xijthe daye beinge Tuesdaye and ye fyrst Ladye even or Lee fayre his even in yo after noone of that daye.
Jonye wyfe of Robert Speight of Chickenlaye was buried the xvjtho daye beinge Satterday after ye first Lee fayre.
Katheryne wyfe of John Boothe buried yt daye.
John sonn of Rycharde Smithe alias Thorpe baptised the xxiijth daye being tenthe Sondaye after Trinity Sonday and Barthlemewe daye.
Uxor Boye alias Rychardsonn buried ye xxxthe and Satterday after Barthlemewe day.
Stephen sonn of Rychard Hall buried yt daye in ye after noone.
Christopher Bunche buried yo last daye being Sonday after Barthlemewe daye.

September.

Uxor Lanscarre of Chickenlaye was buried yo first daye.
Issabell wyfe of Thomas Acrode late of Dewsburie deceased was buried on Tuesdaye beinge the second daye and Tuesdaye before ye latter Ladye daye.
Phillippe Berrye and Grace Cowpas maried ye ixth daye beinge Tuesdaye after ye latter Ladye daye.
Grace daughter of Valentyne Speight baptised the tenthe daye.
A yonge childe of Robert Tomsons buried yt daye.
John Robinsonn of Ossett was buried yo xiijth daye.
Robert sonn of John Parker yonger buried yo xviijth daye being Thursdaye in ye after noone.

---

* The Earl of Gowrie was executed in April, 1584, for his part in a rising against the King of Scotland, afterwards James I. of England. The Earl had organized a revolution in August, 1583, and having secured the King in Ruthven Castle, he assumed, with his associates, the exercise of the royal authority.

1623.

Julitho daughter of Michaell Bentlaye buried ye xviijth daye being Tuesdaye after St. Mathew daye.
Jeffraye Acrode an oulde man was buried ye xviiijth daye.
Thomas Lauscarie was buried ye xxvjth daye beinge Frydaye before Michellmas daye.
Uxor Tolde of Ossett was buried ye xxviijth daye being Sondaye and Mychellmas even.
Mathew sonn of Robert Pickerde baptised yt daye.
Christopher sonn of Josephe Lister baptised yt daye.
Edwarde Willsonn of Myrffelde and Ellen Newson alias Jackeson maried ye xxixth day michellmas day and Monday that yeare.
Uxor Arrandell wyfe of Willme Arrandell deceased buried on Tuesdaye being daye after Michelmas daye and ye xxxth daye.
A yonge sonn of Rychard Archer not baptised buried yt day in the alter noone.

October.

Josephe Cryer of Honley within Allmanburie parishe and Alice Owldroide of this parishe were maried ye vijth daye.
Anne wyfe of John Fell buried ye ixthe day Thursdaye a weeke and odde dayes before St. Luke daye.
Margerie wyfe of Thomas Secker was buried the xjth daye beinge Satterday before St. Luke day.
John sonn of Thomas Cartar baptised ye xijth daye Sonday before St. Lukes daye.
John sonn of Willme Whitlaye of ye Carre baptised the xiiijth daye.
Uxor Ashtonn under ye hill was buried ye xvth daye then beinge Wednsdaye before St. Luke his daye.
Thomas Awtye of ye Hill toppe was buried ye xvijth day being Fryday and St. Luke his even.
John Cowpas was buried ye xxvijth day being Monday and Symon day and Jude his even.
Dorithe daughter of John Otlayo baptised ye xxvjth day beinge Sonday before Symon and Jude his daye.
Willme Hall and Elizabethe Rawsonn maried ye xxvijth day beinge Tuesdaye and Symon and Jude daye.
Sibell Slacke was buried ye xxixth day beinge Wednsdaye.
Elizabethe wyfe of John Grayve yonger buried ye xxxth daye beinge ye last daye of this monethe and All Sanctes or All Hallowe his even.
Ellen daughter of Thomas Grayve yonger buried yt day.

November.

Lawrance Saxtonn and Mereye Owldroide of this parishe maried ye thirde daye.
Lyehaide Cartar of Chickenlaye was buried ye xiijth daye being Thursdaye after St. Martyns daye.
James sonn of James Speight baptised ye xvijth day.
Robert Robinsonn was buried the xvijth daye.
George Netherwoode of Caverlaye parishe and Marye Peace of this parishe maried ye xviijth day.

1623.

Elizabethe wyfe of John Cowpas latelie deceased was buried ye xxvjth daye Wednesdaye before Sancto Andrewe daye.
Willme sonn of Willme Westerman buried ye xxixthe daye beinge St. Andrewe his even and Satterdaye.
John sonn of Willme Hall baptised ye xxxth day being St. Andrewe daye.

December.

George Saxton and Grace Lea maried ye first day beinge Tuesdaye* after Andrewe daye.
John sonn of Willme Hall buried ye vijth daye Sondaye.
Grace daughter of Josephe Cryer was baptised ye xiiijthe daye beinge Sonday and ye day after St. Lucye daye.
Ann daughter of Robert Stansfelde baptised yt daye at eveninge prayer.
Issabell wyfe of Humphrye Waterhouse buried ye xvth daye.
Thomas Balmfforthe dyinge at Nicholas Wheatlays was buried on Mondaye being ye xxijth daye.
John Wurmall was buried the xxiiijth daye.
Marye wyfe of Willme Speight late of Earles Heaton deceased was buried that daye.
Gilbert Wholewright an oulde man of Gawthorpe was buried ye xxvjthe daye being Fryday and St. Stephen his daye in Christenmas Holye dayes.
Uxor Awtye wyfe of Rycharde Awtye deceased was buried the xxxthe daye beinge Tuesdaye.

Jenuarie.

Jenett daughter of Josephe Walker baptised ye first day being newe yeares day at eveninge prayer and Thursdaye that yeare.
Grace daughter of Mathewe White baptised ye iiijthe daye.
John sonn of Peter Thornton baptised ye tenthe day.
Robert Walker of Gawthorpe and Jane Lands of ye same towne within this parishe maried ye xith daye being Sonday and in the morninge of that daye.
Jennett daughter of Josephe Walker buried ye xvijthe daye beinge Satterdaye at nighte.
Jonathan son of James Pickerd baptised the xxvth daye being Sonday and St. Paule daye.
Jenet daughter of Thomas Langefelde buried ye xxixth daye Thursdaye before Candlemas day in ye after noone.
A yonge childe of George Pickeringe not baptised buried ye xxxthe daye beinge Frydaye before Candlemas day in the after noone.
And the sayd George Pickering buried his wyfe mother of the same childe at Horburie on Sonday next after.

Februarye.

Michaell Speight and Jenett Bedforthe maried ye ixthe daye being Shrove Mondaye or colloppe Mondaye.

---

* Should be Monday.

1623.

Josua sonn of John Sharpe alias gornall baptised the xth daie beinge Tuesdaie and fastens even.*
Rychard Fell buried that daye in ye after noone.
Robert Bradforthe of ye Street buried his wyfe the xijth day beinge Thursday after Shrove Tuesdaye.
Sibell wyfe of Thomas Langcffelde of Sowood Grene buried the xiijth daye and Frydaye before St. Valentyne daye.
Juditho daughter of John Ellis buried ye xxiijth daye beinge Mondaye before St. Mathias daye.
Elizabethe wyfe of Willme Sheplaye buried ye xxvijth daye.
Dorithie daughter of Willme Roydes baptised the last day in the after noone at eveninge prayer.

Marche 1623.

John Sykes late Parsonn of Kyrtonn in the countye of Notingham departed this lyfe there ye tenthe of December ano Dni. 1623 who being borne in oure towne of Ossett the sonn of Willme Sykes there gave at his deathe tenn poundes to ye towne of Ossett ye profitt wherof to be distributed to ye pore of the sayd towne for ever: recorded ye vthe daye of this monethe of Marche 1623 ano Jacobi regis vicessimo primo.
Michael Bentlaye son of John Bentlay late of Dewsburie deceased dyinge at Grantham in Lyncolneshire was buried there on Frydaye beinge the vthe daye of this monethe of Marche ano Dni. 1623.
George Bocmar was buried ye xjth daye beinge Thursdaye before Care Sondaye.
Elizabethe daughter of John Tayler baptised the xiiijth daye beinge Care Sonday or Sonday before Palme Sondaye.
John Hurst vnder ye Hill ye elder was buried ye xvthe daye.
Josua sonn of John Sharpe alias Gurnall was buried the xxijth daye.

Aprill 1624.

Margrett daughter of Willme Aerode of Earles Heaton baptised ye iiijth daye Low Sondaye.
Josephe son of Nicholas White baptised ye vth daye.
A yonge daughter of John Dixon not baptised buried ye viijth daye.
Edwarde Hurst vnder ye Hill buried ye xvijth daye.
Dorithie daughter of Willme Westerman baptised the xviijthe day Sonday before St. Marke daye.
Jenet daughter of Roger Hurst baptised ye same daye.

Maye.

John Phillippe of Ossett buried his wyfe the vijthe daye beinge Satterdaye after ye Ascention daye or Holye Thursdaye.
Elizabethe daughter of Nicholas Wheatlay baptised ye ixth daye.
John Greye of Penniston and Alice Boothe of this parishe maried the tenthe daye.

* i.e., The even before the fast of Lent. Shrove Tuesday was called Fastens or Fassens Tuesday.

1624.

Martha daughter of Nicholas Mitchell baptised ye xiijth daye beinge Thursdaye before Whitsondaye.
Ellen daughter of John Tilsonn baptised yt daye.
Dorithie daughter of George Whelowright baptised ye xvjth daye Whitsondaye.
Dorithie daughter of Michaell Speight baptised xxth daye Thursdaye before Trinitye Sondaye.
Rychard Hurst alias Fox buried ye xxvth daye.
A yonge daughter of Roger Beatsonn not baptised buried the xxvijth daye.

June.

Thomas Musgrayve and Francis Owldroide maried the first daye.
Ellen daughter of Willme Wrighte baptised ye vjthe daye beinge Sondaye before St. Barnabye daye.
Ann daughter of Thomas Netletonn of Hanginge Heaton baptised the viijth daye.
Rachell wyfe of Robte Netletonn of Chidsell was buried the ixth daye.
A yonge childe of Willme Speight of Chidsell not baptised was buried that daye.
Thomas son of Thomas Firthe buried yt daye.
Ann daughter of Robte Stansfelde buried ye xiijth daye Sondaye after St. Barnabye daye.
Jenet beinge a widowe dyinge at Nicholas Wheatlaye his howse was buried the xixth daye Satterdaye before midsmer daye.
Rycharde Kippus a stranger beinge slayne in a colepitt within the newe parke was buried ye same daye in ye after noone.
Uxor Speight of Chidsell was buried ye xxvth daye.
Robert Bradforthe elder of Ossett and Jane Smithe of ye same maried ye xxixth day beinge Peters daye and Tuesdaye.

Julye.

Robert Roodes and Elizabethe Marshall maried the vjthe daye.
Rycharde sonn of Robert Wheatlaye baptised ye xjth daye.
Robert sonn of Anthonye Armitedge baptised that day beinge the seaventhe Sondaye after Trinitye Sonday.
Willme Dobsonn and Elizabethe Burton maried the xxijth day Tuesdaye before St. Swithune daye.
Dorithie daughter of James Broadlaye baptised yt daye being Tuesdaye before St. Smithune* daye wche was on ye Thursdaye next after.
John Phillippe and Issabell Bellett maried ye xxth daye beinge St. Margerett day and Tuesdaye before St. James daye.
Alice daughter of Henrie Barbar deceased buried the xxijth beinge Thursdaye and Marye Magedelene daye.
Willme Swallowe and Marye Harrisonn yonger was maried that daye.
Thomas sonn of George Woode baptised ye xxvth daye beinge Sonday and St. James day.
Emar Fox buried that daye.
Robert Lee of Dewsburie More Syde buried ye xxvijth day being yt daye Tuesdaye after St. James daye.

* So in Register.

August 1621.

Henrie Nowell an owlde man was buried ye vjth daye beinge Frydaye and ye day after ye Kynge bodye daye of Gowrye conspemeye in Scotlande.
Alice daughter of Mychaell Wheatlay baptised ye viijth day beinge Sonday before ye first Lee fayer.
John Fell and Susan Hurst maried ye teuthe daye beinge Tuesdaye before the first Lee fayer.
Sara daughter of John Cowper baptised ye xvth daye being Sondaye after ye first Ladye daye at eveninge prayer.
Elizabethe daughter of George Saxtone baptised ye xxijth daye.
Thomas Oxelaye an oulde man buried the xxvijthe daye.
Ellen daughter of Nicholas Gunsonn baptised ye xxixth daye.
Willme sonn of Philemon Dixon baptised ye xxxth daye.
Jennett daughter of Roger Hurst buried ye last daye beinge Tuesdaye before ye latter Lee fayer.

Jacobi regis 22. September.

John sonn of Willme Newsome alias Jackeson baptised ye vthe daye beinge ye latter Lee fayer his even.
Josephe son of John Murton a tyneler (tinker) of Leedes borne at widowe Beckowithe her howse in Dewsburie baptised yt day at eveninge prayer.
A yonge sonn of Thomas Musgrayve of Hanginge Heaton not baptised was buried ye ixthe daye beinge Thursday and the day after ye latter Ladye daye.
John Brooke of Burstall and Jenett Fearnlaye of this parishe maried the xiiijth daye beinge Tuesdaye and Holy roode daye.
Willme Brooke and Agnes Ashton bothe of this parishe maried here that daye.
Elizabethe daughter of Thomas Woode baptised ye xxixth daye Sondaye before St. Mathew daye.
Elizabethe daughter of Marmaduke Longelay baptised yt day.
Elizabethe daughter of Marmaduke Longelaye buried ye xxiijthe daye.
Susanna daughter of Rycharde Longelaye baptised the xxiijthe daye.
A yonge childe of John Clayton not baptised buried ye xxiiijth daye.
Henrie son of John Aerode baptised ye xxixth daye.
Jane wyfe of John Sonyare of Bowderoide buried the xxxth daye.

October.

Marye daughter of John Gill baptised ye thirde daye.
Mathewe Cockell of Wakeffelde and Alice Dey of this parishe maried ye vth daye.
Robert sonn of John Fletcher baptised that daye.
Willme Hurst of Ossett was buried ye vjth daye Wednsdaye after Michelmas daye.
Henrie Tilsonn and Dorithie Briggs maried the teathe daye bye a licence.
A yonge childe of Henrie Darwyn not baptised buried the xjth daye.
Thomas sonn of Thomas Milner alias Shepperde baptised the vijth daye.

1624.

Uxor Blagburne of Ossett buried the xvjth daye.
Marye Bull daughter of Averie Bull was buried the xixthe daye beinge Tuesdaye and ye daye after St. Luke his daye.
Ellen daughter of Willme Speight of Earles Heatonn elder baptised yt daye.
Roger sonn of John Fox baptised ye xxiiijth daye beinge Sonday before Symon daye and Jude.
Elizabethe wyfe of Wilme Hall of Ossett buried the xxvth day.
Marmaduke Ashtone and Jane Hurst maried ye xxvjth daye Tuesdaye before Symonde daye at Jude.

November.

Robert son of Robert Barbar baptised ye first daye beinge then Mondaye and All Sayntes daye.
Rycharde son of John Hattye baptised ye vijth daye.
Rycharde son of Thomas Greave baptised yt daye beinge Sondaye then before Martynmas daye.
Robert Dey and Ann Brooke maried ye ixth day.
Margrett mother of Willme Lee of Bowderside buried ye xijth day.
Lawrance Rafe and Dorithie Bland maried ye xvijth daye.
Isaacke Firthe an oulde man buried ye same day at nighte.
Christopher son of Edwarde Fayrbarne of Osset baptised the xxijth daye.
Edwarde Miglebrouke and Margrett Medlay maried the xxiijth day.
John Dobsonn and Alice Aerode maried ye xxviijth daye.
Willm sonn of John Whitley baptised the xxviijth daie being Sundaie before St. Andrew thapostle.
Robert Speight of Chickenlaye and Marye Teters sall of the Streete Side both of this parish maried the xxixth daye.
Edwarde Dickeson of Thornhil Lees and Sara Wamerslaye of the Street Side within this parish married the xxxth daye beinge St. Andrewes day.
Willm Richardinson and Elizabeth Hopkinson married by a licence the same daye by Mr Sonyare.

December.

Robert Sharphowse and Mawde Riddall maried the vijth daye.
Willme Dixon of Leedes and Alice Owldroide of this parishe maried that daye.
Marye daughter of Robert Owldroide baptised ye xijth daye being St. Lueye her even.
John Bayldon of Kyrke Heaton and Elizabethe Milnes of this parishe maried ye xiiijth daye.
Mereye daughter of Carey Morishe baptised ye xxth day being Monday and Innocents daye.
John son of Rycharde Archer baptised ye xxviijth day being Tuesdaye and Innocents daye.
Elizabetha daughter of John Nayler of ye Streete baptised that daye.
John Sonyeare of Upper Bowderoide buried the last daye.

Januarye 1624.

John son of John Medlay baptised ye seconde day.
Henrie Woode and Elizabethe Stubley maried yt daye bye a licence.
Henrie son of John Acrode buried ye same daye.
Perigrene Wilkenson buried ye third daye.
Thomas Woode was buried ye vjth daye beinge Thursdaye and ye twelfe daye or ye Epiphanye.
Thomas Wooler an oulde man buried yt daye beinge Thursdaye and ye twelfe daye.
Marye wyfe of James Claytonn buried on Thursdaye ye xiijth daye beinge St. Hillarye daye.
A yonge childe of George Brealhead not baptised buried the xxiiijth daye beinge Monday and St. Paule his even.
Elizabethe daughter of Rycharde Dawsonn yonger baptised the xxvth daye beinge Tuesday and St. Paule daye.
Marye daughter of Nicholas Avyarde alias Jallinge buried the xxixth day.
Rebecca daughter of Willme Acrode of Dewsburie baptised the xxxth daye beinge Sondaye being Candlemas daye at eveninge prayer.
Dorithie daughter of Josephe Walkar baptised that daye at eveninge prayer.

Februarye.

George Whitelaye servant to Robert Netletonn yonger of Chidsell was buried ye vijth daye beinge Mondaye before valentyne daye.
Elizabethe daughter of Rycharde Dawson yonger buried the xijth daye.
Moses son of Josephe Owldrojde baptised ye xiijth daye being Septuagesima Sondaye.
Averie son of John Claytonn buried ye xxijth daye beinge Wednesdaye and St. Mathie his even.
Agnes wyfe of Lawrance Pickeringe buried yt daye in ye after noone.
John Hage of Huddersfelde parishe and Jane Robinsonn widowe of this parishe of Dewsburie maried at Osset Chappell within this parishe on Shrove Mondaye the last daye of Februarye.

A mundi creatione 5587. Jacobi regis, &c. 22.

Marche 1624.

Elizabethe daughter of John Battye se (i.e. senior) baptised the first daye beinge Shrove Tuesdaye alias fastinge his even.
Robert son of Robert Tonnsonn baptised that daye then beinge Shrove Tuesdaye.
Sara daughter of Thomas Robinsonn elder of the Moresyde baptised that daye in the after noone.
Issabell Davison a maide buried the vthe daye.
Robert sonn of John Hall of Gawthorpe within this parishe was baptised ye vjth daye beinge first Sondaye in Lent or after Shrove Tuesdaye.
Alice daughter of Willme Dixon of ye water yate yen (then) baptised yt daye at ye eveninge prayer.
A yonge sonn of Mr. Hemyngeway not baptised buried the xxijth daye beinge Tuesdaye before ye Ladye daye in Lent or ye annunciation of oure Ladye.
Ann daughter of Willme Acrode of Earles Heaton buried ye xxiiijth daye beinge Thursdaye and ye Ladye her even beinge ye Annunciation of ye Virgyn Marye or ye Ladye daye in Lent.

1624.

Elizabethe daughter of John Battye elder buried yo xxvthe daye beinge ye Ladye daye in Lent.
Ann daughter of Rycharde Hall baptised ye xxvijth day.
James sonn of Robert Barton baptised yt daye.
Rychard Grene an oulde man buried ye xxviijth day.
A yonge sonn of John Ollaye not baptised buried ye xxixthe daye.
Jane daughter of John Howldsworthe baptised ye xxxth daye.

Caroli regis primo. April 1625.

Thomas son of Thomas Gamble baptised ye third daye beinge Care Sondaye 1625.
Thomas son of John Stapleton baptised yt daye.
Issabell daughter of ye same John Stapleton baptised that daye.
Thomas sonn of Edwarde Pickerde baptised ye vijth daye.
Agnes daughter of Willme Gill of the towne of Ossett was buried ye xvijth daye beinge Easter daye in ye after noone.
Rycharde son of Edwarde Allan baptised ye xixth daye Tuesdaye in Easter Holidayes.
Elizabethe daughter of Robert Roydes of Chidsell was that daye baptised.
Ann Wymerslay widowe wyfe of Willme Wymerslay late deceased was buried ye xxtie day beinge ye daye after Easter Holye dayes.
Elizabethe daughter of Willme Hall baptised ye xxvthe daye beinge Monday and St. Marke day.

Ano Dni. 1625. Caroli regis, &c., primo.

May.

Roger sonn of Thomas Marshall baptised ye first daye beinge Sondaye and May daye or St. Philippe and Jacobe theyr daye.
Ellenn wyfe of James Cossen buried ye seconde day.
Rycharde Baxner of Hartsheade and Grace Speight of this parishe maried ye thirde day Tuesday and Saynt Ellen daye.
A yonge sonn basse borne of Grace Lynslay begotten of her bye Willme Westerman of Rodwell parishe not baptised was buried ye iiijth day.
Thomas Nayler of Ossett yonger and Susane Seeker of the same towne within this parishe maried the viijthe daye beinge Sondaye after May daye.
Elizabethe daughter of Rycharde Smithe baptised yt daye.
Marye wyfe of George Broadheade buried ye tenthe daye.
Willme sonn of Robte Cartar baptised ye xijthe daye.
Rycharde sonn of Edwarde Deneso baptised ye xvth day.
Willme sonn of Bryan Healde baptised yt day at the eveninge prayer.
John Manusfeldo and Margrett Rawsonn maried ye xvjthe daye beinge Mondaye before St. Dunstons day.
George Pickeringe and Grace Mallinson maried ye xixth daye beinge St. Dunstone daye.

1625.

Josephe sonn of Thomas Robinsonn of Bowderoide baptised the xxijth daye.
Elizabethe daughter of Robert Barbar buried ye xxiijth.
Ann daughter of John Knowles baptised ye xxixthe day Sondaye after ye Ascention day.

June.

Edwarde Roydes of Ossett yonger was buried the vth daye beinge Whitsondaye.
Martha daughter of Robert Walker baptised ye vijth daye.
John sonn of Willme Speight yonger of Earles Heaton baptised ye xijth daye beinge Trinity Sondaye.
Alice daughter of Philippe Derrye baptised yt day at the eveninge prayer.
Alice daughter of Nicholas Secker of Ossett buried the xiijthe daye.
Thomas sonn of Willme Leadbeater alias Shepperde buried ye xvjth Thursdaye after Trinitye Sonday and daye after ye first day of exercise at Dewsburie.
John Savile of Burstall dyinge at Willme Roodes his son in lawe of Dewsburie his howse was buried the xvijth day.
James sonn of Robert Bartonn buried ye xvijth daye.
Samuell Allan of Wakefielde and Marye Lands (Lande or Lanes) of this parishe maried ye sixthe daye.
John Harisonn of Rothewell and Ann Fox of oure parishe maried ye same daye.
Henrye sonn of Rychard Wilkenson baptised ye xxvjth daye.
James sonn of James Pickerde buried ye xxvijth daye.
Elizabethe daughter of John Gurnall alias Sharpe baptised the xxixth daye beinge St. Peters daye.

Julye.

Alice daughter of Willme Rychardson alias Boy baptised the third daye.
Elizabethe daughter of Willme Dey baptised ye xth daye.
James sonn of Rycharde Dawsonn baptised ye xixth daye.
Marye daughter of George Towlsonn baptised ye xxiiijth day.
Marye daughter of Averie Pickerde baptised yt daye.
John Gurnall alias Sharpe dyinge ye xxiiijth day at night being Sondaye at St. James his even was buried the xxvjth daye.
Marye daughter of Abrahame Grenewoode baptised the xxvth daye St. James day.
James sonn of Willme Speight of Chidsell baptised yt day.
Jennett daughter of John Boulde baptised ye last day at eveninge prayer and Lammas his even.

August.

Henrie sonn of Henrie Grayve baptised ye vijth daye.
Dorithie daughter of Rycharde Fernlay baptised yt daye beinge Sondaye after Lamas daye.

1625.

Elizabethe daughter of Rycharde Smithe buried ye xijthe daye.
Thomas son of Thomas Peace baptised ye xiiijth daye.
John sonn of George Lambert of Leedes dyinge at Alexander Netleton his howse was buried ye xvjth daye.
Robert sonn of George Pickeringe baptised ye xxjth day.
Alice daughter of John Parker yonger baptised the xxviijthe daye at eveninge prayer.

September.

Thomas sonn of Thomas Langfelde of Sowsel Grene buried ye firste daye Thursdaye before ye later Ladye daye or ye seconde Lee fixer daye.
Thomas son of John Awdelaye baptised ye vjth daye.
John son of Marmaduke Longelay baptised yt daye.
Thomas son of Thomas Milner alias Shepperd buried ye xiijth daye.
John sonn of Thomas Musgrayve baptised ye xviijthe daye.
Abraham son of Rycharde Waynewright baptised yt day.
Robert Bradforthe elder buried ye sixthe daye.
Elizabethe daughter of Robert Cartar buried ye xxijth day.
Marye daughter of Edwarde Higgyns baptised ye xxvth day.
Josephe son of Thomas Fivthe baptised ye xxixth day.
Marye daughter of John Taylier baptised yt daye.

October.

Willme Wilson and Alice Clayton maried ye xjth daye.
John Boothe buried ye same day at nighte.
Issabell daughter of Willme Brouke of ye More Syde baptised ye xvjth day.
Thomas Pickersgill and Francis Radcliffe marieIve xviijth daye beinge Tuesdaye and St. Luke daye.
Margrett daughter of Willme Knowles baptised ye xxiijth day.
Jervice sonn of Robert Stansfelde baptised ye xxxth daye Sondaye before All Sayntes daye at eveninge prayer.
Rycharde son of Robert Robinson of Dewsburie towne baptised yt daye at eveninge prayer.

November.

John son of Willme Leadbeater alias Shepperde baptised the vjth daye Sondaye before Martynmas day.
Ann daughter of Nicholas Steade baptised ye xxth day at eveninge prayer.
Jenye wyfe of Rycharde Fell buried ye xxjth daye.
Margrett daughter of Willme Knowles buried ye last daye being St. Andrewe day and Wednesdaye.

December.

Elizabethe daughter of John Sharpe alias Gurnall deceased buried ye third daye.

1625.

Willmo Longelay of Horburie dyinge at Willmo Dixon his howse here at Dewsburie was buried ye fourthe daye.
Andrew son of Edward Midlebrouke baptised yt daye.
Gilbert Bentlaye was buried ye viijth daye.
Grace daughter of Willmo Westerman baptised ye xviijth daye.
A yonge sonn of Roger Hurst not baptised buried ye xxjth daye St. Thomas daye in the after noone.
Thomas son of John Dobsonn baptised ye xxvjth day being St. Stephen his daye in Christenmas holye dayes in the after noone.
Easter daughter of John Horsforthe baptised the xxvijth day on St. John day in Cliristenmas holy dayes at eveninge prayer.

Januarye.

Ann daughter of Robert Harroppe baptised ye eight daye beinge Sondaye after ye twelfe day in ye after noone.
John Wilsonn and Agnes Milnes maried ye xth daye.
Alice daughter of Robert Nayler baptised ye xijth daye and the same Alice was buried ye xiiijth daye.
Willmo son of Willmo Whitlaye baptised ye xvth daye.
A yonge daughter of George Saxton not baptised buried that daye.
Md. (Mem.) that tow yonge daughters of Mr. Henryugewayo not baptised buried ye xvijth daye.
Willmo Ashton of this parishe and Susann Childe of Burstall parishe maried there ye same daye.
A yonge daughter of Thomas Pickersgill not baptised buried ye xviijth day
John sonn of Willmo Awdslay of Ossett baptised xixth day.
Robert Nayler buried his wyfe the xxijth daye.
Sara daughter of John Cowpar buried yt day at ye eveninge prayer.
Andrewe son of Edwarde Midlebrouke buried ye xxvjth daye beinge Thursdaye before Candlemas daye 1625.

Februarye.

Edmonde son of John Hage of Ossett baptised yo seconde daye beinge Thursdaye and Candlemas daye 1625 and ye same Coronation daye of Kynge Charles nuo Dni. dicto: from ye worldes creation 5575: Noahe floude 3919.
James son of James Pickerde baptised yt day.
Synce Yorke was builte 2592; and Yorke Minster built 907: and Londonn was built 2734: Caroli regis &c. primo.
A yonge childe beinge a daughter not baptised of Edwarde Walker and Marye Clayton basse borne buried ye vjthe daye.

An° Ætatis Caroli regis &c. Novemb. 19—24.
A conquæsto (conquæstu) Angliæ 558: and synce ye Israelites departed out of Egipto 3553.

Myles Cooke and Issabell Nowell maried ye xijth day beinge Soulaye Sexagesima or Sunday before Shrove Sondaye an° Dni 1625: an° regis dni. dicto: primo: a mundi creatione 5575: synce ye begininge of Quene Elizabethe her raigne 68.

1625.

John Fogall and Ellen Handlaye maried ye xxvth day beinge Shrove Mondaye.
Rychard sonn of Edwarde Newsome alias Jackeson baptised ye xxjtie daye beinge Shrove Tuesdaye in ye after noone.
Thomas son of Mathewe Hepworthe baptised yo xxvjth daye.

Marche 1625.

James Pickerde buried ye vijth daye.
Marie daughter of John Otlaye baptised ye xijth daye.
Henrie Robinson buried yo xvth daye.
Ann daughter of Edwarde Fayrbarne elder beinge drowned in Calder was buried ye same xvth day in yo after noone.
Josephe sonn of Edwarde Fayrbarne of Sowoode Groene baptised ye xixth daye Sonday before Caro Sondaye 1625.
Henrie son of Philemon Dixon baptised ye xxiijth daye being Thursday before ye Ladye day in Lent 1626.
Edmonde son of Thomas Nayler Ju. baptised ye xxvjth day Care Sondaye.
Thomas son of Thomas Jewithe baptised yo xxixth day beinge Wednsdaye before Palme Sondaye 1626.

Aprill 1626.

Rychard son of Rycharde Castlehowse baptised ye second daye Palme Sonday at eveninge prayer.
Robert Robinson of Earles He ton dying of Easter daye was buried on Mondaye yo tenthe daye in Easter holie dayes.
Rychard Firthe and Jane Stublaye yo xiijth day maried.
Henrie son of John Tilsonn baptised yo xxth day.
John sonn of Willmo Thornes baptised ye xxvth day being then Tuesday and St. Marks daye.

Maye.

Edmonde Tattersall and Dorithie Nayler maried ye xvjth daye.
Elizabethe wyfe of John Wood of Earles Heaton buried yo xxtio daye.
Willmo Williamson and Jane Wilkenson maried yo xxjth daye.
Willmo son of Francis Gill baptised ye same daye.
Sara daughter of John Speight baptised yt day.
Mereye daughter of Willmo Nowell baptised yt daye.
Rychard son of Rychard Dawson Ju. baptised ye xxiiijth daye.
Ann daughter of Thomas Curtar baptised ye xxviijth daye being Whitsondaye.

June.

Edwarde sonn of Robert Smithson Ju. baptised ye viijth daye.
Thomas son of Thomas Wurmall baptised ye xjth daye.
John son of Nicholas Aveycarde alias Jullinge baptised the same day at morninge prayer.
Grace daughter of Nicholas White baptised yt daye at the evening prayer.
Grace daughter of Nicholas Gunsonn baptised yo xviijth day.

DEWSBURY PARISH REGISTERS. 113

1626.

Willme sonn of Robert Robinson of Earles Heaton
deceased baptised yt daye at eveninge prayer.
John Warde of Ossett buried ye xxvth daye.
Thomas Spenceleye and Marie Oxelay maried yo
xxvijth daye.
John Nayler and Dorithie Bawlinge maried yt dayo.
John Fernlaye and Marie Earle maried yt day.

Julie.

Josephe sonn of Rycharde Spurre baptised ye
seconde day.
Elzabethe daughter of Robert Burtonn baptised yt
daye.
John Sonyare of Bowderoide buried ye third daye.
Mathew sonn of Mathew White baptised yo xvjth
daye.
Henrie sonn of John Acrode baptised yt dayo also
at ye eveninge prayer.
Willme Smitheson and Alice Bunche maried ye
xviijth daye.
Marye wyfe of Thomas Poplewell buried yo xixth
daye.
Francis Wilkinson and Ann Nabbe maried yo
xxiiijth day.
Jane daughter of George Mawde baptised yo xxvth
daye St. James daye.
Sara daughter of Thomas Robinsonn of yo More
Side the yonger buried yo xxxth day.

August.

Robert Hepworthe of Thornhill and Dorithie
Milnes of this parishe maried the last day of Julie
beinge Monday and Lammas even and yo assisses
(Assizes) weeke then at Yorke.
Anthonye Eeamlaye and Grace Pighells maried ye
xvth daye beinge Tuesdaye and ye first Ladye daye.
Marye Rawbe buried yo xxiijth day beinge Wed-
te daye and St. Barthelmewe his even.
John Dege and Elizabethe Whitakers maried ye
xxvijth daye.
John son of John Gill baptised yo xxvijth day.
John sonn of John Maumsfelde baptised ye same
day.
Thomas son of John Battye elder baptised yo same
daye.
Alice daughter of Rycharde Smithe baptised yt
daye.
These were baptised in ye fore noone of that daye.
John Farrer and Elizabethe Walker maried yo
xxixth daye.

September.

Marye daughter of Willme Wilson baptised yo
tenthe day.
Mrs. Wilkinsonn dyinge ye ixth daye at Chidsell
was buried at Allmanburie the xjth day beinge
Moonlaye after ye latter Ladye daye or Lee fayor
day.
Elizabethe daughter of Michaell Speight baptised
ye xijth day.
Thomas Lee and Alice Fox maried ye xixth daye.

October 1626.

Thomas Marcer and Issabell Yeoman maried yo
tenthe daye.
Thomas sonn of Rycharde Hemyngewaye baptised ye xviijth day beinge Wednesdaye and St.
Luke daye in ye after noone.
Rycharde Kyrkman of Rothewell and Sibell Gill
of this parishe maried ye xxijth daye.
Jane wyfe of Thomas Leadbeater alias Shepperde
late deceased buried ye xxvth daye.

November.

Issabell wyfe of Anthonye Hurst buried ye xijth
day.
Ann daughter of John Dixon baptised yt day at
evening prayer.
Alice daughter of Willme Ashton baptised yt day
at eveninge prayer.
John Woode and Sara Preisthaye maried yo xiiijthe.
Thomas Crabtree and Jennet Robinson maried ye
xixth daye.
Thomas son of Willme Acrode ju: baptised that
daye.
Sara daughter of Anthonye Armitage baptised yt
daye.
Averie sonn of Rycharde Kyrkeman baptised yo
xxvjth daye.

December.

Abraham sonn of Samuell Allen baptised yo
seconde daye.
Elizabethe daughter of Thomas Lee baptised yo
thirde daye at morninge prayer.
John Slacke buried ye vijth daye.
Francis daughter of John Arrowsmithe baptised ye
vijth daye.
Humphrye Waterhowse buried ye ixth daye.
Ann daughter of Rycharde Firthe baptised yo xth
daye at eveninge prayer.
John Hudsonn of Leeds and Beatrice Longelaye of
this parishe maried there at Leedes yo xijth daye.
Samuell sonn of Roberte Wade baptised yo xiijth
daye St. Lucye daye.
A yonge sonn of Roberto Wheatlaye not baptised
buried the xvth daye.
John sonn of John Battye baptised ye xvijth day.
Elizabethe daughter of Thomas Shepperde bap-
tised yt day.
Thomas son of Rycharde Hemyngwaye buried yo
xviijth daye.
Elizabethe daughter of John Fell baptised yo
*xxiijth day Thursday and St. Thomas day.
Uxor Denison buried yo xxiiijth day Chrytenmas
even and Sonday.
John sonn of Carey Morise baptised yt day.
Ann daughter of Willowe Robinson of Earles
Heaton buried yo xxvjth day beinge St. Stephen's
daye.
Faythe daughter of George Woode baptised yo
xxxith day being Sonday and new years even or yo
circumcision.

Januarie.

Elizabethe daughter of James Speight baptised ye
first day.

* So in Register, but evidently a mistake for 21st.

1626.

Robert Parker was buried yᵉ ixth daye.
Grace daughter of John Fox baptised yᵉ xiiijth day.
Isabell daughter of Rychard Sunderland baptised the same daye.
Jenet wyfe of James Cressery buried yᵉ xvth daye.
Willmᵉ Hall buried yᵉ xviijth daye.
Allexander Nettetonn buried yᵉ xxiijth daye.
Alice daughter of Willmᵉ Ashtonn buried yᵉ xxviijth daye.
Michaell sonn of George Wheelewright baptised yt day.
Willmᵉ sonn of John Naylor of yᵉ Street baptised yt day.
Nicholas Hargrayve and Jonye Midlebrouke maried yt day.
At eveninge prayer that daye was Ashton's childe buried.

Februarie.

Marye daughter of Peter Thornton baptised yᵉ second day and Candlemas day.
Thomas son of Thomas Marshall of Ossett baptised the fourth day beinge Shrof Sundaie.
Elizabeth daughter of Richard Meakendall of Ossett baptised yt day.
Sara daughter of William Halle baptised that daie.
Grace daughter of George Saxton of Gawthorpe baptised that daie.
John Claye of Ealand and Marie Rychardson of this parisho maried here yᵉ vth daye beinge Shrove Mondaye or Colloppe Mondaye.
Uxor Bowlinge of Sothill comon was buried yᵉ ixth daye.
Robert Boothe an oulde man of Gawthorpe buried yᵉ tenthe daye.
Marie daughter of Edwarde Denise buried yᵉ xijth daye in the after noone.
Vallentyne sonn of Willmᵉ Wright baptised yᵉ xviijth day.
Willmᵉ son of Willmᵉ Wright baptised yt daye.
Lidia daughter of Nicholas Mitchell baptised yᵉ xxijth daye beinge Thursdaye after vollantyne day.
John sonn of Thomas Crabtree baptised yᵉ xxiijth daye St. Mathias daye.
John sonn of Symeon Grenewoode baptised yᵉ xxvijth daye.

Marche.

John sonn of Robert Kaye of Myrffelde buried yᵉ seconde daye.
Mr. Higginsonn minister and preacher at Hartsheade within this parisho dying on Satterdaye beinge the third daye and Midlents Sondaye his even was buried there yᵉ vth day.
Alice daughter of Anthonye Fearnlay baptised yᵉ vijth daye.
John sonn of Robert Roydes baptised yᵉ viijth beinge Thursdaye before Care Sondaye.
Alice daughter of Anthonye Fernlay buried yᵉ xjth being Care Sondaye in the after noone.
Mercye Lasse daughter of Willmᵉ Tomsonn of Thornell and Jennett Hall of this parisho baptised yᵉ xiiijth day beinge Wednsdaye before Palme Sonday anᵒ Dni. 1626.

1627.

Robte Roydes of this parishe and Elizabethe Iingelaye of Thornhill parishe maried here bye a licence yᵉ xxijth daye beinge Shire Thursdaye 1627.
Rycharde Naylor of Ossett buried yᵉ xxviijth day being Satterday and Easter even anᵒ Dni 1627.
Robert Mowlsonn of Thornhill parishe and Grace Woode of yᵉ same parishe maried here at Dewsburie yᵉ xxvjth daye 1627.
Thomas sonn of Thomas Jewithe buried yt daye 1627.

Aprill 1627.

Jane wife of Thomas Carter under yᵉ Hill was buryed thᵉ xjth daye beinge Wednesdaye.
Samuell sonn of Edmonde Tattersall baptised yᵉ xvth daye.
Alice wyfe of Willmᵉ Sheaffelde curate of Ossett buried yᵉ same daye in yᵉ after noone at eveninge prayer.
Wynefryde daughter of Willmᵉ Musgrayve buried yᵉ xvjth daye.
Nicholas Allen of Thornhill and Dorothie Houthroide maried here bye a license yᵉ xviijth daye.
Samuell son of Edmonde Tattersall buried yᵉ same day in yᵉ after noone at nighte.
Samuell son of Nicholas Wheatlay baptised yᵉ xxvth daye St. Marke daye.

Maye.

Edwarde son of John Dey baptised yᵉ first day yᵉ Ascention even.
Jane daughter of Robert Owldroide baptised yᵉ vjth daye.
Uxor Burnett Robert Tomsonn of Ossett his wyfe mother was buried on Thursdaye before Whitsonday yᵉ tenthe day.
Willmᵉ Gill elder buried yᵉ xiijth daye being Whitsondayᵉ.
Francis daughter of Willmᵉ Musgrayve buried yᵉ xvth day.
Alice daughter of Willmᵉ Casson baptised yᵉ xxjth daye.
Willmᵉ son of Willmᵉ Speight of Earles Heaton elder baptised yᵉ xxiiijth daye.
Robert son of Willmᵉ Speight of Chidsell baptised yt day.
Francis Whitlay was buried yᵉ xxvjth daye.
Elizabethe daughter of Thomas Robinsonn buried yt day.
Elizabethe Tillye wyfe of one Tillye buried yᵉ xxviijth day.
Elizabethe daughter of Michaell Speight buried yᵉ xxxjth daye.
Elizabethe wyfe of Averie Pickerde buried yt daye.

June.

Martha Whitakers was buried yᵉ seconde daye.
Thomas Fox and Marye Burnlaye maried yᵉ vth daye.
Abrahame Grenewoode buried yᵉ vijth daye.
Thomas Stanlaye and Alice Ball maried yᵉ xjth daye.
A yonge daughter of Robert Tomson not baptised buried yᵉ same daye in the afternoone, this is Tomson of Ossett, and yt day was Sancte Barnabye day yt yeare.

1627.

Walter Cordinglaye was buried yo xiiijth daye.
Marye daughter of Rycharde Archer baptised yt daye.
George Kay of Churcheaton and Dorythic Binns of Thornhill maryed here by a licence the xv daye by *Samuell Pearson, Clarke, preacher at Dewsburye of God's worde.
John son of John Nayler yonger baptised ye xvijth daye.
Faythe daughter of John Ellis baptised yt daye.
Alice daughter of John Parker yonger buried yt daye.
Thomas Smithe and Judithe Moyses maried ye xixth daye.
Thomas Crabtre was buried ye xxjth daye.
Ellen wyfe of Willme Gill of Ossett Towne buried ye xxiiijth day at ye after noone.
Thomas sonn of Thomas Gamble buried yt day in ye after noone.
Marye daughter of Mr. Hemyngewaye baptised ye xxiiijth daye beinge Midsmer daye.

Julye.

John basse sonn of Abraham Townende and Alice Goodall baptised ye vjth daye in the after noone.
Henrie Knowles buried ye eighte daye.
Agnes daughter of John Dickenson baptised yt daye in ye after noone.
John sonn of Phillippe Berrye baptised yt day at eveninge prayer.
Sara daughter of Willme Knowles baptised ye xvth day beinge Sonday and St. Swithune daye.
Abrahame Hutchinsonn of Leedes parishe and Grace Milnes of this parishe maried here ye xvjth daye.
Willme sonn of Thomas Grayve yonger baptised ye xxixth day.
Willme sonn of Fraunces Gill buried ye same daye at eveninge prayer.

August.

Jennett wyfe of Robert Linthewayte buried ye secconde daye.
Ann daughter of Rycharde Firtho buried ye tenthe daye beinge Fryday and St. Lawrance daye.
Sara daughter of Roger Lee, baptised ye xijth daye beinge Sonday at eveninge prayer.

---

*The Rev. Samuel Pearson became Vicar of Dewsbury in July, 1612, and was buried 6th October, 1650. He brought an action against the Vicars of Huddersfield, Almondbury, Kirkheaton, Kirkburton, and Bradford, to recover the pensions payable by them to him as Vicar of Dewsbury; and the dispositions in this action, taken in Michaelmas Term, 1653, are printed in the 26th and 27th Articles on Dewsbury Parish Church, which appeared some years ago in the *Dewsbury Reporter*. Mr. Pearson is said to have been ejected from his living by the Puritans, but if so, he must have been allowed to return, for he obtained an order dated 4th November, 1651, from the Committee for Plundered Ministers, for £30 a year, to be paid for increase of his maintenance, out of the impropriate tithes of Hartshead, &c.; this allowance continued to be made until some time in the year 1655, when we find Mr. Pearson petitioning the Commissioners for managing Estates under sequestration that the allowance may be continued to him and the arrears paid. See Royalist Composition Papers, 1st Series, Vol. 50, page 317. The above-mentioned tithes used to be part of the property of the Rectory of Dewsbury, which, in 1848, was appropriated to St. Stephen's College, Westminster.

1627.

A yonge daughter of Edwarde Midlebroughe not baptised buried the xiijth daye being Mondaye and ye first Lee fayer daye.
John sonn of Willme Dixeson baptised ye xvth daye being then Wednesdaye and ye first Ledye daye or Lee fayer.
James Milner alias Shepperde and Issabell Wilson were maried ye sixth daye.
Peter Milner and Alice Seeker maried the xvjth daye.
Sara daughter of Rycharde Whitlaye of ye Carre baptised that daye.
Willme sonn of John Houldsworthe baptised ye xxvjth day.
Ann wyfe of Thomas Wright of Sowoode Greene in Ossett was buried yt daye at eveninge prayer.

September.

Dorithye daughter of John Fletcher baptised ye second daye.
Rycharde Beamonde of Allmanburie parishe and Rosamond Acrode of this parishe were lawfullie maried bye a licence ye vjth daye being Thursdaye and ye later Lee fayer daye.
Edwarde Phillippe of Ossett buried ye ixth daye at eveninge prayer.
Rycharde son of Edwarde Newsome alias Jackson buried yo xjth daye.
Mercye daughter of Willme Acrode of Dewsburie baptized ye xvth daye in ye after noone.
Ann daughter of ye same Willme Acrode baptised being then Satterday before St. Mathew daye.
Willme Nussye of Thornhill and Marye Poplewell of this parishe maried ye xvjth daye Sonday before St. Mathew day.
Marye daughter of Edwarde Allan baptised yt day.
Issabell wyfe of Willme Pasleye beinge an excommunicated Parson (person) and soo dyinge was secretlye unknowne to me ye Vicker on Sunday beinge ye xvjth daye in ye night buried bye her frendes.
Elizabethe daughter of John Boulde baptised ye xxiijth daye beinge Sonday after St. Mathew daye at eveninge prayer.
Robert Gill and Marian Crowdshawe maried here bye a licence ye xxiiijth day.
Elizabethe daughter of Michaell Wheatlay baptised ye xxvjth daye.
Mercye daughter of Willme Acrode buried ye xxixth day.
Ann daughter of ye same Willme Acrode buried together then the same daye.
John Brouke and Abilene Armistede maried ye same daye.
Josua son of Josephe Owldroide baptised ye xxxth daye.

October.

Grace daughter of John Stapletonn baptised ye vjth daye.
Faythe daughter of John Ellis of Ossett was buried the 13 daye.
Henrie sonn of Thomas Robinsonn of ye Moresyde baptised ye xxjth daye.
Thomas son of Thomas Woode baptised yt day.

1627.

Roberte Thornes and Ann Pickerde maried on Monday after St. Luke his day beinge yo xxijth daye.
John Otlaye of Ossett was buried yo xxvth daye.
Easter daughter of George Towlsonn baptised the xxviijth being Sondaye and also Symon day and Jude.

November.

Uxor Robinsonn of Ossett was buried yo first day beinge All Saynetes daye and Thursdaye.
Rycharde son of Henrie Grayve baptised yo fourthe daye.
Anthonye Hurst and Alice Cryer maried the vjthe day.
A yonge sonn of Rycharde Hall not baptised buried the viijth daye in the after noone.
Robert son of Thomas Netleton of yo Hoyle Milne baptised yo xviijth day.
Rychard son of John Woode baptised yt daye.
Charles son of Philemon Dixon baptised yo xxth day in yo after noone.
John son of Willme Dey baptised yo xxvth day.
George Howson and Easter Ashton maried yo xxvjth day.
Jennett daughter of Robert Thornes baptised yo xxvijth day.

December.

Sara basse daughter of Edwarde Walker and Mary Clayton baptised yo second day Sonday after Saynt Andrewe daye being Advent Sondaye.
Margrett daughter of Thomas Wright buried that daye at eveninge prayer.
Averie Pickerde and Mereye Tharpe maried yo thirde daye Monday after Andrewe daye.
Marye daughter of Edwarde Pickerde baptised yt day.
Marye daughter of John Fell buried on Satterday senight after St. Andrewe daye being ye eight day of this monethe December.
A yonge daughter of Rycharde Dawson of Batlay Cairo not baptised buried yt daye.
George Illinsall of Thornhill and Ann Cordinglay maried the xjth daye by Mr. Allensonn.
A yonge sonn of Miles Coke not baptised buried yo xiijth daye beinge Thursdaye and St. Lucye day in yo after noone.
A yonge daughter of Thomas Awdslaye not baptised buried the xiijth daye beinge Fryday and yo day after St. Lucye daye.
Abrahan sonn of Robert Walker of Gawthorpe baptised yo xvjth day Sondaye before St. Thomas daye.
Willme Tenande of Leeds parishe and Jane Nayler of this parishe maried at Ossett on Wednsdaye the xixth daye being Wednsdaye before St. Thomas day bye Mr. Adam Cocke Minister at Leedes.
Jennett daughter of John Townende baptised yo xxth daye being Thursdaye and St. Thomas his even.
Elizabethe daughter of Thomas Peace baptised yo xxiijth day Sonday before Christenmas day.
Edwarde Middlebrouke buried yt daye being Sonday before Christenmas day wch was on Tuesday after in yt yeare.

1627.

John son of Thomas Pearson a stranger borne at John Medlay's of Ossett baptised yo xxxth day.
Robert son of Thomas Houldsworthe baptised yo last day being Monday and New years even.

Jannarie.

Philemon son of Marmaduke Longelaye baptised yo first daye being Tuesday and New year's daye.
Martha daughter of Robert Walker buried yt daye.
Susann wyfe of Thomas Wurnnall buried yo vjth daye.
Agnes Robinson daughter of Ambrosse Robinson buried the viijth daye.
Willme sonne of Willme Fell of Ossett was buryed the ix daye.
Anne wife of Richard Ilcaison of Ossett was buryed the same daye.
Thomas Wurnnall buried yo xiiijth daye being Mondaye and yo daye after Hillarye daye in yo after noone.
Robert Bedforthe elder buried yo xvth daye beinge Tuesday.
Robert Awdslaye of Chidsell and Jennett Bowlinge of the same maried yt daye.
Willme Kent buried yo xvth daye.
Rycharde Pughells and Elizabethe Waughe were lawfullye maried here at Dewsburio bye a licence yo xixth daye beinge Satterdaye after Hillarye daye.
Willme son of Thomas Jewithe baptised the xxth daye.
A yonge son of Nicholas Hargraive buried yt day.
Willme son of John Wilsonn baptised yt day at eveninge prayer.
Edmonde Sonyaro buried his wyfe the xxijjth day Wednsdaye before St. Paule daye.
Elizabethe wyfe of Robert Barbar buried that day.
John sonn of John Nayler youngest buried ye xxvjth daye at night.
Robert Roydes of Chidsell buried yo xxvij daye in the after noone.

Februarye.

Willme son of Rycharde Fornlaye baptised yo third day beinge Sondaye and yo day after Candlemas daye.
Willme son of John Speight baptised ye tenthe daye.
Ann daughter of James Shepplye baptised yt daye.
Nicholas Seeker was buried yo xvjth daye at night.
Elizabethe daughter of John Parker yonger baptised yo xvijth daye.
Thomas Barbar was buried yo xixth day.
Willme Tainnforthe and Ann Kaye maried the xxvthe daye and being Mondaye and St. Mathias daye and Colloppe Mondaye.
Robert sonn of John Maunsfolde baptised ye xxiiijth daye being Shrove Sondaye.
Robert sonn of Robert Wright alias Greave baptised that daye at morninge prayer.
Ann daughter of Robert Cartar baptised the xxvth daye being Colloppe or Shrove Mondaye in yo after noone.
Ruthe daughter of Willme Speight Jn. baptised that daye in the after noone.

1627.

Ann daughter of James Shepperde buried ye xxvijth day beinge Ashwednsdaye at night.
John son of Thomas Shepparde buried yt day at night.

Marche 1628.

Ann daughter of Robert Phillippe deceased buried ye first day.
Anthonye sonn of Thomas Musgreave baptised ye second daye.
John sonn of Willme Ashtonn baptised yt daye at morninge prayer.
Agnes wyfe of Francis Fernlaye buried ye vtho daye beinge Wednsdaye and ye exercise daye.
Josepho sonn of John Talier baptised ye ixth day.
Ann daughter of Robert Smithson baptised yt day at the eveninge prayer.
Willme son of Michaell Owldroide baptised ye xijth day.
A yonge childe of Anthonye Fernlaye not baptised buried ye xvijth daye.
Edwarde Cowpar a younge man buried ye xviijth daye.
Ann daughter of Michaell Speight baptised ye xxth day.
Uxor Hutchinson wyfe of Nicholas Hutchinson deceased buried the same day at night.
Robert sonn of Robert Barton baptised ye xxiijth day.
Alice daughter of Willme Dickeson buried ye xxvijth daye.
Grace daughter of Willme Westerman buried ye xxviijth daye Frydaye before Passion or Care Sondaye.
Ellen daughter of John Greave yonger buried ye last daye beinge Mondaye before palme Sondaye.

Aprill.

Mychaell Walker buried ye second daye.
John Slade alias Ilage buried ye thirde day.
Thomas sonn of Willme Thornes baptised ye vth day.
A yonge sonn of the same Willme Thornes buried yt day in afternoone.
Thomas sonn of Willme Thornes buried ye vijth day.
Tymothie sonn of Robert Wheatlaye baptised ye xvth day beinge Tuesdaye in Easter holidayes.
Elizabethe daughter of George Mawde of Ossett buried the xvijth daie.
Anthonye Hurst buried ye xxth daye beinge Lowe Sonday or first Sondaye after Easter Holye dayes.
Edmonde sonn of Edmonde Tattersall baptised yt day at morninge prayer.
Elizabethe daughter of Rycharde Firthe baptised ye xxjth day Mondaye after Low Sondaye and ye festinge day.
Elizabethe daughter of Rycharde Firthe buried ye xxvijth day.
Peter Wilkocke and Susann Hurst maried yt day.
Sara daughter of Nicholas Gunsonn baptised yt day at morninge prayer.

Mayo.

Rycharde Beatsonn and Jane Bradforthe maried ye ivjth day.

1628.

Edwarde son of John Dawson buried ye xjth daye.
Robert sonn of Xpofer Easton baptised yt day.
Thomas son of Lawrence Saxton baptised yt day.
Sara daughter of John Speight buried ye xiijth day.
Susan daughter of John Knowles baptised ye xxijth day then beinge Thursday and Accention or holye Thursday.
John Mitchell and Margrett Midlebrouke maried ye xxvijth daye.

June.

Alice daughter of John Whitlaye baptised ye seconde day.
Sara daughter of John Otlaye deceased baptised ye xvth daye.
Robert Barghe and Alice Lee maried ye xvijth day.
Katheryne wyfe of Rycharde Robinson of Far Heaton buried yen the xxth daye.
George sonn of Rycharde Castle baptised ye xxijth day in yo after noone.
Josephe sonn of John Boothe baptised ye xxiijth day.
Moreye daughter of Willme Whitlaye baptised ye xxixth being St. Peters daye.

Julye.

Thomas son of Thomas Nayler baptised ye vjth day.
Elizabethe daughter of Peter Milner baptised yt daye at eveninge prayer.
Edwarde Bowlinge and Rosamonde Ward maried the vijth daye.
Edwarde son of Edwarde Newsome alias Jackson baptised ye xiijth daye at eveninge prayer.
Elizabethe daughter of Robert Roydes baptised ye xxth day yen Sondaye before St. James daye in affore noon.
Marye daughter of Henrie Netleton baptised ye same daye at morninge prayer.
Charles sonn of Philemon Dixon buried ye xxjth daye in the afternoone.
Elizabethe daughter of Willme Dransfelde baptised the xxvijth daye at evening prayer.

August.

A yonge daughter of Samuell Foxcroft not baptised was buried ye first daye at night being Thursday and Lammass day.
John Jagger of Ossett and Marie Grene within Clifton within the Chappelrie of Hartshede within this parishe was maried there the first day 1625 beinge Tuesdaye per Mr. Sonyare.
Roger sonn of Roger Hurst baptised ye tenthe day being St. Lawrance day.
Roger son of Willme Awdslaye baptised yt daye at morning prayer.
Jane daughter of Robert Owldroide buried ye xxijth daye.
Rycharde Battye of Hunslett and Elizabethe Swyfte maried at Ossett within this parishe on ye xxvijthe daye.
Robert Dickson of Thornhill and Margrett Tolle of this parish was maried here the 28 daye.

September 1628.

James son of Robert Wade baptised ye iiijtho daye.
Robert sonn of Jorge Hooran was baptised the vijth daye beinge Sondaye at eveninge prayer.
Nicholas Walker was buried the ix day.
Alice wyfe of John Goodall buried ye xijth daye.
Marye Awtye daughter of Thomas Awtie se. buried ye xvjth daye.
Jane Sugden widowe buried ye xixth day.
Robert Beatson and Elizabethe Lee maried ye xxjth day beinge St. Mathew day.
Uxor Pickerde of Ossett buried ye xxiiijth daye.
Edwarde Smithe and Mereye Berrye maried yt daye.
Ellen daughter of Edwarde Bowlinge baptised yo xxviijth day.
John Coninghamo and Jane Smithe maried yo xxixth daye.

October.

Mereye daughter of Thomas Fox baptised ye vth daye.
John Crowder of Durstall and Elizabethe Peace maried ye xvth daye.
Robert Bradforthe buried ye same daye.
Josua son of Josephe Owldroide buried ye xvjth daye.
Issabell Dawson widowe late wyfe of Robert Dawson deceased buried ye xviijth.
Arthure Cowoode and Cicelie Burball maried yo xxth day.
Thomas Wilson and Elizabethe Saxton maried yt daye.
Michaell Walker and Jenett Crabtre maried the xxjth daye.
Jane daughter of Averie Milnes buried ye xxiiijth daye.
Elizabethe daughter of Willme Awdslay of Gawthorpe baptised ye xxiijth day.
Susan daughter of George Pickerd baptised yt day.

November.

Margerie basse daughter of Willme Smithe and Jennett Cowpas baptised ye first day.
Katheryne wyfo of Willme Newsome alias Jacksonn buried the viijth daye.
Agnes daughter of John Nailer yonger of Ossett baptised the ixth daie.
Bridget daughter of Thomas Gamble baptised the same daie.
John Robinson and Anne Greaves were maried the xjth daie.
Issabell daughter of Willme Boy baptised ye xvth daye.
Isaacke Wilson buried ye xxjth daye.
James son of John Loye baptised ye xxiijth day.
Averie son of Averie Pickerd baptised ye last day.
Willme son of Rycharde Tawson Ju. baptised yt daye of Hatlay Carre.

December.

Willme Fox and Alice Hocbucke maried yo xth day.
Rychardo Wilkenson of Chidell was buried ye xiijth daye.
Rycharde Robinson and Marie Lanscarre maried ye xvjth daye.

1628.

Not baptised this basse son of John Greaves Ju. and Elizabethe Owldroide. This child not baptised at all.*
Jennett Hall was buried ye xxvth daye beinge Christenmas daye and Thursdaye In yo after noone.
A basse son of John Greave yonger and Elizabethe Owldroide not baptised was buried ye xxvijth daye.
Rosamonde daughter of John Hage of Ossett baptised ye xxvijth daye beinge Saynct John day in Christenmas holy dayes.

Januarie.

Willme son of Josephe Walker baptised ye vjth daye beinge Tuesdaye and ye twelfe daye or Epiphanye in Christenmas holydayes.
John son of James Speight of Ossett deceased buried ye vijth daye.
Henrie basse son of Henrie Ellmsall and Alice Robinson baptised ye xvth daye.
George basse son of Ann Jewithe and John Bootheroide of Ealande dyinge within this parishe was buried here the xvjth daye beinge Fridaye and ye second daye of yo sessions at Wakefielde at Christenmas.
Marie daughter of Rycharde Beamonde of ye Deane Howse in Allmanburie parishe baptised here at Dewsburie ye xxijth daye.
Grace daughter of Robert Harrope buried ye xxvjth day.
Rachell Houlde buried ye xxviijth daye.
Robert son of Robert Robinson of Heaton deceased buried the xxixth daye.
Averie Sonyare buried yo same daye.
Issabell daughter of Robert Harroppe buried ye last daye.
Marye wyfe of John Tilson dyinge on Thursdaye ye xxixth daye was buried on Satterdaye xxxjth daye.

Februarye.

Willme son of Thomas Shepperde baptised ye first daye.
Ann daughter of Robert Dey baptised ye vth daye.
Jane Robinsou daughter of John Robinson late of Ossett deceased buried ye vjth day.
Marie daughter of John Fletcher buried ye xth day.
Thomas Robinson of the More syde yonger buried his wyfe yt daye.
John son of John Robinson late of Ossett deceased buried the xijth daye.
Rycharde son of Henrie Greaxe buried ye thirteenthe daye.
Richard sonne of Willme Wilson of the More side baptised the xvth daye.
Richard sonne of Richard Mckindale of Ossett baptised yt daye.
Roger sonne of Robert Beatsonn of Ossett baptised yt day.
Willme Newsome and Marie Musgreave maried ye xvjth daye being Colloppe Mondaye.
Rosamond daughter of Averie Pickerde buried yt day.

---

* This entry is partly made over an erasure, and several words are carefully obliterated.

1628.

Grace daughter of Anthonye Fernlaye baptised yo xvijth daye beinge Shrove Tuesdaye.
Agnes daughter of Willme Deyo deceased buried yo xxjthe daye.
Thomas sonn of Thomas Awtie of ye water yate baptised yo xxiiijth daye.
Marye daughter of Peter Thornton buried yt daye.
John sonn of Thomas Robinson of Ossett buried the 25 daye.

Marche Ano Dni. 1628.

James sonne of Mathewe Hepworthe baptised the first daye at eveninge prayer.
Willme son of Willme Hall baptised ye eight daye.
Edward son of Thomas Robinson of Ossett buried yt day at the morninge prayer.
Sara daughter of Nicholas Gunsonn buried yo 12th day.
Susan daughter of Anthonye Armitedge baptised yo xvth daye.
Jonye daughter of Carey Morishe baptised at home ye xvjthe daye.
Agnes wyfe of Bryan Healde buried ye xvijth daye.
Christopher Bronke sa (senior) buried ye xviijth day.
Willme Dishforthe of Gawthorpe buried yt daye 1629.
Stephen son of Nicholas Hargreave baptised yo xxvth day beinge Wednsdaye and yo Ladye daye in Lent yt yeare 1629.
Robert son of Robert Thornes baptised yo xxixth daye then Palme Sondaye 1629.
Thomas Son of John Coningham baptised yt day at the eveninge prayer ano Dni. 1629.

Aprill 1629.

A yong son of John Horsforthe not baptised buried ye seconde daye beinge Shere Thursdaye in ye night.
Rosamond wyfe of Edwarde Wurmall buried yo fourth day then Easter even.
Samuell son of John Burche of Caverlay parishe baptised ye vijth daye.
Willme son of Thomas Marshall baptised yo xijth daye then beinge Lowe Sondaye.
Ann wyfe of Robert Phillippe deceased buried ye xvth daye.
John son of Willme Newsome alias Jackson buried the xvjth daye.
Marie daughter of Willme Speight of Chidsell baptised ye xixth daye.
Alice daughter of Robert Tomson baptised yt day at the eveninge prayer.
Thomas son of John Coninghame buried ye xxijth daye.
Thomas Gill of Ossett buried yo xxiijthe.
Alice wyfe of John Medlaye buried yo xxiiijth daye.
Ruthe daughter of Willme Speight yonger buried ye 29th day.
Henrie basse sonn of Henrie Elmesall and Alice Robinson was buried ye xxixth daye.

May.

Robert Barber and Jane Kaye was married the fourth daye at Mirffeilde.

1629.

Rosamonde daughter of Myles Cooke baptised ye vth daye.
James son of John Townend baptised yo vjth day Wednsdayo and then the exercise daye.
Lawrance Bull was buried ye tenthe daye Rogation Sondaye.
Margret daughter of Thomas Ewinge baptised yt day.
Thomas son of Robert Barghe baptised ye xijth daye.
Elizabethe wyfe of Rycharde Wilson buried ye xiiijth day.
Elizabethe daughter of Francis Gill baptised ye xvijth day.
A yonge son of Rychard Hall not baptised buried ye xxiijth daye in ye after noone.
George Woode buried his wyfe being an excomunicated person at the tyme of her deathe the same daye in ye after noone.
John sonne of Mr. Abraham Hemingewaye baptised ye xxiijth daye beinge Whitsundaye.
Marye daughter of Robert Gibson baptised ye xxvth daye.
Alice daughter of Phillippe Berrie buried ye xxvjth daye.
John sonne of Peter Thornton buried the xxviijth daye.
John Nayler of East Ardslay and Jenet Westerman of Rothwell were here lawfullie maried by a licence the xxixth.

June.

Charles sonne of Simeon Greenwood buried the xjth daye.
Willme son of John Arroswithe (? Arrosmithe) baptised ye xiijth daye.
Willme son of Willme Westerman baptised ye xviijth daye.
John Walker of Ossett was buried ye xxiijth daye.
Timothie son of Willme Acrode of Earles Heaton baptised ye xxvijth daye.
Thomas Tomson of Myrffelde and Sara Gill of this parishe were maried ye xxxth daye.
James Sonyare of this parishe and Brigett Ferglaye of Thornhill were maried there yo xxixth day.

Julie.

Grace daughter of Rycharde Whitlaye Junior buried ye fourth of Julie.
John Walker and Ann Beckwithe maried yo vth day.
John basse son of Abrahame Towened and Alice Goodall buried the xjth daye in ye after noone being drowned.
Ann daughter of Thomas Wilson baptised yo xijth daye.
Sara daughter of Willme Wright baptised yt daye.
Beniamen (Benjamin) son of Willme Leadbeater alias Shepperde was baptised yo xiijth daye in ye after noone.
Sibell daughter of Robt Oates base begotten with one Alice Walton of Ossett baptised the xiiijth daie this childe was buried ye xxiijth day of this monethe afterwards.
John Wadsworth and Anne Nailer married at Ossett Chapell the xiiijth daie.

1629.

Sara daughter of Robert Tompson baptised that daye this is Robert Tomson of Ossett.
Beniamen Acrode and Anne Claytonn married the xvth daie.
Thomas Nayler of Ossett yonger buried ye xviijth day.
Sibell basse daughter of Robert Oates and Alice Walton [*was not] buried that day this childe was buried ye xxijth day.
Jane daughter of Willme Acrode of this Towne was Baptised the xviijth day in the after noone.
James son of James Shepperde alias Milner baptised ye xixth daye.
Willme son of ye same James Shepperde baptised yt daye.
James son of James Shepperde buried ye xxiiijth at night.
Willme son of said James Shepperde buried yt daye.
Christopher son of John Speight buried ye xxvjth daye.
Willme Wroe and Juditho Roydes maried ye same daye.
Alice daughter of Willme Tillye buried yt day at eveninge prayer.
Willmo son of John Speight buried ye xxviijth day.

August.

Anthonye son of Samuell Foxcroft baptised ye second day.
†Joseph daughter of Josephe Owldroide baptised yt daye.
Willme Hepwortho and Margerie Walker maried ye vth day.
Elizabethe daughter of Edwarde Smithe baptised ye vjth day.
Dorithy daughter of John Burche buried the viijth daye.
John sonn of John Mannsfelde buried ye xijth day.
Mercye daughter of Thomas Fox buried ye xviijth daye.
Elizabethe daughter of George Towlsonn buried ye xixth daye.
Willme son of Willme Williamson baptised yt daye.
Willme son of Thomas Shepperde buried yt day.
Marye Wife of John Clayton buried the xxjth daye being an excommunicated parson in my absence yt day.
Mathewe son of Willme Thornes baptised ye xxiijth daye.
Ann daughter of John Dixon buried ye xxxth daye.

September.

Margrett daughter of Thomas Ewinge buried ye vth daye.
Rachell daughter of Robert Owldroide baptised ye vjth day Sonday and ye first (latter) Ladye day ye even.
Robert Osburne and Sibell Chambers maried ye

* The words in brackets are interlined.
† "Joseph" is written over "Lidia" which has been truck out.

vijth day beinge Mondaye and ye latter Ladye day.
Thomas Wade and Jonye Liversedge of this parishe were maried here ye xxtie daye.
Grace daughter of Michaell Owldroide baptised ye xxijth day.
Agnes daughter of the same Michaell Owldroide baptised that daye.
John Dawson of Dewsburie elder buried ye xxxth daye.

October.

Grace daughter of Michael Owldroide buried ye third daye.
Thomas sonn of Robert Smithesonn yonger baptised ye iiijth daye.
Thomas son of John Boulde baptised then at eveninge prayer.
Easter daughter of Mathew White baptised yeu at eveninge prayer.
Agnes daughter of John Dickensonn of Ossett buried ye vjth day in the after noone.
George Broadheade buried ye vijth daye.
John Dey and Ann Phillippe maried ye xjth daye.
James basse son of James Hurst and Jenet Shepperd alias Leadbeater baptised yt day at eveninge prayer.
Grace daughter of Nicholas Wheatlay baptised ye xxvth day.
Willme son of Robert Jewitho baptised yt day at eveninge prayer.
Phillippe Berrie buried ye xxvjth daye.
Thomas Collier and Susan Nayler maried ye xxvijth daye.
Edmonde Jepson buried ye xxxjth daye.

November.

Beniamen son of Willme Leadbeater alias Shepperde buried ye first daye All Sayntes day at evening prayer.
John Phillippe dyinge at ye Hugges wthin ye parishe of Wakefielde was buried here at Dewsburie ye iiijth day.
Christopher Blackeburn of Leedes and Grace Owldroide of this parishe maried ye xjth daye being Wednsdaye and Saynt Martyn his daye.
Grace wyfe of Edwarde Owldroide buried ye xiiijth day.
Elizabeth wife of Robert Wade buried the xviijth daye.
Elizabethe daughter of Robert Harrope baptised ye xxjth daye at eveninge prayer.
James Broadlaye buried ye xxvth daye.
Robert son of Willme Newsome alias Jackeson baptised ye xxixth daye.
Dorithie daughter of Robert Robinson baptised yt day bothe of them at eveninge prayer.
John Brase and Margrett Hanley married the xxxth daye.

December.

Mathewe son of Philemon Dixon baptised ye thirde day.
Marye daughter of Henrie Netleton baptised at Ossett Chappell there by Mr. Wilde preacher then there ye same day.

1629.

Elizabethe wyfe of Robert Gill buried the fourthe daye.
Ursula daughter of Widowe Sharphouse of Gawthorpe buried that daye.
Edwarde son of Robert Smithson yonger buried ye eight day.
Edwarde son of Edwarde Newsome alias Jackson buried ye xijth dayo.
Alice daughter of Thomas Greave Junior baptised ye xiijth day beinge St. Lucye day.
Robert son of Bryan Brooke baptised ye xxth day.
Agnes daughter of Henrie Greave baptised yt day.
Sara daughter of Rycharde Archer baptised ye xxviijth day beinge Innocentes daye or ye last of Christenmus first holie daye.

Januarie.

Rycharde son of Rycharde Firthe baptised ye third day at evening prayer.
Abraham son of Willme Nowell baptised ye vjth day.
Thomas Wilbore and Alice Bull married the xth day.
Grace daughter of Richarde Robinson baptised that daye.
Robert sonne of John Walker baptised the xvijth daye.
George Feelden and Elizabeth Wright both of Ossett married the xxiiijth daie.
Elizabeth daughter of Willme Knowles buried the 20th dayo.
John Nayler of Ossett Senior buried the xxixth day.
Mercye daughter of John Wood baptised the xxxjth day.

Februarye.

Willm Midlebrough and Sara Rawson both of Ossett married the seconde daie.
James Senior (? Sonior) and Isaboll Coodale married ye same daie.
John son of Thomas Peace baptised the same daie also.
James Bradley and Elizabeth Roodes married the fourth daie.
Dorithye daughter of Willmo Doye buried the 5th day and Shrove Mondaye.
Thomas Grayson and Jane Hall married the 9th daye beinge Shrove Tuesday.
Samuell sonne of Michaell Wheatley baptised the xjth daye.
Marye Robinson widdowe buried the xiijth daye.
John Greave senior buried the xiiijth daye.
Edward son of Edward Allan baptised that daye.
Dorythy daughter of James Speight of streete baptised that daye.
Grace daughter of Marmaduke Longleye baptised the xxjth daye.
Grace daughter of Jorge Wheelewright baptised yt daye.
Edwarde sonne of John Stapleton baptised the xxviijth daye.
Elizabeth daughter of Thomas Peace of Ossett beinge a poore man in the towne baptised that daye also.

1629.

George sonn of George Feelden baptised that daye at Ossett Chappell by Mr. Wilde.
Martha daughter of Mr. Richarde Wilde preacher at Ossett Chappell baptised that daye also By Mr. Wilde.

Marche.

Marye daughter of John Foxe of Ossett baptised the thirde daye beinge Wednesdaye and the exercise daye.
Willme Robucke of Ossett buried the fourthe daye.
Elizabeth wife of Roger Beatson of Ossett buried yt daye.
A yonge daughter of Robert Awdsley of ye Hagbecke buried the vth daye being not baptised.
Samuell son of Nicholas Mitchell buried ye vjth daye.
Grace daughter of John Cunningham baptised the 7th day.
John sonn of Phillipp Berrie deceased buried the 9th day.
Elizabeth daughter of John Fell buried the xiijth day.
Robert sonne of Richard Smithe baptised the xiiijth day.
Winifroide daughter of the same Richard Smithe baptised that daye.
Dorithye Nayler of Ossett widdow buried the xvth day.
Lidia daughter of Michaell Walker baptised the xxjth day Palm Sondaye.
John sonne of Peter Thornton baptised the xxviiijth daye.
Richard sonne of Robert Phillipp buried the xxxth daye.

April 1630.

Willme sonn of Willmo Speight Ju. baptised the first daye.
Winfroide daughter of Richard Smithe buried the seconde daye.
Robert sonn of Richard Smythe buried the fourth daye being Sondaye after Easter daye.
Willme Leadbeater alias Shopperde buried his wife the xiijth daye.
John Garnull and Alice Middlebrooke married the xxvth daye.
Margerie daughter of John Cowpas deceased was buried the same day.
Jane daughter of Jo: Speight baptised the 28th daye.
Robert Browne buried the xxixth day.

May.

John Akeroyd and Alice Hirst maried the thirde daye.
Ann wife of Willme Doy buried the same daye.
Thomas sonn of Willme Wroe baptised the sixt daye.
Thomas Lee and Elizabeth Pickard maried the xjth day.
Robert Nettleton and Alice Dawson maried the xijth day.
Elizabeth daughter of Willme Dixon baptised that daye.
Ann daughter of the same baptised that day also.

1630.

Edward sonn of Thomas Robinson, Sr. baptised the xvijth day being Tuesday in Whitsun weeke.
Alice daughter of Nicholas Gunson baptised the xxiijth day.
Willme bas-e sonn of Willme Banton and Jonye Walshe baptised the same day at eveninge prayer.
Alice daughter of Nicholas Hargreaves baptised the 30th day.

June.

Robert sonn of James Sonyare baptised the sixte daye.
Dorithie wife of Edmond Tattersall buried the xijth daye.
A yonge childe basse begotten of Henry Dawson wth one Ann Kent not baptised buried the same daye.
Jane wife of Robert Wright of Ossett buried the xiijth daye in the after noone.
Richard sonn of Willme Newsome alias Jackeson buried the xxjth daye.

Julie.

Isaacke sonn of Robert Walker baptised the xjth daye.
A yonge sonn of Willme Casson of Ossett not baptised buried the xxjth daye.
John Gibson was buried the xxvijth daye.

August.

Thomas Terrie and Grace Boothe married the thirde daye.
Ann daughter of Thomas Wilson buried the third daye.
Jorge Hoosan was buried the 9th daye.
Ann Warde buried the xijth daye Lee fayer even.
Tobie sonn of Willme Lee buried the xvth day.
Willme son of Thomas Musgrayve baptised yt daye.
Robert Sharphouse of Gawthropp buried the xviijth day.
Ellen Speight an ould woman buried the same daye.
Grace wife of Henrie Atkinson buried the same daye.
Ann daughter of Michaell Speight buried the xxjth daye.
Alice daughter of Richard Crowdar of Batley baptised here at Dewsburie the 22th daye Sonday in ye afternoone.
Mereye daughter of Tho: Foxe baptised that daye.
Jorge Westerman and Elizabeth Hemingway married the xxvth daye.
Roger sonn of Willme Audsley of Ossett buried the 29th day.

September.

Faythe daughter of Jorge Wood of Ossett buried the vth daye.
Marye daughter of Mr. Abraham Hemingway buried the viijth day.
Grace daughter of Robert Wheatleye baptised the xjth daye.
A yonge childe of Edward Bowlinge not baptised was buried the xvjth daye.
Elizabeth daughter of Simion Greenwoode baptised the xxiijth daye.

1630.

A yonge childe of Willme Middlebroughe of Ossett not baptised buried the xxiiijth daye.
Elizabethe daughter of James Sonyare baptised the xxixth daye.

October.

Susan daughter of Willme Speight senior baptised the thirde daye beinge Sondaye.
Elizabethe daughter of Ed: Allen buried the sixte daye Wednesdaye.
Willme Barton and Grace Rayner maried the vijth daye.
Elizabeth daughter of Richard Fearnley baptised the tenthe day.
Joyce daughter of Tho: Shepherde of Ossett baptised the same day.
Elizabethe daughter of James Sonyare buried the xvjth daye.
Allen Ellerie of Ossett was buried the xxth daye.
John son of John Tayler baptised the xxiijth daye.
Easter daughter of Jorge Hoosan deceased baptised the xxiijth daye.
Rachell daugnter of Robert Oldroyde buried that daye.
Willme Sacker of Ossett was buried the xxvjth daye.
Robert Mitchell and Ann Oldroyde maried the xxvjth daye.
John sonn of George Mawde of Ossett baptised the xxviijth daye.
Judithe daughter of Edward Pickarde of Ossett baptised the xxxjth daye.

November.

Ellen daughter of John Nayler of Ossett baptised the fourthe daye at Ossett Chappell by Mr. Richard Wilde preacher of God's word there.
John sonn of Robert Bedforthe baptised the xjth daye.
Robert Whitakers and Elizabeth Hollewell married the xvijth daye.
Elizabethe wife of Richarde Acrode buried the xxijth daye.
Marye daughter of James Bradley baptised that daye.
Edward sonne of Thomas Robinson buried the xxiijth day.
Jane wife of Thomas Wood deceased buried the xxvth daye.
Easter wife of Mathewe White buried the xxviijth daye.
Margrett wife of John Battie of Ossett buried that daye.
Thomas Whitakers and Marye Liversidge married the xxxth daye beinge Tuesdaye.

December.

Rachell daughter of Mr. Muereye Acrode vicar was buried on Satterdaye the fourthe daye.
Marye wife of Robert Brooke of Ossett buried the same daye.
Uxor Walton of Ossett towne was buried the vijth daye Sonday.
Jorge Birridge of Ossett was buried the xjth daye Satterday.

1630.

Alice Sharphouse of Gauthropp widdow buried the xth daye Friday.
Annes Littlewood widdow buried the xijth daye Sondaye.
Ellen wife of Thomas Archer buried the xiijth daye Mondaye.
John son of John Dey of Ossett buried that daye.
Samuell sonn of Nicholas Mitchell baptised the xiiijth day Tuesdaye.
A yonge sonne of Richarde Hall not baptised of Ossett buried the xvth day Wednesdaye.
John sonn of George Westerman baptised the xixth day Sondaye.
Edward sonn of Edward Newsome alias Jackson baptised that daye.
John son of John Doye baptised the xxvijth daye.

Januarie.

James basse son of James Hirst and Jennett Shepperde alias Leadbeater buried the vth daye.
Thomas sonn of Averie Pickarde of Ossett baptised the ixth daye.
Mathewe White and Marie Barbar married the xviijth daye.
Marye daughter of Edward Wormall of ye Haigh becke buried on Sondaye the xxiijth daye.
James sonn of John Foxe of Ossett buried the xxvth daye.
Sara daughter of Richarde Dawson of Dewsburie townshippe baptised the xxxth daye.

Februarie.

Nicholas Fell and Issabell Peace maried at Ossett Chappell the seconde daye.
A yonge daughter of Mr. Sam. Peirson not baptised was buried the same day.
Samuell son of John Burche buried the same day.
Elizabeth wife of Thomas Gill of Ossett deceased was buried the fourthe daye.
Thomas sonn of Anthonye Armitadge of Ossett buried the xijth daye.
John son of John Carnell of Ossett buried the xxth daye.
Sara daughter of Robert Barbar senior baptised the same daye at eveninge prayer.
Jane Foxe widdowe buried the xxijth day.
Sara daughter of Robert Barbar senior buried the xxijth daye.
Jonas sonn of Willmo Ashton baptised the xxiiijth daye.

Marche.

Easter daughter of Mathew White buried the fourthe daye.
Edward Oldroyde of Earlesheaton an oulde man buried the xjth daye.
Grace daughter of Averie Goodall baptised the xijth daye.
Henrie son of Willmo Westerman baptised the xxth daye.
Sara daughter of Willmo Hall of Ossett buried that daye.
John sonn of Anthonye Fearnleye baptised the xxiijth daye.
Elizabeth Dishforthe of Ossett was buried the xxvijth daye beinge Care Sondaye.

1630.

Susan daughter of Michaell Bentley deceased was buried the xxxjth daye beinge the last daye.
*Richard sonn of Thomas Woode of Ossett baptised at Ossett Chappell the thirde daye of October 1630 By Mr. Wilde preacher of Gods worde there 1630.
*Alice daughter of Nicholas Beaumont of Ossett baptised yt daye there at Ossett Chappell 1630.
*Dorithie daughter of James Shepperde alias Milner baptised that day at Ossett Chappell all by Mr. Richardo Wilde 1630.

Aprill 1631.

Willmo basse son of Willmo Benton and Jony Warmbie buried the vth daye.
Edward Smythe buried the 8th day Good Fridaye.
Annes daughter of Robert Barghe of Ossett baptised the xjth daye.
Ann Beaumont of Ossett buried the xvjth day.
Elizabeth daughter of John Townende baptised the xxthe daye.
Uxor Wood widdow buried the same daye.
Thomas son of Thomas Autye Junior baptised the xxjth daye.
Elizabeth daughter of the same Thomas Autye baptised the same daye.
Sara daughter of John Harrison beinge a traveller baptised the xxiiijth daye beinge Sondaye.
Willmo son of Mathow Hepworthe baptised that daye.
Christopher Brooke Ju. of Ossett buried that daye.
Elizabeth daughter of Michaell Bentley deceased was buried the xxixth daye.

Maye 1631.

Thomas sonn of Thomas Grayson baptised the first daye beinge Phillipp and Jacob his daye.
Ann daughter of Thomas Terrie of Gauthroppe baptised the same daye.
Marke son of Thomas Whitakers baptised the seconde daye.
Nathaniell Stirke and Elizabeth Walton married the viijth daye.
Thomas son of Thomas Awtye Ju. buried the xth daye.
Willmo Haighe and Margrett Dixon married the xjth daye.
Marye daughter of Robert Beatson of Ossett baptised at Ossett Chapell the xvth daye.
Willmo Kent and Katherin Hazlewood married the xixth daye.
Issabell daughter of Laurence Saxton baptised the xxijth daye.
Christopher son of Willmo Audsleye baptised yt day alsoe.
A yonge childe of Rycharde Mekindale not baptised buried the xxiijth daye.

June.

Rosamond daughter of Jorge Pickarde baptised the sixth daye.

---

* These three entries are at the bottom of a page, and a line has been drawn above them to separate them from the preceding entries for March.

1631.

Samuell son of Robt Wade buried the xxiith daye.
Thomas son of Richard Castlo baptised the xxiijth daye.

Julye.

Alice daughter of Edmondo Somaro buried the 4th daye.
Jorge son of Richard Castles buried the 7th daye.
Annes Beutleye of Gauthroppe widdowe buried the xiijth daye.
A yonge childe of Michaell Oldroyde, buried the xvijth daye.
Samuel son of Jorge Towlson baptised the xxiiijth daye.
A yonge childe of Jo. Parker Ju. buried that daye.
Aluereye son of Aluerey Pickarde buried the xxvjth daye.
Elizabeth daughter of Willme Broadleye baptised the xxxjth daye.

August.

Ann wife of John Booth deceased an ould woman was buried the first daye.
John son of John Deye of Ossett baptised the xiiijth daye.
John sonn of Willme Neusome alias Jackson baptised the same daye at eveninge prayer.
Elizabeth wife of Robt Roydes of Ossett buried the xvjth daye.
Elizabeth daughter of Aluerey Pickarde of Ossett buried the xvijth daye.
Jane daughter of Mr. Richarde Wilde preacher of the worde of God at Ossett Chappell was baptised there by him tho xxjth daye.
Marie daughter of Robert Peaker baptised the xxiiijth daye.
Thomas sonn of Willme Speight of Chidsell baptised the xxviijth daye.

September.

Dynise wife of Jo. Parker yonger buried the vth daye.
Mathew Robinson and Ann Ledgearde married the xijth daye.
Thomas Archer and Elizabeth Manusfielde both of this parishe was married here by a licence from the Court of Yorke directed they was married on Tuesdaye the xxth daye
Willme Antie alias Anderton and Alice Robinson married the xxijth daye.
Richard Harrishe buried his wife the 24th daye.

October.

Willme son of Willme Autie baptised the second daye
Marie daughter of John Aikroide in the Preist (Priest) lane baptised the same daye.
Richard son of Robert Barton of Chidsell baptised the ixth daye.
Willme son of Robert Deye of Ossett baptised that daye
Issabell daughter of Robert Whittakers of Earles Heaton baptised that daye alsoe.
Willme son of Willme Kent of Earlesheaton baptised the same daye at eveninge prayer.

1631.

Willme son of Willme Middlebroughe of Ossett baptised the xiijth daye.
Margrett wife of Edwarde Roydes of Ossett buried the xixth daye.
Willme Shepleye buried the xxth daye.
Henric Roades and Grace Thorppe married by a license the xxjth daye.
John Manusfelde of Ossett buried the same daye.
Joyce daughter of Thomas Shepperde of Ossett buried that daye.
John Laye and Alice Boulinge married the xxiiijth daye.
Mario daughter of Tho. Firthe of Gauthroppe baptised the 30th daye.

November.

Willme son of Robert Oldroide baptised the sixte daye beinge Sondaye.
Thomas Jaggar Junior and Jennett Birridge married the vijth daye.
Robert son of John Jagger of Ossett baptised the xijth daye.
Mr. George Fearnleye clarke Mr. of Arte (Master of Arts) and Marie Tilson of our Parish of Dewsburie married here by a license on Tuesdaye the xxijth daye.
Robert Broaro of Hanginghoaton buried the xxiijth daye in the afternoone.
Katherin daughter of Carey Morrice baptised the 24th daye.
Elizabeth daughter of Thomas Marshall of Ossett baptised the xxvijth daye.

December.

Willme Soniare and Mereye Robinson married the fourthe daye.
John Woodheade of Thornhill and Jennett Gill of this parishe married the vthe daye at Ossett Chappell.
Willme son of Jorge Saxton of Gauthroppe baptised the xjth daye
Ann daughter of Michaell Speight of Ossett baptised the xiijth daye.
Issabell daughter of Robert Whitakers of Earles heaton buried the same day.
Jorge son of Willme Wrighte of Ossett baptised the xvijth daye.
A yonge childe of John Carnell of Ossett not baptised buried the xixth daye.
John sonn of James Soniare of ye water yate baptised ye xxjth daye.
Jeremy Roades and Alice Roades married by a license the 22th daye.
Robert son of Robert Bedfortho baptised the 28th daye.
Thomas son of Thomas Wilson of Ossett baptised ye same day circa hora duodecima.

January.

Dorithie daughter of Robert Tompson of Ossett baptised the first day.
John son of John Hirst a yonge infant buried the third daye.
Elizabeth daughter of Mr. Abraham Hemingwaye baptised the seaventhe day beinge Satterdaye circa hora duodecima.

1631.

Jonas son of Willme Ashton buried the same day.
Richard Hall of Ossett buryed the eight daye.
Alexander Hartley of Birstall beinge drowned in Calder the xvijth daye was here buryed the xviijth daye.
Robert son of Mathew Robinson baptised the xxijth daye in the fornoone.
Nathaniell son of Nathaniell Stirke of Ossett baptised the same day.
Alice daughter of Edward Dowlinge baptised that daye.
John Tilson and Winifreide Barbar married here by a licence on Tuesdaye the xxiiijth daye.
Anthonye Curtisse and Agnes Nayler married that daye.
Willme Lee the yonger and Ann Brooke married the 26th daye.

Februarye.

Robert Chadwicke and Francis Barghe married the seconde daye.
Elizabeth daughter of Jorge Nayler of Ossett baptised the vth daye.
Edward son of Robert Barbar senior baptised the same daye at eveninge prayer.
John son of Willme Neusome alias Jackson buried the same daye at eveninge prayer.
Joseph Maude a poore man beinge a stranger dying at the Haghbecke within this parish was buried here the sixto daye.
Robert son of Robert Bradforth of Ossett baptised the xijth daye.
Ann daughter of Jo. Robucke of Ossett baptised that daye.
Ann daughter of the same Jo. Robucke buried the xiiijth day.
Aluereyo Bull buried the xvjth daye.
Thomas son of John Dubbell beinge a stranger baptised here the xixth daye.
John son of Willme Roydes of this Towne baptised that daye.

Marche.

Mario wife of Robert Speight of the Street side buried the first daie.
Thomas Archer buried the thirde daye.
Robt son of Mathew Robinson buried the ninetho daye.
Josua son of John Fell baptised the xjth daye.
Easter wife of Jorge Hoosan deceased was buried the xijth daye.
Uxor Fell of Ossett buried the xvtho daye.
Jenaett basse daughter of ——* and Rosamonde Roydes of Ossett baptised here the xviijth daye and Care Sondaye.
Nicholas Nayler of Birstall was buried here in the Churche the 20th daye.
Uxor Whitakers of Earles Heaton buried that daye.
Jennett basse daughter of ——* and Rosamond Roides of Ossett was buried here the 22th daye.

* Blank in Register.

Aprill 1632.

Samuell son of Mr. Samuell Peirson clerke baptised the xjth daye.
Jennett daughter of Anthonye Armitadge of Ossett baptised the xvth daye.
Margerie basse daughter of Willme Smythe and Jennett Cowpas was buried the xviijth daye.
Ann daughter of Willme Hall of Ossett baptised the xxijth daye.
Edward Wood of Churcheaton and Mary Ellerye of this parish married at Ossett Chappell the 23th daye.
Elizabeth daughter of Philemon Dixson baptised the xxvth daye.
Issabell wife of Edwardo Phillippe deceased was buryed the xxvijth daye.
Ellen daughter of Willme Nowell of Gauthroppe baptised the 29th daye.
Willme Milner and Elizabeth Middlebroughe marryed the 30th daye.

Mayo.

Marke sonn of Willme Williamson baptised the first daye.
Elizabeth daughter of Henrie Broke baptised that daye.
Willme Rodleye and Issabell Ellis married the seconde daye.
Alice daughter of John Holdsworth baptised the fifte daye.
Sara daughter of Nicholas Gunson baptised the sixte daye beinge ye Rogation Sundaye.
Marye daughter of James Sonyare of Earlesheaton baptised the same day at eveninge prayer.
This Childe was buryed ye seaventh daye.
Eliz. daughter of Willme Hall buryed the 9th daye.
John son of Willme Soniare baptised the tentho daye beinge tho Ascention daye.
Thomas Maupsfeilde buried the xjth daye.
Easter daughter of Jorge Hoosan deceased buried the xvijth daye.
Michaell Bentleye and Grace Speighte both of this parish married here by a lycencee on Satterdaye the sixth daye.
Eliz. daughter of Willme Thornes of Ossett baptised ye xxth daye beinge Whitsundaye.
Richard Acrode the yonger and Alice Beckwith married the xxjth daye.
Robt Roydes and Ellen Gill married the xxiiith daye.
Issabell wife of Mr. Aluereye Acrode vicar dyinge on Trinitie Sundaye the 27th daye was buryed on Mondaye the xxviijth daye.

June.

John son of Edward Phillippe deceased buryed the thirde daye beinge Sondaye in the afternoone.
Robert son of Thomas Jewithe of Gauthroppo baptised the tenthe daye.
A yonge childe of Joseph Oldroide not baptised buried the sixth daye.
Aluereye Acrode buried the xxijth daye.

Julye.

Sara daughter of Michaell Bentleye of this Towne baptised the 4th daye beinge Wednesdaye and our exercise dayo.

1632.

Ri. son of Ro. Cartar deceased baptised the 8th daye.
Addam Jessuppe and Issabell Milnes married the tenthe daye.
Susan daughter of Edmonde Soniare baptised the xvth daye.
Robert Broadleye and Marye Speight married the xviijth daye.
Ann daughter of Robt Burbar junior baptised the xixth daye.
Willmo son of Willmo Autic alias Anderton baptised the xxijth daye.

August.

Ann daughter of Jo. Kaye of Chidsell baptised the vth daye.
Eliz. daughter of Francis Gill of Ossett buried the xijth daye.
Willmo son of Willmo Gill of Ossett baptised the xixth daye.
Thomas son of John Cuningham baptised that daye.
Marye daughter of Michaell Oldreide baptised that daye.
Eliz. basse daughter of Jacob Wood and Eliz. Ashton buried the xxijth daye.
A yonge childe of Jo. Walker not baptised buried ye same daye.
Martha daughter of John Nettleton yonger of Hangingheaton baptised the xxvjth daye.
Francis daughter of Ro. Gilson baptised that daye.
Richard basse son of Edwarde Townende of Netherton and Marye Ellis of Ossett baptised the xxxth daye in the afternoone.

September.

Sibell daughter of Thomas Greave Ju. baptised the seconde daye.
Henrie son of Robert Smithson Ju. baptised that daye.
Martha daughter of Jo. Nettleton Ju. buryed the thirde daye.
John son of Marmaduke Longleye buried the same daye.
Edward Walker and Rosamonde Reades married the 4th daye.
Maryo daughter of Nicholas Hargreaves baptised the ninthe daye.
Elizabethe daughter of Marmaduke Longleye baptised the same daye.
Edmonde Brooke and Martha Fearnleye married by a lycence the ninthe daye beinge the same daye of these christenings above written.
Thomas Sallett and Alice Oldroide married the xiijth daye.
Robert Goodall and Ann Burnbye married the xvjth daye.
Maryo daughter of Robert Smytle of Ossett baptised the same daye.
Willmo Dickson buried the xviijth daye.
Ann wife of Robt Thornes of Ossett buryed the xxijth daye.
A yong son of Robt Audsleye of the Haigh becko not baptised buried the same daye in the afternoone.

1632.

Mathew son of Robt Walker of Gauthroppe baptised the xxiijth daye.
Henrie son of Bryan Brooke baptised the 29th daye.

October.

James son of James Fearnleye baptised the thirde daye.
Samuell son of Willmo Aikreble of Earlesheaton baptised the seaventh daye.
Prudence daughter of John Wood of Earlesheaton baptised the xith daye.
Robt son of George Naude buried the same daye.
Eliz. daughter of Willmo Whitleye of the Carre baptised the xvth daye.
Fraunces son of John Stapleton of Earlesheaton baptised ye xxjth daye.
Elizabeth daughter of John Carnell of Ossett baptised the same daye.
Elizabeth Wooler of Ossett widdowe buried the xxiijth daye.
Josepho son of John Speight of Ossett baptised the xxviijth daye.
Willmo son of Robt Harroppe baptised the same daye.
Arthure Kaye and Dorithie Walker married the xxixth daye.
Ann daughter of Willmo Dickson deceased buried that daye.

November.

Annes daughter of Thomas Peace of Ossett baptised the fourthe daye.
Henrie son of Bryan Brooke buried the same daye.
Michaell Yudell and Elizabeth Sacker married the eighte daye.
Annes wife of Thomas Oldroide of Squrrell Hall buryed the xiiijth daye.
A yonge childe of John Boulde not baptised buryed the xvth daye.
Mris Oglethorppe of Earlesheaton buried the xvijth daye.
Dorithie daughter of John Burche baptised the xviijth daye.
Eliz. daughter of John Nayler of Ossett baptised that daye.
Dorithie wife of Willmo Speight of this townshippe buried ye xxth daye.
Josepho son of Willmo Ashton baptised the xxvth daye.
Henrye son of John Tilson baptised the xxvijth daye.
John Bargho and Margrett Mannsfeilde married at Ossett Chappell the same daye by Mr. Ri. Wilde preacher there.

December.

Ellen daughter of Robt Whitakers of Earlesheaton baptised the seconde daye.
Issabell wife of Robt. Smythson senior buryed the same daye.
A yonge childe of Willmo Brooke of Ossett not baptised buryed the thirde daye.
Jennett wife of Willmo Deye deceased buryed the vijth daye in the afternoone.

---
* So in Register.

1632.

Grace daughter of Anthonie Curtisse baptised the ninthe daye.
Ann daughter of Raphe Dod a traveller baptised the xjth daye.
Henrye son of Tilsen* buryed the xiiijth daye.
Elizabeth daughter of Jo. Nayler of Ossett baptised there ye xvjth daye.
Margrett wife of Richarde Castleye of this towne was buryed the xxth daye.
Willme Aikroyde of Earlesheaton buryed the xxiiijth daye.
Michael Walker of this townshippe buryed the xxvth daye beinge Tuesdaye and Christmas daye.

Januarye.

John son of Marmaduke Fletcher base begotten with one Alice Wilkinson of Chidsell baptised the seconde daye.
Grace wife of John Oldroide of the Mooreside buryed the same daye.
Leonarde son of Henrye Greaves of Ossett baptised the sixte daye.
Margrett daughter of Willme Lee of Bouthroide baptised the same daye.
Sara daughter of Willme Musgraye buried that daye.
James son of James Fearnleye buryed the xth daye.
Francis son of Thomas Robinson of the mooreside baptised the xiijth day.
Elizabeth daughter of James Speight of the Streete side buryed the xiiijth daye.
Brene daughter of Symeon Greenwood of Soothill Hall baptised the xvth daye.
Ann daughter of Richarde Archer baptised the xvijth daye.
Robert son of Thomas Jewitt buryed the xixth daye.
John son of Edwarde Denys buryed the xxjth daye.
John Kaylie servant to Nicholas Wheatleye was buryed the xxijth daye.
Elizabeth Oldroyde of Earlesheaton buryed the xxiiijth daye.
Jorge son of Willme Westerman of Hanginghenton baptised the xxvjth daye.
Alice daughter of the same Willme Westerman baptised the same day.
Thomas Hanson of Ossett buryed the same day.
Alice daughter of Willme Rolleye baptised at home in the night beinge the 26th daye and Satterday by Mr. Peirson.
Thomas son of Thomas Foxe baptised the xxvijth daye.
Alice wife of Richarde Acrede yonger buried yt daye.
A yonge childe of the same Ri. Acrode buried that daye wth his wife.
Alice daughter of Willme Rolleye buryed the xxviijth daye.
Willme Speight of Ossett and Elizabeth Hall of ye same maryed the xxixth daye.
Ann daughter of Willme Broadleye of this towne baptised the same daye.

*I think that this is J. Tilson, but it is difficult to say, the J is badly formed and runs into the T.—S. J. C.

Februarye 1632.

Elizabeth daughter of Thomas Walker base begotten with one Jennett Leadbeater alias Shepperde baptized the seconde daye.
Edwarde Bull of Ossett buryed the fourth daye.
Marke son of Willme Williamson buryed the seaventh daye.
Anthonye son of Richard Fearnleye of Gauthroppe baptised the tenthe daye.
Martha daughter of Robt Goodall baptized the same daye.
Willme Castleye and Ellen Liversedge marryed the xiiijth daye.
Rebecca daughter of James Bradleye of Chidsell baptised the xixth daye.
Grace daughter of John Doye of Hanginghenton baptized the xxiiijth daye.
Thomas Fisher and Jane Chamber both of the parish of Thornhill married here the xxvth daye.
John Doye and Elizabeth Ashton marryed the xxvjth daye.

Marche.

Martin Parker and Alice Whitakers, marryed the fourthe daye beinge Colloppe Mondaye.
Jennett daughter of Edwarde Allen of Earlesheaton baptised the tenthe daye.
George son of Anthonye Fearnleye of Hangingheaton baptised the xiiijth daye.
Marye daughter of Robt Barghe of Ossett baptized the xvjth daye.
Marye Wilbie of this towne buryed the same daye.
Thomas son of Richard Mckindale of Ossett baptized the xvijth daye.
John son of Willme Milner of the same baptized that daye.
Ann daughter of Tho. Audsleye of Chickenley baptized the same daye.
Rycharde Nensome of this towne buryed the xviijth daye.
Ann daughter of Michaell Oldroyde buryed the xixth daye.
John son of Arthure Kaye baptized the xxiiijth daye.
Samuell son of James Sonyare alias Peace beinge of Earlesheaton baptized the same daye 1632.
A yonge childe of Thomas Awtye of the mooreside yonger not baptized buryed the xxvjth daye beinge Tuesdaye 1633.
Grace daughter of Willme Wilson baptized the xxxjth daye beinge 4th Sondaye in Lent 1633.
Marye daughter of John Robucko of Ossett baptized at Ossett Chappell there the same daye by Mr. Richarde Wylde preacher of Gods Word there.

Aprill 1633.

Elizabethe daughter of Thomas Whitakers of this towne baptized the first daye beinge Mondaye.
John son of Aluerie Goodall baptized the sixte daye.
Marye daughter of Mr. Richarde Wilde baptized the seaventhe daye at Ossett Chappell by him the said Mr. R. Wilde.
Ellen daughter of Mathowe Robinson of Earlesheaton baptized the xith daye.
Thomas son of Thomas Terrie of Gauthroppe baptized the xviijth.

1633.

Willmo Shepleye of Wakefeilde and Sibell Roydes of this parish married the xxijth daye.
Henrie son of Willme Newsome baptized the xxiijth daye.
Susan daughter of Mathew Hepworthe baptized that daye.
Willme Speight of Ossett buryed the 28th daye.
Robert son of Willme Richardson alias Boye baptized yt daye.
Uxor Hirste an ouble woman buried the 60th daye.

Maye.

Frauncis son of John Walker deceased buried the fourthe daye in the afternoone.
Alice daughter of Willme Westerman buryed that daye.
Alice daughter of Roger Dawson buryed the vijth daye.
Richarde Robinson of Earlesheaton buried the viijth daye.
Ellen daughter of Robert Whitakers of Earlesheaton buried ye tenthe daye.
Robt Scoorer of Ossett buryed the xiiijth daye.
John son of Jorge Wheelewrighte baptized the sixth daye.
Robert Breare of Birstall and Marye Mitchell of this Townshippe married here by a Lycense the xxijth daye.
Grace daughter of Jorge Wheelewrighte of Ossett buryed the xxvth daye.
Rychard Aikroide yonger and Annes Medleye of Ossett marryed the xxvijth daye.
Elizabethe wife of Robt Whitakers of Earlesheaton buryed the same daye.
Mychaell Robinson of the parishe of Leeds and Jonye Wilcocke of this parish marryed the xxviijth daye.
Katherin daughter of John Dawson baptized that daye.

June.

Willmo son of Thomas Nettleton of Gauthroppe baptized the sixte daye.
Dorithie daughter of Willme Westerman of Hanyngheaton buried the eighte daye.
John son of Careye Morrico of the Haighbecke buryed the same daye.
James Fearnleye wife was buryed in Birstall Churcheyerde the xiijth daye.
Anthonie son of John Taylier of Hanyngheaton baptized the xvjth daye.
Grace daughter of Thomas Milner of Ossett baptized yt daye.
Thomas son of Henrye Robinson deceased buryed the xxjth daye.
Robt Wright of Ossett and Sara Walker of the same marryed the 29th daye.

Julye.

Willmo Audsleye of Gauthroppe buryed the sixte daye.
Ann wife of John Hepworthe of Mirffeilde being drowned in the Calder betwixt the milles on Fridaye at night beinge the vth daye was buried here in the Churchyerde the xjth daye beinge Thursdaye.

1633.

Sara basse daughter of ——* Walker of Ossett and Marye Clayton buried the xvjth daye.
John son of John Haighe of Ossett baptized the xviijth daye.
Christopher Smythe of Batleye and Agnes Phillippe of Ossett marryed the xxijth daye.
Willme Castle of the parishe of Leedes and Ann Ellis of this parishe married the 29th daye.

August.

Thomas sonu of Thomas Musgreave of Hangingheaton baptized tho third daye.
Margrett daughter of Willme Barton of Hanging heaton baptized the fourthe day.
James Dyson and Elizabeth Speight of Ossett marryed the tenthe daye.
Jennett daughter of John Haighe of Ossett baptized the xjth daye.
Judith daughter of Edwarde Pickcarde of Ossett buryed the xiiijth daye.
A yonge childe of Willme Middlebroughe of Ossett not baptized buried tho xvth daye.
John son of Edwarde Newsome baptised the xviijth daye.
Elizabeth daughter of Jorge Feilden of Ossett baptized the same daye.
Elizabeth wife of Christopher Brooke of Ossett buryed the xxijth daye.
Josephe son of Thomas Nayler of Ossett buryed the xxiijth daye.
Edmonde Speight of ye parishe of Birstall and Judith Lee of this parisho married yo xxviijth day.
Richarde son of Thomas Savile basse begotten with one Elizabeth Barbar baptized the 29th daye.

September.

Robert Harroppe buryed the first daye.
Sara daughter of John Nettleton of Hangingheaton baptized the fourthe daye.
Marye daughter of Richarde Dawson of Dewsburie townshippe baptized the eighte daye.
John base son of John Okerd and Alice Goodall baptized ye ixth daye.
James son of Robt Broadleye of this townshippe of Dewsburie baptized ye xjth daye.
Josephe son of John Doye of Ossett baptized the xvth daye.
Alice daughter of John Nullie (? Nuttie) of Gauthroppe baptized the same daye.
Willme son of Josephe Arnitadge of Ossett baptized the xxijth daye.
Willmo Mansfeilde of the parish of Wakefeilde and Susann Beatson of Ossett married at chappell of Ossett the xxiiijth daye by Mr. Audsleye.
A yonge childe of Myles Coote of Ossett not baptized buried the xxvth daye beinge Wednesdaye this childe is a man childe.
Sara daughter of Josephe Nayler baptised that daye.
Grace daughter of Robert Tomson of Ossett buried ye xxvjth day.
Susan daughter of Roger Lee of this townshippe of Dewsbury baptized the 29th daye.

---
* Blank in Register.

DEWSBURY PARISH REGISTERS. 129

October 1633.

Elizabethe daughter of Henrie Broke of Ossett buried the first daye.
Thomas Carter and Ellen White married the seconde daye.
Elizabeth daughter of Richarde Speight baptized the sixte daye.
Elizabethe daughter of John Dobson baptized the same daye at eveninge prayer.
Sara daughter of Nyman Coulten of Gauthroppe buried the same daye after eveninge prayer.
John son of Robert Hoydes of Ossett baptized the xxth daye.
Annes daughter of Thomas Woode of Ossett baptized the same daye.
John Wilbie of Cleckeheaton and Issabell Dickson marryed the xxiijth daye.
Henrye son of Willme Speighte of Chidsell baptized the xxiiijth daye.
Marye daughter of Robert Bradforthe of Ossett baptized the 27th daye.
Elizabeth daughter of John Tilson baptized the xxxth daye.

November.

Rebecca daughter of Josephe Oldroyde baptized the thirde daye.
Marye daughter of Bryan Brooke baptized that daye.
Michaell Berrie and Marye Robinson marryed the sixte daye.
Edward son of Edwarde Walker baptized the xth day.
Richarde son of John Walker baptized that daye.
John Phillippe of Ossett and Jennett Cowpas of this townshippe marryed the xijth daye.
Robert son of Michaell Wheatlaye of this towne baptized the xvijth daye.
Willme son of Willme Autye alias Anderton buryed the xxvth daye.
Luke Wrighte and Margrett Fletcher marryed that daye.
Marye daughter of Rychard Dawson of this townshippe buryed the 29th daye.

December.

Thomas Blackburne of Mirffeilde and Marye Midwoode of this parish marryed the thirde daye.
Sara daughter of Willme Autye senior baptized the vth daye.
Willme Brooke buryed the same daye.
Francis wife of Ambrose Robinson buryed the seaventhe daye.
Sara daughter of Willme Autye senior buried that daye.
George son of George Pickarde of Ossett baptized the xvth daye.
Willme son of Willme Audsleye of Ossett baptized the xxijth daye.
Marye daughter of Thomas Sallett baptized that daye.
Alice wife of Thomas Sallett buryed yo same daye at nighte.
Jane daughter of Willme Williamson baptized at home the xxijth daye.
Richarde Harrishe buryed the xxiiijth daye.
Thomas Gamble buryed the same daye.

1633.

Jane daughter of Willme Williamson buryed the xxviijth daye.
Thomas son of Thomas Batlaye base begotten with one Alice Robinson of this townshippe of Dowsburie baptized the same daye.
Judyth daughter of Robte Wrighte of Ossett baptised the 29th daye beinge first Sondaye after Christmas daye.
Elizabeth wife of John Deye of the streete buryed the 30th daye.

Januarye.

Marye daughter of Tho. Sallett buryed the first daye.
Marye daughter of Robt. Barbar senior baptized the same daye.
A yonge childe of Edmonde Tattersall of Ossett townshippe not baptized buryed the seconde day.
Ann daughter of James Senykye of this townshippe of Dewsburie baptized the xijth daye.
Thomas Greave of Earleshoaton junior buried the xiiijth daye.
Robert son of Lauranco Saxton of Earleshoaton baptized the xixth daye.
Grace wife of Jorge Pickeringe buryed the xxvijth daye.
Jorge son of Willme Westerman of Hanging Heaton buryed the 29th daye.

Februarye.

Marye daughter of Willme Rodleye of this towne baptized the seconde daye.
Alice daughter of Philemon Dickson baptized the sixte daye.
Josua son of Alnerye Pickarde of Ossett baptized the ninthe daye beinge Sondaye after morninge prayer.
John son of John Townende of this townshippe of Dewsburio buried the xiiijth daye.
Willme son of Willme Foxe of Ossett baptized the xvjth daye.
Robert Bull of Ossett and Alice Stirto married that daye.
Thomas son of Willme Castleye of this townshippe of Dowsburie baptized the xviijth daye.
An daughter of Edwarde Bowlinge baptized that daye.
Uxor Nousome an oulde woman buryed the xxijth daye.
Betterisse wife of Willme Casson of Ossett buryed the xxiijth daye.
Rychard son of Thomas Autye of the mooreside yonger baptized the xxvjth daye.
Rycharde sonn of John Hall of the moorside baptized the xxvijth daye.

Marche.

Sara daughter of John Full baptized the seconde daye.
Marye daughter of John Jagger of Ossett junior baptized the xxiijth daye.
Elizabeth daughter of Mr. Henrie Addam baptized the xxvth daye.
Willme son of Michaell Yudall baptized that daye.
Richarde Castley of this towne buryed the xxvjth daye.

1633.

Marye daughter of Michaell Bentleye deceased was buryed the 29th daye beinge Sattenlaye 1634.
John son of Willme Gill of Ossett baptized the xxxth daye beinge Sondaye before Easter daye 1634.
Franscis daughter of Robt Robinson of this towneshippe baptized the same daye at eveninge prayer 1634.

April 1634.

Willme son of Rychard Dawson of Earlesheaton baptized the seconde daye.
Robert Daylden an oulde man buryed the xiijth daye.
Elizabeth daughter of Michaell Bentleye of this towne baptized the xvjth daye.
Susan daughter of Richarde Acrode junior of this towne baptized the xxth daye.
Annes wife of Thomas Ashton of Soothill Towneshippe buryed the xxiijth daye.
Elizabeth wife of Willme Acrode of this towne buried the 28th daye.

May.

Sibell daughter of Thomas Greave of Earlesheaton deceased buryed the first daye.
Marye daughter of Thomas Wardelasse begotten with one Susan Northe buryed the third day.
Margrett wife of John Jagger buried that same daye.
John Robert and Anu Scoorer married the 4th daye.
John Roades of Ossett and Elizabeth Freckleton of the same marryed the sixte daye.
Marye daughter of Richarde Firthe baptized the vijth daye.
Winifreide daughter of John Townende baptized the eight daye.
Willme Acrode of this towne buryed the 9th day.
Marye daughter of Richarde Firthe buryed the xjth daye.
Thomas son of Thomas Nayler of Ossett yonger baptized the xiijth daye in Ossett Chappell.
Alice daughter of Robert Penker baptized the xvth daye.
Jennett daughter of Nicholas Gunson baptized the xviijth daye.
Stephen Sagar of Ossett townshippe buried that daye.
Elizabeth daughter of Thomas Eatocke* of Ossett baptized the xxijth daye.
Marye daughter of Tho. Hepworthe of Ossett baptized the xxvjth daye.
Marye daughter of Robt Bedforthe of Dewsburie towneshippe baptized the xxvijth daye.
Uxor Alice Broadheade buried the same daye.
Susan daughter of Mathew Hepworth buried the 30th daye.
Thomas son of Thomas Nayler of Ossett yonger buryed the xxxjth daye.

June.

John son of George Nayler of Ossett baptized the first daye.
John son of John Boulde baptized ye same daye.

---
* This name has been altered and is not easy to make out.

1634.

Franscis Nettleton of this parish and Alice Bradleye of the parish of Rothwell married there yo seconde daye.
Elizabeth wife of Robt Bentson of Ossett buryed the 4th daye.
Elizabeth daughter of Mychaell Bentley of Gauthroppe baptized the vth daye.
John son of George Nayler of Ossett buryed the same daye in tho after noone.
Henrye son of Thomas Jewith of Gauthroppe baptized the eight daye.
Mathew son of John Speight of ye same baptized the same daye.
Thomas son of Willme Wroo of Ossett buryed the xjth daye.
Robert son of Edwarde Pickearde of Ossett baptized the xvth daye.
Thomas Ashton of Dewsburie townshippe buried the 23th daye.
Thomas Shepleye of Mirffeilde and Elizabeth Dawson of this parishe of Dewsburie married here the 24th daye by a lycence directed from the Courte of Yorke.
Marye daughter of Martin Parker of this towne of Dewsburie baptised the xxvth daye.
James Fearnley of this parish and Eliz. Rayner of Batley parish married there the same daye.

July.

Robert son of Thomas Carter of Earlesheaton baptized the xiijth daye.
John son of Marmaduke Fletcher of Earlesheaton baptized the xvijth daye.
Michaell Speight of Ossett son of Richard Speighte of Earlesheaton deceased buried the xxjth daye.
Elizabethe daughter of Henrye Barbar baptized the 29th daye.

August.

Thomas son of Mr. Samuell Pearson baptized the sixte daye.
Sara daughter of John Wilbie baptized the xvjth daye.
Elizabeth daughter of Willme Hall of Ossett baptized the xvijth daye.
Thomas Robinson of the mooreside buryed the xxth daye.
George Lickeringe and Issabell Millner marryed the xxvjth daye.

September.

John Ellis of Ossett and Elizabeth Gleadall of the same married the seconde daye beinge Tuesdaye before the latter Lee fayre.
Thomas Nettleton of this parishe and Ann Saltingstall of the parish of Hallifax married there the thirde daye beinge Wednesdaye before the Latter Lee fayre.
Joseph son of Robert Thornes of Ossett baptized the seaventh daye.
Marye daughter of Nathaniell Stirte of Ossett baptised the 21th daye.
Marye wife of John Gill of Ossett buryed that daye.
A yonge infant or childe of John Barghe of Ossett not baptized buryed the 25th daye.

1634.

Willme Speighte buryed the 24th daye.
Thomas son of Willme Kent baptized the xxviijth day.

October.

Willme son of Robert Smithson junior baptized the vth daye at eveninge prayer.
Thomas Acrode and Ellen Dickson marryed the eight daye.
Alice daughter of Thomas Phillippe of Ossett baptized the xijth daye.
Ann daughter of Michaell Speight deceased buryed the 18th daye.
Marye daughter of Willme Beamounte of Ossett townshippe baptized the xixth daye.

November.

Thomas son of Willme Castleye buryed the seconde daye.
James Hirst and Alice Johnson marryed the third day.
Aluery Walker and Elizabethe Richardson married the fourthe daye.
John Millnes and Marye Dowson married the vth daye.
Nynian son of Nynian Coulten baptized the ninthe daye.
Christopher son of Willme Wrighte baptized that daye.
Elizabeth wife of Richard Pollarde of Ossett buryed the xvjth day.
Edwarde son of John Phillippe of Ossett baptized the xvijth daye.
Susan daughter of Willme Broadleye of this townshippe baptized the xxvjth daye.
Henrye son of Richarde Dawson baptized the xxxth daye beinge Sondaye and Anders (Andrew's) daye.
Robert son of Robert Roydes of Ossett baptized that day.
Robert son of Robert Barghe of the same baptized that day.

December.

An daughter of James Seniare of this townshippe of Dewsburie buryed the thirde daye.
Elizabeth daughter of Willme Thornes of Ossett buryed the xjth daye.
Rycharde son of Willme Kitson baptized the xiiijth daye.
Humphreye Dickson of Ossett buryed the xvijth day.
Uxor Charles Walton of Ossett townshippe buryed the xixth daye.
Sara daughter of Michaell Oldroyde baptized the xxviijth daye.

Januarye.

Willme son of Willme Millner of Ossett baptized the first daye.
Elizabeth Snawden widdowe buryed the sixte daye.
Alice daughter of Robt Gibson of Gauthroppe baptized the xjth daye.
Jane Joye of Soothill townshippe buryed the xvth daye.

1634.

Nicholas Gunson of Soothill townshippe buryed the xxjth daye.
Robert Mortimar of this towne buryed the xxijth daye.
Mereye daughter of Marmaduke Longley baptized the xxvth daye.
Josua son of Willme Middlebroughe of Ossett baptized the same daye.

Februarye.

Grace wife of Henrye Barbar deceased buryed the fourth daye.
Elizabeth daughter of Jeremye Pratt of London buryed here the seaventh daye.
Thomas son of Willme Nowell of Gauthroppe baptized the eighte daye.
Sara daughter of Willme Williamson baptized the xth daye.
Josias son of Willme Ashton baptized the xvth daye.
Willme son of Willme Seniare baptized that daye.
Elizabeth daughter of Anthonye Armitadge baptized that daye.
Thomas son of Thomas Whitakers baptized the xxjth daye.
Jonas son of Willme Autye of the mooreside baptized the xxvijth daye.

Marche.

Thomas son of Myles Cooke of Ossett baptized the first daye.
Judith daughter of James Fearnleye of the moreside baptized the seaventh daye.
Robert Mitchell of Chidsell buryed the same daye.
Willme son of John Roades baptized the viijth daye.
Rachell daughter of Francis Nettleton baptized the tenthe daye beinge Tuesdaye before Care Sondaye.
Margerye daughter of Luke Wrighte baptized the xviijth daye.
Robert son of Robert Broadleye baptized the xxjth daye beinge Satterdaye and Palme Sondaye even.
Jonas son of Willme Autye buried the xxijth daye beinge Palm Sondaye.
Thomas son of Myles Cooke buryed the 24th daye beinge Tuesdaye and the Annunciacon of Marye even.
Dorithie daughter of Willme Walker buryed the xxvth daye beinge Wednesdaye and Annunciacon of Marye comonlye called the Ladye daye 1635.
Ann daughter of John Ellis of Ossett baptized the 29th daye beinge Easter daye and Sondaye 1635.
Robert Audsleye of Ossett buryed the 30th daye.
Edward Goodall and Alice Clegge maryed the 31th daye.

Aprill 1635.

Elizabeth daughter of Willme Wroe baptized the vth daye beinge Lowe Sondaye 1635.
Elizabeth daughter of John Cuningham baptized the same daye at eveninge prayer 1635.
Arthure Kaye was buryed the vijth daye beinge Tuesdaye.
John Tompson of Earlsheaton buryed the xiiijth daye.

1635.

John son of Mathew Hepworth baptized the xixth day.
Annes wife of Willmo Wilbye of Ossett buryed the xxth daye beinge Mondaye 1635.
Francis Nelthorppe and Annes Pickearde marryed the xxijth daye.
Dorithie late wife of Edwarde Hirst deceased buryed the xxiijth day.

May.

George Greake a collier dyinge at Ossett was buryed here the seconde daye.
Edwarde Kaye buried the vjth daye.
Rycharde Oldroyde and Sara Brookesbanke marryed the vijth daye.
Margrett wife of John Aikroyde buried the 8th daye.
John son of Willmo Westerman of Hangingheaton baptized the xjth daye.
George son of the same Willmo Westerman baptized that day.
Katherin wife of Willmo Westerman buryed ye same daye.
Rycharde Harrison and Dorithye Nettleton marryed the xiiijth daye by a Lycence.
Grace daughter of Robert Dickson of Hanging Heaton baptized the same daye.
Rycharde Aikroyd senior of Dewsburie townshippe buryed the xvth daye.
Dorithye wife of Abraham Bowlinge of Ossett townshippe buryed the xviijth day.
Martha daughter of Henrye Bull buryed the xxjth daye.
Christopher son of Robert Deye of Ossett baptized the xxiijth daye.
Marmaduke Denison buryed the same daye.
Tymothye son of Henrye Brooke of Ossett baptized at Ossett Chappell the xxviijth daye by Mr. Peirson.

June.

Winifreide wife of Robert Barton of Chidsell buryed the first daye.
John Moore of the parish of Caresworth and Sara *Shemclde of the parish of Wakefoilde was here marryed the seaventhe daye.
Rosamonde daughter of Willmo Casson of Ossett buryed the same daye.
Eliz. daughter of Edwarde Hirst buryed the same daye at eveninge prayer.
Willmo Burnleye and Katherin Robinson marryed the tenthe daye beinge Wednesdaye at Woodchurche by Mr. Peirson.
Edwarde Moore of Ossett buryed the xjth daye.
Robert Boothe of the Haighbeeke within Soothill townshippe buryed the xvth daye.
Susan daughter of Anthonye Fearnleye of Hangingheaton baptized the xvjth daye.
Edwarde Dawson of this townshippe and Jenuott Bull of the same marryed the xvjth daye.
Alice daughter of Willmo Autye alias Anderton baptized the xxjth daye.
John son of Willmo Westerman buried that daye.

---

* It is doubtful whether this is the correct reading. I think there is a sign of abbreviation between the S and the h, so that there may be another syllable in the name.—S. J. C.

1635.

Edmonde Haighe a stranger dyinge in this towne was here buryed the 24th daye.
Jane daughter of Charles Walton deceased buryed the 27th daye.
Roger son of Franscis Nelthorppe of Ossett baptized the xxviijth daye.
Obadiah son of Willmo Lee baptized the same daye.
Jennett daughter of Anthonye Armitadge of Ossett buryed the 30th daye.

July.

Matthew Speight of Gauthroppe and Dorithie Middlebroughe of Ossett married here the first daye.
An wife of Henrye Robinson deceazed buryed the seconde daye.
Josephe son of Robert Walker of Gauthroppe baptized the vth daye.
Lawrence Pickeringe of Ossett buryed the same daye at the eveninge prayer.
Marye daughter of Robert Barghe of Ossett buryed the sixte daye.
John Foxe of Ossett buryed the eight daye.
Marye daughter of Robert Barbar junior baptized the nintue daye.
Jennett daughter of Rychard Mekindale of Ossett baptized the xijth daye.
Nicholas Westerman of Hangingheaton buryed that daye at the eveninge prayer.
James Wilson and Sara Peace marryed here the x4th daye.
Robert Whitakers and Issaboll Gunson marryed the xvth daye.
Christopher Brooke of Ossett junior and Jane Hunter marryed the same daye.
Edwarde Wilson and Alice Kaye marryed the xxijth daye.
Willmo son of John Carnell of Ossett baptized the xxvjth daye.
Marye daughter of James Sonyare of this townshippe baptized the 29th daye beinge Wednesdaye.

August.

Josephe son of John Deye of Ossett buryed the first daye.
Ann daughter of James Hirst baptized the seaventhe daye.
Sara daughter of Josephe Nayler buryed the xiijth daye.
Thomas son of Anthonye Curtice baptized the xvjth daye.
John son of John Claughton baptized that daye.
John son of John Dawson baptized the xixth daye.
Robert Speight buryed the xxth daye beinge Thursday.
Rycharde son of Rycharde Hanson base begotten with one Ann Bull baptized the xxijth daye.
Abraham Bowlinge and Mabell Harrison marryed the xxiiijth day.
Jane daughter of Willmo Castleye baptized the xxxth daye.

September.

Willmo son of Willmo Foxe of Ossett buryed the first daye.

1635.

Elizabeth daughter of Robert Beckwth deceazed buryed the same daye.
John son of John Millns junior baptized the sixte daye.
Elizabeth daughter of John Doye baptized that daye.
Edwarde Aikroyde of this towne buryed the eighte daye.
Margrett wife of Willme Walker of this towne buryed the sixth daye.
Mychaell son of Robert Thorpe buryed the xxth daye.
Mereye daughter of James Sonyare of Earlesheaton baptized the same dayo at the eveninge prayer.
Ann late wife of Edwarde Hull of Ossett deceazed buryed the xxjth daye.
Ann wife of Tho. Rodleye of this towne buryed that daye.
Elizabeth late wife of Rycharde Hirst of Earlesheaton deceazed buryed the xxijth daye.
A yonge infant or childe of Willm Nensome of this townshippe of Dewsburie not baptized buryed the 23th daye.
Henrye son of Henrye Bull of this towne buryed the xxvjth daye.
John son of Thomas Ellis basse begotten with one Ann Wormall baptized the xxvijth day.
Ann daughter of James Hirst buryed the 28th daye.
Alice daughter of John Speight of Ossett baptized the 29th daye.

October.

A yonge infant or childe of Rychard Oldroyde of the moreside still borne buryed the seconde daye.
Rycharde son of Rychard Dishforth of Gauthroppe the yonger buryed the thirde day.
Marye daughter of Willm Copleye basse begotten with Ann Autye baptized the thirde daye beinge Satterdaye.
Emor Addye and Ann Lancaster was marryed the eighte daye by a Lycense directed from the Courte of Yorke they was marryed the 8th daye.
Sara daughter of Thomas Nayler of Ossett yonger buryed the tenthe daye.
John son of Thomas Foxe of Soothill townshippe baptized the xjth daye.
Marye daughter of Robert Bradforth son of Tho. Bradforth of Ossett baptized the same daye.
Willme son of Thomas Peace of Ossett baptized the same daye at Ossett Chappell at eveninge prayer.
Robert Millns and Easter Barbar marryed by a license the xith daye.
Willme son of Thomas Wood of Ossett baptized the xviijth daye.
Edwarde Autye and Alice Tebb marryed the xxvjth daye.
Elizabeth daughter of Mychaell Bentley of this towne buryed the 30th day.
Willm Cooke of Leedes parish and Jane Hall of this parish marryed the last daye.
Thomas Oldroyde of Dewsburie townshippe was buryed the same daye in the afternoone.

November 1635.

Alice daughter of Rycharde Archer Laptized the first day.
Elizabeth daughter of John Robucke of Ossett baptized the thirde daye.
Elizabeth daughter of John Robucke of Ossett buryed the vth daye.
Rycharvl son of John Taylier of Hanginghcaton baptized the xxijth daye.
Robert son of John Stapleton of Earlesheaton baptized the same daye at the eveninge prayer.
Mathew Speight and Alice Wilkinson marryed the xxiijth daye.
Josephe son of Robert Walker of Gauthroppe buryed the xxvth day.
June wife of Michaell Walker of Ossett deceazed buryed the xxviijth daye.

December.

Marye wife of Thomas Whitakers of this towne buryed the first daye.
Susan daughter of Thomas Nettleton of this towne baptized the thirde daye.
Grace daughter of Willme Whitleye baptized the vth daye.
John son of Josephe Nayler of Ossett baptized the sixto daye.
Grace daughter of Thomas Terrye of Gauthroppe baptized the same daye.
Grace daughter of Willme Whitleye buryed the seaventh daye.
Thomas son of Robert Smithson of this towne buryed the xijth daye.
John son of Josephe Nayler buried the same daye.
A yonge infant of Willme Foxe of Ossett still borne buryed the same daye alsoo.
Ann daughter of Mr. Addam baptized the xvijth daye.
Rycharde Bridge dyinge in this towne was buryed here the 20th daye at the eveninge prayer.
Jennett wife of George Speight buryed the xxiiijth daye.
Alucrey Millnes buryed the same daye.
Jennett Leadbeater alias Shepperde buryed the 29th daye.

Januarye.

Rycharde son of Thomas Audsleye of Chickenleye baptised the first daye.
Thomas son of John Barghe baptized the same daye.
Jennet wife of Robert Audsleye of the Haighbecke buryed the thirde daye.
John son of Rycharde Fearnley baptised that daye.
John Peace of Ossett buryed the seaventh daye.
Josephe son of Willme Ashton buryed the thirteenthe daye.
Ellen daughter of Willme Roades of Ossett baptized the xvijth daye.
Alice daughter of Aluereye Goodall baptized that day.
Elizabeth daughter of Aluereye Walker baptized the same daye.
A yonge childe of Robt Bull of Ossett not baptized buryed the xviijth daye.
Elizabeth daughter of Michaell Bentleye of Gauthroppe buryed the xxijth daye.

1635.

John son of John Nettleton of Hanginghoaton baptized the xxiijth daye.
A yonge infant or childe of Edwarde Autye still borne buryed the 24th daye.
John Sykes and Elizabeth Walker marryed the xxvth daye.
Alice wife of Robert Bull of Ossett buryed the xxrjth daye.
Peter Toulinge and Susan Barton marryed the xxvijth daye.
Ellen daughter of Willm Gill baptized the xxxjth daye.
Willmo Shoaffeilde curate at Ossett Chappell buryed the last daye of this month.

Februarye.

John Hardcastle and Annes Steade marryed the seconde daye.
Ann daughter of Robert Barbar junior was buryed the tenthe daye.
Dorithie daughter of Robert Bradforthe of Ossett baptized the xiiijth daye.
Elizabethe daughter of Rycharde Aerode was baptized the same daye at the eveninge prayer.
Mychaell son of Mychaell Bentleye of this towne baptized the xvijth daye.
Grace daughter of Mathewe Speight of Chidsell baptized the same daye.
Debora daughter of James Bradleye of Chidsell baptized the xviijth daye.
Elizabethe wife of John Tompson deceased buryed the xxjth daye.
A yonge childe of Marmaduke Fletcher still borne buryed the xxijth daye.
John Nayler and Marye Soothill marryed the xxiijth daye.
Elizabeth Grayve widdowe buryed that daye.
John son of Marmaduke Fletcher buryed the xxiiijth daye.
Robert son of Robert Broadley buryed the xxvth daye.
Elizabeth daughter of John Jagger of Ossett baptized the xxvijth daye.
Rycharde son of Jorge Pickeringe baptised that day.
Thomas Whitakers and Dorithye Soniare was marryed the xxixth daye beinge Collop Mondaye.

Marche.

Easter daughter of Edwarde Wilson of Gauthroppe baptised the eight daye.
John Bentleye of Gauthroppe buryed the ninthe daye.
Samuell son of John Tilson baptized the tenthe daye.
Willme son of Willme Wilson buryed the xjth daye.
Thomas son of Thomas Eacocke of Ossett baptized the xiijth daye.
Mychaell son of Philemon Dickson buryed that day.
A yonge daughter of Robert Oldroide not baptized buryed the same daye.
Mathewe son of John Speight buryed the 6th daye.
Roger son of Robert Thornes of Ossett baptized the xxth daye.

1635.

Thomas son of Michaell Yudall baptized that daye.
Grace daughter of Rycharde Whitley of this towne junior baptized the same daye alsoe.
Thomas son of Michaell Yudall buryed the xxvth daye beinge Frydaye and the Annunciacon of the Virgin Marye comonlye called the Ladye daye 1636.
Jane Doye of Hanginghcaton widdowe buryed the xxvjth daye 1636.
Henrye son of Thomas Musgreave baptized the 27th daye.
Margrett daughter of Robert Barbar of this towne senior baptized the same daye.
John Townend buryed the 29th daye 1636.
Sara daughter of Willm Burnleye baptized the 31th daye.

Aprill 1636.

Elizabeth daughter of Willme Speight of Chidsell baptized the seconde daye.
Alice daughter of Willme Ludge of Ossett base begotten with one Rosamonde Thornes baptized the thirde daye.
Jorge Speight buryed the fourth daye.
Elizabethe wife of Marmaduke Fletcher buryed the vth daye.
Elizabeth daughter of Willme Speight buryed the xiiijth daye.
Ann Taylier widdowe buryed the xvjth daye.
James son of James Wilson of Ossett baptized the xixth daye.
John son of Christopher Brooke baptized that daye.
Robert Bull and Marye Sladin marryed the xixth daye.
John son of Christopher Brooke buryed the xxth daye.
Henrye son of Henrye Barbar baptized the same day.
Grace wife of Almereye Millns buryed the xxvth daye.

Maye.

John Battye of Ossett buryed the fourthe daye.
Edward Wood of Ossett buryed the viijth daye.
Elizabeth daughter of John Sykes base begotten with Jennett Walker baptized the same daye.
John Parker senior of this towne buryed the ixth daye.
Mathew son of Willme Thornes of Ossett buryed the same day.
Robert Hartley and Edithe White married the xjth daye.
Ann Terrie of Gauthroppe widdowe buryed the same daye.
Mereye daughter of John Graive of Earlesheaton deceased buryed the xiijth daye.
Sara wife of Willme Speight of Chidsell buryed the xvijth daye.
Thomas son of Willme Kent buryed the xviijth daye.
Willm Steade and Eliz. Forrest married the xxijth daye.
John Walker and Eliz. Westerman married that day.
Eliz. daughter of Willm ——— buried the 23th daye.
Susan Forrest of Ossett buryed the same daye.

June 1636.

Robert Walker of Gauthroppe buryed the ixth daye.
Jennett wife of John Oldroid of Hanging heaton buried the xjth daie.
Richard Rouse and Alice Burnley married the xijth daie.
Thomas son of Robert Whitakers baptized the same daie also.
Joseph son of John Daye of Ossett baptised the same day also.
Alverie Acrode vicar here buried the xiijth daie being Monday.
Abraham Hemingway of Gauthroppe buried his wife the xiiijth daye beinge Tuesdaye.
Robt son of Tho: Carter buryed the same daye.
John Dobson of this towne buryed the xvijth daye.
Jane wife of Robt Walker of Gauthroppe latelye deceased buryed the xxjth daye beinge Tuesdaye.
James Ellam and Annes Thornes marryed that daye.
Edwarde son of John Phillippe buryed the 23th daye.
Rycharde Firthe buryed the same daye alsoo.
Mychaell Wheatleye the yonger beinge drowned in ye Calder the same daye was buryed the xxvth daye.
A yonge infant or childe of Robt Roades buryed the 27th daye.
Edward son of Henrye Greaves of Ossett baptized at Thornhill Churche the 26th daye for want of a lawfull minister within the parish of Dewsburie.
Grace daughter of Rychard Rouse baptized at Batleye Churche the same daye.

July.

Richard Farrande and Eliz Hargreaves married here the first day.
Ellen wife of Robert Roades of Ossett buryed the first daye beinge Fridaye after Peters daye.
Robert Gill of the same buryed the same daye.
Edwarde Walker of this towne buried the second day.
Thomas Wheelwright buried the ixth daye.
Robert son of John Foxe of Ossett deceased buried the same daye in the afternoone.
Abraham Hemingwaye of Gauthroppe buried the xth daye.
John Oldroyde of Hangingheaton buried the xvjth daye.
Marie Speight of the Street buried the xviijth daie.
Alice daughter of Thomas Phillip of Ossett buried the xxvjth day.
A man child of Nynion Cowton of Gawthroppe still borne buried the xxxth daie.
Mychaell son of Edward Newson baptized the last daie.
Thomas son of Willm Wilson baptized the last daie.
An infant of George Pickard of Ossett buried ye last daie also.

August.

Marie daughter of Tho Nailer yonger baptised the vijth daie.
Marie daughter of Tho Marshall baptised the same daie also.
Anne wife of Richard Dawson buried the xijth daie.

1636.

John Gill of Sow wood in Ossott buried the xiiijth daie.
Frauncis wife of John Dickinson of Ossett buried ye xviijth day.
Isabell wife of Tho: Dargh of Ossett buried the xixth daye.
Susan wife of John Fletcher buried the xxjth daie.
Anne wife of George Wheelewright buried ye 22th day.
Tobie son of Richard Oldroid baptized the xxviijth daie.
John sonne of George Wheelewright buried ye xxixth daie.
Robert Linthwet buried the laste daie.

September.

Elizabeth daughter of Robert Bedforth baptized ye first daie.
George Wheelewright of Ossett buried the viijth daie.
Thomas son of John Walker baptized the xjth daie.
Dorithie daughter of Robert Westerman baptized the same day.
Marie daughter of George Nayler baptized the same day also.
Alice wife of Robt Nettleton of Chidsell buried the xijth daie.
Marie daughter of Robert Barbar buriel ye xiijth daye.
Edward son of Robert Barber buried the xiiijth daye.
Henrie Dunwell buried the xvth daie.
Alice wife of Richard Whitley buried the xixth daie.
Tho: late son of John Battie of Ossett buried the same daie also.
Jonas son of John Fell buried the xxjth.
Marie late wife of Richard Robinson buried the xxvjth daie.
Lucie daughter of John Nailer of Ossett baptized the xxviijth daie.
Hanna daughter of James Fearnley baptized ye 29th day.

October.

John Dickinson of Ossett buried the first daie.
John sonne of James Hirste baptized the seconde daie.
John son of Robert Bargh of Ossett baptized the same daie also.
Dorithie wife of Richard Fearnley of Gawthrope buried the 3 daie.
John Terrie and Elizabeth Acrode married the iiijth daie.
A man child of John Dishforth of Gawthrope still borne buried the vijth daie.
Sara daughter of Mathew Speight of Gawthrope baptised the ixth daie.
Robert Dey of Ossett buried the same daye.
Alice late wife of Willm Roebucke of Ossett buried ye xiijth day.
Robert late son of Tho: Gamble of Ossett buried the xvth daie.
Marie wife of Willm Lee of this towne buriel the xvjth daie.
James Wightman and Alice Thornes married the xviijth daie.

1636.

Willm Ellis and Mercie Bull married the xxvjth daie.
Eden Roydes of Hanginghcaton buried the same daie also.
Joseph Walker of the prest (priest) lane buried the xxxth daie.
Robert Roodes and Marie Greave married ye last daie.
Marie daughter of Will'm Pasley baptized the last daie.

November.

Sara daughter of Richard Gibson baptized the fyfto daie beinge the Kinges Holidaie.
Symon son of Bryan Brooke of Earles heaton baptized the vjth daie.
Anna daughter of Thomas Hepworth baptized the vjth daie also.
Hellen wife of Michaell Bentley of Bouthroid buried the viijth daie.
John Woode and Betrice Wormall married the ixth daie.
Aron son of Joseph Oldroid of the mooreside baptised the xiijth daie.
A man child of Willm Myres of the Street side still borne buried the xiiijth daie.
Richard Thornes thelder of Ossett buried the xvth daie.
Christopher Jagger and Elizabeth Milner married the xvjth daie.
Josua son of Willm Awtie of the mooreside baptized the same daie also.
Willm Lee of this towne buried the xxijth day.
Susan daughter of John Hirste of this towne buried the xxvth daie.
Robert son of Thomas Whitakers baptized the laste daie.

December.

Abraham son of Mr. Samuell Pearson baptised the first daie.
Alice wife of Willm Musgreave buried the fourth daie.
Agnes wife of Thomas Audsley of Ossett buried the viijth daie.
James son of Richard Speight of Ossett baptized the xjth daie beinge Sundaie and a faire snowe.
Alice daughter of John Roobucke baptised the same daie also.
A woman child of Phillope Udalle still borne buried the xliijth daie beinge Wedensdaye.
Sara daughter of Joseph Nailer baptized the xviijth daie.
Agnes daughter of Willm Audsley of Ossett baptized the 26th day.
Isabell Greene widdowe of the Street side buried the xxviijth daie.

Januarie.

Elizabeth daughter of George Westerman of Earlsheaton baptized the first daye.
Alice daughter of Thomas Warmall and Elizabeth Thornton borne before marriage baptized the same daye.
Thomas Robinson of Ossett buried that third daye.
James son of Richard Speight of Ossett buried the sixt daie.

1636.

John Tottie a rough mason buried the xviijth day.
Sara daughter of Willm Beaumont of the Street side in Ossett baptized the xxijth daie.
Dorithie daughter of John Nailer of Ossett baptized the same daie.
Alice daughter of Willm Rodley of this towne baptized the same daie also.
George Woode and Anne Deye married the xxiiijth day.
Elizabeth daughter of Edward Dawson baptized the xxixth daie.

Februarie.

Thomas Wormall and Elizabeth Thornton both of Ossett married the seconde daie.
Willm Beatson and Elizabeth Harpin both of Chidsell married the same daie.
Michaell Sacker and Ann Antie married the vth day.
Richard Roodes and Agnes Ashton married ye same day.
Margerie daughter of Luke Wright of Earles Heaton buried the viijth daie.
Elizabeth daughter of Willm Jackson alias Newsome baptized the xijth daie.
Grace daughter of Willm Steade of Gawthrope baptized the xvth daie.
John Bedforth thelder buried the xviijth daie.
Sara daughter of Mathew Robinson of Earlesheaton baptized the sixth daie.
Margret wife of John Sugden of Ossett buried the xxiiijth daie.

Marche.

John Ellis thelder of Ossett buried the first day.
Rebeca late daughter of Willm Fell of Ossett deceased buried the fourth daie.
Henrie son of Laurence Saxton of Earlesheaton baptized the vth daie.
Joseph son of John Dey of Ossett buried yo same daie.
Alice wife of Richard Goodale of Soothill Mill was buried the xjth daie beinge Saterdaye.
Willm son of Fra: Nettleton of Earles-heaton baptized the xijth daie.
Henrie son of Willm Nowell of Gawthrop baptized the same daie.
Susan daughter of John Holdsworth of Bouthroid baptized the same daie.
Elizabeth daughter of Francis Nelthorpe of Ossett baptized the same daie also.
John Croste of Ossett buried the xviijth daie.
Sibell daughter of Robt Wright of Ossett baptized the sixth daie.
Marie daughter of Edward Boulinge baptized ye 19th day.
Obadiah son of Daniell Simpson of Gawthrope buried the same daie also.
Elizabeth daughter of Wm Newsom buried the xxijth daie.

April 1637.

Mercie daughter of Edw Awtie baptized the second daye.
Jane Firth widdowe buried the iiijth daie.
Samuell son of Robt Peaker baptized the vjth daie.

1637.

Jennet wife of John Richardson of Ossett buried the nynth daie beinge Easter daye.
Robert Nettleton and Alice Bedforth married ye xxth day.
Agnes daughter of Robert Stansfield buried ye xxvijth daie.
Anne wife of John Walker buried the xxixth daie 1637.

Maie.

Grace daughter of Willm Ingham baptized ye first day.
Grace daughter of John Stead buried the same daie.
Elizabeth daughter of Michaell Bentley of Chickenley baptized the iiijth daie.
Michaell Bentley and Marie Linthwet married ye xth daie.
George son of Willm Westerman buried the xjth daie 1637.
Hellen daughter of Willm Gill of Ossett buried ye same daye.
Willm sonne of Willm Kitson baptized the xiiijth daie.
Robert Mansfield buried the xvjth daie.
Margret daughter of Wm Sonier baptized ye xviijth daie.
A man child of Willm Beatson still borne buried the xxvth daye.
John son of Willm Beatson baptized the same daie.
Alice daughter of Tho: Wormall buried ye xxvjth daie.

June.

Richard Dishforth of Gawthrope buried the first daie.
Margret daughter of Willm Sonier buried the iiijth daie.
Edward Lee of Wakefield and Grace Musgreave married here by lycence the vijth daie.
John Walker of this towne buried the same daie.
Anne wife of Tho: Phillip of Ossett buried the viijth daie.
Michaell Sharpe and Anne Michell married the same daie.
Elizabeth wife of Robert Bradforth buried the xvijth daie.
Robert Roodes and Jennett Speight married yt daie.
Elizabeth daughter of Joseph Armitage baptized ye xviijth day.
Eliz daughter of Robt Gibson of Gawthrop baptized yt daie.
Marie daughter of Willm Halle of Ossett baptized the xxvth day.
John sonne of Robert Speight buried the xxixth daie.

July.

Beatrice daughter of James Speight buried yo ixth day.
A man child of Willm Myres of Ossett rubaptized buried the xxth daie.
Christabell wife of George Mawde of Ossett buried the xxjth daie.
Willm son of Willm Ellis baptized the xxiiijth daye.
Richard Beateman and Margrot Ellis married ye xxvjth daie.
Samuell son of Marmaduke Longley buried the xxviijth daie.

1637.

Elizabeth late daughter of Edward Smyth deceased buried the xxixth daie.

August.

Marie daughter of Nicholas Batley baptized ye second daye.
Marie daughter of Edward Stephenson of Ossett baptized the sixt daie.
Richard late son of Tho: Greaves of Earlesheaton buried the ixth daie.
Robert Pickard of Ossett buried the xixth daie.
John son of John Sikes baptized the xxth daie.
Willme son of Xpofer Brooke of Ossett yonger baptised yt daie.
Mercie daughter of Alverie Pickard baptized yt daie.
Bridget Hunt widdowe buried the xxvth daie.
Jane daughter of Tho: Autie yonger baptised ye xxvjth day.
Michaell son of Martin Parker baptized the xxvijth daie.
Marie daughter of Roger Lee baptised yt daie.
Marie daughter of Xpofer Jagger baptized yt daie.
Easter daughter of Edward Wilson buried the xxvijth daie.

September.

Marie daughter of John Phillipe of Ossett baptized ye viijth day.
Robert Bradforth and Rosamunde Thornes both of Ossett married the xijth daie.
Willm Ashton and Dorithie Lee married the xiijth daie.
Elizabeth daughter of Willm Foxe of Ossett baptized the xvijth daye.
Thomas Peace of Ossett buried ye xviijth daie.
Mercie daughter of John Claughton of Ossett baptized the xxiiijth daie.
Susan daughter of John Fell of Bouthroid baptized yt daie.
A daughter of Peter Richardson still borne buried the same daie in the after noone.
John Forrest and Dorithie Nailer both of Ossett married the xxvijth daie.
Mathew sonne of Ninian Coulton of Gawthrop baptized the xxixth day.

October.

John son of John Walker of Ossett baptized ye first daie.
Judeth daughter of George Field of Ossett baptised yt daie.
Jennett daughter of Tho: Autie of Soothill base begotten with one Jennett Armestronge of Gawthrope baptized yt daye.
John son of Henrie Sikes of Ossett baptized the 8th daye.
John son of Edward Chaster baptized the same daie.
Thomas son of Anthonie Fearnley baptized the xjth daie.
Michaell son of Michaell Oldroid baptized the xvth daie.
Rosamunde daughter of Willm Milner of Ossett baptized yt daie.
Edward son of Willn Kent baptized yt daie.
James son of James Somer baptized the xxijth daie.
Luke son of Thomas Carter baptised ye same daie.

1637.

George Glover and Jennett Fairebarne married yo 30th daye.
Willm Westerman and Alice Hoult both of this parishe married the last daie.

November.

Robert Greene of the parishe of Mirfield and Sibell Wilkinson of this parishe was married with a lycense the first day.
Marie daughter of John Woode of Earlesheaton baptized the firste daie beinge the Kinge daie.
Richard Brooke and Anne Scotte both of Ossett married the vijth daie.
John Robinson and Mercie Beckwth married yo viijth daie.
John Hollamle of Leedes and Judith Roe of Ossett married the xvth daie.
Winfrede daughter of Richard Bateman baptized yt daie.
John son of John Terrie of Gawthrope baptized yo xixth daie.
Mercie daughter of Robert Dickson of Hangingheaton baptized the xxiijth daie.
Marie daughter of Robert Gunson of Earlesheatonn baptized the xxvjth daie.
Agnes daughter of Willm Ashton of Earlesheatonn baptized that daie.

December.

Gregorie son of Tho Jagger of Ossett buried yo iiijth daie.
Mercie daughter of Marmaduke Longley buried the 5th day.
Robert son of Willm Westerman baptized the ixth daie.
Elizabeth daughter of Richard Acrode buried the xjth daie.
Thomas Booth of Ossett a poore man buried the xijth daie.
James son of James Senior of the Mill buried the xvth day.
Alice daughter of John Dishforth baptized the xvijth daie.
Grace daughter of Willm Gill of Ossett baptized yt daie.
Michaell son of Michaell Sacker baptized yt daie.
Thomas Acrode of this towne buried the xviijth daie.
John Speight of Ossett buried the sixth daie.
Anne daughter of Robert Netleton of Chidsell baptized yo xxjth daie.
Jennett late wife of Anthonie Armitage of Liverseidge Halle buried here the xxiijth daie.
Willm son of Willm Castley baptized the xxvijth daie.
Henrie Robinson buried the same daie.

Januarie.

Willm sonne of Tobie Sill of Soothill baptized the third day.
John son of Robert Goodale of Chidsell baptized the vijth daie.
Thomas son of Anthonie Feam'ey buried ye viijth day.
A man child of Luke Wright still borne buried yt daie.

1637.

Agnes wife of Richard Acrode buried the ixth daie.
Margret wife of Joseph Oldroid buried the xijth daye.
Thomas son of John Forrest yonger baptised yo xxviijth day.
Willm son of John Dey of Ossett baptized the same daie.
Marie daughter of John Milnes baptized yt daie.
Thomas son of John Bargh of Ossett buried yt daie.
Willm son of Mathew Speight baptized ye xxxth day.

Februarie.

Robert son of John Bould baptized the iiijth daie.
John son of Marmaduke Longley baptized ye vjth day.
Thomas Jewet of Gawthrop buried the ixth day.
Marie daughter of John Stapleton baptized ye xjth day.
Willm late son of Robt Dey of Ossett buried yo xvjth daie.
Elizabeth wife of George Toulson buried yo xxijth daie.
Sara daughter of Richard Whitley yonger baptized the xxiiijth daie.

March.

Thomas son of Thomas Netleton baptized ye first daie.
Dorithie daughter of John Fletcher buried yo third daye.
John son of John Cuningham baptized the iiijth daie.
Alverie son of Tho: Netleton of ye hole-mill buried ye sixth day.
Grace daughter of George Pickard baptized ye xjth daie.
Alice daughter of Richard Bateman base begotten with one Elizabeth Wormall baptized the same daie in ye after nooue.
Elizabeth daughter of Michaell Bentley baptized the xiijth daie.
Henrie late son of Tho: Robinson buried the xiiijth daye.
A daughter of Ric Roods still borne buried the same daie.
Essan daughter of Jo Ellis basse begotten with one Eliz Gaukeroger baptized the xvijth daie.
John son of John Sugden of Ossett buried yt daie.
Robert son of George Beatson of Ossett baptized ye xviijth daie.
Elizabeth daughter of Tho Walker of Thornhillees basse begotten wth one Jennett Leadbeater buried the xxth daie.
Grace wife of Alverie Truelove buried yo xxijth day.
Jonas son of John Brooke of Ossett buried the xxxth daie.

April 1638.

Grace daughter of James Senior baptized ye first daie.
Richard son of George Pickringe buried the vjth daie.
Anthonie son of Edward Goodale baptized ye viijth.
Thomas Sacker a millner buried the xiijth daie.
Robert son of Robert Bradforth of Ossett baptized the xvth daie.

1638.

A man child a baster still borne begotten wth one Elizabeth Bargh of Ossett by Tho Jagger yonger buried ye xvijth daie.
Nicholas Beamounte of Ossett buried the xxijth daie.
John Greenewoode of Ossett batchler buried the xxijth daie.
Laurence Bull and Jennett Richinson married ye xxvth daie.
George Clarko and Sara Medley married the xxviijth daie.
Elizabeth wife of John Halle buried the same daie also.
Sara daughter of Willmo Ashton baptized the xxixth daie.
Symion son of Thomas Foxe baptized the laste daie.

Maye.

Marie daughter of John Wood of Earlesheaton buried ye first daie.
Elizabeth daughter of Willm Lee of ye moore side baptized ye vjth day.
Isabell daughter of John Ellis of Ossett baptized yt daie.
Elizabeth Greave of Earles-heaton spinster buried ye same daie.
Edmonde son of Richard Sharpe baptized yt daie in ye after noone.
John son of Alverie Goodalle of Earles-heaton buried yo vijth day.
Richard son of Robert Robinson of this towne buried the ixth daie.
Elizabeth daughter of John Woode baptized ye xiiijth daie.
Elizabeth daughter of Willm Dey buried the xxiijth daie.
John Ellis and Elizabeth Gaukeroger married the xxiiijth daie.
James Hutton and Dorithie Kaye married the xxxth daie.

June.

Thomas Cofin and Grace Pickard married the iiijth daie.
John Robinson and Grace Allen married the vjth daie.
Lidia daughter of Michael Walker deceased buried the xjth day
Winifred daughter of Robert Barber baptized the xiiijth daie.
Jervice son of Robt Stansfield buried the xixth daie.
Grace daughter of George Pickarde buried ye xxth day.
Thomas son of John Dey of Earles-heaton baptized the xxiiijth daie.

July.

Thomas Hemingwaie and Marie Speight married the seconde daie.
John Robinson of Earles-heaton buried the vjth daie.
Willm son of Peter Richardson baptized yt daie also.
Edward son of John Tailer baptized the viijth daie.
Thomas Autie and Marie Aerode married yo ixth daye.

1638.

Marie daughter of John Milner of Ossett buried the xvijth day.
Isabell daughter of John Ellis of the same buried the same day.
Susan daughter of Tho Nettleton of the Hole mill buried the xxijth daie.
Agnes daughter of John Jagger of Ossett baptized ye xxijth daie.
Agnes daughter of the said Jo Jagger buried ye 23th daie.
Willm son of Peter Richardson buried the xxvth daie.
Anne daughter of Tho: Whitakers baptized the xxviijth daie.

August.

Marie daughter of Willm Willmson of Bouthroid baptized the iiijth daie.
Henrie son of Richard Dawson buried ye viijth daie.
Sara daughter of ye said Ric Dawson buried yt day.
Anthonie son of Anthonie Curtice of Ossett baptized the xijth daie.
John son of John Carnell of Ossett baptized yt daie also.
Richard son of Richard Dawson buried the sixth daie.
Susan daughter of John Tilson baptized ye xxth daye.
Thomas Pasley son of Willm Pasley baptized the same day.
Richard and Jennett son and daughter of Richard Speight of Ossett being twins baptized the xxvjth daie.
Alice daughter of Averie Goodalle buried yo xxviijth day.
John son of James Wilson of Ossett baptized ye xxxth daie.
Jennett daughter of Richard Speight buried ye last daie.

September.

Susan wife of Tho Nettleton of ye Hole-mill buried the first daie.
Willm son of Willm Speight of Chidsell baptized the seconde daie.
Willm son of Richard Brooke of Ossett baptized yo same daie.
Winifried daughter of Richard Bateman buried the same daie in the after-noone.
Hellen wife of Robert Tompson of Ossett buried yo xijth day.
Parcevell son of Thomas Terrie of Gawthrope baptized the xvjth daie.
Alverie Trueloye of Earlesheaton buried ye xvijth day.
John son of Robert Bargh buried the xviijth day.
Marie daughter of Robert Bargh baptized yo xxijth day.
Marie daughter of the said Robert Bargh buried ye xxiiijth day.
Willm son of Nathaniell Stirke of Ossett baptized the last daie.

October.

Elizabeth wife of John Sikes buried the second day.
Robert Sugden and Grace Freckleton married yo vijth daie.

1638.

A daughter of John Hargh of Ossett still borne buried the same daie.
Anne daughter of Edward Dawson of this towne baptized yt daie.
Richard late son of Robt Carter of Ossett buried that daie.
Josua Crotto and Grace Gill married the xth daie.
Samuell son of John Nettleton baptized the same daie.
Jennett daughter of John Hagbe buried the same daie.
John son of James Wilson of Ossett buried yt daie also.
Anne daughter of Robt Westerman baptized ye xth daie.
Grace late daughter of Nicholas Gunson buried the xiijth daye.
Roger son of Mr. Raphe Walkeden preacher of the word of God at Ossett buried the xvth daie.
Marie daughter of Willm Burnley of Soothill baptized the xxvijth daie.
Thomas son of Tho: Nailer of Ossett yonger baptized the xxviijth daie.

November.

Joseph late son of John Speight of Ossett buried ye third daie.
Jennett wife of Thomas Jagger of Ossett yonger buried ye xjth daie.
John son of Richard Poole of Ossett baptized the xiijth daie.
Willm son of Xpfor Brooke of Ossett yonger buried the same day.
A daughter of George Glover of Ossett still borne buried the xviijth daie.
Thomas son of John Forrest yonger of Ossett buried the xxjth day.
Dorithie daughter of Nicholas Wheatley buried ye xxiijth daie.
John son of Robert Bradforth of Ossett baptized the xxvth daye.
Marie daughter of Willm Roods of Chickingley baptized yt daie also.
Willm Rayner and Dorithie Jewett married the xxvjth daie.
John son of Tho: Audsley of Gawthrop baptized ye xxviijth day.

December.

Thomas son of Tho: Antie of Soothill baptized the second daie.
Tho: son of ye said Tho: Antie of Soothill buried the iiijth daie.
John son of John Dynison yonger of Soothill buried the xiiijth daie.
John son of Willm Burtwistle of Hunslett buried the same daie.
Symion son of Anthonie Fearnley baptized the xxijth daie.
Tymothie late son of Willm Acrode of Earlesheaton deceased buried the xxvijth daie.
Richard son of Robert Sonier base begotten with one An Toulson baptized the xxviijth daie.
Thomas Jagger and Isabell Speight married the last day.

Januarie 1638.

Marie daughter of John Stapleton buried the iiijth daie.
Sara daughter of Tho: Clacke of Ossett baptized the vjth daie.
Margret daughter of Alverie Walker baptized ye xiijth daie.
Willm son of Richard Dawson of ye car-heade buried the xvjth daie.
Willm son of Willm Kitson of Earlesheaton buried the xvijth daie.
Agnes daughter of Willm Steade baptized the same day also.
John son of Richard Rouse of Soothill baptized the xixth daie.
Robert son of Robert Whitakers baptized the xxth daye.
A man child of Robert Bedforth still borne buried ye xxijth daie.
A man child of Richard Roods yonger still borne buried the xxiijth daie.
Marie daughter of Tho Musgreave baptized the xxvijth daie.
Alice late wife of Sympson of the newe parke buried the xxviijth daie.
Henrie Scolfield and Alice Dishforth married ye xxixth daie.

Februarie.

Agnes daughter of Robert Thornes of Ossett baptized the third daye.
A woman child of Richard Dawsons still borne buried ye iiijth daie.
Thomas Nayler of Ossett yonger buried the vjth daye.
Thomas Bollande and Jennett Pickard married the vijth daie.
Robert son of John Bould of this towne buried the same day.
John son of Mathew Speight of Gawthrope baptized the xiiijth daie.
John son of the above said Mathew Speight buried the xvth daye.
Grace daughter of Robert Broadley baptised ye xvjth daie.
Willm Tompson late servant to Anthonie Fearnley buried the same daie.
Thomas son of Willm Ellis baptized the xvijth daie.
Elizabeth daughter of John Wildman baptized the same daie.
Alverie son of Robt Barber baptized yt daie also.
Thomas Rodley of this towne buried the xixth daie.
James late son of Tho: Haumshey of Barsland (? Barkisland) buried the xvijth daie.
Laurence son of Laurence Bull baptized the xxiiijth daie.

March.

Elizabeth late wife of Xpofer Brooke of Ossett buried ye vth daie.
Marie wife of Robert Broadley buried the same daie.
James son of James Fearnley baptized ye vijth daie.
Elizabeth daughter of Edward Newsome baptized ye xth daye.
Grace daughter of Michaell Vdalle baptized yt daye.
Mercie daughter of Robert Sugden of Ossett baptized the xxiiijth daie.

1638.

Willm son of John Dison base begotten with one Anne Holdsworth baptized the same daie.
Anno wife of Benjamen Ackroid buried yt daie also.

April 1639.

John son of Richard Gibson baptized the vjth daie.
Laurence son of Laurence Bull buried the viijth daie.
Alice daughter of Willm Westerman baptized yo xjth daie.
Edward Dickson and Grace Melley married yo xxiijth daie.
George Allen aud Elizabeth Dawson married by lycence the xxiiijth daie.
Samuell Coultman late servante to Willm Castley slayne in a coale pitt buried the xxvth daie beinge St Mks daie.

Maie.

Willm Anderton of ye mooreside buried the seconde daie.
Sara daughter of Willim Audsley of Osset buried the fourth daie.
Isabell daughter of John Robinson of ye mooreside baptized the vth daie.
A woman child of Peter Richardson still borne buried the xjth daie.
Anne daughter of Joseph Harison of Ossett baptized the xijth daie.
A man child of Robt Nettleton of Chidsell still borne buried the xvijth daie.
Richard son of Richard Dyson of Ossett baptized the xxvjth daie.
Willm son of Willm Wilson baptized ye same day.

June.

Alice daughter of Robert Barton of Chidsell buried the vth daie.
Agnes daughter of Edward Fairebarne of Ossett buried the vijth daie.
Friswide wife of Edward Dynins (? Dynnis) buried yo same daie.
Easter daughter of James Hirst baptized yo ixth daie.
Joseph son of Willm Sonier baptized the xvjth daie.
Sara daughter of Willm Whitley baptized yt daie also.
Elizabeth daughter of Joseph Nailer of Ossett baptized the xxth daie.
Agnes late wife of Willm Gill of Sowood in Ossett buried the xxiiijth daie being Midsomer daie.
Elizabeth daughter of John Cuningham buried ye 25th daie.

July.

Xpofer Jagger of Ossett buried the iiijth daie.
John Wright and Anne Ellis both of Ossett married yo vijth daie.
Grace daughter of Alverie Goodale buried the xiijth daie.
Jane daughter of John Nailer of Ossett baptized the xxjth daie.
Jane daughter of John Ellis of Ossett baptized the same daie.
Richard son of Richard Terrie of Gawthrope baptized yo xxixth daie.

August 1639.

Alice daughter of Willm Foxe of Ossett baptized ye first daie.
Alice wife of ye said Willm Foxe buried the same daie.
Sara daughter of Willm Ridlesden of Hanging heaton baptized the iiijth daie.
Elizabeth daughter of Mr. Raphe Walkeden Minister and preacher of the word of God at Ossett baptized the vjth daie.
Anne daughter of George Westerman baptized yo xth daie.
Josua son of Willm Nowell of Gawthrope baptized ye xjth dayo.
John son of John Nailer of Ossett baptized yt daie also.
Marie daughter of James Hutton baptized yt daie also.
Azariah son of Richard Oldroid baptized yo xxviijth daie.
Hellen wife of Richard Dawson of Earlesheaton buried the xxviijth daie.

September.

Xpofer Wrongham and Eliz Sonier married yo iiijth daie.
Willm son of Xpofer Jagger late of Ossett deceased baptized the viijth daie.
Abraham Greenewod and Easter Savile married by lyceence the xiiijth daie.
Joseph son of Willm Beamounte of the street side baptized the xiiijth daie.
George Tonkson buried the xxth daie.
Robert son of Francis Netleton baptized the xxjth daie.
John son of Tho: Autie yonger baptized that daie also.
Dorithie daughter of John Jagger baptized ye xxijth daie.
Mercie late wife of Robt Thorpe buried the xxiijth daie.
Dorithio daughter of John Jagger buried ye xxiiijth daie.
Willm Sikes and Elizabeth Acrode married the xxvth daie.
Marke Robinson late son of Thomas Robinson buried the xxvjth daie.
Willm Brooke son of Christofer Brooke of Ossett baptized the xxixth daie.

October.

Isaac sonne of Samuell Pierson preacher baptized the 2d daie.
Mr. Robert Armitage and Elizabeth Cuiton married by a licence the thirde day.
Samuell Fearnside and Elizabeth Castley married the 2d day.
Richard sonne of George Naylor of Ossett baptized the same day.
Susan daughter of Thomas Hepworth of Ossett baptized the xjth day.
——— sonne of Henrie Greaves of Ossett baptized the 9th day.
Marie daughter of Henrie Greaves buried the same daie.
Abraham Cowlinge and Jennett Taylor married the same daie.

October 1639.

Robert Tharpe clarke buried the xth daie.
Robert sonne of William Ingam of Ossett baptized the xiijth day.
Martha daughter of John Cobacke baptized the same daie.
Robert Sugden of Ossett buried the same daie.
Susan daughter of Thomas Hepworth of Ossett buried xvj day.
Susan daughter of Willm Beatson of Ossett baptized xx day.
Robert son of Tho: Nettleton buryed the 21th daye.
Elizabeth daughter of Willm Rayner baptized the 24th dayo.
A yonge son of Cocking Tonge not baptized buryed the xxvth day.
Ambrosse Robinson and Margret Ashton maried 27 day.

November.

Ellen daughter of Mathew Robinson buried the seaventh dayo.
Edward son of Edward Wilson baptized the xth dayo.
Dorithie daughter of James Clayton basse begotten wth one Alice Goodall baptized the same dayo.
Sara daughter of Mathew Robinson buryed the xjth daye.
Thomas Jagger and Issabell Speight married the xvth day.
Henry son of Henrye Ellis baptized the xvijth dayo.
Lucy daughter of John Wood baptized the same day.
John son of Thomas Hemingway baptized the 20th dayo.
Mercye basse daughter of Willm Tompson buried the 23th day.
Elizabeth daughter of John Forrest baptized the 24th dayo.
* daughter of Miles Cooke baptized the same daye.
John Dey and Elizabeth Harrison maried the xxvth daye.
Robert Richardson and Jennett Walker maryed the xxiiijth day.
Raphe Battye and Mercye Robinson married xxxth dayo.

December.

Marye daughter of Robert Bargh of Ossett baptized first daye the same Marye buryed the fourth daye
Grace wife of John Hollinrake buryed the xjth daye.

Januarye.

Mercye daughter of Robert Gibson baptized the 6th daye.
John son of Robert Peaker baptized the xijth daye.
Edward Wormall buryed the xiijth daye.
Marye daughter of Willm Pasley buryed the xvjth day.

* Name illegible.

1639.

Alvereye son of Robert Barbar buried the xvijth daye.
A yonge son of Rychard Roydes not baptized buried 23th day.
Thomas son of Bryan Brooke baptized the xxvjth dayo.
A man child of Willm Ashtons still borne buried the 28th day.
Elizabeth wife of William Dey buried the same day.
*John Bradforth and Marye Grayson maryed the xxixth day.

* The second volume of the Register ends with this entry. The following notes are entered at the foot of the last page and on a fly leaf :—

Henrie Adam was inducted vicar of Dewsburie the xijth date of July 1636 by Roger Audsley vicar of Batley anno R.Re Caroli Anglie &c. duodecimo.
Franscis Ireland beinge deade was brought throughe our towne of Dewsburie the xth of June, 1634, 1634.
John Lee of Ardsley and Marje Nettleton of this parishe married at Ardsley the xvijth of June, 1634.

Caroli regis sexto. Sep. ix 1630.
John Lord Savile beinge one of his Majesty's Lordes of the Privie Council at London was buried at Batley in the Churche on Thursday the ixth of September 1630, 1630.
Christopher son of Willme Audsleye of Ossett baptized the xxijth daye of Maye 1631.
Judith daughter of Edmond Tattersall baptized the xxvjth of Feb. by Mr. Wilde at Ossett Chappell 1631.
Richard Shepley and Alice Kaye maried the xvjth of August 1632.
Tho Nayler of Ossett Ju. and Dorithie Brooke of Otloye married there the third daye of September 1633.
Jo Nayler of Ossett had a child baptized there the xvj of Decem. beinge Sondaye 1632 named Elizabeth.

August 1631.

Jeremye Hoile dyinge at Wakefeilde the sixth daye of August was there buried the same daye 1631.
.... the sixte daye of Feb. upon the stone in our .... at Dewsburye 1631, 1631, 1631.

Caroli regis octo.

.... (Shea) rde pishe Clarke of Mirffeilde was buried there .... aye of August beinge Fridaye 1632.

Caroli regis, &c., quarto.

.... dar vicar of Mirffeilde was
.... August 1628 beinge
.... his day 1628
.... ffeilde
.... gust
.... vicar of
.... Monday.

END OF THE SECOND VOLUME.

DEWSBURY PARISH REGISTER.

VOLUME III.

The Regester Booke belonging to the Parishe of Dewsburye of all Mariages christeninges and buriulls: 1639.

Februarye 1639. Caroli regis xvth.
Willme Foxe and Eliz. Middleton marryed the 3 day.
Roger Son of George Pickard of Osset baptized the 5th day.
John son of Michaell Bentleye baptized the sixt daye.
Thomas son of Henrye Sykes of Ossett baptized the 9th day.
Hugh son of John Dey of Ossett baptized the xviiith daye.
An daughter of John Wight baptized the   day.
Marye daughter of Mathew Speight baptized 23 day.
Elizabeth daughter of Rychard Whitley baptized xxvth day.
John Milnes Se. buryed the xxvith daye.
Elizabeth daughter of Willm Dickson deceased buried 28th day.

Marche.
Rychard son of Rychard Dawson baptized the first day.
Agnes daughter of Willm Gill of Ossett baptized that daye.
Sara daughter of Willm Milner of Ossett baptized that daye.
Marye daughter of Thomas Carter baptized that daye.
Joseph son of Willm Sonyare buryed the thirde daye.
A yonge son of Tho. Autye stillborne buryed that daye.
Agnes wife of Crerye Coulton and a child with her buryed the fourth daye.
John son of Thomas Whitakers baptized the vth daye.
Agnes daughter of Jo. Walker baptized the . . . day.
The said John [*i.e.* John Whitakers] buryed the sixt daye.
Mary daughter of John Claughton of Ossett baptized the eight daye.
Katherin wife of Bryan Brooke buried the xiiith daye.
John son of John Dishforth of Gauthroppe baptized the xvth daye.
Easter daughter of Robert Wright of Ossett baptised the same daye.
Agnes daughter of Thomas Wormall of Ossett baptised the same daye.
Isaac son of Laurence Bull baptized that day.
John son of Thomas Nettleton baptized the sixth daye.
Willm son of Willm Kitson baptized xxith daye.
Mary daughter of Anthony Auty baptized the xxiiith daye.

1639.
Winifreide daughter of Robett Dickson of Hanginge Heaton baptized the xxvth daye.
Isaac son of Lawrence Bull buryed the xxviith daye.
Elizabeth daughter of Mathew Speight baptized the 31th day.

Aprill 1640.
Sara daughter of Jorge Allen baptized the second daye.
Grace daughter of Michaell Stubley base begotten with one Alice Anderton baptized the 7th day.
Robert sonne of Rbt. Nettleton of Chidsell baptized the 9th day.
Edward son of Thomas Wilbie of Ossett baptized the 11th day.
Alice daughter of John Cuningham baptized the xiith day.
Paul Ramsden and Jane Olley marryed the xiiiith day.
A yonge daughter of Willm Newsome buried xvith day.
Dorithie daughter of Edward Barbar deceazed buried the sixth daye.
Aaron son of John Ellis baptized that daye.
Samuell son of Michaell Bentley of this towne baptized the xxii daye.
Thomas son of Tho. Walker buried the 24th daye.
Sara daughter of Alverey Goodall baptized the xxvth day.
John son of John Wood of Gauthroppe . . . . the xxvith daye.
. . . . ger deceased . . . . daye 1640.
Christoper son of Michaell Oldroide baptized the tenthe daye.
John son of Alverey Pickeard of Ossett baptized the same day.
Marie daughter of Willm Pasley baptized the 13th day.
A yonge son of Peter Rychardson not baptized buryed the xviith daye.
Sara daughter of Robert Bedforde baptized the xxith daye.
Benjamin Acrode buryed the xxiith daye.
Mary daughter of John Ellis buryed that daye.
Elizabeth daughter of John Terrye of Ganthrope baptized the xxiiith daye beinge Whitsundaye.
Grace daughter of Michaell Stubleye base begotten with Alice Anderton buryed the same daye.
Thomas Slacke of Ossett buryed that daye.
John son of Laurence Saxton baptized the xxvth daye.
Grace daughter of John Millns baptized that daye.
Elizabeth wife of Thomas Wilson of Ossett buryed the xxvith daye.
Katherin Wife of John Crofte of Ossett deceazed buryed the xxvijth daye.
Israell son of Willme Autye baptized last daye.

June 1640.
Thomas Hartleye and Elizabeth White married the thirde daye.
Marye daughter of Rychard Brooke of Ossett baptized the seaventhe day.
Rychard son of Edwarde Denys buried the eight daye.

1640.

Ann wife of Mathew Robinson buryed the xith daye.
Bryan Gibson and Margrett Briggs married the xviijth daye.
Edward Sonyare and Easter Newsome maried xxjth daye.
John Acrode of the Preist lane buried the xvijth daye.
Sara daughter of Joseph Oldroide Ju. baptised the xxviijth daye.
John son of James Sonyare of Earlesheaton baptised the same day.
John son of Michaell Sacker baptized that daye.

Julye.

John Hallila and Issabell Acrode maried first daye.
Margrett daughter of John Millnes deceazed buried the seconde daye.
Marye daughter of John Bradforth of Ossett baptised the vth daye beinge Sondaye.
Sara daughter of Edwarde Autye of this towne baptized the xij daye.
Elizabeth daughter of Edward Sonyare base begotten with An Towleson baptized the xvjth daye.
Alice wife of Edwarde Chaster buryed the xviijth daye.
A yonge daughter of Jorge Wood of Ossett not baptised buried the first day of August.
Robert son of Rychard Sharpe of Earlesheaton baptized the seconde day.
Marye daughter of Willme Castleye baptized the eight daye.
Thomas Robinson and Ann Tyar (? Tyas) maried the xjth daye.
Edwarde son of Edward Fayrbarne of Ossett buried the xijth daye.
Joseph sou of Thomas Foxe baptized the same daye.
Joseph Phillippe and Jennett Armstronge maried the sixth daye.
Abraham son of Abraham Greenwood baptized the 26th daye.
John son of Robert Stanfeilde buried the 30th daye.

September.

John son of Thomas Webstar baptized the seconde daye.
Elizabeth wife of John Broodley of Chidsell buried thirde daye.
Elizabeth daughter of Robert Bradforth of Ossett baptized the sixt daye beinge Sondaye in the forenoone.
An daughter of Rychard Bateman baptized the xijth daye.
Jusua son of James Wilson of Ossett baptized the 21th daye.
John Goodall of Ossett buried the last daye.

October.

Rycharde son of Rychard Poole of Ossett baptised the 4th daye.
Elizabeth daughter of Edward Dickson of Ossett baptized the eleventhe daye.
Sara daughter of Martin Parker baptized that daye.

1640.

Thomas son of Henry Ellis deceazed buried xvjth daye.
Marye daughter of Robert Bradforth of Ossett buried xvijth daye.
Thomas son of William Ashton baptized the xviijth daye.
Marye daughter of John Tompson baptised that daye.
Agnes daughter of George Beatson of Ossett baptized the same daye.
A yonge son of George Pickard of Ossett not baptized buried 19th daye.
Alvereye Whitleye and Margrett Warde maired the xxjth daye.
Jonye daughter of Bryan Gibson of Gauthroppe baptized the xxvth daye.
Elizabeth daughter of Robert Rychardson baptized that daye.
A yonge daughter of Joseph Phillippe of Gauthroppe not baptized buryed the xxxjth daye.

November.

John Mitton buryed the seconde daye.
Mary daughter of John Mytton buryed the fourthe daye.
Thomas son of Mr. Wareinge buryed the sixte daye.
John son of Willme Roades buryed the nynthe daye.
Thomas Carre and Margrett Wheatley married the xij daye.
Josua son of George Gloover baptized the 29th daye.

December.

Issabell daughter of Thomas Hartley baptized vth daye.
Willm son of Willm Foxe baptized the 6th daye.
Rychard Bull buryed the seaventhe day Mondaye.
Alice wife of the said lly. Bull buryed the same daye.
Robert son of Willme Souvare baptized eight daye.
Katheringe daughter of John Dawson buryed the nynthe daye.
An basse daughter of Issabell Robinson baptized the xijth daye.
Edward son of Mr. Wareinge buryed the fourteenth daye.
Eliz. daughter of Thomas Hepworth baptized the 13th daye.
Susan daughter of Willme Lee baptized the xxiijth daye.
Margrett wife of John Bargh of Ossett buryed at Horburye the 24th daye.
Thomas son of Franscis Neltuorpe baptized the 26th daye.
Willme Roydes buryed the xxixth daye.

Januarye.

Dorithie daughter of Stephen Rouse of Ossett baptized 2 daye.
Alice daughter of Edward Dawson baptized sixt daye.
Dorithie daughter of the said Stephen Rouse buryed at Horburie the thirde daye.
. . . . wife of Mr. Burdett of Walton buryed that daye beinge the sixte daye.

DEWSBURY PARISH REGISTERS.

1640.

John son of John Dawson buryed the eight daye.
John son of John Robinson Ju. baptized the tenth daye.
. . . . Dawson buryed the xjth daye.
Rychard son of Robt. Souyaro basse begotten with An Towleson buryed the xiijth daye.
John son of Thomas Etocke baptized the xvijth daye.
Jonnett daughter of John Jaggor baptized that daye.
A yongo child of Henry Ellis not baptized buryed the xvjth daye.
Sara daughter of Nich. Hargreaves baptized 18th daye.
Edward Speight of Gauthroppe buryed the xvijth daye.
Parcivell Terryo and Mary Neusome married the xxth daye.
Bryan Brooke and Alice Robinson married the xxvith daye.
Willme Broadhead and Alice Boulde marryed the xxvijth daye.
Grace daughter of Joseph Tryar (? Fryar) buryed the xxixth daye.
An Wife of Jorge Wood buryed at Ossett the same duye.
Jane wife of Rychard Beatson of Ossett buryed the xxxith daye.

Februarye.

John Broadley and Dorithye Harrison married 2 day.
A yongo son of John Dawson not baptized buryed the same daye.
John Parker Se. buryed the thirde daye.
Robert Touleson and Alice Autye married the xth daye.
Robt. Booth of Ossett base borne buryed the xith daye.
Elizabeth daughter of Willme Stead, baptized xiiijth daye.
Josua son of James Fearnleye baptized the xiijth daye.
Jane daughter of Robert Barber Se. baptized 14th daye.
James Speight of Batleye and Elizabeth Steade married the xvijth daye.
Mateson Jackson and Ann Musgreave married the same daye
Thomas Nettleton and Alice Dobson maried that daye.
John son of Tho. Robinson baptized the xviijth daye.
Jorge son of Jorge Westerman baptized the xxjth daye.
Robt. son of Samuell Pickeard baptized the same daye.
Sibell daughter of Tho. Terrie baptized that daye.
Edward Claster and Jane Hardcastle marryed the same daye.
Edward son of Willme Kent buryed the xxijth daye.
Dyna daughter of George Feeble baptized xxviijth daye.
Thomas son of John Deye baptized the last daye.
Ann daughter of John Preanay of Gauthroppe baptized the same day.

Marche 1640.

Katherin wife of Thomas Wilson buried v daye.
Issabell daughter of Laurence Bull baptized the seaventh day beinge Shrove Sunday.
Thomas Moxon and Dorithie Breare married the eight daye beinge Shrove Monday at Ossett by Mr. Walkeden a curate there.
Isaacke son of Robert Crofte baptized the xth daye.
Thomas son of Thomas Carre baptized xvijth daye.
Marye daughter of Michaell Speight baptised the xxth daye.
Marye daughter of Michaell Speight buryed 21th daye.
Robert son of Edward Goodall baptized that daye.
. . . n daughter of Thomas Nettleton of the hoyle
. . . buryed the xviiijth daye.
. . . . xvth . . .
A yonge son of Willme Ellis still borne buryed xxvjth daye.
Mathow son of Willme Speight of Chidsell baptized the xxviijth daye.

Aprill 1641.

John son of Michaell Bentleye deceazed buryed the first daye.
Elizabeth wifo of Thomas Archer deceazed buried 2 daye.
James son of James Sympson buryed the vth daye.
Rychard son of John Hallilah baptized the seaventhe daye.
Agnes daughter of Thomas Wormall of Ossett buryed the xijth daye.
Jane daughter of Robt. Smytheson baptized the xvijth daye.
Ann daughter of James Beaumont of Gautbroppe baptized the xviijth daye beinge Palme Sondaye.
John son of Robt. Larghe of Ossett baptized the xixth daye.
A yonge childe of Willm Ashton of Soothill township still borne buryed the same daye.
Marye daughter of Willme Willimson buryed that daye.
Willme son of Willme Burnley baptized the 21th daye.
Elizabeth wifo of Bryan Phillippe Ju. buryed xxijth daye.
Thomas son of John Deye buryed the same daye.
John Ashley and Issabell Tompson maryed xxvijth daye.

Maye.

Easter daughter of James Sonyaro baptized the first daye.
Mr. Rapho Walkeden preacher and curate at Ossett Chappell buryed the seconde daye Sondaye.
Margrett wife of Luke Wright buryed the vijth daye.
Rychard Walker buryed the eight daye.
Rychard son of Rychard Rouse baptized the xijth daye.
James son of James Hirst baptized the xvjth daye.
Elizabeth daughter of Robert Goodall baptized that daye.
Symon Dalton and Eliz. Gill marryed the xxvth daye.
Robert Roydes and Grace Ingham married that daye.

1641.

Robert Sonyare and Ann Ellis married the 26th daye.
Elizabeth daughter of Edward Dawson buried 27th daye.
John son of Joseph Harrison of Ossett baptized the xxxth daye.

June.

Robert Sharpe and Sara Hill married the xijth daye.
John Lylye and Grace Sugden married by a lycense the xvth daye.
Thomas son of Robert Bedforde baptized the xvjth daye.
Willme son of Robert Bradforthe of Ossett baptized the xxth daye.
Ellen Brooke buryed the xxjth daye.
George Childe and Ann Wilkes married the xxiijth daye.
John son of John Sykes buryed the same day.

July.

John son of Robt. Westerman baptized the xviijth daye.
James Moore and Ann Tompson married the same daye.
John son of John Nettleton baptized the xxjth daye.
Elizabeth daughter of Willme Steade of . . . . townshippe buryed the 29th daye.

August.

James son of Mr. Raphe Walkden deceazed baptized the fourthe day.
Dorithye wife of Jo. Westerman deceazed buryed eight day.
Margret Sunderland vid (widow) buryed the xjth daye.
Marye daughter of Nicholas Hargreave buryed xvth daye.
Marye daughter of Thomas Antye of Soothill township baptized the same daye.
Thomas Hepworthe and Alice Ditche married 18th day.
Henrye Bull buryed the xxth daye.

September.

Elizabeth daughter of Willme Fletcher baptized the xijth daye.
Dorithye daughter of Thomas Whitaker baptized the xviijth daye.
Willme son of Anthonye Curtice of Ossett baptized the xxvjth daye.
John son of George Pickard of the same baptized that daye.
Nicholas White buryed the 29th daye.

October.

John Parker and Alice Bull marryed the sixt daye.
Rycharde son of Willme Roades of Chickenleye baptized the ninthe daye.
John Bargho and Issabell Thorppe married the xijth daye.
Thomas son of Edwarde Wilson of Gauthrope baptized the xvijth daye.
Elizabeth daughter of Robt. Touleson baptized that daye.

1641.

George son of George Westerman buryed the xxijth daye.
Elizabeth daughter of Joseph Phillippe of Gauthroppe baptized the xxiijth daye.
Issabell daughter of John Wildman of Ossett baptised that daye.
A yonge child of Rychard Jackson base begotten with Marye Dalton not baptized buryed the xxvjth daye.
Grace daughter of Willme Kent baptized last day.

November.

Robert Smythson buryed the first daye.
Jennet wife of Robert Stansfeild buryed the vth day.
Katherin wife of Willme Ingham of Ossett buryed that day.
Susan daughter of Willme Wilson baptized the seaventhe day beinge Sondaye at evening praier.
Thomas son of John Dey of Earlesheaton buryed ixth daye.
Thomas son of Rychard Gibson baptized xiiijth daye.
Parcivall son of Parcivall Terrye of Gauthroppe baptized the xxjth daye.
Rychard son of Willme Newsome baptized that daye.
George Wood and Sibell Sacker married the 23 day.
John son of Henrye Ellis baptized the last daye.

December.

John son of George Pickeard of Ossett buried first day.
Ann daughter of Edward Chaster . , . . .
A yonge son of Rychard Roydes not baptized buryed that daye.
Thomas son of John Wright of Ossett baptized vth daye.
John son of Abraham Hemingwaye baptized the eight daye.
Thomas son of Anthonye Fearnleye baptized the xvjth daye.
Marye daughter of Willme Kitson baptized the xixth daye.
A yonge daughter of Willme Broadhead not baptized buried yt daye.
Thomas Wilson of Gauthroppe buryed the last daye.

Januarye.

Samuell son of James Sonyare of Earlesheaton buryed the sixte daye.
Robt. son of Robt. Stansfeilde buryed the 8th daye.
A yonge son of Mr. Cockinge Tonge not baptized buryed the xijth daye.
John Antye and Ann Hirde married the xvjth daye.
James son of James Hutton baptized the 23rd daye.

Februarye.

Michaell Stubley and Alice Anderton married second day.
Eliz. daughter of James More of Ossett baptized sixte day.
Judith daughter of John Hoyslande of ye same bapt. that daye.

1641.

Ann daughter of Willme Beaumont of the same bapt. that daye.
Marmaduke Longleye buryed the seaventhe daye.
Sara daughter of John Taylier baptized the xth daye.
Thomas Brooke and Margret Graive married the xijth daye.
Michaell son of Thomas Musgrave baptized the 13th daye.
John son of Abraha. Greenwood baptized the same daye.
Anthony son of Willme Millner of Ossett baptized the same daye.
Eliz. daughter of Tho. Wilbye of Ossett baptized the xxth daye.
Thomas Bradforthe of Ossett buryed the xxjth daye.
Thomas son of Anthonye Fearnleye buryed the xxijth daye.
Elizabeth wife of Edward Speight of Gauthroppe deceazed buryed the xxiijth daye beinge Ashwednesdaye.
Willme son of Robt. Bradforth of Ossett Ju. buryed the same daye.
Ellen daughter of George Allen, baptized the 24th daye.
Willme son of Willme Riddlesden baptized xxvjth daye.
Elizabeth daughter of Willim Pasley baptized that daye.
Ann daughter of Joseph Harrison buryed the 26th daye.
Rychard Dickenson and Annes Pickeard married by a lycense the xxviijth daye.

Marche.

Edward Woodheade and Sara Cowper married by a licence the first daye.
John son of John Haigh of Ossett baptized sixt daye.
Joseph son of John Nayler baptized the same daye.
Michaell son of John Deye baptized the same daye.
Dorithie daughter of Chr. Brooke of Ossett Ju. baptized the xijth daye.
John son of John Haigh of Ossett buryed the same daye.
Thomas son of John Deye of Ossett baptized the xiijth daye.
Ellen daughter of Joseph Nayler of the same baptized that daye.
Marye daughter of Robt. Sonyare baptized that day.
Dorithie daughter of Chr. Brooke of Ossett Ju. buryed the xvth daye.
Sara daughter of Rych. Oldroide baptized the xvjth daye.
Marye daughter of Mathew Boamer baptized the xxth daye.
Thomas son of Robt. Bedforde buryed the xxijth daye.
Marye daughter of Robt. Sonyare buryed 26th daye.
John son of John Robucke of Ossett baptised the 27th daye.
Rychard son of Bryan Phillippe of the same baptized the same daye.

1641.

Eliz. daughter of Robt. Roydess baptized the same daye.
Marye daughter of Tho. Hemingwaye baptized 28th daye.
Thomas Langfeild of Ossett buried the 29th daye.
Jane wife of Chr. Brooke of Ossett buried the last day.

Aprill 1642.

Thomas Wilson buryed the first daye.
Edward Whitleye buryed the same daye.
Ann daughter of Michaell Spaight bap. second day.
Thomas son of Michaell Sacker baptized the 3 daye.
Josua son of Thomas Brooke of Ossett baptized the 4th daye.
Elizabeth daughter of Willme Fletcher buryed eight day.
Elizabeth daughter of Edward Sonyare base begotten with Ann Towleson buryed the same daye.
Willme son of Willme Booth of the New Parke baptized the xijth daye.
John son of Nicholas Mitchell buryed the xvth daye.
Thomas son of Thomas Audsleye of Gauthroppe baptized the xviijth daye.
Willme Booth of the New Parke buryed the same daye.
Elizabeth daughter of Mr. Samuell Pierson baptized the xxth daye.
Joseph son of Joseph Abbat of the parish of Batley baptized here the same daye.
Alice daughter of John Speight of Ossett deceazed buryed the xxijth daye.
Marye daughter of Franscis Nettleton, baptized the xxvth daye.
Rychard son of John Hallilah buryed the xxvjth daye.
Agnes wife of John Whitleye of Ossett buried the 29th daye.

Maye.

Nicholas Hargraive of Ossett buried the third daye.
Phillippe son of John Udall, buried the fourthe daye.
Elizabeth daughter of Rychard Dawson baptized that daye.
A yonge son of George Childe of Ossett not baptized buried the eight daye.
Addam son of Willme Nowell of Gauthrop baptized at Batleye the same daye at even praier.
Sara wife of Henric Sykes of Ossett buryed the xjth daye.
Michaell son of Michaell Stubley baptized xvth daye.
Elizabeth daughter of Thomas Wornall of Ossett baptized the same daye.
George son of Thomas Cartar baptized that daye.
Robt. Fairbarne and Elizabeth White married with a license the xvijth daye.
Rychard Bagson of Ossett buryed the xixth daye.
Robert son of Mathew Speight baptized that daye.
Jane daughter of John Cuningham baptized the same daye.
Thomas son of Thomas Hartleye baptized the 29th daye.

1642.

John son of Darbye Mullinn of the parish of Westardesleye baptized the 30th daye.
A yonge Son of Peter Rychardson not baptized buried yt daye.

June.

Parcivall son of Parcivall Terrio buryed the sixt daye.
Ann daughter of John Ashleye baptized the eight daye.
Sara daughter of Robt. Thornes of Ossett baptized the 12th daye.
Judith daughter of John Horslande buried the xviijth daye.
Susanna daughter of Bryan Brooke baptized xixth daye.
John son of Thomas Antye buryed the xxvith daye.
Robt. Fisher and Jonye Hargraive married the 29th daye.

Julye.

Grace daughter of John Wood baptized thirde daye.
Mary daughter of Edward Sonyare baptized that daye.
Elizabeth daughter of Robt. Sharpe baptized the xth daye.
Rosamond daughter of Henrye Graive buried the xijth daye.
Robt. Stansfeild and Jennett Walker married 13th daye.
Rychard Deute and Elizabeth Crofte married the xxth daye.
Danyell son of Robt. Greenwood base begotten with Mereye Sykes baptized the xxith daye.
Sara daughter of John Breareye of Gauthroppe baptized the same daye alsoe.
Michaell son of John Parker baptized the 24th daye.
Marye wife of Mathew White buried the 29th daye.
Willmo son of John Claughton of Ossett baptized last daye.
John son of Alverey Whitley of same baptized that daye.

August.

A yonge daughter of Willmo Ashton not baptized buryed the first daye Mondaye and Lamas daye.
Marye daughter of Willmo Wilson buryed sixt daye.
Rychard son of Joseph Walker deceased buryed ixth daye.
Jennett Huott of Ossett vid. (widow) buryed the tenthe daye.
George son of Robt. Nettleton baptized the xjth daye.
Margrett wife of John Stockes buryed the xviijth daye.
Elizabeth daughter of Nathaniell Stirke of Ossett baptized the xxviijth daye.

September.

Alice daughter of Willmo Musgrave buried vth daye.
Agnes wife of Joseph Walker deceazed buried the 7th day.

1642.

Thomas son of Bryan Brooke buried that daye.
John son of John Broadbent base begotten with one Susan Hemingwaye buryed the xvjth daye.
Susan daughter of John Ellis of Ossett baptized the 18th day.
Michaell son of Thomas Antye Ju. baptized the xxvth day.
Sara daughter of William Stoade boptized the 18th day.
John son of Alvereyo Pickeard of Ossett buryed same day.

October.

Mereye daughter of Michaell Bentleye of Overbouthroide Ju. baptized the first daye.
Luke son of Thomas Carter buried eight daye.
John son of Robt. Rychardson baptized the ix daye.
Thomas son of Rychard Poole of Ossett township baptized the xijth daye.
Eliz. daughter of John Hallilah baptized that daye.
Willmo Sharphouse and Issaboll Harroppo married the xvijth daye.
Joseph son of Willmo Gill of Ossett baptized 23 day.
Robert Barton and Susan Willkinson married the xxiijth daye.
John Wood of Gauthrope buried the 26th daye.
Marye daughter of Robt. Goodall buried that daye.
A yonge daughter of Michaell Parker base begotten with Alice Whitley buried the last daye.

November.

Marye wife of Willmo Pollard buried second day.
Willmo Musgraive buryed the nynthe daye.
A yonge son of John Terrie of Ossett buried 12th day, this childe was not baptized.
John Shearde and Ann Udall married the 13th daye.
Alice daughter of Rycharde Brooke of Ossett baptized the same daye.
Thomas son of John Robinson baptized the xxth daye Sondaye.
Alice daugher of Willmo Ingham of Ossett baptized the same daye.
Michaell Broadleye buryed the xxijth daye.
Willmo son of John Walker of Ossett baptized the 27th daye.
Willmo son of Alverey Goodall baptized the same daye.
Mereye wife of Willmo Ellis buried the xxviijth daye.
Willmo Broadley and Mereye Hemingwaye married the 29th daye.
Sara daughter of John Ellis baptized the last daye

December.

Willmo son of Willmo Broadhead baptized 7th day.
Willmo son of Robt. Bargh of Ossett baptized xjth daye.
Marye daughter of Robert Bradforth of the same baptized the same daye.
Dorithie daughter of Willmo Castleye baptized the same daye alsoe.
Thomas son of Edward Chester baptized 8th daye.
Agnes wife of Bryan Phillip buried that daye.

DEWSBURY PARISH REGISTERS. 149

1642.

Robt. son of James Wharleworthe base begotten with Marye Wilbe baptized xxjth daye.
Mereye daughter of Willme Sonyare baptized that daye.
Mathew son of Nicholas Baxstar base begotten with Ann Bull baptized the xxijth daye.
Joseph son of Joseph Oldroide Ju. baptized 26th daye.
Mathew son of Nicholas Baxstar base begotten with Ann Bull buryed the same day alsoo.
. . . . of Willme Beatson of Ossett baptized the same daye alsoe.
Rychard son of Rychard Whitleye baptized xxvijth daye.
Josuah son of James Fearnleye buryed that daye.
Margret daughter of James Sonyare baptized the xxviijth daye.
A yonge son of George Wood of Ossett still borne buryed the same daye.
Mereye daughter of Willme Sonyare buryed the xxxth daye.

Januarye.

Robert son of George Pickeard of Ossett baptized the first daye.
Alice daughter of Robt. Fisher of the same baptized the same daye alsoe.
Thomas Jagger Se. of the same buryed that daye.
Willme son of Thomas Foxe baptized the vth daye.
George Lee and Elizabeth Musgreaive married 9th daye.
Roger son of Thomas Carre baptized the xvth daye.
Jennet daughter of Robt Gibson baptized that daye.
John Forrest of Ossett Se. buried the xvjth daye.
Thomas son of John Barghe of Ossett baptized 23th daye.
Roger son of Thomas Carre buried the xxvth daye.
John Breare and Elizabeth Jagger married the 29th daye.
Agnes daughter of George Nayler of Ossett bap. that daye.
Marye daughter of Robt. Fayrbarne of ye same bap. that day.
Elizabeth daughter of Robt. Peaker baptized that daye.
Alvereye son of Laurence Bull baptized the same daye.
Christopher Usley and Jennit Oddy married then.

Februarye 1642.

Marye daughter of Thomas Carter buried the 4th daye.
Alvereye son of Alvereye Pickeard baptized the vth daye.
Anthonye son of Anthonye Autye baptized the same daye.
Gamaliell Goodall and Ann Rychardson married sixt daye.
Joseph son of Michaell Oldroide baptized eight daye.
Martha daughter of Mathewe Speight baptized xijth daye.
Marye daughter of Laurence Saxton baptized that daye.
Sara wife of Edward Langfeilde, buried the 14th daye.

1642.

Edward son of Edward Dawson baptized the 19th daye.
Elizabeth wife of Willme Beatson buried the xxth daye.
Dorithie wife of John Broadleye buried the 21th daye.

Marche.

Grace daughter of Willme Westerman baptized the first daye.
Grace daughter of the said Westerman buried the thirde day.
Eliz. daughter of Roger Pickeard of Ossett baptised vth daye.
Thomas son of Robert Bedforde baptized the nynth day.
John son of James Fearnleye baptized the same daye.
A yonge childe of Stephen Rouse of Ossett not baptized buried the xiijth daye.
Elizabeth daughter of Roger Pickeard of Ossett buried the xvijth daye.
Sara daughter of Thomas Hepworth of Ossett baptized the 19th day.
Sara daughter of Thomas Autye baptized that daye.
Agnes wife of John Parker deceased buried the xxth daye.
George son of John Jagger of Ossett baptized 21th daye.
James son of Willme Hinde baptized the xxvth daye.
Willme son of Robt. Barton baptized the same daye.
Willme son of John Claughton buried that daye.
Robt. son of Robt. Naylor base begotten with Eliz. Lockwood baptized the same daye 1643.
John son of George Beatson of Ossett baptized 27th daye.
Eliz. daughter of John Bradforth of Ossett bap. that day.
Ann wife of Rychard Roydes buried the 29th daye.

Aprill 1643.

Samuell son of Thomas Allen base begotten with Eliz. Wade baptized the seconde daye.
The said Samuell buried the thirde daye.
Rychard Castleye and Alice Woomersleye married that daye.
Michaell son of Joseph Phillipp baptized the 4th daye.
Emanuell son of John Autye baptized the same daye.
Marye daughter of Anthonye Autye buried the 7th daye.
Jennett wife of John Dawson deceazed buried the ixth daye.
Marye wife of Thomas Hemingwaye buried the 13th day.
Thomas son of John Bradforth of Ossett bap. the xvjth daye.
John son of Robt. Barbar baptized the same daye.
Thomas son of Willme Ellis buried the xxith daye.
Susan daughter of Willme Fletcher bap. xxiiith daye.

1643.

Michaell Parker and Alice Whitley married 27th daye.
Jennet Grayson buried the same daye.

Maye.

James son of Michaell Udall baptized the vijth daye.
Thomas Allen and Elizabeth Wade married eight day.
Jeremye son of Nicholas Batleye baptized the ixth daye.
Edward son of John Deye buryed the xijth daye.
Ann daughter of John Harrison of Woodchurch bap. 14th daye.
Marye daughter of Hue Mateson base begotten with Elizabeth Hirst baptized the same daye.
A yonge childe of Thomas Whitaker still borne buryed the xxijth daye Mondaye.
James son of Symon Dalton of Ossett baptized the xxiijth daye tuesdaye.
Margret daughter of James Senyare bap. that day.
Robt. son of George Pickeard buried the 24th daye.
John Stockes and Alice Acrode married the 29th daye.

June.

George son of John Nelson of Woodchurch baptized the fourth daye Sondaye 1643.
Jane daughter of John Breare of Ossett baptized that daye.
Thomas son of John Walker deceased buried the 7th daye.
Avarias son of Rychard Oldroide buried the 9th daye.
Dorithie daughter of Willme Hall of Ossett baptized the xith daye.
Sara daughter of Christopher Brooke of Ossett baptized the same daye alsoe.
Marye daughter of Willme Castleye buried the xijth daye.
Hue Mateson and Ellen Smythe married the 14th daye.
Roger son of John Sugden buryed the same daye.
John son of Robt. Rychardson buryed the 17th daye.
Elizabeth daughter of John Fell baptized the 18th daye.
John Broadleye and Jane Thornton married the 19th daye.
Robt. son of James Wharlewoth base begotten with Marye Wilde buried the xxth daye tuesdaye.
Marye daughter of George Gloover of Ossett baptized the xxvth daye 4 Sondaye after trinitye.
Elizabeth daughter of John Fell buryed the same daye.
John Aticke and Agnes Oggell married the xxvjth daye.

Julye.

Martin son of Martin Parker baptized the vth daye.
Timothie basse son of Bartholomew Boamer buried that daye.
Sara daughter of John Breareye buried that daye.
Elizabeth daughter of Thomas Shepleye baptized 6th daye.

1643.

John Popleton* a souldier and sergeant under Sir George Waintworth dyinge at Ganthroppe buried here the 8th daye.
Isabell daughter of John Sugden buryed that daye.
Franscis daughter of John Dymon of Batley bap. that daye.
Thomas Haigh of Brotherton and Issabell Barker married by a lycense the xiijth daye.
John son of George Beatson of Ossett buried that daye.
Elizabeth daughter of John Dishforthe baptized that daye.
Thomas son of Robt. Dickson baptized the xvth daye.
Thomas son of Edward Chaster buried 16th daye.
Alice daughter of Henrye Scolefeilde bap. 16th daye.
James Synypson buryed the xxijnd daye.
John son of John Holdsworthe buried the 24th daye.
Franscis wife of Rych. Hemingwaye buried that daye.
James son of John Millnes baptized the xxvth daye.
George Atkinson and Ann Hill married the xxvjth daye.
Marye wife of John Marsh of Birstall buried that daye.
Judith daughter of Mr. Cockinge Tonge baptized 27th daye.
Grace daughter of Willme Lee baptized that daye.
Marye daughter of Tho. Hemingwaye buried 28th daye.
Ann Holdsworth buried the 30th daye.
Elizabeth daughter of John Dishforthe buried the 31th daye.

August.

Philemon Dickson buried the first daye.
Judith daughter of Mr. Cockings Tonge buried eight daye.
Grace daughter of Willme Lee buried nynthe daye.
Marye wife of Henrie Barbar buried the tenthe daye.
Susan daughter of Willme Fletcher buried 12th daye.
Anthonye Fearnleye buryed the 14th daye.
Willme son of Alvereye Goodall buryed the 18th daye.
Ann wife of Franseis Gill buried the xxijth daye.
A yonge childe of Peter Richardson still borne buried that day.
James son of James Lobleye baptized the same daye.
Rychard Hemingwaye buried the 26th daye.
Ann daughter of John Shearde baptized 27th daye.
James son of James Lobleye buried the 28th daye.
Cockinge Tonge buried the 29th day.

September.

Susan wife of Willme Ashton buried first daye.
Christopher son of Christopher Usleye baptized the 3 daye.

---

* Possibly wounded at the Battle of Wakefield on the 21st May, 1643.

1643.

Robt. son of Robt. Sonyare baptized that daye.
Edward Sonyare buryed the eight daye.
A yonge daughter of George Allen not baptized buried the xijth daye.
Edward Lee and Margret Applebye maried the 13 daye.
Rychard Kaye and Alice Robinson maried that daye.
Grace daughter of Willme Kent buried that daye.
Ann daughter of John Sheard buried the 14th daye.
John Morehouse Se. buried the xvth daye.
Michaell Oldroide buried the xvjth daye.
Willme Phillippe and Ann Gomersall married the xviijth daye.
Ann daughter of John Allerton of Westardsleye baptized the xxth daye.
Sarah daughter of Edward Dickson of Ossett baptized the 24th daye.
A yonge son of Thomas Allen still borne buryed the 28th daye.

October.

A yong daughter of William Milnes unbaptized buried the second daye.
A yong son of William Kitson unbaptized buried the same daye.
James Clayton buryed the fourth daye.
John Grayve buryed the fifth daye.
Joshua Hepworth buryed the eight daye.
Peter son of Thomas Aticke of Ossett bap. that day.
Michael son of Tho. Musgreave buryed xith day.
Elizabeth daughter of William Hall buryed xvth day.
Ann daughter of William Beaumont buried the same daye.
Thomas son of Henry Ellis baptized xxijth daye.
Henry son of James Clayton buryed 29th daye.

November.

Ann daughter of Robt. Towleson baptized vth day.
Isabel wife of John Morehouse buryed the xjth day.
Anthony son of James Hirst baptized xijth day.
William Richardson buryed the xiijth daye.
Ann wife of Thomas Autye buryed the xxijth daye.
Elizabeth wife of Nicholas White buryed 23th daye.
Marye wife of John Taylier buryed xxvth daye.
Elizabeth wife of Mich. Wheylwright buried that daye.
Thomas Nowell and Grace Foxe married 26th daye.
Jonas son of Willme Sonyare baptized that daye.
John son of Rych. Kaye baptized that daye.
Issabell wife of Chr. Audsleye buried that daye.

December.

Grace daughter of Tho. Carre baptized xth daye.
A yonge son of John Terrye not bap. buried that daye.
Susan daughter of Willme Autye baptized 14th daye.

1613.

Elizabeth wife of John Dyre buried the same daye.
Martha daughter of John Nettleton baptized 16th daye.
John son of Edward Swifte. base begotten with Susan Dickson baptized the 17th daye.
Rychard Hemingwaye of Earlesheaton buried 20th daye.
A yonge son of John Bargh not bap. buried that daye.
Eliz. daughter of John Autye baptized the 24th daye.
Jouye wife of Tho. Aticke buried the 26th daye.
Dorithye wife of Willme Ashton buryed 29th daye.
Tho. son of George Lee baptized the last daye.

Januarye.

Franscis Fearnleye buried the first daye.
Margret daughter of Robt. Wright baptized ye 7th daye.
A yonge childe of Rych. Castley not bap. buried 7th day.
Sara daughter of George Fielden baptized that daye.
Robt. son of John Walker deceazed buried 19th daye.
Robt. son of Willme Roydes deceazed buried the 21th day.
Mary daughter of Edward Wilson baptized that day.
Robt. Wright buried the same daye.
Abraham Broadley and Ellen Parker married the 23th daye.
Michaell son of Michaell Parker baptized the 28th daye.
Marye daughter of Thomas Terrye of Gaulthroppe baptized the same daye.
Willme Ashton and Elizabeth Whewell married the 30th daye Tuesdaye.

Februarye.

Edward Bowleing buryed the third daye.
Richard Spurre buryed the same daye.
Elizabeth wife of Nicholas Hirst buried the sixth day.
Richard son of William Burnley baptized ye xjth day.
Anthony son of Anth. Fearnley deceazed bapt. xvth day.
Elizabeth daughter of John Bolland base begotten with Mary Whitleye bapt. 18th daye.
Robt. son of Robt. Goodall baptized the 24th day.

March.

Elizabeth daughter of Tho. Aticke buried first daye.
William Brooke and Ann Crowther marryed by a lycense the thirde daye.
Tho. son of John Broadley baptized the 17th day.
Michael son of Oates Thornes baptized ye same day.
Bryan Phyllip sen. buried the same day.
Elizabeth daughter of Robt. Turner bapt. 18th daye.
Richard son of Bryan Phillip buried ye xxth.

1643.

Margret daughter of Robt. Wright buried that day.
William Naylor buried the xxiijth daye.
Robt. son of Bryan Hudson baptized ye 24th daye.
Mary daughter of Parcivel Terrye baptized the same daye.
Robt. son of John Fletcher buried ye same daye.

Aprill 1644.

William son of Laurence Saxton buried ye first day.
Margret wife of Humphrey Dixon buried yo fourth day.
Thomas son of Edward Chaster baptized ye 7th day.
A yong child of Bryan Brookes not bapt. buried ye 8th day.
Ann daughter of Thomas Coozen bapt. xvth day.
John Denyson and Esther Thornes marryed the 23th day.
Thomas Bradforth and Jennett Fearnley married 25th day.
Matthew Whyte buried the 28th daye.
Christopher son of Christopher Usley buried the 29th day.
Richard Clayton buried the 30th daye.

Mayo.

Richard son of John Doye baptized the fifth daye.
Elizabeth daughter of John Holland base begotten with Marye Whitleye buried the sixth daye.
Jonas Holdsworth and Sara Gill married ye 9th day.
Grace daughter of William Rhodes baptized yo 12th day.
Mereye daughter of Abraham Broadley bapt. 13th day the said Mercy buried the fourteenth daye.
Sara daughter of George Pickard baptized ye 19th day.
Richard son of Abraham Hemingway baptized the 22th day.
James son of Marmaduke Longley buryed the 25th daye.
Leonard son of Henry Greaves buryed the 28th day.

June.

William son of Robt. Richardson baptized the second day.
Ann daughter of John Dickenson buryed the 7th daye.
Sara daughter of William Beament buried the 8th day.
Nicholas son of Nicholas Aveyard baptized the 9th day.
Thomas son of John Robinson buryed the thirteenth day.
Two chibdren of Will Beaumont not bap. buried 17 day.
John Bradforth buried the 15th daye.
Sara daughter of Chr. Brooke buried 22th daye.
Sara wife of Will Beaumont buried 26th daye.
Ann wife of Rych. Brooke buried that daye.
Sara daughter of Rychard Dawson baptized last daye.

Julyo 1644.

Martha daughter of Abraham Greenwood baptised 3 daye.
Robt. son of Bryam Hudson buried the 6th daye.
Robt. son of Robt. Sharpe baptized 7th daye.
Eliz. daughter of George Wood of Osset bap. that daye.
Marke Banne and Grace Westerman married 9th daye.
Dorithye daughter of Willme Hall buried that daye.
Danyell son of Edward Autye baptized 13th daye.
Marye daughter of John Cuningham bap.14th daye.
Robt. son of Tho. Barber deceazed buried 24th daye.
Grace daughter of Willme Lee bap. the 25th daye.
Robt. Stansfeilde buried the 27th daye.
Robt. son of Nicholas Aveycarde bap. the 28th daye.
Eliz. daughter of Rych. Oldroide bap. that daye.
Alice daughter of Willme Robinson base begotten with Eliz. Stansfeilde bap. that day.

August.

Eliz. daughter of George Allen bap. first daye.
Nich. Beetye a souldier buried the 4th daye.
John Doy and Rosamond Longley married the 5th daye.
Eliz. wife of Will. Hall buried the 7th daye.
Sarah daughter of Will. Speight bap. xjth daye.
Tho. base son of Eliz. Brooke bap. that daye.
Ann Wife of Jo, Robt. buried the 21th daye.
Dorithie daughter of James Hutton bap. 25th daye.
Marye daughter of Willme Ingham bap. that daye.
Willme Audsleye buryed the 26th daye.
Margret wife of Mr. Hemingwaye buried that daye.

September.

Eliz. daughter of Tho. Allen bap. the first daye.
Robt. son of Rych. Poole bap. that daye the saide Robt. buried the thirde daye.
Eliz. Hirst of Ossett vid. buried the 4th daye.
Eliz. daughter of Robt. Peater buried the 6th daye.
John son of Rych. Kaye buried the 14th daye.
Rich. son of Abraham Hemingwaye buried xvth daye.
Eliz. daughter of John Breare bap. that daye.
John son of John Sheard bap. the same daye.
Eliz. daughter of Tho. Marshall buried 16th daye.
Tho. son of Edward Chaster buried 19th daye.
Henrie son of Rich. Gibson bap. 22th daye.
Rych. son of Robt. Barghe bap. 25th daye.
Issabell daughter of John Robinson Ju. buried the 26th daye.
Alice Richardson buried the same daye.
Thomas son of Tho. Carter baptized 29th daye.
Elizabeth daughter of Tho. Allen buried that day.
John son of Hugh Mateson buried last daye.

October.

John son of Alvereye Whitley buryed the sixt daye.
Willme Dickson and Marye Cookeson married 9th daye.
George Towleson buryed the xjth daye.

1641.

Agnes Gibson of Gauthrop vid. buried the 13th daye.
John Fell buryed the same daye.
Willme Ellis and Ann Peace maried the 16th daye.
Martin Binnes and Grace Roydes maried 21th daye.
A yong daughter of Robt. Nettleton not bap. buried that day.
Edward son of Mich. Sacker baptized the 27th daye.
Tho. son of Tho. Wilbye of Ossett baptized that daye.
A yong son of John Robucke not bap. buried that day.
Joseph Jepson and Eliz. Millus maried the 30th day.
Ann daughter of Robt. Bedford baptized 31th daye.
Ann daughter of Peter Robinson of Woodchurch baptized the same daye.

November.

Ann wife of Abraham Hemingwaye buried second day.
Alice daughter of Willme Robinson base begotten with Eliz. Stansfilde buried third daye.
Eliz. daughter of Robert Fairbarne of Ossett baptized the vth daye.
Hanna daughter of Edward Haigh of Woodchurch baptized the vijth daye.
Eliz. daughter of Samuell Lee deceazed buryed the ninthe daye.
James son of James Lebleye baptized the xth day.
Willme son of Willme Ashton of Moreside baptized the same daye.
Marye daughter of Rych. Tailier buried that day.
Ann wife of John Robucke of Ossett buried xvth day.
John son of Anthonie Sheard baptized 17th daye.
A yong daughter of Willme Steade not bap. buryed the xviijth daye.
Henrye Graive buryed the 23th daye.
Willme son of Robt. Tompson buried the 24th day.
Susan daughter of Willms Autye buried the xxvth daye.
Willme son of Willme Autye buried 28th daye.

December.

Ann daughter of James Sonyare of Dewsburie baptized the eight daye.
Robt. son of Willme Foxe of Ossett baptized the same daie.
Grace daughter of John Claughton of the same baptized that daie.
Willme son of John Bargh Osset baptized xjth daye.
Robt. Hall and Alice Megson married that daye.
Franscis son of Franscis Nettleton bap. xijth day.
Thomas son of Willme Ashton of Dewsburie buryed the xiijth daye.
Ann wife of Henrie Graive of Ossett buried the 11th day.
Thomas son of Thomas Nettleton of Dewsburie buried the 23th daye.
Rychard Whitleye buried the 26th daye.
Elizabeth daughter of Bartholomewe Bridge of Woodchurch baptized the same daye.

1641.

Willme Middlebrough buryed 27th daye.
John son of Willme Kitson baptized 31th daye.

Januarye.

Alice wife of John Carwell buried the 3 daye.
Robt. and Josuah children of Thomas Musgraive baptized the 4th daye.
Robt. son of Thomas Musgraive buried the 6th daye.
Josuah son of Tho. Musgraive buried the 8th day.
Willme Graive and Eliz. Watsone marryed ye 12th day.
Marye daughter of Tho. Bolland baptized that daye.
George son of Willme Broadhead bap. same daye.
Eliz. wife of Robt. Pickard buried the 14th daye.
Jane daughter of Robt. Barker buried that daye.
Sara daughter of Tho. Autye of Soothilltownship buried the same daye.
Marye daughter of Edward Nelson buried xvth day.
Tho. Williams buried the xvijth day.
Edward son of Edward Walker buried xixth day.
Samuell son of Michaell Mitchell buried the 21th day.
Jeremy son of Jonas Holdsworth o bap. 23th . . .
Tho. son of John Fletcher buryed the 27th . . .
Robt. son of Tho. Whittaker buried the 29th . . .
Willme son of Robt. Sayile buried that daye.

Februarie.

Edward son of Robt. Bradforth Osset baptized 2d day.
John son of John Hallilah baptized the vth day.
John son of John Nayler of Osset baptized the 8th daye.
Mary daughter of Laurence Bull, bap. the 16th daye.
John Whitleye and Ann Ingrathorpe maried the 17th daye.
Edward Whitleye and Mary Wheelewright maried that daye.
Marye daughter of Mathewe Speight bap. 18th daye.
Edmonde Sonyare buried the 19th daye.
A yonge daughter of Thos. Nowell not bap. buried 25th daye.
Sara daughter of Christopher Vslye bap. 27th day.

Marche.

Thomas son of Thomas Robinson of Osset bap. second daye.
Elizabeth daughter of Michaell Speight bap. that daye.
Elizabeth daughter of Edward Bridge bap. same daye.
Robt. Sonyare buried the thirde daye.
Thomas son of Joseph Phillippe baptized the 4th daye the said Thomas buryed the vth daye.
Willme son of Willme Ashton baptized the 9th daye.
Elizabeth daughter of Willme Castley bap. xijth daye.
Thomas Autye of Wateryate buried the 14th daye.
Grace daughter of Anthonye Autye baptized 16th daye.

1644.

Alice daughter of John Robinson Ju. bap. that daye.
Elizabeth daughter of Isaiah Oldroide bap. 19th daye.
Thomas son of Robt. Bedford buried same daye.
Alice wife of Rych. Thornes buried 21th daye.
John son of Michaell Parker baptized 23th daye.
Thomas son of John Breare of Osset baptised that day.
James son of Anthonye Curtice of Osset bap. samo daye.
Lydiah daughter of Mathewe Speight bap. 26th daye.
Sarah daughter of George Fielden buried 30th daye.
Parcivall son of John Terrie baptized last daye.
Marye daughter of Thomas Wormall bap. that daye.

Aprill 1645.

Elizabeth wife of Michaell Bentley buried first day.
A yonge daughter of Stephen House not bap. buried yt day.
Alice daughter of Robt. Fisher buried the vth daye.
John son of John Parker baptized the 7th daye.
James Cowpar and Ann Mortimar maried eight daye.
Willme son of Robt. Richardson buried 9th daye.
Edward son of Robt. Barbar bap. the 13th daye.
Rychard son of James Sonyare baptized 20th daye.
George Dawson and Marye Chadwicke maried xxijth day.
Grace wife of Thomas Nowell buried same daye.
Willme Megsom and Elizabethe Applebye maried that daye.
Issabell wife of George Pickeringe buried 25th day.
Alice wife of Robt. Tompson buried 28th daye.
Jonye wife of Willme Knowles buried the 29th daye.

Maye.

Ellen daughter of Edward Goodall bap. first day.
Henrie son of Rich. Gibson buried same daye.
Hellen daughter of Willme Fletcher bap. the 4th daye.
Sara daughter of Rich. Dawson buried same daye.
Mereye daughter of Willme Richardson buried 12th day.
Willme Pollard and Jennet Stansfeilde maried 14th day.
A yonge child of Robt. Bradford not bap. buried 17th day.
Michaell son of Robt. Barton baptized 20th daye.
A yonge daughter of Christopher Brooke of Osset Ju. not bap. buried the 21th daye.
Michaell son of Robt. Barton buried 24th daye.
Marye daughter of James Hatton buried that daye.
Sara daughter of Christopher Usley buried the 28th daye.

June.

Mereye daughter of John Jagger baptized 2 daye.
Ann daughter of Abraham Broadley baptized the 4th daye.
John son of Mr. Tharpe baptized the vth daye.

1645.

John Browne and Grace West maried 8th daye.
James son of John Wildeman baptized same daye.
Phillipp Brooke buried the xjth daye.
Mereye daughter of Willme Westerman bap. 11th daye.
John Maude and Ellen Acrod maried the 16th daye.
Patriarch Heye buried the 18th daye.
Tho. son of Tho. Foothergill baptized 21th daye.
Marye daughter of Nicholas White buried that daye.
Two sons of James Hirst not bap. buried 25th daye.
George son of George Westerman bap. 28th daye.
Hugh son of Hugh Mateson baptized the 29th daye.

Julye.

Franscis Ashton and Ann Bull maried the first daye.
John Armitadge and Agnes Kighley maried that daye.
Timothie Kitson and Eliz. Archer maried same daye.
Marye daughter of Tho. Whitaker bap. 2 daye.
Mereye daughter of Willme Westerman buried 3 day.
Robt. son of Tho. Foxe buried same daye.
Willme Simpson and Eliz. Roades marricd at Lightlife chappell wthin parish of Halifax the 9th daye.
Nicholas Nayler and Marye Greenwood maried 14th daye.
A yonge daughter of Will. Gill stilborne buried 18th day.
Marmaduke Dey and Eliz. Fletcher maried 19th daye.
Ann daughter of Robt. Gibson bap. same daye.
A yonge son of Simeon Greenwood Ju. not bap. buried yt. day.
Thomas son of Will. Gill Osset bap. 20th daye.
Rychard son of Michaell Stubley baptized yt daye.
Edward Ellis and Eliz. Hemingwaye maried 28th day.
Jeremye son of Nicholas Batley buried 29th daye.

August.

Tho. son of Nicholas Wheatley buried 4th daye.
A yonge son of Alverey Whitley not bap. buried 8th day.
Robt. son of Robt. Graive of Westerton bap. 9th daye.
Paull Ramsden buried the same daye.
Henrye son of Willme Ellis baptized xth daye.
John Cowpar and Sara Oldroide maried xjth daye.
Ann wife of Willme Riddlesden buried 13th daye.
A yonge child of James Wilson stilborne buried xvth daye.
Tho. son of Richard Gibson buried 16th daye.
George Maud Osset buried that daye.
Rosamond wife of Edward Bowleinge deceased buried 19th day.
Edward Oldroide and Mary White maried xxvth day.

September.

Alvery son of Philemon Dickson buryed xth day.
Edward son of Robt. Taylier baptized 14th daye.

1645.

John Moorehouse and Alice Wheatley maried xvth day.
Thomas Wilbye of Osset buryed same daye.
Charles son of Charles Hall base begotten with Grace Denis baptized the 17th daye.
Henrye son of Willme Neusome buried 18th daye.
A yonge childe of Tho. Allen not bap. buried that daye.
Martha daughter of Thomas Hepworth baptized the 19th day.
Mereye daughter of Laurence Saxton bap. 22th daye.
A yonge son of James Moore of Osset not bap. buried 30th day.

October.

Jonas Woodhead buried third daye.
Elizabeth daughter of Robt. Nettleton bap. that day.
Willme Ashton Soothill Township buried that day.
Abraham son of John Ellis baptized that daye.
George son of Edward Chaster baptized 9th daye.
Susan daughter of Joseph Oldroid Ju. bap. xith daye.
Marye daughter of Willme Pollard bap. xijth day.
Willme Riddlesden and Alice Roades maried 16th daye.
Henrie Jepson and Grace Oldroid maried 20th day.
Abraham Hemingwaye and Eliz. Barbar maried that day.
Willme son of Willme Antye bap. same day.
Samuell son of Tho. Audsley bap. 21th daye.
Christabell wife of Tho. Armstronge buried 22th day.
Tho. son of Tho. Shepleye baptized 23th daye.
Tho. son of John Autye baptized same daye.
Joseph son of John Autye baptized 26th daye.
Tho. son of John Autye buried 28th daye.
Marye daughter of Rich. Kaye bap. same daye.
Willme Neusome and Ann Wheatley maried 30th daye.

November.

Mary daughter of Willm Phillip baptized the 2d day.
Easter daughter of Henrie Ellis bap. 8th daye.
Edward son of John Taylier buried xith daye.
Abraham Haighe and Susan Benson married the 13th day.
Richard Royds and Sara Wood maried xvth daye.
Robt. Bradley and Jane Barbar maried same daye.
Rych. son of Rich. Taylier baptized 18th daye.
Ann daughter of Robt. Bedford buried 20th daye.
Edward son of Robt. Taylier buried 21th daye.
Eliz. daughter of Martin Parker bap. 22th daye.
Martha daughter of Michaell Bentley bap. 27th day.

December.

John Richardson and Marye Wilson maried 1th day.
Willme Heluish and Eliz. Robert maried 2 daye.
Christopher Gunson and Mercye Acrode maried the 6th day.
Symon son of Symon Dalton baptized 7th day.
Ann daughter of Bryan Gibson buried 17th daye.

1645.

Rychard son of Martin Bynnes bap. 27th daye.
Elizabeth daughter of John Medley buryed the 30th day.

Jannarye.

Elizabeth daughter of Willm Megsonn baptized the i day.
Marye daughter of Robt. Westerman bap. i daye.
Proscilla daughter of John Speight of Osset bap. 4th day.
Vid. Wood of Osset buryed the xvjth daye.
Stephen Mitchell buryed the 21th daye.
John son of Rychard Dawson buried 30th daye.
Peter son of Tho. Aticke buried that daye.
Elizabeth daughter of Michaell Speight buried 31th daye.

Februarye.

Jeremy son of James Fearnley bap. first daye.
Willme Bentson and Sara Middlebroughe married the seconde daye.
Robt. Wade and Marye Walker married the 4th daie.
Ellen daughter of Robt. Touleson bap. that daye.
Henrie Simpson and Easter Pickard married 5th daie.
Robt. Healde and Marye Fletcher married same daye.
Allexander son of Willme Neusome buried 9th daye.
Thomas Nowell and Grace Street maried that daye.
Thomas son of Willme Ashton bap. the xth daye.
A yonge son of Timothie Kitson not bap. buried xjth daie.
Abraha son of Robt. Peaker bap. the 14th daye.
Edward son of Robt. Bedforde bap. the 18th daye.
Issabell daughter of John Taylior base begotten with Issabell Robinson baptized the 19th daye.
Nicholas Walker buried the xxvth daye.
Issabell daughter of John Taylior base begotten with Issabell Robinson buried 26th daye.

Marche.

A yonge childe of John Millns not bap. buried vth daye.
Vid. Ellis of Ossett buried that daye.
Eliz. daughter of Marmaduke Deye baptized 7th daye.
Rosamonde daughter of Mich. Smyth of Osset bap. 8th daye.
Lucye daughter of George Pickard of Osset bap. xth daye.
John son of Rich. Calloye of Ossott bap. xvth daye.
Tho. son of George Fieldon of Ossett bap. 19th daye.
Martha daughter of Rich. Bateman bap. xxvth daye.

Aprill 1646. Oar. 22th.

Richard son of Robt. Stansfeild buried 4th daye.
Easter daughter of Henrie Jepson baptized that daye. The said Easter buried vth daye.
Thomas son of Francis Ashton bap. same day.
Willme son of Willme Dawson bap. sixt daye.

1646.

A yonge child of Ed. Dawson base begotten with Ann Towleson not bap. buried the 7th daye.
Eliz. daughter of Willme Whitley buried that daye.
Thomas Hemingwaye and Alice Acroglo married 9th daye.
Ann daughter of Rich. Dawson baptized xjth daye.
John Haigh of Osset buried the xvth daye.
Rich. Wheatleye and Marye Booth married 22th day.
Tho. son. of Tho. Nettleton baptized the 23th daye.
Ann Towleson buried the same daye.
Robt. Copley and Easter Sonyare married 26th daye.
A yonge childe of John Knowles not bap. buried 27th day.

Mayo.

Eliz. daughter of Edward Wilson baptized 7th daye.
Martin son of Joseph Tayler baptized same daye.
. . . . . of Tho. Musgraive baptized 13th daye.
Eliz. wife of John Dishforth buried the 14th daye.
Eliz. daughter of John Dishforthe baptized that daye.
Henrie Dickson and Eliz. Taylier married 18th daye.
Alice daughter of Tho. Carro bap. 23th daye.

June.

Michaell Wheatley and Dorithie Speight married 4th day.
Robt. son of Joseph Phillippe baptized 6th daye.
A yonge son of Rych. Gibson not bap. buried 8th daye.
Edward son of Edward Ellis Ju. baptized the xith daye.
Henrie son of Mich. Bentleye baptized the 13th daye.
Alice wife of George Kighleye buried 18th daye.
John son of Christopher Gunson bap. the 20th daye.
Rich. son of Parcivall Dishforthe bap. 21th daye.
John Carnell and Susan Nayler married 22th daye.
Alice wife of Henrie Bull deceazed buried that daye.
Willme son of John Deye of Osset buried 30th daye.

Julie.

Ann daughter of Abraham Hemingway baptized the i daye.
Marmaduke Greenfield and Grace Fearneley married the 2 day.
Alice daughter of James Hirst baptized the 4 day.
Willm Hall and Elizabeth Thornetou married ye 7th day.
A young childe of John Whitley Ju. of Ossett buried yt day.
Richard Rawson and Mary Grave married yo 8th day.
Elizabeth Birch buried that day.
John son of Alverie Pickard baptized the xith day.
Robert son of Thomas Fox baptized ye 15th day.
Richard son of Michaell Parker baptized ye same day.
Ann Peace of Osset wid. buried the 4 day.

August 1646.

Francis daughter of Willim Ingham of Osset baptized yo 9th day.
Mary daughter of Willim Sonjar buried the 11th day.
Margret daughter of Christopher Brooke of Osset baptized the 29th day.

September.

John White and Marie Walker married the 2 day.
Grace daughter of Richard Dickinson of Osset buried ye 3 day.
George Pickering and Alice Goodale married the 4th day.
John Carter and Isabell Stappleton married yo 5th day.
Richard Wilson and Mary Burkeheade married that . . .
Elizabeth daughter of Willim Green baptized ye 8 day.
An daughter of Richard Kighley baptized the 12 day.
Jeremiah son Jonas Holdsworth buried ye 15th day.
Sara daughter of John Ashley baptized the 16th day.
John son of Edward Dickson baptized the 17th day.
Susan daughter of Isiah Oldroyde baptized ye 19th day.
Elizabeth daughter of John Fozard baptized the same day.
John son of Richard Gallie buried the 20th day.
Thomas Armitage and Rosamund Wade married the 22th day.
Thomas Ellis and Susanna Tomlison married the 23 day.
Mary daughter of John Bradforth of Osset buried the 23 of September.
Sara daughter of Nicholas Hargrave buried the same day.
Rebecca daughter of Mr. Cudworth buried the 26th day.
Robert Robinson and Ann Smithson married the 29th day.

October.

John son of John Tennand of Westerton baptized the first day.
Elizabeth daughter of Thomas Stapleton baptized the 3 day.
Richard son of Willim Heluish of Osset baptized the 4th day.
Henrie Barbar and Elizabeth Jerison of Wakefeild married the 5th day.
Grace daughter of Willm Rodes buried the same day.
John Morewood and Easter Hopefull married the 6th day.
Mary daughter of Richard Rodes of Earlsheaton baptized the same day.
Gennit daughter of Thomas Allen baptized the same day.
Mary daughter of John Nettleton baptized the 7th day.
Thomas Atacke and Elizabeth . . . . . of Osset married yt day.

1646.

Martha daughter of William Burnley baptized the 10th day.
A childe of Willm Newsome unbaptized buried the same day.
John Browne and Margrett Walker maried the 12th day.
Elizabeth wife of Marmaduke Ashton buried the 15th day.
Thomas son of Brian Hudson of Gawthrop baptized the 20th day.
John Awdsley and Ann Wormall married the 21th day.
John son of John White baptized the 24th of October.
Rbt. son of Rbt. Fox of Westerton baptized ye same day.
Timothie son of Willm Kitson baptized ye same day.
Jane daughter of John Nalor junior of Ossett baptized the same day.
Martin Barbar and Elizabeth Laugstar married the 27th day.
Alice the daughter Marke Robinson baptized the same day.
Mary daughter of Thomas Wormall buried yt day.

November.

2 children of John Walkars of Osset buried the 3rd day.
Josua Rodes and Elizabeth Saxton married the 5th day.
Robert son of John Brearey baptized ye 7th day.
Sara daughter of Robt. Bull of Ossett baptized the same day.
Elizabeth daughter of John Barge baptized yt day.
Sara daughter of Thomas Nowell of Osset baptized the 8th day.
Jane daughter of Joseph Nalor baptized the 12th day.
Mary the daughter of Willm Johnson of Ossett baptized the 15th day.
Sarah daughter of Willm Steade buried ye 17th day.
Thomas Liverseige and Mary Nottleton of Westerton maried the 18th day.
Mary daughter of Mr. Richard Thorpe baptized ye 19th day.
Elizabeth daughter of John Forest baptized the 23 day.
John Scolefeild and Rebecca Acrode married 24th day.
Jeffera Pratt and Margrett Breer maried the 25th day.

December.

Sara daughter of John Forrest baptized yo 2 day.
John son of Willme Simpson baptized the 3d day.
John son of Rbt. Heald baptized the 5th day.
A daughter of Nicholas Nalor unbaptized buried yo 6 day.
Jeremie son of Henry Sympson of Ossot baptized yt day.
Timothie Cawthorne of Horberie and Margrett Acrode of this pish married yo 15th day.
Elizabeth daughter of Tho. Carter baptized the 16th day.

1646.

Thomas son of Abraham Greenwood baptized yo 23 day.
John son of Robt. Wade baptized the 31th day.
Elizabeth daughter of Robt. Bargh baptized yo same day.

Januarie.

Ester daughter of Anthonie Sheard baptized the 2 day.
Thomas son of Paul Sharpe of Woodchurch baptized yo 3 day.
Agnes wife of John Milner buried yt day.
Henry Acrode son of John Acrode buried the 11th day.
Samuell Denton and Joine Holdsworth married the 12th day.
Alice Hartley buried the 14th day.
Thomas son of John Awty baptized the 17th day.
John Terrie of Gawthrop buried yt day.
Thomas Soothill buried the 19th day.
John Sunderland buried that day.
Mary daughter of John Breere of Osset baptized the 23 day.
John son of John Dey ju. baptized the 26th day.
Willm son of Steven Rouse baptized the 27th day.
Thomas son of Thomas Hemmingway baptized the 28th day.
A childe of Willm Speight's unb. buried yt day.
Joseph son of Willm Lee baptized the 29th day.
Grace daughter of Willm Knowles junior base begotten with Sara Milnes baptized the 30th day.
Richard son of Willm Wilson buried the 31 day.

Februarie.

Jennitt Townend buried the 3 day.
Nicholas son of Michaell Seccar baptized yt day.
Elizabeth daughter of Hugh Watson bap. the sixth day.
Robt. son of Thomas Hartley baptized the 7th day.
Josua son of Willm Middlesden baptized the 13th day.
Thomas son of Rbt. Sharpe baptized the 14th day.
Timothie son of Willm Kitson buried the 17th day.
Sibill wife of George Woode buried the 19th day.
Elizabeth daughter of John Ellis of Ossett baptized yo 20th day.
Marie daughter of John Shearde baptized yo same day.
Grace daughter of Richard Ouldred baptized the 24th day.
Grace daughter of Marmaduke Greenfeilde baptized yo same day.
Edward Walker and Grace Acroyd married the 25th day.
A childe of Tho. Cosens of Ossett buried the 26th day.
A childe of Willm Westerman's buried the same day.
Henry son of Henry Dixon baptized yo 27th day.
Elizabeth daughter of John Mores baptized yo same day.

March.

Christopher Brooke and Ellin Bradley married the first day.
John son of Rbt. Fairborne baptized the same day.
John son of Willm Broadheade baptized the 2 day.

1646.

Jonas son of Richard Holdsworth baptized the 4th day.
Willim son of James Hutton baptized the same day.
Alvery son of John Millnes baptized the 6th day.
Rbt. Green of Chidsell buried that day.
John son of James Mitchell baptized ye 11th day.
Ellin daught. of Michaell Speight of Osset buried the 13th day.
Abhm North and Elizabeth Dickson married ye 17th day.
Edward son of Edward Chagter baptized the 18th day.
Henrie son of Willim Castlehouse baptized the 20th day.
Thomas son of George Whiteheade buried ye 24th day.
Elizabeth daughter of Laurence Bull bapt. ye 27th day.

Aprill 1647.

George Scott and Rebecca Tailor married the 6th day.
Jonas sonne of Brian Brooke of Chidsell buried the same day.
Elizabeth daughter of Samuell Pickard buried 7th day.
John son of Rbt. Fairbarne buried the 14th day.
Elizabeth White buried the 15th day.
Easter daughter of John Bradforth of Ossett baptized the 19th day.
Joshua son of John Knowles baptized the same day.

May.

John son of John Speight of Osset baptized the first day.
James son of James Cowper baptized the 8th day.
Marie daughter of Rbt. Goodale baptized the 15th day.
Elizabeth daughter of Bryan Philip of Osset baptized yo same day.
John Langfeild and Elizabeth Walkar married the 18th day.
Lawrence Whittaker and Mary Broadley married ye 19th day.
Jonas son of Jonas Holdsworth of Osset baptized yo 20th day.
Grace daughter of John Carter baptized ye 28th day.
Edward son of John Richison baptized the 30th day.

June.

Christopher Sanderson and Cennit Richison married the first day.
Sara daughter of John Claughton baptized the 6 day.
Elizabeth wife of Rbt. Wroe buried the 10th day.
Thomas son of John Tinson jn. baptized the 11th day.
James son of James Soniar baptized the 15th day.
..... Forrest buried the 19th day.
Benjamin Holmes and Dorithie Broadley married ye 23 day.
John Nettleton sen. buried the 24 day.

1647.

Abraham son of James Soniar baptized the 26th day.
John Tennand and Mary Peace married the 29th day.
John son of Francis Nettleton of Osset baptized ye 30th day.

Julie.

Thomas son of Jefera Pratt baptized ye 6th day.
Avery Tomlison buried the 7th day.
Elizabeth daughter of Rbt. Talor baptized the 11th day.
Marmaduke Dey buried the 17th day.
Sara daughter of John Hardcastle bapt. ye 18th day.
Winyfred daughter of Richard Dixon baptized ye 20th day.
James Hutton and Dorathie Rodes maried ye 24th day.
Samuell Glover and Ann Kirke married the 25th day.

August.

Francis Cunningham and Anna Preistley married ye 3 day.
Thomas son of Thomas Ellis baptized ye 4 day.
A man childe unbaptized of Abraham Broadleye's buried ye 5th day.
Jeremy Dunwell and Ann Pollard married the 8th day.
Alice daughter of Rbt. Bedforth bapt. the 11th day.
Elizabeth daughter of Aboll Garret of Osset bapt. ye 12th day.
Mary daughter of John Nettleton buried ye same day.
Mary daughter of Gamaliell Brearie buried ye 13th day.
James son of George Foild of Battley baptiz. ye 14th day.
Elizabeth daughter of Rbt. Barbar bapt. ye 21 day.
A boy (unbaptized) of Josua Rodes buried ye samo day.
Willim Beatson buried the 23 day.
Margret daughter of Thomas Wormall of Osset baptized the 25th day.
Ann daughter of Parcivell Terrie bapt. ye 28th day.
John Dey and Ann Broadley maried 30th day.

September.

Reginald Fyrth and Mary Soniar married ye 5th day.
Robert Truelove and Elizabeth Dey married yo 6th day.
Susan Allen buried the same day.
John son of Thomas Stead bapt. ye 8th day.
Elizabeth daughter of Willim Soniar baptized yo 11th day.
John son of Thomas Steade buried the 12th day.
Richard son of Edward Goodale baptized yt day.
Alice daughter of Martin Barbar bapt. ye same day.
Elizabeth daughter of John Tilson buried ye 15th day.
Susan daughter of Henry Jepson baptized the 16th day.

1647.

Christopher son of Willm Ellis baptized yt (the 16th) day.
Mary daughter of Willm Fletcher baptized ye 19th day.
John son of Samuell Pickard buried the 20th day.
Susan daughter of Rbt. Barbar buried ye same day.
Elizabeth B[eck]with [?]* wid. buried the ..... 21th day.
Gennit daughter of Thomas Bolland baptized ye 22th day.
John son of John Awdseley baptized the 23 day.
Edward Hurst buried ye 23 day also.
Michaell son of Henrie Ellis baptized the 29th day.
Samuell sonne of Thomas Awdsley buried ye 30th day.

October.

Samuell Whiteley buried ye first day.
Martha daughter of Thomas Abbison baptized ye 3d day.
James Dixon and Grace Boulton married the 6th day.
William Knowles and Susan Fell married the 7th day.
Richard Brooke and Mary Taylor married the 11th day.
John sone of Edward Ellis ju. baptized ye 16th day.
Richard son of Rbt. Robinson baptized the 18th day.
Mary daughter of Rbt. Dicon baptized the 19th day.
John Musgrave and Isabell Tompson married ye 20th day.
John son of Mathew Speight baptized the 24th [?] day.
Willm sonne of the sde Mathew baptized ye same day.
Grace daughter of Nicholas Wheateley buried the 28th day.

November.

Martha daughter of Michaell Bentley buried ye 9th day.
Elizabeth daughter of Lawrence Hepworth baptized the 11th day.
Elizabeth daughter of John Bargh buried ye 14th day.
A son of John Whitley unbaptized buried the same day.
Dorothie daughter of Willm Castley buried the 16th day.
Elizabeth daughter of Abie Garret buried the 21 day.
Abraham son of John Ellis buried the 22th day.
Elizabeth daughter of Hugh Matson buried yo 26th day.
Josua son of Thomas Musgrave buried the same day.
Thomas Wilson and Grace Stapleton married the 29th day.
Abraham Beardsell and Elizabeth Stringer married the same day.

* A blot.

1647.

Robert Beewith and Gennitt Townend married yo 30th day.

December.

Richard Gunson and Elizabeth Stappleton married the first day.
Henrie son of Rbt. Barbar baptized the 3 day.
Edward son of John Richardson buried the 5th day.
Willm son of Willm Newsom baptized the 11th day.
Robert son of Nichus Naylor baptized and buried the 13th day.
Martha daughter of Israell Oldroyde baptized the 15th day.
Abraham Myres of Churwell and Mercie Croft married ye same day.
Ellin daughter of Rbt. Towlson buried ye 16th day.
George son of Thomas Cantar buried ye 20th day.
Jonas son of Willm Fox buried ye 22th day.
Tobie son of George Lee baptized the 28th day.
Henry son of Willm Preistley baptized ye same day.
Rosamund daught. of Michaell Smith buried ye 29th day.
Alice daughter of Rbt. Bedforth buried ye same day.

January.

Mary daughter of Richard Taylor baptized ye i day.
Thomas son of Rbt. Sharpe buried the same day.
Reginall Preist and Francis Copley married the 6th day.
Alice daughter of Martin Parker baptized ye same day.
Ambrose Ellis buried yt day also.
John son of John Auty ju. baptized the 9th day.
James son of Rbt. Barbar [or Barker ?] baptized yt day.
Josua son of Willm Rodes baptized the 10th day.
John son of Willm Soniar buried the —— 14th day.
Elizabeth daughter of Edward Whitley baptized the 20th day.
Ralph son of Francis Cunningham baptized yo 24th day.
Jane daughter of Nichus Gunson buried yo 27th day.
A male childe of Richard Gibson unbaptized buried ye 28th day.

Februarie.

Willm son of Willm Broadheade buried ye 2 day.
Mary wife of Thomas Hepworth buried ye 3 day.
John Browne and Elizabeth Dickson married yo 9th day.
Mary daughter of John Haileley baptized ye 12 day.
Thomas Moyens buried ye 14th day.
Joseph son of Rbt. Nettleton baptized ye 17th day.
Willm son of Willm Winterton of Westerto baptized ye 17th day also.
Tho. Ashton buried the 18th day.
Elizabeth daughter of Thomas Cartar buried ye 20th day.

1617.

Rbt. Smithson and Anne Tompson married ye 23 day.
Mathew son of Mithael Parker baptized the 26th day.
Mary daughter of Christopher Sanderson baptized ye 28th day.
Elizabeth wife of Willim Fox buried ye 29th day.
Edward son of John Stappleton buried ye same day.

March.

Willim Newsom and Mary Johnson married ye 2 day.
Thomas Cartar buried ye 3 day.
Ann daughter of Richard Dawson buried the 4 day.
Grace daughter of Edmunde Copley baptized ye 7th day.
Richard Rodes buried the 10th day.
Sara daughter of Rbt. Woode baptized ye 11th day.
Roger son of Willim Carre baptized ye 15th day.
Richard son of Abraham Hemmingway baptized ye 16th day.
Marjary wife of Willim Kitson buried the same day.
Josua son of Willme Lee baptized the 18th day.
Elizabeth daughter of Martin Bins baptized the 30th day.

April 1618.

Joseph son of Joseph Aticke baptized ye 4th day.
Sarah daughter of Willim Sugden baptized ye same day.
Marie daughter of Willim Wilson baptized yt day.
Mary daughter of Thomas Whittakers buried yt day.
Alice Whitley buried ye 6th day.
Samuell Ellis and Mary Bothomley married ye 8th day.
Robert son of John Parker baptized ye 9th day.
John son of Willim Steade baptized ye 10th day.
Elizabeth Turner buried ye 15th day.
Elizabeth wife of George Allen buried ye same day.
Ellin wife of Thomas Milner buried ye 16th day.
Wid. Ann Peace buried the 21th day.
Ester daughter of Francis Nelthorp baptized ye 24th day.
George son of Rbt. Westerman baptized ye 29th day.

May.

James Lee and Margret Brooke married ye 1 day.
Sara daughter of Rbt. Fairebarne baptized the same day.
Elizabeth daughter of Thomas Wilson baptized the 7th day.
Willim Megson buried the 12th day.
Margret Saxton buried the 13th day.
Mathew son of Mathew Boomer [?] baptized yo same day.
Joseph son of — Aticke baptized ye 14th day.
John Grave and Easter Whitley married ye 15th day.
Willim Fox and Sara Beatson married ye 17th day.
Alice wife of Thomas Futhersgill buried ye 20th day.
Edward son of Rbt. Bedforth buried ye same day.
Grace daughter of Rbt. Truelove baptized ye 22th day.

1618.

Willim son of John Ashley baptized the 23 day.
Willim Casson and Isabell Robinson married ye same day.
Dorothie daughter of Thomas Bradforth baptized the 28th day.

June.

Avery son of Francis Ashton baptized ye 3 day.
Robt. son of Richard Rodes baptized ye 4th day.
Edward son of Willim Speight baptized ye 8th day.
Henry son of Willim Dawson baptized ye 10th day.
Robt. Scott and Agnes Morse married ye 12th day.
Mary daughter of Christopher Gunson baptized the 15th day.
Mary daughter of Xstopher Gunson buried ye 17th day.
Sara daughter of Willim Phillip baptized ye 18th day.
Richard son of Abraham Hemmingway buried the 19th day.
An infant of Lawrence Whittaker's unbaptized buried ye 24th day.
Thomas Peace and Sara Naylor married ye 26th day.
James son of Mr. Samuell Pierson baptized the 29th day.

Julie.

John son of James Hutton baptized ye 1 day.
Christopher Saxton and Mary Whitley married ye 11th day.
Rbt. son of Samuell Pickard buried ye 20th day.
Roger son of Willm Gill baptized ye 25th day.
Mary daughter of Anthonie Awty baptized ye 30th day.

August.

Priscilla daughter of John Speight buried ye 2 day.
Willim Kitson and Sara Hanson married ye 17th day.
John sonne of John Dey baptized ye 19th day.
Nichus Mitchell buried the 20th day.

September.

Ann Jaggar of Osset buried ye first day.
Jonie daughter of Carie Morris buried ye 3 day.
Thomas Hepworth and Judith Burrough married the 12th day.
Thomas Futhorgill and Gennit Thornes married the 18th day.
Christopher Dickson and Dorothie Armitage mied the same day.
Abraham son of Abraham Beardsill baptized ye 22th day.
Joyce Edge buried the 22th day.
Rbt. Walkar and Sara Lee married ye same day.
Ann daughter of Christopher Brooke baptized the 24 day.

October.

Timothie son of Timothie Kitson baptized ye 4th day.
John son of Josua Rodes baptized the same day.
Grace daughter of Thomas Carr baptized ye same day.
Richard son of Rbt. Bedforth baptized ye 6th day.
Mary daughter of Edward Chaster baptized ye 7th day.

1648.

Grace daughter of Edward Wilson baptized ye 6th day.
Elizabeth daughter of John Musgrave baptized ye 9th day.
Mathew son of Mathew Boomer [?] buried the 11th day.
Mary daughter of John Hurst of Osset baptized ye 14th day.
Edmunde son of Symon Dalton of Osset baptized ye 15th day.
Michaell Bentley buried ye 24th day.
Josua son of Isiah Ouldroyde baptized the 25th day.
Thomas son of John Nalor of Ossett baptized 30th day.
Margret daughter of Willim Dey of Osset baptized ye same day.

November.

Christopher Saxton buried ye 3d day.
James Dixon and Hester Hopkinson of Wakefeild married the 6th day.
Ellin daughter of Willim Awty baptized the 11th day.
James Dawson and Elizabeth Mitchell married ye 14th day.
Rbt. Dixon buried ye 17th day.
Margrett Dixon his wife buried ye 17th day.
Isabell wife of Thomas Audsley buried ye 19th day.
Ann daughter of John Terrie baptized ye 19th day.
Sara daughter of Richard Huntington baptized ye same day.
Susanna daughter of John Grave baptized the 25th day.
John Steade buried the same day.

December.

John son of Willim Cauthorne baptized ye 3 day.
Gabriell Morris buried ye 5th day.
Mary daughter of Abraham Broadley baptized ye 13th day.
Richard Maunsfeild buried the 16th day.
Anu daughter of Willim Ridlesden baptized ye same day.
Elizabeth daughter of Thomas Hemmingway baptized ye 15th day.
Willim Lee buried ye 20th day.
Thomas Awdsley buried the 23 day.
Michaell Dey buried ye 25th day.
Sybill daughter of Mathew Speight baptized the 26th day.
Christopher Fairbarne and Elizabeth Makinder married the same day.
James Armitage and Ann Binns married ye same day.
Alice daughter of John Ellis baptized ye 27th day.
Mary daughter of John Nettleton baptized ye 28th day.
Sibill daughter of Mathew Speight buried ye 30th day.
Edward Autie of Upper Sootill buried ye 31 day.

Januarie.

Jonas Dey and Mary Lee married ye 2 day.
Susan daughter of Henry Jepson buried yo same day.

1618.

John son of John Walsha baptized the 4th day.
Judith daughter of Willim Ingham baptized ye same day.
Alice wife of Mathew Speight buried ye 5th day.
Margret daughter of Richard Kay baptized ye 6th day.
Mary daughter of James Dixon baptized ye same day.
Thomas Awdsley buried ye same day.
Sara daughter of Rbt. Wood buried ye 12th day.
Rebeceah daughter of Joseph Ouldroyd ju. baptized ye 13th day.
Mary daughter of Hugh Matson baptized ye 17 day.
Abraham son of Joseph Phillips baptized ye 18th day.
Sara daughter of John Speight baptized the 21th day.
Rbt. son of Robert Beewith baptized the 24th day.
Mary daughter of Nichus Naylor baptized ye 25th day.
Richard son of Richard Proistley baptized ye 28 day.
Grace White buried ye 30th day.
Rbt. Wade son of Rbt. Wade of Osset bapt. ye same day.
Elizabeth Nalor buried ye same day.

Februarie.

John son of Thomas Hartley baptized ye 3 day.
Willim son of Willim Whitley buried the same day.
Dorothie daughter of George Nalor of Osset baptized ye 4th day.
Josua son of Thomas Fox baptized ye 10th day.
Elizabeth daughter of Michaell Wheatley baptized the 12th day.
George son of John Moros baptized ye 15th day.
Elizabeth Bargh buried ye 17th day.
Robert Dickenson and Elizabeth Beamond married the 20th day.
Mary wife of Rbt. Rodes buried the 22th day.
Nicholas son of John White baptized yt day.
Isiah sonne of Willim Lee buried ye 25 day.

March.

Sara daughter of Anthonie Sheard baptized ye 1 day.
Thomas Robinson buried yt day.
Michaell son of Joseph Phillip buried ye 3 day.
Richard son of Richard Ouldrod baptized ye 5th day.
Samuell son of Rbt. Barton baptized ye 10th day.
Mary daughter of John Breer buried ye 13th day.
Mathew Hepworth buried ye 15th day.
John son of Willim Cawthorne buried ye 17th day.
Elizabeth daughter of Thomas Rodes buried ye 18th day.
Lidia daughter of Israell Ouldroyde baptized ye 25th day.
Rbt. son of Willm Casson baptized ye 27th day.

April 1649.

Dorothie daughter of John Breer of Osset baptized ye first day.
John son of Edward Dickson buried the 10th day.

1649.

Mary daughter of John Barghe baptized the 19th day.
Umphrey son of Nicholas Scotson buried ye 23d day.
James sonne of James Soniar buried ye 27th day.
A son of John Sheard buried the 28th day.

May.

Rbt. Rodes and Rosamunde Dey married the 1 day.
Lidia daughter of Richard Wheatley baptized ye same day.
Joseph Spurre [?] and Ann Sharphouse married the 2 day.
Rosamund daughter of George Glover baptized yo 3 day.
Thomas son of Thomas Peace baptized ye 7 day.
John Broer buried ye 10th day.
Joseph White and Mary Acrode married the 14th day.
Dinas daughter of John Richardson baptized ye same day.
John son of Joseph Nalor baptized the same day.
John son of Francis Justice buried ye 18th day a bastard with Ellin Gunson.
John son of John Bradforth baptized ye 21th day.
Williu son of Willim Kent buried yt day.
Thomas Grave buried ye 24th day.
Mercie daughter of Henry Hawkshaw and Mary Pickard of Osset base begotten baptized the 29th day.
James Speight and Elizabeth Whittaker married yo 30th day.

June.

Mercie wife of Rbt. Heald buried ye first day.
Elizabeth and Mary daughters of Willim Chapman baptized the 4th day.
Sarah daughter of Christopher Fairbarne baptized the 20th day.
John Rodes and Mary Ambler married ye 25th day.
Thomas Steado buried the 26th day.
Michaell Howroyd and Ann Soniar married yo 27th day.
Richard son of Richard Bateman baptized yo 30th day.

Julie.

Dorothie daughter of John Breer buried ye 2 day.
Richard son of Richard Holdsworth baptized ye 7th day.
Willim son of Thomas Nowell baptized ye 8th day.
Elizabeth daughter of Willim Milner baptized yo same day.
George son of Richard Gunson baptized ye 11th day his brother unbaptized buried ye same day.
Jonas son of Richard Holdsworth buried yo 13th day.
Thomas son of James Hyrst baptized ye 14th day.
John Richardson buried the same day.
Willim Beamont and Elizabeth Norfolke married ye 22th day.
Michaell Stubley buried the 28th day.
Hugh son of Thomas Whittakers baptized ye 30th day.
Gennet wife of John Udall buried ye 31 day.

August 1649.

Hugh son of Thomas Whittaker buried ye 1 day.
John Spur and Mary Hage married the 5th day.
Sarah daughter of Tho. Stappleton baptized yt day.
Rbt. Ball a childe baptized yo same day.
. . . . . of Rbt Bull baptized ye same day.
Josiah son of Tho. Hepworth baptized ye 6th day.
Tho. Rodes and Elizabeth Stubley married ye 8th day.
Edward Worrncall buried ye 16th day.
Willim Walker ju. buried the 23 day.
A man childe of James Lee of Osset unbaptized buried ye 28th day.
Mary daughter of Christofor Saxton baptized yo 30th day.

September.

Alice daughter of Abraham Hemingway baptized ye 5th day.
Rbt. Wroe buried ye 9th day.
Abraham Hemingway buried yo 12th day.
John Milner buried ye same day.
. . . . . daughter of John Breer buried yo same day.
Susan wife of Rbt. Ellis buried yo 13th day.
Martha daughter of Will. Kitson baptized yo 15th day.
Elizabeth daughter of Richard Dickson baptized yo 22th day.
Elizabeth Raynor buried ye 28th day.

October.

Willim Fox of Osset buried the first day.
Tho. Robinson and Elizabeth Mogson married ye 8th day.
Elizabeth daughter of Rbt. Dickinson baptized ye 9th day.
Anne daughter of George Allen baptized ye 10th day.
Willim Wilbie of Osset buried ye 13th day.
The son of John Breer buried ye same day.
Willim son of Willim Nowell buried ye 19th day.
Sara daughter of Jefera Prat baptized the 24th day.
Elizabeth wife of John Sharpe buried yo 21th (sic) day.
Rbt. Naylor buried the 26th day.
George Otley and Elizabeth Dawson married ye 30th day.
A man childe of Michaell Dawson's unbaptized buried the same day.
Rbt. son of Christopher Gunson baptized yo 31 day.

November.

Sarah daughter of Willim Ellis baptized ye 4th day.
A man childe of Michaell Dawson buried ye 6th.
Elizabeth daughter of Willim Milner buried yo 7th day.
Rbt. Heald and Elizabeth Townend married ye 8th day.
Elizabeth wife of Umferey Beamont buried yo 9th of . . . . ber.
Martha daughter of Jonas Dey baptized the 10th day.
Elizabeth daughter of James Soniar baptized yo same day.

November 1649.

Mary daughter of Samuell Ellis baptized ye 11th day.
Joseph son of Lawrence Whittaker baptized ye same day.
Mary wife of Lawrence Whittaker buried the 13th day.
Joseph son of Lawrence Whittaker buried ye same day.
Ellen wife of Henry Witman buried ye 14th day.
A man childe of ye sde Henry buried ye same day.
Richard son of Rbt. Bedforth buried the same day.
A woman childe of Edward Ellis ju. buried ye 18th day.
Prudence wife of Tho. Sharpehouse buried ye 19th day.

December

Tho. son of John Jaggar baptized ye 3 day.
Ann and Elizabeth daughters of John Claughton baptized the same day.
Alice daughter of Richard Phillip buried ye 6th day base begotten wth Grace Wright.
Ann daughter of Abraham Greenwood baptized ye 8th day.
Richard Dawson buried the 15th day.
Willim son of James Hutton buried ye 26th day.
Willim Walkar buried ye 26th day.
John son of Henry Dickson baptized ye same day.
Elizabeth daughter of Willim Buruley baptized the same day.
Isaac son of Rbt. Goodale baptized the 31th day.

Januarie.

Martha daughter of Thomas Bolland baptized ye 1 day.
James son of James Soniar baptized the 5th day.
Mathew son of Henry Ellis baptized ye same day.
Mathew son of Henry Ellis buried the 15th day.
Richard son of Michaell Speight baptized the 19th day.
Robert son of Michael Secear baptized the 20th day.
Robert son of Christopher Gunson buried the 23 day.
Adam Wheatley and Mercie Webster married ye 30th day.
Thomas Allen buried the last day.

Februarie.

Joseph son of Jeremy Radcliffe buried ye 6th day.
Mercie daughter of Martin Barbar baptized ye 9th day.
Robert son of Robert Tator baptized ye 16 day.
Robt. son of John Parker buried ye 17 day.
Martin son of Willim Broadhead baptized ye 27 day.
John Oxley buried the 28 day.

March.

Robert son of Rbt. Barbar baptized the 3 day.
Mathew son of Michaell Parker buried the 6 day.
Elizabeth Dalton wife and Emond son of Symon Dalton buried ye 9 day.
Mary wife of Michaell Bentley buried the 16 day.
Alice daughter of Willim Green baptized yt day.

1649.

Alexander son of Willim Newsom baptized ye 17 day.
Josua son of John Milnes baptized the 23 day.
Daniell son of John Autie baptized ye 24 day.
Mathew son of Michaell Parker baptized the same day.
Henry Weetman and Thomazin Jackson married ye 26 day.
Marmaduke Ashton buried the 29th day.
Mary daughter of Francis Cunningham baptized ye 31 day.
Ann daughter of James Armitage of Greasbrough baptized yt day.

Aprill 1650.

Rebecca daughter of Willim Lee baptized the 6th day.
John son of Jonas Holdsworth baptized ye 7th day.
Richard son of Nicholas Ellis baptized ye 11th day.
John Knowles buried yt day.
Mercie daughter of Thomas Abison baptized ye 15th day.
Mathew son of John Knowles baptized ye 18th day.
Richard Shefeild and Sarah Crowder married the 21th day.
Mary daughter of John Robinson baptized the same day.

May.

George son of John Mores buried the 5th day.
Mary daughter of Joseph Spur alias Maira baptized the 6th day.
Rbt. son of Rbt. Robinson baptized ye 16th day.
Rbt. son of Rbt. Robinson buried the 17th day.
Annah daughter of Rbt. Walkar . . . . . the same day.
John son of Thomas Terrie baptized ye 22 day.
Rbt. son of Brian Phillip baptized ye same day.
Elizabeth daughter of Thomas Allen baptized ye 26th day.
Lidia daughter of Willim Ashton baptized ye 28 day.
Elizabeth wife of Rbt. Truelove buried the said day.

June.

Elizabeth daughter of Marke Whittakers baptized ye 8th day.
Thomas Barras and Ellin Metcalfe married ye 12th of June.
Ann wife of Nichus Wheatley buried ye 14th day.
Grace daughter of Thomas Futhergill baptized ye 16th day.
John son of James Cowper baptized the 20th day.
Anne daughter of Marmaduke Greenfeild baptized the same day.
John son of John Smith baptized the 29th day.

Julie.

Rbt. Reyner and Mary Brooke married the 2 day.
Joseph Ellis and Elizabeth Robinson married the same day.
Anne daughter of Tho. Shepley baptized ye 12 day.
Agnes daughter of Francis Ashton baptized 15th day.

1650.

John son of John Marian alias Spurr baptized the 14th day.
Rbt. son of James Hutton baptized the 15th day.
Richarde son of Willim Castlehouse baptized the 17th day.
John son of John White baptized the 18th day.
Abraham Hemingway and Elizabeth Kitson married ye 19th day.
Ann daughter of George Ottley baptized the 20th day.
John son of Willim Seniar baptized the 21th day.
Willin Dey of Earlsheaton buried the 25th day.
Christopher Fairbarne of Osset buried the 28th day.

August.

Francis Denton and Ann Marshall married ye 6th day.
Thomas Bargho buried the same day.
Elizabeth daughter of Marmaduke Dey buried ye 14th day.
John Bargh buried the 16th day.
Gennet daughter of Christopher Sanderson baptized the 17th day.
John son of Thomas Wilson baptized the 18th day.
John son of Michaell Howroyde baptized ye same day.
George Broadheade buried the same day.
Dorothie daughter of Elizabeth Hemingway buried ye same day.
Thomas son of John Bargh buried ye same day.
John Medley and Grace Hepworth married ye 20 day.
Martha daughter of Tempest Wheatley baptized yo 24th day.
Alice daughter of Martin Barber buried ye 25th day.
Sarah daughter of Francis Nelthorp baptized 27th day.
Elizabeth daughter of Richard Taylor baptized the 31th day.

September.

A man childe of James Wilson unbaptized buried ye 4 day.
Thomas son of Thomas Robinson baptized ye 8th day.
Thomas son of Richard Gibson baptized yt day.
Grace daughter of Willim Rodes baptized the 11th day.
Wid. Isabell Cartar buried the 13 day.
Joseph Fairbarne buried the 23 day.
Edward son of Rbt. Bedforth baptized the 24th day.
Thomas son of Henry Jepson baptized ye 25th day.

October.

A man childe unbaptized of John Sheard's buried the 5th day.
John son of John Cartar baptized the 8th day.
Ellen daughter of Rbt. Woode baptized the 13th day.
Sarah daughter of John Rodes baptized yo 2 . . .
Mercie daughter of Willim Sugden baptized yo . .
Agnes daughter of Marmaduke Greenfalde buried 31th day.

November 1650.

Rbt. Armitage and Elizabeth Ellis married ye 3 day.
Mercie wife of Edward Newsom buried ye 5th day.
Ruth daughter of Rbt. Nettleton baptized the 6th day.
Edward Fairbarne buried yo 11th day.
Grace daughter of Francis Nettleton baptized yo 14th day.
Thomas son of Thomas Wormall baptized ye 17th day.
Mary daughter of Martin Bins baptized the 20th day.
Sarah daughter of James Lee baptized ye 23 day.
Rosamund daughter of John Ellis baptized ye 24 day.

December.

Willim Marstin and Elizabeth Greenwood married the 3 day.
James Speight buried the 8 day.
Mary daughter of John Gill baptized the 11th day.
Dorithie Medley buried the 12th day.
James son of John Barrows baptized the 14th day.
Elizabeth daughter of John Speight baptized ye 21th day.
Elizabeth wife of Michaell Udall buried the 22th day.
Abraham Tilson and Elizabeth Hemingway married ye 23 day.
John son of Richard Rodes baptized the 26 day.
. . . . Hall . . . . married the same day.
Robert Copley buried the 31th day.

Januarie.

Rbt. Truelove and Ellin Carter married ye 7th day.
Sarah daughter of Isiah Ouldroyde baptized ye 9th day.
Jane wife of Thomas Marshall buried the 12th day.
John son of John Dey buried the 13th day.
Hannah daughter of Adam Wheatley baptized ye 16th day.
Thomas son of Thomas Autie baptized the same day.
Mary daughter of Jusua Rodes baptized ye 20th day.
Josiah son of John Autie baptized the 26th day.
Benjamin son of Abraham Harrison baptized the 29th day.

Februarie.

Jane daughter of Edmund Copley baptized ye 3 day.
Rbt. son of James Dixon baptized the 4th day.
Martha daughter of James Dixon baptized ye same day.
Rbt. sonne of Rbt. Towlson baptized the 5th day.
Mary daughter of John Hardcastle baptized the 8th day.
Wilfera Bull and Mercie Morris married the 13th day.
George son of Rbt. Fairbarne baptized ye 15th day.
Elizabeth daughter of Thomas Bradforth baptized the same day.
Edward son of Edward Whitley baptized ye 19th day.
Lidia daughter of Richard Ouldroyde baptized the 22th day.

1650.

Elizabeth wife of James Fearneley buried yo same day.
Sarah daughter of Willim Eluish baptized ye 23 day.
An infant unbaptized of John Wilbie of Ossett buried the same day.
Henry son of Rbt. Heald baptized the same day.
James Lambert and Susan Oldroyde married ye 26 day.

March.

Josua son of George Lee baptized the first . . .
. . . . . . Joseph Phillip baptized the 9th day.
. . . as son of Henry Wightman baptized the same day.
Mary daughter of John Barghe buried ye 16th day.
Anne Hemingway buried the 22th day.
Robert son of Rbt. Sharpe buried ye 28th day.
John Dickson Sen. buried the 30th day.
John son of John Ashley baptized the 31th day.
Henry son of Thomas Hemingway baptized ye same day.
Sara daughter of Willim Steade baptized ye same day.
Susanne daughter of Christofer Gunson baptised yo same day.

April 1651.

Thomas Oates and Mary Brooksbank married ye 3 day.
John Hurst buried the same day.
John Awdsley and Mary Maunsfield married ye 7th day.
Francis Ellis and Grace Bolde married ye 10th day.
James son of Cristofer Dickson baptized ye 15th day.
James son of Xtofer Dixon buried ye 17th day.
Esther daughter of Thomas Hepworth baptised ye 20th day.
Joseph sonne of Tho. Thornes baptised ye 26th day.

May.

Andrew son of Henry Ellis baptized ye 3 day.
Edward son of Edward North baptized ye 10th day.
George Pickard buried ye 13th day.
George Glodall and Sarah Fox married ye 14th day.
John Fletcher and Marie Priestley married ye 20th day.
Edward son of Willim Newsom baptized ye same day.
Robt. son of John Musgrave baptized ye same day.
John Walsha and Elizabeth Cawthorne married ye 28th day.
Willim son of William Hall baptized ye 29th day.
The sde William Hall ju. buried ye 31th day.

June.

Elizabeth daughter of Rbt. Brewith baptized ye 12th day.
Jonas son of Jonas Dey baptized ye 21th day.
Thomas Appleby buried ye 28th day.

Julie.

Alice daughter of Martin Barbar buried the first day.

1651.

John son of Richard Gunson baptized ye 2 day.
Elizabeth daughter of Thomas Carr baptized ye 5th day.
Josua sone of Josua Awdesley baptised ye 8 day.
An infant unbaptized of William Sympsons buried yo 9th day.
Francis wife of Thomas Dickinson buried the 19th day.
James White and Elizabeth Scholefield married ye 21 day.

August.

Elizabeth Mitchell buried the 9th day.
Rbt. son of John Parkar baptised ye 10th day.
Joseph son of Michaell Bentley baptized ye 13:h day.
John son of William Riddlesden baptized ye 16th day.
Willim son of Willim Scurrer and Alice Ellis bastard baptized ye 30th day.
Mathew sonne of Mathew Speight baptized ye 31th day.

September.

Joseph son of John White baptized the 4th day.
Miles son of John Aticke baptized ye 7th day.
Sarah daughter of Willim Ellis buried ye 9th day.
Elizabeth daughter of Hugh Matson baptised ye 13th day.
Gennett daughter of John Sheard baptized ye 25th day.
Elizabeth wife of Samuell Pierson Vicar of Dewsburie buried the 27th day.
John White and Betteris Speight married the same day.

October.

Rbt. son of Gamaliell Breer baptized the 6th day.
John Bailie and Ann Norfolke married the same day.
Martha daughter of James Dixon buried ye 10th day.
Alice Wife of Willim Westerman buried ye 16th day.
Michaell Bentley buried ye 18th day.
Elizabeth Matson daughter of Hugh Matson buried yt day.
George Pickering buried ye 19th day.
Martha daughter of John Brevrie baptised yt day.
Josua son of Joseph Ouldroyde baptised ye 22th day.
An infant unbaptized of Joseph Talors buried ye same day.
Elizabeth daughter of James Armitage of Greasbrough baptized the 23 day.
Joseph son of Jefera Pratt baptized the 30th day.

November.

Ellin wife of John Broddey buried ye first day.
An infant of Francis Nolthorpe buried yt day.
John son of John Tompson baptized ye 2 day.
Thomas Crosley and Margret Walker married ye 5th day.
Thomas Bould and Mary Hyrst married yt day.
Judith wife of John Bolland of Ossett buried the 10th day.
Lawrence Whittakers and Mary Archer married yo 11th day.

1651.

John son of Nicolas Naler baptized the 12th day.
Anthonie Musgrave and Ellin Aveyard married yo 19th day.
Thomas son of James Dixon buried the same day.
Ann daughter of John Richardson baptized yo 22th day.
Richard Hanson and Ellen Tilson married the 27th day.

December.

Thomas Armstrong buried the 5th day.
Sara daughter of Anthonie Auty baptized yo 7th day.
Josua son of Wilferd Hull baptized the 10th day.
Jane daughter of Authonie Sheard baptized ye 11th day.
Anne wife of Robt. Bedforth buried the 17th day.
Mary wife of Michaell Smith of Osset buried yt day also.
Mary daughter of Edward Chaster buried yo 26th day.

January.

Dynas wife of Tho. Hawkey [?] buried the 3 day.
Abraham Charlesworth and Aun Hopton married yo 6th day.
Margret daughter of George Allen baptized yo 8 day.
John son of John Ellis baptized yo 11th day.
James Whittakers buried the same day.
Edward son of Edward Chaster buried ye . . .
Ann daughter of Israell Oldroyd baptised yo 14th day.
A man child unbaptised of Tho. Allen's buried . .
Philemon son of Richard Dixon baptized yo 24 day.
Willim son of John Awdsley baptized yt day.
Sarah daughter of George Otley baptized yt day also.
John son of Robt. Dickinson baptized ye 28 day.
Sarah daughter of George Glover baptized that day.
Willim son of John Walsha baptized yt day also.
Avery Pickard buried the 26th day.

February.

Robert son of Edward Ellis junior baptized yo 1 day.
Willim Smith and Ellin Dodgson married yo 2 day.
James son of William Ellis baptised the same day.
Rbt. son of Rbt. Robinson baptized yt day also.
Sarah daughter of Abraham Greenwood baptized yo 4th day.
Ellin daughter of Henry Barbar baptized yt day.
Thomas Fox buried the 6th day.
James son of Francis Ellis baptized the 8 day.
An infant unbaptized son of Tho. Peace buried yt day.
Joseph son of Willim Shepheard baptized ye 12th day.
Robt. } sons of Christopher Brooke baptized yt day.
John }
John basebegotten of Mary Pickard baptized yt day.
An infant unbaptized of John Wilbie's of Osset buried yo 14th day.
Michaell son of Michaell Udall baptized yt day also.

1651.

George Ellis and Alice Chadwicke married yo 14th day.
Alice Bedforth buried yo 20th day.
Elizabeth wife of Richard Whitley buried yt day.
Willin son of John Awdsley buried yt day also.
Joseph Hepworth and Elizabeth Wrosindale married ye 23 day.
Thomas Oxley and Grace Justice married yo 24 day.
A man child unbaptized of Joseph Spurr buried yt day.
Willim son of James Speight baptized yo 28th day.
John son of Willim Ingham baptized yo 29th day.
Connet daughter of Christopher Saxton baptized yt day also.
Elizabeth daughter of Rbt. Barbar baptized yt day.
An infant of yo sde Rbt. Barbar buried yt day.

March.

Ann daughter of Richard Kay baptized the 2 day.
Willin Brooke and Elizabeth Brooke married yt day.
Martha daughter of Rbt. Wade baptized ye 3 day.
Elizabeth daughter of Rbt. Barbar buried ye 3 day.
Henry son of John Knowles ju. baptized ye 6 day.
Mary daughter of Thomas Stappleton baptized yo 7th day.
An infant of Rbt. Truelove unbaptized buried yt day.
John basebegotten of Mary Pickard buried yo 8th day.
An infant of Francis Ashton unbaptized buried 11th day.
Isabell daughter of Tho. Ellis baptized yt day.
Francis daughter of John Torrie baptized yo 14th day.
Ann daughter of Tho. Webster ju. baptized yo 18th day.
Anne daughter of Michaell Dawson buried yt day.
Mary daughter of Nicholas Ellis baptized yo 20th day.
John Talor and Grace Fearneley married yo 23 . .
Elizabeth daughter of Michaell Bentley of . . this townshippe (?) buried the 25th day.
Mary daughter of Martin Barbar baptized ye 27th day.
Robert son of John Musgrave buried yo 28th day.
John son of William Whitley buried yo 30th day.
John White buried yo same day.

Aprill 1652.

Joseph Hyrst and Elizabeth Roe [?] married ye 6th day.
Gilbert Sharpe and Elizabeth Seniar married ye 7th day.
Christopher son of Christopher Dixon baptized yt day.
Dorothie daughter of Mark Whittaker baptised the 14th day.
Grace Daughter of Francis Nettleton buried yo 21 day.
John Audsley and Elizabeth Brooksbanke married 24th day.
William son of John Walshaw buried yo 27th day

May 1652.

Joseph son of Joseph White baptized the first day.
Elizabeth daughter of Richard Chaster baptized yt day.
Michaell son of Michaell Udall buried ye 3 day.
Rbt. Lee and Ann Knowles married the 6th day.
Sarah daughter of Thomas Neilson baptized ye 8th day.
Martha daughter of John Taler baptized ye 12th day.
John Bedforth buried ye 14th day
Martha daughter of William Brooke baptized ye 15th day.
Gennett daughter of John Speight baptized yt day.
Martha Taler buried ye 18th day.
Elizabeth base-begotten of Elizabeth Soniar baptized ye 21th day.
James Hyrst buried yt day.
Rbt. son of Henry Dixon baptized ye 23 day.
John son of Xtopher Brooke buried ye same day.
Ann daughter of Thomas Johnson baptized ye 27th day.
Elizabeth daughter of Richard Wheattakers bapt. 28th day.
Rbt. son of Rbt. Bull baptized ye 30th day.

June.

John Son of Richard Archer buried the . . . day.
An infant unbaptized of Rbt. Goodales buried ye 9th day.
Margret daughter of Richard Kay buried ye same day.
Elizebeth daughter of Willim Hall baptized ye 19th day.
John Watson and Jane Ashton married ye 20th day.
John Woodheade and Ann Jepson married ye 30th day.

July.

Thomas son of Laurence Bull baptized the fourth day.
Mary daughter of James Hutton bapt. the tenth day.
Ann daughter of William Simpson bapt. the eleventh day.
Mary base begotten of Elizabeth Ashton bapt. ye same day.
Susanna Jackson buried the thirteenth daye.
William son of John Newsome bapt. the 15th day.
William Stead buried the 21th day.
William Ashton buried the 25th day.
Gennet wife of Thomas Nettleton buried yt day also.
Wid. Gennet Nettleton buried the 28 day.

August.

Samuell son of John Milne baptized the 7th day.
Ann daughter of Marmaduke Greenfeild baptized yt day.
George son of Rbt. Fairberne buried ye 8th day.
John Towne and An. Hardwick married ye 11th day.

1652.

Margret daughter of Edward Chaster baptized the 15th day.
John son of Willim Phillip baptized the 22th day.
Thomas son of Thomas Bold baptized the 28th day.
Daniell son of John Bradforth baptized ye 29th day.

September.

Rbt. Mansfeild buried ye 2 day.
Willm Hemingway and Mary Bingley married ye 3 day.
Thomas son of Lawrence Whittakers baptized ye 11th day.
Ruth daughter of John Wilbie baptized yt day.
Jeremiah son of Francis Cuningham baptized ye 12th day.
Alice daughter of Willim Casson baptized yt day.
John son of John Hust baptized the 19th day
Tempest Pollard and Ann Peace married ye 21 day.
Nathaniell Stirke and Sara Hancocke married ye 29th day.
Gennet wife of Tho. Naylor buried ye 30th day.

October.

Hellinor daughter of Abraham Tilson baptized ye 6th day.
Ellin daughter of Alice Beamont base begotten baptized ye 11th day.
Mary daughter of John Hardcastle buried ye 11th day.
Henry Issott and Grace Curteouse married ye 12th day.
Willim son of James Dixon baptized the 13th day.
Margret daughter of Edward Chaster buried ye 13th also.
Alice daughter of John Awty baptized the 17th day.
Mary daughter of Willim Newsome baptized ye 24th day.
Ann daughter of Willim Sympson buried ye 28th day.

November.

Thomas son of Thomas Abyson baptized ye 2 day.
Joseph Paget and Ester Moulson married ye 5th day.
John son of Willim Castlehouse baptized ye 17th day.
Jane wife of Rbt. Breadley buried ye 18th day.
Mary daughter of Charles Shymeld baptized ye 25th day.
Ann daughter of Willim Smith baptized the 26th day.
An infant unbaptized of Francis Nelthorp's buried the 26th day.
Joseph son of Joseph Spur baptized ye 27th day.
Ann daughter of Margrett Howroyde baptized yt day.
Elizabeth daughter of Francis Nelthorp buried yt day also.

December.

Tho. Nettleton of Gawthorp buried ye 9th day.
James son of Michael Seckar baptized the 12th day.

1652.

Robert son of Mathew Speight baptized ye same day.
An infant unbaptized of Richard Rodes buried ye 20th day.
Sara daughter of Michaell Parker [or Packer?] baptized ye 28 day.

Januarie.

Margret daughter of Isiah Oldroyd baptized ye 5th day.
Elizabeth wife of Robert Healde buried yt day also.
Martha daughter of Robt Ould . . . . . the 6th day.
Bartholomew Stead and Am. Walkar married . . . . .
Mercie Brodeley buried the 8th day.
Rebecca daughter of Sam. Colbecke baptized ye 10 day.
Martha daughter of Joseph Talor baptized ye 13th day.
Martin son of Martin Tenand baptized the 16th day.
Elizabeth daughter of Martin Musgrave baptized yt day.
Richard son of Edward Newsom baptized ye 20th day.
Samuell son of John Milnes buried yt day.
Henry Woode and Mary Peaker married the 23 day.
Sara wife of Rbt. Sharpe buried ye 27 day.
Mary daughter of John Audsley baptized ye last day.

February.

Willim son of John Wilbie baptized ye 2 day.
John son of Bryan Phillip baptized the same day.
Thomas son of Rbt. Barbar baptized yt day.
Grace daughter of John Awty Sen. baptized ye 3d day.
Ann daughter of Robert Lee buried the 4th day.
Adam Wheatley buried the 5th day.
Isabell daughter of John Robinson baptized yt day.
Richard Longley and Elizabeth Brooke married the 6th day.
Rbt. son of Mathew Speight buried yt day.
An infant of Richard Gunson's unbaptized buried ye 9th day.
Thomas son of Robert Barbar buried ye 10th day.
John Speight buried the 13th day.
Sarah daughter of Christofer Ostler baptized 17th day.
Willim son of Willim Parsley baptized the 10th day.
Mary daughter of John White baptized ye 19th day.
Ann wife of Thomas Robinson buried ye 20th day.
Joseph son of Joseph Paget baptized yt day also.
John son of John Tompson baptized ye 26th day.
Elizabeth daughter of Rbt. Lynley baptized yt day.
Robert son of Rbt. Bull baptized the 27th day.

March.

Mary wife of Edward Antie buried ye 2d day.
Sara daughter of Christofer Ustler buried yo 4th day.

1652.

Jane daughter of Hugh Matson baptized ye 14th day.
John son of Willim Castlehouse buried yt day.
George son of Josua Rodes baptized ye 16th day.
Grace daughter of George Lee baptized ye 19th day.
Another man childe of his unbaptized buried yt day.
Elizabeth daughter of Edward Whitley buried yt day.
Sara wife of James Wilson buried the 20th day.
Sara daughter of James Wilson baptized yt day.
Grace daughter of George Lee buried ye same day.
Mary daughter of Richard Oldroyd baptized ye 23 day.
John Soniar and Elizabeth West married yt day.

1653.

Sara daughter of Jonas Holdsworth baptized ye 25th day.
John Shillito and Ellin Sampson of Wakefeild married ye 27th day.
Tho. Savile and Ann Claton married ye 28th day.
John Hill and Alice Johnson married ye 29th day.

Aprill 1653.

George son of Rbt. Fairbarne baptized ye 2 day.
Hannah daughter of Tho. Robinson baptized ye 2 day.
Richard son of Willim Rodes baptized ye 11th day.
Ann daughter of John Musgrave baptized the 12th day.
Mary daughter of Joseph Spurr baptized ye 19th day.
Mary daughter of Tho. Peace baptized ye 19th day.
Jennet wife of Thomas Bradforth buried the 15th day.
Ellin daughter of William Auty buried the 22nd day.

May.

Elizabeth daughter of George Wood buried the third day of May.
Samuell son of Michaell Audley buried ye 11th day.
James son of Michaell Speight baptized the 8th day.
Mathew son of John Gill baptized ye 29th day.
Susanna daughter of Willim Soniar baptized ye 25th day.
Thomas son of John Walshe baptized ye 7th day.
Sarah daughter of Joseph Phillips baptized yt day.
Thomas son of Edward Anson [?] baptized ye 26th day.

August.

Rosamund daughter of John Ellis buried ye 21st day.
John Hogge and Anne Oxley married the 28th day.
Collected within ye pish of Dewsbury for Mabury in Wiltshire ye summe of——18s.—8d.

June.

Joseph son of John Barrough baptized ye 4th day.
Samuell Watteras [Waterhouse] and Grace Mitchell married ye 19th day.
Rebecca daughter of Thomas Wheateley baptized the 7th day.

1653.

Thomas Woode and Alice Wilbie married the 6th day.
Thomas Wilkinson and Grace Dennis married the 8th day.
Henrie son of Michaell Bentley. ng. [? for ju.] buried the 10th day.
Rbt. Heald and Jane Newsom married the 22th day.
George Feild and Elizabeth Bickliffe married the 24th day.
Grace daughter of Christopher Sanderson baptized the 25th day.
John son of Rbt. Barton buried the 26th day.
James Hopwoode and Mary Bedforth married the 28th day.

Julie.

John Musgrave buried ye 3 day.
John Dinison buried ye 4th day.
Thomas son of Rbt. Nettleton baptized ye 5th day.
Robert Googdale buried the 10th day.
Rbt. son of Richard Talor baptized the 17th day.
Samuell son of Willm Toulson baptized the same day.
Josiah Clapam and Jane Wilkinson married 3th day.
Mercy daughter of Persevell Terry baptized ye 21th day.
Willm Harrison and Elizabeth Armitage married yt day.
Samuell son of John . . . .
Robert Sharpe and Mary Gunson married the 24th day.
Christopher Newsom and Elizabeth Preostley married same day.

August.

[G]ilbert Booth and Elizabeth Firth married the 21th day.

September.

. . . . . . [daugh]ter of Hugh Watson.
Elizabeth daughter of Richard Jepsen baptized the 14th day.

1653.

Willm Carr and Mercie Wheatley married the same day.
Michaell Broadley and Alice Tetley married ye 18th day.
Jonas Robart and Elizabeth Longley married the 20th day.
Gennit wife of Xtopher Sanderson buried the 23 day.
John Spibey and Mary Webster married ye 30th day of September.

October.

Ann daughter of Rbt. Beckwith baptized ye first day.
Ester daughter of James Soniar buried the 8th day.
A man childe of Edward Mosleyes unbaptized buried the same day.
Elizabeth daughter of Edmund Copley baptized the 10th day.
Thomas son of Thomas Dowld buried ye 16th day.

November.

Michaell son of Edward Newsom buried ye 2 day.
Robert son of John Bedforth baptized ye 5th day.
Martha daughter of George Allen baptized 10th day.
Isabell wife of Thomas Jaggar buried the 12th day.
Thomas Wilbie and Maybee Winter married 15th day.
Rebecca daughter of Edward Lee baptized the 16th day.

---

* Mary d. of John Faweet about 1640.

---

* This entry is written in a comparatively modern hand on a blank page at the end of the volume.

END OF VOLUME 3.

Since the first volume of the Registers was printed, a few loose leaves of an old copy have been found and restored to the Church. They are in a hand of the latter part of the 16th century, and are probably the "copy" which Dr. Hemingway refers to in his copy. It differs in many cases from the original, but in some instances it serves to fill up a blank caused by wear and tear or other injury, and therefore it has been thought best to print it in full. Where it differs from the original it will probably be best to accept the latter as correct, as in many instances it is quite evident that the copyist has been careless.

The monith of Julij.

Robarte Longeley had a child buried the first day named William.
Richard Nettilton buried his wife xj day named Genitt.
John Audesley was buried the xijt day of Julij.
Alis Baldon was buried the same daye.

The monithe of November Anno di 15 xxxviijt.

Inprimis Mathew Speight had a child Xined the vijt day named Alice.
William Boltone and Elizabeth Monsfeld weare maried the xxtj day.
Nicholis Walker had a child Xined the same day named Joanna.
Edward Tomsone had a child Xined the xxx day named Henry.

The monithe of December.

Benyt Medley had a child Xined the vijt day named Richard.
Wilferay Walker had a child Xined the ix day named Sybell.
Stewine (Stephen) Tomsone had a child Xined the xxixth day named Richard.

* The monithe of Januarij.

Thomas Browne was buried the xvijt day of Januarij.
Robarte Longeley and Agnes Gibsone weare maried ye xix day.
Annes Turton widowe was buried the xxviijt daye.

The monithe of Februarij.

William Richardsone and Margaret Kickeley were maried ye first day.
Richard Speight had a child Xined the iijt day named Elizabeth.
William Audesley had a child Xined the iiijt day named William.
Edwarde Biarle had a child Xined the x day named Allexsaunder.

* Here is written in a later hand "1571:" the real date being 1538-9.

Syr Henry Savill knighte had a child Xined the xrjt day Edward.
Willm Wormall had a child Xined the xxiijt d named Robarte.
Ellis Greyne had a child Xined the xxiiij day named John.
John Boy had a child Xined the xxvti d. named Johan.

The monithe of Marche.

Gylbert Wilkinsone had a child Xined the second d. named Issabell.
Thomas Mawlame *aliter* Fladder had a child Xined ye vij d. named John.
Thomas Stede had a child Xined the x day named John.
Richard Aldersone had a child Xined the same day John.
[Edw]ard Biarle had a child buried the xx day named . . . . .
. . . . . . Fladder had a child buried the same day named Margarit.
. . . . . . Greine had a child Xined the xxñijt day named Allexsaunder.

The monithe of Aprioll.

Robarte Baulle had a child Xined the first day named Williame.
John Disfoorthe had a child Xined the x day named James.
John Blakborne had a child Xined the xjt day named Elizabethe.
Margaret Wilkinsone had a child Xined the xiiijt day Allexsander.

Hereafter followth the names of every person weddinge Xtined and buried wthin the parishe of Dewisburie maid sins the xv day of Aprioll in the year of our lorde God 15 xxxixt recorded by the wardens of the said churche that is Richard Byrkeby William Richardsone Thomas Medley Robarte Janinge *aliter* Hawyerd* Richard Wormell and Thomas Gomersaill in the xxxjti yeare of the Reigne of King Henryo viijt.

Aprioll.

Robarte Le of Gawthropp had a child Xtined [altered to buried] the xx day named Robart.
Alyce Ramesdem [? Ramsden] widow were buried the xxxti day of Aprioll.

The monithe of May.

Robarte Wright and Jenit Tomson weare maried the iiijt day.
Richard Browne and Agnes Sikes weare maried the same daye.
John Secker had a child Xined the viijt day named Allexsander.
John Nayler weare buried the xiijt day of Maye.
James Robarte had a child buried the xiiijt day named Agnes.
Mathew Speight had a child buried the xxiijt day Alice.
Edward Hucchinssone had a child Xined the ye same day named E . . . . .
John Fladder had a child Xined the xxiiijt day named Allexsander.

* Elsewhere spelt "Haworthe."

The monithe of June (1539).
Robarte Lo of Sotchill common had a child buried the xxv day of June named John.
Annes Bradforthe widow weare buried the xxvj day.

The monithe of Auguste (? 1540).
Anne Oxeley wife of William Oxeley was buried ye third day.
John Forest had a child Xined the xiijt day named Richard.
John Boyll yonner [younger] had a child Xined the xvjt day named Lawrance.
Thomas Barbar had ij children Xined the one named Agnes and the other named Johanna which was Xined upon the xxij day.

The monithe of September.
Johanna Disforth had a child Xined which weare baise-begotten ye xiiijt day Richard.
Annes Robinsone laite wife of William weare buried the xvj day.
Johanna Disforth afforesaid had her child buried the xviijt day Richard.
Robarte Lo of Sotchill common had a child Xined the xvjt day named John.

The monithe of October.
Stowine Tomson had a child Xined the second day named Elizabeth.
Rychard Kitchinge and Elizabethe Rosen were maried the third day.
Robarte Bingeleye and Elizabethe Richardsone were maried ye same day.
John Walker had a child Xined the vijt day named Johanna.
Kaitherine Tyas wife of Thomas weare buried ye tente day.
John Peace and Elizabithe Disforthe were maried the xt day.
Richard Browne had a child buried the xxt day named Elizabethe.
William Tyas had a child buried the xxjti day named Agnes.
Syr John Gillot priest weare buried the xxijti day.
Johanna Broke laite wife of Robarte weare buried the xxiiijt day.
John Towncend had a child Xined the xxvj day named John.

The monith of November.
Richard Disshefourth had a child Xined the xix day named Margaret.
Margaret Hill was buried the xxijt day of November.
Johanna Broke widow laite wife of Robarte weare buried the xxixt day.
Jaimes Robarte had a doighter buried the xxxti day named Anna.

The monithe of December.
Robarte Goodefelow alias Broughte had a child Xined the xixt day Johanna.
Mathew Speight had a child Xined the xxijt day named Robarte.

Thomas Musgrave had a child Xined the same day named Anna.
Richard Speight had a child Xined the xxxti day named Sybell.
Robarte Baull had a child Xined the same day named Agnes.
Jayne Scotte wife of John Scote was buried the same daye.

The monith of Januarij*.
Xoper [Christopher] Nailor was buried the first day of January.
Alice Robinsone wife of John Robinsone weare buried the viij day.
Robarte Lo of Sotchill common had a child buried the xiijt day named John.
Kaitherine Disforth weare buried the xxijti day of Januarij.
Elizabeth Haigo weare buried the xxiijti day of Januarij.
Jenyt Sykes widow laite wife of Thomas Sikes was buried the xxvijt day.
Thomas Nowill had a child Xined the same day named Essabell.
William Gibsone had a child Xined the xxixti day named Thomas.
John Alland had a child Xined the xxx day named Helyngo.

The monithe of Februarij.
Nicholis Whitley and Alce Haulsdworthe [sic] weare maried the first day.
Richard Alldersone had a child Xined the seconnd day named Thomas.
John Raner and Alice Bayldon weare maried the sext day.
Richard Hurst and Elizabethe Dickinsone weare maried the vijt day.
Thomas Haulle had a child Xined the viijt day named James.
Charles Baldon had a child Xined the xij day named Agnes.
Juliana Scarbroughe had a child Xined the xxvjt day which weare baise begotten named Willyame the xxvj day of February.

The monithe of Marche.
Williame Kitsone of Ossit weare buried the seconnd daye.
Gilberte Wilkinsone had a child Xined the vj day named Alice.
Edwarde Wrighte was buried the xxti day of Marche.
Alice Haull wife of John Haull wife predict. [sic] was buried the same [day].
Richard Dransfeld had a child Xined the same day named Elizabeth.
John Groine had a child Xined the xxvti day named Thomas.
Nicholis Whitley had a child Xined the xxvj day named Agnes.
Annes Wrighte laite wife of Robarte weare buried the xxxti day.

* In the same hand as before is added, erroneously, "1576."

The monithe of Apriell.

John Robinsone of Newparke had a child Xined the xj named Agnes.
The said John Robinsone did burie his said child named Agnes ye xvj [day].

Hearcafter folowth the names of everye weddinge Xined burialls wthin the parishe of Dewisburie from the xxvijt day of Apriell in the year of oure lorde God 15xljti Recorded by the churche wardens of the said church of Dewisburie than beinge that is Richard Haull Richard Wod Thomas Methley Robarte Ganinge* *alias* Haworthe John Allande and Richarde Wormemall in the xxxiijti yeare of the Reigne of Kinge Henry the eight supreame head of the churche of Ingland &c.

Apriell anno di 15xljt.

Henry Robinsone had ij children Xined the xxixti day the one named Thomas and ye other named Jeynet.
John Ellingesone had a child Xined the same day named Richarde.

The monithe of May.

Robarte Janinge [?] *aliter* Haworth had a child Xined the secomnd day John.
Thomas Bradfourthe had a childe Xined the viij day named Dorite.
John Baildone and Jenyt Wormemall was maried the ix day of May.
John Forest th' elder was buried the same day of Maye.
Richard Kitsone had a child Xined the xixt day named Edwarde.
Robarte Wrighte had a child Xined the xxvj day named Esabell.

The monithe of June.

John Ackeroid had a child Xined the fowert day named Johanna.
John Medley had a child Xined the xj day named Williame.
Nicholis Tempest Esquier had a child Xined the the xxiiijti day named Gayne (Jane).

The monithe of July.

Henry Robinsone had a child buried the third day named Johanna.
Gilbert Ollered had a child Xined the vijt day named Annes.
John Baildon yonner [younger] had a child Xined the xv day named Elizabethe.
Item William Oxeley and Jane Bruke were maried the xixt day.
Richard Hirst had a child Xined the same day named Thomas.
Richard Kitson had a child buried ye xxti day named Margaret.
John Sykes had a child Xined the xxvti day named Richarde.
William Tayler had a child Xined the xxxjti day named William.

* Elsewhere spelled "Janinge"; *cf* "Gayne" for "Jane."

The monithe of August.

Nor [Christopher] Scotte and Johanna Scavernsley weare maried the vij day.
Richarde Fairebarne weare buried the xvijt day of August.
Willyame Whitehead weare buried the xviijt day.
John Raner had a child Xined the xxti day named Margaret.
James Woodd and John [*sir*] Dishefourthe was maried the xxviijti day.
Thomas Steede had a child Xined the xxx day of August named Anna.

The monithe of September.

Williame Williamsone had a child Xined the third day named . . . . .
Hughe Monsfeld weare buried the ix day of September.
Gilbert Wodd had a child Xined the same day named Richard.
Richard Dransfeld had a child buried the xxijti day . . . .
Edward Barle had a child Xined the xxiiijt day named . . . .
John Fladrier had a child Xined the same daye named Richard.
Richard Tomsone yonner [younger] was buried the xxvti day.
John Carter foole to Sir James Whaites sometyme of Pomfrett weare buried the xxviijti day of the monithe of September.

The monithe of October.

Elizabeth Hirst was buried the xjt day of October.
Edward Greyne and Jenyt Haull were maried the xvjt day.
Edmunde Hey and Margaret Browne weare maried the same daye.
John Ackeroid had a child buried the xxvti day named John.

The monithe of November.

Annes Metheley wife of Thomas Methley weare buried ye second [day].
Thomas Greine had a child Xined the same day named Thomas.
John Dawsone had a child Xined the third day named William.
Briande Bradforthe jentill man begatte a child with Alice Gaunge [?] which weare Xined the xv day named Thomas.
Richard Fallay and Elizabethe Grifen weare maried ye xiiijt day.
Alice Nowell widow late wife of Robarte weare buried ye xixt [day].
William Tailer and Sybell Haulle weare maried the xxt day.
John Hall and Agnes Broke weare maried the xxjt day.
Briande Horton had a child Xined the xxiiijt day named John.
John Secker had a child Xined the xxvti day named Richard.
Rogar Thornes and Alice Hesleye weare maryed the xxvjt day.
Briande Bradfourth gentylman had a child Xined the xxvij named Thomas.

The monythe of December.

Richarde Brown had a child buryed the second day named John.
John Dishforth had a child Xined the xxixti day named Elizabeth.

The monythe of Jauuarij.*

Thomas Ramsdeyne and Elizabeth Methley weare maryed ye xvth day.
[Ro]barte Longeley had a child Xined the xixt day named Betteris.
Willyame Whittykers had a child Xined the xx day named Elizabeth.
Edward Hucchinsone had a child Xined the xxxjtye named Nicholis.

The monithe of Februarij.

Thomas Symsone and Margaret Tomsone was maryed the iiijt day.
Benyt Medley had a child xined the vjt day named Robarte.
Lawrance Waltone was buryed the xxvj day of Februarij.
Wylliam Peace had a child Xined the xxvijt day Dortye.

The monythe of Marche.

John Bradforthe the yonner [younger] had a child Xined the x day, named Edwarde.
William Tyas had a child Xined the xijt day named Thomas.
Nicholis Walker had a child Xined the xxjt day named Elizabeth.
Wylliam Audesley had a child Xined the xxij day named Rychard.
John Bradforthe had a child buryed the xxv day named Edwarde.
Edward Thompsone had a child Xined the xxvj nay named Edwarde.
John Peace of Sawwoode was buried the xxviijt day.
John Carlyngchow was buried the xxixt day.
Wylliam Brooke had a child Xined the xxx day named John.

The monythe of Apryell.

Nicholis Secker had a child Xined the secound day named Doryte.
John Broke had a child Xined the third day named Johanna.
Wyllm Rychardsone had a child Xined the viijt day named Annes.
James Wodd had a child Xined the ix daye named Alce.
John Peace had a child Xined the xixt day named Richarde.
Edwarde Greyne had a child Xined the xxti day named Edwarde.

Hereafter folowethe the names of every persone beynge wedded Xined and buried wthin the parrishe of Dewisburye frome the xviijt day of Apryell in the yeare of our lorde God a thousand v hunderithe xlijti in the xxxiiijti year of King Henry the eighte.

*In the same hand as before is added, erroneously, "1577."

Benyt Medley had a child Xined the xxiiijty day named Dorytye.
John Browne weare buried the the xxvtye day of Apryell.

The monythe of Maye.

James Browne son of Thomas weare buryed the fyrst daye of Maye.
Edward Tomsone had a child buryed the xt day named Edward.
Ellys Greyne had a child Xined the xijt day named Agnes.
Stewene Tomsone had a child xined the xiiijt day named Eizabel [?].
Jenyt Tomsone widow laite wife of Richard Tomsone had a child Xined the xvijt day named Agnes.
Mathew Speight had a child Xined the xxjti day named Issabel.
Elizabeth Hollynwell [?] had a child Xined the the xxiijt daye named Johanna beynge base begotten as yt is said Richard Ell .... his faither of ye [same].

The monithe of June.

John Walker had a child Xined the ix day of June named .....
Rychard Dransfield had a child Xined the xijt day named .....
John Byrkes and Kaitherine Hansone weare maryed the xx [? day].
John Hinceeloyfe and Elizabethe Kitsone was maryed the xxix [? day].

The monythe of Julij.

Margaret Dysheforthe widow laite wife of Willm weare buried .....
Thomas Ramesdeyne had a child Xined the xxj daye John and the said child was buryed the same daye.

The monithe of August.

Willyame Richardsone had a child Xined the xxvjt day named Agnes.
Willm Taylor of Batley carre had a child Xined the xxxti daye named Rychard.

The monythe of September.

Rychard Browne had a childe Xined the fowerth day named Johanna and the same child weare buryed the same daye.
Nycholis Whytley had a child buryed the xxtie day named Margaret.

The monythe of October.

Willyame Barbar and Elyzabeth Hanll weare maryed the first day.
Willyame Gaunte had tow children Xined the sext daye the one of them named Issabell and the other named Margaret.
Olde John Robingesone smythe was buryed the xiijt day.
John Audesley had a child Xined the eight day named James.
Rogar Aland being a baistarde sone of Richard Tattersall weare buryed the xxt day of October.

Thomas Nettyltone had a child Xined the xxx day named William.

The monith of November.

Annes Bradforth wydow late wife of Thomas weare buryed the viijt day of the monythe of November.
Thomas Clayton and Elizabethe Dawsone weare maried ye xi day.
John Tomsone and Alyce Robyngesone weare marryed ye xxiij day.
John Towneende *alyter* Robinsone had a child Xined the xxvt day named Richarde.
Margaret Greyne widow late wife of Thomas weare buryd the same day of the monythe of November.
William Dycksone had a child Xined the xxviij day named Alyce.
Haymere Foxe and Elizabeth Broke weare maryed the xxix day.
John Towneend *alyter* Robynsone had a child buryed ye same daye Richard.
Rogar Swallow had a child Xined the xxxti day named Rogar.

The monythe of December.

William Smythe had a child Xined the xiiijt daye named Elyzabeth.
Margaret Barker layte wyfe of William Barker weare buryed ye xix day.
Thomas Symsone had a child Xined the xxti day named Gayne.
Thomas Sykes had a child Xined the xxijtye day named Thomas.
Anna Wytcheade widow laite wyfe of of Willyame Whitcheade weare buried the xxxtye day.

The monythe of Januarij.

Elizabethe Bradforth wife of John Bradforthe was bureyd ye seconnd day.
Robarte Goodefelow *aliter* Broughte had a child Xined the viijt day named Rog[er].
Robarte Whittykers had a child Xined the xjt day named Anne.
Robarte Baull had a child Xined the xiijt day named Nycholis.
Robarte Wrighte had a child Xined the same day named Agnes.
Adame Tyngeley and Elizabethe Fairebarne weare maryed the xvjt day.
William Gaunte had a child buryed the xvijt day named Margaret.
Robarte Robynsone and Agnes Robingesone weare maryed the xxtye day.
Richarde Wedd had a child Xined the same daye named Allexsander.
John Mylnes had a child Xined the xxviijti day named Robarte.

The monythe of Februarij.

Robarte Lee of Dewisbury had a child Xined the secound day named Aryce.
Rogar Dawsone had a child Xined the xt day named Robarte.
Rycharde Hurst had a child Xined the xiijt day named Robarte.
John Baldone had a child Xined the xxvjt day named Agnes.

Thomas Claytone had a child Xined the xxiijtye day named Roger.

Heare folowth the names of every person beynge maryed Xined and buried within the parrishe of Dewisburye from the fyrst day of Apryell in the xxxiiijtie yeare of the Reigne of Kynge Henry the eighte of famous memory and in the yeare of oure Lord God a thousand v hunderithe fortye and three recorded by the churchwardnes [*sic*] of Dewisbury. Anno Di 1543.

The monithe of Aprioll.

Alyce Ollered had a child Xined the first day named Margaret.
Benyt Medley had a child Xined the xt day named Jeferay.
Thomas Nayler had a child Xined the xijt day named Annis.
John Fairebarne and Dorytye Nayler weare maryed the xv daye of the monithe of Aprill.
Rychard Baulle had a child Xined the xvijt day named Robarte.
Wylliam Boythe and Elizabeth Goodedall weare maried the xxijt day.
Nycholis Whitley had a child Xined the xxiij [?] day named Thomas.
Betteris Le wyfe of Rychard Le weare buryed the xxix daye of Aprioll.
Thomas Steade had a child Xined the xxx day named Gaine (Jane).

The monythe of Maye.

[Jo]hn Medley had a child Xined the first day named Elizabethe.
John Aickerondd [?] had a child Xined the third day named Geferay.
William Rychardesonne had a child Xined the xix day named Alyce.
Edwarde Tomsone had a child Xined the xx day named Agnes.
John Ollerede and Elizabethe Wilkinsone weare maried xxvijti day.
John Saxtone had a child Xined the xxviijt day named Johanna and the same child weare buryed the same day.

The monythe of June.

Hamar Foxe had a child Xined the first day named Agnes.
Willeray Walker and Jenyt Boythe weare maryed the thirde day.
Alce Hurst widow laite wife of William Hurst weare buryed the vijt day of the monithe of June.
William Wormell had a child Xined the xxjti day named Elyzabeth.
Gylberd Ollerede had a child Xined the xxiiijt day named Dorytye.
William Tayler had a child Xined the xxvijt day named Nycholas.

The monythe of July.

Robarte Smythe and Elizabeth Bradforthe weare maryed the first day of the monithe of July anno di 1542 [*sic* but appears to be an error for 1543].

DEWSBURY PARISH REGISTERS. 175

The monithe of Auguste.

Robarte Janynge *aliter* Haworthe haid a child Xined the ix day . . . . .
Richard Browne had a child Xined the xvjt daye named . . . . .
John Bradforth yonner [younger] had a child Xined the xxiijt day named . . . . .
William Tyas had a child Xined the xxiijt day named Margaret.

The monythe of September.

John Boylle yonner [younger] haid a child Xined the sext day named Robarte.
Rychard Disheferthe had a child Xined the xxvijth day named Agnes.

The monythe of October.

Nycholis Clarke had a child Xined the first daye named Jaine.
John Ward had a child Xined the same day named John.
John Le had a child Xined the viijt day named George.
Robarte Le of Gawthrop had a child Xined the xjt day named Agnes.
John Townend *aliter* Robinsone had a child Xined the xiijt day.
Edwarde Ramesdeine and Elizabethe Gagar [? Jagger] weare maryed ye xiiij^t day.
Willyame Broke had a child Xined the xxv day named Johanna.

The monythe of November anno Di. M.D. xliij.

Willyame Robynsone had a child Xined the iiijt day named Robarte.
Rychard Haull and Elizabethe Broke weare maryed the same day.
William Tyas had a child buryed the xxiijt day named Margaret.
Thomas Bradforthe had a child Xined the xxvijt day named Anna [?]
A poore woman and a straunger weare buryed the xxv day named Jenyt Hawley.
John Bradforthe and Elizabethe Burrell weare maried ye xx . . . .

The monythe of December.

Christofer Nayler had a child Xined the iij day named Rycharde.
William Robinsone had a child buryed the eighte day named Johanna.
John Peace wife weare buryed the ix day named Agnes.
William Gibsone had a child Xined the xiiijt day named Elizabeth.
Thomas Hyrst had a child Xined the xxiijti day named James.
Rychard Dransfeld had a child Xined the xxvjti [?] marayd Rychard.
[John] Townsend *aliter* Robinsone had a child buryed ye xxxti day Christopher.
William Tayler had a child Xined the same day named Jenyt.

The monyth of January.

Rychard Fladder had a child Xined the sixte day named Rychard.
Margaret Haulle had a child Xined the viijt day named Elizabethe.
John Fairebarne had a child Xined the xxjti day named John.
Robarte Robynsone had a child Xined the xxiijty named Robarte.
John Forrest had a child Xined the same daye named Isabell.
Rychard Dysheforthe had a child buryed the xxvjti day named Agnes.
Margaret wydow [*sic*] was buryed the xxvijti daye of January.

The monythe of February.

Thomas Nowell of the Strete had a child Xined the fourte day named Thomas.
[Roger ?] Dawsone wife widowe weare buryed the fyfte daye.
Roberte Smyth of Dewisbury had a child Xined the sixte day named Robert.
Thomas Graysone was buryed the xiijt daye.
Rychard Addersone had a child buryed the same daye named John.
George Servytheley [?] was buryed the xviijt daye.
Mathewe Speighte had a child Xined the xvij day named Nycholis.
Wylliam Whittykers had a child Xined the xixt day named Dorytye.
Gylberte Wod of Ossit had a child Xined the xxjti day named Alyce.
William Foxe was buryed the xxvjti daye.*

The monyth of Marche.

Henry Robynsone had a child Xined the first day named Elizabeth.
James Wodd had a child Xined the second day named Rychard.
Gylbert Wilkingesone of Ossit had a child Xined the third day Thomas.
William Whittykers had a child buryed the iiijte day named Dorytye.
John Hollerede had a child Xined the same day named John.
Thomas Haull had a child Xined the xvijt day named Nycholis.
Richard Sagar was buryed the xviijt day of Marche.
William Hoythe had a child Xined the same day named Anne.
Willferay Walker had a child Xined the xxxti day named Anne.
. . . . [? Robar]tesone and Margaret Peace was buried [*sic*] the xxixti day.
[Rog]er [?] Tyus and Annes Walker weare buried [*sic*] the same day of October.
. . . . the doighter of Thomas Peykerd was buried the xxxti day.
Peter son of William Barber was Xined the same day of October.

---

* Here is written "Anno Di Mr D. xliij^o"; this has been written after the actual entries, but apparently in the same hand. It should come lower down.

The monithe of November (1556).

Henry Erlingehawe was buried the fower day of November.
John Wilbie had a sonne Xined the same day named George.
Issabell Mankingcholis was buried the xiij day of November.
John Walker had a child Xined the xviijt day of November named John.
Edwarde Gomersaill had a child Xyned the xxxti day named Margaret.

December.

John Bradfourthe had a child Xined the fowert day named William.
Thomas Secker had a child Xined the xiiijt day named Annes.
Robarte Dey had a child Xined the xvijt day named Thomas.
Robarte Ollerede had a child Xined the xxijti day named Sybell.
William Richardsone had a child buried the xxvijt day named Anne.
Richard Haulle had a child Xined the xxix day named Edwarde.

The monithe of January.*

Maister Averay Copley Esquire and Mistris Grace Bradfourthe weare maried the xix day of January by Mr. Rud vicar of D.
Thomas Sykes had a child Xined the xxiijt day named George.
John Arnall and Elizabeth Tyns weare maried the xxvjt day.
Annie Nowell was buried the same day.

The monithe of February.

Nicholis Clarke had a child Xined the second day named Dorytie.
William Burnet was buried the sext daye.
John Disfourthe had a child Xined the viijt day named . . . . .
Anthony Awty and Jenyt Graisone weare maried ye xj day.
Alys Robinsone weare buried the xv day of February.
Annes Secker was buried the xvjt day of February.
Jenyt Haulle was buried the xix day of February.
John Robinsone had a child Xined the xxvjti day named . . . . .
Thomas Sikes had a child Xined the xxvijj named Elizabeth.
The said Thomas had a child buried the same day named John [?]

The month of March.

William Speight of Chidshell weare buried the first day of [March].

* Here is written in a later hand, "1573."

Elizabeth Sykes weare buried ye secound day of Marche.
Thomas Greyne had a sonne Xined the tente day named [John].
Thomas Musgrave was buried the xij day of Marche.
Thomas Sharpehus had a child Xined the xiiijt day named Robarte.
Richard Whitley had a child buried the xv day of March named John.
Christofer Naylor had a child Xined the xxjti day named Michiell.
James Waide had a child buried the same day of Marche named Nicholis.
Annes wife of William Naylor was buried the xxijti day of Marche.
Elizabeth the doighter of John Morvill was buried the same day.
Margret Hollrede was buried the xxiiijt day of Marche.
Michill Naylor sonne of Christofer Nayler was buried the xxvti day.
William Foxe sonne of Amer Foxe weare buried the xxxti day.

The monithe of Aprioll.

John Gowett was buried the first day of Aprioll.
Willyame Musgrave wife was buried the third daye.
John Greyne sonne of Thomas Greine was buried the xj daye.
Christofer Bradfortho weare buried the xxviijt daye.

The monithe of Maye.

John Daye was buried the xv daye of Maye.
Robarte Le was buried the xviijt day of May.
Jenyt wif of John Baldone was buried the xixt daye.
Annes Disforthe weare buried the xxijt daye.

The monithe of June.

John Bradfourth was buried the third day of June.
William Smithe had a child Xined the same day named William.
J[ohn] Koynit [?] was buried the vjt day of June.
Anthony Awtye had a child Xined the same day named Anthonie.
Margaret wife of Rogar Barker weare buried the x day.
Thomas Stannesfeld had a child buried the xijt day named Margaret.
Richard Le had a child buried the xxti day named Robarte.
Gilbert Hollered had a child buried the same day named Thomas.
William Lee had a child Xined the xxijt day named Elizabeth.
John Kent was buried the xxviijt day of June.
Thomas Secker had a child buried the same day Margaret.

THE END.

INDEX.

Abbat—147.
Albison, Abison, Abyson—159, 163, 167.
Acrod, Acrode, Akroid, Aykroyd, Aykrod, Aykrodd, Ayckroul, Ayckerodl, Aickerod, Aickerad, Ayeroidde, Ayerode, Ackrood, Ackroode, Ackeroide, Acroid, Ackroode, Ackeroede, Ackrood, Akeroyd, Aikroide, Aikroyde, Ackroid, Avroyd, Ackeroid, Aickeroudd, Akeroid, Aikroyd, Okerd—6, 7, 9, 14, 16, 18, 19, 22, 23, 24, 25, 26, 27, 28, 29, 30, 31, 34, 37, 38, 39, 40, 41, 42, 45, 49, 50, 51, 52, 53, 54, 55, 56, 57, 59, 60, 61, 62, 63, 64, 65, 66, 67, 68, 69, 70, 71, 74, 75, 76, 78, 79, 82, 81, 85, 86, 87, 88, 90, 91, 92, 95, 96, 110, 102, 103, 106, 107, 108, 109, 110, 113, 115, 119, 120, 121, 122, 124, 125, 126, 127, 128, 130, 131, 132, 133, 134, 135, 138, 139, 140, 141, 143, 144, 150, 154, 155, 156, 157, 162, 172, 174.
Adam, Adame, Addam—17, 45, 62, 129, 133, 142.
Adamson—5.
Adcocke—54, 56, 57, 64.
Addie, Addye—35, 36, 39, 40, 41, 133.
Aglande—97.
Alcoke—16, 17.
Aldersley, Hadlersley, Hayldrysley—12, 21, 49.
Aldersson, Alldersone, Addersone, Aldersone—2, 5, 170, 171, 175.
Allsworth—5 (*see* Holdsworth).
Allanson, Alanson, Allensonn, 11, 22, 116.
Allen, Alen, Aylen, Alan, Alayn, Aylene, Alane, Hallan, Allayn, Allanm, Allande, Alland, Allyne, Aland, Allan, Allin, Alline, Allinn—3, 5, 6, 8, 10, 13, 14, 18, 19, 21, 23, 24, 26, 27, 29, 32, 34, 36, 43, 55, 61, 63, 67, 73, 74, 75, 76, 77, 80, 82, 83, 85, 89, 90, 92, 93, 97, 99, 101, 102, 103, 104, 110, 111, 113, 114, 115, 121, 122, 127, 130, 141, 143, 147, 149, 150, 151, 152, 155, 156, 158, 160, 162, 163, 166, 169, 171, 172, 173.
Allerton—151.
Allott, Alot—22, 63, 65.
Alverey—97.
Ambler, Amblers—55, 162.
Anderson—9, 23.
Anderton, Andertone—59, 72, 124, 126, 129, 132, 141, 143, 146.
Andrue—23.
Anson—168 (*see also* Hanson).
Appleby, Applebye—151, 154, 165.
Archer—39, 42, 45, 49, 54, 59, 60, 61, 62, 69, 74, 80, 90, 95, 97, 101, 107, 109, 115, 121, 123, 124, 125, 127, 133, 145, 154, 165, 167.
Armistade—115.
Armstronge, Arnestronge—137, 144, 155, 166.
Arnytage, Armitedge, Arnitadge, Armitage—37, 38, 40, 42, 43, 47, 54, 55, 61, 67, 68, 72, 108, 113, 119, 123, 125, 128, 131, 132, 137, 138, 141, 154, 156, 160, 161, 163, 164, 165, 169.
Arnold, Arnall, Arnalde, Arnauld, Arnald, Arnoulde, Arnould—20, 21, 24, 27, 54, 66, 67, 83, 176.
Arrowsmithe, Arrosmithe, Arrowwithe—102, 113, 119.
Arundell, Arandell, Arrandell, Arrundell, Arandall—26, 30, 31, 33, 36, 38, 40, 43, 47, 48, 50, 58, 69, 72, 74, 88, 107.
Ashley, Ashleye—61, 145, 148, 156, 160, 165.

Ashton, Asheton, Ashtone, Ashtons, Ashetonne, Ashtonn—22, 26, 35, 36, 38, 42, 43, 44, 45, 46, 47, 53, 51, 57, 63, 64, 66, 68, 85, 94, 98, 99, 107, 109, 112, 113, 114, 116, 117, 123, 125, 126, 127, 130, 131, 133, 136, 137, 138, 139, 142, 144, 145, 148, 150, 151, 153, 154, 155, 157, 159, 160, 163, 166, 167.
Aske—58.
Askehonne—31.
Aspinal, Aspinall—51, 52.
Atacke, Aticke—150, 151, 155, 156, 160, 165.
Atkinson—37, 39, 62, 66, 122, 150.
Audley—168.
Audsley, Andesley, Awdslay, Awdsleye, Haudsley, Hawidsley, Hawdysle, Andysley, Awdslai, Awdysley, Awdesleyc, Hadesley, Austley, Audisley, Auddisley, Audeslay, Awdesley, Awdslaye, Awdesleye, Audeslye, Auddislay, Audesulay, Auddeslay, Awdisley, Audsleyc—1, 4, 7, 8, 11, 12, 15, 17, 22, 23, 21, 25, 27, 28, 29, 30, 31, 32, 33, 34, 36, 39, 40, 41, 42, 43, 44, 47, 50, 51, 52, 54, 55, 56, 57, 58, 59, 60, 61, 62, 63, 64, 68, 70, 72, 73, 74, 75, 78, 80, 83, 87, 97, 99, 101, 103, 106, 111, 112, 116, 117, 118, 121, 122, 123, 126, 127, 128, 129, 131, 133, 136, 140, 141, 142, 147, 151, 152, 155, 157, 159, 161, 165, 166, 168, 170, 173.
Auty, Awtie, Aute, Awtye, Awty, Awtyes, Autye, Autie—2, 4, 10, 18, 20, 21, 30, 33, 35, 36, 38, 39, 40, 44, 46, 47, 53, 59, 61, 62, 67, 69, 70, 72, 73, 78, 79, 80, 82, 83, 84, 85, 86, 89, 92, 94, 95, 96, 97, 98, 99, 103, 107, 118, 119, 123, 124, 126, 127, 129, 131, 132, 133, 134, 136, 137, 139, 140, 141, 143, 144, 145, 146, 148, 149, 151, 152, 153, 155, 157, 159, 160, 161, 163, 164, 166, 167, 168, 176.
Aveyard, Avyarde, Aveyearde. Aveyerde—102, 110, 112, 152, 166 (*see also* Haveyerde).
Awbraye—74.

Backhouse, Bachouse, Bachowse, Backhowse, Backehowso—32, 34, 37, 72, 74, 91, 103.
Bacoun—105.
Baildon, Bayldon, Bayldone, Bayldonn, Baildone, Baldon, Baldone, Beldon—1, 4, 5, 6, 8, 10, 11, 12, 13, 14, 16, 17, 19, 20, 22, 25, 26, 27, 28, 29, 33, 35, 40, 42, 43, 44, 54, 56, 74, 80, 81, 100, 130, 170, 171, 172, 174, 176.
Ball, Bawll, Bolle, Baull, Baulle, Balle—2, 5, 8, 9, 14, 15, 16, 18, 22, 26, 27, 28, 32, 35, 37, 40, 170, 171, 174 (*see also* Bull).
Balmfforthe, Baumforthe—107, 116.
Bankes—77.
Baracloughe—80.
Barber, Berbre, Barbare, Barebar, Barbur, Berber, Barbre, Barbure, Beldon—1, 4, 5, 8, 10, 11, 12, 13, 14, 15, 16, 17, 18, 19, 21, 22, 23, 24, 25, 26, 27, 28, 30, 33, 36, 38, 39, 40, 41, 42, 44, 46, 47, 48, 49, 51, 52, 53, 55, 58, 59, 60, 61, 62, 63, 64, 65, 66, 67, 68, 69, 71, 72, 75, 77, 79, 80, 89, 91, 92, 93, 94, 98, 99, 100, 105, 106, 108, 109, 111, 116, 119, 123, 125, 126, 128, 129, 130, 131, 132, 133, 134, 135, 139, 140, 142, 143, 145, 149, 150, 152, 153, 154, 155, 156, 157, 158, 159, 163, 164, 165, 166, 168, 171, 173, 175.
Bargh, Barghe, Barge—53, 57, 61, 65, 69, 74, 82, 117,

ii.   INDEX.

119, 123, 126, 127, 128, 130, 131, 132, 133, 135, 138,
139, 140, 142, 144, 145, 146, 148, 149, 151, 152, 153,
157, 159, 161, 162, 164, 165.
Barker, Barkar—8, 13, 20, 22, 34, 44, 45, 49, 55, 150,
169, 174, 176.
Barkston, Barkesstone—14, 21.
Barlow, Barlou—47, 49, 50.
Barmbye, Barmeby—42, 43, 64, 66.
Barnard, Barnerd, Barnarde, Barnerde—70, 73, 79, 82,
89, 101, 104.
Barom, Birome—65, 70.
Barras—163.
Barrett—67, 101.
Barrie—79.
Barrough, Barrongs—164, 168.
Barstoe, Barstone—17, 45.
Barton, Bartonn—45, 46, 47, 50, 51, 52, 65, 81, 102, 103,
104, 110, 111, 117, 122, 124, 126, 132, 134, 141, 148,
149, 154, 161, 169.
Bateman, Beateman—137, 138, 139, 141, 155, 162.
Batley, Batlay, Batleye—18, 49, 129, 137, 150, 151.
Battye, Battie—95, 97, 102, 103, 106, 109, 110, 113, 117,
122, 134, 135, 112.
Bawme, Baune—13, 62, 152.
Baxster—149,
Bayley, Baylye, Bayly, Baylie, Bailie—48, 54, 78, 91,
165.
Beards ll, Beardsill—159, 160.
Beatson, Betthson, Betison, Beatcson, Beatsonn—21,
23, 24, 26, 29, 35, 60, 70, 91, 95, 101, 105, 108, 116,
117, 118, 121, 125, 128, 130, 136, 137, 138, 142, 144,
145, 147, 149, 150, 155, 158, 160.
Beaumont, Beaumunde, Beaumonde, Beaumound, Beaumond,
Beaumount, Beaumounte, Beamont—17, 18, 19, 21, 27,
32, 38, 44, 45, 47, 77, 80, 82, 95, 115, 118, 123, 131,
136, 139, 141, 145, 117, 151, 152, 161, 162, 167.
Beckwith, Beckwithe, Bekwithe, Beckwth, Becwith,
Beckewithe—60, 71, 72, 75, 77, 82, 88, 97, 100, 109,
119, 125, 133, 137, 159, 161, 169.
Bectye—152.
Bedford, Badforthe, Bedforde, Bedforth, Bedfourthe—
19, 26, 28, 29, 35, 37, 40, 49, 56, 59, 60, 61, 63, 68,
70, 71, 77, 87, 107, 116, 122, 124, 139, 135, 136, 137,
140, 143, 146, 147, 149, 153, 154, 155, 158, 159, 160,
163, 164, 166, 167, 169.
Beisbey, Beisbye—69, 76.
Beldon—(see Baildon).
Bell—103, 105, 114.
Bellett—153.
Bent—82, 97.
Benson, Bentesone—19, 155.
Bent—28, 72.
Bentley, Bentlay, Bentlaye, Benley, Bentley, Bentleye
—26, 30, 33, 37, 38, 40, 41, 43, 45, 56, 59, 60, 61, 62,
68, 69, 71, 73, 76, 77, 78, 79, 83, 85, 87, 89, 90, 91,
95, 96, 97, 101, 106, 107, 108, 112, 123, 124, 125, 130,
133, 134, 136, 137, 138, 143, 145, 148, 154, 155, 156,
159, 161, 163, 164, 166, 169.
Benton, Beatonn—88, 99, 122, 123.
Berry, Berrye, Berrie—45, 50, 54, 57, 67, 68, 69, 71, 84,
92, 100, 106, 111, 115, 118, 119, 120, 121, 129.
Best—56.
Dickliffe—109.
Bighlay—40.
Bingley, Byngley, Bingelaye, Bingeleye—5, 34, 42, 46,
75, 114, 167, 171.
Binns, Binnes, Bynnes, Bins, 96, 100, 115, 155, 155,
160, 161, 164.
Birch, Burche—119, 120, 123, 126, 156.
Birkby, Byrkeby, Byrkby, Byrkbe, Byrkebie, Byrkabe,
Burkbye, Birkebe, Birkebeye, Byrkeby, Byrkebye—
2, 4, 22, 25, 26, 27, 30, 36, 37, 40, 88, 106, 170.

Birkhead, Byrkcheade, Birkchead, Burkcheade—60,
83, 94, 156.
Birkhill, Birkill—65, 66, 70.
Birle, Byerle, Byarle, Byrele, Byarell, Byerell, Byrle,
Birle, 1, 2, 6, 7, 9, 10, 11, 13, 23, 24, 32, 33, 34, 35,
38, 40, 42, 43, 170, 172.
Birridge—122, 124.
Blackburne, Blakbourne, Blagburne, Blakborne, Blackeburn,
Blakburne—2, 5, 32, 35, 40, 41, 43, 46, 55, 92,
109, 120, 129, 170.
Blacke—39.
Blacker—83.
Blakey—52
Bland—109.
Bleishye, Bleisbee—45, 49, 99.
Bold, Boulde, Bolde, Bowld, Bould—100, 101, 105, 111,
115, 118, 129, 126, 130, 138, 140, 145, 165, 167, 160.
Bolland, Bollande—138, 140, 151, 152, 153, 159, 164,
165.
Bolling—6.
Bolton, Boulton—1, 18, 39, 150, 170.
Bonsar, Bonnar, Bonmar, Boonar—76, 81, 89, 100, 108,
147, 150, 160, 161.
Boot—18.
Booth, Boith, Boyth, Boythe, Both, Bothe, Boithe,
Bout, Boathe, Boithe, Boothe—7, 9, 10, 11, 12, 13,
14, 15, 17, 22, 23, 25, 26, 28, 30, 31, 32, 34, 45, 46,
48, 50, 52, 53, 56, 57, 60, 61, 62, 63, 64, 65, 67, 69,
72, 73, 75, 76, 77, 78, 79, 80, 82, 86, 88, 90, 93, 97,
98, 100, 102, 103, 106, 108, 111, 113, 114, 117, 122,
124, 132, 138, 143, 147, 156, 169, 174, 175.
Boothroble, Boothcroide—114, 118.
Borghe—11.
Bothman, Boytman, Boythman—22, 23, 36, 39.
Bothomlay, Bothomley—86, 160.
Boull—(see Bull).
Boult—10.
Bower—80.
Bowkcht—14.
Bowling, Bowlinge, Boulinge, Bowleinge—60, 68, 73,
79, 95, 113, 114, 116, 117, 118, 122, 124, 125, 129,
132, 136, 151, 154.
Bows—30.
Boy, Boyy, Boye, Boyes—2, 11, 17, 22, 34, 37, 41, 45,
46, 47, 48, 49, 53, 84, 88, 93, 95, 100, 105, 106, 111,
118, 128, 170.
Boyle, Boylle, Boyll—2, 5, 13, 19, 36, 43, 44, 171, 175
(see also Bull).
Bradford, Bradfourthe, Bradforthe, Bradforth, Bradforthe,
Bradfourthe, Bradfourth, Bradforde—2, 3, 4,
5, 6, 7, 8, 9, 12, 13, 15, 16, 17, 18, 19, 20, 21, 22, 23,
24, 26, 29, 30, 31, 32, 34, 35, 36, 39, 40, 42, 43, 45,
46, 47, 48, 51, 53, 54, 55, 56, 57, 59, 60, 61, 62, 64,
66, 67, 68, 72, 75, 76, 77, 78, 79, 80, 83, 86, 87, 89,
92, 94, 95, 96, 97, 98, 108, 111, 117, 118, 125, 129,
133, 134, 137, 138, 140, 142, 144, 146, 147, 148, 119,
152, 153, 154, 156, 158, 160, 162, 164, 167, 168, 171,
172, 173, 174, 175, 176.
Bradley, Bradlay, Bradle, Bradlaye, Bradleye—31, 32,
33, 49, 61, 62, 71, 72, 96, 121, 122, 127, 130, 134, 157.
Bramham—84.
Brase—120.
Brear, Breare, Breer, Breere—81, 85, 103, 124, 128,
145, 149, 150, 152, 154, 157, 161, 162, 165.
Brearey, Brearaye, Brearay, Breareye, Brearie, Breerie,
Breallay—35, 60, 80, 86, 88, 89, 94, 100, 101, 106,
145, 148, 150, 157, 158, 165.
Brent—73.
Brewith—165.
Bridge, Brygg—14, 133, 153.
Briggs, Brygge, Brigge, Brigges—24, 25, 30, 37, 40,
42, 45, 46, 48, 49, 50, 69, 77, 81, 84, 89, 90, 94, 101,
109, 144.

INDEX.   iii.

Bright—2.
Broadbent, Brodebent—12, 118.
Broadhead, Broadheade—89, 95, 96, 103, 110, 120, 130, 145, 146, 148, 153, 157, 159, 163, 164.
Broadley, Brodlaye, Broadlaye, Broadlaye, Broadley, Broadly, Brodeley, Bradley, Breadhay, Broadleye—42, 45, 50, 52, 53, 55, 60, 61, 62, 68, 72, 74, 81, 82, 83, 84, 86, 88, 90, 92, 93, 94, 101, 103, 108, 120, 124, 126, 127, 128, 131, 134, 140, 144, 145, 148, 149, 150, 151, 152, 154, 155, 158, 164, 165, 167, 168, 169.
Brooke, Brake, Broke, Brok, Broike, Bruk, Browke, Brock, Brocke, Brouke, Broukes, Brockes, Broyke, Brouk, Broocke—1, 5, 6, 7, 8, 9, 10, 13, 15, 19, 22, 23, 24, 25, 26, 27, 28, 31, 32, 35, 36, 37, 38, 39, 40, 41, 42, 43, 45, 49, 50, 52, 53, 55, 56, 57, 59, 62, 63, 64, 66, 67, 68, 70, 72, 73, 74, 75, 76, 77, 78, 79, 80, 82, 84, 85, 88, 89, 90, 93, 95, 99, 106, 109, 111, 115, 119, 121, 122, 123, 125, 126, 128, 129, 132, 134, 136, 137, 138, 139, 140, 141, 142, 143, 145, 146, 147, 148, 150, 151, 152, 154, 156, 157, 158, 159, 160, 163, 166, 167, 168, 171, 172, 173, 174, 175.
Brooksbank, Brookesbanke, Brooksbanke—132, 165, 166
Brought, Broughte, Broughe, Browght, Browghat—5, 8, 33, 34, 171, 174.
Brown, Browne, Broune—1, 2, 4, 5, 7, 8, 9, 13, 15, 17, 18, 19, 23, 47, 95, 121, 154, 157, 159, 170, 171, 172, 173, 175.
Brught—4.
Bug—27.
Bull, Boull, Bule, Bulle, Boll—14, 16, 18, 21, 22, 28, 29, 30, 32, 33, 34, 35, 36, 37, 38, 39, 40, 41, 42, 43, 44, 46, 48, 49, 51, 55, 56, 58, 63, 64, 65, 67, 68, 70, 72, 73, 75, 76, 77, 79, 80, 82, 86, 88, 89, 90, 91, 95, 96, 99, 100, 102, 105, 109, 111, 119, 121, 123, 127, 129, 132, 133, 134, 136, 139, 140, 141, 143, 144, 145, 146, 153, 154, 156, 157, 158, 160, 164, 166, 167, 168.
(see also Ball).
Bullman—64.
Bunche—106, 113.
Burball—115.
Burdett—144.
Burghe—26.
Burke, Byrk, Barke, Byrkes—8, 49, 173.
Burlby—21.
Burnell—57.
Barnett, Bunnet, Bernet, Burnete—20, 24, 25, 27, 29, 33, 35, 37, 39, 40, 41, 47, 50, 56, 65, 102, 114, 176.
Burnley, Burnlaye, Burnleye, Burneley—61, 62, 114, 126, 132, 134, 135, 140, 145, 151, 157, 163.
Burrell—80, 175.
Burrough—160.
Burton, Barton, Byrtton, Byrtann, Burtonn—10, 16, 23, 108, 113.
Burtwistle—140.
Butts—67.
Bybson—17.
Byenme—23.
Bylson—17.
Byrkenshey, Byrkyngshey—4, 16.
Byrkinge—30.

Caiton—141.
Cantuar, Cantuar—70.
Capps—67.
Carsforth—36.
Carlynghow, Carlynhall, Carlingehawe, Carlyngehow—3, 7, 14, 19, 173.
Carnell—123, 124, 126, 132, 139, 156.
Curr, Carre—4, 144, 145, 149, 151, 156, 160, 165, 169.
Carrier—71.
Carter, Cartter, Cartar, Cartare—7, 10, 11, 12, 13, 15, 23, 31, 39, 41, 42, 44, 45, 47, 49, 50, 59, 60, 76, 79, 84, 86, 92, 96, 102, 104, 107, 110, 111, 112, 114, 116, 126, 129, 130, 135, 137, 140, 143, 147, 148, 149, 152, 156, 157, 158, 159, 160, 164, 172.
Cartuar—70.
Carwell—153.
Casson, Cassonn—21, 29, 31, 52, 70, 83, 97, 105, 114, 122, 129, 132, 160, 161, 167.
Castle, Castley, Casle, Castleye, Castles—79, 84, 86, 88, 90, 93, 98, 101, 102, 105, 117, 124, 127, 128, 129, 131, 132, 138, 141, 144, 148, 149, 150, 151, 153, 159.
Castlehouse, Castlehowse—112, 158, 164, 167, 168.
Catryne—37.
Cawthorne, Cauthorne—101, 157, 161, 165.
Cay (see Kaye).
Chadwicke—125, 154, 166.
Chambers, Chamber—95, 120, 127.
Chumpney—62.
Chapman—162.
Chappell—67.
Charlesworth—166.
Chester—32, 46, 53, 54, 65, 66, 68, 72, 78, 83, 90, 95, 103, 137, 144, 145, 146, 148, 150, 152, 155, 158, 160, 166, 167.
Chayff. (see Scafe).
Chickeley—39.
Childe, Chylde—22, 24, 112, 146, 147.
Cholfeld (see Scholefield).
Chollar—28.
Chossyn—28.
Clappam, Clapam, Claypam—12, 71, 169.
Clark, Clak, Clarke, Clarke—9, 12, 13, 15, 18, 20, 22, 24, 29, 43, 44, 49, 55, 87, 139, 140, 175, 176.
Clarkson, Clarksonne, Clarkeson, Clarsonn, Clarkesone —16, 39, 35, 40, 52.
Claughton, Claghton—76, 132, 137, 143, 148, 149, 153, 158, 163.
Clay, Claye—67, 114.
Clayton, Clatone, Claytonn, Claton, Clathon, Claiton, Claytton, Claytone—8, 12, 13, 16, 21, 23, 24, 26, 27, 28, 29, 30, 31, 33, 34, 43, 45, 46, 47, 48, 50, 51, 52, 54, 57, 59, 60, 61, 63, 65, 66, 69, 70, 71, 72, 78, 89, 90, 99, 102, 103, 104, 106, 109, 110, 111, 112, 115, 120, 128, 142, 151, 152, 168, 174.
Clegge—131.
Clough—89.
Coa—67.
Cockell—100
Cofin, Cofyne—21, 139.
Colbecke—73, 168.
Collier, Colier, Collyer, Colyer—16, 17, 18, 25, 30, 55, 78, 79, 80, 88, 95, 120.
Colpe—20
Comsmithe—80, 103.
Conyer—24.
Cooke, Coke—76, 77, 79, 112, 116, 119, 131, 133, 142.
Cookeson, 152.
Coosen, Coozen, Cosens, Cosyn, Coosinge, Cowsinge, Cussinge, Cossen, Cossinge, Cossinge—25, 31, 35, 42, 43, 68, 72, 74, 75, 110, 152, 157.
Coossery—114.
Coote—128.
Copley, Coplay, Copleye—11, 19, 22, 59, 62, 80, 83, 133, 156, 159, 160, 164, 169, 176.
Cordingley, Cordinglay, Cordinglayo—13, 46, 49, 60, 104, 105, 115, 116.
Coultmann—141.
Coulton, Coulton—129, 131, 137, 142.
Compa—2.
Coward—47.
Cowlinge—111.
Cowood, Cowoode—44, 44, 118.

iv.   INDEX.

Cowpas—45, 47, 18, 49, 69, 71, 75, 83, 85, 90, 103, 106, 107, 118, 121, 125, 129.
Cowper, Cowpar—66, 87, 90, 95, 98, 109, 112, 117, 147, 154, 158, 163.
Cowton—135.
Crabtree, Crabtre—17, 113, 114, 115, 118.
Craven—35, 48, 50.
Crawshaw, Crowdshawe—96, 115.
Croft, Crofte—47, 68, 69, 76, 84, 90, 140, 143, 145, 148, 169.
Crosbe—10
Crosfeld, Crosfelde—42, 57, 101.
Crosland, Croslande—78, 98.
Crosley, Croslay, Croslaye—55, 93, 94, 165.
Crusto—136.
Crowle—67.
Crowther, Crowder, Crouder, Crother, Crowdar—12, 13, 15, 17, 21, 30, 42, 51, 69, 84, 87, 118, 122, 151, 163.
Cryer—107, 116.
Cudworth—156.
Culpeper—6.
Cunningham, Coningham, Coninghame, Cuningham, Cuningha—118, 119, 121, 126, 131, 138, 141, 143, 147, 152, 158, 159, 163, 167.
Curtice, Curteous, Cutisse, Curteouse—61, 62, 125, 127, 132, 139, 146, 154, 167.
Cyllymbroke—12.

Dallahaye—54.
Dalton, Daulton, Dolton—99, 145, 146, 150, 155, 161, 163.
Darwyn—101, 109.
Davison, Davesonn, Davisonn—86, 87, 91, 110.
Dawson, Dawsson, Dawsone, Dauson, Dowson, Dawsone, Dawsons—1, 7, 8, 9, 13, 15, 16, 20, 22, 23, 24, 25, 27, 29, 30, 31, 32, 33, 34, 35, 36, 37, 40, 43, 46, 49, 50, 52, 54, 55, 57, 59, 60, 61, 63, 66, 68, 69, 70, 73, 74, 77, 78, 81, 82, 86, 90, 93, 94, 96, 102, 110, 111, 112, 116, 117, 118, 120, 121, 122, 123, 128, 129, 130, 131, 132, 135, 136, 139, 140, 141, 143, 144, 145, 146, 147, 149, 152, 154, 155, 156, 157, 160, 161, 162, 163, 166, 172, 174, 175.
Day, Dey, Daye, Deie, Daie, Deye—5, 17, 19, 20, 24, 26, 27, 28, 29, 31, 34, 38, 40, 45, 46, 48, 50, 52, 55, 56, 57, 58, 63, 66, 67, 71, 72, 73, 76, 79, 82, 85, 86, 87, 92, 93, 98, 99, 103, 105, 109, 111, 113, 114, 116, 118, 119, 120, 121, 123, 124, 126, 127, 128, 129, 132, 133, 134, 135, 136, 138, 139, 142, 143, 145, 146, 147, 150, 151, 152, 154, 155, 156, 158, 160, 161, 162, 164, 165, 176.
Denis, Denyse, Denise, Denese, Denys, Dennis, Dynnis—84, 94, 98, 100, 105, 110, 114, 127, 141, 143, 155, 169.
Denison, Dynnyson, Denyson, Dinysone, Dynisone, Dinison, Dynison, Denysonn, Denisons, Denisonn, Denyxon—16, 22, 31, 32, 35, 37, 40, 41, 43, 48, 60, 61, 81, 83, 84, 85, 86, 99, 102, 116, 132, 140, 152, 169.
Dent, Dente—41, 45, 47, 68, 118.
Denton, Dentonn—10, 27, 30, 31, 33, 35, 39, 43, 46, 50, 55, 157, 161.
Dewsberie—50.
Dickenson, Dykanson, Dyrconson, Dickenson, Dyckenson, Diconson, Dyconson, Dycunson, Diconsone, Dickinsone, Diceonsen, Dyckenson, Dickinsonn, Dickynson, Diekyngson, Dickensons, Dickensonn, Dickinson—3, 4, 5, 8, 11, 15, 16, 19, 21, 25, 26, 28, 29, 34, 37, 38, 39, 40, 43, 44, 45, 46, 53, 54, 58, 59, 63, 68, 69, 71, 81, 87, 96, 101, 115, 120, 135, 147, 152, 156, 161, 162, 165, 166, 171 *see also* Dixon'.
Dishforth, Dyshyrth, Dyshforth, Dushford, Dyschforth, Dyscheforthe, Dyshefourth, Disforthe, Disforthe,

Disforth, Dyshefurth, Dysheforthe, Dyshefurthe, Dysfurthe, Disheforthe, Dischforth, Dishforthe, Disshefourth, Dyshforthe, Dyshfurthe, Dysforthe, Dishefourthe—2, 3, 5, 6, 7, 8, 9, 10, 13, 14, 15, 16, 17, 18, 20, 21, 22, 23, 24, 25, 26, 27, 28, 29, 30, 32, 33, 35, 36, 38, 42, 43, 45, 46, 47, 49, 51, 53, 57, 58, 62, 64, 65, 66, 71, 75, 76, 78, 80, 83, 88, 92, 100, 104, 105, 119, 123, 133, 135, 137, 138, 140, 143, 150, 156, 170, 171, 172, 173, 175, 176.
Ditche, Diche, Dych—21, 22, 23, 146.
Diton—15.
Dixon, Dycson, Dixesone, Dieson, Dikson, Dickson, Dixson, Dicksonn, Dixonn, Dixsonn, Dixeson, Dicson, Dycksone, Dicksonn, Dickeson—25, 27, 32, 31, 39, 47, 50, 51, 53, 55, 60, 61, 63, 64, 65, 70, 74, 75, 76, 77, 79, 82, 84, 86, 88, 89, 92, 93, 98, 100, 102, 104, 105, 106, 108, 109, 110, 112, 113, 115, 116, 117, 120, 121, 123, 125, 126, 129, 131. 132, 134, 138, 141, 143, 144, 150, 151, 152, 154, 156, 157, 158, 159, 160, 161, 162, 163, 164, 165, 166, 167, 174 (*see also* Dickerson).
Dobson, Dobsonn—69, 108, 109, 112, 129, 135, 115.
Dod—127.
Dodgson—166.
Downes—81.
Dransfield, Dransfeld, Drancfeld, Drancefeld, Draunccfelde, Dransfelde, Draunsfeld—2, 4, 5, 6, 7, 9, 10, 11, 37, 38, 117, 171, 172, 173, 175.
Draper—53, 57.
Drybecke—83.
Dubbell—125.
Duckeworthe—81.
Dunhill—102.
Dunwell—135, 158.
Duxburie—25.
Dymon—150.
Dynina—141.
Dyson, Dison—34, 61, 128, 141.

Eacocke—134.
Earle—24, 25, 27, 31, 92, 113.
Eastewoode, Estwoode—21, 97.
Eatocke, Etocke—130, 145.
Ecclesfield—16.
Edge—160.
Ellam—135.
Ellery, Ellerie, Ellerye—49, 86, 122, 125.
Ellis, Ellys, Elys, Elyse, Ellies—7, 27, 34, 36, 37, 39, 40, 42, 43, 45, 54, 55, 57, 64, 65, 66, 67, 69, 70, 71, 72, 73, 74, 75, 76, 78, 79, 80, 82, 83, 85, 86, 87, 88, 89, 91, 93, 94, 95, 98, 102, 104, 105, 108, 115, 125, 126, 128, 130, 131, 133, 136, 137, 138, 139, 140, 141, 142, 113, 144, 145, 146, 148, 149, 151, 153, 154, 155, 156, 157, 158, 159, 160, 161, 162, 163, 164, 165, 166, 168.
Ellinsall, Felmesall, Elmesall—35, 43, 116, 118, 119.
Ellyson, Ellingsene—6, 172.
Eluish—(*see* Helvishe).
Elvidge—105.
Erlingehawe—176.
Ewinge—119, 120.
Exam, Excame, Exame, Exsome, Exome—23, 25, 27, 30, 42, 46, 50, 52, 53, 63, 85, 92.
Exley, Exlay—14, 45.

Failvo—10.
Fairbarn, Fayrbarne, Fayrbarn, Ffarbarne, Farbarne, Fayrebarne, Fayrnbarne, Fairebarne, Fayer'arne, Fairbarne, Fayrebarne, Farbarne, Fayrbourne—6, 8, 9, 11, 14, 15, 16, 18, 21, 22, 24, 25, 26, 27, 34, 35, 42, 48, 56, 57, 58, 59, 60, 61, 61, 65, 68, 78, 79, 81, 82, 83, 84, 85, 89, 90, 91, 92, 98, 99, 101, 105, 109, 112, 138, 141, 144, 117, 149, 153, 157, 158, 160, 161, 162, 164, 167, 168, 172, 174, 175.

INDEX. v.

Fallay—7, 172.
Fallinge—105.
Furnell—33, 43, 63.
Farowe—21.
Farrande, Farande, Forrand—15, 17, 26, 41, 135.
Furrar, Farrer—14, 113.
Fawcet—109.
Fearnley, Fernley, Fernlaye, Fernlyc, Fernlay, Fearnleye, Fearnlaye, Fearnlay, Ferneley, Fearneley—12, 16, 26, 32, 42, 43, 44, 46, 48, 51, 53, 55, 60, 61, 62, 65, 72, 73, 74, 77, 80, 86, 95, 97, 100, 104, 105, 109, 111, 113, 114, 116, 117, 119, 122, 123, 124, 126, 127, 128, 130, 131, 132, 133, 135, 137, 138, 140, 145, 146, 147, 149, 150, 151, 152, 155, 165, 166.
Fearnside, Fernsyde—70, 141.
Feather, Feether—43, 44, 48.
Fell, Fells, Felles—42, 44, 77, 80, 82, 85, 87, 88, 89, 90, 91, 95, 96, 97, 98, 99, 103, 107, 108, 109, 111, 113, 116, 121, 123, 125, 129, 135, 136, 137, 150, 153, 159.
Few—53, 54.
Field, Feelde, Feild—137, 145, 158, 169.
Fielden, Feelden, Feilden—121, 128, 151, 154, 155.
Finche, Fynche, Fenche—15, 24, 37, 39.
Firth, Firthe, Farthe, Fyrth—82, 95, 108, 109, 111, 112, 113, 115, 117, 121, 124, 130, 135, 136, 158, 169.
Fisho—68.
Fisher—57, 102, 127, 148, 149, 154.
Flader, Flayther, Filather, Fladder, Flather—2, 4, 7, 9, 17, 21, 70, 170, 172, 175.
Flat—12.
Fletcher—66, 76, 77, 80, 90, 95, 97, 101, 109, 115, 118, 127, 129, 130, 134, 135, 138, 146, 147, 149, 150, 152, 153, 154, 155, 159, 166.
Forrest, Forest—4, 5, 6, 9, 13, 15, 30, 31, 32, 33, 34, 36, 37, 38, 39, 41, 44, 45, 46, 48, 50, 51, 56, 57, 60, 61, 68, 70, 71, 72, 81, 82, 83, 85, 86, 87, 88, 93, 94, 97, 100, 134, 137, 138, 140, 142, 149, 157, 158, 171, 172, 175.
Fournesso—68.
Fox, Foxe—8, 9, 10, 11, 14, 17, 19, 20, 21, 24, 25, 45, 46, 47, 48, 49, 52, 54, 55, 56, 57, 59, 60, 61, 63, 61, 66, 68, 69, 70, 71, 73, 74, 77, 78, 83, 84, 87, 89, 91, 93, 96, 99, 102, 103, 108, 109, 111, 113, 114, 118, 120, 121, 122, 123, 127, 129, 132, 133, 135, 137, 139, 141, 143, 144, 149, 151, 153, 154, 156, 157, 159, 160, 161, 162, 165, 166, 174, 175, 176.
Foxcroft—60, 117, 120.
Fozdll—112.
Fozard—156.
France, Franne—31, 62, 75.
Franckland—99.
Frank, Francke, Franke—11, 12, 13, 15, 17, 18.
Freckleton, Freelton, Frecklton, Freeleton, Freeletoun—40, 45, 46, 48, 61, 79, 80, 86, 91, 100, 130, 139.
Fryar—145.
Futhersgill, Foothergill, Futhergill—154, 160, 163.

Gagar (see Jagger.)
Galleye, Gallie—155, 156.
Gamble, Gamell, Gamoll, Gammell—34, 35, 36, 40, 44, 56, 88, 90, 95, 101, 104, 110, 115, 118, 129, 135.
Ganinge, Genynge, Ginyngs (see Jeninge).
Gardalhe—32.
Garrett, Garrct—39, 158, 159.
Gascoyne—29.
Gaston—21, 24.
Gaukeroger—138, 139.
Gaunge—172.
Gaunt, Gauntt, Gawnte, Gante, Gant, Gaunte, Gawnt—1, 8, 10, 11, 14, 15, 16, 24, 26, 28, 31, 35, 39, 41, 42, 45, 48, 49, 50, 55, 68, 173, 174.
Gawen—88.

Genynge (see Jeninge).
Gest—38.
Gibson, Gibsone, Gybson, Gibsonne, Gibsonn—1, 3, 5, 9, 12, 11, 16, 18, 23, 24, 26, 29, 30, 31, 32, 33, 34, 35, 37, 44, 45, 47, 62, 63, 65, 69, 70, 71, 73, 74, 76, 86, 91, 119, 122, 126, 131, 136, 137, 141, 142, 144, 146, 149, 152, 153, 154, 155, 156, 139, 161, 170, 171, 175.
Gill, Gyll, Gyle, Gylle—8, 13, 21, 26, 30, 32, 34, 37, 39, 41, 42, 44, 45, 47, 48, 50, 51, 52, 53, 54, 56, 57, 58, 59, 60, 61, 62, 63, 65, 66, 68, 69, 70, 71, 72, 73, 74, 75, 76, 79, 81, 82, 84, 90, 91, 97, 98, 99, 100, 101, 103, 109, 110, 112, 113, 114, 115, 119, 121, 123, 124, 125, 126, 130, 134, 135, 136, 137, 138, 140, 141, 142, 145, 148, 150, 152, 154, 160, 164, 168.
Gillome—67.
Gillott, Gillot—5, 171.
Gledall, Gifdall, Gleadall—33, 49, 130, 165.
Glover, Gloover—70, 72, 138, 140, 144, 150, 158, 162, 166.
Godraic—24.
Gomersall, Gomsawlle, Gomersalle, Gomsaill, Gommersall, Gomersaule, Gomersaill—2, 4, 14, 18, 19, 21, 23, 24, 27, 29, 151, 170, 176.
Goodall, Goodayll, Gooddall, Goydall, Goodaill, Goodale, Goodalle, Goodales, Goodedall—9, 32, 33, 35, 38, 39, 41, 42, 44, 59, 60, 61, 67, 68, 70, 71, 73, 75, 78, 79, 82, 83, 87, 88, 89, 102, 115, 118, 119, 121, 123, 126, 127, 128, 131, 133, 136, 138, 139, 141, 142, 143, 144, 145, 148, 149, 150, 151, 154, 156, 158, 163, 167, 169, 174.
Goodfellow, Goodfelow, Goodfeloy, Goodefelow—4, 5, 8, 11, 15, 16, 28, 40, 171, 171.
Goudroyd, Goodroood, Goodrode—46, 48, 51.
Gornall, Gurnall, Girnall, Garnall—42, 44, 48, 53, 108, 111, 121.
Gouldsborowe—72.
Gowett (see Jowett).
Gowrie, Gowrye—106, 109.
Graneson—13.
Granison—9.
Grare—17.
Grawe—33.
Graysu—35.
Grayson, Graisone, Grayfsson, Grayfson, Grayveson, Graysonn, Graysone, Graveson—19, 20, 21, 34, 43, 44, 45, 48, 52, 56, 63, 66, 71, 74, 75, 87, 88, 95, 121, 123, 142, 150, 175, 176.
Greake—132.
Greave, Grayve, Graive, Greaves, Grave, Grayff, Graver—17, 20, 29, 40, 41, 42, 44, 46, 47, 48, 49, 51, 52, 53, 54, 55, 57, 59, 66, 73, 74, 77, 80, 82, 85, 91, 92, 95, 96, 97, 99, 100, 102, 103, 105, 106, 107, 109, 111, 115, 116, 117, 118, 121, 126, 127, 129, 130, 134, 135, 136, 137, 139, 141, 147, 148, 151, 152, 153, 154, 156, 160, 161, 162.
Green, Greyne, Greyn, Grene, Grane, Gren, Grenne, Grayne, Greine, Greene—2, 4, 6, 7, 8, 10, 11, 12, 13, 14, 15, 16, 18, 19, 20, 21, 22, 23, 24, 26, 27, 28, 29, 30, 31, 32, 33, 34, 35, 36, 37, 39, 40, 41, 42, 44, 45, 46, 47, 48, 53, 55, 57, 61, 64, 65, 67, 69, 72, 75, 76, 78, 80, 82, 84, 91, 97, 110, 136, 138, 156, 158, 163, 170, 171, 172, 173, 174, 176.
Greenfield, Greenfeild, Greenfelde, Greenfeilde—155, 157, 163, 164, 167.
Greenwood, Grenwood, Grenewoode, Greenwoode, Grenewoode, Greenewoode, Grenewod, Grenwood, Grenwoode, Grenewode—14, 45, 47, 50, 51, 60, 61, 62, 64, 68, 69, 73, 75, 77, 81, 82, 84, 91, 96, 105, 106, 111, 114, 117, 119, 122, 127, 139, 141, 144, 147, 118, 152, 154, 157, 163, 166.
Grendall—64.
Greye—108.

INDEX.

Griffine, Gryffyn, Grefyne, Gryfyng, Gryfine, Griffinge, Gryfinge, Gryfine, Gryphyn, Grifen, Gryffyne —7, 10, 14, 21, 36, 38, 39, 41, 48, 56, 64, 86, 172.
Grindal—90.
Gripper—57.
Gryme—46.
Grynton -11.
Gunson, Gunsonn, Gunsome—85, 89, 97, 98, 103, 109, 112, 117, 119, 122, 125, 130, 131, 132, 138, 140, 155, 156, 159, 160, 162, 163, 165, 168, 169.
Guyeslay—72.
Gyles—46.

Hadeslay, Haudsley, Hawidsley, Hawdysle (see Audsley).
Haigh, Hagh, Hayge, Haghe, Haighe, Haughe, Hage, Haige—5, 15, 21, 22, 24, 25, 26, 30, 33, 34, 36, 38, 40, 49, 61, 71, 75, 76, 77, 78, 80, 82, 84, 110, 112, 117, 118, 125, 128, 132, 140, 147, 150, 153, 155, 156, 162, 171.
Haines—29.
Haldenn—70.
Hall, Hooll, Haull, Hawle, Hawlle, Haulle, Haule, Halle, Hoole—3, 5, 6, 7, 8, 9, 10, 11, 12, 15, 16, 18, 19, 20, 21, 22, 23, 24, 27, 29, 30, 32, 34, 42, 45, 46, 47, 48, 50, 56, 75, 77, 82, 88, 94, 99, 100, 105, 106, 107, 109, 110, 114, 116, 118, 119, 121, 123, 125, 127, 129, 130, 133, 137, 139, 150, 151, 152, 155, 156, 164, 165, 167, 171, 172, 173, 175, 176.
Halley—13.
Hallila, Hdlilah, Haileley—144, 145, 147, 148, 153, 159.
Haloode, 18.
Hancocke—167.
Handlaye—112.
Hanley—120.
Hanson, Hansonne, Hansonn, Hansone—1, 8, 28, 70, 86, 127, 132, 160, 166, 173 (see also Anson).
Hardcastle—134, 145, 158, 164, 167.
Hardwick—167.
Hardye—98, 101.
Hare—81.
Hargreaves, Hargrayve, Hargraive, Hargreave, Hargrave—114, 116, 119, 122, 126, 135, 145, 146, 147, 148, 156.
Harpin, Harpine—39, 136.
Harrish, Harrishe—63, 68, 73, 79, 92, 96, 104, 124, 126.
Harrison, Harison, Harrisonn, Harisonn—30, 37, 44, 49, 53, 54, 55, 71, 93, 96, 105, 108, 111, 123, 131, 141, 142, 145, 146, 147, 150, 164, 169.
Harrope, Harroppe—50, 95, 97, 104, 112, 118, 120, 126, 128, 148.
Harte—37.
Hartley, Hartleye—125, 134, 143, 144, 147, 157, 161.
Hassard—51, 52.
Haunshey—140.
Haveyard, Haveor, Hayvyerd, Havyord, Haveyardd, Haveyearde—6, 9, 28, 32, 33, 36, 52 (see also Aveyard).
Hawden, Hewden—63, 79, 83, 96, 102.
Hawkesworthe—86.
Hawkshaw—162.
Hawkyeard, Hawkeyerde, Hawyerd—77, 87, 170.
Hawley—9, 175.
Haworth, Hauworthe, Haworthe, Hayworth—30, 41, 44, 45, 62, 170, 172, 175.
Hayll—15.
Haywyerd—2, 3, 4.
Hazlewood—123.
Headeley, Headelay—41, 95.
Heald, Healde—98, 99, 100, 105, 110, 119, 155, 157, 162, 165, 168, 169.
Heape—78.
Hearhold—7.
Helderithe—96.

Helisston—21.
Hellywell, Hellewell, Hollynwell—7, 122, 173.
Helvishe, Elnish, Helves, Heluish—65, 77, 102, 104, 155, 156, 165.
Helyfeld—26.
Hemingway, Hemmyngwaye, Hemyngeway, Hemyngewaye, Hemyngwaye, Hemyngway, Hemmingway, Hemingwaye, Hemingewaye, Hemingwaie—27, 46, 60, 61, 67, 68, 69, 71, 75, 80, 86, 87, 89, 91, 96, 97, 102, 104, 105, 106, 110, 112, 113, 115, 119, 122, 124, 135, 139, 142, 146, 147, 148, 149, 150, 151, 152, 153, 154, 155, 156, 157, 160, 161, 162, 164, 165, 167.
Hepworth, Hepworthe—3, 21, 22, 26, 27, 30, 33, 34, 44, 55, 61, 68, 87, 89, 101, 103, 112, 113, 119, 120, 123, 128, 130, 132, 136, 141, 142, 144, 146, 149, 151, 155, 159, 160, 161, 162, 164, 165, 166.
Hesleye—172.
Hesselwod—13.
Hesshall—4.
Hey, Hay, Haye, Heye—7, 70, 89, 154, 172.
Heywood—85.
Higginsonn—114.
Higgyns, Higgyn—94, 95, 111.
Hill—5, 116, 150, 168, 171.
Hinchcliffe, Hinchlyffe, Hyncheliffe, Hynchlyffe, Hyncliffe, Hinecleyfe, Hynchelyff, Hynchliffe—8, 64, 65, 67, 69, 71, 75, 173.
Hinde—149.
Hindlebronghe—65.
Hirde—146.
Hirst, Hvrst, Heyrst, Heyrste, Hyrstt, Hurst, Hirste, Hust, Hyrste—5, 6, 7, 8, 9, 11, 13, 15, 16, 17, 24, 25, 26, 27, 29, 30, 31, 32, 33, 34, 35, 37, 38, 39, 40, 41, 42, 43, 47, 48, 49, 52, 53, 55, 57, 59, 60, 65, 66, 67, 69, 70, 71, 72, 73, 74, 76, 77, 78, 79, 81, 84, 85, 86, 87, 88, 90, 91, 93, 95, 96, 99, 100, 101, 102, 103, 104, 108, 109, 112, 113, 116, 117, 120, 121, 123, 124, 128, 131, 132, 133, 135, 136, 141, 145, 150, 151, 152, 154, 156, 159, 161, 162, 163, 166, 167, 171, 172, 174, 175.
Hogge—168.
Hokle—99.
Holdsworth, Haldsworth, Aldsworth, Haddesworth, Houldsworthe, Haldsworthe, Howldsworthe, Houldsworthe, Haldisworth, Holdsworthe—3, 5, 15, 26, 60, 62, 68, 69, 78, 88, 92, 97, 102, 109, 110, 115, 116, 125, 136, 141, 150, 152, 153, 156, 157, 158, 162, 163, 168, 171.
Hollinbridge—91.
Hollinraku—142.
Holmes—158.
Holred, Hollered, Holrod, Holrede, Hallrede, Hollerede, Hollored—12, 13, 14, 16, 20, 175, 176 (see also Oldroyd).
Homlay—75.
Hoosan—118, 122, 125.
Hopkinson, Hobkynson, Hobkinson, Hobkyngson—14, 21, 109, 118, 161.
Hopton, Hoptonn—25, 55, 166.
Hopwoode—169.
Horner—14.
Horsfall, Horsfull—17, 156.
Horsforthe, Horsefurth, Horsfortho—27, 49, 69, 102, 106, 112, 119.
Horshaule—146, 148.
Horton—7, 172.
Hoult, Houlte—37, 69, 71, 138.
Howard—6.
Howkey—166.
Howly—82.
Howroyd, Howroyde—162, 164, 167.
Howson, Howsonn—68, 116.
Hoyle, Hoile, Hoyll—41, 43, 47, 51, 106, 142.

INDEX.

Hueden—68.
Hudeswell, 49.
Hudson, Hudsonn—15, 50, 94, 113, 152, 157.
Huett—148.
Hull—82.
Hunt—44, 97, 104, 137.
Hunter—92, 100, 132.
Huntington—161.
Hustlar—19 (*see also* Ostler.)
Hutchinson, Huchinson, Huchodson, Hutchynson, Hochynson, Huchynsone, Huchonson, Hucchinsone, Huchinsone, Huchoson, Huchason, Hucchason, Huchingson, Hintchinsonn, Hucchinssone, Hutchinsonn—2, 7, 10, 14, 15, 17, 18, 25, 26, 28, 31, 33, 36, 39, 40, 42, 51, 54, 55, 58, 61, 65, 66, 71, 73, 74, 76, 87, 90, 101, 102, 104, 115, 117, 170, 173.
Hutton—139, 141, 146, 152, 154, 158, 160, 163, 164, 167.
Hycke—73, 93.

Iles—88, 99.
Illingworthe—76.
Ingram—82.
Ingham, Ingam—137, 142, 145, 146, 148, 152, 156, 161, 166.
Ingle—70, 72.
Ingrathorpe—153.
Innes—97.
Ireland—40, 142.
Issott—88, 167.

Jackson, Jakson, Jacson, Jacksonn, Jacksons, Jackesonn, Jackeson, Jakesonn—13, 32, 38, 41, 44, 46, 48, 51, 52, 71, 73, 75, 77, 81, 84, 88, 91, 93, 94, 95, 97, 100, 104, 107, 109, 112, 115, 117, 118, 119, 120, 121, 122, 123, 124, 125, 136, 145, 146, 163, 167.
Jagger, Jaggar, Jagar, Jegger, Gagar—9, 11, 14, 15, 32, 50, 52, 53, 61, 68, 72, 76, 82, 103, 117, 124, 129, 130, 134, 136, 137, 138, 139, 140, 141, 142, 145, 149, 154, 160, 163, 169, 175.
Jallingo—110, 112.
Jeukinson—43.
Jeninge, Janyng, Janyn, Jannyns, Jannys, Janinge, Janynge, Yanyn, Genynge, Ginyngs, Ganinge—2, 3, 4, 6, 7, 9, 10, 12, 15, 18, 25, 30, 170, 172, 175.
Jepson, Jepsonn, Jepsonne, Jebsone, Gepsonn—28, 30, 50, 51, 52, 53, 56, 59, 62, 86, 87, 100, 101, 120, 153, 155, 158, 161, 164, 167, 169.
Jerison—156.
Jessuppo—120.
Johnson, Johnsonn—49, 131, 157, 160, 167, 168.
Johnston—86.
Jowet, Gowitt, Juet, Jowithe, Juwitt, Jewelthe, Jewithe, Jewith, Gowett, Jewett, Jewet—17, 20, 21, 28, 69, 80, 95, 97, 100, 101, 106, 112, 114, 116, 118, 120, 125, 127, 130, 158, 140, 176.
Joy, Joye—69, 70, 131.
Justice—162, 166.

Kaye, Kay, Cay, Caye—22, 27, 62, 69, 88, 94, 101, 102, 105, 114, 115, 116, 119, 126, 127, 131, 132, 139, 142, 151, 152, 155, 161, 166, 167.
Kaylie (*see* Keighley).
Kealing, Kealinge—70, 72.
Keighley, Kyghley, Kykley, Kighley, Kighleye, Kighlaye, Kickeley, Kythley, Kyghlay, Keighlay, Kaylie—1, 6, 35, 40, 46, 65, 87, 99, 127, 151, 156, 170.
Kellam, Kellann—78.
Kent, Keynit, Kynte, Kente—10, 16, 20, 21, 23, 35, 44, 45, 46, 48, 49, 50, 53, 55, 58, 68, 82, 84, 99, 105, 116, 122, 123, 124, 131, 134, 137, 145, 146, 151, 162, 176.
Kippas—108.

Kirke, Kyrke—39, 81, 68, 89, 90, 92, 158.
Kitchinge, Kytchin—24, 31, 171.
Kitson, Kytson, Kytison, Kitsonn, Kitsonu, Kitsono—4, 5, 6, 8, 11, 14, 17, 19, 31, 34, 38, 40, 59, 60, 62, 63, 67, 93, 91, 95, 102, 131, 137, 140, 113, 146, 151, 153, 154, 155, 157, 160, 162, 164, 171, 172, 173.
Knowles, Knowels, Knolles, Knowcks—23, 26, 31, 33, 34, 40, 48, 49, 51, 55, 59, 80, 82, 87, 88, 93, 94, 96, 97, 99, 101, 103, 111, 115, 117, 121, 154, 156, 157, 158, 159, 163, 166, 167.
Kurton—41.
Kyrkbye—74.
Kyrkman, Kyrkeman—113.
Kytchengman—21.

Lacye—66.
Lambe—54, 55, 56, 57, 63, 66, 68, 71, 72, 75, 81, 98.
Lambert—111, 165.
Lancaster—133.
Lands, Lande—107, 111.
Lanes—111.
Lange—80, 81, 82.
Langfeld, Langefield, Langefeild, Langfeilde, Langfelde, Langefielde, Langfeild, Langefeld, Lankefeld, Laughtfelde, Langefelde, Langfield—22, 52, 33, 45, 48, 49, 50, 53, 51, 57, 60, 82, 87, 95, 107, 108, 111, 147, 149, 158.
Langstar—157.
Lanscarre, Lanscare—44, 45, 46, 49, 53, 92, 99, 106, 107, 118.
Lansfearre—63.
Lasles—25.
Lastlesse—39.
Law, Lawe—39, 41, 42, 49.
Lawley—16.
Layllizar—22.
Leadbeater, Leadebeater, Ledbeater—26, 30, 31, 53, 66, 67, 68, 69, 70, 71, 72, 73, 74, 77, 86, 85, 91, 92, 94, 95, 96, 100, 111, 113, 119, 120, 121, 123, 127, 133, 138 (*see also* Lidbetter).
Leake—67, 80.
Leaver—99.
Leckwithe—82.
Ledgarde, Ledgearde—59, 124.
Lee, Ley, Le, Lea, Leye, Leigh, Leeighe, Laye—2, 3, 4, 5, 8, 9, 10, 11, 13, 14, 15, 16, 17, 18, 19, 20, 22, 23, 24, 25, 26, 27, 28, 29, 30, 31, 32, 33, 34, 35, 36, 37, 38, 39, 41, 42, 43, 45, 46, 47, 48, 49, 50, 51, 52, 53, 54, 55, 56, 57, 58, 61, 63, 64, 65, 66, 67, 69, 71, 73, 74, 75, 76, 79, 80, 81, 82, 83, 84, 85, 86, 87, 88, 89, 90, 92, 96, 97, 98, 102, 103, 104, 107, 108, 109, 113, 115, 117, 118, 121, 122, 124, 125, 127, 128, 132, 135, 136, 137, 139, 142, 144, 149, 150, 151, 152, 153, 157, 159, 160, 161, 162, 163, 164, 165, 167, 168, 169, 170, 171, 174, 175, 176.
Lepton, Leptonn—44, 53, 55.
Lewes—102.
Lidbetter—23 (*see also* Leadbeater).
Liley, Lylye—99, 146.
Limelebroughe—65.
Linley, Linlay, Lynlaye, Lynley, Lynlay—25, 44, 48, 50, 81, 105, 168.
Linthewayte, Linthwcet—115, 135, 157.
Lister, Lyster—56, 58, 59, 61, 66, 76, 107.
Littlewood, Litelwod, Litelwod, Lyttellwood, Lyttellwoode, Lyttellwoode, Lettlewood, Lyttlewoode, Lytllwood, Lytllwooll, Litlewoode, Litlewoodde, Lutllewoode, Lytellwood, Litlewood—30, 31, 32, 33, 35, 36, 37, 38, 40, 41, 44, 45, 46, 49, 52, 56, 58, 63, 67, 72, 77, 96, 123.
Liversedge, Lyversedge, Liversige, Liversidge, Lyusedge—27, 81, 120, 122, 127, 157.
Lobley, Loblcye—50, 150, 153.

viii. INDEX.

Lockwood, Lockwoode, Lockewood—43, 46, 52, 64, 75, 149.
Longley, Longeley, Longely, Longleye, Longelay, Longlay, Longlaye, Longeleye, Langeleye—1, 4, 7, 10, 13, 18, 19, 21, 22, 24, 38, 40, 43, 47, 53, 54, 66, 76, 82, 83, 84, 88, 90, 93, 95, 101, 102, 104, 106, 109, 111, 112, 113, 116, 121, 126, 131, 137, 138, 147, 152, 168, 169, 170, 173.
Lord, Loord—39, 40, 41.
Ludge—134.
Lumble—38.
Lunde—29.
Lyney—13.
Lynslay—110.

Mairn—163.
Makinder—161.
Mallinson, Malinson, Mallinsonn—26, 88, 91, 100, 110.
Man, 73, 76.
Mankingeholis—176.
Mansfeld, Mansfeld, Mawnsfeld, Monnsefeld, Monsfield, Monsfeild, Mannsfeld, Maunsfelde, Mounsfeld, Mannsfelde, Mansfelde, Maunsfielde, Maunsfeilde, Mansfeilde, Monsfeld, Mannsfield, Mannsfeild, Maunsfeld, Mansfeild—1, 20, 28, 29, 30, 31, 32, 34, 43, 46, 47, 52, 56, 59, 63, 67, 69, 73, 74, 75, 77, 83, 88, 89, 92, 110, 113, 116, 120, 124, 125, 126, 128, 157, 161, 165, 167, 170, 172.
Marcer—112.
Mardlay—79.
Margaret—175.
Mariam—164.
Marsh, Marshe—24, 32, 36, 38, 48, 150.
Marshall, Murshalls—26, 27, 47, 57, 59, 60, 61, 63, 66, 70, 73, 74, 78, 82, 86, 87, 88, 89, 90, 94, 99, 101, 104, 106, 108, 110, 114, 119, 124, 135, 152, 164.
Marstin—161.
Mason, Masonn, Masorn, Masson—34, 67.
Massoley, Maid of Mr. Rowland Owans, a washwoman —47.
Mateson, Matson—150, 152, 154, 159, 161, 165, 168.
Mathew, Mathewe—19, 24.
Mathewgill—103.
Matling—2.
Maule, Mawde, Maud—5, 31, 45, 47, 48, 55, 65, 88, 93, 99, 102, 103, 105, 113, 117, 122, 125, 126, 137, 154.
Maukuycholis—19.
Maulcell—20 (see also Monssell).
Maw, Mawe—57, 77, 79, 85, 91, 92, 97.
Mawhume—170.
Mayhall—60.
Medley, Medlaye, Medlay, Medleye, Madley—1, 10, 11, 12, 13, 15, 16, 17, 18, 19, 21, 25, 43, 45, 48, 49, 50, 60, 75, 79, 81, 86, 91, 96, 99, 102, 109, 110, 116, 119, 128, 139, 141, 155, 161, 170, 172, 173, 174.
Megson, Megsonn, Megsom—13, 50, 153, 154, 155, 160, 162.
Mekindale, Meakendall—111, 118, 123, 127, 132.
Metcalfe, Mentcalfe—41, 52, 57, 100, 163.
Methley, Methlay, Metheley—2, 4, 5, 6, 7, 8, 9, 10, 172, 173.
Middlebrooke, Midlebrouke—88, 94, 97, 109, 112, 114, 116, 117, 121.
Midllebroughe, Middbrowe, Middlbrough, Midleboroughe, Middlebroughe, Middlebrough—49, 52, 55, 57, 60, 61, 64, 67, 68, 73, 77, 78, 81, 84, 92, 93, 101, 115, 121, 122, 124, 125, 128, 131, 132, 153, 155.
Middlton, Midltonn- 58, 145.
Midwwde—129.
Milner, Mylner, Myllners, Myllnor, Myl'ner, Millner— 25, 40, 41, 68, 70, 73, 85, 97, 98, 99, 102, 109, 114, 115, 117, 120, 123, 125, 127, 128, 130, 131, 136, 157, 139, 143, 147, 157, 160, 162.

Milnes, Mylnes, Mylne, Millnes, Millns—8, 25, 26, 27, 29, 35, 42, 48, 49, 51, 52, 53, 55, 57, 59, 60, 61, 61, 66, 68, 71, 72, 75, 76, 77, 79, 80, 88, 109, 112, 113, 115, 118, 126, 131, 135, 131, 138, 143, 144, 150, 151, 153, 155, 157, 158, 163, 167, 168, 174.
Mitchell, Mychell, Mitchill, Michell—44, 47, 48, 55, 60, 61, 62, 73, 74, 75, 77, 80, 81, 83, 84, 87, 88, 89, 91, 94, 98, 102, 104, 106, 108, 114, 117, 121, 122, 123, 128, 131, 137, 147, 153, 158, 160, 161, 165, 168.
Mitton, Mytton, Mittonn—81, 95, 144.
Molingdale—61.
Monssell, Mawnsell, Mavnsell—6, 21, 25 (see also Maulcell).
Moore, More—35, 36, 39, 45, 50, 54, 58, 72, 74, 83, 95, 97, 102, 104, 106, 132, 146, 155.
Moorehouse, Morehowse, Morehouse, Moros—79, 81, 84, 87, 151, 155, 157, 161, 163.
Morebye—86.
Morewood—156.
Morris, Morise, Morrice, Merishe, Moris—60, 102, 104, 109, 113, 119, 124, 128, 160, 161, 164.
Mortinnar—131, 154.
Mortonn—55, 92.
Morvell, Morvill—19, 20, 28, 176.
Mosco—160.
Mosseley, Mosleyes—48, 53, 169.
Moulson, Mowlsonn—114, 167.
Mowbraye—53, 79.
Moxon—145.
Moyens—159.
Moyses—115.
Mullion—148.
Murton—109.
Musgrave, Musgrav, Musgreve, Mvsgreve, Musgrayve, Musgreave, Musgreaive, Musgraive—5, 16, 18, 20, 37, 38, 43, 44, 57, 61, 67, 70, 71, 72, 76, 80, 85, 91, 98, 105, 108, 109, 111, 114, 117, 118, 122, 127, 128, 134, 136, 137, 140, 145, 147, 148, 149, 151, 153, 156, 159, 161, 165, 166, 168, 169, 171, 176.
Mylls—22, 23.
Myres—136, 137, 159.
Myrfeild—48.

Nabbe—113.
Naylor, Nailer, Nayler, Naller, Naler, Nayller, Neyler, Nailor, Nalor, Naylers—2, 4, 5, 9, 10, 11, 12, 13, 14, 16, 17, 18, 19, 20, 21, 22, 23, 24, 25, 26, 27, 28, 29, 31, 32, 33, 34, 35, 36, 38, 39, 40, 42, 43, 44, 45, 46, 47, 48, 49, 50, 51, 52, 53, 54, 55, 56, 57, 58, 60, 61, 62, 63, 65, 66, 67, 68, 70, 71, 72, 73, 74, 75, 77, 78, 79, 81, 82, 83, 86, 88, 90, 93, 94, 96, 99, 100, 102, 103, 104, 109, 110, 112, 113, 114, 115, 116, 117, 118, 119, 120, 121, 122, 125, 126, 127, 128, 130, 133, 133, 134, 135, 136, 137, 140, 141, 142, 147, 149, 152, 153, 154, 156, 157, 159, 160, 161, 162, 166, 167, 170, 171, 174, 175, 176.
Neilson—107.
Nelson—150, 153.
Nelthorpe, Nelthorppe, Nelthorp—132, 136, 144, 160, 164, 165, 167.
Netherwoode—107.
Nettleton, Netleton, Nettylone, Neteyllton, Nytylton, Nettylton, Nettiltone, Netteltton, Nettletonn, Nettletone, Nettillton—1, 8, 16, 20, 21, 26, 28, 30, 32, 34, 35, 37, 38, 40, 43, 53, 57, 59, 60, 61, 62, 63, 67, 69, 71, 72, 74, 78, 80, 82, 85, 86, 88, 90, 91, 93, 97, 98, 103, 104, 106, 108, 110, 113, 114, 116, 117, 120, 124, 126, 128, 130, 131, 132, 133, 151, 155, 156, 157, 158, 159, 110, 141, 142, 143, 145, 146, 147, 148, 151, 153, 155, 156, 157, 158, 159, 161, 164, 166, 167, 169, 170, 174.
Newsome, Newsom, Newsome, Newson—35, 37, 41, 44, 48, 64, 66, 68, 69, 71, 74, 75, 77, 81, 84, 89, 91, 94, 95, 98, 100, 104, 107, 109, 112, 115, 117, 118, 119, 120,

INDEX.

121, 122, 123, 124, 125, 127, 128, 129, 133, 135, 136, 140, 143, 144, 145, 146, 155, 157, 159, 160, 163, 164, 165, 167, 168, 169.
Nicolls—53, 56.
Nicolson—45.
Norcliffe—90, 98.
Norfolke—72. 162, 165.
North, Norythes, Northe—13, 28, 99, 102, 130, 158, 165.
Northoppe—25.
Norton, Nortonn—56, 57. 59, 64. 83.
Nowell, Nowwell, Nowill, Newell—4, 5, 7, 9, 10, 11, 13, 14, 15, 17, 19, 20, 30, 33, 43, 45, 50, 53, 54, 55, 56, 57, 78, 86, 100, 109, 112, 121, 125, 131, 136, 141, 147, 151, 153, 154, 155, 157, 162, 171, 172, 175, 176.
Nullic—128.
Nussye—115.
Nutt—49.
Nuttie—128.

Oates, Oits, Otes, Ootes, Octes—15, 24, 25, 58, 65, 67, 119, 120, 165.
Oddy—149.
Oggell—150.
Oglethorpe, Oglethorppe—70, 126.
Oiles—34.
Oke—19.
Okerd (*see* Acrod).
Oldroyd, Olred, Olerede, Oylerhlade, Wholroyde, Olleroyd, Olleroid, Ollredd, Ollerred, Oldrede, Olrood, Oldrood, Olredd, Oldrel, Oldreed, Oldroode, Ouldroyd, Ouldrood, Oulroyd, Ouldroyde, Ouldroide, Owldroyd, Owldroide, Ollerede, Oldroid, Ouldred, Owlroyd, Oldroyde, Oldroide, Ollerrede, Olered, Olroid, Olroyd, Ouldroid, Owldroid, Owlderoide, Ollered (*see also* Holred)—4, 6, 8, 9, 10, 11, 14, 19, 20, 21, 22, 23, 24, 25, 26, 27, 30, 31, 32, 33, 35, 37, 38, 40, 42, 43, 44, 45, 46, 47, 48, 49, 50, 51, 52, 54, 55, 56, 57, 58, 59, 60, 61, 62, 63, 64, 65, 66, 67, 70, 71, 72, 73, 74, 75, 76, 77, 78, 79, 80, 81, 82, 84, 85, 86, 87, 88, 89, 90, 91, 92, 96, 98, 101, 104, 105, 106, 107, 108, 109, 110, 114, 115, 117, 118, 120, 122, 123, 124, 125, 126, 127, 129, 131, 132, 133, 134, 135, 136, 137, 138, 141, 143, 144, 147, 149, 150, 151, 152, 154, 155, 156, 157, 159, 161, 164, 165, 166, 168, 172, 174, 176.
Osburne—45, 120.
Osther, Ustler—168 (*see also* Rustlar).
Otley, Otlaye, Ottley—62, 107, 110, 112, 116, 117, 143, 162, 164, 166.
Ouldfeild—71.
Owen, Owans—34, 36, 38, 41, 42, 45, 47.
Oxley, Oxelay, Oxelaye, Oxeley—2, 5, 6, 72, 73, 76, 106, 109, 113, 163, 166, 168, 171, 172.

Paget—167, 168.
Parker, Packer, Parkers, Parkar, Perker—37, 38, 42, 46, 47, 48, 49, 52, 55, 61, 65, 70, 80, 96, 97, 101, 109, 111, 114, 115, 116, 121, 127, 130, 131, 137, 144, 145, 146, 148, 149, 150, 151, 154, 155, 156, 159, 160, 163, 165, 168.
Parkinsonn—93.
Parsley—168.
Pasley, Pasleye, Paslaye—50, 97, 98, 103, 115, 136, 139, 142, 143, 117.
Patricke—71.
Paule—105.
Peace, Pees, Pese, Paee, Peaze, Pease—5, 7, 9, 10, 13, 15, 16, 17, 28, 30, 31, 33, 34, 36, 37, 40, 43, 44, 52, 53, 56, 57, 59, 60, 62, 63, 65, 66, 69, 71, 72, 73, 77, 78, 81, 84, 85, 101, 105, 107, 111, 116, 118, 121, 123, 126, 127, 132, 133, 137, 153, 156, 158, 160, 162, 166, 167, 168, 171, 173, 175.

Peaker, Pekar—5, 19, 33, 35, 38, 49, 54, 61, 124, 130, 136, 142, 149, 155, 168.
Pearson, Pearsonn, Peirson, Pierson—62, 105, 115, 116, 123, 125, 127, 130, 132, 136, 141, 147, 160, 165.
Peater—152.
Pell—65, 88.
Phillips, Phylype, Philipe, Phylipe, Phillippe, Phillipps, Phillipp, Phillip, Phyllip, Philip, Philyppe, Phillipe—27, 31, 35, 37, 38, 41, 46, 48, 55, 57, 59, 66, 70, 73, 74, 75, 76, 79, 80, 82, 83, 84, 85, 87, 89, 91, 92, 95, 98, 108, 115, 117, 119, 120, 121, 125, 128, 129, 131, 135, 137, 144, 145, 146, 147, 148, 149, 151, 153, 155, 156, 158, 160, 161, 163, 165, 167, 168.
Pickard, Pyckard, Pecarde, Peykerd, Pyckerd, Pyckerde, Pickarde, Pickhard, Pickerd, Pickerde, Pickearde, Pickeard—19, 24, 34, 35, 37, 39, 41, 44, 47, 49, 52, 59, 60, 62, 70, 72, 74, 75, 76, 78, 79, 84, 85, 86, 88, 89, 91, 93, 95, 96, 97, 98, 100, 102, 103, 107, 110, 111, 112, 114, 116, 118, 121, 122, 123, 124, 128, 129, 130, 132, 135, 137, 138, 139, 140, 143, 144, 145, 146, 147, 148, 149, 150, 152, 153, 155, 156, 158, 159, 160, 162, 165, 166, 175.
Pickering, Pyckerrynge, Pyckaryng, Pickeringe, Pickeryng, Pyckeringe, Pickringe—12, 16, 26, 27, 29, 31, 33, 35, 37, 38, 40, 41, 42, 43, 44, 46, 48, 51, 68, 69, 71, 76, 94, 104, 107, 110, 111, 120, 130, 132, 134, 138, 154, 156, 165.
Pickersgill, Piekarsgill—42, 49, 56, 111, 112.
Pighells—56, 57, 59, 64, 67, 68, 70, 75, 80, 85, 90, 113, 116.
Piper—64.
Pollard, Pollerd, Pollerde, Pollarde—18, 53, 60, 74, 76, 99, 103, 131, 148, 154, 155, 158, 167.
Pomlcht—14.
Pook—25
Poolay—54.
Poole—140, 144, 148, 152.
Popleton—150.
Poplewell—113, 115.
Porsonn—88.
Powell—35.
Pratt, Prat—131, 157, 158, 162, 165.
Preist—159.
Priestley, Priestlaye, Preistlaye, Preistley, Preestley, Priestlay—47, 51, 52, 113, 158, 159, 161, 165, 169.
Prince—28.
Proctor, Procter—97, 106.

Quill—26.

Radcliffe—111, 163.
Radleye—80.
Rafe—109.
Ramsden, Ramesden, Ramsdine, Ramesdenn, Ranesdenn, Ramseden, Ramsdeyne, Ramedeyne, Ramesdeine—2, 3, 7, 8, 9, 14, 29, 34, 39, 45, 48, 49, 61, 68, 100, 143, 154, 170, 173, 175.
Ratcliffe, Ratcliff—41, 50.
Rawnslaye, Ronesley, Raunsley, Raunseley, Raundesley 28, 37, 39, 46.
Rawson, Rawsonn, Rosen, Rawsonne—2, 23, 24, 26, 59, 65, 67, 72, 73, 74, 75, 77, 82, 107, 110, 121, 156, 171.
Rayner, Raner, Reynor, Raynor—6, 14, 25, 41, 61, 62, 63, 65, 86, 88, 90, 95, 100, 110, 122, 130, 140, 142, 162, 163, 171, 172.
Renoulde—57, 93.
Rhodes, Royds, Roodes, Rodes, Roades, Roods, Roids, Roydes, Roides, Roydess—4, 42, 45, 48, 51, 52, 54, 55, 57, 59, 60, 61, 62, 64, 68, 70, 71, 72, 73, 74, 75, 77, 78, 81, 85, 86, 87, 88, 89, 91, 94, 95, 96, 97, 101, 104, 108, 110, 111, 114, 116, 117, 120, 124, 124, 125, 126, 128, 129, 130, 131, 133, 134, 135, 136, 137, 138, 140, 142, 144, 145, 146, 147, 149, 151, 152, 153, 154,

x. INDEX.

155, 156, 157, 158, 159, 160, 161, 162, 164, 168.
Richardson, Rychardson, Ryerson, Ricson, Richadson, Rychardsonn, Rycharson, Richinson, Richison, Richardsone, Rychardsone, Rychardesonne, Richardsoun, Richardinson—1, 2, 4, 5, 7, 8, 9, 10, 12, 13, 14, 15, 16, 18, 19, 22, 23, 25, 35, 40, 41, 42, 43, 44, 45, 47, 48, 49, 50, 52, 53, 54, 55, 56, 57, 61, 64, 70, 71, 74, 79, 83, 84, 88, 90, 92, 93, 95, 100, 102, 105, 106, 109, 111, 114, 128, 131, 137, 139, 141, 142, 143, 144, 148, 149, 150, 151, 152, 154, 155, 158, 159, 162, 166, 170, 171, 173, 174, 176.
Richmonde, Rychemend, Rychmond—44, 47, 48, 52, 56, 64, 77.
Riddesdell, Riddessdell—30.
Riddlesden, Ridlesden, Ridlsden, Ridlesdenn, Ridlsdenn—61, 84, 100, 103, 141, 147, 154, 155, 157, 161, 165.
Riplyn—79.
Ritson—157.
Robert, Robarte, Roberd, Robard, Robt, Robart—2, 4, 5, 130, 152, 155, 169, 170, 171.
Robinson, Robynson, Robensone, Robinsone, Robinsonn, Robingesone, Robynsone, Robyson, Robynesone—2, 3, 5, 6, 7, 8, 9, 10, 11, 13, 17, 20, 23, 24, 25, 27, 28, 30, 32, 33, 34, 36, 37, 38, 39, 40, 41, 42, 44, 45, 47, 48, 49, 50, 52, 53, 54, 55, 56, 57, 59, 60, 63, 65, 66, 67, 68, 70, 71, 74, 75, 77, 78, 79, 80, 82, 83, 84, 85, 86, 87, 88, 89, 90, 91, 92, 93, 94, 95, 96, 97, 98, 99, 100, 101, 102, 103, 104, 105, 106, 107, 110, 111, 112, 113, 114, 115, 116, 117, 118, 119, 120, 121, 122, 124, 125, 127, 128, 129, 130, 132, 135, 136, 137, 139, 141, 142, 144, 145, 148, 151, 152, 153, 154, 155, 156, 157, 158, 159, 160, 161, 162, 163, 164, 166, 168, 171, 172, 173, 174, 175, 176.
Rockley—12.
Rodley, Rodlaye, Rodlay, Rodleye—45, 46, 49, 59, 60, 75, 76, 77, 84, 89, 90, 97, 98, 125, 127, 129, 133, 136, 140.
Roebucke, Robucke, Robacke, Roobucke—60, 65, 66, 73, 101, 104, 118, 121, 125, 127, 133, 135, 136, 142, 147, 153.
Roger—27.
Rolland—78.
Romer—5.
Roper—38.
Rosell—5.
Roulles—18.
Rouse, Rowse—48, 51, 53, 54, 57, 59, 64, 65, 67, 73, 76, 135, 140, 144, 145, 149, 154, 157.
Rowbotham, Roebothom—23, 85.
Rudd, Rude, Rud—19, 20, 21, 24, 26, 176.
Rushforthe—46.
Rydall, Riddall, Reedall—35, 44, 109.
Ryding—46.
Rylay, Ryghlay—40, 70.

Sagar—10, 130, 175.
Sallett—126, 129.
Saltinstall, Saltingstall—71, 130.
Sampson, 168.
Sandell, 30.
Sanderson, Sanderson—57, 158, 160, 164, 169.
Sandie—39.
Sanscule—97.
Saville, Savell, Sayvell, Savyll, Sayvill, Savill—2, 6, 8, 18, 21, 24, 43, 48, 49, 51, 52, 53, 57, 68, 111, 128, 141, 142, 153, 168, 170.
Saxton, Saxtonn, Saxstone, Saston—9, 10, 11, 14, 16, 17, 18, 22, 25, 27, 30, 36, 37, 39, 41, 43, 44, 45, 46, 47, 48, 49, 54, 57, 60, 66, 68, 72, 73, 75, 77, 78, 80, 81, 84, 85, 89, 90, 91, 92, 100, 101, 102, 105, 107, 109, 112, 114, 117, 118, 123, 124, 129, 136, 143, 149, 152, 155, 157, 160, 161, 162, 166, 174.
Sayer—52.

Scafe, Schayf, Scayve, Scayfe, Chayfte—20, 22, 23, 26, 35.
Scarbroughe—171.
Scavernelcy—172.
Schupilthorpe—19.
Schelefichl, Scolfelde, Scolofeld, Scolfeld, Scolffelde, Scollfeild, Scolfield, Scolefeilde, Scolefeild, Cholfeld—4, 10, 11, 12, 13, 16, 18, 42, 65, 68, 69, 70, 73, 76, 104, 140, 150, 157, 165.
Scolar—2.
Scooles—66.
Scorer, Scorar, Scoorer, Scurrer—71, 76, 83, 128, 130, 165.
Scotson—162.
Scott, Scot, Scote, Skott, Scotte, Skot—5, 6, 12, 17, 22, 23, 28, 45, 54, 58, 64, 138, 158, 160, 171, 172.
Scriven—80.
Scryvtheley?—175.
Seade—10.
Secker, Sekar, Seccar, Seker, Seckar, Seckers, Sacker, Sacor, Seiker, Sick, Sekker—2, 3, 7, 11, 12, 14, 15, 16, 18, 19, 20, 21, 22, 23, 24, 25, 26, 27, 28, 29, 30, 31, 33, 35, 36, 38, 39, 41, 52, 54, 55, 57, 58, 63. 66, 67, 70, 71, 72, 74, 75, 76, 77, 79, 80, 83, 84, 86, 88, 89, 92, 94, 96, 97, 104, 105, 107, 110, 111, 115, 116, 122, 126, 136, 138, 144, 146, 147, 153, 157, 163, 167, 170, 172, 173, 176.
Sharp, Sharpe—4, 25, 42, 44, 48, 51, 53, 59, 80, 81, 85, 90, 97, 103, 105, 108, 111, 137, 139, 144, 146, 148, 152, 157, 155, 162, 165, 166, 168, 169.
Sharphouse, Scharpus, Sharpus, Sharppus, Sharphowse, Sharpehouse, Sharpous, Sharpehowse, Sharpehus—4, 20, 21, 23, 24, 26, 27, 28, 36, 40, 41, 43, 45, 46, 47, 48, 51, 54, 56, 58, 64, 66, 68, 70, 81, 82, 85, 86, 89, 91, 92, 96, 99, 102, 109, 121, 122, 123, 148, 162, 163, 176.
Sharpulls, Sharpuls, Scharpule—10, 11, 21.
Shaw, Shawe—27, 104.
Sheard, Shearde—38, 61, 142, 148, 150, 151, 152, 153, 157, 161, 162, 164, 165, 166.
Sheffield, Sheafelde, Sheafeilde, Shefeild—48, 114, 134, 163.
Shemelde, Shymeld—132, 167.
Shepherd, Schepherde, Shapherde, Shepparde, Shoppard, Shepperd, Shepheard, Shopperde, Shepard—14, 19, 30, 31, 33, 34, 36, 39, 41, 42, 46, 48, 52, 57, 64, 67, 68, 69, 70, 71, 72, 73, 76, 77, 79, 81, 85, 86, 87, 88, 91, 92, 94, 95, 96, 98, 100, 102, 109, 111, 113, 115, 117, 118, 119, 120, 121, 122, 123, 124, 127, 133, 166.
Shepley, Shepplay, Sheppleye, Shepleye, Sheplay—59, 60, 63, 69, 70, 73, 76, 77, 89, 93, 94, 108, 116, 124, 128, 130, 142, 150, 155, 163.
Shillito, Shillitoe—72, 168.
Shirley, Shirley, Sherlay, Shirllcy, Shyrley, Sherlaye—32, 37, 38, 39, 43, 46, 47, 48.
Shutleworthe, Shutleworthe—46, 47.
Sill—138.
Simpson, Symson, Symnpson, Sympsons, Symsono—7, 8, 16, 61, 136, 140, 145, 150, 154, 155, 157, 165, 197, 173, 174.
Skidlingthorpe—38.
Slack, Slake, Slak, Slacke, Sllacke—14, 16, 17, 18, 22, 24, 33, 36, 44, 45, 47, 49, 52, 54, 55, 56, 58, 63, 64, 75, 77, 92, 93, 101, 103, 104, 106, 107, 113, 143.
Slade—59, 78, 82, 84, 85, 89, 91, 117.
Sladin, Slalenn—61, 134.
Slater, Slator—50, 53, 63, 68, 72.
Sleth—22.
Smith, Smeth, Smyth, Smythe, Smithe—2, 4, 8, 9, 10, 12, 13, 14, 15, 16, 17, 18, 20, 21, 22, 26, 30, 32, 34, 36, 37, 39, 40, 45, 47, 48, 50, 51, 52, 53, 54, 55, 57, 59, 63, 64, 65, 66, 68, 69, 73, 75, 77, 81, 82, 83, 84,

INDEX. xi.

85, 86, 90, 91, 93, 96, 101, 102, 103, 105, 106, 108, 110, 111, 113, 115, 118, 120, 121, 123, 125, 126, 128, 137, 150, 155, 159, 163, 166, 167, 171, 175, 176.
Smithson, Smithsonn, Smitheson, Smythson, Smithesonn—50, 51, 57, 65, 66, 67, 96, 100, 106, 112, 113, 117, 120, 121, 126, 131, 133, 145, 146, 156, 160.
Smyrthett—97.
Snawden—131.
Somer, Somare—121, 121.
Somestar—81.
Soniar, Soniarde, Sunyer, Sunnyart, Sunycar, Sunnyeare, Sonyerd, Sonycar, Sonyare, Synate, Sonnyar, Sonnyare, Sonyar, Sonnyarre, Soniare, Sonier, Sunyeare, Sonyere, Sonyeare—21, 23, 28, 32, 41, 42, 44, 45, 49, 51, 52, 53, 54, 55, 57, 58, 63, 67, 68, 69, 74, 76, 77, 78, 79, 81, 82, 84, 86, 90, 94, 97, 99, 109, 113, 116, 117, 118, 119, 121, 122, 124, 125, 126, 127, 129, 131, 132, 133, 134, 137, 138, 140, 141, 143, 144, 145, 146, 147, 148, 149, 150, 151, 153, 154, 156, 158, 159, 162, 163, 164, 166, 167, 168, 169.
Soothill, Sottell, Sothill—2, 3, 66, 133, 157.
Southe—52.
Soward—47.
Sowood—41.
Speight, Spight, Spigldt, Speyght, Speght, Spyght, Speighte, Spyghti—1, 2, 3, 4, 5, 7, 8, 10, 12, 13, 14, 15, 16, 17, 18, 19, 20, 22, 23, 24, 26, 27, 28, 29, 30, 31, 32, 33, 34, 35, 36, 37, 38, 39, 40, 41, 42, 43, 44, 45, 46, 47, 48, 49, 51, 52, 53, 55, 56, 58, 59, 60, 61, 63, 64, 65, 66, 67, 68, 69, 70, 71, 72, 73, 76, 77, 78, 79, 80, 81, 83, 84, 86, 87, 88, 89, 91, 92, 93, 95, 97, 98, 100, 101, 103, 104, 105, 106, 107, 108, 109, 110, 111, 112, 113, 114, 116, 117, 118, 119, 120, 121, 122, 124, 125, 126, 127, 128, 129, 130, 131, 132, 133, 134, 135, 136, 137, 138, 139, 140, 142, 143, 145, 147, 149, 152, 153, 154, 155, 156, 157, 158, 159, 160, 161, 162, 163, 164, 165, 166, 167, 168, 171, 173, 175, 176.
Spenceleye—113.
Spurr, Spurre, Spur—61, 62, 100, 101, 105, 113, 151, 162, 163, 164, 166, 167, 168.
Spyvie, Spibey—24, 169.
Stable—98.
Staforthe—13.
Stanlaye, Standley—16, 114.
Stanninge—43.
Stansfield, Stansfeld, Stansfeild, Stansffelde, Stansfeible, Stannesfeld, Stannefeld, Stansfelde, Stansfeilde—16, 17, 18, 20, 25, 26, 40, 44, 45, 47, 65, 78, 79, 81, 83, 88, 93, 100, 107, 108, 111, 137, 139, 144, 146, 148, 152, 153, 154, 155, 176.
Stapleton, Stapletonn, Stappleton—96, 100, 105, 110, 115, 121, 126, 133, 138, 140, 156, 159, 160, 162, 166.
Starbrowghtt—5.
Stawnay—6.
Staynecliffe—69, 70, 72, 95.
Stead, Stede, Sted, Steid, Steade, Steede—2, 6, 7, 9, 13, 24, 33, 40, 44, 48, 49, 52, 60, 93, 111, 134, 136, 137, 140, 145, 146, 148, 153, 157, 158, 160, 161, 162, 165, 167, 168, 170, 172, 174.
Stephenson, Stevensonn—53, 137.
Sterkey—12.
Stirke—123, 125, 139, 148, 167.
Stirte—129, 130.
Stocks, Stockes, Stocke—25, 27, 29, 31, 32, 35, 60, 61, 102, 148, 150.
Storye—35, 35, 46.
Stott, Stotte—16, 25.
Street—155.
Stringer, Strynger, Stringar—24, 32, 159.
Stubley, Stublaye, Stubleye—16, 110, 112, 113, 116, 147, 154, 162.
Stuythley—9.
Sugden, Sugdenn—62, 103, 118, 136, 138, 139, 140, 142,

146, 150, 160, 161.
Sunderland—114, 146, 157.
Swallow, Swallowe—8, 11, 34, 108, 174.
Swifte, Swyfte—117, 151.
Swynden—87.
Sydall—51.
Sykes, Syke, Sikes, Syk, Syks, Sickes, Sckes—2, 3, 4, 5, 6, 8, 11, 14, 15, 16, 18, 20, 21, 24, 26, 27, 32, 34, 35, 37, 39, 41, 43, 45, 50, 54, 56, 72, 74, 77, 87, 93, 102, 108, 134, 137, 139, 141, 143, 146, 147, 148, 170, 171, 172, 174, 176.
Sylleswyck—24.
Symme—54.

Tattersall, Tattarsall—8, 60, 101, 109, 112, 114, 117, 122, 129, 142, 173.
Taylor, Tailver, Taylver, Taylyar, Talyer, Talyere, Tayllyer, Tayllyer, Tayller, Tailier, Taylier, Talier, Talior, Talors, Tayler, Tailor, Taler, Tailler, Tailyor—2, 3, 4, 6, 7, 8, 9, 11, 13, 14, 15, 16, 17, 18, 21, 23, 28, 33, 36, 40, 44, 45, 46, 49, 51, 53, 54, 57, 61, 63, 64, 70, 73, 74, 75, 79, 81, 84, 88, 92, 93, 99, 106, 108, 111, 117, 122, 128, 133, 134, 139, 141, 147, 151, 153, 154, 155, 156, 158, 159, 163, 164, 165, 166, 167, 168, 169, 172, 173, 174, 175.
Tebb, Tebbe—60, 63, 64, 117, 133.
Tempest, Tempes—6, 11, 12, 15, 17, 172.
Tenannte, Tenand, Tennand, Tenande—32, 116, 156, 158, 168.
Terry, Tirrye, Terrie, Terrye—59, 61, 70, 71, 73, 77, 82, 87, 92, 99, 100, 105, 106, 122, 123, 127, 133, 134, 135, 138, 139, 141, 143, 145, 146, 148, 151, 152, 154, 157, 158, 161, 163, 166, 169.
Tetley—169.
Thomas—56.
Thomson, Tomsone, Tomison, Tompsonn, Thompsonn, Tomlsonn, Tomsonn, Tompsonn, Tomsons, Thomsonn, Thompsone—1, 2, 3, 4, 5, 7, 9, 10, 11, 12, 13, 16, 17, 19, 20, 21, 22, 24, 25, 28, 30, 32, 33, 34, 36, 39, 41, 43, 44, 50, 54, 56, 60, 63, 65, 76, 77, 78, 79, 80, 85, 87, 89, 97, 98, 100, 101, 102, 106, 110, 114, 119, 120, 124, 128, 131, 134, 139, 140, 142, 144, 145, 146, 153, 154, 159, 160, 165, 168, 170, 171, 172, 173, 174.
Thornes, Thournes—7, 51, 52, 53, 56, 57, 59, 60, 62, 63, 64, 65, 69, 70, 71, 73, 75, 76, 79, 80, 85, 96, 112, 116, 117, 119, 120, 125, 126, 130, 131, 134, 135, 136, 137, 140, 148, 151, 152, 154, 160, 165, 172.
Thornton, Thorneton—37, 99, 107, 114, 119, 121, 136, 150, 156.
Thorpe, Thorppe, Tharpe—11, 58, 59, 63, 66, 67, 69, 73, 74, 76, 77, 82, 86, 98, 101, 102, 106, 116, 124, 133, 141, 142, 146, 154, 157.
Threapland, Threaplande, Threpeland, Threapeland—30, 36, 44, 71, 79, 87.
Tillye—114, 120.
Tilson, Tilsonn—60, 61, 97, 102, 108, 109, 112, 115, 124, 125, 126, 127, 129, 134, 139, 158, 164, 166, 167.
Tingle, Tyngle, Thyngyll—8, 12, 86.
Tobby—30.
Todde—78, 107.
Tolson, Tuson, Toulsonn, Towlson, Towlsonn, Towleson, Toulieson, Toulson—13, 14, 15, 61, 81, 86, 91, 95, 100, 105, 111, 116, 120, 124, 138, 140, 141, 143, 145, 146, 147, 151, 152, 155, 156, 159, 164, 169.
Tomlinson, Tomlinsonn, Tomlison—54, 102, 103, 156, 158.
Tonge—142, 146, 150.
Toothchill, Toithyll—10.
Topcliffe—97.
Tor pod—26.
Totte—21.
Tottie—29, 136.
Tonlinge—134.

INDEX.

Towne—167.
Townend, Townend, Townende, Towneend, Towneende, Townesnd—2, 5, 7, 8, 9, 11, 14, 17, 53, 59, 84, 86, 88, 91, 98, 100, 103, 115, 116, 119, 123, 126, 129, 130, 131, 157, 159, 162, 171, 174, 175.
Truelove—98, 99, 138, 139, 158, 160, 163, 164, 166.
Tryar—115.
Turner—78, 151, 160.
Turpen, Tyrpen—83, 90.
Turton—1, 170.
Tyas, Tyes, Tyese, Tyase, Tins, Tyass, Tyar—3, 5, 7, 9, 11, 12, 14, 15, 17, 19, 20, 21, 23, 43, 50, 51, 54, 58, 64, 67, 68, 69, 71, 73, 78, 82, 85, 89, 91, 92, 105, 144, 171, 173, 175, 176.
Tyngelay—174.

Udall (*see* Yudall).
Unbye—31.
Usley, Usleye, Uslye—149, 150, 152, 153, 154.
Ustler (*see* Oatler).

Vernon, Varnon—51, 52, 53, 54, 55, 56.
Vicars—21.

Wade, Wayd, Waide, Wayde—4, 12, 14, 15, 16, 19, 20, 22, 29, 32, 35, 36, 42, 43, 44, 45, 46, 47, 48, 49, 52, 56, 60, 73, 75, 76, 77, 78, 79, 80, 81, 82, 83, 87, 91, 94, 96, 97, 100, 113, 118, 120, 124, 149, 150, 155, 156, 157, 161, 166, 176.
Wadsworth, Wadesworth—42, 119.
Waintworth—159.
Walkedon, Walkden—140, 141, 145, 146.
Walker, Walkar, Walcar, Walcare, Walkars, Wallker, Walkes—1, 2, 3, 5, 7, 9, 10, 11, 12, 13, 15, 16, 17, 18, 19, 20, 21, 23, 24, 25, 26, 27, 28, 29, 30, 31, 32, 33, 34, 35, 36, 37, 39, 40, 41, 43, 44, 46, 47, 48, 49, 50, 51, 52, 53, 54, 55, 56, 57, 60, 64, 65, 69, 71, 72, 73, 74, 76, 78, 79, 82, 83, 87, 89, 90, 91, 93, 94, 101, 107, 110, 111, 112, 113, 116, 117, 118, 119, 120, 121, 122, 126, 127, 128, 129, 131, 132, 133, 134, 135, 136, 137, 138, 139, 140, 142, 143, 145, 148, 151, 153, 155, 156, 157, 158, 160, 162, 163, 165, 168, 170, 171, 173, 174, 175, 176.
Wallis—12.
Walshe—122, 168.
Walshaw, Walshaie, Walshoye, Wallshay, Welshey, Walshawe, Walshay, Walshma—25, 27, 44, 40, 48, 51, 52, 53, 65, 161, 165, 166.
Walton, Waltone, Waltonn—7, 11, 16, 46, 74, 90, 106, 119, 120, 122, 123, 131, 132, 173.
Wamsley, Wamesley, Wameslaye—4, 50, 53, 56, 63, 92.
Ward, Warde—31, 48, 50, 74, 113, 122, 130, 144, 175.
Warcinge—144.
Warnbie—123.
Warren—46, 55
Waterhouse, Watterhouse, Waterhowse, Watteras—37, 40, 41, 42, 43, 52, 70, 107, 113, 168.
Watson, Watsone—41, 153, 157, 167, 169.
Waughe—110.
Waynwrighte, Waynewright—97, 99, 105, 111.
Webster, Webstar—61, 90, 94, 95, 100, 141, 163, 166, 169.
Welden—20.
West—151, 168.
Westerman, Westermann—51, 54, 57, 59, 60, 61, 62, 64, 69, 75, 80, 93, 99, 102, 107, 108, 110, 112, 117, 119, 122, 123, 127, 128, 129, 132, 134, 135, 136, 137, 138, 139, 141, 145, 146, 149, 152, 154, 155, 157, 160, 163.
Wharkworth, Wharleworthe—149, 150.
Wharton, Warton—20, 21.
Whaytt, Whaittes—7, 173.
Wheatley, Whealtlay, Wheatlaye, Wheatlye, Wheate-

ley, Wheatleye, Wheatlays—42, 49, 59, 60, 61, 62, 75, 78, 89, 85, 86, 90, 93, 95, 98, 102, 103, 104, 105, 106, 107, 108, 109, 113, 114, 115, 117, 120, 121, 122, 127, 129, 135, 140, 144, 154, 155, 156, 159, 161, 162, 163, 164, 168, 169.
Wheelwright, Whelewright, Whelewrighte, Wheelewright, Wheelwrighte, Wheedewrighte—56, 58, 60, 61, 63, 67, 70, 71, 73, 74, 76, 83, 88, 94, 103, 104, 105, 107, 108, 114, 121, 128, 135, 151, 153.
Whewell—151.
White, Wight, Whyte—62, 74, 77, 80, 81, 83, 89, 91, 93, 95, 98, 99, 101, 102, 104, 107, 108, 112, 113, 120, 122, 123, 129, 134, 143, 146, 148, 151, 152, 154, 156, 157, 158, 161, 162, 164, 165, 166, 167, 168.
Whitehead, Whythed, Whiteheade, Whytehead, Whiteheade, Whitehede, Wytcheade, Wythed—6, 8, 12, 29, 41, 48, 51, 54, 56, 57, 59, 85, 91, 158, 172, 174.
Whiteley, Whitley, Wytllay, Wyttley, Whytley, Wytteley, Wytley, Whytley, Whytlaye, Whiteylaye, Whitelaye, Wittelay, Whitlei, Whittley, Whitlaye, Whitlay, Whittlay, Whitleye—3, 5, 6, 8, 9, 10, 11, 12, 13, 15, 17, 18, 20, 21, 22, 23, 24, 25, 28, 31, 33, 35, 36, 37, 38, 39, 41, 42, 43, 45, 47, 49, 51, 52, 55, 57, 59, 60, 61, 62, 63, 65, 70, 72, 74, 75, 76, 77, 79, 80, 81, 84, 87, 90, 91, 92, 96, 99, 100, 103, 105, 107, 109, 110, 112, 114, 115, 117, 119, 126, 133, 134, 135, 138, 141, 143, 144, 147, 148, 149, 150, 151, 152, 153, 154, 156, 159, 160, 161, 164, 166, 168, 171, 173, 174, 176.
Whittaker, Wytakers, Wytaker, Whitaker, Wytakerr, Whyteacres, Whitacres, Wyttakarys, Wytacar, Wyttakar, Wyttacar, Whyttacars, Wittikars, Whitticars, Wyttikars, Witticar, Whittikers, Whiteares, Whyttakeres, Whytikers, Whettykeres, Whitakers, Wheattakers, Wytayker, Whytaker, Whyteres, Wyttacars, Whyttacar, Wyttkars, Witticers, Whytakeres, Whyttieurs, Whyttakers, Whittakers, Whittykers—4, 7, 8, 10, 11, 12, 13, 14, 15, 18, 19, 25, 27, 28, 29, 32, 36, 37, 38, 41, 45, 47, 49, 52, 53, 55, 56, 59, 60, 61, 62, 63, 65, 67, 73, 76, 79, 80, 81, 83, 92, 95, 98, 101, 106, 113, 114, 122, 123, 124, 125, 126, 127, 128, 131, 132, 133, 134, 135, 136, 139, 140, 143, 146, 150, 153, 154, 158, 160, 162, 163, 165, 166, 167, 173, 174, 175.
Wholroyde (*see* Oldroyd).
Wibsye—74.
Wightman—135, 165.
Willbore, Willbore—29, 34, 79, 121.
Wilby, Wylhe, Willie, Willbye, Wilbee, Wilbie, Wilbi, 50, 51, 52, 53, 54, 56, 57, 58, 59, 65, 66, 68, 70, 72, 73, 74, 75, 77, 79, 89, 81, 82, 84, 85, 86, 87, 91, 92, 94, 95, 98, 127, 129, 130, 132, 143, 147, 149, 153, 155, 162, 165, 166, 167, 168, 169, 176.
Wilcocke, Wylcocke, Wilcoke—24, 33, 42, 56, 57, 67, 75, 77, 78, 91, 117, 128.
Wild, Wilde, Wylde—33, 120, 121, 122, 123, 124, 126, 127, 142, 150.
Wildman, Wildeman—140, 146, 154.
Wilkes—146.
Wilkinson, Wilkyngson, Wylkyngson, Wylkynson, Wilkinsonn, Wilkensonn, Wilkinson, Wilkinsone, Wilkingsone, Willkinson, Wykyngson—2, 5, 7, 9, 10, 15, 16, 20, 22, 45, 46, 47, 50, 51, 52, 53, 58, 59, 60, 67, 72, 74, 78, 91, 96, 97, 98, 101, 103, 110, 111, 112, 113, 118, 127, 133, 138, 148, 169, 170, 171, 174, 175.
Williams—89.
Williams, William—24, 153.
Williamson, Willimson, Williamsonn, Wilbsson, Williamsone—6, 61, 62, 67, 93, 112, 120, 125, 127, 128, 131, 136, 145, 172.
Willie, Willie—58, 49.
Wilson, Wylson, Wylsone, Wyllson, Wilsons, Wilsonn

Willsonn—10, 14, 17, 23, 21, 26, 32, 37, 41, 46, 47, 49, 51, 53, 55, 56, 57, 58, 61, 63, 66, 67, 69, 71, 73, 75, 78, 82, 86, 90, 91, 96, 100, 102, 103, 107, 111, 112, 113, 115, 116, 118, 119, 122, 124, 127, 132, 134, 135, 137, 139, 140, 141, 142, 143, 144, 145, 146, 147, 148, 151, 154, 155, 156, 157, 159, 160, 161, 164, 168.
Winter—169.
Winterton—159.
Witman, Westman—163.
Womersley, Winnersley, Wymersley, Wymerslay, Woomersleye, Wamerslaye—58, 62, 65, 67, 71, 109, 110, 149.
Wood, Wode, Wod, Woode, Wodde, Woodde, Woodd, Wodd—3, 4, 5, 6, 7, 8, 9, 10, 11, 13, 14, 16, 17, 18, 20, 21, 22, 24, 27, 33, 34, 35, 36, 37, 38, 39, 40, 42, 43, 44, 47, 48, 50, 52, 54, 55, 65, 74, 77, 85, 98, 99, 101, 102, 103, 105, 108, 109, 110, 112, 113, 114, 115, 116, 119, 121, 122, 123, 125, 126, 129, 133, 134, 136, 138, 139, 142, 143, 144, 145, 146, 148, 149, 152, 155, 157, 160, 161, 164, 168, 169, 172, 173, 174, 175.
Woodhead, Woodheade—76, 124, 147, 155, 167.
Wooler—4, 110, 126.
Wormall, Wormhall, Wormwall, Wormwalt, Wormawill, Werwall, Wormenall, Werwell, Wormemalde, Wornaell, Wormeall, Wurmall, Werhall—2, 4, 6, 9, 12, 14, 15, 17, 21, 22, 23, 24, 26, 27, 29, 30, 31, 32, 34, 37, 38, 41, 42, 44, 45, 46, 47, 49, 53, 58, 59, 60, 64, 65, 66, 69, 72, 73, 76, 78, 81, 82, 85, 91, 96, 99, 107, 112, 116, 117, 119, 123, 135, 136, 137, 138, 112, 143, 145, 147, 151, 157, 158, 162, 164, 170, 172, 174.
Worsdall—62.
Wright, Wrightt, Wryghtt, Wryght, Wrighte—2, 4,

5, 6, 8, 9, 10, 11, 12, 37, 39, 53, 55, 57, 58, 65, 70, 73, 77, 81, 82, 92, 99, 108, 114, 115, 116, 119, 121, 122, 124, 128, 129, 131, 136, 138, 141, 143, 145, 146, 151, 152, 163, 170, 171, 172, 174.
Wroo, Wroo, Roo—44, 86, 88, 98, 103, 120, 121, 130, 131, 138, 158, 162, 166.
Wrongham—141.
Wrosindale—166.
Wynterburne—166.
Wyse—80, 81.

Yanyn—see Jeninge.
Yarwood—66.
Yeaden—51.
Yeoman—113.
Yewden—103.
York, Yhorke—15, 18.
Yudall, Udalle, Vdalle, Udall—126, 129, 131, 156, 146, 147, 148, 150, 162, 164, 166, 167.

IMPERFECT NAMES.

B[eck]with (?)—159.
Ell . . . . . —173.
G . . . . de—23.
Ould . . . . —168.
[? Robar]tesone—175.
White—147.
Worm . . . . ll—23.
. . . . . . llson—23.
. . . . . ecker—23.

www.ingramcontent.com/pod-product-compliance
Lightning Source LLC
Chambersburg PA
CBHW030400230426
43664CB00007BB/681